A Guide to HUMAN RIGHTS

Institutions, Standards, Procedures

Edited by JANUSZ SYMONIDES
and VLADIMIR VOLODIN

Preface by KOÏCHIRO MATSUURA
DIRECTOR-GENERAL OF UNESCO

UNESCO Publishing

The choice of the material contained in this book and the opinions expressed therein do not necessarily represent the views of UNESCO and do not commit the Organization.

The designations employed and the presentation of material throughout this publication do not imply the expression of any opinion whatsoever on the part of UNESCO concerning the legal status of any country, territory, city or area or of its authorities, or concerning the delimitation of its frontiers or boundaries.

Correspondence regarding this publication should be addressed to:
Division of Human Rights and Fight against Discrimination
Sector of Social and Human Sciences
UNESCO
1 rue Miollis, 75732 Paris Cedex 15, France
Fax: (33-1) 45 68 57 26

UNESCO Website:
http://www.unesco.org/publishing (for orders)

Published in 2003 by the
United Nations Educational, Scientific and Cultural Organization
7 place de Fontenoy, F-75352 Paris 07 SP, France
Design: Créagraphie, Paris
Printed by Policrom, Barcelona

ISBN 92-3-103928-8

© UNESCO 2003
All rights reserved
Printed in Spain

Preface

The Constitution of UNESCO stipulates that the mission of the Organization is '…to contribute to peace and security by promoting collaboration among the nations through education, science and culture in order to further universal respect for justice, for the rule of law and for the human rights and fundamental freedoms which are affirmed for the peoples of the world, without distinction of race, sex, language or religion, by the Charter of the United Nations'.

The Organization has always been actively involved in the promotion and protection of those human rights which fall directly within its competence, such as the right to education, the right to take part in cultural life, the right to freedom of opinion and expression, including the right to seek, receive and impart information, and the right to enjoy the benefits of scientific progress and its applications. At the same time, it has always worked for the advancement of all human rights by means of research, education and dissemination of information. UNESCO has contributed to the progressive development of international human rights law by assisting in the drafting of the Universal Declaration of Human Rights, the International Covenant on Civil and Political Rights and the International Covenant on Economic, Social and Cultural Rights and by elaborating its own standard-setting instruments.

UNESCO has always striven to achieve the fullest possible implementation of human rights standards by promoting better knowledge and understanding of them. In the era of globalization, which has created unprecedented wealth and well-being, but has been accompanied by increasing poverty, inequality and exclusion for many individuals and groups, the sensitization of decision-makers and society as a whole on human rights issues has become particularly important.

The present publication has been prepared to raise awareness on human rights. By providing brief information on human rights standards, procedures and mechanisms for their protection, organizations and institutions working for human rights, and major international events, this edition should be useful for all those interested in human rights. The Guide is dedicated to the tenth anniversary of the World Conference on Human Rights (Vienna, 1993), which was a landmark in the long struggle for the promotion and protection of all human rights for all. The Vienna Declaration and Programme of Action, adopted by consensus, reaffirm the principles of universality, interdependence and indivisibility of all human rights – civil, cultural, economic, political and social. The current work of the United Nations agencies in the field of human rights, sustained by an increasing cooperation between UNESCO and the Office of the High Commissioner for Human Rights (OHCHR), is built upon these principles.

I hope that this book, along with other UNESCO publications, will contribute to the joint efforts of the international community and civil society to make all human rights a reality for all.

KOÏCHIRO MATSUURA
Director-General of UNESCO

Introduction

Since the creation of the United Nations system and the adoption of the Universal Declaration of Human Rights, the international framework for the promotion and protection of human rights has been greatly developed. International human rights law now comprises an impressive number of standard-setting instruments adopted by universal and regional intergovernmental organizations, which establish obligations for human rights protection and create mechanisms for encouraging and monitoring their enforcement. Numerous procedures and bodies have been established at universal, regional and national levels. In many countries they have taken the form of human rights commissions, ombudspersons and even human rights ministries. The increasing importance of human rights on the international agenda was confirmed by a number of developments including the proclamation of the centrality of human rights in all activities of the United Nations system, in accordance with the United Nations reform, launched at the end of the 1990s. International days, years and decades have been proclaimed with the vision to ensuring the fullest possible implementation of all human rights for all without discrimination. The long-standing efforts of the international community to ensure that violations of human rights do not go unpunished culminated in the adoption of the Rome Statute of the International Criminal Court in 1998, which entered into force on 1 July 2002.

A great number of non-governmental organizations make an extremely important contribution to the promotion and protection of human rights. They undertake tireless daily efforts to mobilize public opinion against violators and to help the victims of human rights violations, often acting as a catalyst for the progressive development of international human rights law and the strengthening of enforcement mechanisms. Hundreds, if not thousands, of institutions throughout the world specialize in human rights education and research and undertake manifold activities related to the sensitization of decision-makers and the general public on human rights issues.

It can be concluded that a global human rights movement involving various governmental and non-governmental partners and civil society as a whole is emerging. The appearance in the international arena of new, powerful actors such as transnational corporations which are capable of greatly influencing the degree of implementation of human rights in various countries, has led to increased efforts to make business a partner in this global movement. The establishment of codes of conduct ensuring the respect for human dignity and rights which are often neglected in the era of globalization is considered an important step forward in this regard.

Human rights standards can be implemented only if they are known – known by the population at large and known by those who have special responsibilities for their promotion and protection, including decision-makers, lawyers, law enforcement personnel, educators, social workers and media professionals. Education has indeed become an essential means to encourage human rights implementation. The United Nations Decade for Human Rights Education (1995-2004) is aimed at furthering the recognition of human rights education as a human right and an obligation of States, and at making it an integral part of formal and non-formal education at all levels. The Decade is also aimed at developing awareness of human rights standards and procedures and empowering people to defend their own dignity and rights and the dignity and rights of others. Human rights education should constitute a life-long process by which people are also informed on challenges and threats to human rights and are mobilized to respond to them. Education for human rights is both a precondition and the very basis of a culture of human rights.

UNESCO has always played an important role in the endeavours aimed at the advancement of human rights. As an Organization with a special mandate in the field of education it is recognized as a leading agency in the implementation of the Plan of Action for the Decade for Human Rights Education. UNESCO has undertaken numerous efforts, in close cooperation with the Office of the United Nations High Commissioner for Human Rights, which is the Coordinator of the Decade, to advance human rights education. Through the efforts of UNESCO Chairs in Human Rights and the Associated Schools Project Network (ASPnet), convening of regional conferences on human rights education, training of educators, preparation of teaching and information materials and revision of textbooks and curricula, UNESCO is greatly assisting in the attainment of the aims of the Decade.

Bearing in mind the ever-growing volume of data on human rights, it is becoming increasingly difficult for an interested person to steer through the huge amount of available information. Several attempts to assist in this exercise have been made. The work entitled *Encyclopedia of Human Rights* by Edward Lawson (2nd Edition: Taylor and Francis Inc., New York/Philadelphia/Washington/London), an impressive volume of more than 1,700 pages, was published in 1996 and became the most comprehensive reference book on this subject. However, it is primarily of use to those who have already a certain knowledge about human rights rather than to non-specialists. To facilitate the comprehension of various notions and terms in human rights, several dictionaries have been published. These very useful terminological works include: *A Dictionary of Human Rights* by David Robertson (London, Europa Publications Limited, 1997); *Dictionary of International Human Rights Law* by John S. Gibson (Lanham, Md./London, The Scarecrow Press, Inc., 1996); and *A Handbook of International Human*

Rights Terminology by H. Victor Condé (University of Nebraska Press, 1999). Similar editions have also appeared in other languages, notably, *Dictionnaire Pratique du Droit Humanitaire* by Françoise Bouchet-Saulnier (Editions La Découverte & Syros: Paris, 2000). However, until now, a concise comprehensive overview of human rights institutions, standards and procedures has not yet been presented in a single publication.

This Guide has been prepared with a view to providing the reader with an orientation to the overall body of information linked with human rights issues. The first edition of this Guide, designed for limited distribution, received a very positive response and inspired us to produce a revised and updated version for a much wider dissemination. The format and methodology of the first edition have been preserved while new information has been added and a substantive part of the text has been modified to reflect new developments. The present volume includes about 600 entries and presents data on major human rights instruments, human rights monitoring bodies and other mechanisms and procedures for human rights protection, on international days, years and decades, major conferences, key notions, etc. In view of the limited size of this book, the entries are as concise as possible. All efforts have been made to ensure that the text contains the most accurate, up-to-date information possible. For those who may wish to have more ample information, the entries are accompanied, wherever possible, by corresponding Internet addresses. Cross-references (printed in bold) are widely used throughout the publication.

This volume is dedicated to the 10th anniversary of the World Conference on Human Rights convened by the United Nations in Vienna, Austria, from 14 to 25 June 1993. Attended by more than 7000 participants, including delegates from 171 States and 800 non-governmental organizations, the Conference represents a landmark event in the advancement of human rights. The Vienna Declaration and Programme of Action, adopted by consensus at the Conference, provide the international community with a comprehensive plan for strengthening human rights activities throughout the world. The

Declaration reaffirms that all human rights are universal, indivisible and interdependent and interrelated. It confirms that the international community "must treat all human rights globally in a fair and equal manner, on the same footing, and with the same emphasis".[1] The Conference also underlined an inherent link between human rights, fundamental freedoms, democracy and development and declared them interdependent and mutually reinforcing. It was agreed that "while the significance of national and regional particularities and various historical, cultural and religious backgrounds must be borne in mind, it is the duty of States, regardless of their political, economic and cultural systems, to promote and protect all human rights and fundamental freedoms".[2] Furthermore, the Conference recognized that "the existence of widespread extreme poverty inhibits the full and effective enjoyment of human rights; its immediate alleviation and eventual elimination must remain a high priority for the international community".[3] The main areas of further joint action – such as prevention and elimination of discrimination, promotion of the human rights of women and gender equality as well as protection of the rights of children, indigenous peoples, persons belonging to minorities and other vulnerable groups were highlighted by the Conference.

The dedication of this volume to the World Conference was made in order to recall that the conclusions of the Vienna Conference are valid, which is proven by their reaffirmation in the United Nations Millennium Declaration. However much work remains to be done in order to make them a reality.

The editors wish to express their deepest gratitude to the UNESCO partners within the United Nations system, in particular to the Office of the United Nations High Commissioner for Human Rights and to the International Labour Office, to the Council of Europe and other universal and regional intergovernmental

---

[1] Vienna Declaration and Programme of Action, Part I, paragraph 5.
[2] Ibidem.
[3] Vienna Declaration and Programme of Action, Part I, paragraph 14.

organizations, to the members of human rights treaty monitoring bodies and other human rights specialists for their valuable suggestions concerning various entries. The editors are most grateful to the colleagues in UNESCO, as well as to consultants and interns in the Division of Human Rights for their assistance, in particular to Christine Allan, Katja Burow, Sophia Botzios, Yvonne Donders, An Goethals, Barbara Sarx and Konstantinos Tararas. Our special thanks go to Sarah Curtis for her valuable contribution to the preparation of this edition. Furthermore, the editors express their appreciation to all those who have helped them with the previous edition, in particular to Sheila Bennett, Karen Garner, Roxanne Kazancigil, Hagar Ligtvoet, Clarisse Magnékou, Birgit Roth, Henrik Steenstrup, Laia Torras and Wibke Weiss. The editors are especially grateful to Gillian Whitcomb, Chief of the Communication, Information and Publications Section of the Sector of Social and Human Sciences, for her valuable assistance in the preparation of both editions.

We hope that this publication may be useful for all those who are interested in the further advancement of human rights.

JANUSZ SYMONIDES[*]   VLADIMIR VOLODIN[**]

---

[*] Professor of international law and Director of the Division of Human Rights, UNESCO, in 1990-2000.
[**] Chief of Section of Human Rights and Development in the Division of Human Rights, UNESCO.

Table of Contents

Academic freedom 1
Additional Protocol to the American Convention on Human Rights
  in the Area of Economic, Social and Cultural Rights
  – "Protocol of San Salvador" (OAS) 2
African Charter on Human and Peoples' Rights (OAU/AU) 3
African Charter on the Rights and Welfare of the Child (OAU/AU) 4
African Commission on Human and Peoples' Rights (OAU/AU) 5
African Court on Human and Peoples' Rights (AU/OAU) 6
African Union – AU 7
American Bill of Rights 9
American Convention on Human Rights – "Pact of San José" (OAS) 9
American Declaration on the Rights and Duties of Man (OAS) 10
Amnesty International – AI 11
Apartheid 12
Arab Charter on Human Rights
  (League of Arab States) 14
Arab League Educational, Cultural and Scientific Organization
  – ALECSO 15
Asian and Pacific Decade of Disabled Persons – 1993-2002 (UN) 15
Basic Principles and Guidelines on the Right to a Remedy
  and Reparation for Victims of Violations of International
  Human Rights and Humanitarian Law (UN) 17
Basic Principles for the Treatment of Prisoners (UN) 17
Basic Principles for the Use of Force and Firearms by Law
  Enforcement Officials (UN) 18
Basic Principles on the Independence of the Judiciary (UN) 19
Basic Principles on the Role of Lawyers (UN) 20
Beijing Declaration and Platform for Action (UN) 21
Beijing Rules (UN) 22
Berne Convention for the Protection of Literary and Artistic Works 22
Bill of Rights – England, 1689 23
Bill of Rights – United States of America, 1791 23
Bioethics and human rights 24
Body of Principles for the Protection of All Persons under Any Form
  of Detention or Imprisonment (UN) 25

Cairo Declaration on Human Rights in Islam (Islamic Conference
    of Foreign Ministers) 27
Cartagena Declaration on Refugees 27
Charter of Fundamental Rights of the European Union (EU) 28
Charter of Paris for a New Europe (CSCE/OSCE) 29
Charter of the United Nations (United Nations Charter) 30
Cities for Human Rights 31
Civil rights 31
Code of Conduct for Law Enforcement Officials (UN) 32
Code of Sports Ethics (Council of Europe) 33
Commissioner for Human Rights (Council of Europe) 33
Commissioner of the Council of the Baltic Sea States on Democratic
    Development 34
Commission for Social Development (UN) 35
Commission on Crime Prevention and Criminal Justice (UN) 36
Commission on Human Rights (UN) 36
Commission on the Status of Women (UN) 38
Committee against Torture – CAT (UN) 39
Committee on Crime Prevention and Control (UN) 41
Committee on Economic, Social and Cultural Rights
    – CESCR (UN) 41
Committee on the Elimination of Discrimination against Women
    – CEDAW (UN) 43
Committee on the Elimination of Racial Discrimination
    – CERD (UN) 44
Committee on the Protection of the Rights of All Migrant Workers
    and Members of Their Families (UN) 46
Committee on the Rights of the Child – CRC (UN) 47
Communication procedure – "1503" Procedure (UN) 48
Communication procedure – UNESCO 50
Communication procedures of the International Labour
    Organization (ILO) 51
Communication procedures – United Nations system 52
Conference for Security and Cooperation in Europe – CSCE 53
Convention (N° 11) concerning the Right of Association
    and Combination of Agricultural Workers (ILO) 53
Convention (N° 29) concerning Forced or Compulsory Labour (ILO) 54
Convention (No. 81) concerning Labour Inspection in Industry
    and Commerce (ILO) 54
Convention (N° 87) concerning Freedom of Association and Protection
    of the Right to Organise (ILO) 55
Convention (N° 97) concerning Migration for Employment
    – revised (ILO) 56
Convention (N° 98) concerning the Application of the Principles
    of the Right to Organise and Bargain Collectively (ILO) 57

Convention (N° 100) concerning Equal Remuneration for Men
and Women Workers for Work of Equal Value (ILO) 57
Convention (N° 102) concerning Minimum Standards of Social
Security (ILO) 58
Convention (N° 105) concerning the Abolition of Forced
Labour (ILO) 58
Convention (N° 111) concerning Discrimination in Respect
of Employment and Occupation (ILO) 59
Convention (N° 118) concerning Equality of Treatment of Nationals
and Non-Nationals in Social Security (ILO) 60
Convention (N° 122) concerning Employment Policy (ILO) 60
Convention (No. 129) concerning Labour Inspection in
Agriculture (ILO) 61
Convention (N° 135) concerning Protection and Facilities to be Afforded
to Workers' Representatives in the Undertaking (ILO) 62
Convention (N° 138) concerning Minimum Age for Admission
to Employment (ILO) 63
Convention (N° 141) concerning Organisations of Rural Workers
and Their Role in Economic and Social Development (ILO) 63
Convention (N° 143) concerning Migrations in Abusive Conditions
and the Promotion of Equality of Opportunity and Treatment
of Migrant Workers (ILO) 64
Convention (No. 144) concerning Tripartite Consultations to Promote
the Implementation of International Labour Standards (ILO) 65
Convention (N° 151) concerning Protection of the Right to Organise
and Procedures for Determining Conditions of Employment
in the Public Service (ILO) 66
Convention (N° 154) concerning the Promotion of Collective
Bargaining (ILO) 67
Convention (N° 156) concerning Equal Opportunities and Equal
Treatment for Men and Women Workers: Workers with Family
Responsibilities (ILO) 68
Convention (N° 168) concerning Employment Promotion and
Protection against Unemployment (ILO) 68
Convention (N° 169) concerning Indigenous and Tribal Peoples
in Independent Countries (ILO) 69
Convention (N°182) concerning the Prohibition and Immediate Action
for the Elimination of the Worst Forms of Child Labour (ILO) 70
Convention against Discrimination in Education (UNESCO) 71
Convention against Torture and Other Cruel, Inhuman or Degrading
Treatment or Punishment (UN) 72
Convention concerning the Protection of the World Cultural
and Natural Heritage (UNESCO) 73
Convention for the Protection of Cultural Property in the Event
of Armed Conflict (UNESCO) 74

Convention for the Protection of Human Rights and Dignity
  of the Human Being with regard to the Application of Biology
  and Medicine: Convention on Human Rights and Biomedicine
  (Council of Europe) 75
Convention for the Protection of Individuals with regard to Automatic
  Processing of Personal Data (Council of Europe) 76
Convention for the Protection of the Architectural Heritage of Europe
  (Council of Europe) 77
Convention for the Suppression of the Traffic in Persons and
  of the Exploitation of the Prostitution of Others (UN) 77
Convention for the Suppression of Unlawful Acts against the Safety
  of Civil Aviation (ICAO) 78
Convention for the Suppression of Unlawful Seizure of Aircraft
  (ICAO) 79
Convention Governing the Specific Aspects of Refugee Problems
  in Africa (OAU/AU) 79
Convention of Belem do Para (OAS) 80
Convention on Asylum (OAS) 80
Convention on Combating Bribery of Foreign Public Officials
  in International Business Transactions (OECD) 81
Convention on Consent to Marriage, Minimum Age for Marriage
  and Registration of Marriages (UN) 82
Convention on Diplomatic Asylum (OAS) 82
Convention on Human Rights and Biomedicine (Council of Europe) 83
Convention on Offences and Certain Other Acts Committed
  on Board Aircraft (ICAO) 83
Convention on Political Asylum (OAS) 84
Convention on Territorial Asylum (OAS) 84
Convention on the Elimination of All Forms of Discrimination
  against Women (UN) 85
Convention on the International Right of Correction (UN) 86
Convention on the Nationality of Married Women (UN) 87
Convention on the Nationality of Women (OAS) 88
Convention on the Non-applicability of Statutory Limitations to
  War Crimes and Crimes against Humanity (UN) 88
Convention on the Participation of Foreigners in Public Life
  at Local Level (Council of Europe) 89
Convention on the Political Rights of Women (UN) 90
Convention on the Prevention and Combating of Terrorism
  (OAU/AU) 91
Convention on the Prevention and Punishment of Crimes
  against Internationally Protected Persons, including
  Diplomatic Agents (UN) 92
Convention on the Prevention and Punishment of the Crime
  of Genocide (UN) 93

Convention on the Reduction of Statelessness (UN) 94
Convention on the Rights of the Child (UN) 94
Convention on the Status of Aliens (OAS) 96
Convention relating to the Status of Refugees (UN) 96
Convention relating to the Status of Stateless Persons (UN) 98
Convention relative to the Rights of Aliens (OAS) 98
Convention to Prevent and Punish the Acts of Terrorism Taking
  the Forms of Crimes against Persons and Related Extortion
  that Are of International Significance (OAS) 99
Copenhagen Declaration on Social Development and Programme
  of Action (UN) 100
Corruption 100
Council of Europe 101
Court of Justice of the European Communities – CJEC (EU) 102
Cultural heritage 103
Cultural rights 104
Culture of peace (UNESCO/UN) 106
Dakar Framework for Action (UNESCO) 109
Decades for Action to Combat Racism and Racial Discrimination
  – 1973-83; 1983-93 and 1993-2003 (UN) 110
Declaration and Programme of Action on a Culture of Peace (UN) 112
Declaration of Basic Principles of Justice for Victims of Crime
  and Abuse of Power (UN) 113
Declaration of Fundamental Principles concerning the Contribution
  of the Mass Media to Strengthening Peace and International
  Understanding, to the Promotion of Human Rights
  and to Countering Racialism, Apartheid and Incitement to War
  (UNESCO) 114
Declaration of Independence of the United States of America
  – 1776 115
Declaration of Mexico on the Equality of Women and Their
  Contribution to Development and Peace (UN) 115
Declaration of Principles on Tolerance (UNESCO) 116
Declaration of Santiago on Promoting Independent and Pluralistic
  Media and Plan of Action (UN/UNDP/UNESCO) 117
Declaration of the Principles of International Cultural cooperation
  (UNESCO) 118
Declaration of the Rights of Man and of the Citizen – 1789 119
Declaration of Windhoek on Promoting an Independent and
  Pluralistic African Press (UN/UNESCO) 120
Declaration on Crime and Public Security (UN) 121
Declaration on Criteria for Free and Fair Elections (IPU) 122
Declaration on Fundamental Principles and Rights at Work and
  Its Follow-up (ILO) 123
Declaration on Human Rights Defenders (UN) 124

Declaration on Principles of International Law concerning
    Friendly Relations and Co-operation among States in accordance
    with the Charter of the United Nations (UN) 124
Declaration on Race and Racial Prejudice (UNESCO) 125
Declaration on Social and Legal Principles relating to the Protection
    and Welfare of Children, with Special Reference to Foster Placement
    and Adoption Nationally and Internationally (UN) 126
Declaration on Social Progress and Development (UN) 127
Declaration on Territorial Asylum (UN) 128
Declaration on the Elimination of All Forms of Intolerance and
    of Discrimination Based on Religion or Belief (UN) 128
Declaration on the Elimination of All Forms of Racial Discrimination
    (UN) 130
Declaration on the Elimination of Discrimination against Women
    (UN) 131
Declaration on the Elimination of Violence against Women (UN) 131
Declaration on the Granting of Independence to Colonial Countries
    and Peoples (UN) 132
Declaration on the Human Rights of Individuals Who Are not
    Nationals of the Country in which They Live (UN) 133
Declaration on the Participation of Women in Promoting International
    Peace and Co-operation (UN) 134
Declaration on the Preparation of Societies for Life in Peace (UN) 135
Declaration on the Promotion among Youth of the Ideals of Peace,
    Mutual Respect and Understanding between Peoples (UN) 136
Declaration on the Protection of All Persons from Being Subjected
    to Torture and other Cruel, Inhuman or Degrading Treatment
    or Punishment (UN) 136
Declaration on the Protection of All Persons from Enforced
    Disappearance (UN) 137
Declaration on the Protection of Women and Children in Emergency
    and Armed Conflict (UN) 138
Declaration on the Responsibilities of the Present Generations
    towards Future Generations (UNESCO) 139
Declaration on the Right and Responsibility of Individuals, Groups
    and Organs of Society to Promote and Protect Universally
    Recognized Human Rights and Fundamental Freedoms (UN) 140
Declaration on the Right of Peoples to Peace (UN) 142
Declaration on the Rights of Disabled Persons (UN) 142
Declaration on the Rights of Mentally Retarded Persons (UN) 143
Declaration on the Rights of Persons Belonging to National or Ethnic,
    Religious and Linguistic Minorities (UN) 144
Declaration of the Rights of the Child (UN) 145
Declaration on the Right to Development (UN) 146

Declaration on the Use of Scientific and Technological Progress in
  the Interest of Peace and for the Benefit of Mankind (UN) 147
Declarations of the Forty-Fourth and Forty-Fifth Sessions of the
  International Conference on Education and Integrated
  Framework of Action on Education for Peace, Human Rights
  and Democracy (UNESCO) 148
Discrimination 149
Displaced persons 151
Durban Declaration and Programme of Action (UN) 152
Economic and Social Council – ECOSOC (UN) 155
Economic rights 156
Ethnic cleansing 157
Ethno-nationalism 158
European Agreement on the Abolition of Visas for Refugees
  (Council of Europe) 158
European Agreement on Transfer of Responsibility for Refugees
  (Council of Europe) 159
European Agreement (1969) relating to Persons Participating
  in Proceedings of the European Commission and Court
  of Human Rights (Council of Europe) 160
European Agreement (1996) relating to Persons Participating
  in Proceedings of the European Court of Human Rights
  (Council of Europe) 160
European Charter for Regional or Minority Languages
  (Council of Europe) 161
European Charter for the Safeguarding of Human Rights in the City 162
European Charter of Local Self-Government (Council of Europe) 163
European Charter on Sport for All: Disabled Persons
  (Council of Europe) 164
European Code of Social Security and Its Additional Protocol
  (Council of Europe) 164
European Code of Social Security – revised (Council of Europe) 165
European Commission (EU) 166
European Commission against Racism and Intolerance – ECRI
  (Council of Europe) 167
European Commission of Human Rights (Council of Europe) 168
European Committee for the Prevention of Torture and Inhuman
  or Degrading Treatment or Punishment (Council of Europe) 168
European Committee of Social Rights (Council of Europe) 169
European Community – EC 170
European Convention for the Prevention of Torture and Inhuman
  or Degrading Treatment or Punishment (Council of Europe) 171
European Convention for the Protection of Human Rights and
  Fundamental Freedoms (Council of Europe) 171

European Convention on Extradition and Additional Protocols thereto
(Council of Europe) 173
European Convention on Human Rights (Council of Europe) 174
European Convention on Mutual Assistance in Criminal Matters
(Council of Europe) 174
European Convention on Nationality (Council of Europe) 174
European Convention on Offences relating to Cultural Property
(Council of Europe) 175
European Convention on the Academic Recognition of University
Qualifications (Council of Europe) 175
European Convention on the Exercise of Children's Rights
(Council of Europe) 176
European Convention on the Legal Status of Children Born out
of Wedlock (Council of Europe) 177
European Convention on the Legal Status of Migrant Workers
(Council of Europe) 177
European Convention on the Non-applicability of Statutory
Limitation to Crimes against Humanity and War Crimes
(Council of Europe) 178
European Convention on the Protection of the Archaeological
Heritage – revised (Council of Europe) 179
European Convention on the Suppression of Terrorism
(Council of Europe) 180
European Council (EU) 180
European Court of Human Rights (Council of Europe) 181
European Cultural Convention (Council of Europe) 183
European Landscape Convention (Council of Europe) 184
European Parliament 184
European Prison Rules (Council of Europe) 185
European Rules on Community Sanctions and Measures
(Council of Europe) 186
European Social Charter (Council of Europe) 187
European Social Charter – Revised (Council of Europe) 188
European Sport for All Charter (Council of Europe) 189
European Union – EU 190
European Union Charter of Fundamental Rights (EU) 190
Extreme poverty 191
Food and Agriculture Organization of the United Nations – FAO 193
Framework Convention for the Protection of National Minorities
(Council of Europe) 194
Free and periodic elections 195
Freedom from arbitrary arrest 196
Freedom from arbitrary interference with privacy 197
Freedom from compulsory or forced labour 198
Freedom from hunger 199

Entry	Page
Freedom from subjection to torture and to cruel, inhuman or degrading treatment	199
Freedom of association	200
Freedom of movement and residence	201
Freedom of opinion and expression	202
Freedom of peaceful assembly	202
Freedom of scientific research	203
Freedom of thought, conscience and religion or belief	204
Freedom to dispose of natural wealth and resources	205
Freedom to seek, receive and impart information	205
General Comments or General Recommendations of Human Rights Treaty Bodies	207
Geneva Conventions (ICRC)	208
Geneva Convention for the Amelioration of the Condition of the Wounded and Sick in the Armed Forces in the Field – Convention I (ICRC)	209
Geneva Convention for the Amelioration of the Condition of Wounded, Sick and Shipwrecked Members of Armed Forces at Sea – Convention II (ICRC)	210
Geneva Convention relative to the Treatment of Prisoners of War – Convention III (ICRC)	211
Geneva Convention relative to the Protection of Civilian Persons in Time of War – Convention IV (ICRC)	212
Genocide	213
Global Compact (UN)	213
Globalization and human rights	214
Guidelines on the Role of Prosecutors (UN)	216
Guiding Principles on Human Organ Transplantation (WHO)	217
Guiding Principles on Internal Displacement (UN)	218
Guillermo Cano World Press Freedom Prize (UNESCO)	219
Helsinki Final Act (CSCE)	221
High Commissioner on National Minorities – HCNM (OSCE)	222
HIV/AIDS and human rights	223
HIV-infected people or people with AIDS	225
Humanitarian Law	226
Human Rights Committee – HCR (UN)	227
Human Rights Day – 10 December (UN)	228
Human rights education	229
Human rights research and training institutions	231
Human rights treaty bodies (or human rights treaty monitoring bodies)	232
Indigenous people	235
Integrated Framework of Action on Education for Peace, Human Rights and Democracy (UNESCO)	236
Inter-American Charter of Social Guarantees (OAS)	238

Inter-American Commission of Women – CIM (OAS) 238
Inter-American Commission on Human Rights (OAS) 239
Inter-American Convention against Corruption (OAS) 240
Inter-American Convention against Terrorism (OAS) 240
Inter-American Convention on Extradition (OAS) 242
Inter-American Convention on Forced Disappearance of Persons (OAS) ...242
Inter-American Convention on International Traffic in Minors (OAS) 243
Inter-American Convention on the Elimination of All Forms
   of Discrimination against Persons with Disabilities (OAS) 244
Inter-American Convention on the Granting of Civil Rights
   to Women (OAS) 244
Inter-American Convention on the Granting of Political Rights
   to Women (OAS) 245
Inter-American Convention on the Prevention, Punishment
   and Eradication of Violence against Women
   – "Convention of Belem do Para" (OAS) 245
Inter-American Convention to Prevent and Punish Torture (OAS) 246
Inter-American Court of Human Rights (OAS) 248
International Bill of Human Rights (UN) 249
International Charter of Physical Education and Sport (UNESCO) 249
International Civil Aviation Organization – ICAO 250
International Code of Conduct for Public Officials (UN) 250
International Committee of the Red Cross – ICRC 251
International Conferences on Education (UNESCO) 253
International Congress on Education for Human Rights
   and Democracy, Montreal, 1993 (UNESCO) 254
International Congress on Human Rights Teaching, Information
   and Documentation, Malta, 1987 (UNESCO) 255
International Congress on the Teaching of Human Rights,
   Vienna, 1978 (UNESCO) 255
International Convention against Apartheid in Sports (UN) 256
International Convention against the Taking of Hostages (UN) 257
International Convention for the Suppression of Terrorist
   Bombings (UN) 258
International Convention for the Suppression of the Financing
   of Terrorism (UN) 258
International Convention on the Elimination of All Forms
   of Racial Discrimination (UN) 259
International Convention on the Protection of the Rights of All
   Migrant Workers and Members of Their Families (UN) 260
International Convention on the Suppression and Punishment
   of the Crime of Apartheid (UN) 261
International Court of Justice – ICJ (UN) 262
International Covenant on Civil and Political Rights (UN) 263

International Covenant on Economic, Social and Cultural Rights (UN)	264
International Covenants on Human Rights (UN)	265
International Criminal Court – ICC (UN)	266
International Criminal Tribunals (UN)	268
International Criminal Tribunal for Rwanda – ICTR (UN)	269
International Criminal Tribunal for the former Yugoslavia – ICTY (UN)	270
International Day against Drug Abuse and Illicit Trafficking – 26 June (UN)	271
International Day for the Abolition of Slavery – 2 December (UN)	271
International Day for the Elimination of Racial Discrimination – 21 March (UN)	272
International Day for the Elimination of Violence against Women – 25 November (UN)	273
International Day for the Eradication of Poverty – 17 October (UN)	273
International Day for the Remembrance of the Slave Trade and Its Abolition – 23 August (UNESCO)	274
International Day for Tolerance – 16 November (UN/UNESCO)	274
International Day in Support of Victims of Torture – 26 June (UN)	275
International Day of Disabled Persons – 3 December (UN)	276
International Day of Families – 15 May (UN)	276
International Day of Innocent Children Victims of Aggression – 4 June (UN)	276
International Day of Older Persons (UN)	277
International Day of Peace – 3rd Tuesday of September (UN)	277
International Day of Solidarity with the Palestinian People – 29 November (UN)	278
International Day of the World's Indigenous People – 9 August (UN)	278
International Decade for a Culture of Peace and Non-violence for the Children of the World – 2001-10 (UN)	279
International Decade for the Eradication of Colonialism – 1990-2000 (UN)	280
International Decade of the World's Indigenous People – 1995-2004 (UN)	280

International humanitarian law 281
International Labour Organization – ILO 283
International Literacy Day
 – 8 September (UNESCO) 284
International Literacy Year – 1990 (UN) 285
International Organization for Migration – IOM 285
International Refugee Organization – IRO 286
International Research and Training Institute for the Advancement
 of Women – INSTRAW (UN) 286
International Women's Day – 8 March (UN) 287
International Women's Year – 1975 (UN) 288
International Year for Action to Combat Racism and
 Racial Discrimination – 1971 (UN) 289
International Year for the Culture of Peace – 2000 (UN) 290
International Year for the Eradication of Poverty – 1996 (UN) 291
International Year for Tolerance – 1995 (UN) 292
International Year of Freshwater – 2003 (UN) 293
International Year of Mobilization against Racism, Racial
 Discrimination, Xenophobia and Related Intolerance
 – 2001 (UN) 294
International Year of Older Persons – 1999 (UN) 294
International Year of Peace – 1986 (UN) 295
International Year of the Child – 1979 (UN) 296
International Year of the Family – 1994 (UN) 297
International Year of the World's Indigenous People – 1993 (UN) 297
International Youth Day – 12 August (UN) 298
International Youth Year: Participation, Development, Peace
 – 1985 (UN) 299
Inter-Parliamentary Union – IPU 299
League of Arab States/Arab League 303
League of Nations 304
Limburg Principles on the Implementation of the International
 Covenant on Economic, Social and Cultural Rights (UN) 305
Maastricht Guidelines on Violations of Economic, Social and
 Cultural Rights (UN) 307
Magna Carta 308
Management of Social Transformations – MOST (UNESCO) 308
Mexico City Declaration on Cultural Policies (UNESCO) 309
Migrant workers 309
Millennium Development Goals (UN) 310
Minorities 310
Nairobi Forward-Looking Strategies for the Advancement
 of Women (UN) 313
Naples Political Declaration and Global Action Plan against
 Organized Transnational Crime (UN) 314

National human rights institutions – NHRI 315
Non-derogatory human rights 317
Non-governmental organizations in the field of human rights 317
Nuremberg International Human Rights Award 319
Office for Democratic Institutions and Human Rights
  – ODIHR (OSCE) 321
Office of the United Nations High Commissioner for Human Rights
  – OHCHR 322
Office of the United Nations High Commissioner for Refugees
  – UNHCR 323
Older persons 324
Ombudsperson 325
Optional Protocol to the Convention against Torture and other Cruel,
  Inhuman or Degrading Treatment or Punishment (UN) 326
Optional Protocol to the Convention on the Elimination of All Forms
  of Discrimination against Women (UN) 328
Optional Protocol to the Convention on the Rights of the Child
  on the Involvement of Children in Armed Conflict (UN) 328
Optional Protocol to the Convention on the Rights of
  the Child on the Sale of Children, Child Prostitution and
  Child Pornography (UN) 329
Optional Protocol to the International Covenant on Civil
  and Political Rights (UN) 330
Organisation for Economic Co-operation and Development – OECD 330
Organization for Security and Co-operation in Europe – OSCE 331
Organization of African Unity – OAU 334
Organization of American States – OAS 334
Organized crime 336
OSCE Representative on Freedom of the Media (OSCE) 336
Pact of San José (OAS) 339
Paris Convention for the Protection of Industrial Property 339
Paris Principles (UN) 339
Peace and human rights 341
Permanent Forum on Indigenous Issues (UN) 343
Political rights 344
Poverty 345
Principles for the Protection of Persons with Mental Illness
  and the Improvement of Mental Health Care (UN) 347
Principles of International Co-operation in the Detection, Arrest,
  Extradition and Punishment of Persons Guilty of War Crimes
  and Crimes against Humanity (UN) 348
Principles of Medical Ethics relevant to the Role of Health Personnel,
  particularly Physicians, in the Protection of Prisoners and
  Detainees against Torture and other Cruel, Inhuman or Degrading
  Treatment or Punishment (UN) 349

Principles on the Effective Investigation and Documentation
  of Torture and other Cruel, Inhuman or Degrading Treatment
  or Punishment (UN) 350
Principles on the Effective Prevention and Investigation of Extra-legal,
  Arbitrary and Summary Executions (UN) 351
Proclamation of Tehran (UN) 351
Protocol against the Illicit Manufacturing of and Trafficking in Firearms,
  Their Parts and Components and Ammunition (UN) 352
Protocol against the Smuggling of Migrants by Land, Sea and Air (UN) ...353
Protocol Amending the 1926 Slavery Convention (UN) 354
Protocol Instituting a Conciliation and Good Offices Commission
  to Be Responsible for Seeking a Settlement of Any Disputes
  which May Arise between States Parties to the Convention
  against Discrimination in Education (UNESCO) 354
Protocol No. 13 to the Convention for the Protection of Human Rights
  and Fundamental Freedoms, concerning the Abolition of the Death
  Penalty in All Circumstances (Council of Europe) 355
Protocol of San Salvador (OAS) 355
Protocol relating to the Status of Refugees (UN) 356
Protocol to Prevent, Suppress and Punish Trafficking in Persons,
  especially Women and Children (UN) 356
Protocol to the African Charter on Human and Peoples' Rights
  on the Establishment of an African Court on Human and
  Peoples' Rights (AU/OAU) 356
Protocol to the African Charter on Human and Peoples' Rights
  on the Rights of Women in Africa (AU/OAU) 357
Protocol to the American Convention on Human Rights to
  Abolish the Death Penalty (OAS) 358
Protocols Additional to the Geneva Conventions of 12 August 1949,
  and relating to the Protection of Victims of International
  Armed Conflicts (Protocol I) and Victims of Non-international
  Armed Conflicts (Protocol II) (ICRC) 358
Protocols to the European Convention for the Protection of Human
  Rights and Fundamental Freedoms (Council of Europe) 360
Racism 361
Recommendation concerning Education for International
  Understanding, Co-operation and Peace and Education relating
  to Human Rights and Fundamental Freedoms (UNESCO) 362
Recommendation concerning the Status of Higher-Education Teaching
  Personnel (UNESCO) 363
Recommendation concerning the Status of Teachers (UNESCO/ILO) 364
Recommendation concerning the Status of the Artist (UNESCO) 365
Recommendation No. R(92)6 on a Coherent Policy for People
  with Disabilities (Council of Europe) 366

Recommendation on Consent to Marriage, Minimum Age for
  Marriage and Registration of Marriages (UN) 367
Recommendation on Participation by the People at Large in Cultural
  Life and Their Contribution to It (UNESCO) 367
Recommendation on the Development of Adult Education
  (UNESCO) 368
Recommendation on the Status of Scientific Researchers
  (UNESCO) 369
Regional Conferences on Human Rights Education
  (UNESCO) 370
Reports of States as a means of evaluation and control for the
  implementation of human rights standards 371
Right of parents to choose education for their children 372
Right of self-determination 373
Rights of refugees 375
Right to adequate food 376
Right to adequate housing 377
Right to a fair and public hearing 379
Right to a fair trial 379
Right to a healthy environment 380
Right to a just social and international order 382
Right to an adequate standard of living 383
Right to a nationality 384
Right to an effective remedy by tribunals 384
Right to appeal 385
Right to asylum 385
Right to benefit from the protection of the moral and material interests
  resulting from scientific, literary or artistic production 386
Right to be presumed innocent 387
Right to compensation 388
Right to creativity 389
Right to cultural identity 390
Right to democracy 391
Right to development 393
Right to education 394
Right to enjoy the benefits from scientific progress and
  its applications 397
Right to equal access to public service 398
Right to equal pay for equal work 398
Right to equal protection of the law without discrimination 399
Right to form and join trade unions 400
Right to free choice of employment 400
Right to health and medical services 401
Right to highest attainable standard of physical and mental health 402
Right to just and favourable conditions of work 404

Right to just and favourable remuneration 405
Right to leave any country, including one's own, and to return
 to one's own country 405
Right to liberty and security of person 406
Right to life 407
Right to marry and to found a family 409
Right to own property 410
Right to peace 411
Right to recognition as a person before the law 411
Right to rest and leisure 412
Right to security in the event of unemployment or other lack
 of livelihood 413
Right to social security 413
Right to strike 414
Right to take part in cultural life 415
Right to take part in the government 416
Right to the protection of the law against interference and attacks
 on privacy 416
Right to vote and to be elected 417
Right to work 418
Riyadh Guidelines (UN) 418
Rome Statute of the International Criminal Court – ICC (UN) 419
Safeguards Guaranteeing Protection of the Rights of Those Facing
 the Death Penalty (UN) 421
Second Optional Protocol to the International Covenant on Civil
 and Political Rights, Aiming at the Abolition of the Death Penalty
 (UN) 421
Security Council (UN) 422
Slave Route Project (UNESCO) 423
Slavery 424
Slavery Convention (League of Nations) 426
Social rights 427
Special Rapporteurs (UN) 428
Standard Minimum Rules for the Treatment of Prisoners (UN) 429
Standard Rules on the Equalization of Opportunities for Persons
 with Disabilities (UN) 430
Sub-Commission on Prevention of Discrimination and Protection
 of Minorities (UN) 431
Sub-Commission on the Promotion and Protection of Human Rights
 (UN) 431
Supervisory procedures of the International Labour Organisation
 (ILO) 432
Supplementary Convention on the Abolition of Slavery, the Slave
 Trade and Institutions and Practices Similar to Slavery (UN) 433
Terrorism 435

Tokyo Rules (UN) 438
Transnational corporations and human rights 438
Treaty of Amsterdam (EU) 440
UNESCO 441
UNESCO Chairs in Human Rights, Democracy, Peace and Tolerance 441
UNESCO/Madanjeet Singh Prize for the Promotion of Tolerance
and Non-Violence 443
UNESCO Prize for Human Rights Education 444
UNICEF 445
United Nations – UN 445
United Nations Centre for Human Rights – UNCHR 447
United Nations Centre for Human Settlements – Habitat 447
United Nations Charter 449
United Nations Children's Fund – UNICEF 449
United Nations Congresses on the Prevention of Crime and Treatment
of Offenders 450
United Nations Convention against Transnational Organized Crime 452
United Nations Crime Prevention Programme 453
United Nations Day – 24 October 454
United Nations Day for Women's Rights and International Peace 455
United Nations Decade against Drug Abuse – 1991-2000 455
United Nations Decade for Human Rights Education – 1995-2004 455
United Nations Decade for the Eradication of Poverty – 1997-2006 457
United Nations Decade for Women: Equality, Development and
Peace – 1976-1985 458
United Nations Decade of Disabled Persons – 1983-1992 459
United Nations Development Fund for Women – UNIFEM 460
United Nations Development Programme – UNDP 461
United Nations Division for the Advancement of Women – UNDAW 462
United Nations Educational, Scientific and Cultural Organization
– UNESCO 463
United Nations Environmental Programme – UNEP 464
United Nations General Assembly 465
United Nations Guidelines for the Prevention of Juvenile Delinquency
– Riyadh Guidelines (UN) 467
United Nations High Commissioner for Human Rights 467
United Nations High Commissioner for Refugees – UNHCR 468
United Nations International Conference on Human Rights 469
United Nations Literacy Decade – 2003-2012 470
United Nations Millennium Declaration 471
United Nations Population Fund – UNFPA 473
United Nations Principles for Older Persons 474
United Nations Principles relating to the Status and Functioning
of National Institutions for the Promotion and Protection
of Human Rights 475

United Nations Prize in the Field of Human Rights 475
United Nations Rules for the Protection of Juveniles Deprived
  of Their Liberty 476
United Nations Secretary-General 477
United Nations Specialized Agencies 478
United Nations Special Session on Children (UN) 478
United Nations Standard Minimum Rules for Non-Custodial
  Measures – Tokyo Rules 480
United Nations Standard Minimum Rules for the Administration
  of Juvenile Justice – Beijing Rules 481
United Nations System 482
United Nations Year of Dialogue among Civilizations – 2001 482
Universal Children's Day – 20 November (UN) 484
Universal Copyright Convention (1952) and the Universal Copyright
  Convention as revised in 1971 (UNESCO) 484
Universal Declaration of Human Rights (UN) 485
Universal Declaration on Cultural Diversity (UNESCO) 487
Universal Declaration on Democracy (IPU) 488
Universal Declaration on the Eradication of Hunger and Malnutrition
  (UN) 489
Universal Declaration on the Human Genome and Human Rights
  (UNESCO) 490
Universal Forum of Cultures 491
Vienna Declaration and Programme of Action (UN) 493
Vienna Declaration on Crime and Justice (UN) 494
Vienna International Plan of Action on Ageing (UN) 495
Vulnerable Groups 495
Week of Solidarity with the Peoples of Non-self-governing Territories
  – beginning 25 May (UN) 497
Week of Solidarity with the Peoples Struggling against Racism
  and Racial Discrimination – beginning 21 March (UN) 497
World AIDS Day – 1 December (WHO) 497
World Assembly on Ageing (UN) 498
World Conference against Racism, Racial Discrimination,
  Xenophobia and Related Intolerance – WCAR (UN) 498
World Conference of the International Women's Year (UN) 500
World Conference on Human Rights (UN) 500
World Conferences on Women (UN) 501
World Day for Water – 22 March (UN) 503
World Declaration on the Survival, Protection, and Development
  of Children (UN) 503
World Education Forum (UNESCO) 504
World Food Day – 16 October (FAO) 505
World Food Summit (FAO) 505
World Habitat Day – 1st Monday of October (UN) 506

World Health Day – 7 April (WHO) 507
World Health Organization – WHO 507
World Heritage Committee (UNESCO) 508
World Heritage List and List of World Heritage in Danger (UNESCO) ... 509
World Intellectual Property Organization – WIPO (UN) 509
World Mental Health Day – 10 October (WHO) 511
World Plan of Action for the Implementation of the Objectives of
  the International Women's Year (UN) 511
World Plan of Action on Education for Human Rights and Democracy
  (UNESCO/UN) 512
World Population Day – 11 July (UN) 513
World Press Freedom Day – 3 May (UNESCO) 514
World Press Freedom Prize (UNESCO) 514
World Programme of Action concerning Disabled Persons (UN) 515
World Public Information Campaign for Human Rights (UN) 516
World Refugee Day – 20 June (UN) 516
World Social Forum 517
World Summit for Children (UN) 518
World Summit for Social Development (UN) 519
World Summit on Sustainable Development - WSSD 520
World Teachers' Day – 5 October (UNESCO) 521
Youth 523

Annexes

I Universal Declaration of Human Rights 527
II International Covenant on Economic, Social and Cultural Rights ... 535
III International Covenant on Civil and Political Rights 551
IV Vienna Declaration and Programme of Action 577
V List of selected human rights web-sites 621
VI List of abbreviations used in this publication 625

Academic freedom

Academic freedom can be defined as the freedom of researchers, teachers and students to teach, study, and pursue knowledge and research without unreasonable interference or restriction from law, institutional regulations, or public pressure. Academic freedom is closely related to the **right to education** stipulated in Article 26 of the **Universal Declaration of Human Rights** and in Article 13 of the **International Covenant on Economic, Social and Cultural Rights**. It is also closely linked to **freedom of opinion and expression**, **freedom of scientific research** and **freedom to seek, receive and impart information**. The justification for academic freedom lies in its benefits to society, which means that the interests of a society are best served when the educational process leads to the advancement of knowledge and the latter is best advanced without any restraints on inquiry.

UNESCO has contributed to the promotion of academic freedom. This question was dealt with at the **International Congress on Education for Human Rights and Democracy** (Montreal, Canada, 8-11 March 1993). The **Recommendation concerning the Status of Higher-Education Teaching Personnel** adopted by the UNESCO General Conference in 1997 at its 29th session was the first intergovernmental instrument presenting academic freedom in a developed form.

Academic freedom is composed of the following rights: the right to become, on the basis of ability and competence without **discrimination** of any kind, a member of the academic community; the right of members of the academic community with research functions to freely determine the subject and methods of research; the right of members of the academic community with teaching functions to fully determine the content and methods of research; the right of students to study, to choose their field of study, to participate in the organization of the educational process and to receive official recognition of the knowledge and experience acquired; the right of all members of the academic community to seek, receive, obtain and impart information and ideas of all kinds and in all forms; and the right of all members of the academic community to cooperate freely with their counterparts in any part of the world. In the case of restrictions, special facilities and protection shall be granted to members of the academic community carrying out research functions.

Additional Protocol to the American Convention on Human Rights in the Area of Economic, Social and Cultural Rights – "Protocol of San Salvador" (OAS)

The Additional Protocol was adopted by the **Organization of American States** on 17 November 1988. It entered into force on 16 November 1999 and had been ratified by 12 States by the middle of 2003. The Protocol was approved in the spirit that "in accordance with the **Universal Declaration of Human Rights** and the **American Convention on Human Rights**, the ideal of free human beings enjoying freedom from fear and want can only be achieved if conditions are created whereby everyone may enjoy his **economic**, **social** and **cultural rights** as well as his **civil** and **political rights**". Therefore, the instrument deals with the **right to work** (Article 6), just, equitable and satisfactory conditions of work (Article 7), trade union rights (Article 8), and the **right to strike** (Article 8). Furthermore, the Protocol includes the **right to social security** (Article 9), the **right to health** (Article 10), the **right to a healthy environment** (Article 11), the **right to adequate food** (Article 12), as well as the **right to education** (Article 13). In its Article 14, the Protocol proclaims the rights to the benefits of culture, and in its Article 15 the right to the formation and the protection of families. Further on, the instrument stipulates the rights and the protection of the child (Article 16), of the aged (Article 17) and of disabled persons (Article 18).

A second additional protocol to the Convention, the **Protocol to the American Convention on Human Rights to Abolish the Death Penalty**, was adopted in 1990.

African Charter on Human and Peoples' Rights (OAU/AU)

Adopted on 26 June 1981 by the **Organization of African Unity (OAU)**, the African Charter on Human and Peoples' Rights entered into force on 21 October 1986. By the middle of 2003, it had been ratified by 52 States. The instrument is based on both the **Universal Declaration of Human Rights** and on the Charter of the OAU, which stipulates that "freedom, equality, justice and dignity are essential objectives for the achievement of the legitimate aspirations of the African Peoples". Its aims are to protect and promote fundamental human and peoples' rights and freedoms. In particular, the Charter affirms that all peoples are equal, and that they have the right to self-determination, the right to dispose freely of their wealth and natural resources, the right to economic, social and cultural development, the right to national and international peace and security and the right to a general satisfactory environment favourable to their development (Articles 19-24). The African Charter is the first international human rights convention which guarantees in a single instrument the **civil, political, economic**, **social** and **cultural rights** of individuals as well as peoples' rights. Although the Charter offers no definition, "peoples' rights" has been interpreted as the collective rights of people as a group. A separate chapter is dedicated to the duties of every individual towards his family and society, the State and the international community. The Charter obliges States Parties to promote teaching and education in human rights and to ensure that the content of the Charter is understood (Article 25). It also provides for the establishment of an **African Commission on Human and Peoples' Rights** to monitor and ensure the promotion of human rights in Africa.

In 1998, the OAU adopted a **Protocol to the African Charter on Human and Peoples' Rights on the Establishment of an African Court on Human and Peoples' Rights** which had not entered into force by the middle of 2003.

African Charter on the Rights and Welfare of the Child (OAU/AU)

In recognition of the concern of Member States regarding the critical situation of most African children and the fact that children require particular care with regard to health, physical, moral and mental development and legal protection (Preamble), the **Organization of African Unity**, in July 1990, adopted the African Charter on the Rights and Welfare of the Child. It entered into force on 29 November 1999 and, by the middle of 2003, it had been ratified by 22 Member States. The aim of the Charter, which defines "child" as "every human being below the age of 18 years" (Article 2), is to provide protection for the rights of the child in all spheres of life. It stipulates that in all actions concerning the child undertaken by any person or authority the best interests of the child shall be the primary consideration (Article 4). To this end, the Charter imposes on the Member States the duty to ensure the survival, protection and development of the child, and to ensure the enjoyment of rights concerning, *inter alia,* the acquisition of name and nationality, **freedom of association**, thought, conscience and belief, privacy, and education and leisure. The States Parties also have the obligation to prohibit child labour and child abuse and to protect the special rights of handicapped and refugee children. The essential role of the family is also recognized in the Charter. Article 18 underlines that the family "shall enjoy the protection and support of the State for its establishment and development". The instrument furthermore provides for the establishment of an

African Committee on the Rights and Welfare of the Child (Article 32). This Committee shall be entrusted with the promotion and protection of the rights guaranteed under the Charter, in particular, by cooperating with other African, international and regional institutions and organizations and by monitoring the implementation of the Charter and ensuring the protection of the rights enshrined therein (Article 42).

African Commission on Human and Peoples' Rights (OAU/AU)

The African Commission on Human and Peoples' Rights was established in 1987 following the entry into force of the **African Charter on Human and Peoples' Rights**. Its objective is to promote and protect human and peoples' rights. To this end, the Commission carries out studies and research, formulates and lays down principles and rules upon which African governments may base their legislation, considers the measures undertaken by States Parties in implementing the Charter, interprets the provisions of the Charter and promotes cooperation with other African and international institutions working in the same field. The Commission is composed of eleven members chosen "from among African personalities of the highest reputation" (Article 31) and with recognized competence in the domain of human and peoples' rights. Members, of which no two can be of the same nationality, are elected by the Assembly of Heads of State and Government for a six-year period and serve in their personal capacity. The Commission meets twice a year and is serviced in its daily work by the Secretariat situated in Banjul, Gambia. Its activity also consists of the examination of any violation of rights guaranteed by the African Charter which is brought to its attention by means of communications from States Parties, individuals or **non-governmental organizations**, provided all local remedies have been exhausted. In response to such a communication and after carrying out all appropriate investigations and requesting from States Parties relevant information, a report, stating the facts, its findings and recommendations, is forwarded to the Assembly of Heads of State and Government, which decides on the appropriate action. If, after deliberation on a communication, the Commission suspects gross and massive violations of human rights, it draws the matter to the attention of the Assembly of Heads of State and Government, which can request the Commission to undertake in-depth investigation, followed by a report containing appropriate recommendations (Article 58). The Commission has no legal enforcement procedure and therefore the compliance with the provisions of the Charter depends on the will of the Member States.

For more information see: http://www.achpr.org

African Court on Human and Peoples' Rights (AU/OAU)

The **Protocol to the African Charter on Human and Peoples' Rights on the Establishment of an African Court on Human and Peoples' Rights** was adopted on 9 June 1998 at the Summit of Heads of State and Government in Ouagadougou, Burkina Faso. The Court has jurisdiction over cases concerning the interpretation and implementation of the provisions of the Charter and "any other relevant human rights instrument ratified by the States concerned" (Article 3). In accordance with Article 5 of the Protocol, cases shall be referred to the Court by the **African Commission on Human Rights**, by Member States and by African intergovernmental organizations. The Court may receive communications from **non-governmental organizations** with observer status and individuals only in regard of those States which have clearly recognized the competence of the Court to receive such recommendations. Article 14 stipulates that the Court is to be composed of eleven judges elected by the Assembly of Heads of State and Government of the **African Union/Organization of African Unity (AU/OAU)**. The Assembly shall ensure representation of the main regions in

Africa as well as adequate gender representation. The judges are elected for a term of 6 years and may be re-elected only once.

Upon receiving a case, the Court shall hear submissions by all parties and, if deemed necessary, hold an inquiry. The submissions may include written or oral evidence including expert testimony and the Court shall make its decision on the basis of such evidence (Article 26). If the Court finds that there has been a violation of human or peoples' rights, "it shall make appropriate orders to remedy the violation, including the payment of fair compensation or reparation" (Article 27). Pursuant to Article 28, the judgment of the Court must be rendered within 90 days after the completion of deliberation and is not subject to appeal. The Court is required to submit a report on its work during the previous year to each regular session of the Assembly. The report shall specify, in particular, the cases where a State has not complied with the Court's judgement. According to Article 2 and Article 8 the Court shall complement the protective mandate of the **African Commission on Human and Peoples' Rights**.

The Protocol establishing the Court enters into force after being ratified by 15 States. By the middle of 2003, it had not yet entered into force.

African Union – AU

Within the process of further regional integration, the African Economic Community (AEC) was established with the entry into force of the Abuja Treaty in May 1994. The decision to create the African Union (AU) to effectively replace the **Organization of African Unity (OAU)** was adopted at the OAU/AEC Summit (Sirte, Libya, September 1999). The Sirte Declaration, which outlines measures for addressing the new social, political and economic realities in Africa and in the world, aims at promoting a greater unity in conformity with the objectives of the OAU Charter and the Treaty Establishing the AEC, as well as at eliminating of conflicts and improving of living conditions.

The Constitutive Act of the AU entered into force on 26 May 2001, after being ratified by 36 OAU Member States.

The main objectives of the AU are the consolidation of unity and solidarity of African States, and the promotion and protection of human and peoples' rights in accordance with the **African Charter on Human and Peoples' Rights** and the **Universal Declaration of Human Rights**. Furthermore, the AU seeks to promote democracy, popular participation and good governance. It is entitled to encourage the cooperation of African **non-governmental organizations**, civil society, labour unions and business organizations with a view to promoting economic integration, social development and political unity.

The supreme organ of the AU is the Assembly, composed of Heads of State and Government. The Assembly is responsible for determining the common policies of the Union and meets at least once a year in ordinary sessions. The Executive Council, meeting at least twice a year in ordinary sessions, is composed of the Ministers of Foreign Affairs or other officials designated by the Governments of Member States. It coordinates policies in fields of common interest such as foreign trade, energy, industry, agriculture, water resources, environmental protection, humanitarian action and disaster relief, education, culture, health, social security, science and technology as well as nationality, and residence and immigration matters. The AU Constitutive Act also establishes the Pan-African Parliament to ensure "the full participation of African people in the development and economic integration of the continent" (Article 17), the Court of Justice of the Union (Article 18), as well as various financial institutions, including the African Central Bank, the African Monetary Fund and the African Investment Bank. The Economic, Social and Cultural Council to be created under Article 22 is an advisory organ composed of different social and professional groups of the Member States of the Union. Its functions, powers, composition and organization shall be determined by the Assembly.

American Bill of Rights

See **Bill of Rights – United States of America – 1791**.

American Convention on Human Rights – "Pact of San José" (OAS)

The American Convention on Human Rights was adopted by the **Organization of American States (OAS)** on 22 November 1969 and entered into force on 18 July 1978. By the middle of 2003, it had been ratified by 25 Member States. The Convention aims at the protection of human rights in the western hemisphere. Its purpose is: "to consolidate in this hemisphere, within the framework of democratic institutions, a system of personal liberty and social justice based on respect for the essential rights of man" (Preamble). States Parties to this Convention "undertake to respect the rights and freedoms recognized herein and to ensure to all persons subject to their jurisdiction the free and full exercise of those rights and freedoms, without any discrimination" (Article 1). The Convention defines the rights and freedoms to be protected. Among the **civil** and **political rights** are the **right to life**, right to humane treatment, freedom from slavery, right to personal liberty, right to equality before the law, right to participate in government, freedom of conscience, religion and belief, and **freedom of association**. With regard to **social**, **economic** and **cultural rights**, States Parties pledge to adopt measures to achieve, progressively, "the full realization of the rights implicit in the economic, social, educational, scientific, and cultural standards set forth in the Charter of the Organization of American States" (Article 26). Part II of the instrument establishes the means to ensure that the commitments made by the Contracting Parties are fulfilled, namely through the creation of the **Inter-American Commission on Human Rights** and the **Inter-American Court of Human Rights**.

Since its inception, the Convention has been supplemented by two protocols. The first was the **Additional Protocol to the American Convention on Human Rights in the Area of**

Economic, Social and Cultural Rights "**Protocol of San Salvador**", adopted on 17 November 1988. The second additional protocol was the **Protocol to the American Convention on Human Rights to Abolish the Death Penalty**, adopted in 1990.

American Declaration on the Rights and Duties of Man (OAS)

The American Declaration on the Rights and Duties of Man was adopted by the **Organization of American States (OAS)** on 2 May 1948. It still serves as a main source of reference especially for those States which are not Parties to the **American Convention on Human Rights** (1969) but which are signatories to the Charter of the OAS. While it has the virtue of being the first international instrument of its type adopted at this level, it was not approved as a convention as had been hoped. Nonetheless, the Declaration proclaims the will of the American States to protect and promote the essential rights of the individual. The American States recognize that States do not create or concede rights but rather recognize rights that existed prior to the formation of the State, rights that have their origins in the very nature of the individual. The Declaration comprises a Preamble and 38 articles defining the rights protected and the correlative duties. Chapter One contains 28 articles on basic rights including the **right to life**, liberty and personal security, the right to equality before the law, the right to religious freedom and worship, the **right to education**, the **right to work** and to fair remuneration, the **right to social security** and the right of assembly. Chapter Two elaborates in its 10 articles the individual's duties towards society and other persons, including the duty to vote, duty to obey the law, duty to serve the community and the nation and duty to pay taxes. Compliance with the Declaration is monitored by the **Inter-American Commission on Human Rights** which reports to the General Assembly of the OAS on the state of progress in the realization of the goals set forth. The Commission also has the function of advising States Parties on any questions regarding the interpretation and application of the Declaration. In its advisory opinion the **Inter-American Court of Human Rights** states that the American Declaration is a source of international obligations for the Member States of the OAS.

Amnesty International – AI

Amnesty International (AI) is one of the most influential and most famous of numerous **non-governmental organizations** striving to promote and protect the human rights enshrined in the **Universal Declaration of Human Rights** and other international standard-setting instruments. In particular, it campaigns: to free all prisoners of conscience; to ensure fair and prompt trials for political prisoners; to abolish the death penalty, torture and other cruel treatment of prisoners; to end political killings, forced "disappearances" and human rights abuses by governments and opposition groups. AI is also active in human rights research and education. It is impartial and independent of any government, political persuasion or religious creed and is financed largely by subscriptions and donations from its worldwide membership.

AI was launched in 1961 by British lawyer Peter Benenson. His newspaper appeal, "The Forgotten Prisoners", was published worldwide on 28 May 1961 and brought in more than 1,000 offers of support for the idea of an international campaign to protect human rights. Within 12 months the new organization had sent delegations to four countries to make representations on behalf of prisoners, and had taken up 210 cases. The emphasis was placed on the international protection of human rights of individuals.

Today, AI has more than one million members, subscribers and regular donors in more than 140 countries and territories. There are more than 7,800 local, youth, specialist and professional groups in more than 100 countries and territories. There are nationally organized sections in 56 countries, 34 of them in Latin America and the Caribbean, Africa, Asia and the Middle

East and Central Europe. The International Secretariat, headed by the Secretary-General, is in London. It comprises more than 350 permanent posts as well as 100 volunteers from more than 50 countries.

In 1977, AI was awarded the Nobel Peace Prize for its tireless activities in the protection of the freedom of speech, religion and belief, in the fight against torture and **discrimination** and for the release of political prisoners. In 1978, on the occasion of the 30th anniversary of the **Universal Declaration of Human Rights**, it received the **United Nations Prize in the Field of Human Rights** for "outstanding achievements in the field of human rights".

For more information see: http://www.amnesty.org

Apartheid

As determined in the **International Convention on the Suppression and Punishment of the Crime of Apartheid**, the term "the crime of apartheid… shall include similar policies and practices of racial segregation and **discrimination** as practised in southern Africa and shall apply to the following inhuman acts committed for the purpose of establishing and maintaining domination by one racial group of persons over any other racial group of persons and systematically oppressing them: (a) Denial to a member or members of a racial group or groups of the **right to life** and **liberty of person**: (i) By murder of members of a racial group or groups; (ii) By the infliction upon the members of a racial group or groups of serious bodily or mental harm, by the infringement of their freedom or dignity, or by subjecting them to torture or to cruel, inhuman or degrading treatment or punishment; (iii) By arbitrary arrest and illegal imprisonment of the members of a racial group or groups; (b) Deliberate imposition on a racial group or groups of living conditions calculated to cause its or their physical destruction in whole or in part; (c) Any legislative measures and other measures calculated to prevent a racial group or groups from participation in the political, social, economic and cultural life of the country and the deliberate creation of conditions preventing the full development of such a group or groups, in particular by denying to members of a racial group or groups basic human rights and freedoms, including the **right to work**, the **right to form** recognized **trade unions**, the **right to education**, the **right to leave and to return to their country**, the **right to a nationality**, the right to freedom of movement and residence, the right to **freedom of opinion and expression**, and the right to **freedom of peaceful assembly** and association; (d) Any measures including legislative measures, designed to divide the population along racial lines by the creation of separate reserves and ghettos for the members of a racial group or groups, the prohibition of mixed marriages among members of various racial groups, the expropriation of landed property belonging to a racial group or groups or to members thereof; (e) Exploitation of the labour of the members of a racial group or groups, in particular by submitting them to forced labour; (f) Persecution of organizations and persons, by depriving them of fundamental rights and freedoms, because they oppose apartheid." (Article 2)

The system of apartheid, with its institutionalized separation of races as a particular form of **racism** and racial discrimination, existed for almost fifty years in South Africa. The **United Nations General Assembly** had condemned South Africa's racial policies since 1948, when apartheid laws were enacted and racial discrimination was institutionalized, and in 1962 called on Member States to apply economic sancions against South Africa and to break off diplomatic relations. The **United Nations specialized agencies**, in particular **UNESCO**, contributed greatly to the dismantling of the regime of apartheid in South Africa. The **Vienna Declaration and Programme of Action** welcomed the progress made in dismantling apartheid and called upon the international community and the **United Nations system** to assist in this process (Part I, Article 16). In 1994 the first multi-party election based on universal suffrage took place, resulting in the establishment of an interim Government of National Unity headed by Nelson Mandela. Since the abolition of the system of apartheid in South Africa, the United Nations and its specialized agencies, UNESCO among them, implemented activities to assist in the construction of a democratic, non-racial, apartheid-free society in South Africa. On 10 December 1985 the United Nations General Assembly adopted the **International Convention against Apartheid in Sports**. In accordance with the **Rome Statute of the International Criminal Court** the Court has jurisdiction over the crime of apartheid as a crime against humanity (Article 7 (j)).

Arab Charter on Human Rights (League of Arab States)

The Arab Charter on Human Rights was adopted on 15 September 1994 by the Council of the League of Arab States (at the time of its adoption, the League comprised 22 Members: Algeria, Bahrain, Comoros, Djibouti, Egypt, Iraq, Jordan, Kuwait, Lebanon, Libyan Arab Jamahiriya, Mauritania, Morocco, Oman, Palestine, Qatar, Saudi Arabia, Somalia, Sudan, Syrian Arab Republic, Tunisia, United Arab Emirates and Yemen). It reaffirms the principles of the **Charter of the United Nations** and the **Universal Declaration of Human Rights**, the provisions of the **International Covenant on Civil and Political Rights** and of the **International Covenant on Economic, Social and Cultural Rights**, as well as those of the **Cairo Declaration on Human Rights in Islam**. It contains 43 articles enumerating **civil** and **political** as well as certain **economic**, **social** and **cultural rights**. The Charter envisages the creation of a Committee of Experts on Human Rights, composed of seven members nominated by the States Parties to the Charter. The Committee is entitled to consider reports by States Parties. The Charter should enter into force two months after the deposit of the seventh instrument of ratification or accession. By the middle of 2003, there was no information about its entry into force.

Arab League Educational, Cultural and Scientific Organization – ALECSO

ALECSO was established on 25 July 1970 by the League of Arab States. Its primary responsibility is the promotion of educational, cultural and scientific activities in the Arab world. It encourages the development of Arab economic and social sciences and their application to daily issues and contributes to the establishment of an international culture which focuses on the basic human values. It plays an important role in preserving, restoring and safeguarding the Arabic-Islamic heritage in the fields of manuscripts, antiquities and historical sites.

Asian and Pacific Decade of Disabled Persons – 1993-2002 (UN)

The Asian and Pacific Decade of Disabled Persons was proclaimed on 23 April 1992 by the Economic and Social Commission for Asia and the Pacific (ESCAP), and endorsed by the **United Nations General Assembly** on 16 December 1992. The Decade provided an opportunity for the 56 countries and areas of the ESCAP region to consolidate the efforts initiated during the preceding **United Nations Decade of Disabled Persons (1983-92)** through effective new policy initiatives and actions at the national, sub-regional and regional levels. In particular, it provided a context for the strengthening of technical cooperation among developing countries, as well as between the region's developing and developed countries, in the resolution of key issues that affect the lives of people with disabilities, especially in the fields of rehabilitation, education and employment. To achieve the objectives of the Decade, an Agenda for Action for the Asian and Pacific region was elaborated on the basis of the **World Programme of Action concerning Disabled Persons**. The Agenda for Action provided a framework consisting of the major policy categories under which efforts were made for the implementation of the Decade. These basic categories included: national coordination; legislation; information; public awareness; accessibility and communication; education; training and employment; prevention of causes of disability; rehabilitation services; assistive devices; and self-help organizations. To monitor and review the implementation of the Agenda for Action and to advise on means of attaining the aims and objectives of the Decade, the Executive Secretary of ESCAP was called upon to submit biennial reports to the Commission throughout the Decade. In May 2002, ESCAP put forward an initiative to proclaim a second Decade.

Basic Principles and Guidelines on the Right to a Remedy and Reparation for Victims of Violations of International Human Rights and Humanitarian Law (UN)

These Principles were adopted by the **Commission on Human Rights** at its 56th session by its resolution 2000/41. Paragraph 2 of the resolution invites the **United Nations Secretary-General** to circulate to all Member States the text of the Basic Principles requesting they send their comments to the **Office of the United Nations High Commissioner for Human Rights (OHCHR)**.

Parts I and II of the Basic Principles concern the obligation, and its scope, to respect, ensure respect for and enforce international human rights and humanitarian law. Part III is devoted to violations of internationally recognized human rights and norms of humanitarian law that constitute crimes under international law. Part V defines the victims of such violations. Part VI concerns the treatment of victims, Part VII to XI their right to a remedy, which includes their right to access to justice, to reparation and to access to information. Concluding Part XII affirms the principle of non-discrimination in the treatment of the victims of violations of international human rights and humanitarian law.

Basic Principles for the Treatment of Prisoners (UN)

Adopted on 14 December 1990 by the **United Nations General Assembly** (resolution 45/111), on the recommendation of the Eighth **United Nations Congress on the Prevention of Crime and the Treatment of Offenders** (Havana, Cuba,

27 August – 7 September 1990), the Basic Principles for the Treatment of Prisoners is one of a number of instruments that sets important guidelines for States in the treatment of prisoners. While not binding, the eleven-point Basic Principles confirm fundamental prisoners' rights by stipulating, *inter alia*, that except for "those limitations that are demonstrably necessitated by the fact of incarceration", all prisoners should be afforded the human rights and fundamental freedoms set out in the universally recognized international instruments (Principle 5). In other words, all prisoners should be treated with due respect for their inherent dignity and value as human beings (Principle 1) and without **discrimination** of any kind (Principle 2). In particular, the Basic Principles provide that "all prisoners shall have the right to take part in cultural activities and education" (Principle 6), that efforts to abolish solitary confinement should be encouraged (Principle 7), and that prisoners shall have access to health services (Principle 9). By declaring these rights, the Basic Principles for the Treatment of Prisoners complements the provisions of the **Standard Minimum Rules for the Treatment of Prisoners** (1955) and the **Body of Principles for the Protection of All Persons under Any Form of Detention or Imprisonment** (1988).

Basic Principles for the Use of Force and Firearms by Law Enforcement Officials (UN)

The Basic Principles for the Use of Force and Firearms were prepared by the Eighth **United Nations Congress on the Prevention of Crime and the Treatment of Offenders** (Havana, Cuba, 27 August – 7 September 1990). In the Basic Principles, as in the **Code of Conduct for Law Enforcement Officials**, the term "law enforcement officials" includes all officers of the law, whether elected or appointed, who exercise police powers, especially the powers of arrest or detention. The twenty-six Principles include: General Provisions; Special Provisions; Policing Unlawful Assemblies; Policing Persons in Custody or Detention; Qualifications, Training and Counselling; and Reporting and Review Procedures. According to Principle 4, "law enforcement officials, in carrying out their duty, shall, as far as possible, apply non-violent means before resorting to the use of force and firearms". In the case of ineffectiveness, they may resort to violent means but only proportionately to the seriousness of the offence and under several other conditions, which include respecting and preserving human life (Principle 5). With regard to the Special Provisions, rules and regulations on the use of firearms should include guidelines enumerated in Principle 11. In their relations with persons in custody or detention, law enforcement officials shall neither use force nor firearms other than in exceptional cases (Principles 15 and 16). Furthermore, pursuant to Principle 18, it must be ensured that law enforcement officials receive "continuous and thorough professional training" and are "tested in accordance with appropriate proficiency standards in the use of force" (Principle 19), giving special attention to issues of ethics and human rights (Principle 20). Finally, effective reporting and review procedures must be established in favour of persons affected by the use of force and firearms.

Basic Principles on the Independence of the Judiciary (UN)

The Basic Principles on the Independence of the Judiciary were adopted by the Seventh **United Nations Congress on the Prevention of Crime and the Treatment of Offenders** (Milan, Italy, 26 August – 6 September 1985). They were later that year endorsed by the **United Nations General Assembly** (A/RES/40/146) of 13 December 1985. They are based upon draft guidelines elaborated by the **Committee on Crime Prevention and Control**, which the **United Nations Economic and Social Council (ECOSOC)** had submitted to the above-mentioned Congress. This Congress decided that an abbreviated version of the guidelines, containing basic principles, would be more appropriate because of the different judicial systems of the Member States. These Principles should be "taken into account and respected by Governments within the framework of their national legislation and practice and be brought to the attention of judges, lawyers, members of the executive and the legislature and the public in general" (Preamble). They provide for the independence of the judiciary; the freedom of expression and association; qualifications, selection and training; conditions of service and tenure; discipline, suspension and removal; and professional secrecy and immunity. In particular, "the independence of the judiciary shall be guaranteed by the State and enshrined in the constitution or the law of the country" (para. 1). Furthermore, "In accordance with the **Universal Declaration of Human Rights**, members of the judiciary are like other citizens entitled to freedom of expression, belief, association and assembly; ..." (para. 8) and "persons selected for judicial office shall be individuals of integrity and ability with appropriate training or qualifications in law" (para. 10). Finally, the conditions of service and tenure "... shall be adequately secured by law" (para. 11) and, regarding discipline, suspension and removal, proceedings shall be enforced "... in accordance with established standards of judicial conduct" (para. 19).

Basic Principles on the Role of Lawyers (UN)

The Eighth **United Nations Congress on the Prevention of Crime and the Treatment of Offenders** (Havana, Cuba, 27 August – 7 September 1990), adopted the Basic Principles on the Role of Lawyers. They have been formulated to assist Member States in their task of promoting and ensuring the proper role of lawyers, and are subdivided into the following: Access to Lawyers and Legal Services (Principles 1 to 4); Special Safeguards in Criminal Justice Matters (Principles 5 to 8); Qualifications and Training (Principles 9 to 11); Duties and Responsibilities (Principles 12 to 15); Guarantees for the Functioning of Lawyers (Principles 16 to 22); Freedom of Expression and Association (Principle 23); Professional Associations of Lawyers (Principles 24 and 25); and Disciplinary Proceedings (Principles 26 to 29). Governments shall ensure the appropriate requirements for effective legal services and the equal access to them.

Beijing Declaration and Platform for Action (UN)

The Beijing Declaration and Platform for Action were adopted by the Fourth **World Conference[s] on Women** (Beijing, China, 4 – 15 September 1995). The participating governments recognized that, while the status of women had improved in the previous decade, progress had been uneven and inequalities persisted. They reaffirmed their commitment to achieve gender equality. The Platform for Action is "an agenda for women's empowerment" (para. 1), which aims at eliminating obstacles to the active and equal participation of women in the decision-making process in the economic, social, cultural and political spheres and to strengthening the implementation of the Nairobi Forward-Looking Strategies for the Advancement of Women adopted at the Third World Conference on Women in 1985. The Platform for Action, underlining the importance of the **Convention on the Elimination of All Forms of Discrimination against Women**, should be carried out at national, regional and international levels. Its strategic objectives for the elimination of **discrimination** against women include: access to education; equal development; measures to prevent and eliminate violence and all forms of traffic to which women are subject; advancement of women's **economic rights**; elimination of job discrimination; access to and full participation in all levels of decision-making; *de jure* and *de facto* equality and non-discrimination; full implementation of all human rights instruments; and the implementation of the Convention. The Platform places emphasis on the elimination of discrimination against girls and makes explicit linkages between the empowerment of women, equality and human rights of women.

The Beijing Declaration and the Platform for Action were endorsed by the **United Nations General Assembly** in December 1995 (A/RES/50/203), which called upon States, the **United Nations system, non-governmental organizations** and other actors to take effective action for their implementation.

In June 2000, the General Assembly, pursuant to its resolutions 52/100 of 12 December 1997 and 52/231 of 4 June 1998, held a special session on "Women 2000: Gender Equality, Development and Peace for the Twenty-First Century". It assessed the progress achieved in implementing the Beijing Declaration and Platform for Action and the Nairobi Forward-Looking Strategies. It adopted a Political Declaration and a document entitled "Further actions and initiatives to implement the Beijing Declaration and Platform for Action" aimed at ensuring the full realization of the goals of gender equality, development and peace, *inter alia*, through mainstreaming a gender perspective into all policies and programmes and promoting full participation and empowerment of women, as well as strengthened international cooperation in the field.

Beijing Rules (UN)

Common name for the **United Nations Standard Minimum Rules for the Administration of Juvenile Justice**.

Berne Convention for the Protection of Literary and Artistic Works

The Berne Convention was adopted in 1886 to guarantee international protection of the rights of authors in their literary and artistic works. By the middle of 2003, it had been ratified by about 150 States. Both the **Paris Convention for the Protection of Industrial Property** (1883) and the Berne Convention led to the creation of an international bureau called the United International Bureaux for the Protection of Intellectual Property, best known by its French name *Bureaux internationaux réunis pour la protection de la propriété intellectuelle* (BIRPI). In 1967, the

World Intellectual Property Organization (WIPO) succeeded BIRPI.

Bill of Rights
– England, 1689

The English Bill of Rights, formally called "An Act Declaring the Rights and Liberties of the Subject and Settling the Succession of the Crown", passed by Parliament in 1689, is one of the basic instruments of the British Constitution. Resulting from the struggle between the royal power, the people and Parliament, the Act aimed at protecting the rights of Parliament by preventing the monarch from exercising "the pretended power of suspending of laws" or "the pretended power of dispensing with laws". Concerning civil liberties, the English Bill of Rights – despite its common name – did not delineate any new **civil rights** and did not even attempt to impose revolutionary ideas. Demands for individual freedoms were restricted to protecting the fairness of the judicial system. Since the Act was not an entrenched code of rights, it did not play the same role as the **American Bill of Rights**.

Bill of Rights
– United States of America, 1791

The first ten Amendments to the Constitution of the United States of America, ratified on 15 December 1791 as a single unit by all states, are also called the **American Bill of Rights**. It is aimed at guaranteeing the country's citizens their rights as well as certain protection against their violation. The American Bill of Rights covers a wide range of the most important civil liberties and individual rights as they were interpreted at the end of the 18th century and imposes limitations on federal and state governments. The First Amendment provides freedom of speech, whereas the Fourth Amendment protects against illegal search and arrest, and the Fifth Amendment guarantees the right to silence in criminal trials. The American Bill of Rights can be traced back to the **Magna Carta** (1215) and the English **Bill of Rights** (1689).

Bioethics and human rights

The bioethics reflection aims at setting out ethical and legal principles to ensure that life sciences develop in a way that is respectful of human rights and fundamental freedoms. The Nuremberg Code (1947), pioneer in contemporary bioethics law, was followed by many other instruments adopted inside and outside the **United Nations system**. These are, for example, the Recommendation Guiding Physicians in Biomedical Research Involving Human Subjects (Declaration of Helsinki) adopted in 1964 by the World Medical Association (WMA), the International Ethical Guidelines for Biomedical Research Involving Human Subjects, adopted in 1993 (revised and updated in 2002) by the Council for International Organizations of Medical Sciences (CIOMS) and the **World Health Organization (WHO)**, and the **Universal Declaration on the Human Genome and Human Rights**, the first universal instrument in the field of bioethics and human rights, adopted in 1997 by **UNESCO**. These instruments focus on the respect for human dignity, the prohibition of **discrimination** based on personal genetic data and the prohibition of the commercialization of the human body. They also protect other basic human rights such as the right to confidentiality of personal data, the **right to health and medical services**, the right not to be submitted to any intervention without the informed consent of the person concerned, the right to know or not to know the result of a medical examination, etc. A number of general human rights instruments adopted by the **United Nations** are particularly relevant in this field, e.g. the **Universal Declaration of Human Rights** (1948), the **International Covenant on Civil and Political Rights** (1966) and the **International Covenant on Economic, Social and Cultural Rights** (1966).

In 1993, UNESCO created the International Bioethics Committee (IBC). A unique body within the United Nations system, it is composed of 36 leading figures in biology, medicine, law, philosophy or sociology the world over. It is entrusted with examining crucial ethical issues raised by genetic research and its applications and, in particular, with identifying practices that could be contrary to human dignity. It is also responsible for encouraging action to heighten awareness among the general public, specialized groups and public and private decision-makers, and for advising on the follow-up of the Universal Declaration on the Human Genome and Human Rights. The IBC holds annual sessions and its reports, state-of-the-art presentations and round table debates are published in the proceedings of these sessions.

For more information see: http://www.unesco.org/ibc

Body of Principles for the Protection of All Persons under Any Form of Detention or Imprisonment (UN)

On 9 December 1988, the **United Nations General Assembly** adopted the Body of Principles for the Protection of All Persons under Any Form of Detention or Imprisonment (A/RES/43/173). The 39 Principles and one general clause contained in the instrument are designed to ensure that all persons under any form of detention or imprisonment are treated in a humane manner with respect for the inherent dignity of the human person (Principle 1). These Principles are to be applied to all persons within the territory of any given State, without distinction of any kind (Principle 5). The Principles provide that arrest, detention or imprisonment shall only be carried out in accordance with the law and by persons authorized for that purpose (Principle 2). It further provides that anyone who is arrested shall be informed at the time of his arrest of the reason for his arrest (Principle 10) and that such persons shall be subject to treatment appropriate to their unconvicted status. For example, arrested persons shall, whenever possible, be kept separate from imprisoned persons (Principle 8). The Body of Principles urges States to prohibit by law any act contrary to the rights and duties contained in these Principles and to make any such act subject to appropriate sanctions (Principle 7). These acts include compelling a detained or imprisoned person to confess, to incriminate himself/herself otherwise or to testify against any other person (Principle 21) or to subject a detained or imprisoned person to any medical or scientific experimentation which may be detrimental to his/her health (Principle 22). States are also urged to conduct impartial investigations of complaints (Principle 7) and to have a competent authority, distinct from the authority directly in charge of the administration of the place of detention or imprisonment, regularly visit such places to ensure strict observance of relevant laws and regulations (Principle 29).

Cairo Declaration on Human Rights in Islam (Islamic Conference of Foreign Ministers)

The Cairo Declaration was adopted on 5 August 1990 at the 19th Islamic Conference of Foreign Ministers at its Session of Peace, Interdependence and Development. In its Preamble, it recognizes the importance of issuing a document on human rights in Islam to serve as a guide for Member States in all aspects of life. The Declaration expresses the belief that fundamental rights and freedoms according to Islam are an integral part of the Islamic religion. It contains 25 articles which affirm the principles of non-discrimination (Article 1), proclaim the **right to life** (Article 2), the **right to education** (Article 9), the **right to own property** acquired in a legitimate way (Article 15), the right to equality before the law (Article 19) and various other rights. Article 24 states that all the rights and freedoms stipulated in the Declaration are subject to the Islamic Shari'ah.

Cartagena Declaration on Refugees

The Cartagena Declaration on Refugees was adopted by the Central American States, joined by Mexico and Panama, at a colloquium held at Cartagena, Colombia, from 19 to 22 November 1984. The Declaration seeks to provide protection to refugees in Central America, Mexico and Panama. Although not formally binding, the Cartagena Declaration on Refugees has become the basis of refugee policy in the region and has brought international protection to people who may not be covered by the 1951 **Convention relating to the Status of Refugees** and its 1967 Protocol. The Declaration fully reaffirms the principles enshrined in those international instruments and urges States "... to carry out, if they have not yet done so, the constitutional procedures for accession to the 1951 Convention and the 1967 Protocol relating to the Status of Refugees" (para. (a)). It also calls upon States Parties to the 1969 **American Convention on Human Rights** to implement this instrument when dealing with refugees who are in their territories (para. 10). In response to regional considerations, the Declaration extends the definition of a refugee as contained in the 1951 Convention and in the 1967 Protocol. Hence it includes among refugees "persons who have fled their country because their lives, safety or freedom have been threatened by generalized violence, foreign aggression, internal conflicts, massive violation of human rights or other circumstances which have seriously disturbed public order" (para. 3). It also invites the countries of the region to set a minimum standard of treatment for refugees, on the basis of the provisions of the 1951 Convention, the 1967 Protocol thereto and the 1969 American Convention on Human Rights, with a view to ensuring the full enjoyment by refugees of their **economic**, **social** and **cultural rights** (para. 8 to 11). In particular, the Declaration calls for the full observance of the following principles: the principle of non-refoulement (para. 5), according to which people may not be returned against their will to a territory where they may be exposed to persecution; the voluntary and individual character of repatriation of refugees (para. 12); the principle of reunification of families (para. 13). The Declaration also stresses the importance of close coordination and cooperation between national, non-governmental, international organizations and the **United Nations High Commissioner for Refugees (UNHCR)** in order to strengthen the international protection of refugees.

Charter of Fundamental Rights of the European Union (EU)

See **European Union Charter of Fundamental Rights (EU)**.

Charter of Paris for a New Europe (CSCE/OSCE)

In November 1990 in Paris, 34 Heads of State or Government adopted the Charter of Paris for a New Europe aimed at proclaiming common values and freedoms for the post-Cold War period. The Charter of Paris marked the beginning of the transformation of the **Conference on Security and Co-operation in Europe (CSCE)** from a series of conferences (as its name implies) to an operational institution, reflecting the changes in Europe and the challenges in a new international environment. The CSCE was renamed **Organization for Security and Co-operation in Europe (OSCE)** in 1994 (with effect from 1995). The Charter of Paris underscores the resolve of the participating States to strengthen democracy and establish market economies across the region, and stresses the need to promote human rights. It further states that democracy is the best safeguard of freedom of expression, tolerance of all groups of society, and equality of opportunity for each person.

New Guidelines for the Future were formulated and the CSCE's first permanent institutions were created: the Secretariat in Prague, the Conflict Prevention Centre in Vienna and the Office for Free Elections in Warsaw. The Charter also set up three main political consultative bodies: the Council of Ministers, comprising foreign ministers from the Participating States; a Committee of Senior Officials to assist the Council and manage day-to-day business; and regular summit meetings of Heads of State or Government. Meanwhile, newly independent States from Central and Eastern Europe and the former Soviet Union joined the CSCE and the number of CSCE (now OSCE) participating States expanded to 55. In the framework of the CSCE/OSCE process, several measures have been adopted aimed at strengthening security and stability throughout Europe as well as promoting human rights, including: the signature in 1990 of an important arms control treaty – the Treaty on Conventional Armed Forces in Europe (CFE); the establishment the same year of the **Office for Democratic Institutions and Human Rights (ODIHR)** which succeeded the Office for Free Elections; the creation in 1992 of the Forum for Security cooperation (FSC) and of the post of the **High Commissioner on National Minorities (HCNM)**; the creation of the Court of Conciliation and Arbitration under the OSCE Convention on Conciliation and Arbitration adopted in 1992; and the creation in 1997 of the position of the Representative on Freedom of the Media.

Charter of the United Nations (United Nations Charter)

The Charter of the **United Nations** was signed on 26 June 1945 at the conclusion of the United Nations Conference on International Organization, held in San Francisco. It entered into force on 24 October 1945. Since this date, 24 October is universally celebrated as **United Nations Day**. The United Nations Charter is the constituting instrument of the Organization, defining the rights and obligations of Member States, and establishing the United Nations organs and procedures. The Statute of the **International Court of Justice**, the principal judicial organ of the United Nations, forms an integral part of the Charter. As it is an international treaty, the Charter codifies the major principles of international relations. The Preamble to the Charter expresses the determination of Member States to "… reaffirm faith in fundamental human rights, in the dignity and worth of the human person, in the equal rights of men and women…". The Charter describes the purposes of the United Nations: to maintain international peace and security; to develop friendly relations among nations based on respect for the principle of equal rights and self-determination of peoples; to cooperate in solving international economic, social, cultural and humanitarian problems, and in promoting or encouraging respect for human rights and fundamental freedoms for all without distinction as to race, sex, language, or religion; and to be a centre for harmonizing the actions of nations in attaining these common goals. The United

Nations Charter reflects the awareness of the close relationship between the maintenance of international peace and the promotion of international economic and social stability, as well as the safeguarding of human rights and fundamental freedoms.

For complete text see:
http://www.un.org/aboutun/charter/index.html

Cities for Human Rights

Cities are playing an increasingly important role in ensuring the implementation of human rights standards. The movement "Cities for Human Rights" emerged following the First European Conference held in Barcelona, Spain (October 1998). This meeting has adopted the "Barcelona Agreement" which was aimed at guaranteeing the enjoyment of human rights by city residents. This agreement was signed by 40 European Cities from 11 Countries. It was further elaborated and signed in May 2000 under the title "**European Charter for the Safeguarding of Human Rights in the City**" by 96 cities. The Charter is the legal basis of the movement "Cities for Human Rights" which is aimed at guaranteeing the enjoyment of human rights and participation in the decision-making process of all inhabitants of the cities without **discrimination** and exclusion. The movement unites (as of May 2003) 235 cities from 21 countries.

Civil rights

Together with **political rights**, civil rights are called by some specialists "first generation" rights, since they already appeared in **Magna Carta** (1215), the **Declaration of the Rights of Man and of the Citizen** adopted by the French National Assembly (1789) and the **American Bill of Rights** (1791). Civil rights include: the right to **freedom of movement and residence** within the border of the State; the **right to leave any country, including one's own, and to return to one's own country**; and the rights to nationality, to marriage and choice of spouse, the **right to own property** alone as well as in association with others, the right to inherit, the right to **freedom of thought, conscience and religion**, the right to **freedom of opinion and expression**, and the right to **freedom of peaceful assembly** and **association**. Civil rights are by and large of an individualistic character and are immediately applicable. Moreover, they are guaranteed by States to their citizens, whereby it is implied that a government should not arbitrarily act to infringe them for political reasons. The legal instruments whose very purpose is either to proclaim civil rights or to guarantee them include the **Universal Declaration of Human Rights** (1948), the **American Declaration of the Rights and Duties of Man** (1948), the **European Convention for the Protection of Human Rights and Fundamental Freedoms** (1950) and its Additional Protocols N° 1 (1952) and N° 4 (1963), the **International Covenant on Civil and Political Rights** (1966) and the **American Convention on Human Rights** (1969), together with a number of specific instruments concerning particular civil rights, such as the **Convention on the Nationality of Married Women** (1957).

Code of Conduct for Law Enforcement Officials (UN)

The Code of Conduct was adopted by the **United Nations General Assembly** (A/RES/34/169) on 17 December 1979. In addition to 8 Articles, which set out a series of principles that ensure the humane performance of law enforcement functions, it contains commentaries providing information to facilitate the use of the Code within the framework of national legislation or practice. It admonishes all law enforcement officials to perform their tasks "consistent with the high degree required by their profession" (Article 1), in full respect for and compliance with the human rights of all persons (Article 2). Pursuant to Article 3, the use of force should only be exceptional, matters of confidential nature should be kept confidential (Article 4) and according to Article 5, "no law enforcement official may inflict, instigate or tolerate any act of torture or other cruel, inhuman or degrading treatment of punishment". Furthermore, law enforcement officials shall secure medical attention (Article 6), any act of corruption is prohibited (Article 7) and the personnel shall "respect the law and the present Code… and prevent and rigorously oppose any violations of them" (Article 8).

Code of Sports Ethics (Council of Europe)

See **European Sport for All Charter**.

Commissioner for Human Rights (Council of Europe)

The idea of instituting an Office of the Commissioner for Human Rights appeared in October 1997 and subsequently the Resolution (99)50, setting out the terms of reference, was adopted at the 104th session of the Committee of Ministers of the **Council of Europe** held in Budapest, Hungary, in May 1999. The Commissioner is elected for a non-renewable term of six years by the Parliamentary Assembly of the Council. He/She shall be an eminent personality of high moral character and have recognized expertise in the field of human rights. The first Commissioner for Human Rights was appointed in November 1999.

The Commissioner is responsible for furthering human rights education and awareness in Member States and ensuring full and effective respect of normative instruments of the Council of Europe. The Commissioner, in exercising his/her functions with complete independence and impartiality, provides advice and relevant information on the protection of human rights and the prevention of human rights violations, however does not handle individual petitions.

Among other activities, the Commissioner undertakes official visits to the Member States, issues recommendations, opinions and reports and organizes seminars.

For more information see:
http://www.Commissioner.coe.int

Commissioner of the Council of the Baltic Sea States on Democratic Development

The mandate of the Commissioner of the Council of the Baltic Sea States on Democratic Development was adopted by the Council of the Baltic Sea States (CBSS) at its 9th Ministerial Session in June 2000. The post of the Commissioner on Democratic Development replaced the post of the Commissioner on Democratic Institutions and Human Rights, including the Rights of Persons Belonging to Minorities, which was created in March 1992. The Commissioner is an instrument for promoting and consolidating democratic development, based upon respect of human rights, in the Member States (there were 12 members as of March 2003: Denmark, Estonia, Finland, Germany, Iceland, Latvia, Lithuania, Norway, Poland, Russian Federation, Sweden and the **European Commission**). The Commissioner is appointed for a term of three years. He/she acts independently, guided by the provisions of the **United Nations Charter**, the standards of the **Council of Europe** and the **Organization for Security and cooperation in Europe (OSCE)**, as well as other standards relevant for democracy and human rights. The Commissioner is also called upon to cooperate closely with national institutions for the promotion of human rights and democracy, the Council of Europe, the OSCE, the **Office of the United Nations High Commissioner for Human Rights (OHCHR)**, as well as other relevant international institutions. The Commissioner's mandate allows him/her to receive and handle communications from individuals, groups and organizations regarding functioning of democratic institutions and human rights concerns. In this respect, his/her functions are comparable to those of an **Ombudsperson**. On the basis of such communications, the Commissioner may propose concrete measures to assist the Member States. The Commissioner is also in charge of studying and reporting to the Council on matters covered by his/her mandate, provides the Council with advice on these issues and follows up when appropriate. The Council may decide to make publicly available Commissioner's reports. It meets once a year in the country of the CBSS Chairman.

For more information see:
http://www.cbss-commissioner.org/

Commission for Social Development (UN)

In 1946, the **Economic and Social Council (ECOSOC)** established the Social Commission as its functional body (ECOSOC resolution 10 II of 21 June 1946). In 1966, it was renamed the Commission for Social Development by ECOSOC resolution 1139 XLI of 29 July 1966 which increased its responsibilities for the whole range of social development issues. The Commission was mandated to provide ECOSOC with recommendations concerning: global social policies; practical measures aimed at improving social development; measures necessary for the coordination of activities in the social field as well as regarding relevant international instruments. At present, the Commission comprises 46 members elected by the ECOSOC for a four-year term and meets annually for a period of eight working days.

In 1995, ECOSOC (resolution 1995/60) entrusted the Commission with the primary responsibility for following-up and reviewing the implementation of the outcome of the **World Summit for Social Development** convened by the United Nations in Copenhagen, Denmark, in 1995. This World Summit was the first major United Nations conference focusing on social development issues. At its conclusion, governments adopted the **Copenhagen Declaration and Programme of Action** which renewed their commitment to placing the improvement of the human condition at the centre of development strategies. The World Summit's core themes were the eradication of poverty, the achievement of full employment and the promotion of secure, stable and just societies. States were assigned the major role in the implementation of the Summit agreements with strong support from relevant **United Nations** agencies.

In June 2000, the **United Nations General Assembly** convened a special session in Geneva to evaluate the overall implementation of the Copenhagen Declaration and Programme of Action, and to plan further action.

For more information see:
http://www.un.org/esa/socdev/csd/index.html

Commission on Crime Prevention and Criminal Justice (UN)

The Commission on Crime Prevention and Criminal Justice, a functional commission of the **Economic and Social Council (ECOSOC)**, was established on 7 February 1992 following the dissolving of the **Committee on Crime Prevention and Control**. It consists of 40 members, elected by the ECOSOC on the basis of equitable geographical distribution. Meeting annually since its first session in Vienna in April 1992, the Commission's main functions are: to provide policy guidelines to the **United Nations** in the field of crime prevention and criminal justice; to develop, monitor and review the implementation of the **United Nations Crime Prevention Programme**; to facilitate and help to coordinate the activities of the inter-regional and regional institutes on the prevention of crime and the treatment of offenders; to mobilize the support of Member States; and to prepare the **United Nations Congress[es] on the Prevention of Crime and the Treatment of Offenders**.

For more information see:
http://www.undcp.org/odccp/crime_cicp_commission.html

Commission on Human Rights (UN)

A subsidiary body of the **Economic and Social Council (ECOSOC)** and one of the principal organs of the **United Nations** in the field of human rights, the Commission is a functional body which meets once a year in Geneva, for a period of six weeks. It was established by ECOSOC on 16 February 1946 in pursuance of Article 68 of the **Charter of the United Nations**. Charged with the task of drawing up an **International Bill of Human Rights** to define the human rights and freedoms referred to in the Charter, and determining ways and means for its effective implementation, the mandate of the Commission led eventually to the drafting of the **Universal Declaration of Human Rights** in 1948 and of the **International Covenants on Human Rights** in 1966. Beginning in 1967, the powers of the Commission were extended to include studying situations revealing a consistent pattern of violations of human rights, and reporting and making recommendations to ECOSOC. In 1979, the Council added the following provision to its mandate: "The Commission shall assist the Economic and Social Council in the co-ordination of activities concerning human rights in the **United Nations system**". In addition to emphasizing the importance of preparing standard-setting instruments and establishing national and local human rights institutions, the Commission has also sought to foster greater knowledge and awareness by the peoples of the world of their human rights. Recent actions taken by the Commission reflect this goal. It has emphasized the central role of grass-roots efforts in promoting human rights, undertaken and disseminated studies on various aspects of human rights, and urged all Governments to consider action to facilitate publicity regarding United Nations human rights activities. Moreover, in pursuance of its mandate to consider publicly situations concerning violations of human rights and fundamental freedoms in any part of the world, the Commission on Human Rights is also the body primarily responsible within the United Nations for dealing with the complaints of individuals and organizations alleging such violations. The membership of the Commission has been increased over the years and now comprises 53 Member States. The **Sub-Commission on the Promotion and Protection of Human Rights** (formerly the **Sub-Commission on Prevention of Discrimination and Protection of Minorities**) is a subsidiary body of the Commission.

For more information see:
http://www.unhchr.ch/html/menu2/2/chr.htm

Commission on the Status of Women (UN)

The Commission on the Status of Women was established by the **Economic and Social Council (ECOSOC)** on 21 June 1946 to prepare recommendations and reports to the Council on promoting women's rights in political, economic, civil, social and educational fields. The Commission was also called upon to make recommendations to the Council on urgent problems in the field of women's rights with a view to implementing the principle that men and women shall have equal rights, and to develop proposals to give effect to such recommendations. On 26 May 1987, the mandate of the Commission was broadened to include promoting the objectives of equality, development and peace, monitoring the implementation of measures for the advancement of women, and reviewing and appraising the progress made at the national, sub-regional, regional, sectoral and global levels. The members of the Commission, whose number has increased over the years from 15 to 45, are elected by ECOSOC for a period of 4 years, with due respect to the principle of equitable geographical distribution. Its annual regular sessions are attended not only by members and their alternates, but also by observers of Member States of the **United Nations** and representatives of bodies and agencies of the **United Nations system**, and intergovernmental and **non-governmental organizations**. The Commission, apart from resolutions and decisions, has adopted a number of draft documents on the basis of which the **United Nations General Assembly** approved: the **Convention on the Political Rights of Women** (1952); the **Convention on the Nationality of Married Women** (1957); the **Convention on Consent to Marriage, Minimum Age for Marriage and Registration of Marriages** (1962); **Declaration on the Elimination of Discrimination against Women** (1967); and the **Convention on the Elimination of All Forms of Discrimination against Women** (1979), as well as the **Optional Protocol** to this Convention (1999). As the preparatory body for the **World Conference[s] on Women** in Beijing in 1995 the Commission was mandated by the General

Assembly to play a central role in reviewing the implementation of the **Beijing Declaration and Platform for Action**.

The Commission also has a mandate to receive confidential and non-confidential communications relating to the status of women. The **communication procedure[s]** authorizes the Commission to appoint a Working Group on Communications that considers the complaints (communications) and the replies of governments. Through their examination, the Working Group will bring to the attention of the Commission those communications that "appear to reveal a consistent pattern of reliably attested injustice and discriminatory practices against women". Subsequently, the Commission recommends to ECOSOC any action to be taken on emerging trends and patterns that are revealed through these communications. The main purpose of this procedure is to provide a source of information about violations against women that can assist the Commission in policy formulation and development of further strategies for the advancement of women. It does not result in the adoption of views and recommendations relating to individual cases, as provided for by the procedure under the **Optional Protocol to the Convention on the Elimination of All Forms of Discrimination against Women**.

For more information see:
http://www.un.org/womenwatch/daw/csw

Committee against Torture – CAT (UN)

Established on 26 November 1987 in accordance with Part II, Articles 17-24, of the **Convention against Torture and Other Cruel, Inhuman or Degrading Treatment or Punishment** (1984), the Committee against Torture monitors the implementation of the provisions of the Convention. Composed of ten experts elected by States Parties to the Convention for a term of four years, it began its functions on 1 January 1988 and held its first session in April 1988. Since 1989, it holds two regular sessions each year. The Committee elects from among its members a

Chairman, three vice-Chairmen and a Rapporteur. The terms of reference of the Committee are as follows: to monitor the progress made in the implementation of the Convention, and in particular to consider the reports submitted by States Parties on the measures they have taken to ensure their undertakings within the Convention; to make such general comments on these reports as it considers appropriate; to receive and consider written communication from individuals who claim to be victims of a violation of the provisions of the Convention by a State Party (which recognizes the competence of the Committee) and who have exhausted all available domestic remedies, and from States Parties claiming that another State Party (which recognizes the competence of the Committee) is not fulfilling its obligations under the Convention. By the middle of 2003, more than 40 States had recognized the competence of the Committee to consider individual and State-to-State communications. Another three States had recognized the competence of the Committee to consider State-to-State communications only. The Committee reports on its activities annually to the **United Nations General Assembly**. In addition, the Committee, when it receives reliable information indicating that torture is being practised systematically in the territory of a State Party, also has the authority to nominate one or more of its members to make confidential inquiries. Such inquiries may include, in agreement with the State Party concerned, visits to the State's territory. After examining the findings of the inquiry, the Committee then transmits them to the State Party concerned together with its comments or suggestions. Although all such proceedings are confidential, the Committee may decide to include a summary account of them in its annual report. On 18 December 2002, the General Assembly adopted the **Optional Protocol to the Convention Against Torture and Other Cruel, Inhuman or Degrading Treatment or Punishment**, providing for the establishment of a Sub-Committee of the Committee against

Torture, which shall carry out the functions laid down in the Protocol.

For more information see:
http://www.unhchr.ch/html/menu2/6/cat.htm

Committee on Crime Prevention and Control (UN)

The Committee on Crime Prevention and Control was first established as an *ad hoc* advisory committee of experts by the **United Nations General Assembly** on 1 December 1950. In 1971, the Committee was authorized by the **Economic and Social Council (ECOSOC)** to advise the **United Nations Secretary-General**, the **Commission for Social Development**, the **Commission on Human Rights**, and other concerned bodies in devising and formulating programmes for study on an international basis and policies for international action in the field of crime prevention and criminal justice. Its members were elected by ECOSOC for a term of four years, with half the membership elected every two years, from among experts with the necessary qualifications nominated by Member States. It normally met in March of alternate years in Vienna.

Following a major re-organization in 1992, the Committee on Crime Prevention and Control was abolished by ECOSOC resolution 1992/1, replacing it with a 40 member intergovernmental **Commission on Crime Prevention and Criminal Justice**, which is the principle standard setting body for the United Nations in this field.

Committee on Economic, Social and Cultural Rights – CESCR (UN)

Unlike the other **human rights treaty bodies**, the Committee on Economic, Social and Cultural Rights was not established by its corresponding instrument, the **International Covenant on Economic, Social and Cultural Rights**. It was established by the **Economic and Social Council (ECOSOC)** in 1985 to monitor the implementation of the Covenant.

The Committee is thus a subsidiary organ of ECOSOC and derives its formal authority from that body. The Committee was set up to assist ECOSOC in fulfilling its responsibilities under Articles 21 and 22 of the Covenant. These provisions stipulate that ECOSOC may submit reports to the **United Nations General Assembly**, including general recommendations and information of States Parties concerning measures they have adopted to implement the Covenant.

Under articles 16 and 17 of the Covenant, States Parties undertake to submit periodic reports to ECOSOC, outlining the legislative, judicial and other measures which they have taken to ensure the enjoyment of the rights contained in the Covenant. These reports should be submitted within two years since the entry into force of the Covenant for a given State Party, and thereafter once every five years. In fact these reports are submitted to the Committee which examines them along with relevant information from **United Nations specialized agencies** and **non-governmental organizations**. It strives to develop a constructive dialogue with States Parties to determine to what extent the norms of the Covenant are being adequately applied and how the implementation of the Covenant could be improved. The Committee identifies positive aspects, but also subjects of concern and difficulties impeding the implementation of the Covenant, as well as suggestions and recommendations. A report on its considerations of the State reports is annually submitted to ECOSOC. In addition, the Committee has adopted 15 **general comments** based on the various articles and provisions of the Covenant with a view to assisting the States Parties in fulfilling their reporting obligations. The Committee is also expected to bring to the attention of other organs, bodies and agencies of the **United Nations**, any matter arising from the State reports that may assist these bodies in deciding on international measures aimed at the effective progressive implementation of the Covenant.

The Committee holds two regular three-week sessions, in May and November/December in Geneva and may have, if authorized by ECOSOC, extraordinary sessions. The Committee is composed of 18 experts with recognized competence in the field of human rights, who serve in their personal capacity, not as representatives of Governments. Members of the Committee are elected by ECOSOC for a term of four years, and are eligible for re-election. Candidates are nominated by States Parties to the Covenant. The principles of equitable geographical distribution and the representation of different social and legal systems guide the selection process. The Committee itself elects its chairperson, three vice-chairpersons and a rapporteur.

For more information see:
http://www.unhchr.ch/html/menu2/6/cescr.htm

Committee on the Elimination of Discrimination against Women – CEDAW (UN)

Since 16 April 1982, the Committee on the Elimination of Discrimination against Women, a treaty body established in accordance with the **Convention on the Elimination of All Forms of Discrimination against Women** (Part V), has assumed the task of monitoring measures taken by Governments to put an end to **discrimination** on the grounds of gender. The Committee is composed of 23 members, elected by the States Parties for a term of two years. It normally meets once a year, for a period of two weeks, preceded by a one-week pre-sessional working group to prepare the list of issues to be taken up with the representatives of those Governments whose reports are scheduled for consideration at the session. In order to create as complete a picture as possible regarding the implementation of the Convention and the progress achieved in the realization of the rights contained therein, the Committee: considers the reports of States Parties on the legislative, judicial, administrative and other measures which they have adopted in achieving observance of the Convention; prepares suggestions and general recommendations based on the reports and other information received from States Parties; invites specialized agencies to submit reports on the implementation of the Convention in areas falling within the scope of their activities; and reports, through United Nations **Economic and Social Council (ECOSOC)**, annually to the **United Nations General Assembly** on its activities. The suggestions are usually directed at **United Nations** entities, while general recommendations are addressed to States Parties to the CEDAW. Since 1986, the Committee has formulated 24 general recommendations dealing, *inter alia*, with reporting by States Parties on temporary special measures, violence against women, equal remuneration, female circumcision, equality in marriage and family relations.

The **Optional Protocol to the Convention on the Elimination of All Forms of Discrimination against Women** established a procedure whereby individuals and groups of individuals have the right to complain to the Committee about violations of the rights contained in the Convention.

For more information see:
http://www.unhchr.ch/html/menu2/6/cedw.htm

Committee on the Elimination of Racial Discrimination – CERD (UN)

The Committee on the Elimination of Racial Discrimination was established on 10 July 1969, pursuant to Article 8 of the **International Convention on the Elimination of All Forms of Racial Discrimination** (1965), to monitor the implementation of the Convention. The Committee is composed of 18 elected members of acknowledged competence and impartiality, who serve in their personal capacity as experts for a term of four years. After holding its first session in New York in January 1970, the normal pattern has since called for two public sessions of three weeks' duration each year. The terms of reference of the

Committee, as set out in Part II of the Convention, are as follows: to review the periodic reports submitted by States Parties on measures taken to give effect to the provisions of the Convention; to make suggestions and general recommendations to the States Parties and to the **United Nations General Assembly** on ways in which the Convention could be more effectively implemented; and to report annually to the United Nations General Assembly on its activities. Since 3 December 1982, the Committee has also been authorized to receive communications from individuals or groups claiming to be the victim of a violation of the Convention (the Committee may not receive communications concerning a State Party which has not recognized the Committee's competence in this regard) and to make recommendations, which are transmitted both to the individual or group concerned and to the State Party. Furthermore, all States Parties to the Convention recognize the competence of the Committee to receive a complaint by one of them that another is not giving effect to the Convention. This procedure provides for the establishment of an *ad hoc* conciliation commission, which shall prepare a report embodying such recommendations as it thinks proper for the amicable settlement of the dispute. In addition, Part II of the Convention assigns to the Committee certain advisory responsibilities relating to the attainment of the principles and objectives of the Convention in Trust and Non-Self-Governing Territories. The Committee is developing measures aimed at the prevention of racial **discrimination**. These include: early-warning measures to prevent existing problems from escalating into conflicts; the preparation of guidelines with a view to combating prejudices which lead to racial discrimination; confidence-building initiatives towards strengthening racial tolerance; and "on the spot" missions to areas of particular concern.

For more information see:
http://www.unhchr.ch/html/menu2/6/cerd.htm

Committee on the Protection of the Rights of All Migrant Workers and Members of Their Families (UN)

The Committee shall be established in conformity with Articles 72-78 of the **International Convention on the Protection of the Rights of All Migrant Workers and Members of Their Families**, which entered into force on 1 July 2003. The Committee is entrusted with the monitoring of the implementation of the Convention. It shall consist of ten experts at the time of entry into force of the Convention and of fourteen experts after the entry into force of the Convention for the forty-first State Party. Members of the Committee shall serve in their personal capacity and be elected by secret ballot by the States Parties at their meeting convened by the **United Nations Secretary-General**. The initial election shall be held no later than six months after the entry into force of the Convention. The members of the Committee shall serve for a term of four years. However, the terms of five members elected in the first election shall expire at the end of two years. The members of the Committee shall be eligible for re-election. The necessary staff and facilities for the effective performance of the functions of the Committee shall be provided by the United Nations Secretary-General. The Committee shall normally meet annually.

States Parties undertake to submit a report on the legislative, judicial, administrative and other measures they have taken to give effect to the provisions of the Convention. These reports should be submitted within one year after the entry into force of the Convention for the State concerned and thereafter every five years or if the Committee so requests. The Committee has the competence to consider communications from individuals and/or disputes between States relating to the non-fulfillment of obligations under the Convention. However, these procedures are applicable only to those States Parties which have made declarations in this regard in conformity with Articles 77 and 76 respectively. The Committee shall present to the **United Nations General Assembly** an annual report on the implementation of the Convention, containing its own considerations and recommendations, based, in particular, on the examination of the reports and any observations presented by States Parties.

Committee on the Rights of the Child – CRC (UN)

The Committee on the Rights of the Child, established on 27 February 1991 in accordance with Part II of the **Convention on the Rights of the Child** (1989), is a body entitled to monitor the implementation of the provisions of the Convention. Its first session took place in the fall of 1991. The Committee is responsible for examining and identifying positive aspects as well as principal concerns in the periodic reports submitted by States Parties on the legislative, judicial, administrative or other measures they have taken to implement the Convention, and forwarding suggestions and recommendations to the concerned States Parties. The Committee also transmits requests and indicates needs for technical advice and assistance arising from States' reports. Before meeting with the delegation of a State Party, the Committee's Pre-sessional Working Group meets with national (and international) **non-governmental organizations** (NGOs) and **United Nations specialized agencies** like the **United Nations Children's Fund (UNICEF), United Nations Educational, Scientific and Cultural Organization (UNESCO), United Nations High Commissioner for Refugees (UNHCR), World Health Organization (WHO)** and the **International Labour Organization (ILO)** to discuss the information they have submitted on the implementation of the CRC in the State Party concerned. After this meeting the Committee sends a request for updated information (list of issues) to the State Party. The written replies to this request allow for a dialogue with the State Party at the session based on the most recent information. In this process UNICEF plays a crucial role in promoting the implementation of the Convention by *inter alia* supporting not only governments through various processes but also NGOs e.g. on their awareness-raising campaigns. The Committee is also authorized to recommend to the **United Nations General Assembly** that studies on specific issues relating to the rights of the child be undertaken by the **United Nations Secretary-General**. The first such study was carried out in 1995 on children in armed conflict (Graca Machel study). A second one on violence against children started in February 2003. A decision to increase the membership of the Committee from 10 to 18 independent experts has been adopted by the United Nations General Assembly on 21 December 1995 (A/RES/50/155). This amendment to Article 43 to the Convention has been formally accepted by the required two thirds of the States Parties. Election for this new 18 member Committee took place in February 2003 and the 33rd session in May 2003 was the first meeting of this expanded Committee.

For more information see:
http://www.unhchr.ch/html/menu2/6/crc

Communication procedure – "1503" Procedure (UN)

In 1967, the United Nations **Economic and Social Council (ECOSOC)** authorized the **Commission on Human Rights** and the **Sub-Commission on Prevention of Discrimination and Protection of Minorities** (now **Sub-Commission on the Promotion and Protection of Human Rights**) to examine information relevant to gross violations of human rights and fundamental freedoms in all countries. The Commission was allowed, in appropriate cases: "to make a thorough study of situations which reveal a consistent pattern of violations of human rights", report, and make recommendations on these violations to the Council. In 1970, the Council adopted a "procedure for dealing with communications relating to violations of human rights and fundamental freedoms" (known as the "1503" procedure because it had been approved by ECOSOC resolution 1503 (XLVIII) of 27 May 1970).

The "1503" procedure concerns situations that affect a large number of people over a protracted period of time. The working method is that every month members of the Sub-Commission on the Promotion and Protection of Human Rights receive from the **United Nations Secretary-General** a list of communications, with a short description in each case, together with any replies submitted by governments. This list is also distributed to the members of the Commission on Human Rights. During two weeks every year a five-member Working Group of the Sub-Commission meets to consider all the communications and governments' replies, and to select for the attention of the Sub-Commission cases where there seems to be reliable evidence of a consistent pattern of gross violations of human rights and fundamental freedoms. The Sub-Commission then considers the communications and decides whether to refer situations of apparently consistent patterns of human rights violations to the Commission on Human Rights which determines whether a thorough study of a particular situation is needed and may also decide to appoint an *ad hoc* committee to make an investigation.

The Sub-Commission has drawn up rules of procedure to decide what communications may be accepted for examination. The communication must not be inconsistent with the principles of the **United Nations Charter**, the **Universal Declaration of Human Rights** and applicable human rights treaties. The communications can be sent by individuals or groups who claim to be victims of human rights violations or by any person or group of people who have direct, reliable knowledge of violations. Each communication must describe the facts, the purpose of the petition, and the rights that have been violated. All actions which are connected with the "1503" procedure remain confidential until a situation is referred to ECOSOC. Since 1978, the Chairman of the Commission on Human Rights announces in public sessions the names of countries which have been under examination, but makes a distinction between countries where the Commission continues to keep the human rights situation under review, and those where it has been decided to take no further action. Sometimes ECOSOC decides, on its own initiative, that secrecy can be lifted. The Commission works through direct contacts with Governments of countries where human rights violations have allegedly occurred in order to establish a dialogue. The authors of communications are not involved at any stage of its treatment.

Communication procedure
– UNESCO

Under Article 1 (para. 1) of its Constitution, **UNESCO**'s purpose is "… to contribute to peace and security by promoting collaboration among the nations through education, science and culture in order to further universal respect for justice, for the rule of law and for the human rights and fundamental freedoms which are affirmed for the peoples of the world, without distinction of race, sex, language or religion, by the **Charter of the United Nations**". Accordingly, in 1978, the Executive Board of UNESCO laid down a confidential procedure for the examination of communications (complaints) received by the Organization concerning alleged violations of human rights in its field of competence, namely education, science, culture and information. The procedure is set out in 104 EX/Decision 3.3 of the Executive Board, entitled "Study of the procedures which should be followed in the examination of cases and questions which might be submitted to UNESCO concerning the exercise of human rights in the spheres of its competence, in order to make its action more effective: Report of the Working Party of the Executive Board". According to this decision, individuals, groups of individuals and **non-governmental organizations** may submit communications to UNESCO. The Committee on Conventions and Recommendations, which is a subsidiary body of the Executive Board, examines communications in private sessions. In the first instance, it examines their admissibility. In paragraph 14(a) of the Decision, ten conditions concerning admissibility are stipulated. For example, the communication must not be anonymous; it must not be manifestly ill-founded and must appear to contain relevant evidence; it must be neither offensive nor an abuse of the right to submit communications; and it must be submitted within a reasonable time-limit following the facts which constitute its subject-matter or within a reasonable time-limit after the facts have become known. Once a communication has been declared admissible, the Committee proceeds to examine the substance of the allegations put forward. The procedure is set out in paragraph 14(b) of the Decision. If violations of human rights or fundamental freedoms are massive, systematic or flagrant, they should be considered by the Executive Board and the General Conference in public meetings (para. 18 of 104 EX/Decision 3.3). Since the Committee is not in any way an international tribunal, it endeavors to resolve the problem in a spirit of international cooperation, dialogue, conciliation and mutual understanding.

The procedure laid down in 104 EX/Decision 3.3 has specific characteristics in comparison with similar procedures in other organizations of the **United Nations system**. The right to present communications does not result from any specific human rights instruments adopted by UNESCO. A complaint may be directed at any Member State without any additional commitment on its behalf for the simple reason that it is a member of UNESCO.

For more information see:
http://www.unesco.org/general/eng/legal/hrights/procedure.shtml

Communication procedures of the International Labour Organization (ILO)

See **Supervisory procedures of the International Labour Organization**.

Communication procedures
– United Nations system

Every year, communications (complaints) concerning alleged violations of human rights reach the **United Nations system**. By these means, individuals, groups or States in a written statement may submit to the attention of an international organ an alleged violation of a human right. A number of procedures have been established by human rights instruments and their handling has become a major function of several international organs, such as the **human rights treaty bodies** (or **human rights treaty monitoring bodies**) as well as the **Commission on Human Rights**, its **Sub-Commission on the Promotion and Protection of Human Rights** (formerly the **Sub-Commission on Prevention of Discrimination and Protection of Minorities**), and the **Commission on the Status of Women**. Procedures have thus been adopted by **United Nations** organs such as the **Economic and Social Council (ECOSOC)**, the **United Nations General Assembly** and the **Security Council**, and **United Nations specialized agencies** such as the **International Labour Organization (ILO)** and **UNESCO**.

The **International Covenant on Civil and Political Rights** and its **Optional Protocol** entered into force on 23 March 1976. By the middle of 2003, more than 90 States had accepted the competence of the **Human Rights Committee** to deal with individual complaints under the Optional Protocol. This means that the States Parties to the Optional Protocol have bound themselves to accept a specific procedure of examining claims brought against them. A communication must not be anonymous and it must come from a person, or persons who live under the jurisdiction of a State which is party to the Optional Protocol. It should be submitted by the individual who claims that his or her rights have been violated by the State. Before the Committee, or its Working Group, decides whether a communication is admissible or not, the alleged victim or the State concerned may be asked to provide additional written information or observations for which a time limit is set. The Committee shall not consider any communication from an individual until it has ascertained that the same matter is not being examined under another procedure of international investigation or settlement. Moreover, the communication may be considered only if the individual has exhausted all available domestic remedies.

The victim and the State are informed of all actions taken by the Committee or its Working Group. The victim has the opportunity to comment on any written submission by the State.

There are some other procedures available for people who believe their human rights are being violated. Those established under the **International Convention on the Elimination of All Forms of Racial Discrimination** and the **Convention against Torture and Other Cruel, Inhuman or Degrading Treatment or Punishment** are dealt with by the **Committee on the Elimination of Racial Discrimination** and the **Committee against Torture** respectively. The **Committee on the Elimination of Discrimination against Women** and the **Commission on the Status of Women** are also authorized to consider communications.

Conference for Security and Cooperation in Europe – CSCE

See **Organization for Security and Co-operation in Europe (OSCE)**.

Convention (N° 11) concerning the Right of Association and Combination of Agricultural Workers (ILO)

The Convention (N° 11) concerning the Right of Association and Combination of Agricultural Workers was adopted by the General Conference of the **International Labour Organization (ILO)** on 12 November 1921. Since entering into force on 11 May 1923, it had been ratified by the middle of 2003 by 121 States. According to the Convention, each Contracting Party "undertakes to secure to all those engaged in agriculture the same rights of association and combination as to industrial workers, and to repeal any statutory or other provisions restricting such rights in the case of those engaged in agriculture" (Article 1).

Convention (N° 29) concerning Forced or Compulsory Labour (ILO)

The Convention (N° 29) concerning Forced or Compulsory Labour was adopted by the General Conference of the **International Labour Organization (ILO)** on 28 June 1930 and entered in force on 1 May 1932. It had become binding for 162 States by the middle of 2003. For the purposes of the Convention, the term "forced or compulsory labour" means "all work or service which is extracted from any person under the menace of any penalty and for which the said person has not offered himself voluntarily" (Article 2). The Convention provides for the suppression of such labour in all its forms (Article 1), subject to exceptions relating to compulsory military service, normal civic obligations, convict labour and minor communal services (Article 2). Similarly, the objectives it contains do not apply to "any work or service exacted in cases of emergency" (Article 2). Pursuant to Article 22 of the Constitution of the ILO, Contracting Parties agree to provide to the ILO annual reports on the measures they have taken to give effect to the provisions of this Convention. These provisions were further developed in the **Convention (N° 105) concerning the Abolition of Forced Labour**, adopted in June 1957.

Convention (No. 81) concerning Labour Inspection in Industry and Commerce (ILO)

The Convention was adopted by the International Labour Conference on 11 July 1947 and entered into force on 7 April 1950. By the middle of 2003, 129 countries had become parties to it. The issue of labour inspection is crucial to the full realization of **economic** and **social rights** at work. Article 1 of the Convention stipulates that each Member State of the **International Labour**

Organization (ILO) for which Convention No. 81 is in force "shall maintain a system of labour inspection in industrial workplaces". The system of labour inspection "shall apply to all workplaces in respect of which legal provisions relating to conditions of work and the protection of workers while engaged in their work are enforceable by labour inspectors" (Article 2). The Convention sets out specific and detailed requirements concerning the functions and organization of the system of labour inspection, including powers of labour inspectors. Part II of the Convention provides for an obligation to maintain a system of labour inspection in commercial workplaces. Any Member State which ratifies this Convention may, by a Declaration appended to its ratification, exclude Part II from its acceptance of the Convention (Article 25).

Convention (N° 87) concerning Freedom of Association and Protection of the Right to Organise (ILO)

The Convention (N° 87) concerning Freedom of Association and Protection of the Right to Organise, adopted on 9 July 1948, is a major **International Labour Organization (ILO)** instrument concerning **freedom of association** and trade union rights. Coming into force on 4 July 1950, the Convention had been ratified by 142 States by the middle of 2003. The guarantees to which it requires States Parties to give effect include the rights of "workers and employers, without distinction whatsoever ... to establish and, subject only to the rules of the organization concerned, to join organizations of their own choosing without previous authorization" (Article 2). The Convention also provides for certain rights and guarantees permitting these organizations, and any federations or confederations they may establish, to draw up their own constitutions and rules, to organize their administration and activities, and to formulate their programmes, without any interference from the public authorities which would restrict this right (Article 3). Similarly, provisions to protect workers against anti-union **discrimination**, and to afford workers' and employers' organizations adequate protection against acts of interference by each other or each other's agents or members in their establishment, functioning or administration, are also contained in the Convention (Article 4). The right to establish and join federations and confederations and to affiliate with international organizations or workers and employers is further recognized (Articles 5 and 6). In exercising the rights listed in the Convention, workers, employers and their organizations should respect the law of the land, but the law of the land should not impair, or be applied to impair, the guarantees provided for in the Convention (Article 8).

Convention (N° 97) concerning Migration for Employment – revised (ILO)

The Convention (N° 97) concerning Migration for Employment (Revised) was adopted by the **International Labour Organization (ILO)** on 1 July 1949 and entered into force on 22 January 1952. By the middle of 2003, it had been ratified by 42 States. Its Article 6, paragraph 1, states that: "Each Member ... undertakes to apply, without **discrimination** in respect of nationality, race, religion or sex, to immigrants lawfully within its territory, treatment no less favourable than that which it applies to its own nationals" concerning remuneration, hours of work, overtime arrangements, holidays with pay, restriction on home work, minimum age for employment, apprenticeship and training, women's work and the work of young persons; membership of trade unions and enjoyment of the benefits of collective bargaining; accommodation, social security, etc. Article 1 envisages that States Parties shall present, at the request of the ILO and its Member States, information on measures undertaken to implement the Convention. The ILO Conference is to conduct a general discussion on migration in 2004 to examine all ILO means of action in this area, including whether its standards remain up to date.

Convention (N° 98) concerning the Application of the Principles of the Right to Organise and Bargain Collectively (ILO)

Freedom of association in regard to trade unions and the freedom to join them for the protection of one's interests, is provided for in the **Universal Declaration of Human Rights** (Article 23), in the **International Covenant on Civil and Political Rights** (Article 22) and in the **International Covenant on Economic, Social and Cultural Rights** (Article 8). Trade union rights are also defined, in greater detail, in the **International Labour Organization (ILO)** instruments, and, in particular, in the Convention (N° 98) concerning the Application of the Principles of the Right to Organise and Bargain Collectively which was adopted on 1 July 1949 and came into force on 18 July 1951. By the middle of 2003, it had been ratified by 153 States. This Convention contains provisions regarding the protection of workers against acts of anti-union **discrimination**, in particular in regard to employment and dismissal (Article 1), and the protection of organizations of employers and workers from mutual interference in the activities of their establishment, functioning or administration (Article 2). Those States Parties to the Convention agree to establish appropriate machinery to ensure respect for these rights (Article 3) and to take measures to encourage and promote voluntary negotiation between employers or employers' organizations and workers' organizations (Article 4).

Convention (N° 100) concerning Equal Remuneration for Men and Women Workers for Work of Equal Value (ILO)

Adopted on 29 June 1951 by the **International Labour Organization (ILO)**, the Convention (N° 100) concerning Equal Remuneration for Men and Women Workers for Work of Equal Value entered into force on 23 May 1953. By the middle of 2003, it had been ratified by 161 States. The Convention specifies that "equal remuneration for men and women workers for work of equal value" refers to "rates of remuneration established without

discrimination based on sex" (Article 1). Differential rates between workers which correspond, without regard to sex, to differences as determined by objective appraisal of the work to be performed, shall not, however, be considered as being contrary to this principle (Article 3). Under Article 2 of the Convention, each Member which is bound by the Convention shall, "by all means appropriate to the methods in operation for determining rates of remuneration, promote and ... ensure the application to all workers of the principle of equal remuneration for men and women workers for work of equal value". This principle may be applied by: national laws or regulations; legally established or recognized machinery for wage determination; collective agreements between employers and workers; or a combination of these various means (Article 2). The Convention also provides that measures be taken to promote objective appraisal of jobs on the basis of work to be performed (Article 3).

Convention (N° 102) concerning Minimum Standards of Social Security (ILO)

This Convention was adopted by the **International Labour Organization (ILO)** on 28 June 1952 and entered into force on 27 April 1955. By the middle of 2003, 40 States had ratified it. It defines the persons entitled to various benefits which are enumerated in its Parts II to X: medical care; sickness benefit; unemployment benefit; old-age benefit; employment injury benefit; family benefit; maternity benefit; invalidity benefit; and survivors' benefit. Part XII concerns the equality of treatment for non-national residents.

Convention (N° 105) concerning the Abolition of Forced Labour (ILO)

In response to the existence in the world of vast systems of forced or "corrective" labour employed as a means of political coercion or as punishment for holding or expressing political views, the International Labour Conference adopted, on 25 June 1957, the

Convention (N° 105) concerning the Abolition of Forced Labour. Since entering into force on 17 January 1959, it had been ratified, by the middle of 2003 by 161 States. The aim of the Convention is to abolish "certain forms of compulsory labour constituting a violation of the rights of man referred to in the **Charter of the United Nations** and enunciated in the **Universal Declaration of Human Rights**" (Preamble). Under Article 1, each Member State of the **International Labour Organization (ILO)** which ratifies the Convention undertakes to suppress and not to make use of any form of forced or compulsory labour: for political purposes; as a method of mobilizing and using labour for purposes of economic development; as a means of labour discipline; as a punishment for having participated in strikes; and as a means of racial, social, national or religious **discrimination**. Each State Party also agrees to "undertake effective measures to secure the immediate abolition of forced or compulsory labour as specified in Article 1" (Article 2).

Convention (N° 111) concerning Discrimination in Respect of Employment and Occupation (ILO)

The Convention (N° 111) concerning Discrimination in Respect of Employment and Occupation was adopted on 25 June 1958 by the General Conference of the **International Labour Organization (ILO)** and entered into force on 15 June 1960. It had been ratified by 159 States by the middle of 2003. It defines "**discrimination**" as "any distinction, exclusion or preference made on the basis of race, colour, sex, religion, political opinion, national extraction or social origin, which has the effect of nullifying or impairing equality of opportunity or treatment in employment or occupation" (Article 1). Other grounds can also be added. The Convention requires States Parties "to declare and pursue a national policy designed to promote, by methods appropriate to national conditions and practice, equality of opportunity and treatment in respect of employment and occupation, with a view to eliminating any discrimination in respect thereof" (Article 2). The measures to be taken for the application of such a national policy are enumerated in Article 3, which states that each contracting Member "... shall seek the cooperation of employers' and workers' organizations and other appropriate bodies in promoting the acceptance and observance of this policy" and "to enact such legislation and promote such educational programmes as may be calculated to secure the acceptance and observance of the policy". States Parties further agree "to indicate in their annual reports on the application of the Convention the action taken in pursuance of the policy and the results secured by such action" (Article 3).

Convention (N° 118) concerning Equality of Treatment of Nationals and Non-Nationals in Social Security (ILO)

This Convention was adopted by the **International Labour Organization (ILO)** on 28 June 1962 and entered into force on 25 April 1964. It had been ratified by 38 States by the middle of 2003. According to this instrument, each State Party shall grant to the nationals of other States Parties, as well as to refugees and stateless persons, equality of treatment under its social security legislation with its own nationals (Articles 3 and 10). Both coverage and the right to benefits are concerned in respect of every branch of social security for which the State has accepted the obligations. Accordingly, invalidity benefits, old-age benefits, survivors' benefits, death grants and employment injury pensions should be guaranteed both to the nationals of the given State Party or to nationals of any other State Party (Articles 5 and 6).

Convention (N° 122) concerning Employment Policy (ILO)

Convention No. 122 was adopted by the **International Labour Organization (ILO)** on 9 July 1964 and entered into force on 15 July 1966. By the middle of 2003 it had been ratified by 94 countries. The Convention follows up on the **right to just**

and favourable conditions of work, to free choice of employment and to protection against unemployment, in conformity with the **Universal Declaration of Human Rights**. Under the Convention, each State Party shall declare and pursue, as a major goal, an active policy designed to promote full, productive and freely chosen employment. This policy shall aim at ensuring that: "there is work for all who are available for and seeking work; such work is as productive as possible; there is freedom of choice of employment and the fullest possible opportunity for each worker to qualify for, and to use his skills and endowments in a job for which he is well suited, irrespective of race, colour, sex, religion, political opinion, national extraction or social origin" (Article 1, part 2). The policy "shall take due account of the stage and level of economic development and the mutual relationships between employment objectives and other economic and social objectives" (Article 1, part 3). In the application of the Convention, "representatives of the persons affected by the measures to be taken, and in particular representatives of employers and workers, shall be consulted concerning employment policies, with a view to taking fully into account their experience and views and securing their full cooperation in formulating and enlisting support for such policies" (Article 3).

Convention (No. 129) concerning Labour Inspection in Agriculture (ILO)

In addition to **Convention No. 81 concerning Labour Inspection in Industry and Commerce**, specific standards for the agricultural sector have been established by Convention No. 129, adopted on 25 June 1969. It entered into force on 19 January 1972 and had been ratified by 41 countries by the middle of 2003. Each Member State of the **International Labour Organization (ILO)** for which this Convention is in force shall maintain a system of labour inspection in agriculture. Such a system "shall apply to all agricultural undertakings in which employees or apprentices work, however they may be remunerated and whatever the type, form or duration of their contract" (Article 4). The functions of the system of labour inspection in agriculture are enumerated in Article 6 and include "securing the enforcement of the legal provisions relating to conditions of work and the protection of workers while engaged in their work" and "bringing to the notice of the competent authority defects or abuses not specifically covered by existing legal provisions and to submit to it proposals on the improvement of laws and regulations."

Convention (N° 135) concerning Protection and Facilities to be Afforded to Workers' Representatives in the Undertaking (ILO)

The Convention (N° 135) concerning Protection and Facilities to be Afforded to Workers' Representatives in the Undertaking was adopted by the **International Labour Organization (ILO)** on 23 June 1971 and entered into force on 30 June 1973. By the middle of 2003, it had been ratified by 73 States. For the purposes of the Convention, the term "workers' representatives" means persons recognized as such under national law or practice, whether they are trade union representatives or representatives freely elected by workers in the undertaking (Article 3). Supplementing the terms of the **Convention (N° 98) concerning the Application of the Principles of the Right to Organise and Bargain Collectively (1949)**, this Convention provides that: "Workers' representatives in the undertaking shall enjoy effective protection against any act prejudicial to them, including dismissal, based on their status or activities as a workers' representative or in union membership or participation in union activities, in so far as they act in conformity with existing laws or collective agreements or other jointly agreed arrangements" (Article 1). Workers' representatives must also be afforded such facilities in the undertaking "as may be appropriate in order to enable them to carry out their functions promptly and efficiently" (Article 2).

Convention (N° 138) concerning Minimum Age for Admission to Employment (ILO)

The Convention (N° 138) concerning Minimum Age for Admission to Employment was adopted by the **International Labour Organization (ILO)** on 26 June 1973 and entered into force on 19 June 1976. By the middle of 2003, it had been ratified by 130 States. The Convention summarizes and further develops the provisions of conventions concerning the minimum age of work in various sectors adopted by the ILO between 1919 and 1965. Its Article 1 is designed to ensure the effective abolition of child labour and to raise progressively the minimum age for admission to employment to a level consistent with the fullest physical and mental development of young persons. This age shall not be less than the age of completion of compulsory schooling and, in any case, shall not be less than 15 years (Article 2). Furthermore, Article 3, paragraph 1, states that: "The minimum age for admission to any type of employment or work which by its nature or the circumstances in which it is carried out is likely to jeopardize the health, safety or morals of young persons shall not be less than 18 years". This Convention has recently been supplemented by the entry into force on 19 November 2000 of the **Convention (N°182) concerning the Prohibition and Immediate Action for the Elimination of the Worst Forms of Child Labour**.

Convention (N° 141) concerning Organisations of Rural Workers and Their Role in Economic and Social Development (ILO)

The Convention (N° 141) concerning Organisations of Rural Workers and their Role in Economic and Social Development was adopted by the **International Labour Organization (ILO)** on 23 June 1975 and came into force on 24 November 1977. It was binding on 38 States by the middle of 2003. Under this Convention, all categories of rural workers, whether wage-earners or self-employed, have the right to establish and, subject only to the rules of the organization concerned, to join organizations of their own choosing without previous authorization. Rural workers' organizations, according to the Convention, shall be independent and voluntary in character and shall remain free from all interference, coercion or repression. In order to enable rural workers to play their role in economic and social development, States Parties to the Convention agree to pursue a policy of active encouragement to rural workers' organizations, particularly with a view to eliminating obstacles to their establishment, their growth and the pursuit of their lawful activities.

Convention (N° 143) concerning Migrations in Abusive Conditions and the Promotion of Equality of Opportunity and Treatment of Migrant Workers (ILO)

The Convention (N° 143) concerning Migrations in Abusive Conditions and the Promotion of Equality of Opportunity and Treatment of Migrant Workers was adopted by the **International Labour Organization (ILO)** on 24 June 1975 and entered into force on 9 December 1978. By the middle of 2003, it had been ratified by 18 States. In its Preamble, it states that considering the **right to leave any country, including one's own and to return to one's country**, as set forth in the **Universal Declaration of Human Rights** and the **International Covenant on Civil and Political Rights**, minimum conditions should be enjoyed by migrants in transit and on arrival. It also aims at the elimination of abuses caused by illicit and clandestine trafficking and at the promotion of equality of opportunity and treatment of **migrant workers** at least equal to those of nationals. Article 1 stipulates that each Member State: "… undertakes to respect the basic human rights of all migrant workers". The Convention determines the term "migrant worker" as "a person who migrates or who has migrated from one country to another with a view to being employed otherwise than on his own account and includes any person regularly admitted as a migrant worker" (Article 11, para. 1). Article 3(a) concerns the suppression of clandestine movements of migrants for employment and illegal employment of migrants. Article 9, paragraph 4, lays down that: "Nothing in this Convention shall prevent Members from giving persons who are illegally residing or working within the country the right to stay and to take up legal employment". According to Article 10, States Parties undertake to: "... declare and pursue a national policy designed to promote and to guarantee, by methods appropriate to national conditions and practice, equality of opportunity and treatment in respect of employment and occupation, of social security, of trade union and **cultural rights** and of individual and collective freedoms for persons who as migrant workers or as members of their families are lawfully within its territory". The International Labour Organization (ILO) will conduct a general discussion on migration in 2004 to examine all the ILO means of action in this area, including whether its standards are up to date.

Convention (No. 144) concerning Tripartite Consultations to Promote the Implementation of International Labour Standards (ILO)

The Convention was adopted on 21 June 1976 and entered into force on 16 May 1978. By the middle of 2003 it had been ratified by 110 countries. Each Member State of the **International Labour Organization (ILO)** which ratifies this Convention undertakes to operate procedures, which ensure effective consultations between representatives of the government, of employers and of workers, with respect to the matters concerning the activities of the ILO. Consultations are to be held concerning matters such as "the proposals to be made to the competent authority or authorities in connection with the submission of Conventions and Recommendations pursuant to article 19 of the Constitution of the ILO" (Article 5.b); "the re-examination at appropriate intervals of unratified Conventions and of

Recommendations to which effect has not yet been given, to consider what measures might be taken to promote their implementation and ratification as appropriate" (Article 5.c); and "questions arising out of reports to be made to the International Labour Office under article 22 of the Constitution of the ILO" (Article 5.d).

Convention (N° 151) concerning Protection of the Right to Organise and Procedures for Determining Conditions of Employment in the Public Service (ILO)

The Convention (N° 151) concerning Protection of the Right to Organise and Procedures for Determining Conditions of Employment in the Public Service was adopted on 27 June 1978 by the General Conference of the **International Labour Organization (ILO)**. It entered into force on 25 February 1981 and, by the middle of 2003, had been ratified by 41 States. Recalling that the **Convention (N° 98) concerning Application of the Principles of the Right to Organise and Bargain Collectively** of 1949 does not cover certain categories of public employees and noting the considerable expansion of public service activities in many countries, this Convention seeks to address the need for sound labour relations between public authorities and public employees' organizations (Preamble). For the purposes of the instrument, the term "public employees' organisation" means "any organisation, however composed, the purpose of which is to further and defend the interests of public employees" (Article 3). As outlined in Article 1, the Convention applies to all persons employed by public authorities, except for high-level employees whose functions are normally considered as policy-making or managerial, employees whose duties are of a highly confidential nature, and the armed forces and the police. The Convention provides that public employees shall "enjoy adequate protection against acts of anti-union **discrimination** in respect of their employment" (Article 4), and that public employees' organizations shall enjoy complete independence from public authorities, and "adequate protection against any acts of interference by a public authority in their establishment, functioning or administration" (Article 5). It further provides that settlement of disputes arising in connection with the determination of terms and conditions of employment shall be sought, through negotiation between the parties, or through independent or impartial machinery, such as mediation, conciliation or arbitration (Article 8).

Convention (N° 154) concerning the Promotion of Collective Bargaining (ILO)

Adopted by the **International Labour Organization (ILO)** on 19 June 1981, this Convention entered into force on 11 August 1983. By the middle of 2003, it had been ratified by 34 States. For the purpose of this Convention, the term "collective bargaining" extends to all negotiations which take place between an employer, a group of employers, or their organizations, on the one hand, and the workers' organizations on the other, with the purpose of: "… determining working conditions and terms of employment; and/or regulating relations between employers and workers; and/or regulating relations between employers or their organisations and a workers' organisation or workers' organisations" (Article 2). The provisions of the Convention should be made effective by means of collective agreements, arbitration awards or in such other manner as may be consistent with national practice (Article 4). Article 5 concerns concrete measures aimed at the promotion of collective bargaining. Article 7 stipulates that "Measures taken by public authorities to encourage and promote the development of collective bargaining shall be the subject of prior consultation and, wherever possible, agreement between public authorities and employers' and workers' organisations". Article 8 lays down that: "The measures taken with a view to promoting collective bargaining shall not be so conceived or applied as to hamper the freedom of collective bargaining".

Convention (N° 156) concerning Equal Opportunities and Equal Treatment for Men and Women Workers: Workers with Family Responsibilities (ILO)

The Convention (N° 156) concerning Equal Opportunities and Equal Treatment for Men and Women Workers: Workers with Family Responsibilities was adopted by the International Labour Conference on 23 June 1981 and entered into force on 11 August 1983. By the middle of 2003, it had been ratified by 34 States. It provides that men and women with family responsibilities, whether dependent children or other members of their immediate family who clearly need their care and support, should be able to exercise their **right to work** without being discriminated against because of those responsibilities.

Convention (N° 168) concerning Employment Promotion and Protection against Unemployment (ILO)

This Convention was adopted on 21 June 1988 and entered into force on 17 October 1991. By the middle of 2003, it had been ratified by 6 States. It is aimed at increasing the protection against unemployment in view of new developments which have occurred since the adoption of previous **International Labour Organization (ILO)** instruments concerning unemployment. The Convention contains sections which deal with: promotion of productive employment; contingencies covered; persons protected; methods of protection; benefits to be provided; special provisions for new applicants for employment; and legal, administrative and financial guarantees.

Convention (N° 169) concerning Indigenous and Tribal Peoples in Independent Countries (ILO)

This Convention was adopted by the **International Labour Organization (ILO)** on 27 June 1989 to revise the Indigenous and Tribal Populations Convention and Recommendation of 1957. It entered into force on 5 September 1991 and by the middle of 2003 had been ratified by 17 States. The Convention considers that "… the developments which have taken place in international law since 1957, as well as developments in the situation of **indigenous** and tribal **peoples** in all regions of the world, have made it appropriate to adopt new international standards on the subject with a view to removing the assimilationist orientation of the earlier standards …" (Preamble). It thus provides that "Indigenous and tribal peoples shall enjoy the full measure of human rights and fundamental freedoms without hindrance or **discrimination**…" (Article 3, para. 1). "Special measures shall be adopted as appropriate for safeguarding the persons, institutions, property, labour, cultures and environment of the people concerned" (Article 4, para. 1). The Convention applies to "tribal peoples in independent countries whose social, cultural and economic conditions distinguish them from other sections of the national community, and whose status is regulated wholly or partially by their own customs or traditions or by special laws or regulations" (Article 1, para. 1(a)) and to "peoples in independent countries who are regarded as indigenous" (Article 1, para 1(b)). In applying the provisions of the Convention, Governments shall: "consult the people concerned…" (Article 6, para. 1(a)); "establish means by which these peoples can freely participate … at all levels of decision-making in elective institutions and administrative and other bodies responsible for policies and programmes which concern them" (Article 6, para. 1(b)); and "establish means for the full development of these peoples' own institutions and initiatives, and in appropriate cases provide the resources necessary for this purpose" (Article 6, para. 1(c)). The Convention covers land rights, education, health and other subjects.

Convention (N°182) concerning the Prohibition and Immediate Action for the Elimination of the Worst Forms of Child Labour (ILO)

This Convention was adopted by the **International Labour Organization (ILO)** on 17 June 1999 and came into force on 19 November 2000. By the middle of 2003, it had been ratified by 143 States. The **Convention (N° 138) concerning Minimum Age for Admission to Employment** of 1973 remains the basic instrument on child labour. Convention N° 182 includes among the worst forms of child labour: the sale and trafficking of children; debt bondage; serfdom; forced or compulsory labour; forced or compulsory recruitment of child soldiers; use, procuring or offering of children for prostitution or pornography; use, procuring or offering of children for illegal activities such as the production and trafficking of drugs; all forms of **slavery** and any work which will harm the health, safety or morals of children (Article 3). Therefore, Member States are required to establish and implement immediate action, in consultation with employers' and workers' organizations, in order to effectively eliminate the worst forms of child labour. In particular, such action must take into account the importance of basic education and must provide penal or other relevant sanctions to implement and enforce the principles set out in the Convention (Article 7). To this end, enhanced international cooperation and/or assistance in economic and social development, **poverty** eradication and universal education is also necessary (Article 8). The Convention is complemented by the Worst Forms of Child Labour Recommendation which calls for the compilation of relevant and comprehensive data regarding the nature and extent of child labour in a State. This will help States in effectively struggling against child labour abuses.

Convention against Discrimination in Education (UNESCO)

On 14 December 1960 the General Conference of UNESCO adopted the Convention against Discrimination in Education. The Convention entered into force on 22 May 1962 and had been ratified by 90 Member States by the middle of 2003. For the purpose of this Convention, the term **"discrimination"** includes any distinction, exclusion, limitation or preference which, being based on race, colour, sex, language, religion, political or other opinion, national or social origin, economic condition or birth, has the purpose or effect of nullifying or impairing equality of treatment in education (Article 1). This Convention commits States Parties to formulate, develop and apply a national policy, which will promote equality of opportunity and of treatment in the matter of education and in particular: to make primary education free and compulsory; make secondary education in its different forms generally available and accessible to all; make higher education equally accessible to all on the basis of individual capacity (Article 4). To this end, States Parties undertake to abrogate or modify any statutory provisions and to discontinue any administrative practices which involve discrimination, and also to forbid any different treatment or preferences based solely on the ground that an individual belongs to a particular group (Article 3). The procedures for supervising the execution of the Convention hinge essentially on periodic reports submitted by States to the General Conference of UNESCO (Article 7). In 1965, it was decided, upon recommendation of the General Conference, that the reports submitted by governments shall be examined by a special committee of the Executive Board (70 EX/Decision 5.2.1).

In 1962 a **Protocol instituting a Conciliation and Good Offices Commission to be responsible for seeking the settlement of any disputes which may arise between States Parties to the Convention against Discrimination in Education** was adopted by the General Conference of UNESCO.

Convention against Torture and Other Cruel, Inhuman or Degrading Treatment or Punishment (UN)

This Convention was adopted by the **United Nations General Assembly** (A/RES/39/46) on 10 December 1984 and entered into force on 26 June 1987. By the middle of 2003, it had been ratified by more than 130 States.

For the purposes of the Convention, aimed at the abolition of all forms of torture and other cruel, inhuman or degrading treatment or punishment, the term "torture" means "any act by which severe pain or suffering, whether physical or mental, is intentionally inflicted on a person" for the purposes of coercion or punishment (Article 1). It excludes pain or suffering arising from lawful sanctions.

Under Article 4 of the Convention, States shall ensure that all acts of torture or attempts to commit torture, or complicity or participation in torture are offences under criminal law. States are also called upon to take effective legislative, administrative or judicial measures to prevent and punish acts of torture in any territory under their jurisdiction (Article 5).

Acts of torture are deemed to be extraditable offences in accordance with existing extradition treaties between States Parties. Failing the existence of a treaty, the "State Party may consider this Convention as the legal basis for extradition" (Article 8). No State Party may, however, "expel, return, or extradite a person to another State where there are substantial grounds for believing that he would be in danger of being subjected to torture" (Article 3). States Parties shall ensure that education and information regarding the prohibition of torture is fully included in the training of law enforcement personnel, civil or military, medical personnel and public officials (Article 10). States are required to ensure that their legal systems allow a fair and adequate compensation for the victims of torture, including the means for rehabilitation (Article 14). Part II of the Convention outlines the establishment and functioning of the **Committee against Torture**.

On 18 December 2002, the **Optional Protocol to the Convention against Torture and Other Cruel, Inhuman or Degrading Treatment or Punishment** was adopted by the United Nations General Assembly.

Convention concerning the Protection of the World Cultural and Natural Heritage (UNESCO)

The Convention concerning the Protection of the World Cultural and Natural Heritage was adopted by the General Conference of **UNESCO** on 16 November 1972, and entered into force on 17 December 1974. By the middle of 2003, it had been ratified by about 160 States. The Convention is one of the most universal international legal instruments for the protection of cultural and natural heritage. The Intergovernmental Committee for the Protection of the World Cultural and Natural Heritage commonly known as the **World Heritage Committee**, composed of 21 States, is the main body directly involved in the implementation of the Convention. In accordance with Article 14 of the Convention, the Director General of UNESCO provides a Secretariat for the day-to-day operations of the Convention. The most significant feature of the Convention is that it links together the concepts of nature conservation and the preservation of cultural sites in one single document. It defines international protection of the world cultural and natural heritage as "… the establishment of a system of international cooperation and assistance designed to support States Parties to the Convention in their efforts to conserve and identify that heritage" (Article 7). By signing the Convention, each country makes a pledge to conserve the world heritage sites situated on its territory and also to protect its national heritage. Furthermore, the Convention provides that the World Heritage Committee shall supervise the protection of items recognized by the Convention as those of outstanding universal value from the point of view of history, art, science or aesthetics. The Convention describes its function and explains how the World Heritage Fund is to be used and managed, and under what conditions international financial assistance may be provided. The World Heritage Committee meets once a year to examine applications on the basis of technical evaluations. As stated by the Convention, the Committee shall establish, keep up to date and publish, under the title of the **World Heritage List**, a list of properties forming part of the **cultural heritage** and natural heritage. The applications for a site to be inscribed on the list must come from the country itself and have to include details of how it is managed and protected in national legislation. The criteria for the selection are explained in the Operational Guidelines which are revised regularly by the Committee to match the evolution of the concept of the world heritage itself. As of July 2003, there were 754 properties on the World Heritage List (among them 582 cultural, 149 natural and 23 mixed properties in 128 States Parties).

Convention for the Protection of Cultural Property in the Event of Armed Conflict (UNESCO)

This Convention, also known as The Hague Convention, and the Protocol to it, were adopted in The Hague on 14 May 1954 by an international conference of States convened by **UNESCO**, and entered into force on 7 August 1956. By the middle of 2003, the Convention had been ratified by more than 100 States and the Protocol by more than 80 States. The Convention is based on the idea that the preservation of the **cultural heritage** is not only a matter of preoccupation for the State on whose territory it is located but is of great importance for all peoples of the world and should receive international protection.

It was decided that UNESCO would be the institution in charge of further development of the legal procedures of protection, since its Constitution declares it responsible for the preservation of humanity's natural and cultural heritage. The States Parties undertake to safeguard cultural property of great importance irrespective of its origin or ownership, in the event of armed conflict, as well as to provide special protection for the refuges intended to shelter such property.

A Second Protocol was adopted in The Hague on 26 March 1999. It will enter into force 3 months after its ratification by 20 States. By the middle of 2003, it had been ratified by only 4 countries and had not yet entered into force. This Protocol defines a whole range of crimes which are contrary to either the original 1954 Convention, the Second Protocol, or the provisions of the 1977 **Protocols Additional to the Geneva Conventions** concerning the protection of cultural property. Furthermore, the Second Protocol foresees the creation of a Committee for the Protection of Cultural Property in the Event of Armed Conflict.

Convention for the Protection of Human Rights and Dignity of the Human Being with regard to the Application of Biology and Medicine: Convention on Human Rights and Biomedicine (Council of Europe)

The Convention on Human Rights and Biomedicine is the first international treaty on the new biomedical technologies and the protection of human rights. It was signed on 4 April 1997 and came into force on 1 December 1999, after having received the five required ratifications, including those of four Member States. By the middle of 2003, it was ratified by 15 States.

The aim of the Convention is to guarantee the rights and fundamental freedoms of individuals and, in particular, their integrity in the biomedical sphere. Article 1 asserts the primacy of the human being over the sole interest of science or society. In the event of a conflict, the former must prevail. The whole Convention is infused with the principle of the primacy of the human being, and all its Articles must be interpreted in this light. The Convention affirms at the international level the well-established rule that human beings should consent to any intervention involving themselves, and establishes detailed rules for the protection of persons unable to consent. The Convention also addresses issues such as genetic testing and genetic **discrimination**, non-selection of sex, embryo research, organ transplantation, private life and right to information. Each State Party has the obligation to take the necessary measures to implement its provisions.

Convention for the Protection of Individuals with regard to Automatic Processing of Personal Data (Council of Europe)

This Convention was adopted by the **Council of Europe** on 28 January 1981, and entered into force on 1 October 1985. By the middle of 2003, the Convention had been ratified by 30 Member States. Based on the fundamental rights and freedoms enshrined in the European **Convention for the Protection of Human Rights and Fundamental Freedoms** and especially on the right of everyone to privacy (Article 1), the Convention for the Protection of Individuals with regard to Automatic Processing of Personal Data aims to protect the privacy of individuals, both within the State and internationally, with regard to the growing amount of personal data undergoing automatic processing. The Convention provides general principles for data protection including guidelines for obtaining and processing data, for data storage and use, and for ensuring its accuracy. It also contains special provisions for data concerning health, criminal convictions and sexual life, namely, that such data may only be automatically processed if domestic law provides sufficient safeguards (Article 6). The Convention also envisages measures enabling the data subject to have knowledge of the existence of any data file and to have access to its content (Article 8). This instrument further provides for the establishment of a Consultative Committee (Articles 18-20). The Committee, composed of one representative of each State Party, held its first session in 1986. It is charged with proposing amendments to both domestic law and to the Convention itself, making comments on any amendments proposed by the States Parties, and submitting reports to the Committee of Ministers on its work and on the implementation of the Convention.

Convention for the Protection of the Architectural Heritage of Europe (Council of Europe)

This Convention was adopted on 3 October 1985 and entered into force on 1 December 1987. By August 2003, it had been ratified by 36 States. The Convention recognizes that architectural heritage, defined as monuments, groups and buildings and sites conspicuous for their historical, archaeological, artistic, scientific, social or technical interest (Article 1) constitutes an "irreplaceable expression of the richness and diversity of Europe's **cultural heritage**". The aim of the Convention is to achieve a greater unity and cooperation between its parties for the purpose of safeguarding that common heritage.

In January 2003 the Committee of Ministers of the **Council of Europe** assigned *ad hoc* terms of reference to the Steering Committee for Cultural Heritage to prepare a draft framework convention on european cultural heritage. That instrument, to be elaborated in 2003-04 should take stock of the functions of cultural heritage in a changing Europe and in the context of **globalization**.

Convention for the Suppression of the Traffic in Persons and of the Exploitation of the Prostitution of Others (UN)

Approved by the **United Nations General Assembly** on 2 December 1949 by resolution 317 (iv) and entered into force on 25 July 1951, this Convention consolidated international instruments on the subject prepared under the auspices of the

League of Nations. By the middle of 2003, it had been ratified by 75 States. The States Parties agree to punish any person who "procures, entices or leads away, for purposes of prostitution, another person", or "exploits the prostitution of another person, even with the consent of that person" (Article 1). The Convention also demands the punishment of any person who "keeps or manages, or knowingly finances or takes part in the financing of a brothel", or similar place for the purpose of the prostitution of others (Article 2). Parties to the instrument agree to encourage through their educational, health, social, economic and other related services, measures for the prevention of prostitution and for the rehabilitation of the victims of prostitution (Article 16). They also agree to undertake, in connection with immigration and emigration, to check the traffic in persons of either sex for the purpose of prostitution (Article 17). Parties to the Convention also agree to communicate to the **United Nations Secretary-General** such laws and regulations concerning the application of the Convention which have already been promulgated in their States and thereafter annually such laws and regulations as may be promulgated (Article 21).

Convention for the Suppression of Unlawful Acts against the Safety of Civil Aviation (ICAO)

The Convention for the Suppression of Unlawful Acts against the Safety of Civil Aviation was adopted by the **International Civil Aviation Organization (ICAO)** in 1971 and entered into force on 26 January 1973. Known as the "Montreal Convention", it applies to acts of sabotage such as bombings aboard an aircraft in flight or placement of an explosive device on an aircraft. It makes an offence any act of violence against a person on board an aircraft in flight, if that act is likely to endanger the safety of that aircraft. It requires parties to the Convention to make such offences punishable by "severe penalties" and parties that have custody of offenders to either extradite the offender or submit the case for prosecution. This Convention is one of 12 major instruments aimed at the struggle against **terrorism** and acts affecting in-flight safety adopted under the aegis of the **United Nations** and its specialized agencies.

Convention for the Suppression of Unlawful Seizure of Aircraft (ICAO)

This Convention was adopted by the **International Civil Aviation Organization (ICAO)**, on 16 December 1970 and entered into force on 14 October 1971. Known as "The Hague Convention", it requires States Parties to make hijackings punishable by "severe penalties"; makes it an offence for any person on board an aircraft in flight to "unlawfully, by force or threat thereof, or any other form of intimidation, to seize or exercise control of that aircraft" or to attempt to do so; requires parties that have custody of offenders to either extradite the offender or submit the case for prosecution; and requires parties to assist each other in connection with criminal proceedings brought under the Convention. It is one of 12 major **United Nations** conventions and protocols dealing with **terrorism** and acts affecting in-flight safety.

Convention Governing the Specific Aspects of Refugee Problems in Africa (OAU/AU)

The Assembly of Heads of State or Government of the **Organization of African Unity (OAU)** adopted, on 10 September 1969, the Convention Governing the Specific Aspects of Refugee Problems in Africa. The Convention entered into force on 20 June 1974 and 44 Member States had deposited their instrument of ratification by the middle of 2003. The main objective of the Convention, designed to complement the **Convention relating to the Status of Refugees** adopted by the **United Nations** in 1951 and modified by the **Protocol relating to the Status of Refugees** of 1967, is to improve conditions for refugees in Africa and to promote a humanitarian approach for solving problems in this field. Article 1, paragraph 1, defines the term "refugee" as "every person who, owing to well-grounded fear of being prosecuted for reasons of race, religion, nationality, membership of a particular social group or political opinion, is outside the country of his nationality and is unwilling to return to it". The Convention equally recognizes as a refugee a person who has been compelled to leave his country for reasons of external aggression, occupation, foreign domination or events seriously disturbing public order in either part or the whole of his country of origin or nationality (Article 1, para. 2). States Parties are obliged to use their best endeavours to receive refugees and to ensure their settlement (Article 2), while at the same time preventing refugees residing in their respective territories from carrying out acts that may cause tension, such as fomenting subversion in another State (Article 3). The Convention also contains provisions stating that the granting of asylum is to be considered a peaceful and humanitarian act, that the provisions of the Convention are to be applied without **discrimination** of any kind and that repatriation may only be realized with the full and voluntary consent of the refugee. While the Convention contains no provisions for the establishment of a monitoring mechanism, it does stipulate that in the case of a dispute between States Parties regarding the interpretation or application of the Convention, the question is to be referred to the Committee for Mediation, Conciliation and Arbitration of the Secretariat of the OAU, which shall advise on the matter.

Convention of Belem do Para (OAS)

See **Inter-American Convention on the Prevention, Punishment and Eradication of Violence against Women.**

Convention on Asylum (OAS)

The Convention on Asylum was adopted by the Pan-American Union, the forerunner of the **Organization of American States (OAS)**, on 20 February 1928 and entered into force on

21 May 1929. By the middle of 2003, it had been ratified by 16 of the 35 OAS Member States. This Convention aims at laying down the rules governing the relations between States Parties with regard to asylum. It stipulates that persons requesting asylum on political grounds should be guaranteed such a request to the extent to which it is recognized by the Conventions or by the laws of the granting country, or on humanitarian grounds. It further stipulates that, in addition to State territory, asylum may be granted in legations, warships, and military aircraft or installations, but only in emergencies and only for the limited period of time necessary to ensure the safety of the asylum seeker. Under the Convention, States Parties agree to promptly report to the Minister of Foreign Relations of the concerned State that one of its nationals has sought asylum. The receiving State is also obliged, upon request of the concerned State and after a guarantee of the safety of the asylum-seeker, to deport the asylum seeker. Excluded from the right to enjoyment of the provisions of the Convention are persons who are accused or convicted of common crimes and persons who are deserters from the armed forces. Two later instruments, the **Convention on Political Asylum** (1933) and the **Convention on Territorial Asylum** (1954), complement the Convention of 1928.

Convention on Combating Bribery of Foreign Public Officials in International Business Transactions (OECD)

This Convention was adopted by the **Organisation for Economic Co-operation and Development (OECD)**, uniting the developed countries of the world on 21 November 1997. It entered into force on 15 February 1999. By the middle of 2003, it had been ratified by 34 Member and non-Member States (Argentina, Australia, Austria, Belgium, Brazil, Bulgaria, Canada, Chile, Czech Republic, Denmark, Finland, France, Germany, Greece, Hungary, Iceland, Italy, Japan, Luxembourg, Mexico, Netherlands, New Zealand, Norway, Poland, Portugal,

Republic of Korea, Slovenia, Slovak Republic, Spain, Sweden, Switzerland, Turkey, United Kingdom and United States of America). The Convention is among the first international instruments aimed at the struggle against **corruption**. It includes measures to be taken concerning: the offence of bribery of foreign public officials (Article 1); money laundering (Article 7); mutual legal assistance (Article 9) and extradition (Article 10). To strengthen the combat against corruption, the OECD has set up an Anti-Corruption Unit as well as an Anti-Corruption Network for Transition Economies.

Convention on Consent to Marriage, Minimum Age for Marriage and Registration of Marriages (UN)

Adopted by the **United Nations General Assembly** on 7 November 1962 by resolution 1763A (XVII), and entered into force on 9 December 1964, this Convention is aimed at the abolition of customs and practices of child marriages and the betrothal of young girls. By the middle of 2003, it had been ratified by about 50 States. The Convention provides that no marriage shall be legally entered into without the full and free consent of the partners, that a minimum age of marriage shall be legislatively specified (although the Convention leaves the specification of the minimum age to each State Party, the Recommendation of 1965 adopted by the United Nations General Assembly on this subject states that the minimum age shall in any case not be less than fifteen years) and that no marriage shall be legally entered into by any person under this age, and that all marriages shall be registered in an official register by the competent authorities (Articles 1-3).

Convention on Diplomatic Asylum (OAS)

Based on the Convention on Asylum (1933) and complementing the **Convention on Territorial Asylum** (1954), this Convention was adopted by the **Organization of American**

States (OAS) on 28 March 1954 and entered into force on 29 December the same year. By the middle of 2003, it had been ratified by 14 of the 35 OAS Member States. The aim of the Convention is to define the rules concerning asylum when granted in legations, war vessels and military camps or aircraft located in the territory of another State Party. For the purposes of the Convention, a legation is "any seat of a regular diplomatic mission, the residence of chiefs of mission, and the premises provided by them for the dwelling places of asylees" (Article 1). The Convention applies to persons being sought or persecuted for political reasons or for political offences, with the exception of individuals who are under indictment, under trial or have been convicted for common offences. States are not obliged to grant asylum (Article 2). It is to be granted only in "urgent cases and only for the period of time strictly necessary" (Article 5), that is, until the asylee's safety can be assured, and it is to be respected by the State of the person requesting it. The Convention also contains provisions on the transfer of the asylee from his territorial State to another, the diplomatic procedures to be followed, and the obligation of the granting State to provide the concerned State with information regarding the granting of asylum, and the settlement of the asylee once in the country giving him or her protection.

Convention on Human Rights and Biomedicine (Council of Europe)

See **Convention for the Protection of Human Rights and Dignity of the Human Being with regard to the Application of Biology and Medicine: Convention on Human Rights and Biomedicine**.

Convention on Offences and Certain Other Acts Committed on Board Aircraft (ICAO)

This Convention was adopted by the **International Civil Aviation Organization (ICAO)** on 14 September 1963. It entered into force on 4 December 1969. It is one of the 12 major multilateral conventions and protocols aimed against terrorism and acts affecting in-flight safety adopted under the aegis of the **United Nations** and its specialized agencies.

Convention on Political Asylum (OAS)

This Convention was adopted by the Pan-American Union, the forerunner to the **Organization of American States (OAS)**, on 26 December 1933. It entered into force on 28 March 1935 and, by the middle of 2003, had been ratified by 16 of the 35 OAS Member States. The aim of the Convention is to ensure the rights of aliens to asylum on political grounds. It amends the provisions of the **Convention on Asylum** (1928) in order to bring it in line with the Convention on Extradition (1933). Furthermore, the OAS adopted the **Inter-American Convention on Extradition** in 1981.

Convention on Territorial Asylum (OAS)

As a complement to the **Convention on Political Asylum** (1933) and to the **Convention on Diplomatic Asylum** (1954), the Convention on Territorial Asylum was adopted by the **Organization of American States (OAS)** on 28 March 1954. It entered into force on 29 December 1954 and, by the middle of 2003, had been ratified by 12 of the 35 OAS Member States. In accordance with the Convention, States Parties undertake to recognize and respect the right of every State to "admit into its territory such persons as it deems advisable, without, through the exercise of this right, giving rise to complaint by any other State" (Article 1). It also contains provisions regarding the right of every State to refuse to expel or extradite from its territory persons persecuted for political reasons or offences elsewhere, and the right of the asylee to freedom of expression, thought, assembly and association in the State granting asylum, without the interference of another State. These rights can be restricted if the asylee incites the use of force or violence against the government of another State. In such cases, the offended State may ask the

State granting asylum to watch over or intern the alien at a reasonable distance from its borders. It is important to note that, under the Convention, the asylee can, at any time, inform the State in which he/she resides that he/she wishes to leave its territory.

Convention on the Elimination of All Forms of Discrimination against Women (UN)

This Convention, adopted by the **United Nations General Assembly** on 18 December 1979 (A/RES/34/180), entered into force on 3 September 1981 and is the most significant and comprehensive instrument with regard to furthering the advancement of women and eliminating gender-based **discrimination**. Ratified by more than 170 Member States by the middle of 2003, the Convention confirms standards formulated in earlier conventions and adds new important dimensions and principles. It defines the term "discrimination against women" as "any distinction, exclusion or restriction made on the basis of sex which has the effect or purpose of impairing of nullifying the recognition, enjoyment or exercise by women, irrespective of their marital status, on a basis of equality of men and women, of human rights and fundamental freedoms in the political, economic, social, cultural, civil or any other field" (Article 1). In the broadest terms, the Convention provides that: "States Parties shall take in all fields, in particular in the political, social, economic and cultural fields, all appropriate measures, including legislation, to ensure the full development and advancement of women for the purpose of guaranteeing them the exercise and enjoyment of human rights and fundamental freedoms on a basis of equality with men" (Article 3). It also contains provisions relating to equality in: political and public life (Article 7), representation at the international level (Article 8); questions of nationality (Article 9); education (Article 10); opportunities and conditions of employment (Article 11); as well as before the law (Article 15); and in matters relating to marriage and family relations (Article 16). The Convention contains provisions requiring States to take a wide range of positive and constructive actions designed to advance the status of women in different fields. The implementation of the Convention is monitored by the **Committee on the Elimination of Discrimination against Women (CEDAW)** established under Article 17.

On 6 October 1999, the United Nations General Assembly adopted the **Optional Protocol to the Convention on the Elimination of All Forms of Discrimination against Women**.

Convention on the International Right of Correction (UN)

To guard against the danger to peace and friendly relations between peoples arising from the publication of inaccurate reports, the **United Nations General Assembly** adopted the Convention on the International Right of Correction on 16 December 1952 by resolution 630 (VII). Entered into force on 24 August 1962, the Convention had been ratified by about 15 States by the middle of 2003. Under the Convention, the "Contracting States agree that, when a State contends that a news dispatch capable of injuring its relations with other States or its national prestige or dignity transmitted from one country to another by correspondents or information agencies ... is false or distorted, it may submit its version of the facts to the Contracting State within whose territories such dispatch has been published or disseminated" (Article 2, para. 1). This communiqué must be "without comment or expression of opinion and be no longer than is necessary to correct the alleged inaccuracy or distortion" (Article 2, para. 2). In complying with the Convention, the receiving State is obliged to release the communiqué through the channels customarily used for the release of news concerning international affairs for publication (Article 3, para. 1). The Convention does not, however, impose a legal obligation on the press or other media to publish the communiqué. In the event that the receiving State does not fulfil its obligation, the complaining State may accord, on the basis of reciprocity, similar treatment to a communiqué submitted to it by the defaulting State (Article 3, para. 2). The complaining State also has the right to seek relief through the **United Nations Secretary-General**. In accordance with the instrument, the Secretary-General will give appropriate publicity to the communiqué, together with the original dispatch and the comments, if any, submitted to him by the State complained against (Article 4). The Convention also contains a compromise clause by which disputes not settled by negotiation may be referred to the **International Court of Justice** (Article 5).

Convention on the Nationality of Married Women (UN)

Adopted by the **United Nations General Assembly** on 29 January 1957 by resolution 1040 (XI), this Convention entered into force on 11 August 1958. By the middle of 2003, it had been ratified by about 70 States. The Convention proclaims that women shall have the same rights as men to acquire, change or retain their nationality. It provides that Contracting States agree that neither the celebration nor the dissolution of marriage between one of their nationals and an alien, nor the change of nationality by the husband during marriage, shall automatically affect the nationality of the wife (Article 1). It further stipulates that neither the voluntary acquisition of the nationality of another State, nor the renunciation of his nationality by a husband shall prevent the retention of the nationality by the wife (Article 2). In other words, no change may be made to the nationality of the wife without an expression of desire on her part for such a change. The Convention further provides that the alien wife of one of the nationals of a Contracting State may, at her request, acquire the nationality of her husband through specially privileged naturalization procedures (Article 3). The Convention, however, does not contain specific provisions concerning international mechanisms of implementation.

Convention on the Nationality of Women (OAS)

This Convention was adopted by the Pan-American Union, the forerunner to the **Organization of American States (OAS)**, on 26 December 1933. It entered into force on 29 August 1934 and, by the middle of 2003 had been ratified by 17 of the 35 OAS Member States. It contains one substantive provision stipulating that within Contracting States "there shall be no distinction based on sex as regards nationality, in their legislation or in their practice" (Article 1).

Convention on the Non-applicability of Statutory Limitations to War Crimes and Crimes against Humanity (UN)

The Convention on the Non-Applicability of Statutory Limitations to War Crimes and Crimes against Humanity was adopted by the **United Nations General Assembly** on 26 November 1968 by resolution 239 (XXIII), and entered into force on 11 November 1970. It had been ratified by more than 40 Member States by the middle of 2003. This Convention aims at affirming in international law the principle that there is no period of limitation for crimes against humanity and war crimes. It conveys the idea that certain norms are so basic to humanity and to the international community that grave infringements of these norms in no way lose their criminal character through the passage of time. The Convention states that no statutory limitation shall apply to: war crimes, crimes against humanity whether committed in a time of war or peace (as defined in the Charter of the International Military Tribunal, Nuremberg, of 8 August 1945), eviction as a result of armed attack or occupation and inhuman acts which are the consequences of the policy of **apartheid** or the crime of **genocide** (Article I). The provisions of the Convention apply to "both representatives of the State authority and to private individuals who, as principals or accomplices, participate in, or who directly incite others, to the commission of any of the crimes cited above, or who conspire to commit them" (Article II). States Parties to the Convention agree to adopt all necessary domestic measures, legislative or otherwise, making possible the extradition of such persons as listed above (Article III), and to ensure that statutory or other limitations shall not apply to the prosecution and punishment of international crimes (Article IV).

Convention on the Participation of Foreigners in Public Life at Local Level (Council of Europe)

Adopted by the **Council of Europe** on 5 February 1992, this Convention entered into force on 1 May 1997. By the middle of 2003, it had been ratified by 6 Member States and signed by three others. The Convention aims to secure genuine **civil** and **political rights** for foreign residents in local communities. It is based on the opinion of Member States that the participation of citizens in local government is a fundamental principle of all democratic regimes and, as stated in the Preamble, that the existence of lawfully resident foreigners in the national territory of Member States is a real and common feature. Three measures to enhance the participation of foreigners in public life at the local level and to protect their rights are envisaged in this instrument: the assurance of **freedom of opinion and expression, peaceful assembly** and **association** (Articles 3-4); the establishment of consultative bodies to represent foreign residents at the local level, to provide a forum for discussion and for the formulation of opinions and policies, and to foster their general integration into the life of the community (Article 5); and the guarantee of the right of foreign residents to vote in local elections and to stand for election provided that he or she has been a lawful resident for five years prior to the election (Articles 6-7). To secure the civil and political rights of foreign residents, Member States agree to ensure that no legal obstacles exist to prevent the establishment of the aforementioned consultative bodies and that links between local authorities and such organizations will be formed. Each Contracting State further agrees to keep the Secretary-General of the Council of Europe informed of any legislative measures adopted under the terms of the Convention. No monitoring body is envisaged by the instrument. In order to facilitate the procedures of ratification, Article 1 of the Convention contains provisions making it possible to adopt only parts of the Convention and adhere to the remaining provisions at a later stage.

Convention on the Political Rights of Women (UN)

Upon recommendation of the **Commission on the Status of Women**, the Convention on the Political Rights of Women was adopted by the **United Nations General Assembly** on 31 March 1953 by resolution 640 (VII), and entered into force on 7 July 1954. By the middle of 2003, it had been ratified by about 120 States. The Convention was designed as a further means to promote equality of status of men and women in the enjoyment and exercise of **political rights** in accordance with the provisions of the **Charter of the United Nations** and the **Universal Declaration of Human Rights**. It provides that women, on equal terms with men and without **discrimination**, shall: be entitled to vote in all elections (Article I); be eligible for election to all publicly elected bodies, established by national law (Article II); and be entitled to hold public office and to exercise all public functions, established by national law (Article III). Though the Convention deals only with discrimination against women as far as the implementation of their political rights is concerned, it was the first universal binding instrument creating legal obligations for States Parties. It opened the way for the adoption by the **United Nations** of a series of instruments aimed at the elimination of discrimination against women in all spheres of public and private life.

Convention on the Prevention and Combating of Terrorism (OAU/AU)

The Convention on the Prevention and Combating of Terrorism was adopted on 14 July 1999 by the Member States of the **Organization of African Unity** (now **African Union**). The Convention came into force on 6 December 2002. It was ratified by 24 States by the middle of 2003. The Convention expresses the conviction that "**terrorism** constitutes a serious violation of human rights and, in particular, the rights to physical integrity, life, freedom and security, and impedes socio-economic development through destabilization of States". Furthermore it reaffirms that "terrorism cannot be justified under any circumstances and, consequently, should be combated in all its forms and manifestations, including those in which States are involved directly or indirectly, without regard to its origin, causes and objectives" (Preamble) and aims at promoting cooperation among the Member States to prevent and combat terrorism. It should ensure collective measures to fight terrorism and provides for a greater coordination of national policies, legislative, administrative and enforcement approaches to terrorism pursuant to the principles of international law and the provisions of the Charter of the Organization of African Unity, the **Charter of the United Nations** and the **African Charter on Human and Peoples' Rights**. The Convention contains a detailed definition of a "terrorist act" and prohibits "any promotion, sponsoring, contribution to, command, aid, incitement, encouragement, attempt, threat, conspiracy, organizing, or procurement of any person, with the intent to commit" such an act (Article 1). Article 3 stipulates that "the struggle waged by peoples in accordance with the principles of international law for their liberation or self-determination, including armed struggle against colonialism, occupation, aggression and domination by foreign forces shall not be considered as terrorist acts".

The Convention contains detailed provisions concerning areas of cooperation (Articles 4 and 5), State jurisdiction (Articles

6 and 7), extradition (Articles 8-13), extra-territorial investigations and mutual legal assistance (Articles 14-18).

Convention on the Prevention and Punishment of Crimes against Internationally Protected Persons, including Diplomatic Agents (UN)

This Convention was adopted by the **United Nations General Assembly** on 14 December 1973, and entered into force on 20 February 1977. This instrument is aimed at the struggle against **terrorism**. By the middle of 2003, it had been ratified by about 110 States. It includes in the category of "internationally protected persons": Heads of State or Government; Ministers for Foreign Affairs; and representatives or officials of a State or of an international organization who are entitled to special protection from attack under international law. It requires each State Party to criminalize and make punishable by appropriate penalties which take into account their grave nature: the intentional murder, kidnapping, or other attacks upon the security or liberty of an internationally protected person; violent attacks upon the official premises, private accommodation, or the means of transport of such persons; threats or attempts to commit such attacks and acts constituting participation as accomplices.

The Convention provides that States Parties must establish criminal jurisdiction over offenders (for example, the State(s) where the offence takes place or, in some cases, the State of nationality of the perpetrator or victim). The State Party in whose territory the alleged offender is present shall take the appropriate measures to establish its jurisdiction over the crimes committed or to extradite the offender.

Any dispute between two or more States Parties concerning the interpretation or application of this Convention, which is not settled by negotiation, shall at the request of one of them be submitted to arbitration. If within six months from the date of the request for arbitration, the States Parties are unable to agree on the organization of the arbitration, any one of them may refer the dispute to the **International Court of Justice** by request in conformity with the Statute of the Court.

Convention on the Prevention and Punishment of the Crime of Genocide (UN)

This Convention was adopted by the **United Nations General Assembly** on 9 December 1948 by resolution 260A (III) and entered into force on 12 January 1951. It had been ratified by more than 130 States by the middle of 2003. Under the Convention, Contracting Parties "confirm that **genocide**, whether committed in time of peace or in time of war, is a crime under international law which they undertake to prevent and to punish" (Article I). It defines genocide as "any of the following acts committed with intent to destroy, in whole or in part, a national, ethnical, racial or religious group, as such: (a) killing members of the group; (b) causing serious bodily or mental harm to members of the group; (c) deliberately inflicting on the group conditions of life calculated to bring about its physical destruction in whole or in part; (d) imposing measures intended to prevent births within the group; (e) forcibly transferring children of the group to another group" (Article II). The Convention provides for persons charged with committing genocide, conspiracy to commit genocide, direct and public incitement to commit genocide, attempt to commit genocide or complicity in genocide (Article III) to be tried either by a competent tribunal in the State where the act was committed or by such an international penal tribunal as may have jurisdiction and has been accepted as competent by States Parties to the Convention (Article VI). The Convention also provides that any Contracting Party may call upon the competent organs of the **United Nations** for the prevention and suppression of acts of genocide (Article VIII). No limitation is applied to the crime of genocide as a crime against humanity, in conformity with the **Convention on the**

Non-Applicability of Statutory Limitations to War Crimes and Crimes against Humanity (1968).

Convention on the Reduction of Statelessness (UN)

Taking into account the provision of the **Universal Declaration on Human Rights** that everyone has the **right to a nationality** (Article 15), the Convention on the Reduction of Statelessness was adopted on 30 August 1961, and entered into force on 13 December 1975. By the middle of 2003, it had been ratified by 26 States. This Convention was drawn up to guard against statelessness and to facilitate the exercise of human rights by refugees and stateless persons. It contains provisions for attributing a nationality to persons who would otherwise be stateless and prohibits, subject to certain exceptions, the deprivation of nationality if such deprivation would render persons stateless (Articles 1 and 5-8). States Parties are also prohibited from depriving "any person or group of persons of their nationality on racial, ethnic, religious or political grounds" (Article 9). The Convention further provides that the States Parties promote the establishment, within the framework of the **United Nations**, of a body to which a person claiming the benefit of the Convention may apply for the examination of his/her claim and for assistance in presenting it to the appropriate authority (Article 11). In 1976, the General Assembly, after noting that the **United Nations High Commissioner for Refugees (UNHCR)** was already carrying out the functions described under the Convention, requested the UNHCR to continue to do so.

Convention on the Rights of the Child (UN)

Concerned that the situation of children in many parts of the world remained critical as a result of inadequate social conditions, natural disasters, armed conflicts, exploitation, hunger and disability, and convinced that urgent and effective national and international legislation was called for, the **United Nations General Assembly**, on 20 November 1989 (A/RES/44/25), adopted the Convention on the Rights of the Child based on the **Declaration of the Rights of the Child** (1959). Entering into force on 2 September 1990, the Convention which, by the middle of 2003, had been ratified by a record number of 191 States, recognizes and protects a wide range of rights and liberties of the child. In Article 1, for the purposes of the Convention, the term "child" is defined as every human being below 18 years of age unless, under the State law applicable to the child, majority is attained earlier. The Convention acknowledges the importance of a secure and healthy family or alternative environment, provides for education, leisure and cultural activities, states that children in emergency situations are entitled to special protection and that children in situations of conflict with the law must be guaranteed basic rights, and protects children from any form of exploitation. The following general principles are also enunciated: non-**discrimination**; the obligation to take the best interest of the child into account; respect of the child's opinion; and the **right to life**, survival and development. The Convention also contains a number of provisions concerning its implementation, including the obligations of the States Parties in this regard. The implementation of the Convention is monitored by the **Committee on the Rights of the Child** established in conformity with its Article 43.

On 25 May 2000, the United Nations General Assembly adopted both the **Optional Protocol to the Convention on the Rights of the Child on the Sale of Children, Child Prostitution and Child Pornography** and the **Optional Protocol to the Convention on the Rights of the Child on the Involvement of Children in Armed Conflict**. The first Optional Protocol entered into force on 18 January 2002 (50 ratifications by the middle of 2003) and the second one on 12 February 2002 (52 ratifications by the middle of 2003). States Parties to these Protocols have to submit a report to the Committee on the Rights of the Child within two years after ratification.

Universal Children's Day is observed on 20 November each year and the **International Day of Innocent Children Victims of Aggression** on 4 June.

Convention on the Status of Aliens (OAS)

Complementing the Convention Relative to the Rights of Aliens (1902), the Convention on the Status of Aliens was adopted by the Pan-American Union, the forerunner to the **Organization of American States (OAS)**, on 20 February 1928. The Convention entered into force on 29 August 1929 and had been ratified by 15 of the 35 OAS Member States by the middle of 2003. The aim of the Convention is to ensure the juridical status of aliens. It stipulates that, as a basic principle, aliens should be granted enjoyment of all essential **civil rights** equal to that of nationals or citizens.

Convention relating to the Status of Refugees (UN)

The Convention relating to the Status of Refugees was adopted by the United Nations Conference of Plenipotentiaries on the Status of Refugees and Stateless Persons on 28 July 1951 (resolution 429 (V)), and entered into force on 22 April 1954. It had been ratified by more than 140 Member States by the middle of 2003. According to Article 1.A (2) of the Convention, the term "refugee" shall apply to any person who "As a result of events occurring before 1 January 1951 and owing to well-founded fear of being persecuted for reasons of race, religion, nationality, membership of a particular social group or political opinion, is outside the country of his nationality and is unable or, owing to such fear, is unwilling to avail himself of the protection of that country; or who, not having a nationality and being outside the country of his former habitual residence as a result of such events, is unable or, owing to such fear, is unwilling to return to it". Contracting States undertake to apply the provisions of the Convention without **discrimination** as to race, religion or country of origin (Article 3). The Convention requires that refugees receive treatment at least as favourable as that accorded to the nationals of the State Party concerned with regard to certain rights, such as freedom of religion (Article 4), access to courts (Article 16), elementary education (Article 22) and public relief (Article 23). With regard to other rights, such as wage-earning employment (Article 17) and **freedom of association** (Article 15) refugees are entitled to the most favourable treatment accorded to nationals of a foreign country. In other respects, for example self-employment (Article 18) and freedom of movement (Article 26), refugees receive treatment as favorable as possible and not less favorable than that accorded to aliens in general. Of particular importance for refugees is the principle of non-refoulement, that is, that refugees may not on any account whatsoever be expelled or returned to a country where their life or freedom would be threatened on account of their race, religion, nationality, membership of a particular group or political opinion (Article 33). The application of the provisions of the Convention are supervised by the Office of the **United Nations High Commissioner for Refugees (UNHCR)** which requests that States Parties to the Convention give information concerning: the condition of refugees; the implementation of the Convention and the Protocol; and laws, regulations and decrees which are, or will be, in force relating to refugees (Article 35).

The **Protocol relating to the Status of Refugees** was adopted by the **United Nations General Assembly** on 16 December 1966. It entered into force on 4 October 1967 and, by the middle of 2003, had been ratified by more than 140 Member States. It contains general provisions concerning the modification of the definition of a refugee removing the geographic and time limitations in the Convention (Article 1). Cooperation of the national authorities with the **United Nations** is foreseen in Article 2.

Convention relating to the Status of Stateless Persons (UN)

Adopted on 28 September 1954, and entered into force on 6 June 1960, the Convention on the Status of Stateless Persons had been ratified by more than 54 States by the middle of 2003. The Convention applies to "a person who is not considered as a national by any State under the operation of its law". Two principles are at the basis or this Convention: first, that there should be as little **discrimination** as possible between nationals, on the one hand, and stateless persons on the other; second, that there should be no discrimination based on race, religion or country of origin among stateless persons (Article 3). The Convention requires that stateless persons receive treatment at least as favourable as that accorded to nationals of States Parties with regard to certain rights, such as freedom of religion (Article 4), the right of association (Article 15), access to courts (Article 16), elementary education (Article 22) and public relief (Article 23). With regard to such rights as wage-earning employment (Article 17) and self-employment (Article 18) stateless persons should enjoy treatment not less favourable than that accorded to aliens generally in the same circumstances. In accordance with Article 33, States Parties are obliged to "communicate to the **United Nations Secretary-General** the laws and regulations which they may adopt to ensure the application of this Convention".

Convention relative to the Rights of Aliens (OAS)

The Convention relative to the Rights of Aliens was adopted by International Union of American Republics, a predecessor to the Pan-American Union and a forerunner to the **Organization of American States (OAS)**, on 29 January 1902. By the middle of 2003, the Convention had been ratified by 5 States: Bolivia, Dominican Republic, El Salvador, Guatemala and Honduras. The Convention stipulates that aliens shall enjoy all **civil rights** pertaining to citizens, and make use thereof in the substance, form or procedure, and in the recourses which result therefrom, under exactly the same terms as citizens, except as may be otherwise provided by the Constitution of each country. It declares that States do not owe to, nor recognize in, favour of foreigners, any obligations or responsibilities other than those established by their Constitutions and laws in favour of their citizens. Therefore, the States are not responsible for damages sustained by aliens through acts of rebels or individuals, and in general, for damages originating from fortuitous causes of any kind, considering as such the acts of war, except in the case of failure on the part of the constituted authorities to comply with their duties. Whenever an alien shall have claims or complaints of a civil, criminal or administrative order against a State, or its citizens, he shall present his claims to a competent Court of the country, and such claims shall not be made, through diplomatic channels, except in the cases where there shall have been on the part of the Court, a manifest denial of justice, or unusual delay, or evident violation of the principles of international law.

Convention to Prevent and Punish the Acts of Terrorism Taking the Forms of Crimes against Persons and Related Extortion that Are of International Significance (OAS)

This Convention was adopted by the **Organization of American States (OAS)** on 2 February 1971 to strengthen the combat against **terrorism**. It enters into force for the States that ratify it when they deposit their respective instruments of ratification (Article 12). By the middle of 2003, the Convention had been ratified by 15 countries. Article 2 states that: "… kidnapping, murder, and other assaults against the life or physical integrity … shall be considered common crimes of international significance, regardless of motive" and Article 8 concerns cooperation in preventing and punishing the crimes contemplated in Article 2.

Copenhagen Declaration on Social Development and Programme of Action (UN)

Adopted by the **World Summit for Social Development** in 1995. See also the **Commission for Social Development**.

Corruption

In the 1990s, corruption, recognized as a threat to democracy, the rule of law and human rights, became a subject of the attention of international and regional organizations. It was put on the agenda of the **United Nations** and regional intergovernmental organizations. The **United Nations General Assembly** and the **Economic and Social Council (ECOSOC)** have adopted a number of resolutions on this matter. The General Assembly also adopted an **International Code of Conduct for Public Officials** which is based on the assumption that a public office, as defined by national law, is a position of trust, implying a duty to act in the public interest. A Charter for European Security was adopted at the Istanbul Summit of the **Organization for Security and Co-operation in Europe (OSCE)** in 1999. It contains a section on "Rule of law and fight against corruption" (para. 33) which states that: "corruption poses a great threat to the OSCE's shared values. It generates instability and reaches into many aspects of the security, economic and human dimensions". Participating States pledge "to strengthen their efforts to combat corruption ... to promote a positive framework for good government practices and public integrity ... and assist each other in the fight against corruption". It emphasizes the duty of public officials to refrain from using "their official authority for the improper advancement of their own and their family's personal or financial interests" and calls for requirements to disclose personal assets and liabilities. A particularly pernicious type of corruption is bribery in international business transactions.

The **Organization of American States (OAS)** adopted the **Inter-American Convention against Corruption (OAS)** in 1996 which entered into force on 3 June 1997 and the **Organization for Economic Co-operation and Development (OECD)** adopted the **Convention on Combating Bribery of Foreign Public Officials in International Business Transactions** on 15 February 1999.

Council of Europe

The **Council of Europe** was established on 5 May 1949, upon signature of its Statute by Government representatives of 10 countries. Its membership has grown over the years and, by the middle of 2003, reached 45 (Albania, Andorra, Armenia, Austria, Azerbaijan, Belgium, Bosnia-Herzegovina, Bulgaria, Croatia, Cyprus, Czech Republic, Denmark, Estonia, Finland, France, Georgia, Germany, Greece, Hungary, Iceland, Ireland, Italy, Latvia, Liechtenstein, Lithuania, Luxembourg, Malta, Moldova, Netherlands, Norway, Poland, Portugal, Romania, Russian Federation, San Marino, Serbia and Montenegro, Slovakia, Slovenia, Spain, Sweden, Switzerland, "The former Yugoslav Republic of Macedonia", Turkey, Ukraine and the United Kingdom). The central aims of the Council include: the protection of human rights; the promotion of pluralist democracy and the rule of law; seeking solutions to problems concerning **minorities**, intolerance, xenophobia, **organized crime**, AIDS, drugs and environmental protection; improving living conditions; working for greater European unity; and strengthening an independent and pluralistic press. The Council is composed of two main bodies: the Committee of Ministers and the Parliamentary Assembly. The Committee of Ministers, which is the decision-making body, comprises the Ministers for Foreign Affairs of the Member States. It meets twice a year but may also hold special sessions. Its Chair changes every six months, following the alphabetical order of Member States. The Parliamentary Assembly is the deliberative body. It comprises 306 representatives appointed by national parliaments of Member States, as well as special guests from certain European non-Member States, and holds four plenary sessions a year, at which it makes recommendations to the

Committee of Ministers on any matter concerning the work of the Council. Another body is the Congress of Local and Regional Authorities of Europe, composed of 582 members, which represents the entities of local and regional self-government within the Member States. Although the Council deals with practically all aspects of European affairs (with the exception of defence), human rights activities constitute one of its most important fields for intervention, this being reflected in a number of ways. First, to achieve membership in the Council a country must abide by Article 4 of the Statute which declares that each Member State must recognize the principle of the rule of law and guarantee its citizens the enjoyment of human rights and fundamental freedoms. Second, a country cannot become a member of the Council until it formally accepts to abide by the provisions of the **European Convention for the Protection of Human Rights and Fundamental Freedoms** (1950) which set up the **European Court of Human Rights** in 1959. Among other binding instruments adopted by the Council in the field of promotion and protection of human rights are: the **European Social Charter** (1961) and **European Social Charter revised** (1996); the **European Convention for the Prevention of Torture and Inhuman or Degrading Treatment or Punishment** (1987) and the **Framework Convention for the Protection of National Minorities** (1995).

The Office of the **Commissioner for Human Rights** was established in 1999 as an independent institution within the Council of Europe to promote the full enjoyment of human rights in all Member States.

For more information see: http://www.coe.int

Court of Justice of the European Communities – CJEC (EU)

The Court of Justice of the European Communities is a common institution to the three European Communities (**European Community**, European Atomic Energy Community and European Coal and Steel Community), with relative autonomy regarding its organization and proceedings. It ensures that community law is uniformly interpreted and effectively applied throughout the community and has wide jurisdiction to give preliminary rulings and to hear various types of action involving Member States, **European Union** institutions, businesses and individuals.

The Court is often called upon to settle questions of major economic significance, such as single market issues and to secure the respect of the four European fundamental freedoms (free movement of goods, capital, persons and services). It also gives an important place to the fundamental principles for the protection of individuals in its case law. For instance, the fundamental rights of individuals have been declared general principles of law to be applied by the Court within the framework of community law. Furthermore, the principle of equality has been interpreted, particularly in the context of equal access to employment and pay for women and men. The CJEC has already begun referring to the new **European Charter of Fundamental Rights**, which extends its competence to the field of civil liberties. It could transform this mainly commercial court to a rival court set against the non-EU **European Court of Human Rights** and the **European Convention for the Protection of Human Rights and Fundamental Freedoms**, in the area of European rights law.

The governments of the Member States appoint by common accord 15 Judges and eight Advocates General for a six-year term, partially renewable every 3 years. The President of the Court is selected by and among the Judges for a term of three years. A Court of First Instance has been attached to the CJEC since 1989.

For more information see: http://curia.eu.int/en/index.htm

Cultural heritage

In 1972, the General Conference of UNESCO adopted the **Convention concerning the Protection of the World Cultural and Natural Heritage**. This instrument defines international protection of the world cultural and natural heritage as "the establishment of a system of international cooperation and assistance designed to support States Parties to the Convention in their efforts to conserve and identify that heritage" (Article 7). The two basic principles of the instrument are: each State Party recognizes its obligation to ensure the conservation of elements of the world cultural heritage situated within its territory; and the international community as a whole recognizes its obligation to cooperate to conserve the heritage which is of a universal character. Furthermore, the Convention provides for the establishment of the **World Heritage Committee** as an intergovernmental committee to supervise the protection of items recognized by the Convention as being of outstanding universal value from the point of view of history, art, science or aesthetics. According to the Convention, the term "cultural heritage" is applied to a monument, group of buildings or site of historical, aesthetic, archaeological, scientific, ethnological or anthropological value. The Convention is based on the belief that the preservation of the cultural heritage is the concern of all and that it should be treasured as a unique testimony of an enduring past. The cultural heritage of humanity is the subject of several universal and regional instruments including the following: **Convention for the Protection of the Architectural Heritage of Europe; European Convention on Offences relating to Cultural Property; European Convention on the Protection of the Archaeological Heritage – revised; Hague International Convention for the Protection of Cultural Property in the Event of Armed Conflict.**

Cultural rights

Cultural rights are specified in several human rights instruments including: the **Universal Declaration of Human Rights** (1948); the **International Covenant on Economic, Social and Cultural Rights** (1966); the **International Covenant on Civil and Political Rights** (1966); the **Declaration of the Principles of International Cultural cooperation** (1966); and the

Universal Copyright Convention (1952) and the Universal Copyright Convention as revised in 1971. Mention should also be made of the following **UNESCO** instruments: the **Recommendation on the Status of Scientific Researchers** (1974), the **Convention for the Protection of Cultural Property in the Event of Armed Conflict** (1954), the **Recommendation on Participation by the People at Large in Cultural Life and their Contribution to It** (1976) and the **Universal Declaration on Cultural Diversity** (2001).

During the last decade of the 20th century, cultural rights have increasing attention from international governmental and **non-governmental organizations** as well as from human rights specialists. Among the various reasons for which they have become a subject of active international debate is the fact that cultural differences can often be among the main sources of internal conflicts. Violations of cultural rights of various groups, rejection of the right to be different, to have different cultural identities have become very dangerous pathologies which fuel aggressive **ethno-nationalism**, xenophobia, racism and anti-semitism. Therefore culture and respect of cultural rights have also been recognized as an essential element in the prevention and resolution of conflicts. This has resulted in increased efforts to the elaboration of and respect for the cultural rights of persons belonging to **minorities, indigenous people** and other **vulnerable groups**.

Nowadays there is also a general recognition of the importance of culture for the development not only in its economic dimension but also for "human development" understood by the **World Summit for Social Development** (Copenhagen 1995) as the social and cultural fulfilment of the individual. Without the implementation of cultural rights – the **right to education**, the **right to take part in cultural life**, and without the freedom of artistic, scientific and intellectual activities and pursuits, human development is impossible. The observance of cultural rights, in particular the right to cultural identity, is considered now as a constitutive element of the respect of human dignity.

Culture of peace (UNESCO/UN)

The culture of peace concept was formulated by the International Congress on Peace in the Minds of Men, organized by the **United Nations Educational, Scientific and Cultural Organization (UNESCO)** in Yamoussoukro, Côte d'Ivoire, in 1989. In 1993, it was adopted as a specific programme of UNESCO. In 1995, the General Conference of UNESCO at its 28th session dedicated the Organization's Medium-Term Strategy for the years 1996-2001 to the promotion of a culture of peace. Subsequently, in 1996, UNESCO launched the Transdisciplinary Project "Towards a Culture of Peace" involving all Sectors of the Organization in the development of innovative projects and activities that foster this culture.

Recognizing the importance of UNESCO's experience concerning a culture of peace, the **United Nations General Assembly** placed this concept on its agenda for the first time in December 1995 by adopting resolution 50/173. The culture of peace thus became a common objective for the entire **United Nations system**, as attested by the General Assembly's proclamation of the Year 2000 as the **International Year for the Culture of Peace** (A/RES/52/15), which designated UNESCO as the focal point for the celebration of the Year. The primary objective of the Year was to establish a global network for a culture of peace by mobilizing public opinion at all levels in a common endeavour towards a global movement. In 1998, the United Nations General Assembly proclaimed the decade 2001-10 as the **International Decade for a Culture of Peace and Non-Violence for the Children of the World** (A/RES/53/25) and, on 13 September 1999, adopted the **Declaration and Programme of Action on a Culture of Peace** (A/RES/53/243). It provides a framework for action to consolidate, at the national, regional and international levels, the initiatives taken and the movement started on the occasion of the International Year.

UNESCO has undertaken a number of activities promoting the concept of the culture of peace. Thus, in May 1999, it organized the Pan-African Women's Conference on a Culture of Peace in Zanzibar, United Republic of Tanzania. This meeting adopted the Zanzibar Declaration: Women of Africa for a Culture of Peace, which contains a strong human rights component.

Dakar Framework for Action (UNESCO)

The text of the Dakar Framework for Action was adopted by the **World Education Forum** organized by **UNESCO** in Dakar, Senegal, from 26 to 28 April 2000. The Framework is a collective commitment to action. Governments have an obligation to ensure that "Education for All" goals and targets are reached and sustained. This is a responsibility that will be met most effectively through broad-based partnerships within countries, supported by cooperation with regional and international agencies and institutions. It reaffirms the vision of the World Declaration on Education for All (Jomtien, Thailand, 1990) that "all children, young people and adults have the human right to benefit from an education that will meet their basic learning needs in the best and fullest sense of the term, an education that includes learning to know, to do, to live together and to be... an education geared to tapping each individual's talents and potential, and developing learners' personalities, so that they can improve their lives and transform their societies" (Preamble). The Dakar document welcomes the commitments made by the international community to basic education throughout the 1990s, notably at the **World Summit for Children** (1990), the Conference on Environment and Development (1992), the **World Conference on Human Rights** (1993), the World Conference on Special Needs Education: Access and Quality (1994), the International Conference on Population and Development (1994), the **World Summit for Social Development** (1995), the Fourth **World Conference on Women** (1995), the Mid-Term Meeting of the International Consultative Forum on Education for All (1996), the Fifth International Conference on Adult Education (1997), and the International Conference on Child Labour (1997).

Decades for Action to Combat Racism and Racial Discrimination – 1973-83; 1983-93 and 1993-2003 (UN)

On 2 November 1972, the **United Nations General Assembly** designated "the ten-year period beginning on 10 December 1973 as the Decade for Action to Combat Racism and Racial Discrimination", and invited Governments, **United Nations** organs, specialized agencies and other intergovernmental and **non-governmental organizations** to participate in the observance of the Decade. The ultimate goals of the Decade were: "to promote human rights and fundamental freedoms for all, without distinction of any kind on grounds of race, colour, descent or national or ethnic origin, especially by eradicating racial prejudice, **racism** and racial **discrimination**; to arrest any expansion of racist policies, to eliminate the persistence of racist policies and to counteract the emergence of alliances based on mutual espousal of racism and racial discrimination; to resist any policy and practices which lead to the strengthening of the racist regimes and contribute to the sustainment of racism and racial discrimination; to identify, isolate and dispel the fallacious and mythical beliefs, policies and practices that contribute to racism and racial discrimination; and to put an end to racist regimes" (**United Nations General Assembly** resolution 3057 (XXVIII) Annex, para. 8). To this end, the United Nations vigorously pursued a worldwide campaign of information designed to dispel racial prejudice and enlighten and involve world public opinion in the struggle against racism and racial discrimination. This campaign emphasized the importance of the education of **youth** for human rights and dignity and worth of the human person and against theories of racism and racial discrimination.

Two World Conferences to Combat Racism (1978 and 1983), were organized during the first decade (see **World Conference against Racism, Racial Discrimination, Xenophobia and Related Intolerance**). On 22 November 1983, the United

Nations General Assembly proclaimed the Second Decade to Combat Racism and Racial Discrimination, beginning on 13 December 1983. The Assembly also approved the Programme of Action for the Second Decade and called upon all States to cooperate in its implementation. By the same resolution, Governments, **United Nations specialized agencies**, bodies and other interested international governmental organizations, as well as **non-governmental organizations**, in consultative status with the **Economic and Social Council (ECOSOC)** were invited to intensify their efforts to ensure the rapid elimination of racism and racial discrimination. The basic objectives of the Second Decade were: to promote human rights and fundamental freedoms for all without distinction as to race, colour, descent or national or ethnic origin; to eliminate prejudice and racial discrimination; and to abolish regimes and policies based on racism. Publications, seminars, training courses and workshops were among the activities undertaken during the Second Decade. At the mid-point of the Decade, on 10 December 1988, the **United Nations General Assembly** launched a **World Public Information Campaign for Human Rights**. The fight against racism, racial discrimination and **apartheid** and the struggle for equality had a central place in the implementation of the various activities of the World Campaign.

On 20 December 1993, the United Nations General Assembly proclaimed the 10-year period beginning in 1993 as the Third Decade to Combat Racism and Racial Discrimination and adopted a Programme of Action. The goals and objectives of the Third Decade are those adopted by the General Assembly for the First Decade.

The resolution 48/91 declared once again that "all forms of racism and racial discrimination, whether in their institutionalized forms, such as apartheid, or resulting from official doctrines of racial superiority and/or exclusivity, such as ethnic cleansing, are among the most serious violations of human rights in the contemporary world and must be combated by all available means" (para. 1). Governments were urged to take measures to combat new forms of racism, in particular, in legislative, administrative, educational and information fields (para. 4) and the **United Nations Secretary-General** was requested to continue the study of the effects of racial discrimination on the children of **minorities**, particularly those of migrant workers, and to submit recommendations for combating those effects (para. 8). The Programme of Action for the Third Decade (A/RES/48/91, Annex) foresees actions against racism and racial discrimination at the international (paras. 9-18), regional and national levels (paras. 19-23), involving basic research and studies (para. 24), coordination and reporting (paras. 25-26), and system-wide consultations (paras. 27-29). The Plan also outlines measures to ensure a peaceful transition from apartheid to a democratic, non-racial regime in South Africa (paras. 3-5) and measures to remedy the legacy of cultural, economic and social disparities left by apartheid (paras. 6-8). The World Conference against Racism, Racial Discrimination, Xenophobia and Related Intolerance (Durban, South Africa, 31 August-8 September 2001) was the major event within the Third Decade. Moreover, the year 2001 was proclaimed by the United Nations General Assembly as the **International Year of Mobilization against Racism, Racial Discrimination, Xenophobia and Related Intolerance.**

Declaration and Programme of Action on a Culture of Peace (UN)

The Declaration and Programme of Action on a **Culture of Peace** were adopted on 13 September 1999 by the **United Nations General Assembly** (A/RES/53/243). The text of the Declaration defines a culture of peace as a set of values, attitudes, traditions and modes of behaviour, and ways of life that inspire social interaction based on the principles of freedom, justice, democracy, tolerance, solidarity, cooperation, dialogue, understanding among peoples and within and among nations, pluralism, and cultural diversity. Education at all levels, in particular **human rights**

education, is seen as one of the principal means to build a culture of peace (Article 4). To this end, governments, all actors of civil society, the media and **non-governmental organizations** are called upon to fully participate in the process.

The Programme of Action on a Culture of Peace, among other things, serves as the basis for activities within the **International Year for the Culture of Peace** (2000) proclaimed on 20 November 1997 (General Assembly resolution 52/15) and for the **International Decade for a Culture of Peace and Non-Violence for the Children of the World** (2001-10) proclaimed on 10 November 1998 (General Assembly resolution 53/25). The Programme of Action identifies the major areas of action to promote and strengthen a culture of peace, which include education, sustainable economic and social development, human rights, equality between women and men, democratic participation, advancing understanding, tolerance and solidarity, participatory communications and free flow of information and knowledge. According to the Programme of Action, the **United Nations Educational, Scientific and Cultural Organization (UNESCO)**, should continue to play its important role in and make major contributions to the promotion of a culture of peace (para. 5). Effective implementation of the Programme also requires activities at national, regional and international levels mobilizing all partners to contribute to the objectives of the International Year and of the International Decade. The International Year was to serve as the launching point for the process of promoting a culture of peace which will be further consolidated during the International Decade.

Declaration of Basic Principles of Justice for Victims of Crime and Abuse of Power (UN)

This Declaration was adopted by the **United Nations General Assembly** (A/RES/40/34) on 29 November 1985 on the recommendation of the Seventh **United Nations Congress[es] on** the Prevention of Crime and the Treatment of Offenders. It defines "victim" as "any persons who, individually or collectively, have suffered harm, including physical or mental injury, emotional suffering, economic loss or substantial impairment of their fundamental rights, through acts or omissions that are in violation of criminal laws operative within Member States, including those laws proscribing criminal abuse of power" (para. 1). The Declaration recommends measures to be taken at the national, regional and international levels to improve access to justice and fair treatment (paras. 4-7), restitution (paras. 8-11), compensation (paras. 12-13) and social assistance (paras. 14-17) for victims of crime. It outlines the main steps to be taken to proscribe abuses of power and to provide remedies to victims of such abuses (paras. 18-21). To implement the Declaration, A Guide for Practitioners Regarding the Implementation of the Declaration was published in 1989 with the assistance of the Helsinki Institute for Crime Prevention and Control.

Declaration of Fundamental Principles concerning the Contribution of the Mass Media to Strengthening Peace and International Understanding, to the Promotion of Human Rights and to Countering Racialism, Apartheid and Incitement to War (UNESCO)

This Declaration was adopted by the General Conference of **UNESCO** on 28 November 1978 at its 20th session. It affirms the commitment and importance of the mass media in promoting the values of peace and the advancement of international understanding (Article III). In its Preamble, the Declaration recalls the provisions of international conventions which oblige States Parties to adopt immediate and positive measures assigned to eradicate all incitement to, or acts of, racial **discrimination**, and to prevent any encouragement of the crime of **apartheid** and similar segregation policies or their manifestations. The Declaration seeks to underpin the efforts of **United Nations**

specialized agencies and bodies, particularly UNESCO, to create the conditions necessary for a freer, broader and more balanced flow of information (Article I). It aims at: assisting journalists and news reporters in the exercise of their functions (Article II); assisting people who train agents of the mass media to attach special importance to the principles of this Declaration (Article VIII); and establishing the conditions and resources necessary to enable the mass media in developing countries to gain strength and expand thus helping to correct inequalities in the flow of information to and from developing countries (Article VI).

Declaration of Independence of the United States of America – 1776

The Declaration of Independence of the United States of America was drafted by Thomas Jefferson in June 1776 and presented to Congress which, on 2 July, officially declared the new State free and independent. After reviewing the draft, the Congress adopted the final text on 4 July 1776. The document contains the political philosophy and principles, which are still in force and serve as a symbol of liberty for the country. The document claims that all men are created equal and are endowed with unalienable rights, including life, liberty and the pursuit of happiness. The philosophy expressed in the Declaration influenced the adoption of the 1791 **American Bill of Rights** and of various national and international human rights instruments.

Declaration of Mexico on the Equality of Women and Their Contribution to Development and Peace (UN)

The Declaration was adopted by the **World Conference of the International Women's Year**, held in Mexico City from 19 June to 2 July 1975. It proclaims that it is the responsibility of all States to guarantee equality between women and men in all spheres of life, as well as the integration of women in the development process. The Declaration stresses that equality between women and men means equality in their dignity and worth as human beings as well as equality in their rights, opportunities and responsibilities. It calls for concrete action to ensure equality between women and men in family life; full and equal access to education and training; equal pay for work of equal value; equal opportunities for advancement in work; equal participation of women in the political life of their countries and of the international community, etc. Pursuant to the World Conference (1975), the **United Nations General Assembly** proclaimed the **United Nations Decade for Women: Equality, Development and Peace – 1976-1985**. The very existence of this Decade for Women was important bearing in mind that women had not before been taken into consideration in debates on development.

Declaration of Principles on Tolerance (UNESCO)

The Declaration of Principles on Tolerance was adopted by the **UNESCO** General Conference on 16 November 1995 at its 28th session. It emphasizes the responsibilities of Member States to promote tolerance and to develop and encourage respect for human rights and fundamental freedoms for all, without distinction as to race, gender, language, national origin, religion or disability. The Declaration stresses, in particular, that tolerance "is not concession, condescension or indulgence"; it is "above all, an active attitude prompted by recognition of human rights and fundamental freedoms of others" and "the responsibility that upholds human rights, pluralism, democracy and the rule of law" (Article 1). Article 2 states that tolerance at the State level requires just and impartial legislation, law enforcement and judicial and administrative process as well as making available to each person, without distinction, economic and social opportunities. The Declaration asks States to ratify existing international human rights conventions, and draft new legislation where necessary to ensure equality of treatment and of opportunity for all groups and individuals in society (Article 2). Education, as stated in Article 4, is the most effective means of preventing intolerance. States are invited to support and implement programmes of social science research and education for tolerance, human rights and non-violence by "devoting special attention to improving teacher training, curricula, the content of textbooks and lessons, and other educational materials including new educational technologies, with a view to educating caring and responsible citizens open to other cultures, able to appreciate the value of freedom, respectful of human dignity and differences, and able to prevent conflicts or resolve them by non-violent means" (Article 4). The day of the adoption of the Declaration is observed annually as the **International Day for Tolerance** – 16 November.

Declaration of Santiago on Promoting Independent and Pluralistic Media and Plan of Action (UN/UNDP/UNESCO)

The Declaration of Santiago and its Plan of Action were endorsed by the participants of the **United Nations/ UNESCO/United Nations Development Programme** "Seminar on Media Development and Democracy in Latin America and the Caribbean", held in Santiago, Chile, from 2 to 6 May 1994. It is based on Article 19 of the **Universal Declaration of Human Rights**, which states that "Everyone has the right to **freedom of opinion and expression**; this right includes freedom to hold opinions without interference and to seek, receive and impart information and ideas through any media, and regardless of frontiers". It affirms that freedom of expression is the cornerstone of democracy and that democracy is a prerequisite for peace and development. The aim of the Declaration of Santiago is to promote the greatest possible number of newspapers, magazines, videos, radio and television stations reflecting the widest possible range of opinion in the community (para. 5). To this end, it encourages all States of the region to provide constitutional guarantees for freedom of expression, freedom of the press for all forms of media, **freedom of association** and freedom for media trade unions (para. 2). It further states that no journalist should be forced to reveal his or her sources of information (para. 7) and that access to and the practice of journalism must be free, and not limited by any means (para. 8). The Declaration also calls for the creation of a **World Press Freedom Prize**, to be awarded annually, to honour individuals, organizations or institutions that have contributed significantly to the advancement of freedom of information, irrespective of the medium (para. 10). This prize was instituted in 1997.

The Plan of Action adopted by the Seminar proposes the following measures: to promote community media in rural, indigenous and marginal urban areas (Part 1); to promote and support the training of journalists, broadcasters and other media professionals (Part 2); to encourage the reading of both community and national newspapers in school as learning tools (Part 2); to promote free press and the safety of journalists (Part 3); and to request UNESCO and the International Telecommunication Union (ITU), together with professional organizations, to advise small media, especially in rural and marginal urban areas, on available technology optimal for their needs (Part 4). The Plan of Action also aims at encouraging media organizations, universities, research institutions and governmental and intergovernmental agencies to conduct research on the impact of communication technology development on indigenous communities, with a view to maintaining their cultural identity (Part 5, para. A). It recommends that UNESCO, in cooperation with professional organizations, conduct a comparative study of legislation affecting media (Part 5, para. B).

Declaration of the Principles of International Cultural cooperation (UNESCO)

This Declaration was proclaimed by the General Conference of **UNESCO** on 4 November 1966 in order to strengthen international cultural cooperation. The opening articles of the Declaration assert that each culture has a dignity and value which must be respected and preserved, that every people has the right and the duty to develop its culture (Article I) and that nations shall endeavour to develop the various branches of culture side by side so as to establish a harmonious balance between technical progress and the intellectual and moral advancement of mankind (Article III). The aims of international cultural cooperation shall be: (I) to spread knowledge, to stimulate talent and to enrich cultures; (II) to develop peaceful relations and friendship among the peoples and bring about a better understanding of each other's way of life; (III) to contribute to the application of the principles set out in the various United Nations Declarations that are recalled in the Preamble of this Declaration; (IV) to enable everyone to have access to knowledge, to enjoy the arts and literature of all peoples, to share in advances made in science in all parts of the world and in the resulting benefits, and to contribute to the enrichment of cultural life; and (V) to raise the level of the spiritual and material life of man in all parts of the world (Article IV). The Declaration states that a broad dissemination of ideas and knowledge, based on the freest exchange and discussion, is essential to creative activity, the pursuit of truth and the development of the personality (Article VII). It also declares that cultural cooperation shall be particularly concerned with the moral and intellectual education of young people in a spirit of friendship, international understanding and peace (Article X).

Declaration of the Rights of Man and of the Citizen – 1789

The Declaration of the Rights of Man and of the Citizen, one of the first instruments in the field of human rights, was approved by the National Assembly of France on 26 August 1789 during the French Revolution. Containing 17 Articles, the Declaration represents one of the basic charters of human liberties and is characteristic of 18th century French thought, which strove to specify principles that are fundamental to man and therefore universally applicable. The main principle of the Declaration was that: "Men are born and remain free and equal in rights ..." (Article 1), which were specified as the rights to "... liberty, property, safety and resistance to oppression" (Article 2). Article 4 stipulates: "Liberty consists in the freedom to do everything which injures no one else. Hence the exercise of the natural rights of each man has no limits except those which assure to the other members of the society the enjoyment of the same rights. These limits can only be determined by law". Article 6 states that: "Law is the expression of the general will. Every citizen has a right to participate personally, or through his representative, in its foundation. ... All citizens, being equal in the eyes of the law, are equally eligible to all dignities and to all public positions and occupations ...". It is stipulated in Article 7 that: "No person shall be accused, arrested, or imprisoned except in the cases and according to the forms prescribed by law". Article 9 proclaims the presumption of innocence. Article 10 provides for **freedom of opinion** and religion and Article 11 proclaims freedom of expression. Article 16 provides that: "A society in which the observance of the law is not assured, nor the separation of powers defined, has no constitution at all". The final Article 17 proclaims the **right to property** as "an inviolable and sacred right". The Declaration has served as a basis and an inspiration for the elaboration of numerous human rights instruments in force today.

Declaration of Windhoek on Promoting an Independent and Pluralistic African Press (UN/UNESCO)

This Declaration was adopted on 3 May 1991 by a joint **United Nations/UNESCO** seminar held in Windhoek, Namibia. Its main purpose is to encourage the development of an independent and pluralistic press, which is defined as "a press independent from governmental, political or economic control" (para. 2). A pluralistic press means "the end of monopolies of any kind and the existence of the greatest possible number of newspapers, magazines and periodicals reflecting the widest possible range of opinion within the community" (para. 3). The Declaration envisages conducting research on obstacles to developing an independent and pluralist press in Africa. It contains, in an Annex, a list of initiatives and projects identified at the seminar with a view to achieving the aims of the Declaration. In 1993, 3 May, the day of the adoption of the Declaration of Windhoek was proclaimed **World Press Freedom Day** by the **United Nations General Assembly**. The day of the adoption of the Declaration is also the occasion for the awarding of the **World Press Freedom Prize**.

Declaration on Crime and Public Security (UN)

The Declaration on Crime and Public Security was adopted by the **United Nations General Assembly** in its resolution 51/60 of 12 December 1996. It aims at strengthening crime prevention and promoting public security. The Declaration urges Member States to "protect the security and well-being of their citizens and all persons within their jurisdictions by taking effective measures to combat serious transnational crime, including **organized crime**, illicit drug and arms trafficking, smuggling of other illicit articles, organized trafficking in persons, terrorist crimes and the laundering of proceeds from serious crimes" (Article 1). In particular, Member States will develop measures for mutual cooperation and assistance to apprehend and prosecute persons guilty of serious transnational crimes (Articles 2 and 3). Member States will also adopt measures to: extradite or prosecute transnational criminals; combat and prohibit **corruption** and bribery; and prevent criminal organizations from operating in their territories. The Declaration urges States that have not yet done so to become parties to the principal international treaties against **terrorism** and to international drug control conventions as soon as possible. States

Parties to these instruments are called upon to effectively implement the provisions of these instruments (Articles 5 and 6).

Declaration on Criteria for Free and Fair Elections (IPU)

The Declaration on Criteria for Free and Fair Elections was unanimously adopted by the Inter-Parliamentary Council (the policy-making body of the **Inter-Parliamentary Union**) on 26 March 1994. It is based on the **Universal Declaration of Human Rights** (Article 21) and the **International Covenant on Civil and Political Rights** (Article 25), which establish that the authority to govern shall be based on the will of the people as expressed in periodic and genuine elections. In Part 1, the Declaration states that "in any State the authority of the government can only derive from the will of the people as expressed in genuine, free and fair elections held at regular intervals on the basis of universal, equal and secret suffrage". Part 2 of the instrument outlines voting and elections rights, including the right of every adult citizen to vote in elections, on a non-discriminatory basis, the right of every voter to equal and effective access to a polling station in order to exercise his or her right to vote, and the right to vote in secret. The Declaration also outlines the right of everyone to take part in the government of their country and to have an equal opportunity to become a candidate for election, and the right of everyone to join, or together with others to establish, a political party or organization for the purpose of competing in an election (Part 3). Similarly, the Declaration outlines the rights of candidates and political parties (Part 3). In the final section, the Declaration stipulates the rights and responsibilities of States with regard to free and fair elections. Accordingly, States should take the necessary "legislative steps and other measures, in accordance with their constitutional process, to guarantee the rights and institutional framework for periodic and genuine, free and fair elections" (para. 1). In particular, States are asked to: establish an effective, impartial and non-discriminatory procedure for the registration of voters; provide for the formation and free functioning of political parties; initiate or facilitate national programmes of civic education to ensure that the population is familiar with election procedures and issues; and take all necessary and appropriate measures to ensure that the principle of the secret ballot is respected, and that voters are able to cast their ballots freely, without fear or intimidation.

Declaration on Fundamental Principles and Rights at Work and Its Follow-up (ILO)

The International Labour Conference adopted the Declaration on Fundamental Principles and Rights at Work and its Follow-up on 18 June 1998 at its 86th session. In its Preamble, it underlines that economic growth is essential but not sufficient to ensure equity, social progress and the eradication of poverty, confirming the need for the **International Labour Organization (ILO)** to promote strong social policies. The instrument reaffirms the obligation of the Member States "… even if they have not ratified the fundamental Conventions … to respect, to promote and to realize, in good faith and in accordance with the Constitution …" the right of workers and employers to **freedom of association** and the effective rights to collective bargaining, the elimination of all forms of forced or compulsory labour, the effective abolition of child labour, and the elimination of **discrimination** in respect of employment and occupation (para. 2). The Declaration includes a promotional Follow-up (para. 4) aiming at "… encouraging the efforts made by the Members of the Organization to promote the fundamental principles and rights enshrined in the Constitution of the ILO and the Declaration of Philadelphia in 1944 and reaffirmed in this Declaration" (para. 1 of the Follow-up). Global reports focus annually on one of the four categories of rights, and governments that have not ratified the ILO's basic Conventions on these subjects are required to report every year on their efforts to implement the Principles concerned. On the whole, the Declaration and its annual Follow-up gives the ILO the means to address the social impact of phenomena such as **globalization** and liberalization of international trade, and marks a turning point in the struggle to achieve social justice.

Declaration on Human Rights Defenders (UN)

A common name for the **Declaration on the Right and Responsibility of Individuals, Groups and Organs of Society to Promote and Protect Universally Recognized Human Rights and Fundamental Freedoms** adopted in 1998.

Declaration on Principles of International Law concerning Friendly Relations and Co-operation among States in accordance with the Charter of the United Nations (UN)

The Declaration on Principles of International Law Concerning Friendly Relations and Co-operation among States was adopted by the **United Nations General Assembly** on 24 October 1970 by resolution 2625 (XXV). It is aimed at promoting international peace and security and the development of friendly relations and cooperation among States in accordance with the **United Nations Charter.**

The Declaration proclaims that "every State has the duty to refrain in its international relations from the threat or use of force against the territorial integrity or political independence of any State, or in any other manner inconsistent with the purposes of the **United Nations**" (Principle 1). States "shall seek early and just settlement of their international disputes by negotiation, inquiry, meditation, conciliation, arbitration, judicial settlement, resort to regional agencies or arrangements or other peaceful means of their choice". The Declaration obliges States to respect the principles of territorial integrity and political independence. All States shall enjoy sovereign equality and have equal rights and duties and are equal members of the international community. Every State has the duty to promote the realization of the principles of equal rights and self-determination of peoples.

Declaration on Race and Racial Prejudice (UNESCO)

The General Conference of **UNESCO** adopted the Declaration on Race and Racial Prejudice on 27 November 1978 at its 20th session. The Declaration provides that **racism** includes "racist ideologies, prejudiced attitudes, discriminatory behaviour, structural arrangements and institutionalized practices resulting in racial inequality as well as the fallacious notion that discriminatory relations between groups are morally and scientifically justifiable" (Article 2). It states that all human beings belong to a single species and are descended from a common stock; that they are born equal in dignity and rights and all form an integral part of humanity (Article 1). It also proclaims that "all individuals and groups have the right to be different, to consider themselves as different and to be regarded as such" and that this right may not, in any circumstances, serve as a pretext for racial prejudice (Article 1). States are called upon, in the Declaration, to "take all appropriate steps, *inter alia*, by legislation, particularly in the spheres of education, culture and communication, to prevent, prohibit and eradicate racism, racist propaganda, racial segregation and **apartheid** and to promote mutual respect among groups, and to encourage the dissemination of knowledge and the findings of appropriate research in natural and social sciences on the causes and prevention of racial prejudice and racist attitudes" (Article 6). Similarly, the mass media and those who control or serve them are urged to "contribute to the eradication of racism, racial **discrimination** and racial prejudice, in particular by refraining from presenting a stereotyped, partial, unilateral or tendentious picture of individuals and of various human groups" (Article 5).

Moreover, due to the fact that disequilibria in international economic relations contribute to the exacerbation of racism and racial prejudice, all States are also urged to contribute to the restructuring of the international economy on a more equitable basis (Article 9).

Declaration on Social and Legal Principles relating to the Protection and Welfare of Children, with Special Reference to Foster Placement and Adoption Nationally and Internationally (UN)

In recognition of the problems that could arise in the case of inter-country movement of children and the need to safeguard the rights of all concerned, particularly those of the child, the **United Nations General Assembly** adopted this Declaration on 3 December 1986 (A/RES/41/85). The Declaration sets out guidelines to assist governments in the implementation of the Principles established in this instrument. Nine principles are related to general family and child welfare, three principles regard fostering placement and twelve concern adoption, bearing in mind that in all foster placement and adoption procedures the best interests of the child should be the paramount consideration (Article 5) and that the child should grow up in an atmosphere of affection and moral and material security. In particular, the principles state that persons responsible for foster placement or adoption procedures should have professional or other appropriate training (Article 6) and that Governments should determine the adequacy of their national child welfare services and consider appropriate actions (Article 7). The Declaration also affirms that such placement should be regulated by law and that a competent authority or agency should be responsible for supervision to ensure the welfare of the child (Article 12).

Declaration on Social Progress and Development (UN)

The Declaration on Social Progress and Development, adopted by the **United Nations General Assembly** on 11 December 1969 by resolution 2542 (XXIV), is designed to help each State acquire a fair and comprehensive realization of **economic**, **social** and **cultural rights**. Particularly important for the realization of this aim are the following principles proclaimed in the Declaration: elimination of all forms of **discrimination**, inequality, colonialism, **racism**, nazism, **apartheid** and exploitation of peoples and individuals; respect for national sovereignty and territorial integrity of States and non-interference in their domestic affairs; adoption of measures for continuous and comprehensive industrial and agricultural growth and assurance of the **right to work** for all; fair, equitable distribution of national wealth and income among all members of society; elimination of inequality, **poverty**, hunger and undernourishment, as well as assurance of adequate housing for all; achievement of high standards of medical care and medical service free whenever possible; eradication of illiteracy with free education at all levels and general access to culture; elaboration of measures for the protection and improvement of the environment; development of international cooperation with the aim of international exchange of information, knowledge, and development; and the achievement of general and complete disarmament (Articles 10-13). Among instruments relating to general development questions this Declaration is unique, as it contains a great number of provisions which deal with human rights in a very technical sense. The achievement of these objectives, the Declaration states, requires the mobilization of the necessary resources by national and international action including the effective participation of all elements of society in the preparation and execution of national plans and programmes of economic and social development (Article 15(a)) and the formulation of policies to avoid "brain drain" and obviate its adverse affects (Article 21(d)).

Declaration on Territorial Asylum (UN)

The **United Nations General Assembly** adopted the Declaration on Territorial Asylum on 14 December 1967 by resolution 2312 (XXII). The Declaration, while not proclaiming a right to be granted asylum (Article 1 states that "it shall rest with the State granting asylum to evaluate the grounds for the grant of asylum"), goes beyond the provisions of the **Universal Declaration of Human Rights** by stating that the situation of persons entitled to invoke Article 14 of the Universal Declaration is, without prejudice to the sovereignty of States, of concern to the international community. The Declaration further provides that a person coming under Article 14 of the Universal Declaration shall not be subjected to contradictions to the basic humanitarian principles of non-refoulement, according to which no person shall be rejected at the frontier or expelled or compulsorily returned to any State where he/she may be subjected to persecution (Article 3). In addition, the Declaration lays down a series of fundamental principles with regard to territorial asylum. It states that the granting of asylum "is a peaceful and humanitarian act and that, as such, it cannot be regarded as unfriendly by any other State" (Preamble). Moreover, where a State finds difficulty in granting or continuing to grant asylum, other States "individually or jointly or through the **United Nations** shall consider, in a spirit of international solidarity, appropriate measures to lighten the burden" (Article 2).

Declaration on the Elimination of All Forms of Intolerance and of Discrimination Based on Religion or Belief (UN)

On 25 November 1981, the **United Nations General Assembly** (A/RES/36/55) adopted and proclaimed the Declaration on the Elimination of All Forms of Intolerance and of

Discrimination Based on Religion or Belief. In its Article 1 the Declaration reaffirms the right of everyone to "**freedom of thought, conscience and religion**" and states that "freedom to manifest one's religion or belief may be subject only to such limitations as are prescribed by law and are necessary to protect public security, order, health or morals or the fundamental rights and freedoms of others." Article 2 defines "intolerance and **discrimination** based on religion or belief" as "any distinction, exclusion, restriction or preference based on religion or belief and having as its purpose or as its effect nullification or impairment of the recognition, enjoyment or exercise of human rights and fundamental freedoms on an equal basis". The Declaration makes an important clarification concerning the content of the rights specified in this definition, providing that it shall include the right to: worship or assemble in connection with a religion or belief, and to establish and maintain places for these purposes; write and disseminate relevant publications in these areas; teach a religion or belief in places suitable for these purposes; solicit and receive voluntary financial and other contributions from individuals and institutions; and observe days of rest and celebrate holidays and ceremonies in accordance with the precepts of one's religion or belief (Article 6). The Declaration also provides the right of parents or guardians to organize life within the family in accordance with their religion or belief, bearing in mind the moral education in which they believe their children should be brought up (Article 5). The Declaration requests from States effective measures to prevent and eliminate discrimination on the grounds of religion or belief in all fields of civil, economic, political, social and cultural life and all efforts to enact or rescind legislation, where necessary, to prohibit any such discrimination or intolerance (Article 4).

Declaration on the Elimination of All Forms of Racial Discrimination (UN)

The Declaration on the Elimination of All Forms of Racial Discrimination was proclaimed by the **United Nations General Assembly** on 20 November 1963 by resolution 1904 (XVIII). The Declaration provides that no "State, institution, group or individual shall make any **discrimination** whatsoever in matters of human rights and fundamental freedoms in the treatment of persons, groups of persons or institutions on the ground of race, colour or ethnic origin" (Article 2). It also calls upon States "to take effective measures to revise governmental and other public policies and to rescind laws and regulations which have the effect of creating and perpetuating racial discrimination", to pass laws "prohibiting such discrimination", and to take "appropriate measures to combat those prejudices which lead to racial discrimination" (Article 4). In particular, it stipulates that effective steps be taken in the fields of teaching, education and information, with a view to eliminating racial discrimination and prejudice and promoting understanding, tolerance and friendship among nations and racial groups (Article 8), and that "immediate and positive measures" be taken "to prosecute and/or outlaw organizations which promote or incite to racial discrimination, or incite to or use violence for purposes of discrimination based on race, colour or ethnic origin" (Article 9). The Declaration also provides that the **United Nations**, its specialized agencies, States and **non-governmental organizations** shall "study the causes of racial discrimination with a view to recommending appropriate and effective measures to combat and eliminate it" (Article 10). The text of the Declaration served as a basis for the **International Convention on the Elimination of All Forms of Racial Discrimination**, adopted in 1965. The **International Day for the Elimination of Racial Discrimination** is observed on 21 March each year.

Declaration on the Elimination of Discrimination against Women (UN)

The Declaration on the Elimination of Discrimination against Women was adopted by the **United Nations General Assembly** on 7 November 1967 by resolution 2263 (XXII) and represents an important milestone in the work of the **United Nations** for the advancement of women. It defines **discrimination** against women "fundamentally unjust" and proclaims it "an offence against human dignity" (Article 1) and calls for measures to be taken to ensure universal recognition of the principle of equality between men and women. Particularly, the Declaration recommends "to abolish existing laws, customs, regulations and practices which are discriminatory against women" (Article 2) and "to educate public opinion … towards the eradication of prejudice and the abolition of customary and all other practices which are based on the idea of the inferiority of women" (Article 3). Furthermore, women shall have the same rights as men concerning voting (Article 4), nationality (Article 5), civil and penal law (Articles 6 and 7), education (Article 9) and concerning their economic and social life (Article 10). According to Article 8, "all forms of traffic in women and exploitation of prostitution of women" shall be combated. The Declaration served as the basis for the elaboration of the **Convention on the Elimination of All Forms of Discrimination against Women**, adopted by the United Nations in 1979.

Declaration on the Elimination of Violence against Women (UN)

Recognizing that "violence against women constitutes a violation of the rights and fundamental freedoms of women and impairs or nullifies their enjoyment of those rights and freedoms" and "alarmed that opportunities for women to achieve legal, social, political and economic equality in society are limited, *inter alia*, by continuing and endemic violence" (Preamble), the **United**

Nations General Assembly (A/RES/48/104) proclaimed the Declaration on the Elimination of Violence against Women on 20 December 1993. The Declaration aims to provide a clear and comprehensive definition of violence against women and to ensure its elimination. For the purposes of this Declaration, the term "violence against women" means "any act of gender-based violence that results in, or is likely to result in, physical, sexual or psychological harm or suffering to women, including threats of such acts, coercion or arbitrary deprivation of liberty, whether occurring in public or in private life" (Article 1). The Declaration urges States to condemn violence against women and to pursue by all appropriate means a policy of eliminating such violence. To this end, States should: exercise due diligence to prevent, investigate and punish acts of violence against women, whether those acts are perpetrated by the State or by private persons; work to ensure that women subjected to violence have specialized assistance, such as rehabilitation, assistance in child care and maintenance, treatment and counselling; take measures to ensure that law enforcement officers and public officials responsible for implementing policies to prevent, investigate and punish violence against women receive training to sensitize them to the needs of women; adopt all appropriate measures, especially in the field of education, to eliminate prejudices, customary practices and all other practices based on the idea of the inferiority or superiority of either of the sexes; and facilitate and enhance the work of the women's movement and **non-governmental organizations** (Article 4).

The **International Day for the Elimination of Violence against Women** is observed on 25 November each year.

Declaration on the Granting of Independence to Colonial Countries and Peoples (UN)

Proclaiming the necessity of bringing to a speedy and unconditional end colonialism in all its forms and manifestations, the **United Nations General Assembly** adopted the Declaration on the Granting of Independence to Colonial Countries and Peoples on 14 December 1960 by resolution 1514 (XV). It states, in its paragraph 7, that: "All States shall observe faithfully and strictly the provisions of the **Charter of the United Nations**, the **Universal Declaration of Human Rights** and the present Declaration" (paragraph 7). It declares in its paragraph 1 that: "The subjection of peoples to alien subjugation, domination and exploitation constitutes a denial of fundamental human rights... and is an impediment to the promotion of world peace and cooperation". It particularly stipulates the right of all peoples to self-determination (paragraph 2), their right to complete independence (paragraph 4) and the integrity of their national territory (paragraphs 4 to 6).

Declaration on the Human Rights of Individuals Who Are not Nationals of the Country in which They Live (UN)

This Declaration was adopted by the **United Nations General Assembly** (A/RES/40/144) on 13 December 1985. Its aim is to promote the protection of human rights and fundamental freedoms provided for in international instruments for individuals who are not nationals of the country in which they live (Preamble). For the purposes of this Declaration, the term "alien" applies to "any individual who is not a national of the State in which he or she is present" (Article 1). Under Article 5, aliens shall enjoy the **right to life** and security of person; the right to protection against arbitrary or unlawful interference with privacy, family, home or correspondence; the right to be equal before all organs and authorities administering justice; the right to **freedom of thought, opinion, conscience and religion**; the right to manifest their religion or beliefs; the right to retain their own language, culture and tradition; and the right to transfer abroad earnings, savings or other personal monetary assets. Although the Declaration does not restrict the right of any State to promulgate laws and regulations concerning the entry of aliens and the terms and conditions of their stay or to establish differences between nationals and aliens, it does state that an alien may be expelled only in pursuance of a decision reached in accordance with law and that individual or collective expulsion of aliens on grounds of race, colour, religion, culture, descent or national or ethnic origin is prohibited (Article 7). Article 8 stipulates the right to safe and healthy working conditions, to fair wages and equal remuneration for work of equal value without distinction of any kind; the right to join trade unions; and the **right to health** protection, medical care, **social security**, social services, **education, rest and leisure**.

Declaration on the Participation of Women in Promoting International Peace and Co-operation (UN)

This Declaration was adopted by the **United Nations General Assembly** (A/RES/37/63) on 3 December 1982. Recalling that women have a vital role to play in the promotion of peace in all spheres of life – in the family, the community, the nation and the world – the Declaration proclaims: "Women and men have an equal and vital interest in contributing to international peace and cooperation. To this end women must be enabled to exercise their right to participate in the economic, social, cultural, civil and political affairs of society on an equal footing with men" (Article 1). The Declaration affirms that: "The increasing participation of women in the economic, social, cultural, civil and political affairs of society will contribute to international peace and cooperation" (Article 3). It appeals for special national and international measures "… to increase the level of women's participation in the sphere of international relations, so that women can contribute, on an equal basis with men, to national and international efforts to secure world peace and economic and social progress and to promote international cooperation" (Article 5).

In its Articles 6 to 13, the Declaration appeals for the adoption of all appropriate measures to ensure women's participation in all spheres of life, to pay tribute to their participation in the promotion of international peace and cooperation, to promote their equitable representation in governmental and non-governmental functions, to promote equality of opportunities for women to enter diplomatic service, etc. Article 14 urges governments, international organizations, including the **United Nations system**, **non-governmental organizations** and individuals to do all in their power to promote the implementation of the principles contained in the Declaration.

Declaration on the Preparation of Societies for Life in Peace (UN)

This Declaration on the Preparation of Societies for Life in Peace was adopted by the **United Nations General Assembly** (A/RES/33/73) on 15 December 1978. It is aimed at maintaining and strengthening international peace and security and eliminating the threat of war. The Declaration invites all States to observe the principles set out in this instrument while recognizing the supreme importance and necessity of establishing, maintaining and strengthening a just and durable peace for present and future generations. Among these principles are the individual's inherent **right to life** in peace (Principle 1); the prohibition by international law of war of aggression (Principle 2); the duty of every State to promote all-round, mutually advantageous and equitable political, economic, social and cultural cooperation with other States (Principle 4); their duty to respect the rights of all peoples to self-determination, independence, equality and sovereignty (Principle 5); and their duty to discourage all manifestations and practices of colonialism, **racism**, racial **discrimination** and **apartheid** (Principle 7). Finally the instrument recommends that the governmental and **non-governmental organizations** concerned as well as the **United**

Nations and its specialized agencies initiate appropriate actions towards the implementation of this Declaration.

Declaration on the Promotion among Youth of the Ideals of Peace, Mutual Respect and Understanding between Peoples (UN)

The Declaration on the Promotion among **Youth** of the Ideals of Peace, Mutual Respect and Understanding between Peoples was proclaimed by the **United Nations General Assembly** on 7 December 1965 by resolution 2037 (XX). The Declaration is based on the conviction that "the education of the young and exchanges of young people and of ideas in a spirit of peace, mutual respect and understanding between peoples can help to improve international relations and to strengthen peace and security" (Preamble). The Declaration encourages States to ensure that its young people are brought up in "the knowledge of the dignity and equality of all men, without distinction as to race, colour, ethnic origins or beliefs, and in respect for fundamental human rights and for the right of peoples to self-determination" (Principle III). In Principles IV and V, the Declaration outlines measures that should be taken to achieve this goal. It calls for the encouragement and facilitation among young people of exchanges, travel, tourism, meetings and national and international associations, of foreign language study and the twinning of towns and universities.

Declaration on the Protection of All Persons from Being Subjected to Torture and other Cruel, Inhuman or Degrading Treatment or Punishment (UN)

This Declaration was adopted by the **United Nations General Assembly** on 9 December 1975 by resolution 3452 (XXX). An act of torture is defined in Article 1 as "any act by which severe pain or suffering, whether physical or mental, is intentionally inflicted by or at the instigation of a public official on a person for such purposes as obtaining from him or a third person information or confession, punishing him for an act he has committed or is suspected of having committed, or intimidating him or other persons". It recommends that States take effective measures to prevent torture and other cruel, inhuman or degrading treatment or punishment (Articles 4, 6, 7). The instrument further recommends the training of law enforcement personnel and of other public officials (Article 5). Article 8 provides that "any person who alleges that he has been subjected to torture or other cruel, inhuman or degrading treatment or punishment by or at the instigation of a public official shall have the right to complain to, and to have his case impartially examined by, the competent authorities of the State concerned". The Declaration paved the way for the elaboration and adoption of the **Convention against Torture and Other Cruel, Inhuman or Degrading Treatment or Punishment** (1984).

Declaration on the Protection of All Persons from Enforced Disappearance (UN)

On 18 December 1992, the **United Nations General Assembly** (A/RES/47/133) adopted the Declaration on the Protection of All Persons from Enforced Disappearance. As stated in the Preamble, "enforced disappearance undermines the deepest values of any society committed to respect for the rule of law, human rights and fundamental freedoms and the systematic practice of such acts is of the nature of a crime against humanity". The Declaration proclaims, not only that no States shall practise, permit or tolerate enforced disappearances (Article 2), but also that they shall take effective legislative, administrative, judicial or other measures to prevent and terminate acts of enforced disappearance in any territory under their jurisdiction (Article 3) and shall make all such acts punishable by penalties which take into account their extreme seriousness (Articles 4 and 5). To address the concern relating to the involuntary disappearance of persons subject to detention or imprisonment, the Declaration states that any person deprived of liberty shall be held in an officially recognized place of detention and that accurate information on the detention of such persons and their place or places of detention shall be made promptly available to their family members and their counsel (Article 10). The Declaration stresses that no circumstances whatsoever, whether a threat of war, a state of war, internal political instability or any other public emergency, or instruction from any public authority, civilian, military or other, may be evoked to justify enforced disappearances (Articles 6 and 7).

Declaration on the Protection of Women and Children in Emergency and Armed Conflict (UN)

In proclaiming on 14 December 1974 by its resolution 3318 (XXIX) the Declaration on the Protection of Women and Children in Emergency and Armed Conflict, the **United Nations General Assembly** expressed its concern for the plight of women and children in emergency situations. The Declaration states: that "attacks and bombings on the civilian population, inflicting incalculable suffering, especially on women and children ... shall be prohibited, and such acts shall be condemned" (para. 1); that "all efforts shall be made by States involved in armed conflicts ... to spare women and children from ravages of war ..." (para. 4); and that "all forms of repression and cruel and inhuman treatment of women and children, including imprisonment, torture, shooting, mass arrests, collective punishment, destruction of dwellings and forcible eviction, committed by belligerents in the course of military operations or in occupied territories shall be considered criminal" (para. 5). It furthermore stipulates that "women and children belonging to the civilian population and finding themselves in circumstances of emergency and armed conflict ... or who live in occupied territories, shall not be deprived of shelter, food, medical aid or other inalienable rights" (para. 6).

Declaration on the Responsibilities of the Present Generations towards Future Generations (UNESCO)

The General Conference of **UNESCO** adopted the Declaration on the Responsibilities of the Present Generations Towards Future Generations on 12 November 1997 at its 29th session. The Conference stressed that full respect for human rights and ideals of democracy constitute an essential basis for the protection of the needs and interests of future generations. Thus, the Declaration is based on the conviction that there is a moral obligation to formulate behavioural guidelines for the present generations within a broad, future-oriented perspective. Article 1 proclaims the responsibility of present generations to ensure "... that the needs and interests of present and future generations are fully safeguarded". The freedom of choice concerning political, economic and social systems is confirmed in Article 2. The present generation "should strive to ensure maintenance and perpetuation of humankind with due respect for the dignity of the human person" (Article 3). Its members have "the responsibility to bequeath to future generations an Earth which will not one day be irreversibly damaged by human activity" and "to ensure that future generations benefit from the richness of the Earth's ecosystems" (Articles 4 and 5). Furthermore, the Declaration is aimed at protecting the human genome and biodiversity (Article 6) and also cultural diversity and **cultural heritage** (Article 7). Article 8 stipulates that present generations may use the common heritage of humankind provided that this does not compromise it irreversibly. Finally, the instrument stipulates that "present generations should ensure that both they and future generations learn to live in peace, security, respect for international law, human rights and fundamental freedoms" (Article 9). Article 10 states, *inter alia*, that education is an important instrument for the development of human persons and societies. Article 11 stresses that present generations should refrain from taking any action, which would lead to or perpetuate any form of **discrimination** for future generations.

Declaration on the Right and Responsibility of Individuals, Groups and Organs of Society to Promote and Protect Universally Recognized Human Rights and Fundamental Freedoms (UN)

After thirteen years, the **Commission on Human Rights** completed its work on this instrument, commonly known as the **Declaration on Human Rights Defenders** and transmitted it to the **United Nations General Assembly**. On 10 December 1998, the General Assembly (A/RES/53/144) adopted the Declaration, which reaffirms the importance of the **Universal Declaration of Human Rights** and the **International Covenants on Human Rights** and of the observance of the purposes and principles of the United Nations Charter for the promotion and protection of all human rights and fundamental freedoms for all persons in all countries of the world. The Declaration stresses that "... all members of the international community shall fulfil, jointly and separately, their solemn obligation to promote and encourage respect for human rights and fundamental freedoms for all without distinction of any kind ..." (Preamble). Its Article 1 states that: "Everyone has the right, individually, and in association with others, to promote and to strive for the protection and realization of human rights and fundamental freedoms at the national and international levels". Article 5 ensures the right to meet or assemble peacefully; to form, join and participate in **non-governmental organizations**, associations or groups; and to communicate with non-governmental or governmental organizations. The right to develop and discuss new human rights ideas and principles and to advocate their acceptance is laid down in Article 7. In Article 8, paragraph 2, it is stated that: "Everyone has the right, individually and in association with others, to submit to governmental bodies and agencies or organizations concerned with public affairs criticism and proposals for improving their functioning …". Furthermore the Declaration contains an enumeration of different legal guarantees if there is a human rights violation, in particular the right to an effective remedy and protection, public hearings, independent judicial authorities and compensation. The right to complain by petition, to attend important public discussions and decisions, to communicate with international bodies and the possibility for the lawful exercise of occupation or profession should also be guaranteed. The right for peaceful activities against violations of human rights and fundamental freedoms is granted. The possibility to solicit, receive and utilize resources is also envisaged as an important element for the activities related to the protection of human rights. With regard to all these guarantees, human rights defenders have the duty to protect and promote human rights peacefully, in accordance with domestic law consistent with the **Charter of the United Nations**. In this connection, Article 2 states: "Each State has a prime responsibility and duty to protect, promote and implement all human rights and fundamental freedoms, *inter alia*, by adopting such steps as may be necessary to create all conditions necessary in the social, economic, political and other fields". The State "shall take all necessary measures to ensure, individually and in association with others, the protection by the competent authorities of everyone … against any violence, threats, retaliation, *de facto* or *de jure* adverse **discrimination**, pressure or any other arbitrary action …" (Article 12, para. 2) and "ensure and support, where appropriate, the creation and development of further independent national institutions for the promotion and protection of human rights and fundamental freedoms" (Article 14, para. 3).

Declaration on the Right of Peoples to Peace (UN)

Approved by the **United Nations General Assembly** (A/RES/39/11) on 12 November 1984, this Declaration reaffirms that the principal aim of the **United Nations** is the maintenance of international peace and security. It also expresses the conviction that "... life without war serves as the primary international prerequisite for the material well-being, development and progress of countries and for the full implementation of the rights and fundamental human freedoms proclaimed by the United Nations" (Preamble). The Declaration solemnly proclaims that the peoples of our planet have a sacred right to peace and that the preservation of this right and its implementation constitute a fundamental obligation of each State (paras. 1 and 2). The Declaration emphasizes that "ensuring the exercise of the right of peoples to peace demands that the policies of States be directed towards the elimination of the threat of war, particularly nuclear war, the renunciation of the use of force in international relations and the settlement of international disputes by peaceful means on the basis of the **Charter of the United Nations**" (para. 3).

All States and international organizations are called upon to do their utmost to assist in implementing the right of peoples to peace through the adoption of appropriate measures at both the national and the international level (para. 4).

Declaration on the Rights of Disabled Persons (UN)

On 9 December 1975, the **United Nations General Assembly** proclaimed the Declaration on the Rights of Disabled Persons by resolution 3447 (XXX) and called for national and international action to ensure that it would be used as a common basis and frame of reference for the protection of the rights set forth therein. The Declaration defines the term "disabled person" as meaning "any person unable to ensure by himself or herself, wholly or partly, the necessities of a normal individual and/or social life, as a result of a deficiency, either congenital or not, in his or her physical or mental capabilities" (para. 1). It provides that organizations of disabled persons be consulted in all matters regarding the rights of such persons (para. 12) and calls for disabled persons, their families and communities to be fully informed of the rights contained in the Declaration (para. 13). The Declaration sets out the following principles: disabled persons have the same fundamental rights, including **civil** and **political rights**, as their fellow citizens of the same age (para. 3 and 4); disabled persons are entitled to the measures designed to enable them to become as self-reliant as possible (para. 5); disabled persons have the right to medical, educational and other services which will enable them to develop their capabilities and skills to the maximum (para. 6); disabled persons have the right to secure and retain employment or to engage in a useful, productive and remunerative occupation and to join trade unions (para. 7); and disabled persons shall be protected against all exploitation, all regulations and all treatment of a discriminatory, abusive or degrading nature (para. 10). The **International Day of Disabled Persons** is observed on 3 December each year.

Declaration on the Rights of Mentally Retarded Persons (UN)

On 20 December 1971, by resolution 2856 (XXVI), the **United Nations General Assembly** proclaimed the Declaration on the Rights of Mentally Retarded Persons and called for national and international action to ensure that the Declaration would be used as a common basis and frame of reference for the protection of rights set forth therein. The Declaration is based on the tenet that the mentally retarded person shall have, to the maximum degree of feasibility, the same rights as other human beings (para. 1). To achieve this tenet the Declaration sets forth the following principles: the mentally retarded person has a right to proper medical care and education as will enable him/her to develop his/her ability and maximum potential (para. 2); the mentally retarded person has a right to economic security, to perform productive work, and to a decent standard of living (para. 3); the family with which a mentally retarded person lives should receive assistance (para. 4); and the mentally retarded person has the right to protection from exploitation, abuse and degrading treatment (para. 6). The Declaration further stipulates that whenever mentally retarded persons are unable, because of the severity of their handicap, to exercise all their rights in a meaningful way or it should become necessary to restrict or deny some or all of these rights, the procedure used for that restriction or denial of rights must contain proper legal safeguards against every form of abuse (para. 7). This procedure, according to the Declaration, must be based on an evaluation of the social capability of the mentally retarded person by qualified experts and must be subject to periodic review and to the right of appeal to higher authorities (para. 7).

Declaration on the Rights of Persons Belonging to National or Ethnic, Religious and Linguistic Minorities (UN)

The Declaration on the Rights of Persons Belonging to National or Ethnic, Religious and Linguistic Minorities, adopted by the **United Nations General Assembly** (A/RES/47/135) on 18 December 1992, recognizes the need to ensure more effective implementation of international human rights instruments with regard to the rights of persons belonging to **minorities**. The Declaration is based on the conviction that the promotion and protection of the rights of persons belonging to such minorities contribute to the political and social stability of States in which they live (Preamble). The Declaration proclaims that States shall protect the existence and the national or ethnic, cultural, religious and linguistic identity of minorities within their respective territories, encourage conditions for the promotion of that identity, and adopt appropriate legislative and other measures to achieve those ends (Article 1). In accordance with the Declaration, persons belonging to national or ethnic, religious and linguistic minorities have the right to enjoy their own culture, to profess and practise their own religion and to use their own language; the right to participate effectively in cultural, religious, social, economic and public life as well as in the decision-making process concerning the minority to which they belong; and the right to establish and maintain their own associations (Article 2). To eliminate any misinterpretation, the Declaration provides that: "Nothing in the present Declaration may be construed as permitting any activity contrary to the purposes and principles of the **United Nations**, including sovereign equality, territorial integrity and political independence of States" (Article 8, para. 4). The Declaration foresees measures to be taken by States to ensure that persons belonging to minorities may exercise fully and effectively all their human rights and fundamental freedoms. States should, where appropriate, take measures to encourage knowledge of the history, traditions, language and culture of minorities existing within their territory and enable persons belonging to minorities to participate fully in economic progress and development in their country (Article 4). The Declaration does not, however, provide a definition of the term "national or ethnic, religious and linguistic minorities".

Declaration of the Rights of the Child (UN)

The **United Nations General Assembly** decided that the special needs of children necessitated the adoption of an international instrument on this issue. On 20 November 1959, the Assembly by resolution 1386 (XIV) proclaimed the Declaration of the Rights of the Child which contains ten principles aiming at special safeguards and care, including appropriate legal protection, for the benefit of the child. Pursuant to Principle 1, every child shall be entitled to the rights set out in this Declaration without any **discrimination**. Concerning these rights, the instrument provides that the child shall enjoy special protection (Principle 2) and the benefits of social security (Principle 4), and is entitled to receive education (Principle 7). Every child has the right to a name and nationality at birth. Regarding children who are physically, mentally or socially handicapped, special treatment and care required by their particular condition shall be given (Principle 5). Furthermore, the Declaration outlines that a "child, for the full and harmonious development of his personality, needs love and understanding" (Principle 6) and that the child "shall in all circumstances be among the first to receive protection and relief" (Principle 8). This protection is further specified in Principles 9 and 10. The Declaration paved the way for the elaboration and adoption of the **Convention on the Rights of the Child** (1989).

Declaration on the Right to Development (UN)

The **United Nations General Assembly** (A/RES/41/128) adopted the Declaration on the Right to Development on 4 December 1986. The Declaration proclaims that the "**right to development** is an inalienable human right by virtue of which every human person and all peoples are entitled to participate in, contribute to, and enjoy economic, social, cultural, and political development, in which all human rights and fundamental freedoms can be fully realized" (Article 1). It further proclaims that human beings are the central subject of development and thus should be the active participants and beneficiaries of the right to development, that an appropriate political, social and economic order for development should be promoted and protected, and that States have the right and the duty to formulate appropriate national development policies and ensure the fair distribution of the benefits resulting therefrom (Article 2). The Declaration reaffirms the indivisibility and interdependence of all human rights (Article 6).

The **Vienna Declaration and Programme of Action** (1993) reaffirmed the right to development as "a universal and inalienable right and an integral part of fundamental human rights" (Part I, para. 10). This right is specifically mentioned in the **Copenhagen Declaration on Social Development and Programme of Action** adopted by the **World Summit for Social Development** (1995). In recent years the **Commission on Human Rights** and the United Nations General Assembly have adopted a number of resolutions concerning this right. States are called upon to undertake further concrete actions at the national and international level to remove the obstacles to the realization of the right to development.

Declaration on the Use of Scientific and Technological Progress in the Interest of Peace and for the Benefit of Mankind (UN)

The Declaration on the Use of Scientific and Technological Progress in the Interest of Peace and for the Benefit of Mankind, proclaimed by the **United Nations General Assembly** on 10 November 1975 by resolution 3384 (XXX), contains a number of provisions aimed at the promotion and protection of human rights and fundamental freedoms. The Declaration provides that "... all States shall take appropriate measures to prevent the use of scientific and technological developments, particularly by State organs, to limit or interfere with the enjoyment of human rights and fundamental freedoms of the individual as enshrined in the **Universal Declaration of Human Rights**, the **International Covenants on Human Rights** and other relevant international instruments" (para. 2). The Declaration calls upon all States to take necessary measures to ensure that the results of scientific and technological progress are used exclusively in the interests of international peace and security (para. 1), for the benefit of all sectors of the population (para. 3) and for promoting and encouraging universal respect for human rights and fundamental freedom without any **discrimination** whatsoever on the grounds of race, sex, language or religious beliefs (para. 7). The Declaration also envisages that: "All States shall cooperate in the establishment, strengthening and development of the scientific and technological capacity of developing countries with a view to accelerating the realization of the **social** and **economic rights** of the peoples of those countries" (para. 5).

Declarations of the Forty-Fourth and Forty-Fifth Sessions of the International Conference on Education and Integrated Framework of Action on Education for Peace, Human Rights and Democracy (UNESCO)

The Forty-Fourth International Conference on Education, held in Geneva in October 1994 on the theme "Appraisal and Perspectives of Education for International Understanding", unanimously adopted a Declaration. This Declaration is a reflection of the political commitment of the ministers of education of **UNESCO** Member States to give the highest priority to activities in favour of the encouragement of understanding, solidarity and tolerance between people, between ethnic, social, cultural and religious groups, and between nations. The widespread distribution of the text of this Declaration is an important means for training citizens and for the social supervision of its implementation. The Conference also took note of an Integrated Framework of Action on Education for Peace, Human Rights and Democracy which was then adopted by the UNESCO General Conference at its 28th session and widely disseminated.

The Forty-Fifth session of the International Conference on Education, held in Geneva in October 1996 on the theme "Strengthening the Role of Teachers in a Changing World", also concluded with the adoption of a declaration and recommendations. The Declaration emphasized implementing integrated policies to make schools the key to social cohesion and instrumental in the teaching of democratic values. It also stresses strengthening the role, functions and status of teachers in partnership with educational professionals and society as a whole.

The Forty-Sixth International Conference on Education was held in Geneva in September 2001 on the theme "Education for All for Learning to Live Together". Its final conclusions and proposals for action emphasized the need of strengthening and reinforcing dialogue and cooperation to improve the quality of education and promote sound educational policies.

Discrimination

The term "discrimination" was defined by the **Human Rights Committee** during its 37th session in 1989 in its general comment as "any distinction, exclusion, restriction, or preference which is based on any ground such as race, colour, sex, language, religion, political or other opinion, national or social origin, property, birth, or other status, and which has the purpose or effect of nullifying or impairing the recognition, enjoyment or exercise by all persons on an equal footing, of all rights and freedoms". Discrimination is the very negation of the principle of equality and an affront to human dignity. One of the purposes of the **United Nations Charter** (1945), as stipulated in Chapter I, Article 1, is "… to achieve international cooperation in solving international problems of an economic, social, cultural, or humanitarian character, and in promoting and encouraging respect for human rights and for fundamental freedoms for all without distinction as to race, sex, language, or religion …". Subsequently, the provisions concerning the struggle against all forms of discrimination have been developed and included in human rights instruments: Articles 2 and 7 of the **Universal Declaration of Human Rights** (1948), Article 2 of both the **International Covenant on Civil and Political Rights** (1966) and the **International Covenant on Economic, Social and**

Cultural Rights (1966), Article 1 of the **Convention against Torture and Other Cruel, Inhuman or Degrading Treatment or Punishment** (1984), Article 2 of the **Convention on the Rights of the Child** (1989) and others. Questions linked with the prevention and elimination of discrimination are permanently dealt with by the **United Nations General Assembly**, the **Economic and Social Council (ECOSOC)**, the **Commission on Human Rights** and the **Sub-Commission on Prevention of Discrimination and Protection of Minorities** (now **Sub-Commission on the Promotion and Protection of Human Rights**). The achievement of equality not only *de jure* but also *de facto* demands sometimes that an affirmative action be taken by States to diminish or eliminate conditions which cause discrimination of individuals or groups. Reverse discrimination can also exist and is called "positive discrimination". This term can be understood as "selecting people for merits or employment on the basis of their membership in oppressed groups, even if a member of a more privileged group is better qualified". It is worth mentioning that the enjoyment of human rights and fundamental freedoms on an equal footing does not mean identical treatment in every instance. Human rights instruments allow in some cases differentiation, as is foreseen for example in Articles 6 and 25 of the International Covenant on Civil and Political Rights.

The principle of non-discrimination is the cornerstone of the human rights protection system after the Second World War. It has become an indispensable element of efforts aimed at the promotion and protection of human rights by means of education. This principle, enshrined in the United Nations Charter, has become the very core of all human rights instruments. A number of human rights instruments are specially designed to prevent discrimination in specific fields or against specific groups or populations, for example the **Convention on the Elimination of All Forms of Discrimination Against Women** and the ILO **Convention (N° 111) concerning Discrimination in Respect of Employment and Occupation**.

The **World Conference on Human Rights** (Vienna, 14-25 June 1993) confirmed the importance of the principle of non-discrimination for the implementation of human rights. It declared that "respect for human rights and for fundamental freedoms without distinction of any kind is a fundamental rule of international human rights law" (**Vienna Declaration and Programme of Action**, Part I, para. 15).

Three **Decades for Action to Combat Racism and Racial Discrimination** have been proclaimed by the **United Nations**, as well as the **International Year of Mobilization against Racism, Racial Discrimination, Xenophobia and Related Intolerance (2001)**. The **World Conference against Racism, Racial Discrimination, Xenophobia and Related Intolerance** (Durban South Africa, 31 August – 8 September 2001) was the main event within the Year and adopted the **Durban Declaration and Programme of Action**. The **International Day for the Elimination of Racial Discrimination** is observed on 21 March every year.

Displaced persons

Displaced persons may be described as such persons who have been deported against their will from, or have been obliged to leave their country of nationality or former habitual residence. Distinction can be made between internally displaced persons, who have been forced to leave their homes or have been forcibly removed from their homes to another part of their country, and externally displaced persons who are outside their country of nationality and for whom the term "refugees" is normally used. Internally displaced persons are among the most vulnerable groups in need of protection and assistance. In 1992, at the request of the **Commission on Human Rights**, the **United Nations Secretary-General** appointed a Representative to study the causes and consequences of internal displacement, the status of internally displaced persons in international law, the extent of the coverage accorded to them within existing international institutional arrangements, and ways in which their protection and assistance could be improved, including through dialogue with Governments and other pertinent actors. The **Guiding Principles on Internal Displacement** were completed in 1998. They are aimed at addressing the specific needs of internally displaced persons worldwide by identifying rights and guarantees relevant to their protection. The Principles reflect and are consistent with international human rights law standards and the norms of **international humanitarian law**.

Durban Declaration and Programme of Action (UN)

The Durban Declaration and Programme of Action was adopted at the **World Conference against Racism, Racial Discrimination, Xenophobia and Related Intolerance** held in Durban, South Africa (31 August – 8 September 2001). The Declaration recognizes that **racism**, racial **discrimination**, xenophobia and related intolerance "constitute serious violations of and obstacles to the full enjoyment of all human rights and deny the self-evident truth that all human beings are born equal in dignity and rights" (Preamble). A global fight against racism, racial discrimination, xenophobia and related intolerance is therefore recognized as a matter of priority for the international community (para. 3). The Declaration reaffirms "that everyone is entitled to a social and international order in which all human rights can be fully realized for all, without any discrimination" (para. 10). Its 5 sections, which correspond to the 5 themes of the Conference, concern: sources, causes, forms and contemporary manifestations of racism (paras. 13–30); victims (paras. 31–75); measures of prevention, education and protection aimed at the eradication of racism, racial discrimination, xenophobia and related intolerance at the national, regional and international levels (paras. 76–97); provision of effective remedies, recourse, redress, and compensatory and other measures at national, regional and international levels (paras. 98–106); and strategies to achieve full and effective equality, including international cooperation and enhancement of **United Nations** and other international mechanisms (paras. 107–122). The Declaration affirms "the solemn commitment of all States to promote universal respect for, and observance and protection of, all human rights, economic, social and cultural, civil and political, including the **right to development**, as a fundamental factor in the prevention and elimination of racism, racial discrimination, xenophobia and related intolerance" (para. 78). It also recognizes that "education at all levels and all ages, including within the family, in particular **human rights education**, is a key to changing attitudes and behaviour based on racism…and to promoting tolerance and respect for diversity in societies" (para. 95).

The Programme of Action aims at translating the objectives of the Declaration into a practical and workable plan. It contains five sections corresponding to the five themes identified in the Declaration. States are urged to take all necessary measures, legislative, judicial, regulatory, administrative and other, to redress discriminatory practices and to work for their eradication in particular with regard to certain groups that have been and continue to be victims of racism and racial discrimination (Africans and people of African descent; **indigenous peoples**; migrants; refugees; and other victims). Particular attention is attached to the role of independent **national human rights institutions** in combating racism (para. 90), as well as to the role of the media (paras. 140-147). A call is launched for the strengthening of cooperation among States and intergovernmental organizations, while special mention is made of the contribution of civil society (paras. 210-212) and **non-governmental organizations** (paras. 213-214) to the fight against racism.

The Durban Declaration and Programme of Action invite various actors, including **United Nations specialized agencies**, and in particular **UNESCO** and the **International Labour Organization (ILO)**, to undertake concrete action within their fields of competence giving effect to the provisions of the documents. The overall responsibility to follow up the Durban Declaration and Programme of Action is entrusted to the **Office of the United Nations High Commissioner for Human Rights (OHCHR)**.

Economic and Social Council – ECOSOC (UN)

The Economic and Social Council (ECOSOC) was established on 13 January 1946 as one of the six principal organs of the **United Nations**. It pursues the aims of the United Nations in the field of international economic and social cooperation, namely to promote: "(a) higher standards of living, full employment and conditions of economic and social progress and development; (b) solutions of international economic, social, health, and related problems; and international cultural and educational cooperation; and (c) universal respect for, and observance of, human rights and fundamental freedoms for all without distinction as to race, sex, language, or religion" (Article 55 of the **Charter of the United Nations**). ECOSOC's principal functions are determined in Chapter X of the Charter which states that it: "may make or initiate studies and reports with respect to international economic, social, cultural, educational, health and related matters and may make recommendations with respect to any such matters to the **United Nations General Assembly**, to the members of the United Nations and to the specialized agencies concerned" (Article 62, para. 1); "may make recommendations for the purpose of promoting respect for and observance of human rights and fundamental freedoms for all" (Article 62, para. 2); "may prepare draft conventions for submission to the United Nations General Assembly with respect to matters falling within its competence" (Article 62, para. 3); and "may call, in accordance with the rules prescribed by the United Nations, international conferences on matters falling within its competence" (Article 62, para. 4).

In addition, ECOSOC is responsible for coordinating the activities of the specialized agencies through consultation with and recommendations to those agencies and through recommendations to the United Nations General Assembly and members of the United Nations, and for considering applications for the granting of consultative status to **non-governmental organizations**. Under Article 61 of the Charter as originally adopted, ECOSOC was to consist of 18 Members of the United Nations elected by the United Nations General Assembly. However, Article 61 has been twice amended, most recently on 20 December 1971 to increase the number of Members to 54. According to its rules of procedure, ECOSOC holds an organizational session and two regular sessions each year (Rule 1). However, special sessions may be held at its request or at the request of the United Nations General Assembly or the **Security Council** (Rule 4). The rules also provide for the participation of non-members of ECOSOC in its deliberations without the right to vote (Rules 72-78).

Of ECOSOC's subsidiary bodies, those most directly concerned with human rights questions are: the **Commission on Human Rights**, the **Commission on the Status of Women**, the **Sub-Commission on the Promotion and Protection of Human Rights** (formerly the **Sub-Commission on Prevention of Discrimination and Protection of Minorities**) and the **Committee on Economic, Social and Cultural Rights**.

For more information see:
http://www.un.org/esa/coordination/ecosoc

Economic rights

Economic rights include a number of rights such as the **right to work, to free choice of employment** and **to just and favourable conditions of work**; the **right to form and join trade unions**, including the **right to strike**; and the **right to social security**. The realization of economic rights is provided for in Chapter IX of the **United Nations Charter**, entitled "International

Economic and Social cooperation". It states that among the primary goals of the **United Nations** are "higher standards of living, full employment, and conditions of economic and social progress and development; solutions of international economic, social, health related problems; and international cultural and educational cooperation" (Article 55). An extended list of economic rights is contained in the **Universal Declaration of Human Rights** (1948). Economic rights are further laid down in the **International Covenant on Economic, Social and Cultural Rights** (1966) and in various **International Labour Organization (ILO)** conventions on a variety of aspects of labour relations and working conditions. Protection of economic rights is envisaged in a number of regional instruments, such as: the **European Social Charter** (1961) and the **European Code of Social Security** (1964); the **American Declaration of the Rights and Duties of Man** (1948); the **American Convention on Human Rights** (1969); and the Arab Labour Standards Convention (1967).

Ethnic cleansing

Ethnic cleansing can be defined as a process in which one ethnic group expels persons belonging to other ethnic groups from towns and villages in order to create "ethnically pure" territories. Often refugees of an ethnic group previously "cleansed" from their homes by other ethnic group are made to live in a freshly "cleansed" territory of that other ethnic group. The vengeance they feel explains the cruelties to which such a situation can lead.

The most abhorrent cases of ethnic cleansing occurred in former Yugoslavia and Rwanda. In order to punish those guilty of the crime of ethnic cleansing, an **International Criminal Tribunal for the former Yugoslavia** and an **International Criminal Tribunal for Rwanda** have been set up by the **United Nations**. The **International Criminal Court** has jurisdiction over: the crime of **genocide**; crimes against humanity; war crimes; and the crime of aggression (**Rome Statute of the International**

Criminal Court, Part 2, Article 5). Deportation or forcible transfer of population is acknowledged as a crime against humanity (Part 2, article 7).

Ethno-nationalism

Ethno-nationalism can be characterized as aggressive extreme nationalism and/or chauvinism. In order to achieve a dominant position, ethno-nationalists utilize either forced assimilation, imposition of a dominant cultural identity, language and religion or exclusion of members or other ethnic groups from the national society by the denial and deprivation of citizenship or by ethnic cleansing. Ethno-nationalism provokes internal ethnic conflicts and massive and flagrant violations of human rights like **genocide** in Rwanda and **ethnic cleansing** in the former Yugoslavia. Such movements have a strong irrational component which contributes to their strength and, at the same time makes them less susceptible to political compromise or acceptance of the rights of other cultural groups. Thus, ethno-nationalism creates many dangers for human rights, peace and security. Means aimed at eliminating the sources of ethno-nationalism are the following: full respect of various cultural, national, ethnic, religious and linguistic minorities including acceptance of multi-culturalism and cultural autonomy; intercultural formal and non-formal education; internal self-determination; and procedures and criteria guaranteed by the international community, the **United Nations** and regional organizations to evaluate claims to external self-determination, to secession and independence.

European Agreement on the Abolition of Visas for Refugees (Council of Europe)

The European Agreement on the Abolition of Visas for Refugees was adopted on 20 April 1959 and entered into force on 4 September 1960. By the middle of 2003, it had been ratified by

20 States. It aims at facilitating travel for refugees residing in the territories of the Contracting States.

European Agreement on Transfer of Responsibility for Refugees (Council of Europe)

Adopted by the **Council of Europe** on 16 October 1980, the European Agreement on Transfer of Responsibility for Refugees entered into force on 1 December 1980. By the middle of 2003, it had been ratified by 12 States. The Agreement aims to improve the situation of refugees by specifying the conditions and making uniform the regulations, under which responsibility for issuing a travel document is transferred from one Contracting Party to another. For the purposes of the Agreement, a "refugee" is any person who falls within the definition contained in Article 1 of the 1951 **Convention Relating to the Status of Refugees** of the **United Nations** and modified by the 1966 **Protocol Relating to the Status of Refugees**. Accordingly, the transfer of responsibility for issuing a travel document takes place when the refugee, carrying travel documents from the first State, has stayed in the second State with the consent of the authorities for a period of two years, or earlier if the second State permits the refugee to remain in its territory. The Agreement defines a "first State" as a Contracting Party "which has issued such a travel document" and a "second State" as another Contracting Party "in which a refugee, holder of a travel document issued by the first State, is present" (Article 1). When a transfer has taken place, the second State takes over responsibility in matters relating to the refugee, for example the issue of new travel documents and the reunification of his/her family. The Agreement ensures the **rights of refugees** to be readmitted to the territory of the first State at any time, even after the expiry of the travel document, in such cases where the transfer of responsibility has not taken place.

European Agreement (1969) relating to Persons Participating in Proceedings of the European Commission and Court of Human Rights (Council of Europe)

Adopted by the **Council of Europe** on 6 May 1969, this Agreement entered into force on 17 April 1971. By the middle of 2003, it had been ratified by 26 Member States. The Agreement aims to protect all persons, whether they are agents or advisers of the Contracting Parties, representatives of persons taking part in the proceedings, persons chosen by the delegates of the Commission to assist them, or witnesses and experts called upon to participate in proceedings of the **European Commission** or the **European Court of Human Rights** (Article 1), with the goal of ensuring the freedom of speech and the independence necessary for the discharge of their functions, tasks or duties, or the exercise of their rights in relation to the Commission and the Court (Article 5). To achieve this, the Contracting Parties undertake to ensure all such persons certain immunities and facilities, including: immunity from legal process in respect of any oral or written statement made or documents or other evidence submitted by them (Article 2); the right to correspond freely with the Commission and with the Court, in particular relating to persons under detention (Article 5); and the right to free movement and travel for the purpose of attending or returning from proceedings (Article 4).

European Agreement (1996) relating to Persons Participating in Proceedings of the European Court of Human Rights (Council of Europe)

This Agreement was adopted by the **Council of Europe** on 5 March 1996. It entered into force on 1 January 1999 and, by the middle of 2003, it had been ratified by 29 Member States. This Agreement, based on the 1969 **European Agreement Relating to Persons Participating in Proceedings of the European**

Commission and Court of Human Rights, was designed to adapt the 1969 Agreement to the reforms that had subsequently taken place in the European system for protecting and promoting human rights, namely the transformation of the **European Commission** and the **European Court of Human Rights** into a single body. The 1996 Agreement leaves the aim and content of the 1969 Agreement unchanged and simply deletes the word "Commission", as well as all provisions concerning matters involving the Commission.

European Charter for Regional or Minority Languages (Council of Europe)

The European Charter for Regional or Minority Languages was adopted by the **Council of Europe** and opened for signature on 5 November 1992. It entered into force on 1 March 1998. By the middle of 2003, the Charter had been ratified by 17 Member States. As stated in its Preamble, the Charter embraces the ideals of a Europe founded on cultural diversity. Its aim is thus to halt the decline of regional and minority languages and to promote their use, both in their written and spoken forms, in public life and in social, economic and cultural contexts, as well as to encourage people to teach and learn them. "Regional or minority languages", as defined in the Charter, are languages that are "traditionally used within a given territory of a State by nationals of that State who form a group numerically smaller than the rest of the State's population, and different from the official language(s) of that State" (Article 1). The Charter outlines several objectives and principles on which the Parties should base their policies, legislation and practice in relation to all regional or minority languages used on the State's territory (Article 7). More specifically, the Charter contains concrete provisions requiring the Contracting Parties to promote the use of such languages in the field of education, in the media, in cultural activities, in matters involving the judicial and administrative authorities, in economic and social life and transboundary exchanges. The Parties are, however, given the right to exercise a certain degree of choice among these provisions in accordance with the situation of each language. The instrument provides for the establishment of a monitoring body, consisting of one independent expert from each State Party appointed for a period of six years. The Charter obliges States Parties to submit periodic reports for review, initially one year after the entry into force of the Charter for a given Party, and thereafter at three-year intervals. The Committee of Experts is responsible for forwarding to the Committee of Ministers its evaluation on the way in which the Charter is implemented in each State Party and recommendations for improving the application of the Charter in States Parties.

European Charter for the Safeguarding of Human Rights in the City

The First European Conference for Human Rights in the City, held in Barcelona in October 1998, resulted in the 'Barcelona Agreement', signed by 40 European Cities. This document was further elaborated, and, under its actual title, signed in May 2000 by the 96 Cities that participated in the Second European Conference in Saint-Denis, France. The Charter is the basis for the movement **"Cities for Human Rights"** which by May 2003 involves 235 Cities from 21 countries.

The Charter is divided into 5 parts. According to the General Provisions (Part 1), the city is "a collective space which belongs to all those who live in it, who have the right to find there the conditions for their political, social and ecological fulfilment, at the same time assuming duties of solidarity". **Civil** and **political rights**, enshrined in Part II of the document, include the right of political participation, the right of association, meeting and demonstration, the right to a private and family life, and the right to information. Part III of the Charter deals with **economic, social** and **cultural rights**, which include the general right to the public services of social protection, the **right to education**, the **right to work**, the right to culture, the right to a proper, safe and healthy home, the **right to health**, the **right to a healthy environment**, the right to harmonious and sustainable city development, the right to circulation and tranquillity in the city, the right to rest and leisure, and consumers' rights. Part IV entitled "Rights Relative to the Local Democratic Administration" concerns the efficiency of public services and guarantees that citizens must be able to know their political and administrative rights and obligations and that, for this purpose, municipal regulations, which must be comprehensible and regularly brought up to date, should be available. Part V of the Charter concerns local administration of justice, accessibility of local police, warning mechanisms (social or district mediators, the municipal Ombudsman or Defender of the People), and taxation and budgetary mechanisms. The Final Provisions call for each signatory city to create a commission entrusted to establish, every two years, an evaluation of the application of the rights recognized by this Charter, and to make such evaluation public.

European Charter of Local Self-Government (Council of Europe)

Adopted by the **Council of Europe** and opened for signature on 15 October 1985, the European Charter of Local Self-Government entered into force on 1 September 1988. By the middle of 2003, it had been ratified by 38 Member States and signed by three others. The Charter is based on the right of citizens to participate in the conduct of public affairs as stipulated, *inter alia*, in the **Universal Declaration of Human Rights** (Article 21) and the **International Covenant on Civil and Political Rights** (Article 25). It is also based on the assumption of Member States that local self-government, and thus decentralization of power, is one of the main foundations of any democratic regime. The Charter sets out the constitutional and legal basis for local autonomy, the principles governing powers, finance and supervision, which should be respected by any local government system. It provides for the protection of local boundaries, for the establishment of appropriate administrative structures, and for the allocation of adequate human and financial resources enabling local authorities to effectively undertake their duties. Local authorities have the right to associate and to cooperate in order to realize projects of common interest. The Charter also expects Member States to incorporate in domestic legislation the principle of self-government and its definition.

European Charter on Sport for All: Disabled Persons (Council of Europe)

This Charter was adopted by the Committee of Ministers of the **Council of Europe** on 4 December 1986. It aims at ensuring that the governments of the Member States of the Council take the necessary steps to ensure that public authorities and private organizations are aware of the sporting and recreational wants and needs of all disabled persons, not only those who are physically disabled and mentally handicapped but also those who suffer from an organic or psychosomatic disorder. Such persons should have adequate opportunities to take part in physical activities which will encourage their feeling of well-being and/or improve their physical condition. In accordance with the Charter, policies designed to sensitize the general public on sport for disabled persons should be developed.

European Code of Social Security and Its Additional Protocol (Council of Europe)

The European Code of Social Security and Protocol thereto were opened for signature by the Member States of the **Council of Europe** on 16 April 1964 and entered into force on 17 March 1968. By early 2003, the Code had been ratified by 18 States and the Protocol by 7 States. The Code aims at encouraging the development of social security in all Member States of the

Council of Europe in order that they may gradually reach the highest level possible. Therefore, the Code, consisting of fourteen Parts, an Annex and two Addenda, defines norms for social security coverage and establishes minimum levels of protection. The Code contains provisions relating to the nine traditional branches of social security: Medical care (Articles 7-12); Sickness benefit (Articles 13-18); Unemployment benefit (Articles 19-24); Old-age benefit (Articles 25-30); Employment injury benefit (Articles 31-38); Family benefit (Articles 39-45); Maternity benefit (Articles 46-52); Invalidity benefit (Articles 53-58); and Survivors' benefit (Articles 59-64). Articles 65-67 deal with standards to be complied with by periodical payments. Following the same structure, the Protocol provides for a standard of social security higher than the level established in the Code and constitutes the desirable "European level" of social security that all Council of Europe Member States should endeavour to attain. Subsequently in 1990 the Council of Europe adopted the **European Code of Social Security – revised**.

European Code of Social Security – revised (Council of Europe)

The European Code of Social Security (revised) was opened for signature by the Member States of the **Council of Europe** on 6 November 1990. By early 2003, 14 States had signed the instrument. The revised Code was drawn up with a view to improve the standards of the **European Code of Social Security and its Additional Protocol** of 1964 and to introduce greater flexibility when it was recognized that a certain number of provisions of these instruments had become, at least partially, incompatible with certain emergent legislative trends and with the different social security practices applied in certain countries. In comparison with the 1964 Code and Protocol, the revised Code provides for increased levels of coverage, as well as for a larger scope; it also sets higher standards for the level and the duration of cash benefits as well as new benefits, and defines more precisely those provided for in the 1964 Code.

European Commission (EU)

The European Commission is one of the main institutions of the **European Union (EU)**. It comprises 20 Commissioners from the 15 EU Member States, who act in their personal capacity. The President of the Commission is chosen by the Heads of State or Government meeting after consultation with the **European Parliament**. The Commission is based in Brussels. It meets once a week to adopt proposals, finalize policy papers and discuss the evolution of its priority policies. When necessary, it holds special sessions in addition to these weekly meetings.

The Commission's work ensures that the EU can attain an ever-closer union of its members and that the benefits of integration are balanced between countries and regions, between business and consumers and between individuals. One of its main tasks is to secure the free movement of goods, services, capital and persons throughout the territory of the EU. The Commission initiates community policy and represents the general interest of the EU. However, it is not the EU's main decision-making body, this responsibility being shared with the Council of the European Union and the European Parliament. The Commission acts as the guardian of the EU treaties to ensure that EU legislation is applied correctly by its Member States. As the EU's executive institution, it is responsible for managing policies and negotiating international trade and cooperation agreements. The Commission works in a close partnership with other European institutions.

In order to promote human rights and democratization in 1992 the European Union launched the Phare and Tacis Democracy Programmes. These programmes seek to promote the use of democratic principles and procedures in different spheres of life. Their aim is to provide practical assistance and expertise to help the countries of Central and Eastern Europe to restructure their political and economic systems.

The European Commission now in charge of these programmes, presents a framework for all activities in the area of human rights. Since 1995, it has issued a series of communications to the **European Council** and the European Parliament. These communications set out strategies aimed at enhancing the consistency and effectiveness of the human rights and democratization approach of the European Union. The communication of May 2001 concentrates mainly on "The EU's Role in promoting Human Rights and Democratisation in Third Countries".

For more information see:
http://europa.eu.int/comm/index_en.htm

European Commission against Racism and Intolerance – ECRI (Council of Europe)

The European Commission against Racism and Intolerance (ECRI) was established by the first Summit of Heads of State and Government of the Member States of the **Council of Europe** (Vienna, October 1993). ECRI is an independent human rights mechanism for monitoring issues related to **racism** and racial **discrimination**. Its members serve in their individual capacity and are independent and impartial in fulfilling their mandate. ECRI's action covers all necessary measures to combat violence, discrimination and prejudice faced by persons or groups of persons, on grounds of race, colour, language, religion, nationality and national or ethnic origin. Its programme of activities comprises three aspects: country-by-country approach; work on general themes; and relations with civil society. In the framework of its country-by-country approach, ECRI monitors the phenomena of racism and racial discrimination by closely examining the situation in each of the Member States of the Council of Europe. It draws up reports containing suggestions and proposals as to how each country could deal with the problems identified. The country-by-country work takes place in four/five year cycles, covering nine/ten countries per year. As part of its work on general themes, ECRI adopts general policy recommendations addressed to all Member States, covering the main areas of racism and intolerance and providing basic guidelines for the development of comprehensive national policies. As to ECRI's relations with civil society, this part of its programme aims to ensure that its anti-racism message filters down to the whole of civil society, and also to involve the various sectors of society in an intercultural dialogue based on mutual respect.

For more information see:
http://www.coe.int/t/E/human_rights/ecri

European Commission of Human Rights (Council of Europe)

The European Commission of Human Rights was a separate entity within the **Council of Europe** until 1 November 1998 when Protocol N° 11 to the **European Convention for the Protection of Human Rights and Fundamental Freedoms** was adopted. This Protocol replaced the two monitoring and enforcement institutions of the Council of Europe, namely the part-time **European Court of Human Rights** and the European Commission of Human Rights, by a full-time new European Court of Human Rights with compulsory jurisdiction.

European Committee for the Prevention of Torture and Inhuman or Degrading Treatment or Punishment (Council of Europe)

The European Committee for the Prevention of Torture and Inhuman or Degrading Treatment or Punishment (CPT) was established by the **European Convention for the Prevention of Torture and Inhuman or Degrading Treatment or Punishment** adopted by the **Council of Europe** on 26 November 1987. The Committee, which began its work in 1989, was established to ensure compliance with the Convention and to strengthen the protection of individuals deprived of their liberty. Its membership consists of a number equal to that of the Member

States having ratified the Convention (44 by the middle of 2003) and is comprised of experts with recognized competence in the field of human rights who serve in their personal capacity. The Members are elected for a period of four years by the Committee of Ministers. According to Article 7 of the Convention, the Committee is entitled to have its members visit the territory of a Contracting Party where persons deprived of their liberty are being held. It has a mandate to carry out such visits on a regular basis or where special circumstances make it necessary. Although the Committee must notify the government of a State Party of an intended visit, it does not have to provide details regarding the arrival of the mission. The Member States are required to cooperate with the members of the Committee, allow them access to all places where persons are deprived of their liberty and to provide them with any information they may request. After each visit, a report is written containing the findings of the Committee and possible recommendations to improve the situation of persons in detention. The Committee does not seek to condemn States but rather to cooperate with them to strengthen the protection of persons deprived of their liberty. Although the Convention provides that all information is to be confidential unless the Member State refuses to cooperate (Article 11), the Committee's reports, with the permission of the Party concerned, have often been published.

For more information see:
http://www.cpt.coe.int/en/about.htm

European Committee of Social Rights (Council of Europe)

The European Committee of Social Rights (ECSR) was set up under Article 25 of the **European Social Charter**. It examines the annual reports submitted by States parties to the Charter indicating how they implement the Charter in law and practice. The Committee decides whether or not the situations in the countries concerned are in conformity with the Charter and publishes these decisions, known as consultations, annually. The ECSR is composed of thirteen independent, impartial members who are elected by the Council of Europe's Committee of Ministers for a period of six years, renewable once.

If a State takes no action on a Committee decision to the effect that it does not comply with the Charter, the Committee of Ministers addresses a recommendation to that State, asking it to change the situation in law or in practice. The Committee of Ministers' work is prepared by a Governmental Committee comprising representatives of the governments of the States Parties to the Charter, assisted by observers representing European employers' organizations and trade unions.

European Community – EC

The European Economic Community (EEC) was created by the Treaty of Rome which was signed by six European States on 6 March 1957 and entered into force on 1 January 1958. After the entry into force of the Treaty of Maastricht on 1 November 1993, it changed its name to the "European Community". The EC now comprises fifteen States (Austria, Belgium, Denmark, Finland, France, Germany, Greece, Ireland, Italy, Luxembourg, Netherlands, Portugal, Spain, Sweden and the United Kingdom) with 365 million citizens. Its objectives are to: promote European unity; establish a common market and an economic and monetary union; improve living and working conditions for citizens; and to preserve peace and freedom. The EC is the largest structure of the **European Union**. At the Copenhagen **European Council** (12-13 December 2002) it was decided to enlarge the membership and to admit 10 new members in 2004 (Cyprus, the Czech Republic, Estonia, Hungary Latvia, Lithuania, Malta, Poland, the Slovak Republic, Slovenia).

European Convention for the Prevention of Torture and Inhuman or Degrading Treatment or Punishment (Council of Europe)

This Convention was signed by the Member States of the **Council of Europe** on 26 November 1987 and entered into force on 1 February 1989. By the middle of 2003, it had been ratified by 44 Member States. The Convention refers to the **European Convention for the Protection of Human Rights and Fundamental Freedoms** which stipulates that "no one shall be subjected to torture or to inhuman or degrading treatment or punishment" (Article 3). To ensure compliance with the Convention, and based on the conviction of Member States that "the protection of persons deprived of their liberty against torture and inhuman or degrading treatment or punishment could be strengthened by non-judicial means of a preventive character" (Preamble), the Convention calls for the establishment of a **European Committee for the Prevention of Torture and Inhuman or Degrading Treatment or Punishment**.

Two Protocols to the Convention have been adopted. Protocol N° 1 of 4 November 1993 opens up the Convention so that non-Member States may adhere to its provisions. Protocol N°2, also of 4 November 1993, relates to the term of office of the members of the Committee. Both Protocols entered into force in March 2002.

European Convention for the Protection of Human Rights and Fundamental Freedoms (Council of Europe)

Commonly called the **European Convention on Human Rights**, this Convention was adopted by the **Council of Europe** on 4 November 1950. It entered into force on 3 September 1953. By the middle of 2003, it had been ratified by 44 Member States. The Convention sets out the inalienable rights and freedoms of each individual and obliges States to guarantee these rights to everyone within their jurisdiction without **discrimination** on any grounds (Article 14). The provisions of this instrument concern principally **civil** and **political rights**: the **right to life**, the **right to liberty and security of person**, freedom from slavery and torture, freedom from unlawful arrest and detention, the **right to a fair trial**, the right to privacy and family life, **freedom of thought, conscience and religion, freedom of expression**, freedom of assembly and the **right to marry** (Section I). Since the entry into force of Protocol 11 (1 November 1998), Section II of the Convention provides for the establishment of a full-time **European Court of Human Rights** with compulsory jurisdiction (replacing two original enforcement institutions, the part-time Court and the European Commission of Human Rights). States and individuals may refer alleged violations of the rights and freedoms guaranteed by the Convention to the European Court of Human Rights (Articles 33 and 34). Section III of the Convention deals with miscellaneous provisions.

As of December 2002, the European Convention on Human Rights has been modified or developed by 13 Protocols. These Protocols enhance the protection afforded by the Convention, either by extending the list of guaranteed rights or by improving existing procedures.

An Additional Protocol, adopted on 20 March 1952, adds to the Convention, *inter alia*, the **right to vote** in free elections (Article 3), the **right to education** (Article 2) and the right to peaceful enjoyment of one's own possessions (Article 1). Protocol N° 4 of 16 September 1963, which entered into force on 2 May 1968, added to the Convention the right to liberty of movement, freedom to choose one's residence, freedom to leave any country and the right to enter one's own country. Protocol N° 6 of 28 April 1983 concerns the abolition of the death penalty. Protocol N° 7 of 22 November 1984 ensures, *inter alia*, certain guarantees to foreigners from expulsion from the territory of a State Party (Article 1), the right to have a conviction of a criminal offence reviewed by a higher tribunal (Article 2) and the **right to compensation** to persons who have suffered punishment on false grounds (Article 3). Protocol N° 11 "Restructuring the Control Machinery Established thereby" of 4 May 1994 entered into force on 1 November 1998. By the middle of 2003, it had been ratified by 44 States.

Protocol N° 12 of 4 November 2000 concerns mainly the general prohibition of discrimination to ensure the fundamental principle according to which all persons are equal before the law. By the middle of 2003 it had not entered into force. Protocol N°13 is banning the death penalty in all circumstances including crimes committed in times of war and imminent threat of war. Opened for signature on 3 May 2002, this Protocol entered into force on 1 July 2003 and had been ratified in August 2003 by 17 States.

European Convention on Extradition and Additional Protocols thereto (Council of Europe)

The European Convention on Extradition was adopted on 13 December 1957 and entered into force on 18 April 1960. By the middle of 2003, it had been ratified by 45 States. It includes provisions determining extraditable offences (Article 2), political offences (Article 3), military offences (Article 4), fiscal offences (Article 5) and extradition of nationals (Article 6).

The Convention is accompanied by two Additional Protocols. The first was adopted on 15 October 1975 and entered into force on 20 August 1979. By the middle of 2003, it had been ratified by 31 States. The Protocol was elaborated to supplement the Convention and to thus strengthen international cooperation in the struggle against criminality.

A second Additional Protocol was adopted on 17 March 1978. It adds fiscal offences to those giving grounds for extradition under the Convention. The second Protocol also contains provisions on judgements *in absentia* and amnesty.

European Convention on Human Rights (Council of Europe)

See European Convention for the Protection of Human Rights and Fundamental Freedoms (Council of Europe).

European Convention on Mutual Assistance in Criminal Matters (Council of Europe)

The Convention was adopted on 20 April 1959 and entered into force on 12 June 1962. By the middle of 2003, it had been ratified by 42 States. It lays down provisions for letters rogatory, the service of writs and records of judicial verdicts and the appearance of witnesses, experts and prosecuted persons. The Convention has been complemented by two Additional Protocols (1978 and 2001).

European Convention on Nationality (Council of Europe)

On 14 May 1997, the Committee of Ministers of the **Council of Europe** adopted the European Convention on Nationality and opened it for signature on 6 November 1997. It came into force on 1 March 2000 and, by the middle of 2003, it had been ratified by 9 States. With the development of human rights law, there is an increasing recognition that States must, in matters of nationality, take into account the fundamental rights of individuals. This Convention, which consolidates, in a single text, the important issues relating to nationality, reflects the demographic and democratic changes, in particular migration and State succession, which have occurred in Central and Eastern Europe since 1989. Therefore this text, which constitutes an important standard in the field of nationality, aims at contributing to the progressive development of international law. The term "nationality" is defined in the Convention (Article 2) as the legal bond between an individual and a State and does not indicate a person's ethnic origin. As far as multiple nationality is concerned, the text, in general, allows States to take into account their own particular circumstances in determining the extent to which multiple nationality is to be allowed. The Convention embodies principles and rules applying to all aspects of nationality. It is designed to make easier acquisition of a new nationality and recovery of a former one, to ensure that nationality is lost only for good reason and cannot be arbitrarily withdrawn, to guarantee that the procedures governing applications for nationality are just, fair and open to appeal, and to regulate the situation of persons in danger of being left stateless as a result of State succession. It also covers military obligations and cooperation between States Parties. Some of the essential principles behind the text are the prevention of statelessness, non-discrimination (in regulating questions of nationality, States must avoid all **discrimination** on grounds of sex, religion, race, colour, national or ethnic origin) and respect for the rights of persons habitually resident on the territories concerned.

European Convention on Offences relating to Cultural Property (Council of Europe)

This Convention was adopted in Delphi, Greece, on 23 June 1985. By the middle of 2003, it had not yet entered into force. The Convention was drawn up based on the belief that a greater unity between the Member States of the **Council of Europe** is founded to a considerable extent on the existence of a European cultural heritage. Articles 4-5 concern the protection of cultural property and Articles 6-11 the restitution of cultural property. The list of objects comprising the **cultural heritage** is to be found in Appendix II and the offences – acts and omissions – are enumerated in Appendix III.

European Convention on the Academic Recognition of University Qualifications (Council of Europe)

This Convention was adopted on 14 December 1959 and entered into force on 27 November 1961. By the middle of 2003, it had been ratified by 28 States. It lays down in its Article 3 that academic recognition shall be granted to university qualifications conferred by a university situated in the territory of another Contracting Party. Article 4 concerns examination requirements for a foreign university qualification and the necessity to pass an official language test if studies have been pursued in another language. The Convention is also aimed at ensuring **academic freedom**.

The Convention will in due time be replaced by the **Council of Europe/UNESCO** Convention on the Recognition of Qualifications Concerning Higher Education in the European Region, which by the middle of 2003 had been ratified by 32 States and signed by a further 11.

European Convention on the Exercise of Children's Rights (Council of Europe)

This Convention was opened to signature on 25 January 1996 by the **Council of Europe** and entered into force on 1 July 2000. It had been ratified by 8 Member States by the middle of 2003. The Convention aims to protect the best interests of children. It provides a number of procedural measures to allow children to exercise their rights. It sets up a Standing Committee which shall keep under review problems relating to this Convention.

The Convention provides for measures which aim to promote the rights of children, in particular in family proceedings before judicial authorities. The judicial authority, or person appointed to act before a judicial authority on behalf of a child, has a number of duties designed to facilitate the exercise of rights by children. Children should be allowed to exercise their rights (for example, the right to be informed and the right to express their views) either themselves or through persons or bodies.

Among the types of family proceedings of special interest for children are those concerning custody, residence, access, questions of parentage, legitimacy, adoption, legal guardianship, administration of property of children, care procedures, removal or restriction of parental responsibilities, protection from cruel or degrading treatment, and medical treatment.

Each State Party is required to specify at least three categories of family proceedings to which this Convention is to apply. It is worth noting that all Member States of the Council of Europe are also Parties to the **Convention on the Rights of the Child**, adopted by the **United Nations**.

European Convention on the Legal Status of Children Born out of Wedlock (Council of Europe)

This Convention was opened to signature on 15 October 1975 and entered into force on 11 August 1978. By the middle of 2003, it had been ratified by 20 States. The Convention aims at reducing the differences between the legal status of children born out of wedlock and that of those born in wedlock which are to the legal or social disadvantage of the former. Article 2 states that the maternal affiliation of every child born out of wedlock shall be based solely on the fact of the birth of the child, whilst Article 3 states that the paternal affiliation of every child born out of wedlock may be evidenced or established by voluntary recognition or by judicial decision. Article 6 lays down that the father and mother of a child born out of wedlock shall have the same obligation to maintain the child as if it were born in wedlock. States Parties undertake to ensure the conformity of their laws with the provisions of the Convention and to notify the Secretary General of the **Council of Europe** of the measures taken for that purpose (Article 1).

European Convention on the Legal Status of Migrant Workers (Council of Europe)

This Convention was adopted by the Member States of the **Council of Europe** on 24 November 1977 and entered into force on 1 May 1983. By the middle of 2003, it had been ratified by 8 Member States. The Convention enshrines the principle of equality of treatment for migrant workers and nationals of the host country. As defined under the Convention, a "migrant worker" is "a national of a Contracting Party who has been authorized by another Contracting Party to reside in its territory in order to take up paid employment" (Article 1). Excluded from enjoyment of the provisions of this Convention are frontier workers, artists and sportsmen, seamen and persons undergoing training. With regard to migrant workers, the Convention stipulates rules concerning admission into the territory of a Contracting Party, recruitment, work contracts, residence and work permits, travel, working conditions and family reunion, housing, schooling and social security, taxation and access to the courts. The application of the Convention is monitored by a Consultative Committee, consisting of one representative appointed by each State Party. The Committee held its first session in April 1984 and has since met at least once every two years. The Committee examines proposals for improving the application of the Convention and makes recommendations on amendments to it. It is also responsible for submitting to the Committee of Ministers periodic reports containing information on the laws and regulations in force in the Member States on matters provided for in the Convention. It is the Committee of Ministers which then decides on what, if any, action should be taken.

European Convention on the Non-applicability of Statutory Limitation to Crimes against Humanity and War Crimes (Council of Europe)

Adopted on 25 January 1974, the European Convention on the Non-Applicability of Statutory Limitation to Crimes against Humanity and War Crimes has not yet entered into force. The Convention aims to ensure that previously decided statutory limitations will not prevent the prosecution of individuals accused of committing crimes against humanity and war crimes. It applies to such crimes as specified in the **Convention on the Prevention and Punishment of the Crime of Genocide** (1948), and in the **Geneva Conventions** of 1949. The Convention, furthermore, sets out provisions allowing Member States to extend its scope of application to encompass "any other violation of a rule or custom of international law which may hereafter be established and which the Contracting State concerned considers (...) as being of a comparable nature" (Article 1). The Convention applies to offences committed after its entry into force as well as to those committed before in cases where the statutory limitation period had not expired at that time (Article 2).

European Convention on the Protection of the Archaeological Heritage – revised (Council of Europe)

The European Convention on the Protection of the Archaeological Heritage (Revised) was adopted in Valletta, Malta, on 16 January 1992. It entered into force on 25 May 1995. By the middle of 2003, it had been ratified by 27 States. It took note of the **European Cultural Convention** (1954), the **Convention for the Protection of the Architectural Heritage of Europe** (1985) and the **European Convention on Offences relating to Cultural Property** (1985) and recalled that the archaeological heritage is essential to acknowledge of the history of mankind. In its Article 1, para. 1, the Convention established that its main purpose is: "… to protect the archaeological heritage as a source of the European collective memory and as an instrument for historical and scientific study". It identifies the heritage and measures for its protection (Articles 2-4), envisages mutual technical and scientific assistance among States Parties (Article 12), as well as the collection and dissemination of scientific information (Article 7) and the promotion of public awareness of the value of the archaeological heritage and threats to it (Article 9). The Convention also contains provisions concerning the prevention of the illicit circulation of elements of the archaeological heritage (Article 10), as well as those concerning the control of the application of the Convention (Article 13).

European Convention on the Suppression of Terrorism (Council of Europe)

The European Convention on the Suppression of Terrorism was adopted on 27 January 1977 and entered into force on 4 August 1978. By the middle of 2003, it had been ratified by 39 States. The aim of the Convention is to ensure the prosecution and punishment of perpetrators of acts of terrorism. The Convention enumerates a number of particularly serious offences (hijacking, kidnapping, taking of hostages, armed attacks, etc.), which are 'depoliticized' for the purposes of extradition and mutual assistance. The Parties undertake not to regard them as political offences. Extradition cannot therefore be refused on that ground (Article 1). The States Parties to the Convention shall afford one another mutual assistance in matters concerning the struggle against terrorism (Article 8), as also laid down in the **European Convention on Mutual Assistance in Criminal Matters** (1962).

European Council (EU)

The European Council brings together the Heads of State or Government of the fifteen Member States of the **European Union** and the President of the **European Commission**.

It was formally established in 1987 by Article 23 of the Single European Act. It is now a body of the European Union in conformity with Article 4 of the Treaty on European Union.

At least twice a year the European Council is hosted by and takes place in the Member State holding the Presidency of the Council of the European Union, and punctuates the political life and development of the European Union. The function of the European Council is to establish policy guidelines for European integration in relation to both the **European Community** and the European Union.

The European Council seeks to bring the European Union closer to its citizens, to strengthen the Union's democratic character, to facilitate this decision-making capacity and the ability to act as a coherent and unified force in the international system by ensuring the principles of the European Common Foreign and Security Policy. The European Council decided to establish the **European Union Charter of Fundamental Rights**.

The European Council presents the Annual Report on Human Rights, which serves as a basis to make the European Union's human rights policy more consistent and effective. The Report is a result of teamwork of the European Council Secretariat, human rights experts of the fifteen Member States and the European Commission.

The European Council should not be confused with the Council of the European Union, which is an institution of the European Community and exercises the legislative powers conferred by the Treaty establishing the European Community (Art. 202 of the EC Treaty), coordinates the economic policies of the Member States and constitutes, together with the **European Parliament**, the budgetary authority of the European Community.

European Court of Human Rights (Council of Europe)

The European Court of Human Rights was established in 1959 by the **Council of Europe** under the terms of the **European Convention for the Protection of Human Rights and Fundamental Freedoms**. On 1 November 1998, Protocol N° 11 to the Convention entered into force replacing the two original enforcement institutions, the part-time Court and the **European Commission of Human Rights**, by a full-time Court with compulsory jurisdiction. The Court ensures compliance with the principles and ideals enshrined in the Convention. The Court's jurisdiction, as stated in Article 32 of the Convention, extends "to all matters concerning the interpretation and application of the Convention and the protocols thereto". It is composed of judges, in equal number to that of the States Parties. The judges are elected by the Parliamentary Assembly of the Council of Europe for a term of six years with a possibility of re-election, and serve in their personal capacity. Under the new system in force since 1 November 1998, the new European Court deals with individual and inter-State cases.

Following a preliminary examination, each case is assigned either to a Committee of three judges or directly to a Chamber of seven judges, depending on the complexity of the case, which will examine whether or not the case should be examined on the merits. The requirements for a case to be admissible include notably for the applicant to be personally and directly the victim of a breach of the rights enshrined in the Convention, to have exhausted all domestic remedies, to file the application within six months from the final domestic decision, and for the application not to be manifestly unfounded (Articles 34 and 35 of the ECHR). For a case to be rejected by a Committee, there must be a unanimous decision. If a Committee does not reject a case, it is then referred to a Chamber. In the event that a Chamber decides to admit a case, it will then proceed to an examination on the merits of the case. It may invite the Parties to submit further evidence and written observations and to attend a hearing, which will be public – unless, in exceptional circumstances, the Chamber decides otherwise. During the procedure on the merits, negotiations aimed at securing a friendly settlement may be conducted through the Court; such negotiations are confidential. Where serious questions of interpretation and application of the Convention arise, the Chamber, or any party, may request that the case be referred to the Grand Chamber, composed of 17 judges. The Chamber will decide in a public judgement, by a majority vote, on whether or not there has been a violation of the Convention. Compensation and costs can be awarded to the applicant where a violation has been found. The procedure before the Court is public and adversarial and there is no appeal against its judgements.

The Court's final judgements are binding on respondent States and their execution is supervised at regular intervals by the Committee of Ministers. The execution of judgements includes the payment of pecuniary just satisfaction awarded by the Court, the adoption of specific individual measures to erase the consequences of the violations found (such as striking out of impugned convictions for criminal records, re-opening of domestic judicial proceedings, etc.) and of general measures to prevent new similar violations (e.g. constitutional and legislative reforms, changes of domestic case-law, of administrative practices, etc.

For more information see: http://www.echr.coe.int

European Cultural Convention (Council of Europe)

The European Cultural Convention was adopted on 19 December 1954 and entered into force on 5 May 1955. By the middle of 2003, it had been ratified by 48 States, including 3 non-Member States of the **Council of Europe**. Its aim is to achieve greater unity for the safeguarding and realizing of the ideals and principles which are part of the common European heritage. The Contracting Parties shall encourage the study by their nationals of the languages, history and civilization of the other Contracting Parties and grant facilities to promote such studies (Article 2). They shall undertake concerted action to promote cultural activities of European interest (Article 3) and shall, insofar as may be possible, facilitate the movement and exchange of persons as well as objects of cultural value (Article 4). They shall regard objects of European cultural value placed under their control as integral parts of the common cultural heritage of Europe and shall ensure their safeguarding and reasonable access thereto" (Article 5).

European Landscape Convention (Council of Europe)

Adopted in Florence, Italy, on 20 October 2000 in the framework of the **Council of Europe** Campaign "Europe, a common heritage", the European Landscape Convention aims to promote the protection, management and planning of European landscapes to organize European cooperation on landscape issues. By the middle of 2003 it had been ratified by 7 States and had not yet entered into force. It is the first international treaty to be exclusively concerned with the protection, management and enhancement of European landscape. The Convention applies to the States Parties' entire territory and covers natural, rural, urban and peri-urban areas. It deals with ordinary or degraded landscapes as well as those that can be considered outstanding. The Convention represents an important contribution to the implementation of the Council of Europe's objectives, aimed at promoting democracy, human rights and the rule of law and at finding common solutions to the main problems facing European society today. By taking into account landscape, cultural and natural values, the Council of Europe seeks to protect the quality of life and well-being of Europeans.

European Parliament

The European Parliament is one of the five main bodies of the **European Union**. It represents in the words of the Treaty establishing the **European Community**, signed in Rome on 25 March 1957: "... the peoples of the States brought together in the European Community". By the middle of 2003, the European Parliament represents more than 375 million citizens of its 15 Member States through 626 representatives, elected every five years through direct universal suffrage. The first direct elections by the European Parliament were held in June 1979. Its plenary sessions are held in Strasbourg, while the additional sessions and the sessions of its Committees take place in Brussels.

One of the priorities of the European Parliament is to maintain links with national parliaments through regular meetings with chairpersons and with parliamentary committees. Over the years, the European Parliament has evolved from a purely consultative assembly into a legislative body, having powers similar to those of national parliaments. It now shares decision-making powers in a number of fields with the **European Commission** and the Council of the European Union. A Conciliation Committee (consisting of an equal number of members of the European Parliament and of the Council of the European Union) may seek compromises on texts that both bodies may subsequently endorse. The European Parliament can reject a proposal if there is no agreement.

Every year, it approves the European Union's budget and can propose modifications and amendments to the **European Commission**'s initial proposals and to the position taken by Member States in the Council of the European Union. The European Parliament exercises overall political supervision on the executive power in the European Union, shared between the European Commission and the Council of the European Union. It also has the right to ratify or reject international agreements. It can therefore use this power to request that non-Member States improve their human rights situation. In 199 the European Parliament put forward an initiative which brought together a series of budget headings specifically dealing with the promotion of human rights. Its official title is European Initiative for Democracy and Human Rights (EIDHR).

For more information see: http://www.europarl.eu.int

European Prison Rules (Council of Europe)

In 1973, the Committee of Ministers of the **Council of Europe** adopted the Standard Minimum Rules for the Treatment of Prisoners. Considering it necessary to adapt these Rules to modern developments in prison management and treatment of offenders, the Committee adopted a revised version of these standards under the title of "European Prison Rules". They are contained in Recommendation N° R(87)3, adopted on 12 February 1987. The Rules seek to establish minimum standards for all those aspects of prison administration that are essential to humane conditions and treatment. They should serve as a stimulus to prison administration to develop policies and practice based on principles of equity, to encourage professional attitudes of prison staff and to provide basic criteria against which prison administration and those responsible for inspecting the conditions of prisons can make judgements of performance and measure progress towards higher standards.

The Rules enumerate principles on such matters as the management of prison systems, staff policy, education programmes, prison work, and constructive pre-release work. Special rules apply to specific categories of prisoners, such as untried prisoners, insane and mentally handicapped inmates.

European Rules on Community Sanctions and Measures (Council of Europe)

Many Member States of the **Council of Europe** have introduced and expanded recourse to non-custodial penal sanctions. With a view to developing international norms for the adoption and implementation of such sanctions, the Committee of Ministers of the Council of Europe adopted Recommendation N° R(92)16 on the European Rules on Community Sanctions and Measures on 19 October 1992. The aim of these new rules, conceived as a parallel instrument to the **European Prison Rules** (1987), is to establish a set of standards to enable national legislators and practitioners concerned to provide a just and effective application of non-custodial sanctions and measures as well as guarantees against the infringement of the human rights of offenders subject to such sanctions and measures, and to lay down rules of conduct for the persons responsible for their implementation. The 90 Rules are grouped in 11 chapters dealing with: the legal framework for defining, adopting, and applying such sanctions and measures; judicial guarantees and complaints procedures; respect for fundamental rights; cooperation and consent of the offender; human and financial resources required for making non-custodial sanctions and measures work, community involvement and participation; the management aspects of community sanctions and measures; the conditions and methods of implementation and the consequences of non-compliance; and research on the operation of community sanctions systems, including their regular evaluation.

European Social Charter (Council of Europe)

The European Social Charter was signed by Member States of the **Council of Europe** on 18 October 1961 and entered into force on 26 February 1965. The Charter, considered as the counterpart of the **European Convention for the Protection of Human Rights and Fundamental Freedoms**, protects fundamental human rights in the social and economic fields. Three Protocols have been added to the Charter (1988, 1991 and 1995). The Additional Protocol of 1988 adds to the Charter the right of all workers to equal opportunities of employment and the right of every elderly person to social protection. This Protocol had been ratified by 10 Member States by the middle of 2003.

The reporting system defined in the Charter was amended by the Protocol of 1991. By the middle of 2003, it had been ratified by 18 States, but will only enter into force upon ratification by all parties to the Charter. It provides for the monitoring of the Charter by the **European Committee of Social Rights (ECSR)**. The Committee is composed of nine independent and impartial experts who have recognized competence in international social issues. The experts are elected for a mandate of six years renewable once. Upon reception of reports that States Parties are required to submit at regular intervals on selected articles, the Committee decides, from a legal point of view, on the conformity of domestic law and practice with the provisions of the Charter. Its conclusions are then forwarded to the Governmental Committee that selects those that should be the subject of a recommendation by the Committee of Ministers.

The Additional Protocol to the European Social Charter Providing for a System of Collective Complaints of 9 November 1995, entered into force on 1 July 1998. It has an optional character and by the middle of 2003, it had been accepted by 11 States. European as well as national trade unions and organizations of employers and certain international **non-governmental organizations** may lodge complaints against States Parties on alleged violations of the Charter. The complaints are examined for admissibility by the ECSR whose decision is transmitted to the Committee of Ministers whose task is to adopt a recommendation if a violation of the Charter has been found.

European Social Charter – Revised (Council of Europe)

The **European Social Charter** was revised in 1996 and entered into force in 1999. It is gradually replacing the initial instrument. It protects fundamental human rights in economic and social spheres and goes further than the initial instrument in the protection of the **right to** housing, **social security, health, education** and employment. It is aimed at reducing the number of homeless persons and ensuring access to decent housing for all; at guaranteeing accessible and effective health care facilities to the entire population; at ensuring free primary and secondary education for all and free vocational guidance services; at guaranteeing the right to social security, social welfare and social services, as well as the right to be protected against **poverty** and social exclusion. Moreover, it envisages that the principle of non-**discrimination** is applied in respect to all of these rights, thus protecting equal treatment of women and men as well as nationals and legal residents.

The revised Charter embodies in a single instrument the rights guaranteed by the Charter of 1961, the rights guaranteed by the Additional Protocol of 1988 and some further rights relating mainly to: the better protection of maternity and social protection of mothers; the better social, legal and economic protection of employed children (under the new instrument the work of children under the age of 15 is forbidden); and the better protection of handicapped people. It adds the following new rights: the right to protection in cases of termination of employment (Article 24), the right of all workers to protection of their dignity at work (Article 26), the right of workers with family responsibilities to equal opportunities and equal treatment (Article 27), the right of workers' representatives to protection in the undertaking and facilities to be accorded to them (Article 28), the right to protection against poverty and social exclusion (Article 30), and the right to housing (Article 31).

By the middle of 2003 it had been ratified by 32 of 45 Member States of the **Council of Europe** and another 11 States had signed but not yet ratified it.

European Sport for All Charter (Council of Europe)

The Committee of Ministers of the **Council of Europe** adopted the European Sport for All Charter and the **Code of Sports Ethics** on 24 September 1992. The aims of the Charter, in accordance with the Code, are to enable every individual to participate in sport (Article 1). Article 4, para. 1, states that no **discrimination** on the grounds of sex, race, colour, language, religion, political or other opinion … shall be permitted in the access to sports facilities or to sports activities. Special provisions concern top level and professional sport. Article 10 lays down that: "Ensuring and improving people's physical, social and mental well-being from one generation to the next requires that sporting activities … be carried out in accordance with the principles of sustainable development …". The Charter ends by stating that cooperation at the European and international levels is also necessary for the fulfilment of its aims (Article 13, para. 2).

European Union – EU

The European Union (EU) was established on 1 November 1993 following the entry into force of the Treaty on European Union (Treaty of Maastricht) which was signed on 7 February 1992 by 12 States, subsequently joined by another 3. The EU does not replace the European Communities (the European Coal and Steel Community, the European Community and the European Atomic Energy Community) but it is considered as the roof of a three pillar construction, where the EC is the first pillar, the common foreign and security policy the second pillar, and the cooperation in justice and home affairs the third pillar. The common institutional system of the EU comprises the **European Parliament**, the Council of the European Union, the **European Council**, the **European Commission**, the **Court of Justice of the European Communities** and the European Court of Auditors.

The EU's creation marks a new stage in the process of European integration which began with the settlement of the European Communities. The main aims of the EU are: to strengthen contacts between its Member States and their peoples; to promote economic and social progress; to assert the identity of the EU on the international scene; to introduce European citizenship; to develop an area of freedom, security and justice; and to maintain and build on established EU law. The Treaty of Maastricht confirms the attachment of the Member States to the principles of liberty, democracy and respect of human rights and fundamental freedoms and applies them as criteria for the admission of new members.

For more information see: http://europa.eu.int

European Union Charter of Fundamental Rights (EU)

The Charter, officially called the Charter of Fundamental Rights of the European Union was solemnly proclaimed by the Presidents of the **European Council**, of the **European Parliament** and of the **European Commission** on 7 December 2000 in Nice. Despite the initial intentions, neither the Charter nor any reference to it was included in the new Treaty approved in Nice by the European Council (meeting of the Heads of State or Government and the President of the European Commission, organized at least twice a year).

The Charter combines, for the first time at the European level in a single text, the **civil**, **political**, **economic**, **social** and **cultural rights** which are common to the Member States of the **European Union (EU)**. This instrument was adopted in order to make human rights more visible and to make people more aware of human rights values in Europe. It contains seven chapters: "Dignity", "Freedoms", "Equality", "Solidarity", "Citizens Rights", "Justice" and "General Provisions".

Though the new Charter has no binding force, the European Council envisages its wide dissemination amongst the citizens of the European Union, and the **European Court of Justice** has already referred to it in its rulings. In accordance with the European Council's conclusions (Cologne, 3-4 June 1999), the question concerning the binding force of the Charter will be considered later. A further meeting on the future of the European Union foreseen in Nice for 2004, could lead to a "constitutional pact" and this Charter may become an integral part of it.

Extreme poverty

According to **United Nations** statistics, more than 1.2 billion people live on less than US$1 per day, which prevents them from satisfying their basic needs and realizing their fundamental rights. This phenomenon, defined as "extreme **poverty**", has received growing attention from the international community since the early 1990s. The **World Conference on Human Rights** (Vienna, Austria, 1993) affirmed that "... extreme poverty and social exclusion constitute a violation of human dignity and that urgent steps are necessary to achieve better knowledge of extreme poverty and its causes, including those related to the problem of development, in order to promote the human rights of the poorest, and to put an end to extreme poverty and social exclusion and to promote the enjoyment of the fruits of social progress" (**Vienna Declaration and Programme of Action**, Part I, para. 25). It underlined that: "The existence of widespread extreme poverty inhibits the full and effective enjoyment of human rights; its immediate alleviation and eventual elimination must remain a high priority for the international community" (Vienna Declaration and Programme of Action, Part I, para. 14). Extreme poverty is a main obstacle to the realization of all human rights – civil, cultural, economic, political and social. Its destructive consequences for human rights and fundamental freedoms are described in the report on human rights and extreme poverty prepared by the **Special Rapporteur[s]** nominated by the **Sub-Commission on Prevention of Discrimination and Protection of Minorities** (now **Sub-Commission on the Promotion and Protection of Human Rights**). The **Commission on Human Rights** keeps the question of extreme poverty under consideration and has nominated an independent expert on this subject.

The **United Nations** proclaimed the **International Year for the Eradication of Poverty** for 1996 and the first **United Nations Decade for the Eradication of Poverty** for the period from 1997 to 2006. The eradication of poverty and extreme poverty is now a priority for many organizations, bodies and programmes of the **United Nations system**, including **UNESCO**, as well as for other intergovernmental and **non-governmental organizations**. Moreover, poverty reduction strategies are increasingly formulated in human rights terms.

In the **United Nations Millenium Declaration** (2000), the commitment to "spare no effort to free our fellow men, women and children from the abject and dehumanizing conditions of extreme poverty…" was reaffirmed by the Heads of States and Governments (para. 11). They also expressed their resolve "to halve, by the year 2015, the proportion of the world's people whose income is less than one dollar a day…" (para. 19).

Food and Agriculture Organization of the United Nations – FAO

The **Food and Agriculture Organization of the United Nations (FAO)** was the first specialized agency of the **United Nations system** established after the Second World War. At the **United Nations** Conference on Food and Agriculture, held in 1943, 44 nations agreed to work together to banish hunger and establish a stable world agriculture. FAO officially came into being with the signing of its Constitution on 16 October 1945 and was formally brought into relationship with the United Nations as a specialized agency when the **United Nations General Assembly** approved the Agreement between the two organizations on 14 December 1946. The FAO comprises 183 Member States and the **European Community** (Member Organization). The purposes of FAO are set forth in the Preamble to its Constitution: (i) raising the levels of nutrition and standards of living of the peoples; (ii) securing improvements in the efficiency of the production and distribution of all food and agricultural products; (iii) bettering the condition of rural populations; and thus (iv) contributing towards an expanding world economy and ensuring humanity's **freedom from hunger.** Among the functions of the FAO, as described in Article 1 of its Constitution, are the collection, analysis, interpretation and dissemination of information relating to nutrition, food and agriculture, the promotion of national and international action to improve education and administration relating to nutrition, food and agriculture, and the furnishing of technical assistance to governments in these fields. The goal of eliminating **poverty**, hunger and malnutrition by promoting agricultural development and the pursuit of food security is also reflected in numerous resolutions of FAO bodies. Among the milestones are: the International Undertaking on World Food Security (1974); the establishment of the Technical Cooperation Programme (1976); the observance since 1981 of **World Food Day – 16 October**; the establishment of AGROSTAT, the world's most comprehensive source of agricultural information and statistics (1986); the ratification in 1991 of the International Plant Protection Convention with 92 signatories; the **World Food Summit** which brought together Heads of State or government from 185 countries and the European Community (Rome, Italy, 1996). The follow-up summit was organized in Rome in June 2002, reaffirming the commitments assumed at the previous summit and calling for an international alliance to accelerate action to reduce world hunger.

For more information see: http://www.fao.org

Framework Convention for the Protection of National Minorities (Council of Europe)

Following the 1993 Vienna Summit of Heads of State and Government, the **Council of Europe** adopted the Framework Convention for the Protection of National Minorities on 10 November 1994. Opened for signature on 1 February 1995, the Framework Convention entered into force on 1 February 1998. By the middle of 2003, it had been ratified by 35 States. The Framework Convention is based on the ideals and principles of individual rights and freedoms, mutual understanding and cultural diversity and on the provisions against discrimination stipulated in the **European Convention for the Protection of Human Rights and Fundamental Freedoms** and other international instruments. The main purpose of the instrument is to ensure the protection of the rights of persons belonging to national minorities and to promote conditions in which it is possible to preserve and develop their culture "within the rule of law, respecting the territorial integrity and national sovereignty of States" (Preamble). The Framework Convention contains principles to which States Parties adhere as well as objectives that they undertake to pursue through legislation and appropriate policies. It ensures the following fundamental rights and freedoms: the right to choose to be treated or not as a person belonging to a national minority; the right to **freedom of thought, expression, conscience, religion** and association; the right to use one's name; the right to use one's language, both in private and public; and the **right to education** and the fostering of knowledge of their national minority. In 1998, the monitoring mechanism of the Framework Convention, including an Advisory Committee of 18 independent experts, was established. According to this mechanism, the States Parties have to report on the measures they have taken to implement and apply the Convention. The first State reports were submitted in February 1999. State reports are made public and examined by the Advisory Committee, which prepares an opinion on the measures taken by each reporting State. Having received the opinion of the Advisory Committee, the Committee of Ministers adopts, in a resolution, conclusions and, where appropriate, recommendations in respect of the State Party concerned. As of January 2003, 23 opinions of the Advisory Committee have been adopted and 14 resolutions have been adopted by the Committee of Ministers.

Free and periodic elections

Both the **Universal Declaration of Human Rights** (Article 21) and the **International Covenant on Civil and Political Rights** (Article 25) provide that the authority to govern shall be based on the will of the people as expressed in periodic and genuine elections. The **American Convention on Human Rights** (1969), recognizes the right of every citizen "to vote and to be elected in genuine periodic elections" (Article 23, para.1b). The **United Nations General Assembly** took up the subject of periodic and genuine elections and adopted resolution 43/157 on

8 December 1988. Recalling that "all States enjoy sovereign equality and that each State has the right freely to choose and develop its political, social, economic, and cultural system" (Preamble), the General Assembly stressed its conviction that periodic and genuine elections were a necessary and indispensable element of sustained efforts to protect the rights and interests of the governed, and that the right of everyone to take part in the government was a crucial factor in the effective enjoyment by all of a wide range of other human rights and fundamental freedoms (para. 2). It also declared that determining the will of the people required an electoral process accommodating distinct alternatives and providing an equal opportunity for all citizens to become candidates and put forward their political views (para. 3). Additionally, the resolution called upon the **Commission on Human Rights** to consider appropriate ways and means of enhancing the effectiveness of the principle of periodic and genuine elections (para. 5). Responding to this request, the Commission on Human Rights, on 7 March 1989, recommended that the United Nations General Assembly adopt a framework for future efforts in this field containing the following chapters: (i) The will of the people expressed through periodic and genuine elections as the basis for the authority of Government; (ii) The activities of candidates for public office; (iii) Operational aspects: national institutions; and (iv) Cooperative activities of the international community. The subject of free and fair elections has been elaborated by the **Inter-Parliamentary Union** in the 1994 **Declaration on Criteria for Free and Fair Elections**. Substantive work in order to encourage free and periodic elections has been carried out by the **Organization for Security and Cooperation in Europe (OSCE)**, and particularly the **Office for Democratic Institutions and Human Rights (ODIHR).**

Freedom from arbitrary arrest

This freedom is proclaimed in the **Universal Declaration of Human Rights**, which in its Article 9, stipulates: "No one shall be subjected to arbitrary arrest, detention or exile". The **International Covenant on Civil and Political Rights** defines this freedom in detail: "Everyone has the **right to liberty and security of person**. No one shall be subjected to arbitrary arrest or detention. No one shall be deprived of his liberty except on such grounds and in accordance with such procedures as are established by law" (Article 9, para. 1); "Anyone who is arrested shall be informed, at the time of arrest, of the reasons for his arrest and shall be promptly informed of any charges against him" (Article 9, para. 2); "Anyone arrested or detained on a criminal charge shall be brought promptly before a judge or other officer authorized by law to exercise judicial power and shall be entitled to trial within a reasonable time or to release. It shall not be the general rule that persons awaiting trial shall be detained in custody, but release may be subject to guarantees to appear for trial, at any other stage of the judicial proceedings, and, should occasion arise, for execution of the judgment" (Article 9, para. 3); "Anyone who is deprived of his liberty by arrest or detention shall be entitled to take proceedings before a court, in order that that court may decide without delay on the lawfulness of his detention and order his release if the detention is not lawful" (Article 9, para. 4); and "Anyone who has been victim of unlawful arrest or detention shall have an enforceable **right to compensation**" (Article 9, para. 5).

The freedom from arbitrary arrest is also guaranteed by regional human rights instruments.

Freedom from arbitrary interference with privacy

Freedom from arbitrary interference with privacy is proclaimed in the **Universal Declaration of Human Rights** which stipulates: "No one shall be subjected to arbitrary interference with his privacy, family, home or correspondence, nor to attacks upon his honour and reputation. Everyone has the right to the protection of the law against such interference or attacks on privacy" (Article 12). This freedom is also provided for in the **International Covenant on Civil and Political Rights**: "No one shall be subjected to arbitrary or unlawful interference with his privacy, family, home or correspondence, nor to unlawful attacks on his honour and reputation" (Article 17, para. 1) and "Everyone has the right to the protection of the law against such interference or attacks" (Article 17, para. 2).

This freedom is also protected by regional human rights instruments.

Freedom from compulsory or forced labour

Freedom from compulsory or forced labour is provided for in Article 8 of the **International Covenant on Civil and Political Rights**: "No one shall be held in servitude" (para. 2); and "No one shall be required to perform forced or compulsory labour" (para. 3a). The latter paragraph shall not be held to preclude, in countries where imprisonment with hard labour may be imposed as a punishment for a crime, the performance of hard labour in pursuance of a sentence to such punishment by a competent court (para. 3b).

Article 8, para. 3c, further explains that the term 'forced or compulsory labour' shall not include: (i) Any work or service, not referred to in subparagraph (b), normally required of a person who is under detention in consequence of a lawful order of a court, or of a person during conditional release from such detention; (ii) Any service of a military character and, in countries where conscientious objection is recognized, any national service required by law of conscientious objectors; (iii) Any service exacted in cases of emergency or calamity threatening the life or well-being of the community; (iv) Any work or service which forms part of normal civil obligations.

Freedom from compulsory or forced labour is also provided for in Article 4, paras. 2 and 3, of the **European Convention for the Protection of Human Rights and Fundamental Freedoms**.

Freedom from hunger

Freedom from hunger is provided for in the **International Covenant on Economic, Social and Cultural Rights** which, confirming Article 25 of the **Universal Declaration of Human Rights**, stipulates that: "The States Parties to the present Covenant recognize the right of everyone to an adequate standard of living for himself and his family, including adequate food, clothing and housing, and to the continuous improvement of living conditions" (Article 11, para. 1). In conformity with the Covenant, the States Parties "… recognizing the fundamental right of everyone to be free from hunger, shall take, individually and through international cooperation, the measures, including specific programmes, which are needed: (a) To improve methods of production, conservation and distribution of food by making full use of technical and scientific knowledge, by disseminating knowledge of the principles of nutrition and by developing or reforming agrarian systems in such a way as to achieve the most efficient development and utilization of natural resources; (b) Taking into account the problems of both food-importing and food-exporting countries, to ensure an equitable distribution of world food supplies in relation to need" (Article 11, para. 2).

Freedom from hunger is recognized in the Preamble of the Constitution of the **Food and Agriculture Organization of the United Nations (FAO)**, which established as its major goal to contribute to "… ensuring humanity's freedom from hunger".

Freedom from subjection to torture and to cruel, inhuman or degrading treatment

Freedom from subjection to torture and to cruel, inhuman or degrading treatment is provided for in both the **Universal Declaration of Human Rights**, Article 5: "No one shall be subjected to torture or to cruel, inhuman or degrading treatment or punishment", and in the **International Covenant on Civil and Political Rights**, Article 7: "No one shall be subjected to torture or to cruel, inhuman or degrading treatment or punishment. In particular, no one shall be subjected without his free consent to medical or scientific experimentation". The **Convention against Torture and Other Cruel, Inhuman or Degrading Treatment or Punishment**, adopted in 1984, is aimed at the abolition of all forms of torture and other cruel, inhuman or degrading treatment. Part II of the Convention envisages the establishment and functioning of the **Committee against Torture**. The **Optional Protocol** to the Convention, which establishes a system of regular visits by independent, international and national bodies to places where people are deprived of their liberty, was adopted in December 2002 and by the middle of 2003 had not yet entered into force.

This freedom is also confirmed in a number of regional human rights instruments: including the **European Convention for the Protection of Human Rights and Fundamental Freedoms** (1950); the **American Convention on Human Rights** (1969); and the **African Charter on Human and Peoples' Rights** (1981).

Freedom of association

Freedom of association is provided for in both the **Universal Declaration of Human Rights** which stipulates that: "Everyone has the right to **freedom of peaceful assembly** and association" (Article 20, para. 1) and "No one may be compelled to belong to an association" (Article 20, para. 2). The **International Covenant on Civil and Political Rights** develops further this right by stating that: "Everyone shall have the right to freedom of association with others, including the right to form and join trade unions for the protection of his interests" (Article 22, para. 1); "No restrictions may be placed on the exercise of this right other than those which are prescribed by law and which are necessary in a democratic society in the interests of national security or public safety, public order (ordre public), the protection of public health or morals or the protection of the rights and freedoms of others. This Article shall not prevent the imposition of lawful restrictions on members of the armed forces and of the police in their exercise of this right" (Article 22, para. 2). It further stipulates that nothing in this Article shall authorize States Parties to the **Convention (No.87) concerning Freedom of association and Protection of the Right to Organise**, adopted by the **International Labour Organization** in 1948, to take legislative measures which would prejudice, or to apply the law in such a manner as to prejudice the guatantees provided for in that Convention (Article 22, para.3). Freedom of association, as formulated by the International Covenant, is also mentioned in the **European Convention for the Protection of Human Rights and Fundamental Freedoms** (Article 11, para. 1). The **African Charter on Human and Peoples' Rights** declares that: "Every individual shall have the right to free association provided that he abides by the law" (Article 10, para.1). This right is enshrined in other universal and regional standard-setting instruments.

Freedom of movement and residence

Freedom of movement and residence is proclaimed in the **Universal Declaration of Human Rights** which stipulates that: "Everyone has the right to freedom of movement and residence within the borders of each State" (Article 13, para. 1) and "Everyone has the **right to leave any country, including his own, and to return to his country**" (Article 13, para. 2). The **International Covenant on Civil and Political Rights** guarantees this freedom in the following terms: "Everyone lawfully within the territory of a State shall, within that territory, have the right to liberty of movement and freedom to choose his residence" (Article 12, para. 1); "Everyone shall be free to leave any country, including his own" (Article 12, para; 2); "The above-mentioned rights shall not be subject to any restriction except those which are provided by law, are necessary to protect national security, public order (ordre public), public health or morals or the rights and freedoms of others, and are consistent with the other rights recognized in the present Covenant" (Article 12, para. 3); and

"No one shall be arbitrarily deprived of the right to enter his own country" (Article 12, para. 4).

Freedom of opinion and expression

Freedom of opinion and expression is closely linked with **freedom to seek, receive and impart information**. It is proclaimed in the **Universal Declaration of Human Rights**, which states: "Everyone has the right to freedom of opinion and expression; this right includes freedom to hold opinions without interference and to seek, receive and impart information and ideas through any media and regardless of frontiers" (Article 19). The **International Covenant on Civil and Political Rights** guarantees this freedom: "Everyone shall have the right to hold opinions without interference" (Article 19, para. 1); "Everyone shall have the right to freedom of expression; this right shall include freedom to seek, receive and impart information and ideas of all kinds, regardless of frontiers, either orally, in writing or in print, in the form of art, or through any other media of his choice" (Article 19, para. 2); and "The exercise of the rights provided for in paragraph 2 of this Article carries with it special duties and responsibilities. It may therefore be subject to certain restrictions, but these shall only be such as are provided by law and are necessary: (a) for respect of the rights or reputations of others; (b) for the protection of national security or of public order (ordre public), or of public health or morals" (Article 19, para. 3).

Similar provisions are contained in major regional human rights instruments.

Freedom of peaceful assembly

Freedom of peaceful assembly is proclaimed in the **Universal Declaration of Human Rights**, which stipulates that: "Everyone has the right to freedom of peaceful assembly and association" (Article 20, para. 1). The **International Covenant on Civil and Political Rights** guarantees this freedom as follows: "The right of peaceful assembly shall be recognized. No restrictions may be placed on the exercise of this right other than those imposed in conformity with the law and which are necessary in a democratic society in the interests of national security or public safety, public order (ordre public), the protection of public health or morals or the protection of the rights and freedoms of others" (Article 21).

This freedom is also provided for in major regional human rights instruments.

Freedom of scientific research

Article 27, para. 1, of the **Universal Declaration of Human Rights** stipulates that: "Everyone has the right freely to participate in the cultural life of the community, to enjoy the arts and to share in scientific advancement and its benefits". The **International Covenant on Economic, Social and Cultural Rights** proclaims: "The States Parties to the present Covenant undertake to respect the freedom indispensable for scientific research and creative activity" (Article 15, para. 3).

The **Recommendation on the Status of Scientific Researchers** (1974) of **UNESCO** contains several provisions relating to the freedom of scientific research. Member States are recommended to undertake the obligation to encourage conditions in which scientific researchers have the responsibility and right: "to work in a spirit of intellectual freedom to pursue, expound and defend the scientific truth as they see it" (para. 14(a)). Freedom of scientific research is also confirmed by the UNESCO **Recommendation concerning the Status of Higher-Education Teaching Personnel** (1997). The question of the possible both positive and negative effects of scientific and technological developments upon the enjoyment of human rights and fundamental freedoms was for the first time discussed in greater detail during the **United Nations International Conference on Human Rights** (1968). In November 1975, the **United Nations General Assembly** proclaimed the **Declaration on the Use of Scientific and Technological Progress in the Interests of Peace** and for the Benefit of Mankind. It is aimed at strengthening respect for human rights in the field of science and technology. The progress of biotechnology and genetics raised the question of limitation of the freedom of scientific research. It is acknowledged that this principle cannot be absolute and, if necessary, may be limited. Such a necessity arises when research violates respect for human dignity which is the basis of all human rights, including the freedom of scientific research. Focusing on human dignity, the **Universal Declaration on the Human Genome and Human Rights** (1997), adopted by UNESCO in 1997, became the first standard-setting instrument prohibiting the reproductive cloning of human beings.

Freedom of thought, conscience and religion or belief

Freedom of thought, conscience and religion or belief and freedom to change or to manifest religion or belief are proclaimed in the **Universal Declaration of Human Rights**: "Everyone has the right to freedom of thought, conscience and religion; this right includes freedom to change his religion or belief, and freedom, either alone or in community with others and in public or private, to manifest his religion or belief in teaching, practice, worship and observance" (Article 18). The **International Covenant on Civil and Political Rights** guarantees this freedom and defines it in detail as follows: "Everyone shall have the right to freedom of thought, conscience and religion. This right shall include freedom to have or to adopt a religion or belief of his choice, and freedom, either individually or in community with others and in public or private, to manifest his religion or belief in worship, observance, practice and teaching" (Article 18, para. 1); "No one shall be subject to coercion which would impair his freedom to have or to adopt a religion or belief of his choice" (Article 18, para. 2); "Freedom to manifest one's religion or beliefs may be subject only to such limitations as are prescribed by law and are necessary to protect public safety, order, health, or morals or the fundamental rights and freedoms of others" (Article 18, para. 3); and "The States Parties to the present Covenant undertake to have respect for the liberty of parents and, when applicable, legal guardians to ensure the religious and moral education of their children in conformity with their own convictions" (Article 18, para. 4).

Provisions to this effect are contained in regional human rights instruments.

Freedom to dispose of natural wealth and resources

Freedom to dispose of natural wealth and resources is provided for in Article 1, para. 2, of the **International Covenant on Economic, Social and Cultural Rights** which stipulates: "All peoples may, for their own ends, freely dispose of their natural wealth and resources without prejudice to any obligations arising out of international economic cooperation, based upon the principle of mutual benefit, and international law. In no case may a people be deprived of its own means of subsistence". Article 21, para. 1, of the **African Charter on Human and Peoples' Rights** (1981) declares: "All peoples shall freely dispose of their wealth and natural resources. This right shall be exercised in the exclusive interest of the people. In no case shall a people be deprived of it".

Freedom to seek, receive and impart information

Freedom to seek, receive and impart information is provided for in the **Universal Declaration of Human Rights**, Article 19: "Everyone has the right to **freedom of opinion and expression**; this right includes freedom to hold opinions without interference and to seek, receive and impart information and ideas through any media and regardless of frontiers." This freedom is also provided for in the **International Covenant on Civil and Political Rights**: "Everyone shall have the right to freedom of expression; this right shall include freedom to seek, receive and impart information and ideas of all kinds, regardless of frontiers, either orally, in writing or in print, in the form of art, or through any other media of his choice" (Article 19, para. 2). The exercise of this right may be subject to certain restrictions provided by law and necessary for the respect of the rights or reputations of others and for the protection of national security, of public order or of public health or morals. Freedom to seek, receive and impart information is formulated by the following regional instruments: **American Convention on Human Rights** (Article 13); **European Convention for the Protection of Human Rights and Fundamental Freedoms** (Article 10) and **African Charter of Human and Peoples' Rights** (Article 9).

General Comments or General Recommendations of Human Rights Treaty Bodies

The **human rights treaty bodies** can adopt General Comments (**Human Rights Committee, Committee on Economic, Social and Cultural Rights, Committee against Torture, Committee on the Rights of the Child**) or General Recommendations (**Committee on the Elimination of Racial Discrimination, Committee on the Elimination of Discrimination against Women**). General Comments and General Recommendations aim to clarify the content and scope of specific provisions of the instrument concerned. They elaborate on the meaning and implications of a certain provision and outline how States should interpret and implement this provision. Treaty bodies draft General Comments and General Recommendations on the basis of issues emerging from their examination of States Parties reports over a number of years. General Comments and General Recommendations are not legally binding documents. They serve to assist the States Parties in further implementing the instruments and fulfilling their reporting obligations. They provide guidance for the activities of States Parties, **United Nations specialized agencies** and other concerned international organizations aimed at achieving progressively and effectively the full realization of the rights enshrined in the instruments. General Comments can be revised by the treaty bodies in the light of new developments.

The Human Rights Committee, the Committee on Economic, Social and Cultural Rights and the Committee on the Elimination of Racial Discrimination have been most active in adopting General Comments and General Recommendations.

The Human Rights Committee has adopted 30 General Comments, including those on the rights of minorities, the right to participate in public affairs and voting rights, equality of rights between women and men, the rights of the child, the **right to self-determination** and on humane treatment of persons deprived of their liberty. The Committee on Economic, Social and Cultural Rights has adopted 15 General Comments, including those on the **right to education**, the **right to health**, the **right to adequate housing** and on the nature of States Parties' obligations under the Covenant. The Committee on the Elimination of All Forms of Discrimination has adopted 28 General Recommendations concerning **discrimination** against various groups (the Roma, refugees, non-citizens, **indigenous peoples**, etc.) and on the gender related dimension of racial discrimination.

The **Committee on the Protection of the Rights of All Migrants Workers and Members of Their Families** will most likely follow the same practice.

Geneva Conventions (ICRC)

The Geneva Conventions were elaborated by the Diplomatic Conference of 1949, convened by the Swiss Federal Council at Geneva from 21 April to 12 August 1949. They were adopted on 12 August 1949 and entered into force on 21 October 1950. They comprise: **Geneva Convention for the Amelioration of the Condition of the Wounded and Sick in the Armed Forces in the Field – Convention I**; **Geneva Convention for the Amelioration of the Condition of Wounded, Sick and Shipwrecked Members of Armed Forces at Sea – Convention II**; **Geneva Convention Relative to the Treatment of Prisoners of War – Convention III**; **Geneva Convention Relative to the Protection of Civilian Persons in Time of War – Convention IV**.

In 1977, the Diplomatic Conference on the Reaffirmation and Development of **International Humanitarian Law** Applicable in Armed Conflicts adopted two **Protocols Additional to the Geneva Conventions of 12 August 1949, and relating to the**

Protection of Victims of International Armed Conflicts (Protocol I) and Victims of Non-International Armed Conflicts (Protocol II).

The **International Committee of the Red Cross (ICRC)** is the depositary of the four Geneva Conventions and the two Additional Protocols thereto.

Geneva Convention for the Amelioration of the Condition of the Wounded and Sick in the Armed Forces in the Field – Convention I (ICRC)

By the middle of 2003, Convention I was binding on 191 States. The four Geneva Conventions of 1949 contain a number of common Articles. Common Article 3 sets out minimum humanitarian standards which are to be respected in case of conflicts which are not of an international character, and enumerates certain acts which "are and shall remain prohibited at any time and in any place whatsoever". It confirms the principles of non-**discrimination**, corporal well-being (prohibition of murder, mutilation, cruel or humiliating treatment and torture), and personal freedom (prohibition of the taking of hostages and of summary executions). The General Provisions are followed by Chapter II, dealing with the wounded and the sick. Article 13 enumerates the categories of persons put on the same footing as members of the armed forces, and hence entitled to protection under the Convention. Article 12 provides that wounded or sick combatants shall be respected and that medical care is to be given without discrimination, except for medical urgency. The information to be given about wounded captives (Article 16), as well as the duties to the dead have also been defined (Article 17). Convention I further stipulates that medical and religious personnel must not be prevented from performing their functions, but that they must observe strict military neutrality (Article 24). Should they fall into the hands of the enemy, the latter can retain them only if the medical and religious needs of prisoners of war so require (Article 29); otherwise, repatriation is the rule (Article 30). Even under detention such personnel enjoy possibilities for the performance of their functions (Article 29). Other provisions of Convention I concern the immunity of medical buildings and establishments (Article 19), the assignment of medical material (Articles 33-34), the means of transport (Articles 35-37) and the distinctive emblem (Articles 38-44).

Geneva Convention for the Amelioration of the Condition of Wounded, Sick and Shipwrecked Members of Armed Forces at Sea – Convention II (ICRC)

Convention II was binding on 191 States by the middle of 2003. The Maritime Convention, as it is called, is an extension of the Convention I, the terms of which it applies to maritime warfare. The Convention II covers the same field and protects the same categories of persons as Convention I. Following the General Provisions common to the four Conventions, Chapter II protects and guarantees care for the shipwrecked in addition to the wounded and sick, in all circumstances (Article 12). Chapter III, applicable in times of war, deals with Hospital Ships and other relief craft. It states that they shall in no circumstances be attacked or captured (Articles 22, 24 and 27) and that if fighting occurs on board a warship the sick-bays shall be respected and spared as far as possible (Article 28). At sea, medical personnel, on account of conditions prevailing, are given wider protection than on land. Chapter IV concerns medical personnel and crew, and lays down that it is vital that personnel of hospital ships may not be captured during the time they are in the service of the hospital ship, whether or not there are wounded and sick on board (Article 36). Chapter V deals with medical transports and has its parallel in Convention I in that equipment exclusively intended for the treatment of the wounded and sick cannot be captured or seized (Article 38) and that medical aircrafts may not be the object of attack (Article 39). In Chapter VI on the distinctive emblem, provisions exist for the more efficient marking of hospital ships, as a safeguard against air attack (Article 43). Contracting Parties undertake to enact any legislation necessary to provide effective penal sanctions for persons committing or ordering to be committed any grave breaches of Convention II (Article 50).

Geneva Convention relative to the Treatment of Prisoners of War – Convention III (ICRC)

Convention III was binding on 191 States by the middle of 2003. According to Article 4 those persons having a right to be treated as prisoners of war (POWs) include: the regular armed forces, the militia and volunteer corps not part of the regular army, including resistance fighters. Part II of the Convention contains the essential principles which shall, at times and in all places, govern the treatment of such prisoners. It states that prisoners of war have the right to humane treatment in all circumstances and to respect for their persons and honour (Article 13), and that they retain their full civil capacity (Article 14). The Convention lays down detailed provisions on such matters as the beginning of captivity (Articles 17-20), conditions in internment camps (Articles 21-24), labour (Articles 49-57), financial resources (Articles 58-68), relations with the exterior (Articles 69-77) and with the authorities (Articles 78-81), penal and disciplinary sanctions (Articles 82-108), termination of captivity (Articles 109-117) and release and repatriation (Articles 118-119). In particular, these provisions provide that the sole information that a POW is required to supply concerns his surname, first names, age, rank, and regimental number (Article 17), that the places of internment must be salubrious and life must be organized in them in such a way as to maintain the physical and mental health of POWs, including, adequate food (Article 26) and medical care (Article 15), the possibility of practising one's religion (Article 34) and of having intellectual and sports activities (Article 38), and that the detaining Power cannot transfer POWs to the territory of a country which is not a party to the Convention (Article 12). It further provides safeguards against the arbitrary imposition of the death penalty on such prisoners (Articles 100 and 101). In order for POWs to be acquainted with these provisions, the Convention must be posted (Article 41).

Geneva Convention relative to the Protection of Civilian Persons in Time of War – Convention IV (ICRC)

Convention IV, binding on 191 States by the middle of 2003, was drawn up to establish strict standards for civilian protection in areas covered by war and on occupied territories, as well as to ban war offenses and war crimes. Part II contains provisions for hospital and safety zones (Article 14), for neutralized zones (Article 15), for the protection of civilian hospitals (Article 18), for measures on behalf of children (Article 24), and for the exchange of family news (Article 25). Part III defines the status and treatment of protected persons. The most important norm concerning the civilian population is contained in Article 27 which stipulates: "Protected persons are entitled, in all circumstances, to respect for their persons, their honour, their family rights, their religious convictions and practices, and their manners and customs. They shall at all times be humanely treated, and shall be protected especially against all acts of violence or threats thereof and against insults and public curiosity". Furthermore, protected persons must not be compelled to provide information (Article 31), and it is specifically forbidden to cause them physical suffering, to subject them to collective penalties, measures of intimidation or of terrorism, or reprisals (Article 32). Pillage and the taking of hostages are also prohibited (Articles 33-34). In addition, Part III contains a special section relating to the status of aliens in the territory of a Party to the conflict (Articles 35-46) and another very elaborate section on the treatment of the population in occupied territories (Articles 47-78).

The latter section deals with such matters as the prohibition of deportations (Article 49), ensuring food (Article 55) and medical supplies (Article 56) and law enforcement (Articles 64-75). The Convention contains another section devoted to the treatment of internees (Articles 79-82).

Genocide

In conformity with the **Convention on the Prevention and Punishment of the Crime of Genocide** (1948), genocide is defined as "any of the following acts committed with intent to destroy, in whole or in part, a national, ethnical, racial or religious group, as such: (i) killing members of the group; (ii) causing serious bodily or mental harm to members of the group; (iii) deliberately inflicting on the group conditions of life calculated to bring about its physical destruction in whole or in part; (iv) imposing measures intended to prevent births within the group; (v) forcibly transferring children of the group to another group" (Article II). Genocide, whether committed in time of peace or in time of war, is a crime under international law.

The **International Criminal Court**, the Statute of which entered into force on 1 July 2002 has jurisdiction over the crime of genocide, which is classified among the most serious crimes and as a matter of concern to the international community as a whole (Article 5 of the **Rome Statute of the International Criminal Court**).

Global Compact (UN)

First proposed by the **United Nations Secretary-General** at the World Economic Forum in Davos, Switzerland (January 1999) and formally launched in July 2000, the Global Compact calls on companies to embrace universal principles in the fields of human rights, labour standards and the environment. The Global Compact is not a regulatory instrument or a code of conduct, but a value-based platform, which relies on public accountability, transparency and the enlightened self-interest of companies, labour and civil society to initiate and share substantive action in pursuing the principles upon which the Compact is based. At the core of the Global Compact are the Global Compact Office and five other United Nations agencies: the **Office of the United Nations High Commissioner for Human Rights (OHCHR)**; the **United Nations Environmental Programme (UNEP)**; the **International Labour Organisation (ILO)**; the **United Nations Development Programme (UNDP)**; and the United Nations Industrial Development Organization (UNIDO). The Compact involves a variety of social actors including governments, companies, labour, civil society organizations and the **United Nations**.

Through the nine principles, drawn from the **Universal Declaration of Human Rights**, the ILO's **Declaration on Fundamental Principles and Rights at Work** and the Rio Principles on Environment and Development (taken from the Rio Declaration on Environment and Development), the Compact aims at managing global growth in a responsible manner that takes into consideration the concerns of a broad spectrum of stakeholders. Through integrating the Compact and its principles into their corporate strategies and day-to-day activities, over one thousand companies and organizations have joined the initiative to bring the issues of human rights, labour standards and environmental priorities into boardrooms, to company personnel, suppliers, clients and to the public at large with the objective of producing practical solutions to contemporary problems related to **globalization**, sustainable development and corporate responsibility. To participate in the Global Compact, a company must send a letter from the Chief Executive Officer (endorsed by the board) to the United Nations Secretary-General expressing support for the Compact and its principles.

Globalization and human rights

The process of globalization constitutes a powerful and dynamic force that reflects the accelerating interconnection and interdependence driven by the rapid progress of information and communication technology. Globalization concerns the economic, social, political and cultural fields. Economic globalization, for example, means the widening, deepening and liberalization of international trade and finance and the operation of a single, integrated global market.

While globalization offers great opportunities and has created unprecedented wealth and well-being, at present its benefits are very unevenly shared, which has led to increasing **poverty**, inequality and exclusion for many groups and individuals alike, as well as to disregard of human rights, in particular **economic**, **social** and **cultural rights**. Globalization may reduce a State's ability to determine national policies and to implement human rights and a growing number of non-State actors, such as **transnational corporations**, play an increasing role in the promotion of respect for human rights. States, however, still bear the main responsibility for the implementation of human rights. Public economic, social and cultural policies are necessary to correct market failures, to complement market mechanisms and to correct social injustices.

Within the **United Nations system**, many bodies, programmes and specialized agencies are actively working on the subject of globalization and human rights. In 1999, the **Commission on Human Rights** recognized that globalization is not only an economic process but also has social, political, environmental, cultural and legal dimensions that affect human rights and may differ from country to country. Pursuant to this, the **Sub-Commission on the Promotion and Protection of Human Rights** has undertaken a study on the issue of globalization and its impact on the full enjoyment of human rights, which calls for a critical rethinking of policies and instruments of international trade, investment and finance. Furthermore, the **United Nations Secretary-General** presented to the 55th of the **United Nations General Assembly** in 2000 a study on globalization and its impact on the full enjoyment of all human rights. The study concludes that while globalization provides potential for the promotion and protection of human rights through economic growth, increased wealth, greater interconnection between peoples and cultures and new opportunities for development, its benefits are not being enjoyed evenly. It emphasizes that the principles and standards of human rights should be acknowledged as an indispensable framework for globalization. In the **United Nations Millennium Declaration** and in the **Durban Declaration and Plan of Action**, States have declared that the central challenge of today is "to ensure that globalization becomes a positive force for all the world's people". It has been stated that only through broad and sustained efforts to create a shared future based upon the principles of human dignity, equality, equity and diversity, can globalization be made fully inclusive and equitable.

Many **United Nations specialized agencies** are working to achieve this goal. The Medium-Term Strategy of **UNESCO** for 2002-2007 (Document 31 C/4), for example, sets forth the aim "to bring about globalization with a human face". In 2002, the **United Nations High Commissioner for Human Rights** prepared a study on globalization and human rights (E/CN.4/2002/54), which focuses on the liberalization of agricultural trade and its impact on the realization of the **right to development**, including the **right to adequate food**. At its session in April 2003, the Commission on Human Rights adopted resolution 2003/23, in which it endorsed this study and requested the High Commissioner to continue the study on the fundamental principle of non-**discrimination** in the context of globalization, especially with regard to the trade rules of the World Trade Organization (WTO). The Commission also decided to keep the issue of globalization and human rights on its agenda for the coming sessions.

Guidelines on the Role of Prosecutors (UN)

The Guidelines on the Role of Prosecutors were adopted by the Eighth **United Nations Congress on the Prevention of Crime and the Treatment of Offenders**, Havana, Cuba

(27 August – 7 September 1990). They include the following sections: Qualifications, selection and training (Guidelines 1-2); Status and conditions of service (Guidelines 3-7); Freedom of expression and association (Guidelines 8-9); Role in criminal proceedings (Guidelines 10-16); Discretionary functions (Guideline 17); Alternatives to prosecution (Guidelines 18-19); Relations with other government agencies or institutions (Guideline 20); and Disciplinary proceedings (Guidelines 21-24). The Guidelines have been formulated bearing in mind that "prosecutors play a crucial role in the administration of justice" and that the rules should contribute to "fair and equitable criminal justice and the effective protection of citizens against crime". Therefore, prosecutors shall "maintain the honour and dignity of their profession" (Guideline 3) and shall "perform their duties fairly ... and respect and protect human dignity and uphold human rights, thus contributing to ensuring due process and the smooth functioning of the criminal justice system" (Guideline 12). They shall also give due attention to grave violations of human rights and other crimes recognized by international law (Guideline 15).

Guiding Principles on Human Organ Transplantation (WHO)

In 1991, the 44th World Health Assembly of the **World Health Organization (WHO)** endorsed nine Guiding Principles on Human Organ Transplantation in order to provide an orderly, ethical and acceptable framework for regulating the procurement and transplantation of human organs for therapeutic purposes. The Principles state that the term "human organ" includes organs and tissues but does not extend to reproductive tissues, such as sperm, ovaries, or embryos, nor does it concern blood or blood constituents for transfusion purposes. The Principles recommend that organs for transplantation be removed preferably from the bodies of deceased persons. However, they allow organs donations from adult living persons who are genetically related to the recipients and who have given free consent. Recalling that the human body and its parts cannot be the subject of commercial transactions, the Principles prohibit giving and receiving money, as well as any other commercial dealing in this field. However they do not affect payment of expenditures incurred in organ recovery, preservation and supply. To protect minors, the Principles prohibit the removal of organs from the body of living legal minors for the purpose of transplantation. However, exceptions related to regenerative tissues may be allowed by national legislation.

Guiding Principles on Internal Displacement (UN)

These Principles are the result of several years of work by the Representative of the **United Nations Secretary-General** on Internally **Displaced Persons**, in close collaboration with international legal experts, **United Nations** agencies and other organizations. Initially, pursuant to the mandate entrusted to him in 1992 by the **Commission on Human Rights**, the Representative prepared a "Compilation and Analysis of Legal Norms" relevant to the international norms protecting internally displaced persons (in 2003 their number was estimated at over 20 million in more than 40 countries) and submitted them to the Commission. The study concluded that: existing law provides substantial coverage for internally displaced persons but fails, in many fields, to offer an adequate basis for their protection and assistance; existing law are dispersed in many different international instruments and should be consolidated into a specific document. Subsequently, both the **United Nations General Assembly** and the Commission (resolutions 50/195 of 22 December 1995 and 1996/52 of 19 April 1996, respectively) requested the Representative to prepare an appropriate framework for the protection of and assistance to internally displaced persons. Accordingly, the Guiding Principles on Internal Displacement were elaborated and submitted to the Commission on Human Rights in 1998.

The Principles address the needs of internally displaced persons worldwide by specifying rights and guarantees regarding their protection. They apply to the different phases of displacement, providing protection against arbitrary displacement, access to protection and assistance during displacement, as well as during return or alternative resettlement and reintegration. For the purpose of these Principles, internally displaced persons are defined as being persons or groups of persons who have been forced or obliged to flee or to leave their homes or places of habitual residence, in particular as a result of or in order to avoid the effects of armed conflicts, situations of generalized violence, violations of human rights or natural or human-made disasters, and who have not crossed an internationally recognized State border (in this regard, they differ from refugees). Although the Principles are not legally binding, they are based on existing human rights instruments and **international humanitarian law** by analogy, and remedy the deficiencies in existing legal norms in order to improve the protection of internally displaced persons and assistance to them. The Principles aim at guiding the Representative in carrying out his mandate, as well as governments, other competent authorities, intergovernmental organizations and **non-governmental organizations** in their work in favour of internally displaced persons.

Guillermo Cano World Press Freedom Prize (UNESCO)

This Prize was instituted in 1997 in honour of Guillermo Cano Isaza, a Colombian journalist assassinated by the drug cartels on 17 December 1986 in front of the offices of his newspaper *El Espectador* in Bogotá.

See **World Press Freedom Prize**.

Helsinki Final Act (CSCE)

On 1 August 1975, the Heads of the 35 Participating States signed in Helsinki the Final Act of the **Conference on Security and Cooperation in Europe (CSCE)** – which became the **Organization for Security and Cooperation in Europe (OSCE)** in 1995. The Helsinki Final Act seeks to promote cooperation among the Participating States in a number of areas including: science, technology, economic, environmental concerns, humanitarian issues and security. This document is a politically binding agreement adopted on the basis of consensus. All European States, except Albania, as well as Canada and the United States of America were its signatories. The Final Act is divided into three main categories or "baskets" concerning: (1) questions relating to security in Europe with some references to human rights issues; (2) cooperation in the field of economics, science and technology, and the environment; (3) cooperation in humanitarian and other fields. The key issue in the third "basket" is the protection and promotion of human rights, including **freedom of movement and residence**, **freedom of thought, conscience, religion and belief** and **freedom of association**. Thus the Final Act introduced the notion of human rights and fundamental freedoms into the East-West relations, and the Participating States agreed to work together in their effective promotion and protection of those rights and freedoms. Furthermore, the Final Act provides for regular follow-up meetings to review the implementation of CSCE agreements, to set new standards and norms, to expand cooperation and to maintain political dialogue. In the 1970s and 1980s, such meetings were held in Belgrade (1977-78), Madrid (1980-84) and Vienna (1986-89). At these meetings, CSCE Participating States reiterated their commitments concerning the strengthening of human rights, peace and security.

In November 1990, 34 Heads of State or Government adopted the **Charter of Paris for a New Europe** aimed at proclaiming common values and freedoms for the post-Cold War period. The Charter of Paris underscores the resolve of the Participating States to strengthen democracy and stresses the need to promote human rights. It further states that democracy is the best safeguard of freedom of expression, tolerance of all groups of society, and equality of opportunity for each person.

High Commissioner on National Minorities – HCNM (OSCE)

In 1992, the **Conference on Security and Cooperation in Europe (CSCE)** – which became the **Organization for Security and Cooperation in Europe (OSCE)** on 1st January 1995 – decided to establish the post of High Commissioner on National Minorities (HCNM) in order to respond to the challenge of ethnic conflicts as one of the main sources of violence in Europe affecting relations between participating States. The office is located in The Hague. The three-year renewable mandate of the HCNM contains guidelines for determining whether or not he/she should become involved in a particular situation and describes him/her as "an instrument of conflict prevention at the earliest possible stage". The HCNM is empowered to conduct on-site missions and to engage in preventive diplomacy. The conditions for the HCNM's involvement are independence, the political support of the participating States, impartiality at all times and confidentiality. Nevertheless, the mandate contains provisions restricting his/her activities, in particular, the exclusion of consideration of individual cases concerning persons belonging to national minorities and exclusion of engagement in situations involving **terrorism**. It is worth mentioning that the mandate does not include a description or definition of what constitutes a national minority.

In the course of his work dealing with various situations mainly in Central and Eastern Europe and the former Soviet Union, the HCNM has issued a number of specific recommendations. The HCNM has also supported the elaboration of the following generally applicable recommendations: The Hague Recommendations regarding the Education Rights of National Minorities (1996); the Oslo Recommendations regarding the Linguistic Rights of National Minorities (1998); and the Lund Recommendations on the Effective Participation of National Minorities in Public Life (1999). Following the Lund Recommendations, the OSCE **Office for Democratic Institutions and Human Rights** initiated the elaboration of Guidelines to Assist National Minority Participation in the Electoral Process (2001). In addition, the HCNM has issued two reports (in 1993 and 2000) on the situation of Roma and Sinti in the OSCE area, along with a report on the linguistic rights of persons belonging to national minorities in the OSCE area (1999).

For more information see: http://www.osce.org/hcnm

HIV/AIDS and human rights

The AIDS epidemic is spreading at an alarming rate. Unequal access to treatment and care for those living with HIV/AIDS, **discrimination** and stigmatization at work, breaches of confidentiality in disclosure of an HIV-positive status, and vulnerability of women to HIV/AIDS, are among the key human rights issues to be addressed in this connection.

Interrelations between human rights and HIV/AIDS are numerous. An environment in which human rights are fully respected enables those infected and affected by HIV/AIDS to live a life of dignity without discrimination, and contrlbutes to alleviate the personal and societal impact of HIV infection. Vulnerability to HIV/AIDS is higher in an environment where people experience denial of human rights. Moreover, when no specific steps are taken to ensure respect for the rights of people living with HIV/AIDS, they suffer from discriminatory practices.

At both international and national levels, it is increasingly recognized that respect for human rights is a key factor to improve prevention of HIV/AIDS and care of those infected. In September 1996, the International Guidelines on HIV/AIDS and Human Rights were adopted at the Second International Consultation on HIV/AIDS and Human Rights. The Guidelines were published by the **Office of the United Nations High Commissioner for Human Rights (OHCHR)** and the Joint United Nations Programme on HIV/AIDS (UNAIDS). Based on existing international human rights standards, the 12 Guidelines represent a key international policy document on human rights in the context of HIV/AIDS. The Guidelines were elaborated to assist States in creating a positive, rights-based response to HIV/AIDS that is effective in reducing the transmission and impact of HIV/AIDS and is consistent with the protection of human rights and fundamental freedoms. Respect for the principle of non-discrimination, the **right[s] to health**, **education**, information, employment and social welfare, as well as participation in all spheres of life, are at the core of the recommendations of the Guidelines. The responsibility of civil society in disseminating, advocating for and contributing to the implementation of the Guidelines is highlighted throughout the document. In 2002 Guideline 6 was revised and now provides up-to-date policy guidance concerning access to prevention, treatment, care and support. The revised Guideline calls on Governments to establish concrete national plans on HIV/AIDS related treatment.

Efforts at all levels to make human rights an integral element of the response to HIV/AIDS are strongly supported by UNAIDS and its eight co-sponsor organizations: **United Nations Children's Fund (UNICEF)**; United Nations Drug Control Programme (UNDCP); **United Nations Development Programme (UNDP); United Nations Population Fund (UNFPA); United Nations Educational, Scientific and Cultural Organization (UNESCO); World Health Organization (WHO)**; the World Bank and the **International Labour Organization (ILO)**. Within this global framework, UNESCO is taking a lead role to develop culturally and socially sensitive preventive education, to combat complacency, to challenge stigmatization, and to promote more caring attitudes. Given its intellectual mandate, UNESCO also reflects on the ethical dimensions of the HIV/AIDS epidemics, including access to treatment and vaccine trials.

In 1998, 1 December was proclaimed **World AIDS Day**. It is an opportunity for national authorities, organizations of civil society as well as for individuals to demonstrate their commitment to the fight against AIDS and to advocate for more effective human rights protection of people affected by HIV/AIDS.

UNAIDS launched the first year-long World AIDS Campaign (WAC) in 1997. Since then, the WAC has served as a tool to capitalize resources and efforts to achieve a broader and more enduring impact.

For more information see: http://www.unaids.org

HIV-infected people or people with AIDS

In May 1988, the World Health Assembly of the **World Health Organization (WHO)** adopted a resolution entitled "Avoidance of **discrimination** in relation to HIV-infected people or people with AIDS". Among other provisions, this resolution calls on WHO to take all necessary measures to advocate the need to protect the human rights and the dignity of people with HIV/AIDS. In implementing this resolution, WHO has constantly advised Governments that non-discrimination is not only a human right, but is also a prerequisite for ensuring that infected persons are not driven underground, where they may be deprived of the necessary care. WHO has also appealed to: all Member States to review their national HIV/AIDS-related laws and policies, with a view to repealing any that might give rise to discrimination against HIV-infected people and people with AIDS; and to those responsible for policies on AIDS, with the view to promoting the dissemination not only of scientific knowledge, but also of the human rights principle of non-discrimination. Support provided to countries in this field has included information on relevant international principles and policies, as well as on innovative and effective solutions that some countries have developed which could be used as possible models. An international consultation on human rights and people with human immunodeficiency virus (HIV) was held in Geneva from 26 to 28 July 1989. The major objectives of the conference were to promote a better understanding of the human rights dimension of HIV/AIDS policies and laws in such a way as to assure their conformity with international human rights standards. In May 1992, the World Health Assembly declared that there is no public health rationale for any measures that limit arbitrarily the right of the individual, notably measures establishing mandatory screening. Similarly, the **Commission on Human Rights** in its resolutions 2001/51 and 2003/47 recognized the need for intensified efforts to ensure universal respect for and observance of human rights and fundamental freedoms for all so as to reduce vulnerability to HIV/AIDS and prevent HIV/AIDS-related discrimination.

The **United Nations General Assembly** Special Session on HIV/AIDS (June 2001) adopted the Declaration of Commitment on HIV/AIDS which includes several articles that deal specifically with HIV/AIDS and human rights. Among the human rights that are closely related to HIV/AIDS issues, some of the most important are: the **right to life**; the right to non-discrimination and equality before the law; the right to health care and social security; the **right to education**; the **right to work**; the right to freedom of movement and others.

For more information see: http://www.unaids.org

Humanitarian Law

See **International Humanitarian Law.**

Human Rights Committee
– HCR (UN)

The Human Rights Committee was established pursuant to Part IV of the **International Covenant on Civil and Political Rights** at the first meeting of States Parties on 20 September 1976. It is composed of 18 members of recognized competence in the field of human rights, elected by the States Parties for a term of four years. It normally holds three sessions per year, each of three weeks' duration. The Committee monitors the implementation of the International Covenant on Civil and Political Rights (1966) and the **Optional Protocol** thereto (1966), as well as the **Second Optional Protocol** (1989). Its principal objective is to develop a constructive dialogue with reporting States and thereby promote the compliance of States with the provisions of the Covenant. It has four major functions: (a) to receive and study States Parties' periodic reports on actions taken to give effect to the International Covenant on Civil and Political Rights and the Optional Protocol thereto; (b) to study these periodic reports; (c) to elaborate the meaning of individual articles and paragraphs of the Covenant through "general comments" in order to establish the jurisprudence of the Covenant and thus guide the States Parties in their adherence to their obligations under the Covenant and in the preparation of their reports to the Committee; (d) under the Optional Protocol, to consider and produce decisions on communications from individuals claiming to be victims of violations of any of the rights set forth in the Covenant and from States which claim that another State Party is not fulfilling its obligations under the Covenant (provided they have both made a special declaration recognizing this role of the Committee under Article 41). The Committee reports annually on its work to the **United Nations General Assembly** through the **Economic and Social Council (ECOSOC).**

Under Article 41 of this Covenant, a State Party may at any time declare that "… it recognizes the competence of the [Human Rights] Committee to receive and consider communications to the effect that a State Party claims that another State Party is not fulfilling its obligations under the present Covenant" (para. 1). Such declarations shall be deposited by the States Parties with the **United Nations Secretary-General** and may be withdrawn at any time (para. 2). The provisions of Article 41 entered into force on 28 March 1979 when 10 States Parties to the Covenant made declarations recognizing the role of the **Human Rights Committee** under this Article. By the middle of 2003, 55 States have made such declarations. To date, however, no such complaints have been received by the Committee. Should such a communication be received, and provided that both Parties have recognized the Committee's competence in this regard, the Committee can perform certain functions with a view to settling disputes and, when necessary, establishing an *ad hoc* conciliation commission to make available its "good offices" to States Parties involved in a dispute concerning the application of the Covenant, with a view to a friendly solution of the matter on the basis of respect for the Covenant. In each case submitted, the Human Rights Committee prepares a report and communicates it to the States Parties concerned. If a solution is reached, this report is confined to a brief statement of the facts and the solutions reached (para. 2). Should no solution be found, the statement of facts is accompanied by the submission (both written and oral) made by the States Parties concerned.

For more information see:
http://www.unhchr.ch/html/menu2/6/hrc.htm

Human Rights Day
– 10 December (UN)

On 4 December 1950 by its resolution 423 (V), the **United Nations General Assembly**, invited all States and interested organizations to observe 10 December of each year as Human Rights Day. This day is when the **Universal Declaration of Human Rights** was proclaimed in 1948 and is aimed to mobilize increasing efforts in this field. The General Assembly expressed the view that the anniversary of the adoption of the Universal Declaration should be celebrated in all countries as part of a common effort to bring it to the attention of all peoples. Human Rights Day is observed throughout the world and is marked by special events aimed at the promotion of human rights. The **United Nations Secretary-General**, the Director-General of **UNESCO** and the **United Nations High Commissioner for Human Rights** issue a special Human Rights Day message on 10 December.

Human rights education

Knowledge on human rights issues is an indispensable precondition to ensure the enjoyment of human rights. The **Universal Declaration of Human Rights**, recognizing the **right to education**, clarifies that education "shall be directed to the full development of the human personality and to the strengthening of respect for human rights and fundamental freedoms" (Article 26). Human rights instruments contain, as a rule, provisions obliging States Parties to disseminate these instruments and clarify their content. States have therefore an obligation to provide knowledge about human rights standards. With the development of international human rights law, provisions concerning human rights education have become more elaborated and developed. The **Convention on the Rights of the Child** contains the most comprehensive provisions in this regard (Article 29).

Some specialists prefer to use the terms "education for human rights" and "education in human rights" to underline that such education presumes not only dissemination of knowledge, but also the forging of behavioural patterns based upon respect for human rights. **UNESCO** is playing an important role in promoting acknowledgement that education for human rights is itself a human right. The **International Congress on Education for Human Rights and Democracy**, organized by UNESCO in Montreal, Canada (1993), was the first international conference which included this conclusion in its final documents.

The **World Conference on Human Rights** (Vienna, 1993) underlined the importance of human rights education, training and public information for the promotion and achievement of stable and harmonious relations among communities and for fostering mutual understanding and peace. Furthermore, "Governments, with the assistance of intergovernmental organizations, national institutions and **non-governmental organizations**, should promote an increased awareness of human rights and mutual tolerance" (**Vienna Declaration and Programme of Action**, Part II, Paragraph 82). In order to encourage educational and training activities in the field of human rights, the Conference recommended the proclamation of the **United Nations Decade for Human Rights Education**.

The Plan of Action for the Decade (1995-2004) defines human rights education as "training, dissemination and information efforts aimed at the building of a universal culture of human rights, through the imparting of knowledge and skills and the moulding of attitudes and directed to: the strengthening of respect for human rights and fundamental freedoms; the full development of the human personality and the sense of its dignity; the promotion of understanding, tolerance, gender equality and friendship among all nations, **indigenous peoples** and racial, national, ethnic, religious and linguistic groups; the enabling of all persons to participate effectively in a free society; the furtherance of the activities of the **United Nations** for the maintenance of peace" (A/51/506/Add.1, Paragraph 2).

In order to contribute to the implementation of the Plan, UNESCO organized, in cooperation with the **Office of the United Nations High Commissioner for Human Rights**, a series of **Regional Conferences on Human Rights Education** between 1997 and 2001. In the final documents adopted at each conference, concrete recommendations were made to promote human rights education at national and regional levels, to enrich its content and to improve its methodology. Furthermore, the promotion of gender equality and the empowerment of women, children and **vulnerable groups** are recognized as vital to the human rights education process. Human rights education is also promoted through UNESCO networks, such as the Associated Schools Project Network, the network of **UNESCO Chairs in Human Rights, Democracy, Peace and Tolerance** and the network of **Human rights research and training institutions**. Furthermore, best achievements in this field are awarded through the **UNESCO Prize for Human Rights Education**.

Human rights research and training institutions

Human rights research and training institutions play a very important role in the promotion of human rights by means of education, research and information. The **World Plan of Action on Education for Human Rights and Democracy**, adopted in Montreal in March 1993 by the **International Congress on Education for Human Rights and Democracy**, called for "identification, creation and strengthening of national, regional and international research centres and clearing houses on human rights information". The establishment of human rights research and training institutions was further supported by the **World Conference on Human Rights** (Vienna, June 1993) and encouraged by the Plan of Action for the **United Nations Decade for Human Rights Education (1995-2004)**. Such institutions exist now in almost every country of the world. In order to strengthen cooperation between these institutions. **UNESCO** has been publishing since 1987 the World Directory of Human Rights Research and Training Institutions (the 6th edition is to be published in 2003). UNESCO also organized meetings of directors of human rights research and training institutions. These meetings, which were initiated in 1988 (the eleventh took place in January 2001), were aimed at strengthening cooperation among institutions and increasing their contributions to the **United Nations system** efforts to promote and protect all human rights for all, in particular by means of education.

For more information see UNESCO Human Rights Institutes Database: http://www.unesco.org/human_rights/index.htm

Human rights treaty bodies (or human rights treaty monitoring bodies)

This is a general term used for bodies established to monitor the implementation by the States Parties of seven **United Nations** standard-setting instruments in the field of human rights: the **Committee on the Elimination of Racial Discrimination (CERD)**, which monitors the implementation of the **International Convention on the Elimination of All Forms of Discrimination** (1965); the **Human Rights Committee**, which monitors the implementation of the **International Covenant on Civil and Political Rights** (1966); the **Committee on Economic, Social and Cultural Rights**, which monitors the implementation of the **International Covenant on Economic, Social and Cultural Rights** (1966); the **Committee on the Elimination of Discrimination against Women (CEDAW)** which monitors the implementation of the **Convention on the Elimination of All Forms of Discrimination against Women** (1979); the **Committee against Torture**, which monitors the implementation of the **Convention against Torture and Other Cruel, Inhuman or Degrading Treatment or Punishment** (1984); the **Committee on the Rights of the Child** which monitors the implementation of the **Convention on the Rights of the Child** (1989); and the **Committee on the Protection of the Rights of All Migrant Workers and Members of Their Families** which monitors the implementation of the **International Convention on the Protection of the Rights of All Migrant Workers and Members of Their Families** (1990). Unlike the six other human rights treaties bodies, the Committee on Economic, Social and Cultural Rights was not established by its corresponding instrument. It was set up by the **Economic and Social Council (ECOSOC)** in 1985 and is, hence, its subsidiary body. Treaty bodies are composed of independent experts of recognized competence in the respective field.

By becoming parties to each of these treaties, States accept the duty to submit periodic reports to the relevant Committee indicating measures they have taken to implement the provisions of the treaties. Treaty bodies normally examine State reports in the presence of representatives of the government concerned who may answer questions from the experts. The treaty body concludes by formulating observations or comments on the State's performance in respect of its obligations under the relevant treaty.

Furthermore, some treaty bodies are entrusted by their corresponding instrument with the responsibility to receive and examine individual communications related to violations of rights by States Parties: the Human Rights Committee (as provided by the **Optional Protocol to the International Covenant on Civil and Political Rights**); the Committee on the Elimination of Racial Discrimination (as provided by Article 14 of the International Convention on the Elimination of All Forms of Discrimination); the Committee against Torture (as provided by Article 22 of the Convention against Torture and Other Cruel, Inhuman or Degrading Treatment or Punishment); the Committee on the Elimination of Discrimination against Women (as provided by the **Optional Protocol to the Convention on the Elimination of All Forms of Discrimination against Women**) and the **Committee on the Protection of the Rights of All Migrant Workers and Members of Their Families** (as provided for by Article 77 of the International Convention on the Protection of the Rights of All Migrant Workers and Members of Their Families). Pursuant to the **United Nations General Assembly** resolution 38/117 of 16 December 1983, the **United Nations Secretary-General** convened the first meeting of the persons chairing the treaty bodies in order to discuss issues of common concern. Subsequent sessions were convened biannually until 1995 when the meetings became annual. Treaty bodies are serviced by the **Office of the High Commissioner for Human Rights** in Geneva, with the exception of the Committee on the

Elimination of Discrimination against Women, which is serviced by the Division for the Advancement of Women in New York.
    For more information see:
http://www.unhchr.ch/html/menu2/convmech.htm

Indigenous people

Indigenous peoples have received increasing attention in the human rights discourse. The first international legal instrument on the situation of indigenous and tribal populations was adopted by the **International Labour Organisation (ILO)** in 1957 (Convention N° 107). In 1989 the ILO adopted **Convention N° 169 concerning Indigenous and Tribal Peoples in Independent Countries** (1989), which is the revision of Convention 107. ILO Convention 169 is the only international legally binding instrument to protect the rights of indigenous peoples. While it was adopted with an overwhelming majority, by mid March 2003, it had only been ratified by seventeen States.

In May 1982, the ECOSOC established a Working Group on Indigenous Populations to review the developments concerning the promotion and protection of the human rights of indigenous peoples and to formulate standards for the protection of their rights. The Working Group is composed of five independent experts of the **Sub-Commission on the Promotion and Protection of Human Rights**. In 1985 the Working Group started drafting a Declaration on the Rights of Indigenous Peoples. It submitted its draft to the Sub-Commission in 1993, which transferred it unchanged to the **Commission on Human Rights** in 1994. The Commission has established an open-ended working group to study the Draft Declaration. By May 2003, the Commission had not yet adopted a final text.

The **World Conference on Human Rights** (Vienna, Austria, June 1993) recognized the unique contribution of indigenous people to plurality of society and recommended that consideration should be given to the establishment of a permanent forum for indigenous peoples within the **United Nations system**.

The General Assembly endorsed this recommendation in its resolutions 48/163 and 49/214. The first meeting of the Permanent Forum on Indigenous Issues took place in May 2002. The Forum is composed of sixteen independent experts, eight of whom are nominated by States, while the other eight are appointed by the President of the ECOSOC following formal consultations with States on the basis of consultations with indigenous organizations. Another important development with regard to the protection and promotion of the rights of indigenous peoples was the appointment by the United Nations Commission on Human Rights of a **Special Rapporteur[s]** to deal with the situation of human rights and fundamental freedoms of indigenous people (the Rapporteur has been appointed in 2001 for a term of three years).

The **United Nations General Assembly** furthermore proclaimed the **International Decade of the World's Indigenous People (1994-2004)** and adopted a Programme of Action for the Decade. The **International Day of the World's Indigenous People** is on 9 August each year.

Integrated Framework of Action on Education for Peace, Human Rights and Democracy (UNESCO)

The forty-fourth session of the **International Conference[s] on Education** was held in Geneva in October 1994 on the theme "Appraisal and Perspectives of Education for International Understanding". It unanimously adopted a declaration which is a reflection of the political commitment of the ministers of education of **UNESCO** Member States to give the highest priority to activities in favour of the encouragement of understanding, solidarity and tolerance between people, ethnic, social, cultural and religious groups, and between nations. The Conference also took note of a draft Integrated Framework of Action on Education for Peace, Human Rights and Democracy which was adopted in 1995 by the UNESCO General Conference at its 28th session. The

Integrated Framework is intended to give effect to the declaration and, *inter alia*, to the **World Plan of Action for Education for Human Rights and Democracy** and the **Vienna Declaration and Programme of Action**. This document confirms that all human rights are universal, indivisible, interrelated and interdependent and states that strategies for their implementation must take into account specific historical, religious and cultural considerations. The Integrated Framework determines the aims of education for peace, human rights and democracy, stipulating that its ultimate goal is "… the development in every individual of a sense of universal values and types of behaviour on which a culture of peace is predicated" (Part II, para. 6). It also stipulates that "… education must cultivate in citizens the ability to make informed choices, basing their judgements and actions not only on the analysis of present situations but also on the vision of a preferred future" (Part II, para. 10). Education should also serve to promote respect for pluralism, diversity, the **cultural heritage**, protection of the environment, and sustainable development. It should cultivate feelings of solidarity and equity.

The Integrated Framework proposes strategies to reach these aims which, *inter alia*, must be comprehensive and holistic, be applicable to all types, levels and forms of education, be applied on a continuous and consistent basis locally, nationally, regionally and worldwide, and involve all educational partners, including **non-governmental organizations**. The Integrated Framework also determines policies and lines of action related to: content of education; teaching materials and resources; programmes for reading, expression and the promotion of foreign languages; educational establishments; teacher-training; action on behalf of **vulnerable groups**; research and development; higher education; and non-formal education of young people and adults. The Integrated Framework contains a special section dedicated to the promotion of regional and international cooperation to develop education for peace, human rights and democracy.

Inter-American Charter of Social Guarantees (OAS)

The Inter-American Charter of Social Guarantees was adopted as a resolution by the Ninth International Conference of American States in Bogota on 2 May 1948. It was included in the Final Act of the Conference. It aims at encouraging the raising of standards of living in the American continent through economic development and cooperation between workers and employers. The Charter proclaims fundamental principles to protect workers of all kinds and sets forth the rights to which they are entitled in the American States (Article 1). Apart from general principles (Articles 1-5), the Charter deals, among other things, with individual labour contracts (Article 6), collective labour contracts and agreements (Article 7), wages (Articles 8-11), work periods, rest and vacations (Articles 12-15), child labour (Articles 16, 17), the work of women (Article 18), the right of association (Article 26), the **right to strike** (Article 27), the **right to social security** and welfare (Articles 28-34) and rural work (Articles 38, 39).

Inter-American Commission of Women – CIM (OAS)

The Inter-American Commission of Women (CIM), a specialized organization of the **Organization of American States (OAS),** was established at the Sixth International Conference of American States in 1928. It was the first official intergovernmental agency in the world created expressly to ensure recognition of the **civil** and **political rights** of women. CIM comprises 34 Permanent Delegates, one for each OAS Member State, designated by their respective governments. The Assembly of Delegates is held every two years and is CIM's highest authority. It establishes CIM's policies and Plan of Action for the biennium and elects a seven-member Executive Committee. CIM's mission is to promote and protect women's rights, and to support the Member States in their efforts to ensure full exercise of civil, political, **economic**, **social** and cultural rights that make possible equal participation by women and men in all aspects of society, so that women and men share, fully and equally, both the benefits of development and responsibility for the future.

For more information see:
http://www.oas.org/EN/PINFO/OAS/IACW.htm

Inter-American Commission on Human Rights (OAS)

The Inter-American Commission on Human Rights was established in 1959 by the **Organization of American States (OAS)** in accordance with its Charter (Article 106). It held its first session on 25 May 1960. The Commission is one of two organs having competence with respect to the fulfillment of the commitments made by Member States to the **American Declaration of the Rights and Duties of Man** (1948) and the **American Convention on Human Rights** (1969). The **Inter-American Court of Human Rights** is the other organ. The principal function of the Commission is to promote the observance and protection of human rights and to serve as a consultative organ of the Organization in these matters. It is composed of seven members, elected by the OAS General Assembly in their individual capacity for a term of four years with the possibility of one re-election. In order to promote respect for and defence of human rights, the Commission has the mandate to: make recommendations to States Parties for the adoption of progressive measures in favour of human rights; prepare studies and reports on the human rights conditions in OAS Member States; conduct on-site observations; and request the governments of Member States to inform it on the measures adopted by them in matters of human rights. The Commission also has the authority to take action on individual petitions containing complaints on alleged violations of the provisions of the Convention from any person, group of persons or any legally recognized **non-governmental organization**, providing that the

State Party concerned has made a declaration recognizing the competence of the Commission in this respect. Such communications may be admitted and examined only if all remedies under domestic law have been exhausted. When a complaint is found admissible, States Parties are obliged to make available all necessary information to the Commission. Should the Commission fail to seek a friendly settlement, the case can be forwarded to the Inter-American Court of Human Rights by either a State or by the Commission.

For more information see: http://www.cidh.oas.org

Inter-American Convention against Corruption (OAS)

The Inter-American Convention against Corruption was adopted by the **Organization of American States (OAS)** on 29 March 1996. It entered into force on 6 March 1997. By May 2003, it had been ratified by 28 States. According to Article II, the purposes of the Convention are to promote and strengthen the development of mechanisms to prevent, detect, punish and eradicate corruption and to promote, facilitate and regulate cooperation to ensure the effectiveness of relevant measures in the performance of public functions. Article III stipulates the preventive measures to be enforced. Article VI gives a detailed definition of acts of corruption at the national level, while Article VIII concerns transnational bribery and Article IX deals with illicit enrichment. Provisions regarding extradition are laid down in Article XIII. Article XIV covers assistance and cooperation among States Parties. Article XVI stipulates that bank secrecy shall not be invoked by the requested State as a basis for refusal to provide the assistance sought by the requesting State.

Inter-American Convention against Terrorism (OAS)

Adopted by the **Organization of American States (OAS)** on 3 June 2002, the Inter-American Convention against Terrorism entered into force on 10 July 2003. By the middle of 2003 it had been ratified by 6 States.

The purposes of this Convention are to prevent, punish and eliminate **terrorism**. To that end, States Parties agree to adopt the necessary measures and to strengthen cooperation among them, in accordance with the terms of the Convention. According to Article 2, "offenses" mean those which are established in, among others, the **Convention for the Suppression of Unlawful Seizure of Aircraft** (1970); the **Convention for the Suppression of Unlawful Acts against the Safety of Civil Aviation** (1971); the **Convention on the Prevention and Punishment of Crimes against Internationally Protected Persons, including Diplomatic Agents** (1973); the **International Convention against the Taking of Hostages** (1979); the **International Convention for the Suppression of Terrorist Bombings** (1997); and the **International Convention for the Suppression of the Financing of Terrorism** (1999). Each State Party shall endeavour to become a party to the international instruments listed in Article 2, and establish, in its domestic legislation, penalties for the offences described therein.

Measures to prevent, combat and eradicate the financing of terrorism are enumerated in Article 4 of the Convention and include the obligation of States Parties to "institute a legal and regulatory regime to prevent, combat and eradicate the financing of terrorism." This shall include: a regulatory and supervisory regime for banks, other financial institutions, and other entities deemed particularly susceptible to being used for the financing of terrorist activities; measures to detect and monitor movements across borders of cash, bearer negotiable instruments, and other appropriate movements of value; and measures to ensure that the competent authorities dedicated to combating the offences established in the international instruments listed in Article 2 have the ability to cooperate and exchange information at the national and international levels within the conditions prescribed under its domestic law. To that end, each State Party shall establish and maintain a financial intelligence unit to serve as a national centre for the collection, analysis, and dissemination of pertinent money laundering and terrorist financing information.

Under Article 7 of the Convention, States agree to "promote co-operation and the exchange of information in order to improve border and customs control measures to detect and prevent the international movement of terrorists and trafficking in arms or other materials intended to support terrorist activities". The issues of extradition, refugee status claims and asylum are elaborated in Articles 11, 12 and 13 respectively. Article 15 ensures that the measures carried out under the Convention "shall take place with the full respect for the rule of law, human rights and fundamental freedoms".

Inter-American Convention on Extradition (OAS)

This Convention was adopted by the General Assembly of the **Organization of American States (OAS)** on 25 February 1981. It entered into force on 28 March 1992 and had been ratified by 5 States by May 2003. The Convention's purpose is to strengthen international cooperation in legal and criminal matters. Article 3 lays down the conditions under which extradition will be granted, in particular for offences which shall be punishable at the time of their commission, the principle of retroactivity only being applied when it is favourable to the offender. Article 4 establishes various grounds for denying extradition. No provision in the Convention may be interpreted as a limitation on the right of asylum when its exercise is appropriate (Article 6). Nationality may not be invoked as a ground for denying extradition, except when the law of the requested State otherwise provides (Article 7).

Inter-American Convention on Forced Disappearance of Persons (OAS)

Adopted by the **Organization of American States (OAS)** on 9 June 1994, the Inter-American Convention on Forced Disappearance of Persons entered into force on 28 March 1996.

By May 2003, it had been ratified by 10 of 35 Member States. The aim of the Convention is to promote the prevention and the punishment of the crime of forced disappearance of persons, which is defined as "the act of depriving a person or persons of his or their freedom, in whatever way, ... followed by an absence of information or a refusal to acknowledge that deprivation of freedom or to give information on the whereabouts of that person, thereby impeding his or her recourse to the applicable legal remedies and procedural guarantees" (Article II). States Parties to this Convention undertake: not to practise, permit, or tolerate the forced disappearance of persons, even in states of emergency or suspension of individual guarantees; to punish within their jurisdiction those persons who commit or attempt to commit the crime of forced disappearance of persons and their accomplices and accessories; to cooperate with one another in helping to prevent, punish, and eliminate the forced disappearance of persons; to take legislative, administrative, judicial, and any other measures necessary to comply with the commitments undertaken in this Convention (Article I); and to ensure that the training of public law-enforcement personnel or officials includes the necessary education on the offence of forced disappearance of persons (Article VIII). The Convention also stipulates that criminal prosecution for the forced disappearance of persons and the penalty judicially imposed on its perpetrator shall not be subject to statutes of limitations (Article VII). The Convention grants competence to the **Inter-American Commission on Human Rights** to ensure compliance with its provisions (Article XIII).

Inter-American Convention on International Traffic in Minors (OAS)

The Inter-American Convention on International Traffic in Minors was adopted by the **Organization of American States (OAS)** on 18 March 1994 and entered into force on 15 August 1997. By May 2003, it has been ratified by 9 States. The Convention, underlining that this traffic is of universal concern, aims at ensuring comprehensive and effective protection for minors through appropriate mechanisms to guarantee respect for their rights. Article 1 deals with the prevention and punishment of the traffic. Articles 7-11 specify penal aspects and Articles 12-22 civil aspects, including requests for locating and returning a minor to his/her habitual residence. The Convention also envisages the creation of a national authority in each State Party to monitor the problem and to ensure cooperation among States Parties, as well as their cooperation with other States in the region (Articles 4-5).

Inter-American Convention on the Elimination of All Forms of Discrimination against Persons with Disabilities (OAS)

The Inter-American Convention on the Elimination of All Forms of Discrimination against Persons with Disabilities was adopted by the **Organization of American States (OAS)** on 7 June 1999. It entered into force on 14 September 2001. By May 2003, it had been ratified by 12 countries. Article I defines the terms "disability" and "**discrimination** against persons with disabilities". Articles III and IV concern the measures to be taken to achieve the objectives of the Convention, whilst Article VI envisages the establishment of a Committee for the Elimination of All Forms of Discrimination against Persons with Disabilities to follow up on the commitments undertaken by States Parties under the Convention.

Inter-American Convention on the Granting of Civil Rights to Women (OAS)

The Inter-American Convention on the Granting of Civil Rights to Women was adopted during the Ninth International Conference of the American States on 2 May 1948 by the **Organization of American States (OAS)**. It had been ratified by 21 Member States by the middle of 2003. For each State it enters into force on the date of deposit of its instrument of ratification.

The Convention contains only one provision, stipulating that "The American States agree to grant women the same **civil rights** that men enjoy" (Article 1), thus constituting an international legal commitment in the field and contributing to the eradication of **discrimination** against women.

Inter-American Convention on the Granting of Political Rights to Women (OAS)

Adopted during the Ninth International Conference of the American States on 2 May 1948 by the **Organization of American States (OAS)**, the Inter-American Convention on the Granting of **Political Rights** to Women entered into force for each country on the date of deposit of its instrument of ratification. By May 2003, it had been ratified by 24 of the Organization's 35 Member States. It contains only one provision, stipulating that "The High Contracting Parties agree that the **right to vote and to be elected** to national office shall not be denied or abridged by reason of sex" (Article 1). Together with the **Inter-American Convention on the Granting of Civil Rights to Women**, also adopted in 1948, this instrument was a landmark in the promotion of gender equality and the eradication of **discrimination** against women.

Inter-American Convention on the Prevention, Punishment and Eradication of Violence against Women – "Convention of Belem do Para" (OAS)

This Convention, also called the Convention of Belem do Para, was adopted by the General Assembly of the **Organization of American States (OAS)** on 9 June 1994. It entered into force on 5 March 1995 and, by the middle of 2003, had been ratified by 31 Member States. The aim of the Convention is to ensure the right of every woman "to be free from violence in both the public and private spheres" (Article 3). "Violence against women", as defined in Article 1, is "any act or conduct, based on gender, which causes death or physical, sexual or psychological harm or suffering to women, whether in the public or the private sphere". The Convention affirms "the right of women to be free from all forms of **discrimination** and the right of women to be valued and educated free of stereotyped patterns of behaviour and social and cultural practices based on concepts of inferiority or subordination" (Article 6). The States Parties to the Convention agree to condemn all forms of violence against women and to pursue policies to prevent, punish and eradicate such violence (Article 7). To carry out this obligation Contracting States are entitled: to take all appropriate measures, including legislative measures, to amend or repeal existing laws and regulations or to modify legal or customary practices which sustain the persistence and tolerance of violence against women (Article 7); to adopt programmes to promote awareness and observance of the right of women to be free from violence (Article 8); to promote the education and training of all those involved in the administration of justice, police and other law enforcement officials (Article 8); and to provide appropriate specialized services for women who have been subjected to violence (Article 8). Contracting Parties are also obliged to include in their national reports to the **Inter-American Commission of Women** (CIM) information on measures adopted to prevent and prohibit violence against women and to assist women affected by violence, as well as on any difficulties they observe in applying those measures and the factors that contribute to violence against women (Article 10).

The **International Day for the Elimination of Violence against Women** proclamed by the **United Nations General Assembly** is observed on 25 November each year.

Inter-American Convention to Prevent and Punish Torture (OAS)

Adopted by the **Organization of American States (OAS)** on 9 December 1985, the Inter-American Convention to Prevent and Punish Torture entered into force on 28 February 1987. By

May 2003, it had been ratified by 16 Member States. The aim of the Convention is to prevent and punish the use of torture in the Americas. "Torture", under this instrument, shall be understood as "any act intentionally enforced whereby physical or mental pain or suffering is inflicted on a person for purposes of criminal investigation, as a means of intimidation, as personal punishment, as a preventive measure, as a penalty, or for any other purpose" and "the use of methods upon a person intended to obliterate the personality of the victim or to diminish his physical or mental capacities, even if they do not cause physical pain or mental anguish" (Article 2). The Convention determines those who shall be held guilty of the crime of torture: a public servant or employee who, acting in that capacity, or a person who, at the instigation of a public servant or employee, orders, instigates or induces the use of torture, or who directly commits it or who, being able to prevent it, fails to do so (Article 3). Circumstances of war or public emergency do not provide exemption from criminal liability (Article 5). All States Parties to the Convention agree not only to punish severely the perpetrators of torture but also to take effective measures to prevent and punish other cruel, inhuman or degrading treatment within their jurisdiction (Article 6). The Convention also contains provisions on measures to be taken concerning: the education of police officers and other public officials responsible for the custody of persons deprived of their liberty (Article 7); the right of every person to an examination of an accusation of having been subjected to torture within their jurisdiction (Article 8); and the establishment of regulations guaranteeing suitable compensation for victims of torture (Article 9). Although the Convention does not establish a monitoring body, petitions can be submitted to the **Inter-American Commission on Human Rights**, provided the State concerned is a Party to this Convention.

Inter-American Court of Human Rights (OAS)

The **Inter-American Court of Human Rights** was established on 22 November 1969 and brought into being on 18 July 1978 in accordance with Chapter VIII of the **American Convention on Human Rights**. It is an autonomous juridical institution whose purpose is to interpret and apply the provisions of the Convention. Pursuant to Articles 52 and 53 of the Convention, the Court comprises seven judges elected by the General Assembly of the **Organization of American States (OAS)**. The judges, of which no two may be nationals of the same State, serve in their personal capacity and are elected for a term of six years (Articles 52 and 54). The Court has both advisory competence and litigious jurisdiction. All Member States of the OAS can request advice from the Court on any question concerning the interpretation and application of the Convention or concerning any other body or instrument dealing with human rights under the auspices of the OAS (Article 64). The Court's litigious jurisdiction, however, only applies to States Parties who have recognized the jurisdiction of the Court in this regard. Such a declaration "may be made unconditionally, on the condition of reciprocity, for a special period, or for specific cases" (Article 62). The Court's jurisdiction empowers only States Parties and the Commission to submit cases concerning the interpretation and application of the Convention (Article 61), provided that all procedures of the **Inter-American Commission on Human Rights** have been exhausted. If the Court, having examined the complaint, finds that there has been a violation of the provisions of the Convention, it shall ensure for the injured party the enjoyment of his or her right or freedom that was violated (Article 63) and, if necessary, deem a fair compensation to be made. States Parties are obligated to comply with and to implement the judgements of the Court, yet there is no mechanism for the enforcement of the judgements (Article 68). Article 65, however, provides that, in the Court's annual report to the General Assembly of the OAS, it "... shall specify, in particular, the cases in which a State has not complied with its judgment, making any pertinent recommendations".

For more information see:
http://www.oas.org/EN/PINFO/OAS/court.htm

International Bill of Human Rights (UN)

The International Bill of Human Rights encompasses the **Universal Declaration of Human Rights** (1948), the **International Covenant on Economic, Social and Cultural Rights** (1966), the **International Covenant on Civil and Political Rights** (1966) and the two Optional Protocols to the latter, namely the **Optional Protocol to the International Covenant on Civil and Political Rights** (1966) and the **Second Optional Protocol to the International Covenant on Civil and Political Rights, aiming at the abolition of the death penalty** (1989). The International Bill of Human Rights elaborates in detail the general human rights provisions of the **United Nations Charter**. With a view to establishing a worldwide system for the promotion and protection of human rights and fundamental freedoms, the Bill is guided by the principle of equality in rights and non-**discrimination**. It has played a major role in the development of international human rights law.

For more information see:
http://www.unhchr.ch/html/menu6/2/fs2.htm

International Charter of Physical Education and Sport (UNESCO)

This Charter was adopted by the **UNESCO** General Conference at its 20th session on 21 November 1978. It recalls that by the terms of the **Universal Declaration of Human Rights**, everyone is entitled to all the rights and freedoms set forth therein without **discrimination** of any kind. Everyone should be free to develop and preserve his/her physical, intellectual and moral powers and access to physical education and sport should consequently be assured and guaranteed for all human beings (Preamble). Article 1 entitled "The practice of physical education and sport is a fundamental right for all" contains concrete provisions in this regard. The Charter states that physical education and sport programmes must meet individual and social needs (Article 3) and that the protection of the ethical and moral values of physical education and sport must be a constant concern for all (Article 7). It stipulates that international cooperation is a prerequisite for the universal and well-balanced promotion of physical education and sport (Article 11).

International Civil Aviation Organization – ICAO

The ICAO was established in November 1944 by the Convention on International Civil Aviation (also known as the "Chicago Convention") to develop safe, efficient, regular and economical air transport worldwide. It is a specialized agency of the **United Nations** and comprised by the middle of 2003, 188 Member States. The Headquarters of ICAO is located in Montreal, Canada. Several international instruments have been adopted under its auspices concerning such varied questions as damage done by the aircraft to third parties on the surface, the liability of the air carrier to its passengers, crimes committed on board aircraft, etc. The Organization is particularly active in carrying out measures to prevent **terrorism** and air piracy, so as to ensure the safety of international civil aviation.

For more information see: http://www.icao.int

International Code of Conduct for Public Officials (UN)

Concerned with the threat caused by **corruption** to the stability and security of societies, the **United Nations General Assembly** adopted on 12 December 1996 (resolution 51/59) the International Code of Conduct for Public Officials and recommended that States use it as a tool to guide their efforts to fight against corruption. The Code defines a public office as being a position of trust, implying a duty for public officials to act in the public interests of their country, as expressed through the democratic institutions of government. It requires public officials to administer public resources effectively and efficiently and to perform their functions with integrity and impartiality, without preferential treatment or **discrimination**. Furthermore, it prohibits conflicts of interest for public officials and the acceptance of gifts or other favours that might influence their judgement or the performance of their duties. The Code also covers such issues as the disclosure of confidential information and political activity.

International Committee of the Red Cross – ICRC

In February 1863, a committee, initially called the International Committee for Relief to the Wounded, was formed. It soon became known as the International Committee of the Red Cross (ICRC). The basis for its foundation stemmed from the presence at the Battle of Solferino on 24 June 1859 of Henry Dunant, and his attempts to assist the thousands of unattended wounded there. In 1864, the ICRC convened a diplomatic conference and adopted the Geneva Convention for the Amelioration of the Condition of Wounded in Armies in the Field. This instrument marked the birth of modern humanitarian law.

Today, the ICRC works on the basis of a specific mandate which it received from the States bound by the **Geneva Conventions** of 1949 and the 1977 **Protocols Additional to the Geneva Conventions**. Its tasks set out in these instruments include the monitoring of the treatment of prisoners of war and other people detained in connection with a conflict, and the right to offer its services in order to alleviate the suffering of all victims. It also draws attention to violations of **international humanitarian law**, and promotes its further development.

When dealing with conflicts, the ICRC maintains a neutral position and acts as an impartial intermediary between belligerents, caring for the wounded, visiting prisoners of war and persons detained for security reasons, restoring contacts between separated families, protecting the civilian population, and providing food or other assistance to conflict victims. It reminds all States of their collective obligation to ensure respect for international humanitarian law.

The ICRC is an impartial and independent organization forming one of the largest humanitarian networks and is present and active in almost every country of the world. It has set up a network of regional delegations covering practically all countries not directly affected by armed conflict. They have specific tasks which concern operational activities on the one hand, and humanitarian law on the other. These delegations enable the ICRC to undertake rapid humanitarian action when necessary.

To strengthen the standards of international humanitarian law and to increase the protection of human rights, the ICRC adopted a number of instruments that forbid the use and the production of certain arms. These instruments of international law include, in particular, the Convention on the Prohibition of the Use, Stockpiling, Production and Transfer of Anti-Personnel Mines and on their Destruction (1997), which is considered by many specialists as a part of international human rights law. Known as the 'Ottawa Treaty', this Convention outlaws the use of anti-personnel landmines under any circumstances and calls on States Parties to ensure their destruction in accordance with the provisions of the Convention. The 1980 Convention on Prohibitions or Restrictions on the Use of Certain Conventional Weapons Which May be Deemed to be Excessively Injurious or to Have Indiscriminate Effects is aimed at protecting both civilians and combatants from the excess suffering caused by weapons. The 1993 Convention on the Prohibition of the Development, Production, Stockpiling and Use of Chemical Weapons and on Their Destruction, complements and strengthens the 1925 Geneva Protocol for the Prohibition of the Use in War of Asphyxiating, Poisonous or Other Gases, and of Bacteriological Methods of Warfare. This Convention prohibits not only the use of chemical weapons, but their development, production, stockpiling, retention and transfer as well. It requires furthermore the destruction of the weapons and the facilities where they are produced.

For more information see: http://www.icrc.org

International Conferences on Education (UNESCO)

UNESCO has been organizing the International Conferences on Education for many years. Each session, which gathers together ministers of education of UNESCO Member States is dedicated to a subject which has a particular importance in the field of education. The forty-fourth session, held in 1994, was dedicated "Appraisal and Perspectives of Education for International Understanding" and adopted a relevant declaration which led to the adoption of the **Integrated Framework of Action on Education for Peace, Human Rights, and Democracy**.

The forty-fifth session, held in Geneva in October 1996 on the theme "Strengthening the Role of Teachers in a Changing World", concluded with the adoption of a declaration and recommendations. The declaration concentrates on integrated policies to make schools the key to social cohesion and instrumental in the teaching of democratic values. It also stresses strengthening the role, functions and status of teachers in partnership with educational professionals and society as a whole.

The forty-sixth session (2001) addressed the theme "Education for all for learning to live together: contents and learning strategies - problems and solutions". Its main objective was to examine and discuss all aspects connected with the quality of education for all, and to launch a new phase of international dialogue on the content, methods and structures of teaching.

For more information see:
http://www.unesco.org/education/esd/english/international/edconf.shtml

International Congress on Education for Human Rights and Democracy, Montreal, 1993 (UNESCO)

The International Congress on Education for Human Rights and Democracy was held in Montreal, Canada, from 8 to 11 March 1993. It was organized by **UNESCO** in conjunction with the Canadian Commission for UNESCO and in close cooperation with the **United Nations Centre for Human Rights** (now the **Office of the United Nations High Commissioner for Human Rights**). The main aim of the Congress was to contribute to the elaboration of future actions to be taken by UNESCO "... for the promotion of human rights in the political, economic and cultural circumstances that have recently emerged and that call for fresh consideration and debate". Its objective was to highlight the achievements and identify the obstacles to overcome in the field of human rights education; to introduce education for democracy as a complementary aspect; and to encourage the elaboration of tools and ideas, in particular educational methods, pedagogic approaches and didactic materials, so as to give a new impetus to education for human rights and democracy. The Congress adopted the **World Plan of Action on Education for Human Rights and Democracy**, which proposes seven major strategies for concerted actions to promote education for human rights and democracy, including certain activities to be carried out by UNESCO. The Congress concluded that education for human rights is an integral part of education and that the right for **human rights education** is itself a human right. The Plan was noted in the **Vienna Declaration and Programme of Action** (Part II, para. 81) adopted by the **World Conference on Human Rights** (Vienna, Austria, June 1993).

For more information see:
http://www.unesco.org/human_rights/hrfe.htm

International Congress on Human Rights Teaching, Information and Documentation, Malta, 1987 (UNESCO)

The International Congress on Human Rights Teaching, Information and Documentation was organized by **UNESCO** in Malta in 1987 to encourage human rights education. The Congress adopted a series of recommendations noting the progress made in the field of human rights education since the **International Congress on the Teaching of Human Rights** held in Vienna in 1978. It underlined that UNESCO Member States should set up a complete system of human rights teaching and education available to all citizens and all population groups and covering all levels of education, with the broad participation of various public organizations and media. It recommended that the Director-General of UNESCO cooperate with Member States in the development of programmes of human rights teaching and education within the framework of formal and non-formal systems of education, as well as assist Member States in developing new educational methods and materials in this field.

For more information see:
http://www.unesco.org/human_rights/hrfn.htm

International Congress on the Teaching of Human Rights, Vienna, 1978 (UNESCO)

The International Congress on the Teaching of Human Rights, organized by **UNESCO** in Vienna, Austria, in 1978, was the first in a series of congresses devoted to human rights education. For the first time, human rights educators, activists and government officials met to discuss various questions linked to the development of human rights teaching. In its final document, the Congress stressed that human rights education and teaching should be based on the principles which underlie the **United Nations Charter**, the **Universal Declaration of Human Rights**, the **International Covenants on Human Rights**, and other international human rights instruments. **Human rights education and teaching must aim at fostering an attitude of tolerance, respect and solidarity, providing knowledge about human rights and developing the individual's awareness of the ways and means by which human rights can be translated into a social and political reality.** The Congress recommended: the preparation of a six-year plan for human rights education; conducting a preliminary study on the question of the desirability of preparing a UNESCO convention on human rights teaching and education; and setting up a voluntary fund for the development of knowledge of human rights through education and information. A draft plan for the development of human rights teaching (1981-87), foreseen by the Congress, was prepared by a UNESCO expert meeting in 1979. A Voluntary Fund for the Development of Knowledge of Human Rights through Education and Information was also created by the UNESCO Executive Board. After the International Congress in Vienna, UNESCO organized the **International Congress on Human Rights Teaching, Information and Documentation, Malta, 1987**, and the **International Congress on Education for Human Rights and Democracy, Montreal, 1993**. UNESCO takes an active part in the implementation of the Plan of Action for the **United Nations Decade for Human Rights Education** (1995-2004). Within this framework it also organized a series of **regional conferences on human rights education** between 1997 and 2001 and issued a number of educational and information materials in this field.

For more information see:
http://www.unesco.org/human_rights/hrfa.htm

International Convention against Apartheid in Sports (UN)

The International Convention against Apartheid in Sports was adopted by the **United Nations General Assembly** on 10 December 1985 and entered into force on 3 April 1988. By the middle of 2003, it was binding for about 60 Member States. For the purposes of the Convention, the expression "**apartheid**" is defined as "a system of institutionalized racial segregation and **discrimination** for the purpose of establishing and maintaining domination by one racial group of persons over another racial group of persons and systematically oppressing them, such as that pursued by South Africa" (Article 1) and "apartheid in sports" is defined as meaning "the application of the policies and practices of such a system in sports activities, whether organized on a professional or an amateur basis" (Article 1). In compliance with the Convention, States Parties agree to "strongly condemn apartheid and undertake to pursue immediately, by all appropriate means, a policy of eliminating the practice of apartheid in all its forms from sports" (Article 2). With this end in view, Contracting States shall: not permit sports contact with a country practising apartheid (Article 3); refuse to provide financial or other assistance to enable their sports bodies, teams and individual sportsmen from participating in sports activities in a country practising apartheid or with teams or individual sportsmen selected on the basis of apartheid (Article 5); take all appropriate action to secure the expulsion of a country practising apartheid from international and regional sports bodies (Article 8); and undertake appropriate action against their sports bodies, teams and individual sportsmen that participate in sports activities in a country practising apartheid, or with teams representing a country practising apartheid (Article 6). The establishment of a Commission against Apartheid in Sports to monitor compliance with the provisions of the Convention was also envisaged (Article 11).

International Convention against the Taking of Hostages (UN)

This Convention is one of the first universal instruments aimed at the struggle against **terrorism**. Adopted by the **United Nations General Assembly** (A/RES/34/146) on 17 December 1979, it entered into force on 3 June 1983. By the middle of 2003, it had been ratified by about 100 States. The Convention expresses the conviction that "... the taking of hostages is an offence of grave concern to the international community and that, in accordance with the provisions of this Convention, any person committing an act of hostage taking shall either be prosecuted or extradited" (Preamble). States Parties shall cooperate in the prevention of this offence, and take practical measures in this regard at national and international levels. The Convention contains a number of concrete provisions concerning the prosecution and extradition of offenders. However, it is not applied "... where the offence is committed within a single State, the hostage and the alleged offender are nationals of that State and the alleged offender is found on the territory of that State" (Article 13). Article 16 concerns the disputes between two or more States Parties in regard to the interpretation or application of the Convention, and envisages procedures for arbitration.

International Convention for the Suppression of Terrorist Bombings (UN)

The Convention was adopted by the **United Nations General Assembly** (A/RES/52/164) on 15 December 1997 and entered into force on 23 May 2001. By the middle of 2003, it had been ratified by 101 States. The Convention is among a number of standard-setting instruments adopted by the international community in order to prevent, combat and eliminate **terrorism**. In condemning acts of terrorism, the Convention imposes on States Parties the obligation to take action to prosecute and punish those organizing or participating in terrorist bombings. It also serves to enhance international cooperation in this regard.

International Convention for the Suppression of the Financing of Terrorism (UN)

This Convention, adopted on 9 December 1999 by the **United Nations General Assembly** (A/RES/54/109) entered into force on 10 April 2002. By the middle of 2003, it had been ratified by 76 States. The main purpose of the Convention is to mobilize States Parties to take concrete measures at national level and to improve international coordination in order to stop the financing of terrorist activities and prosecute those involved in this practice.

International Convention on the Elimination of All Forms of Racial Discrimination (UN)

The International Convention on the Elimination of All Forms of Racial Discrimination was adopted by the **United Nations General Assembly** on 21 December 1965 by resolution 2106(XX), and entered into force on 4 January 1969. By the middle of 2003, it had been ratified by about 160 States. The Convention defines "racial **discrimination**" as "any distinction, exclusion, restriction or preference based on race, colour, descent, or national or ethnic origin which has the purpose or effect of nullifying or impairing the recognition, enjoyment or exercise, on an equal footing, of human rights and fundamental freedoms in the political, economic, social, cultural or any other field of public life" (Article 1). States Parties undertake "to pursue by all appropriate means and without delay a policy of eliminating racial discrimination in all its forms" and, in particular, "to undertake to amend, rescind or nullify any laws and regulations which have the effect of creating or perpetuating racial discrimination" and "to prohibit and bring to an end, by all appropriate means, including legislation as required by circumstances, racial discrimination by any persons, group or organization" (Article 2). States Parties have further undertaken to adopt measures in the field of teaching, education, culture and information with a view to combating prejudices which lead to racial discrimination (Article 7). The Convention enumerates rights and freedoms to be guaranteed for everyone on the principle of equality and without discrimination. The list contains the **civil, political, economic, social** and **cultural rights** embodied in the **Universal Declaration of Human Rights**, as well as other rights, such as the right of access to any place or service intended for use by the general public, such as transport, hotels, restaurants, cafes, theatres and parks (Article 5). In addition, the Convention opens the possibility of special measures to ensure the advancement of certain racial or ethnic groups (Article 1). The Convention provides for the establishment of a **Committee on the Elimination of All Forms of Racial Discrimination (CERD)** (Article 8) to monitor its implementation and receive and consider communications from individuals or groups of individuals claiming to be victims of a violation of any of the rights set forth in the Convention (Article 14).

International Convention on the Protection of the Rights of All Migrant Workers and Members of Their Families (UN)

In an attempt to prevent and eliminate clandestine movements and trafficking in **migrant workers** and, at the same time, assure the protection of their fundamental human rights, the **United Nations General Assembly**, by its resolution 45/158, adopted on 18 December 1990 the International Convention on the Protection of the Rights of All Migrant Workers and Members of Their Families. This Convention entered into force on 1 July 2003. For the purposes of the instrument, a "migrant worker" is "a person who is to be engaged, is engaged, or has been engaged in a remunerated activity in a State of which he or she is not a national" (Article 2). The Convention establishes, in a number of areas, the principle of equality of treatment with nationals for all migrant workers and members of their families, irrespective of whether they are in a regular or irregular situation. This principle is applicable in areas such as the right to leave any State, including their State of origin (Article 8), the treatment of migrant workers before courts and tribunals (Article 18), their terms of employment (Article 25), access to education for their children (Article 30) and respect for their cultural identity (Article 31). Other provisions deal with rights of migrant workers and members of their families who are documented or in a regular situation (Part IV). In accordance with the Convention, both sending States and States of employment are encouraged to establish procedures or institutions through which account may be taken of special needs of migrants (Article 42). It further stipulates that a State may not expel migrant workers or members of their families except for reasons defined in the national legislation of that State, and subject to the safeguards established in Article 56. For the purposes of monitoring its implementation, the Convention foresees the establishment of a **Committee on the Protection of the Rights of All Migrant Workers and Members of Their Families** (Article 72). Among intergovernmental organizations and bodies committed to solving problems posed by migration, the **International Organization for Migration (IOM)**, situated in Geneva, is one of the most active.

International Convention on the Suppression and Punishment of the Crime of Apartheid (UN)

This Convention was adopted by the **United Nations General Assembly** on 30 November 1973 by resolution 3068 (XXVIII). It entered into force on 18 July 1976 and had been ratified by the middle of 2003 by more than 100 States. The Convention defines the "crime of apartheid" as inhuman acts committed for the purpose of establishing and maintaining domination by one racial group of persons over any other racial group of persons and systematically oppressing them (Article I). Among the inhuman acts mentioned is the denial to a member or members of a racial group or groups of the **right to life** and liberty of person (Article II). States Parties to this Convention declare that **apartheid** is a crime against humanity and that inhuman acts resulting from the policies and practices of apartheid and similar policies and practices of racial segregation and discrimination are crimes violating the principles of international law, in particular the purposes and principles of the **United Nations Charter** (Article I). Such acts include: murder; infliction of serious bodily or mental harm; arbitrary arrest and illegal imprisonment; and deliberate imposition of living conditions calculated to cause physical destruction (Article II). States Parties further declare criminal "organizations, institutions and individuals committing the crime of apartheid" (Article I). According to Article V, persons charged with the acts enumerated in Article II may be tried by a competent tribunal of any State Party to the Convention which might acquire jurisdiction over the accused, or by an international penal tribunal. The Convention also envisages a monitoring system, pursuant to which States Parties submit periodic reports on the measures they have adopted to give effect to the provisions of the Convention (Article VII). These reports were examined by a group comprised of three members of the **Commission on Human Rights** (Article IX).

International Court of Justice – ICJ (UN)

The International Court of Justice (ICJ) is the principal judicial organ of the **United Nations**. All Members of the United Nations are *ipso facto* parties to the Statute of the International Court of Justice which is an integral part of the **United Nations Charter**. Member States have an obligation "... to comply with the decision of the International Court of Justice in any case to which [they are] a party" (Article 94 of the Charter). The Court consists of 15 members, no two of whom may be a national of the same State. Members are elected by the **United Nations General Assembly** and the **Security Council** for nine years, and may be re-elected (Article 3 of the Statute). According to Article 35 of the Statute, only States may be parties in cases before the Court. The Court, however, may be requested by the United Nations General Assembly, by the Security Council and by other organs authorized by the General Assembly, to give an advisory opinion on legal questions (Article 96 of the Charter). The International Court of Justice has thus had occasion to make important pronouncements on questions of human rights, in particular on the right of asylum, the rights of aliens, the rights of the child and reservations concerning the **Convention on the Prevention and Punishment of the Crime of Genocide**. Due to the fact that a great number of United Nations human rights instruments contain provisions whereby any dispute between the States Parties relating to the interpretation, application or fulfillment of the instrument may be submitted to the ICJ, the Court has been involved in contentious cases with regard to human rights.

For more information see: http://www.icj-cij.org

International Covenant on Civil and Political Rights (UN)

By its resolution 2200A (XXI) of 16 December 1966, the **United Nations General Assembly** adopted and opened for signature, ratification and accession the **International Covenant on Civil and Political Rights**. It entered into force on 23 March 1976 and had been ratified by 149 States by June 2003. This Covenant and the **International Covenant on Economic, Social and Cultural Rights** are the first all-embracing, legally binding international instruments in the field of human rights and, together with the **Universal Declaration of Human Rights**, form the core of the **International Bill of Human Rights**.

Article 1 of the Covenant reaffirms the principle that the **right of self-determination** is universal, and calls upon all States to undertake two obligations: to promote the realization of the right of self-determination in all their territories, and to respect that right. Under Article 3, States Parties undertake to reaffirm the principle of equality of men and women as regards human rights, and to make this principle a reality. The Covenant elaborates further the civil and **political rights** and freedoms identified in the **Universal Declaration of Human Rights** which include: the **right to life** (Article 6); the right to privacy (Article 17); the **right to a fair trial** (Article 2); freedom of expression (Article 19); freedom of religion (Article 18); freedom from torture (Article 7); equality before the law (Article 16) etc. Moreover, the Covenant defines the admissible limitations or restrictions on the rights which it sets forth. It provides that the rights and freedoms with which it deals should not be subject to any restriction except those which are provided by law, are necessary to protect national security, public order, public health or morals or the rights and freedoms of others (Article 22). In no circumstances is derogation permitted if it involves **discrimination** on grounds of race, colour, sex, language, religion or social origin or if it involves the following fundamental rights: the right to life, **freedom of thought, conscience and religion**; the right not to be imprisoned solely for inability to fulfil a contractual obligation; and the right not to be held guilty for committing a crime which did not constitute a criminal offence at the time it was committed. The Covenant is legally binding. States are thus obliged to respect the procedures for its implementation, including the submission of periodic reports on their compliance with their obligations under the Covenant. The implementation of the instrument is monitored by the **Human Rights Committee** established under Article 28 of the Covenant.

International Covenant on Economic, Social and Cultural Rights (UN)

The **United Nations General Assembly** adopted the International Covenant on Economic, Social and Cultural Rights on 16 December 1966. It entered into force on 3 January 1976 and had been ratified by 146 States by June 2003. This International Covenant and the **International Covenant on Civil and Political Rights** are the first all-embracing, legally binding international instruments in the field of human rights and, together with the **Universal Declaration of Human Rights**, form the core of the **International Bill of Human Rights**.

Article 1 of the Covenant reaffirms that the **right of self-determination** is universal, and calls upon all States to undertake to promote the realization of the right of self-determination in all their territories, and to respect that right in other States. Under Article 3, States Parties undertake to reaffirm the principle of equality of men and women as regards human rights, and to make that principle a reality. The rights recognized by the Covenant include the **rights: to work** (Article 7), **to form** and join **trade unions** (Article 8), **to social security** (Article 9), **to an adequate standard of living** including adequate food, clothing and housing (Article 11), **to protection of the family** (Article 10), **to the highest attainable standard of physical and mental health** (Article 12), **to education** (Article 13), and **to participation in cultural life** (Article 15). Each Contracting State agrees to take steps "to the maximum of its available resources, with a view to achieving progressively the full realization of the rights recognized" in the Covenant (Article 2). None of the rights protected under the Covenant may be suspended. The body which oversees the implementation of the instrument is the **Committee on Economic, Social and Cultural Rights**, which was established by the **Economic and Social Council (ECOSOC)** in 1985.

International Covenants on Human Rights (UN)

The International Covenants on Human Rights – the **International Covenant on Civil and Political Rights** and the **International Covenant on Economic, Social and Cultural Rights** – were both adopted on 16 December 1966 by the **United Nations General Assembly** and entered into force respectively on 23 March 1976 and 3 January 1976. The Covenants are all-embracing and legally binding international instruments in the field of human rights and, together with the **Universal Declaration of Human Rights**, form the core of the **International Bill of Human Rights**. The United Nations General Assembly appeals to all States to become Parties to the International Covenants, emphasizes the importance of its strictest compliance by States Parties, and urges States to make the provisions of the International Covenants known to the general public by disseminating their texts in as many languages as possible. The **Optional Protocol to the International Covenant on Civil and**

Political Rights (which also entered into force on 23 March 1976) envisages the competence of the **Human Rights Committee** to consider communications concerning alleged violations of human rights. The **Second Optional Protocol to the International Covenant on Civil and Political Rights, aiming at the abolition of the death penalty** entered into force on 11 July 1991.

International Criminal Court – ICC (UN)

The International Criminal Court (ICC) was established by the **Rome Statute of the International Criminal Court** adopted on 17 July 1998 by the United Nations Diplomatic Conference of Plenipotentiaries on the Establishment of an International Criminal Court in which representatives of 120 States participated. The Statute entered into force on 1 July 2002. By the middle of 2003, it had been ratified by 91 States.

The Statute, which comprises 128 Articles divided into 12 Parts, defines the jurisdiction of the Court, its structure and its functions. According to Article 5 of the Statute, four categories of crimes fall under the Court jurisdiction: **genocide**; crimes against humanity; war crimes and aggression. The jurisdiction of the Court extends over both international and internal conflicts and "shall be limited to the most serious crimes of concern to the international community as a whole" (Article 5). It applies only to crimes committed after the entry into force of the Statute.

Part 4 of the Statute concerns the composition and administration of the Court. Its four organs are: the Presidency; the Judiciary; the Office of the Prosecutor and the Registry. The Presidency is composed of the President and First and Second Vice-Presidents, all of whom are elected by an absolute majority of judges for a term of three years (once-renewable) or until the end of their respective terms of office as judges (whichever expires earlier). The Presidency is responsible for the proper administration of the Court excluding the Office of the Prosecutor. The Judiciary, composed of three divisions – a Pre-Trial Division, a Trial Division and an Appeals Division – is responsible for carrying out the judicial functions of the Court. The Office of the Prosecutor is an independent organ of the Court, headed by the Prosecutor who has full authority over the management and administration of the Office, including the staff, facilities and other resources. Cases can be initiated by the Prosecutor following recommendations from a State, the United Nations **Security Council**, an individual, or a **non-governmental organization** on the basis of information received from reliable and credible sources. Vesting the Prosecutor with the full authority to initiate prosecutions free of political interference is central to the establishment of a fair and effective permanent court, and hence to its legitimacy. The Prosecutor is elected by secret ballot by an absolute majority of the members of the Assembly of States Parties for a nine-year term, which is non-renewable. The Registry is responsible for the non-judicial aspects of the administration and servicing of the Court.

Part 5 of the Statute concerns investigation and prosecution and the various duties of the organs of the Court in these processes. Details of the trial set out in Part 6 and Part 7 concern penalties. The maximum penalty is life imprisonment, which is reserved for the most extreme cases. Prison sentences will be served in a State designated by the Court from a list of States which have indicated to the Court their willingness to accept sentenced persons (Article 103). The Court may also impose a fine under the criteria provided for in the rules of Procedure and Evidence or a forfeiture of proceeds, property and assets derived directly or indirectly from that crime. The Statute contains comprehensive measures to ensure confidentiality of sources, witness protection, as well as restitution, compensation and rehabilitation for victims (Article 68). The Statute also provides for the creation of a Victims and Witness Unit (Article 43, paragraph 6). Concerning the offender, the Statute guarantees his/her **right to a fair trial** at every stage of the process, as well as genuine measures aimed at his/her rehabilitation.

Eighteen judges are elected as full-time members of the Court. They shall have 'established competence in criminal law and procedure' or 'established competence in relevant areas of international law such as **international humanitarian law** and the law of human rights' (Article 36, paragraph 3). Judges are elected by secret ballot at a meeting of the Assembly of States Parties. No two judges may be nationals of the same State (Article 36, paragraph 7). The States Parties shall, in the selection of judges, take into account the need within the membership of the Court for: the representation of the principal legal systems of the world; equitable geographical representation and a fair representation of female and male judges (Article 36, paragraph 8). The first 18 judges (7 are women) were elected at the resumed first session of the Assembly of States Parties to the Rome Statute which was held from 3 to 10 September 2002. The Assembly also determined the term of office of the judges: six will serve a full term of nine years, six a term of six years and six a term of three years. The ICC is based in The Hague, the Netherlands.

For more information see: http://www.un.org/law/icc

International Criminal Tribunals (UN)

International Criminal Tribunals were established for the prosecution of persons responsible for grave breaches of the **Geneva Conventions** of 1949 (willful killing, torture, taking of hostages, unlawful deportation, etc.), violations of the laws or customs of war, **genocide** and other crimes against humanity. In 1993, the **Security Council** decided by its resolutions 808 and 827 that such a body shall first be established for the prosecution of persons responsible for "serious violations of **international humanitarian law** committed in the territory of the former Yugoslavia since 1991". The **International Criminal Tribunal for the Former Yugoslavia (ICTY)** must submit an annual report on its activities to the Security Council and the **United Nations General Assembly**. All Member States of the **United Nations** are obliged to cooperate with it. By resolution 955 (1994), the Security

Council then established an **International Criminal Tribunal for Rwanda (ICTR)** to prosecute persons responsible for genocide and other serious violations of international humanitarian law committed on the territory of Rwanda and Rwandan citizens responsible for genocide and other such violations committed on the territory of neighbouring States.

International Criminal Tribunal for Rwanda – ICTR (UN)

The International Criminal Tribunal for Rwanda (ICTR) was established by the **Security Council** of the **United Nations** by its resolution 955 in November 1994 as an enforcement measure under Chapter VII of the **United Nations Charter**, eighteen months after the **International Criminal Tribunal for the former Yugoslavia (ICTY)** had been established. The first phase of the establishment included appointing the Deputy Prosecutor and setting up a core unit of investigators, prosecutors and interpreters. Its seat is in Arusha, Tanzania. In the second phase, judges were elected; practical arrangements for the establishment of the seat were put in place; the staffing was completed; and the Tribunal as a whole became fully operational. Like the ICTY, the ICTR is an *ad hoc* and non-military Tribunal and a subsidiary organ of the Security Council. The ICTR adopted a similar legal approach to that of the ICTY. The six Trial Chamber Judges were elected in June 1995. Both Tribunals share the same Appeals Chamber, whose five judges were elected contemporaneously with the ICTY Trial Chamber Judges, and both have the same Chief Prosecutor. Furthermore, they both have limited temporal and territorial jurisdiction. The ICTR has the mandate to prosecute crimes committed between 1 January and 31 December 1994. Its territorial jurisdiction extends beyond the territory of Rwanda to that of neighbouring States, in respect of serious violations of **international humanitarian law** committed by Rwandan citizens beyond their State's territorial bounds. According to its Statute, the ICTR's jurisdiction applies only to internal armed conflicts and to individuals, but not organizations or States. Like the ICTY, the ICTR applies the principle of *non bis in idem* which rules out prosecution of persons in the domestic criminal justice system of Rwanda who have already been tried by the International Tribunal. Furthermore, it requires the cooperation of States in the investigation and the prosecution of persons accused of committing serious violations of international humanitarian law. The maximum penalty which can be imposed by the ICTR is life imprisonment.

Since 1995 when the ICTR started its work, it has secured the arrest of over 60 individuals accused of involvement in the 1994 genocide and has pioneered advocacy for victim-oriented, restitutive justice (which includes legal guidance, psychological counselling and medical care) in international criminal tribunals – a concept now included in the Statute of the **International Criminal Court**.

For more information see: http://www.ictr.org

International Criminal Tribunal for the former Yugoslavia – ICTY (UN)

This body was established in 1993 by resolutions 808 and 827 of the **Security Council** of the **United Nations**, under Chapter VII of the **Charter of the United Nations**. According to the Statute of the International Tribunal, adopted on 25 May 1993 and amended on 13 May 1998, its purpose is to prosecute persons responsible for serious violations of **international humanitarian law** committed on the territory of the former Yugoslavia since 1991 (Article 1). Articles 2 to 5 of the Statute define the crimes punishable by the International Tribunal. They include serious breaches of the **Geneva Conventions** of 1949 (willful killing, torture, taking civilians as hostages, unlawful deportation, etc.); violations of the laws or customs of war (use of weapons calculated to cause unnecessary suffering, wanton destruction of cities, towns or villages, etc.); and **genocide**, as defined by the **Convention on the Prevention and Punishment of the Crime of Genocide**, and crimes against humanity. The International

Tribunal has jurisdiction over natural persons "... who planned, instigated, ordered, committed or otherwise aided and abetted in the planning, preparation or execution of a crime referred to in Articles 2 to 5 ..." (Article 7). The International Tribunal comprises eleven independent judges elected for a term of four years by the **United Nations General Assembly** from a list submitted by the Security Council, and a Prosecutor nominated by the Security Council. An accused person enjoys all the guarantees of a fair trial and an appeal. The maximum penalty which can be imposed by the ICTY is life imprisonment, to be served in a State designated by it from a list of States which have indicated to the Security Council their willingness to accept convicted persons. The International Criminal Tribunal for the Former Yugoslavia has its seat in The Hague.

For more information see: http://www.un.org/icty

International Day against Drug Abuse and Illicit Trafficking – 26 June (UN)

In 1987, the **United Nations General Assembly** decided to observe 26 June as the International Day against Drug Abuse and Illicit Trafficking as an expression of its determination to strengthen action and cooperation to achieve the goal of an international society free of drug abuse. This Day commemorates the adoption by the International Conference on Drug Abuse and Illicit Trafficking on 26 June 1987 of the Comprehensive Multidisciplinary Outline of Future Activities in Drug Abuse Control. The General Assembly also proclaimed the years 1991-2000 as the **United Nations Decade against Drug Abuse**.

International Day for the Abolition of Slavery – 2 December (UN)

This Day recalls the date of the adoption by the **United Nations General Assembly** of the **Convention for the Suppression of Traffic in Persons and the Exploitation of the**

Prostitution of Others (1949). In 1999, the **United Nations Secretary-General** in his message on the occasion of the Day remarked that: "... there is an urgent need for laws and actions to ensure that new forms of exploitation and oppression are not allowed to occur, and that old forms of **slavery** are eradicated, once and for all" (SG/SM/7242). The **International Day for the Rememberance of the Slave Trade and its Abolition**, proclaimed by **UNESCO**, is observed every year on 23 August.

International Day for the Elimination of Racial Discrimination – 21 March (UN)

The **United Nations General Assembly** proclaimed in 1966, by its resolution 2142 (XXI), 21 March as the International Day for the Elimination of Racial Discrimination and called upon the international community to redouble its efforts to eliminate all forms of racial **discrimination**. The date selected for annual observance commemorates the anniversary of the Sharpeville massacre which occurred on 21 March 1960 when 69 peaceful demonstrators against the **apartheid** "pass laws" were fired upon and killed on the orders of the South African regime of that time. This tragedy focused the attention of the world upon the inherent dangers of racial discrimination, segregation and apartheid, and upon the evils of the philosophy of racial superiority often invoked to support such policies. Since 1967, International Day for the Elimination of Racial Discrimination has been observed each year. The activities, linked with its observance have contributed to the reaffirmation of the need to put an end to racial discrimination, segregation and apartheid, and to the mobilization of public opinion to reach these goals. Since 2003 the Day is also observed at **UNESCO** Headquarters and a special message is issued by the Director-General of UNESCO.

International Day for the Elimination of Violence against Women – 25 November (UN)

On 17 December 1999 The **United Nations General Assembly** (A/RES/54/134) designated 25 November as the International Day for the Elimination of Violence against Women. It invited governments, international and **non-governmental organizations** to organize on that date activities designed to raise public awareness of the problem. Women's activists have marked this day as a day against violence since 1981. The date commemorates the brutal assassination in 1961 of three women political activists in the Dominican Republic, on the order of Rafael Trujillo, the dictatorial ruler of the country at that time.

International Day for the Eradication of Poverty – 17 October (UN)

On 22 December 1992, the **United Nations General Assembly** acknowledging the fact that certain **non-governmental organizations**, on the initiative of the French-based International Movement ATD Fourth World, had in many States observed 17 October as a World Day for Overcoming **Extreme Poverty**, declared that date as the **International Day for the Eradication of Poverty** from 1993 onwards (A/RES/47/196). The observance of the Day aims to promote public awareness of the need to eradicate **poverty** and destitution in all countries – a need which became a priority of development in the 1990s. All States were invited, with the assistance of international governmental organizations and non-governmental organizations, to devote the Day to concrete activities on the eradication of poverty.

International Day for the Remembrance of the Slave Trade and Its Abolition – 23 August (UNESCO)

The Executive Board of **UNESCO** at its 150th session in 1996 noted with interest the support expressed by the **Organization of African Unity (OAU)** for UNESCO's **Slave Route Project** and adopted a decision to observe the International Day for the Remembrance of the Slave Trade and its Abolition on 23 August each year. On this day in 1791, the slaves of the island of Santo Domingo rose in rebellion. This marked the start of the process which led to the abolition of the slave trade. In this manner, UNESCO wishes to inscribe in the memory of all peoples a tragedy that must be remembered, and to pay tribute to the slaves' relentless struggle for freedom.

International Day for Tolerance – 16 November (UN/UNESCO)

On 16 November 1995, the General Conference of **UNESCO** adapted and proclaimed the **Declaration of Principles on Tolerance** and Follow-up Plan of Action for the United Nations Year for Tolerance. Article 6 of the Declaration proclaims 16 November the International Day for Tolerance. It states that "in order to generate public awareness, emphasize the dangers of intolerance and react with renewed commitment and action in support of tolerance promotion and education, we solemnly proclaim 16 November the annual International Day for Tolerance". This day, the anniversary of the signing of the UNESCO Constitution, serves as an annual occasion for discussion of tolerance issues and for related special events, both in educational institutions and among the wider public, in cooperation with the media. On 12 December 1996, the **United Nations General Assembly** adopted resolution 51/95 entitled "Follow-up to the **International Year for Tolerance (1995)**". After recalling that the **Charter of the United Nations** affirms in its Preamble that "to practice tolerance is one of the principles to be applied to attain the ends pursued by the **United Nations** of preventing war and maintaining peace" and reconfirming that "tolerance is the foundation of any civil society and of peace", the resolution invites Member States to observe the International Day for Tolerance annually on 16 November with appropriate activities directed towards both educational establishments and the wider public (para. 6). It also recommends that interested intergovernmental and **non-governmental organizations** and specialized agencies exert efforts in their respective fields to contribute to the long-term follow-up programme for the International Year for Tolerance, including celebration of the International Day for Tolerance, and to consider what further contributions they can make to implement and disseminate the standards affirmed in the Declaration of Principles on Tolerance (para. 8).

International Day in Support of Victims of Torture – 26 June (UN)

The **Universal Declaration of Human Rights**, in its Article 5, proclaims that "No one shall be subjected to torture or to cruel, inhuman or degrading treatment or punishment". The **Convention against Torture and Other Cruel, Inhuman or Degrading Treatment or Punishment**, adopted by the **United Nations General Assembly** (A/RES/39/46) in 1984, urges States to make torture a crime and to prosecute and punish those guilty of it. Bearing in mind that torture is one of the most serious abuses of human rights, the General Assembly (A/RES/52/149) declared 26 June as International Day in Support of Victims of Torture. The observance of the Day aims to focus on helping torture victims and on ending torture. The **United Nations** Voluntary Fund for Victims of Torture, created in 1981, supports financially over 100 programmes treating torture victims in more than 50 countries, giving priority to those providing direct medical or psychological assistance to torture victims. In 2002 over 80,000 victims had been assisted through the fund.

International Day of Disabled Persons
– 3 December (UN)

Noting the importance of developing and carrying out concrete long-term strategies for full implementation of the World Programme of Action of the **United Nations Decade of Disabled Persons** beyond the year 2002, the **United Nations General Assembly** (A/RES/47/3 of 14 October 1992) proclaimed 3 December as the International Day of Disabled Persons. In this resolution, the General Assembly appealed to Member States to highlight the observance of the International Day in order to further integrate people with disabilities into society. Similarly, it invited all Member States and organizations concerned to intensify their awareness-raising and action-oriented measures aimed at the continued improvement of the situation of persons with disabilities and the equalization of opportunities for them.

International Day of Families
– 15 May (UN)

On 20 September 1993, the **United Nations General Assembly** decided that, beginning in 1994 – the **International Year of the Family** – 15 May of every year shall be observed as the International Day of Families. The Day and the Year have the objective of increasing awareness of family issues and improving the capability of nations to tackle family-related problems with comprehensive policies.

International Day of
Innocent Children Victims of Aggression
– 4 June (UN)

On 19 August 1982, at its emergency special session on the question of Palestine, the **United Nations General Assembly**, "… appalled at the great number of innocent Palestinian and Lebanese children victims of Israel's acts of aggression", decided by its resolution ES-7/8 to commemorate 4 June each year as the International Day of Innocent Children Victims of Aggression.

International Day of Older Persons (UN)

On 14 December 1990 The **General Assembly** (resolution 45/106) designated the International Day of Older Persons, which was observed for the first time on 1 October 1991. By designating a special day for older persons, the Assembly is ensuring follow-up to the **Vienna Plan of Action on Ageing** adopted by the 1982 **World Assembly on Ageing** and the **United Nations Principles for Older Persons**. It is giving recognition to the contributions to development made by older persons and is also drawing attention to the necessity to protect their rights, especially when the ageing of the population became a global demographic phenomenon.

International Day of Peace
– 3rd Tuesday of September (UN)

The initiative to proclaim an International Day of Peace was taken by the International Association of University Presidents in July 1981. Reacting to this initiative, the **United Nations General Assembly** (A/RES/36/67) declared in 1981 that the third Tuesday of September (the opening day of its regular session) shall "be officially dedicated and observed as the International Day of Peace and shall be devoted to commemorating and strengthening the ideals of peace both within and among all nations and peoples" (para. 2). The resolution invited all Member States, organs and organizations of the **United Nations system**, regional organizations, **non-governmental organizations**, peoples and individuals "to commemorate in an appropriate manner the International Day of Peace, especially through all means of education, and to cooperate with the **United Nations** observance of that Day" (para. 3).

International Day of Solidarity with the Palestinian People – 29 November (UN)

In 1997, the **United Nations General Assembly** called for the annual observance of 29 November as the International Day of Solidarity with the Palestinian People, as on that day in 1947, the General Assembly had adopted the resolution on the partition of Palestine. On 1 December 1999, the General Assembly reaffirmed that the **United Nations** had a permanent responsibility with respect to the question of Palestine until it was resolved in a satisfactory manner in accordance with international legitimacy.

International Day of the World's Indigenous People – 9 August (UN)

On 23 December 1994, the **United Nations General Assembly** designated 9 August to be observed every year as the International Day of the World's Indigenous People. This date marks the anniversary of the first day of the 1992 meeting of the Working Group on Indigenous Populations of the **Sub-Commission on Prevention of Discrimination and Protection of Minorities** (now the **Sub-Commission on the Promotion and Protection of Human Rights**) of the **United Nations**. It followed upon the proclamation of 1993 as the **International Year of the World's Indigenous People** and of the decade 1994-2004 as the **International Decade of the World's Indigenous People**. The aim is to increase and deepen the awareness of respect for the inherent dignity and rights of **indigenous people**. The main objectives are: to further promote the growing global cooperation among the indigenous peoples of the world and between non-indigenous peoples and indigenous peoples to resolve shared problems and obstacles to self-determination, growth and development; to increase and deepen understanding of the roles and responsibilities of everyone towards preserving, protecting and developing indigenous culture, intellectual properties and knowledge; and to provide venues and opportunities for the various indigenous peoples to know each other, to share their challenges and learn from each other's experiences in dealing with their local problems. The **Permanent Forum on Indigenous Issues** was established in July 2000.

International Decade for a Culture of Peace and Non-violence for the Children of the World – 2001-10 (UN)

Following the proclamation of the **International Year for the Culture of Peace (2000)**, the **United Nations General Assembly** (A/RES/53/25) decided on 10 November 1998, to proclaim the period 2001-10 as the International Decade for a Culture of Peace and Non-Violence for the Children of the World. Member States are invited to take the necessary steps to ensure that the practice of peace and non-violence is taught at all levels in their respective societies, including in educational institutions. The General Assembly called upon the relevant United Nations bodies, in particular **UNESCO** and **UNICEF**, to support the Decade for the benefit of every child of the world. The same appeal was addressed to **non-governmental organizations**, religious bodies and groups, educational institutions, artists, and the media. The resolution underlined that the actions linked to the Decade should contribute to the promotion of a culture of peace based on the principles established in the **Charter of the United Nations** and on respect for human rights, democracy and tolerance, and to the promotion of development, education for peace, the free flow of information, the wider participation of women, and integral approach to preventing violence and conflicts.

International Decade for the Eradication of Colonialism – 1990-2000 (UN)

In 1988, the **United Nations General Assembly** (A/RES/43/47) declared the decade 1990-2000 as the International Decade for the Eradication of Colonialism. In 1991, it declared that the ultimate goal of the Decade was the free exercise of the **right of self-determination** by the peoples of each of the remaining Non-Self-Governing Territories. In endorsing the Plan of Action for the Decade, the General Assembly invited Member States, the **United Nations system**, governmental and **non-governmental organizations** to support and participate in implementing the Plan.

International Decade of the World's Indigenous People – 1995-2004 (UN)

The **International Year of the World's Indigenous People – 1993** raised international awareness about the contribution of and problems faced by **indigenous people** throughout the world. The **United Nations General Assembly**, on 21 December 1993, recognizing the need to build on the results and lessons of the Year, proclaimed the International Decade of the World's Indigenous People and adopted a Programme of Action for the Decade. It also decided that, beginning with the first year of the Decade, one day was to be observed as the **International Day of the World's Indigenous People** (9 August was subsequently selected). The Decade, which has the theme "Indigenous people: partnership in action", was introduced with a view to strengthening international cooperation for the solution to problems faced by indigenous people in such areas as human rights, the environment, development, education and health. To achieve this goal, relevant **United Nations specialized agencies**, organs and programmes were urged, in planning activities for the Decade, to examine how existing programmes and resources might be utilized to benefit indigenous people more effectively, including through the exploration of ways in which their perspectives and activities could be included or enhanced. Similarly, Governments were asked to ensure that activities and objectives for the Decade were planned and implemented on the basis of full consultation and collaboration with indigenous people. The **Permanent Forum on Indigenous Issues** was established in July 2000 by the **Economic and Social Council** resolution 2000/22. The creation of this body was one of the central objectives of the programme of activities for the Decade.

International humanitarian law

International humanitarian law is a set of rules which seek, for humanitarian reasons, to limit the effects of armed conflict. International humanitarian law covers two areas. First, it protects persons who are not participating in the hostilities, such as civilians and medical and religious military personnel, or who have ceased to take part in the fighting, such as wounded, shipwrecked and sick combatants, and prisoners of war. Second, it imposes restrictions on the means of warfare, in particular weapons, and the methods of warfare. International humanitarian law is also known as the law of war or the law of armed conflict. It should be observed not only by States and their armed forces, but also by armed opposition groups and any other parties to a conflict.

The four **Geneva Conventions** of 1949 and the **Protocols Additional to the Geneva Conventions of 12 August 1949, and relating to the Protection of Victims of International Armed Conflicts (Protocol I) and Victims of Non-International Armed Conflicts (Protocol II)** are the principal instruments of humanitarian law. Other international treaties include the **Convention for the Protection of Cultural Property in the Event of Armed Conflict** (1954) and its two Protocols; the Convention on the Prohibition of the Development, Production and Stockpiling of Bacteriological (Biological) and Toxin Weapons and on their Destruction (1972), also known as the Biological Weapons Convention (BWC); the Convention on Prohibitions or Restrictions on the Use of Certain Conventional Weapons which may be deemed to be Excessively Injurious or to have Indiscriminate Effects (1980) and its four Protocols, also known as the Conventional Weapons Convention (CCW); the Convention on the Prohibition of the Development, Production, Stockpiling and Use of Chemical Weapons and on their Destruction (1993), also known as the Chemical Weapons Convention (CWC); and the Convention on the Prohibition of the Use, Stockpiling, Production and Transfer of Anti-Personnel Mines and on their Destruction (1997), also known as the Ottawa Convention. Many provisions of international humanitarian law are now accepted as customary law, that is, as norms binding upon all States.

States have a duty to take legal and practical measures, both in peacetime and in armed conflict, aimed at ensuring full compliance with international humanitarian law, including the translation of international humanitarian law treaties and their dissemination, especially among military personnel but also among the civilian population at large and the prevention and punishment of war crimes, through the enactment of penal legislation.

The **International Committee of the Red Cross (ICRC)** has a specific mandate in implementing international humanitarian law, entrusted to it under the Geneva Conventions and their Additional Protocols.

The **International Criminal Tribunal for the former Yugoslavia (ICTY)**, the **International Criminal Tribunal for Rwanda (ICTR)** as well as the **International Criminal Court (ICC)**, have jurisdiction over serious violations of both international human rights law and international humanitarian law.

International humanitarian law and international human rights law are complementary since they both seek to protect the life, health and dignity of the individual. However, these two bodies of law have developed separately and are contained in different treaties with a different system of implementation. International humanitarian law applies in situations of armed conflict and deals with many issues that are outside the purview of international human rights law, such as the conduct of hostilities, combatant and prisoner of war status and the protection of the Red Cross emblems. International human rights law protects the individual at all times, both in peacetime and in situations of armed conflict (with the exception of certain rights that are derogable in situations of public emergency).

International Labour Organization – ILO

The International Labour Organization (ILO) was established on 11 April 1919 after the end of the First World War, its Constitution becoming part of the Treaty of Versailles. On 10 May 1944 the ILO adopted the Declaration of Philadelphia, whose text was annexed to its Constitution in 1946. It reaffirms the fundamental principles upon which the ILO is based, in particular that: "… labour is not a commodity; freedom of expression and of association are essential to sustained progress; **poverty** anywhere constitutes a danger to prosperity everywhere; the war against want requires to be carried on with unrelenting vigour within each nation, and by continuous and concerted international efforts in which the representatives of workers and employers, enjoying equal status with those of governments, join with them in free discussion and democratic decision with a view to the promotion of the common welfare" (Article I).

On 2 October 1946, ILO became the first **United Nations** specialized agency. Within the **United Nations system**, it has a unique tripartite structure with workers and employers representatives participating as equal partners with governments in its governing organs. The International Labour Conference (the main body of the ILO) establishes, supervises and assists Governments in the implementation of international labour standards. Such standards, in the form of conventions and/or recommendations, are concerned with rights, such as the **right to**

form trade unions and join the trade union of one's choice, **freedom of association**, abolition of forced labour, freedom from **discrimination** in employment and occupation. The ILO also deals with questions concerning conditions of work and occupational safety and health, as well as with child labour. These questions correspond to provisions of both the **International Covenant on Economic, Social and Cultural Rights** and the **Covenant on Civil and Political Rights** and also develop many of the principles in other human rights instruments.

The ILO is recognized as one of the most active **United Nations specialized agencies** in the field of human rights both for its standard-setting activities and for measures to monitor their implementation. It has established **supervisory procedures** in addition to its regular supervision.

For more information see: http://www.ilo.org

International Literacy Day
– 8 September (UNESCO)

Pursuant to its Constitution, popular education is among the main priorities of **UNESCO**. In 1966, The Organization proclaimed 8 September as the International Literacy Day following the recommendation made by the World Conference of Ministers of Education on the Eradication of Illiteracy (Tehran, September 1965). The Day aims at sensitizing and mobilizing international public opinion to develop formal and non-formal learning programmes, which are essential to ensure the **right to education for all**, as recognized by Article 26 of the **Universal Declaration of Human Rights**. As stated in UNESCO's World Education Report 2000 – The **Right to Education**: Towards Education for All Throughout Life, there are more than 800 million illiterate adults in the world today, and nearly 100 million children of primary school age (and an even larger number of children of secondary school age) who are not in school. UNESCO helps its Member States to identify and meet their needs and aspirations in the field of education. In December 2001 the **United Nations General Assembly** (A/RES/56/116) proclaimed the period 2003-2012 as the **United Nations Literacy Decade.**

International Literacy Year – 1990 (UN)

Following the recommendation of the **Economic and Social Council (ECOSOC),** the **United Nations General Assembly** (A/RES/42/104) on 7 December 1987 proclaimed 1990 International Literacy Year. The objective of the Year was to further sensitize the international community regarding the various aspects of illiteracy and to encourage concrete action in favour of its elimination, bearing in mind the necessity to ensure the **right to education.** The General Assembly recognized that education can contribute greatly to achieving economic and social development. As requested by the General Assembly, **UNESCO** assumed the role of lead agency for the Year.

International Organization for Migration – IOM

At the initiative of Belgium and the United States of America, an International Migration Conference was convened in Brussels in 1951. It resulted in the creation of the Provisional Intergovernmental Committee for the Movements of Migrants from Europe (PICMME) which, in 1953, became the Intergovernmental Committee for European Migration (ICEM). In 1980, the Council of ICEM changed its name to the Intergovernmental Committee for Migration (ICM) in recognition of its increasing global role. Finally, in 1989, ICM was renamed International Organization for Migration. As of June 2003, it comprised 101 members. Its headquarters are in Geneva. The central aims of IOM include: organizing the transfer of migrants, refugees, internally displaced persons and other individuals; providing logistical support and medical assistance; providing advisory services on migration questions and on voluntary return migration; and working for the promotion of cooperation and co-ordination of efforts on international migration issues including studies on such issues in order to develop practical solutions. The IOM is composed of three organs: the Council, the Executive Committee and the Administration headed by the Director-General who is responsible to the Council and the Executive Committee.

Since 1951, millions of migrants have received aid from IOM and its predecessors. Currently, 11 million migrants are assisted directly by IOM.

For more information see: http://www.iom.int

International Refugee Organization – IRO

The International Refugee Organization was a temporary agency created by the **United Nations General Assembly** in 1946. In arranging for the care and the repatriation or resettlement of Europeans made homeless by the Second World War, IRO brought to a conclusion part of the work of the United Nations Relief and Rehabilitation Administration (UNRRA). Its goal was to register, protect, resettle and repatriate refugees. IRO was criticized for the controversial character of its operations. It was superseded in 1952, after having resettled approximately one million persons, by the **Office of the United Nations High Commissioner for Refugees (UNHCR)**.

International Research and Training Institute for the Advancement of Women – INSTRAW (UN)

The International Research and Training Institute for the Advancement of Women (INSTRAW) was created by the **Economic and Social Council (ECOSOC)** resolution 1998 (LX) of 12 May 1976 on the recommendation of the **World Conference of the International Women's Year**, held in Mexico City in 1975. INSTRAW is an autonomous body of the **United Nations** which carries out policy-oriented research and training programmes at the international level in order to contribute to the advancement of women as equal partners in all spheres of life; to strengthen their active and equal participation in development; to raise awareness of gender issues; and to create networks worldwide for the attainment of gender equality. Thus, INSTRAW works to improve conceptual and methodological tools, collect and disseminate gender-specific information both within and outside the **United Nations system**, provide training programmes in line with its research results to trainers and policy-makers, and promote measures aimed at the economic and political empowerment of women. In this regard, it focuses on the promotion of the United Nations agenda for gender equality and sustainable development and stimulates further research at the national and international levels and supports institutional building for gender mainstreaming in all sectors.

For more information see: http://www.un-instraw.org

International Women's Day – 8 March (UN)

International Women's Day, dedicated to women and their struggle for equal rights, is traditionally observed on 8 March, in commemoration of a strike by women workers in garment and textile factories in New York City on 8 March 1857.

The celebration of the Day stems from a declaration by the Socialist Party of America. In accordance with this declaration, the first National Women's Day was observed across the United States on 28 February 1909. In 1910, the Socialist International, meeting in Copenhagen, established a Women's Day, international in character, to honour the movement for women's rights and to assist in achieving universal suffrage for women. The proposal was greeted with unanimous approval by the conference of over 100 women from 17 countries. Although no fixed date was selected for the observance, the decision taken at Copenhagen resulted in International Women's Day being marked for the first time on 19 March 1911 in Austria, Denmark, Germany and Switzerland, where more than 1,000,000 women and men attended rallies. In addition to the right to vote and to hold public office, they demanded the **right to work**, the right to vocational training and the right to end **discrimination** on the job.

8 March is commemorated by women's groups around the world and is designated in many countries as a national holiday. International Women's Day is an occasion to encourage coordinated efforts affirming the human rights of women, the struggle for equality of opportunities and for equal participation in political, economic and social life.

In 1975, during the **International Women's Year**, the **United Nations** began celebrating 8 March as International Women's Day. Two years later in December 1977, the **United Nations General Assembly** adopted a resolution proclaiming a **United Nations Day for Women's Rights and International Peace** to be observed every year on a date to be chosen by each Member State.

International Women's Year – 1975 (UN)

On 18 December 1972 the **United Nations General Assembly** endorsed a recommendation by the **Commission on the Status of Women** and proclaimed 1975 International Women's Year. The principal objectives of the Year were: to promote equality between women and men, to ensure the integration of women in all development activities, and to increase the contribution of women to the strengthening of world peace. The **United Nations General Assembly** invited all Member States and all interested organizations to take steps to ensure the full realization of the rights of women and their advancement on the basis of the **Declaration on the Elimination of Discrimination against Women** (1967). The **World Conference of the International Women's Year** which was held in 1975 in Mexico City adopted the **Declaration of Mexico on the Equality of Women and Their Contribution to Development** and Peace as well as the **World Plan of Action for the Implementation of the Objectives of the International Women's Year**. The Plan recommended that governments ensure women and men equality before the law, equality of educational and training opportunities and equality in conditions of employment including remuneration and adequate social security. It was also stressed that, in most regions of the world, women's lower status was essentially due to socio-economic underdevelopment. The Plan drew attention to nine specific areas for national action and made several recommendations for international and regional action. Persuant to the proposals made by the Mexico City Conference, the United Nations General Assembly proclaimed the **United Nations Decade for Women: Equality, Development and Peace - 1976-1985**.

International Year for Action to Combat Racism and Racial Discrimination – 1971 (UN)

On 11 December 1969, the **United Nations General Assembly** designated the year 1971 as the International Year for Action to Combat Racism and Racial Discrimination, and expressed the view that the Year "should be observed in the name of the ever-growing struggle against racial **discrimination** in all its forms and manifestations and in the name of international solidarity with those struggling against **racism**". The General Assembly approved the programme for the observance of the Year prepared by the **United Nations Secretary-General** and appealed to all States to intensify and expand their efforts at the national and the international levels towards ensuring the rapid and total eradication of racial discrimination, including the policy of **apartheid**, and nazism in all of their contemporary forms, as well as other manifestations of racism. The organs of the **United Nations** and its specialized agencies were invited to cooperate and participate in the preparatory work and in the observance of the Year. At the Year's conclusion, the General Assembly recommended that the measures and activities undertaken on the occasion of the Year be continued, developed and enlarged, and that the initiatives which emerged from the observance of the Year should serve as guidelines for action-oriented programmes designed to ensure that the work accomplished in 1971 would be pursued. The period 1973-83 was later proclaimed the **Decade[s] for Action to Combat Racism and Racial Discrimination**. Within the framework of the Third Decade (1993-2003), the **International Year of Mobilization against Racism, Racial Discrimination, Xenophobia and Related Intolerance** was declared for 2001 and the **World Conference against Racism** was organized.

International Year for the Culture of Peace – 2000 (UN)

On 20 November 1997, the **United Nations General Assembly** adopted resolution 52/13 concerning the culture of peace, and resolution 52/15 which proclaimed the year 2000 the International Year for the Culture of Peace. The latter recalls **Economic and Social Council (ECOSOC)** resolution 1997/47 of 22 July 1997 which recommended that **UNESCO** be the focal point for the Year, in as much as this concept was first formulated at the International Congress on Peace in the Minds of Men organized by UNESCO in the Côte d'Ivoire in 1989. In that resolution, the Member States emphasized the impact of such a year by stating their awareness: "... of the need to mobilize public opinion at the national and international levels for the purpose of establishing and promoting a culture of peace and the central role that the **United Nations system** could play in this regard". The main objectives and strategies were to: reflect and inspire social interaction and sharing, based on the principles of freedom, justice and democracy, human rights, tolerance and solidarity; reject violence and endeavour to prevent conflicts by tackling their root causes; to solve problems through dialogue and negotiation; and guarantee the full exercise of all rights and the means to participate fully in the development process of the society.

On 10 November 1998, in its resolution 53/25, the period 2001 to 2010 was proclaimed by the General Assembly as the **International Decade for a Culture of Peace and Non-Violence for the Children of the World**.

On 13 September 1999 the **Declaration and Programme of Action on a Culture of Peace** were adopted by the General Assembly (A/RES/53/243).

International Year for the Eradication of Poverty – 1996 (UN)

On 21 December 1993, the **United Nations General Assembly** proclaimed 1996 the International Year for the Eradication of Poverty. With the theme "**Poverty** can be and must be eradicated throughout the world", the aim of the Year was to support a longer-term, sustained effort to implement fully and effectively the commitments, recommendations and measures undertaken and the basic provisions already agreed upon at major **United Nations** conferences since 1990 as they relate to poverty eradication (para. 3). In its resolution, the General Assembly reaffirmed that the major activities for observing the International Year should be undertaken at all levels to create among States, policy-makers and international public opinion a greater awareness that the eradication of **extreme poverty** is both a complex and multidimensional problem, and is fundamental to reinforcing peace and achieving sustainable development (para. 2). The same resolution requested the **United Nations Secretary-General** to achieve, in consultation with States, specialized agencies and intergovernmental and **non-governmental organizations**, the elaboration of the draft programme concerning the preparations for and observance of the Year (para. 3). Activities during the Year were guided by the following principles: anti-poverty strategies and programmes shall be designed, implemented and monitored with the full and effective participation of people living in poverty; measures shall be adopted to ensure that people living in extreme poverty have access to the resources and opportunities necessary to escape from poverty; access of all people living in poverty to basic social services shall be ensured; anti-poverty strategies and programmes shall be designed with a gender dimension; and targeted programmes shall be developed to meet the special needs of particular social and demographic groups, including young people, disadvantaged **older persons**, persons with disabilities and other vulnerable and disadvantaged groups of persons (para. 4).

International Year for Tolerance – 1995 (UN)

On 20 December 1993, the **United Nations General Assembly**, at the initiative of **UNESCO**, proclaimed 1995 the International Year for Tolerance. This initiative was especially appropriate as it celebrated the 50th anniversary of the **United Nations** and UNESCO by reaffirming the practice of tolerance as one of the guiding principles upon which the United Nations was founded. On 23 December 1994, the General Assembly called upon Member States to cooperate with UNESCO in the observance of national and international programmes and requested UNESCO to prepare for the conclusion of the Year a declaration of principles and a programme of action as a follow-up to the Year. In conformity with its mandate as the responsible agency of the **United Nations system** for the International Year of Tolerance, UNESCO prepared for 1995 a diverse programme of meetings, concerts, broadcasts, festivals, publications, exhibitions and other special events in all regions of the world. The Year's calendar of events included seven regional conferences. Research carried out throughout the world on new forms of **discrimination** and ways of combating them served as a basis for UNESCO's efforts to involve an increasing number of partners in promoting the idea, and above all, the practice of "active" tolerance, which implies the desire to get to know other people, to understand what makes others different and to show respect for those differences. The **Declaration of Principles on Tolerance** was adopted by the General Conference of UNESCO on 16 November 1995. The Plan of Action for the follow-up to the International Year for Tolerance, also adopted by the General Conference, presents the causes and factors contributing to manifestations of intolerance around the world. It states that the aim of the follow-up programme is to transpose the most successful components of the International Year for Tolerance into more enduring strategies and structures by which promotion and sensitization of tolerance may be improved in every region of the world.

International Year of Freshwater – 2003 (UN)

The problem of access to fresh water is very serious nowadays: over one billion people lack clean water, about two and a half have no proper sanitation and more than three million people die from diseases carried by unsafe water. In recognition of the central importance of water resources to the future of the planet, the **United Nations General Assembly** proclaimed the year 2003 as the International Year of Freshwater (A/RES/55/196 of 20 December 2000). It encourages the **United Nations system** and all other actors to take advantage of the Year to increase awareness of the importance of sustainable freshwater use, management and protection. It also calls upon governments, national and international organizations, **non-governmental organizations** and the private sector to make voluntary contributions and to lend other forms of support to the Year. UNESCO is the lead agency for observing the Year.

The publication by the United Nations system of the World Water Development Report will be a major focus of the Year's public information activities. Its first edition was launched at the Third World Water Forum in Kyoto, Japan, in March 2003.

International Year of Mobilization against Racism, Racial Discrimination, Xenophobia and Related Intolerance – 2001 (UN)

In 1998, the **United Nations General Assembly** (A/RES/53/132) proclaimed within the context of the **Third United Nations Decade[s] for Action to Combat Racism and Racial Discrimination (1993-2003)**, the year 2001 as the International Year of Mobilization against Racism, Racial Discrimination, Xenophobia and Related Intolerance. The General Assembly, in proclaiming the International Year, underscored its grave concern that, despite the continuing efforts of the international community, the principal objectives of the two previous Decades had not been attained, and that, on the contrary, **racism** and racial **discrimination** in all their forms and manifestations persist and even grow in magnitude. The main purpose of the International Year was to contribute to the preparation of the **World Conference against Racism, Racial Discrimination, Xenophobia and Related Intolerance** held in Durban, South Africa (31 August-8 September 2001), as well as to the realization of its objectives. The activities within the framework of the International Year were directed towards increasing public awareness about the scourge of racism and encouraging the implementation of the relevant standard-setting instruments, thus giving a new impetus to the political commitment for the elimination of all forms of racism, racial discrimination, xenophobia and related intolerance.

International Year of Older Persons – 1999 (UN)

The **United Nations General Assembly** proclaimed the year 1999 as the International Year of Older Persons (A/RES/47/5 of 16 October 1992). The conceptual framework of a programme for the Year was elaborated by the **United Nations Secretary-General** in 1995 and focused on four dimensions: the situation of older persons; life-long individual development; relationships between generations; and the relationships between development and the ageing of populations. Priority was given to promoting the **United Nations Principles for Older Persons** and the theme "Towards a society for all ages" was adopted as the Year's unifying theme.

In 1997, the Secretary-General elaborated the operational framework for the observance of the Year, also structured along four dimensions: raising awareness (recalling the four conceptual dimensions); looking ahead beyond 1999; reaching out to non-traditional actors including the development community, the media, the private sector and **youth**; and developing cooperation between States and sectors. Furthermore, the operational framework formulated a "Menu of Ideas" concerning national activities. The **International Day of Older Persons** is observed on 1 October each year.

International Year of Peace – 1986 (UN)

The year 1986 was declared the International Year of Peace by the **United Nations General Assembly** (A/RES/37/16 of 16 November 1982). In the proclamation, the General Assembly referred to peace as a universal ideal, the promotion of which was the primary purpose of the **United Nations**. The programme of the Year was designed to promote activities at the international, regional, and national levels aimed at bringing about a sustained increase in understanding of, and support for, the work of the United Nations in the field. It stated that "... the promotion of international peace and security requires continuing and positive action by States and peoples aimed at the prevention of war, removal of various threats to peace – including the nuclear threat – respect for the principle of non-use of force, the resolution of conflicts and the peaceful settlement of disputes, confidence-building measures, disarmament, the maintenance of outer space for peaceful uses, development, the promotion and exercise of human rights and fundamental freedoms, decolonization in accordance with the principle of self-determination, the elimination of racial **discrimination** and **apartheid**, the enhancement of the quality of life, satisfaction of human needs and protection of the environment", and called upon all peoples to join the United Nations efforts to safeguard peace and the future of humanity. The International Year of Peace was observed worldwide by Member States of the United Nations, intergovernmental and **non-governmental organizations**, educational, scientific, cultural and research institutions and the media and highlighted the role of the United Nations in the promotion and maintenance of international peace and security.

International Year of the Child – 1979 (UN)

In its resolution of 21 December 1976, the **United Nations General Assembly** proclaimed the year 1979 the International Year of the Child to mark the 20th anniversary of the adoption of the **Declaration on the Rights of the Child**. Leadership for the Year was provided by the **United Nations Children's Fund (UNICEF)** with the assistance of an advisory group. Essentially a year of action at the national level to improve the situation of children and supported by activities and consultations at the regional and international levels, the International Year of the Child pursued the following general objectives: to provide a framework for advocacy on behalf of children and for enhancing the awareness of the special needs of children on the part of decision-makers and the public; and to promote recognition of the fact that programmes for children should be an integral part of economic and social development plans with a view to achieving the long-term and the short-term sustained activities for the benefit of children at the national and international levels.

International Year of the Family
– 1994 (UN)

On 8 December 1989, the **United Nations General Assembly** proclaimed the year 1994 as the International Year of the Family. The aims of the Year were to increase awareness of family issues and improve the institutional capability of nations to tackle serious family-related problems with comprehensive policies. The General Assembly (A/RES/44/82) recognized the efforts of governments at the local, regional and national levels in carrying out specific programmes concerning the family and in raising awareness, increasing understanding and promoting policies that improve the position and well-being of the family. It also expressed its confidence that the Year would offer a unique opportunity for mobilizing efforts to highlight the importance of the family, promote a better understanding of its functions and problems and strengthen the ability of national institutions to formulate, implement and monitor policies in respect of the family. The major activities for the observance of the Year were designed to create a view, among Governments, policy-makers and the public, of the family as the natural and fundamental unit of society.

International Year of the World's Indigenous People
– 1993 (UN)

On 18 December 1990, the **United Nations General Assembly** (A/RES/45/164) proclaimed the year 1993 as the International Year for the World's Indigenous People with the theme of "Indigenous people – a new partnership". The Year was requested by indigenous organizations and is the result of their efforts to secure their cultural integrity and status in the 21st century. The aim of the Year was to strengthen international cooperation for the solution of the problems faced by **indigenous peoples** in areas such as human rights, the environment, development, education and health and, above all, to encourage a new relationship between States and indigenous peoples, and between the international community and indigenous peoples. The resolution contained a programme of activities for the Year and envisaged that the **United Nations system** would increase co-ordination, cooperation and technical assistance for the solution of problems faced by indigenous peoples; give special emphasis to promoting the ratification and implementation of the international legal instruments related to the objectives of the Year; provide technical assistance to help Governments adopt legislative provisions which recognize and protect the basic human rights of indigenous and tribal peoples; and promote public awareness of the situation of indigenous peoples and the threats to their existence. In preparing the activities for the Year, various organizations of the **United Nations** sought to involve indigenous peoples in the planning, implementation and evaluation of the projects that will improve their living conditions and future. The General Assembly proclaimed an **International Decade of the World's Indigenous People (1995-2004)** and adopted a Programme of Action for the Decade. It also decided that, beginning the first year of the Decade, one day was to be observed as the **International Day of the World's Indigenous People** (9 August was subsequently selected).

International Youth Day
– 12 August (UN)

On 17 December 1999, the **United Nations General Assembly**, adopted resolution 54/120 which endorsed the recommendation made by the World Conference of Ministers responsible for **Youth** (Lisbon, Portugal, 8-12 August 1998) that 12 August be declared International Youth Day. It recommended that public information activities be organized to support the Day as a way to promote better awareness, especially among youth of the World Programme of Action for Youth to the Year 2000 and Beyond, adopted by the General Assembly in 1995 by its resolution 50/81.

International Youth Year: Participation, Development, Peace – 1985 (UN)

On 17 December 1979, the **United Nations General Assembly** designated the year 1985, which marked the 40th anniversary of the **United Nations**, as the International **Youth** Year. The goals of the Year were: to enhance awareness of the needs and aspirations of youth; to make youth activities an integral part of social and economic development; to enhance youth participation in society; and to promote among youth the ideals of peace, mutual respect and understanding among peoples. A highlight of the Year was the endorsement by the General Assembly of guidelines for further planning and suitable follow-up in the field of youth. These guidelines, representing an international instrument providing a global strategy for youth, were contained in the report of the Advisory Committee for the Year, and were endorsed by General Assembly resolution 40/14 of 18 November 1985. The guidelines emphasized human rights and invited Governments "to encourage initiatives and activities aimed at promoting respect for human rights and fundamental freedoms by young people as stated in the **Universal Declaration of Human Rights** and other relevant documents, particularly by giving proper consideration to their education in the field of human rights and its indispensable connection with the preservation of peace".

Inter-Parliamentary Union – IPU

The Inter-Parliamentary Union (IPU), established in 1889 at the initiative of two parliamentarians, William Randal Cremer (United Kingdom) and Frédéric Passy (France), is the world organization of parliaments of sovereign States and, as such, the focal point for worldwide parliamentary dialogue and parliamentary diplomacy.

The IPU, the oldest political multilateral organization, currently has 145 affiliated national parliaments and five associated regional assemblies. Since November 2002, the IPU is a Permanent Observer to the **United Nations General Assembly**, with a special right to have its official documents circulated in the General Assembly.

The promotion of peace and cooperation among peoples and the establishment of representative institutions are the main goals of the IPU. To that end, it fosters contacts and exchanges of experience among parliaments and parliamentarians. It considers questions of interest to the international community and expresses its view thereon with the aim of bringing about parliamentary action.

Convinced that parliaments are guardian of human rights, the IPU contributes to the defence and promotion of human rights, including equal participation of women in political life. The IPU has set up its own human rights mechanism, the Committee on the Human Rights of Parliamentarians, which investigates complaints regarding violations of the human rights of members of parliament.

Through studies and technical assistance, the IPU promotes and brings about improvements in parliamentary institutions. It supports the efforts of the **United Nations** and its specialized agencies (including **UNESCO**) on issues concerning the strengthening of democratic institutions, protection of human rights, promotion of gender equality and other matters. The President of the IPU and the Director-General of UNESCO agreed in 2003 on the establishment of an IPU parliamentary network of focal points in parliaments for matters related to UNESCO.

The IPU cooperates also with other organizations which pursue the same goals. The IPU is financed from public funds. It has two main organs: the Assembly, which expresses the Organization's views on political issues, and the Governing Council. The latter is composed of three representatives, generally of different political views, from each Member Parliament and serves as the IPU's plenary policy-making body, drawing up the annual programme and budget and deciding on membership issues. A number of committees are subordinated to the Council. The Meeting of Women Parliamentarians is a mechanism for co-ordination between women members of parliament. The Executive Committee is a 15-member body which oversees administration and advises the Council; the Secretariat is responsible for carrying out the programme of activities. The IPU Headquarters are situated in Geneva, Switzerland. The President of the IPU is elected by the Council for a single three-year mandate. The Secretary-General is elected by the Inter-Parliamentary Council for a renewable four-year mandate.

For more information see: http://www.ipu.org

League of Arab States/Arab League

The League of Arab States was established on 22 March 1945 upon signature of its Charter by 7 Arab States. Today, with 22 members, it represents more than 200 million people. The League is a regional organization designed to promote the interests of the Member States and the region as a whole through the promotion of political, economic and social programmes, cultural affairs and health. The League serves as both a forum for Member States to coordinate their policy positions and deliberate on matters of common concern, and ways to promote joint Arab action in all fields. The implementation of joint action plans and the coordination of the relations of Member States with regional and universal organizations are the central political functions of the League.

The League of Arab States has four main bodies: the Summit of Heads of State; the Council of Ministers; the Standing Committee; and the Secretariat General.

According to the provisions of the Charter, the Council of the League is the supreme authority within the League system and is composed of the representatives of the Member States, each State having a single vote. The Council is concerned mainly with pursuing the realization of the objectives of the League and following up the implementation of plans and programmes drawn up by the Member States. The Council also takes decision on membership applications and withdrawals, the introduction of amendments to the Charter, and mediates disputes between Member States, or a Member State and a third party. It is also responsible for the appointment of the Secretary-General. The Council meets twice a year, in regular sessions and may convene extraordinary sessions upon the request of two Member States of the League. The permanent seat of the League is in Cairo, Egypt. The Arab League has established several bodies and organizations, including the Arab Labour Organization (ALO) and the **Arab Educational, Cultural and Scientific Organization (ALECSO)**. In 1994 the League adopted the **Arab Charter on Human Rights**. On 22 April 1998 it adopted the Arab Convention for the Suppression of Terrorism, which entered into force on 7 May 1999.

League of Nations

The League of Nations, a universal organization of States, was established at the initiative of the victorious Allied Powers at the end of the First World War. The Covenant of the League, adopted at the Paris Peace Conference in 1919, was the charter of the new international order, aiming at promoting international cooperation and achieving international peace and security. The Covenant established the League's directing organs: an Assembly, a Council and a Secretariat. The programme for the direct prevention of war was set forth in Articles 8 to 19. No reference was made to the rights or freedoms of individuals. However, the League of Nations encouraged the establishment of bilateral agreements aimed at the protection of the rights of minorities (for example the Greco-Bulgarian Conventions of November 1919 and of January 1923 and the Polish-German Agreement of January 1934) which were supervised and monitored by it. The League also adopted several standard-setting instruments having particular reference to human rights. One of the most famous instruments is the **Slavery Convention** of 25 September 1926 which was signed under the auspices of the League of Nations and which entered into force on 9 March 1927. The League had 53 members at the height of its influence. It ceased its activities during the Second World War. In 1946, the League was formally dissolved.

Limburg Principles on the Implementation of the International Covenant on Economic, Social and Cultural Rights (UN)

Established at a meeting of eminent experts in international law in Maastricht, the Netherlands, held from 2 to 6 June 1986, these Principles concern the nature and scope of obligations of States Parties to the **International Covenant on Economic, Social and Cultural Rights**. In an attempt to reach an international consensus on the implementation of the Covenant's provisions, 103 Principles were agreed upon and are regarded as a means of assisting in the development and application of **economic**, **social** and **cultural rights**.

The Principles call on States Parties to take all appropriate measures – legislative, judicial, economic, social and educational – in order to fulfill their obligations under the Covenant. Part 1 of the document, which outlines the nature and the scope of States Parties' obligations to the Covenant, recognizes that economic, social and cultural rights are an integral part of the international human rights law and that these rights may be achieved in a variety of political settings. The participation of **non-governmental organizations** at the national and international level, in promoting the implementation of the Covenant, is encouraged (Principle 9). A number of provisions are aimed at the eradication of **discrimination**. The Principles note that the grounds of discrimination enumerated in Article 2.2 of the Covenant are not exhaustive, and stress the need to guarantee equal rights for men and women, bearing in mind not only the provisions of Article 3 of the Covenant, but of other international instruments including the **Declaration on the Elimination of Discrimination against Women** and the **Convention on the Elimination of All Forms of Discrimination against Women**. Principles 70-73 concern violations of economic, social and cultural rights and Principles 83-91 further clarify the role of the **Committee on Economic, Social and Cultural Rights**.

Maastricht Guidelines on Violations of Economic, Social and Cultural Rights (UN)

On the 10th anniversary of the adoption of the **Limburg Principles on the Implementation of the International Covenant on Economic, Social and Cultural Rights**, a group of more than thirty experts met in January 1997 in Maastricht, the Netherlands, to develop a better understanding of the concept of violations of economic, social and cultural rights with a view to strengthen their implementation. The participants unanimously agreed on a series of guidelines to be used for better understanding and determining violations of **economic**, **social** and **cultural rights**. Recognizing that since the adoption of the Limburg Principles, economic and social conditions have declined for over 1.6 billion people, the 32 Principles seek to establish an international consensus on the implementation of the Covenant in light of legal, economic and political developments.

The Guidelines are divided into 5 sections. Section 1 underlines the significance of economic, social and cultural rights. Sections 2, 3, and 4 are dedicated respectively to the different aspects and the meaning of violations; the responsibility for violations; and the victims of violations. The final section concerns remedies and other responses to violations including adequate reparation, the domestic application of international instruments, the role of **special rapporteurs** and the monitoring of violations.

Magna Carta

Magna Carta, also called "The Great Charter", is the charter of liberties granted by King John in 1215. Although it meant less to contemporaries because of the feudal system at that time than to subsequent generations, it became a symbol of the struggle against oppression. It consists of a Preamble and 63 clauses. The content of Magna Carta may be divided into several groups with clauses concerning: the church; feudal law; subtenants; towns, trade and merchants; reform of the law and justice; control of the behaviour of royal officials; royal forests; and guarantees for the King's adherence to the Charter. It is worth mentioning that some national constitutions which are in force today, such as that of the United States of America, contain ideas and formulations traceable to Magna Carta.

Management of Social Transformations – MOST (UNESCO)

UNESCO's MOST programme was established in 1994 to foster international cooperative policy-relevant social science research. Its overarching objective is to evaluate the impact of research on policy-making and to enhance the relations between the latter. The activities of the programme, involving several regional and international research and policy networks, range from research to capacity-building, through supply of expertise and development-oriented field projects. MOST is mainly focused on policies for the governance of multicultural societies, international migrations, cities and urban development, as well as issues relating to social development and **poverty**.

The MOST programme is steered by an Intergovernmental Council of 35 Member States, and a Scientific Committee of nine international scholars, which has decision-making power on scientific issues. The Council meets every two years and establishes the priority areas to be researched, decides on overall policy and funding questions, and handles the relations with governmental authorities. There are also over 50 MOST National

Liaison Committees which link the programme to local research and policy communities. It is coordinated by the MOST Secretariat at UNESCO Headquarters.

For more information see: http://www.unesco.org/most

Mexico City Declaration on Cultural Policies (UNESCO)

Adopted in 1982 by the World Conference on Cultural Policies organized by **UNESCO**, to promote, *inter alia*, the **right to cultural identity**.

Migrant workers

The question of maltreatment and **discrimination** of migrant workers and their families has for a long time been on the agenda of the **International Labour Organisation (ILO)** and, since the 1970s, on the agenda of the **United Nations**. From 1976 to 1979, the **United Nations General Assembly** adopted a series of resolutions on measures to improve the situation and ensure the human rights and dignity of all migrant workers. The General Assembly called upon the **Commission on Human Rights** and the **Economic and Social Council (ECOSOC)** to consider questions concerning migrant workers. The **International Convention on the Protection of the Rights of All Migrant Workers and Members of Their Families** was adopted by the United Nations General Assembly (A/RES/45/158) and entered into force on 1 July 2003. In Article 2, the Convention explains that the term "migrant worker" refers to a person who is to be engaged, is engaged or has been engaged in a remunerated activity in a State of which he or she is not a national. The Commission on Human Rights called upon all United Nations Member States to consider signing and ratifying or acceding to the Convention as a matter of priority. It also urged countries of destination to review and adopt appropriate measures to ensure that their police forces and competent migration authorities comply with the basic standards relating to the decent treatment of migrant workers. It is worth noting that the **European Convention on the Legal Status of Migrant Workers** entered into force on 1 May 1983.

Millennium Development Goals (UN)

In September 2000, at the **United Nations Millennium Summit**, world leaders agreed to a set of time-bound and measurable goals and targets for combating **poverty**, hunger, disease, illiteracy, environmental degradation and **discrimination** against women. Called now Millennium Development Goals (MDGs), they provide a framework for the entire United Nations system to work coherently together to achieve common ends. The Goals complement the **United Nations Millennium Declaration** which outlines a wide range of commitments to human rights, good governance and democracy.

There are 8 Development Goals to be achieved by 2015: reduce extreme poverty and hunger by half; achieve universal primary education; empower women and promote equality between women and men; reduce children under-five mortality by two thirds; reduce maternal mortality by three quarters; reverse the spread of diseases, especially HIV/AIDS and malaria; ensure environmental sustainability; create a global partnership for development, with targets for aid, trade and debt relief.

The MDGs are monitored through the submission of country reports. These reports, which are often a product of collaboration between a country's government, the private sector and civil society, highlight where countries are on track to meet the Goals. Nearly every developing country is planning to produce its first report by the end of 2004.

Minorities

The protection of minorities and their equal and non-discriminatory treatment became a matter of international concern after the First World War. Treaties between the Allied and Associated Powers and the Central and Eastern European and Balkan States provided for the protection of the rights of ethnic, religious or linguistic minorities. For many decades, the protection of their rights has been a controversial question. Neither the protection of minorities nor the rights of persons belonging to minorities were mentioned in the **United Nations Charter** (1945). The **Universal Declaration of Human Rights** (1948) does not foresee a specific provision on the question of minorities. The European **Convention for the Protection of Human Rights and Fundamental Freedoms** contains a provision (Article 14) in which "... association with a national minority" is listed among a series of grounds upon which discrimination is prohibited. The first international convention adopted after 1945 which includes provisions *expressis verbis* relating to the rights of persons belonging to minorities is the **Convention against Discrimination in Education** (1960) of **UNESCO**. The **International Covenant on Civil and Political Rights** (1966), in its Article 27, states: "In those States in which ethnic, religious or linguistic minorities exist, persons belonging to such minorities shall not be denied the right, in community with the other members of their group, to enjoy their own culture, to profess and practise their own religion, or to use their own language". At its 1967 session, the **Sub-Commission on Prevention of Discrimination and Protection of Minorities** (now **Sub-Commission on the Promotion and Protection of Human Rights**) decided to initiate a study of the implementation of the principles set out in Article 27 of the International Covenant on Civil and Political Rights. This Article, with small alterations, was incorporated in the **Convention on the Rights of the Child** (1989).

In 1992, the **Declaration on the Rights of Persons Belonging to National or Ethnic, Religious and Linguistic Minorities** was adopted. Although it does not define the term "minority", the Declaration urges States and the international community to promote and protect the rights of persons belonging to minorities. The **Vienna Declaration and Programme of Action**, adopted on 25 June 1993 by the **World Conference on Human Rights**, called on the **Commission on Human Rights** to examine ways and means to promote and protect effectively the rights of persons belonging to minorities as set out in the Declaration on the Rights of Persons Belonging to National or Ethnic, Religious and Linguistic Minorities. It proclaims that such protection contributes "… to the political and social stability of the States in which such persons live" (Part I, para. 19 of the **Vienna Declaration and Programme of Action**).

The **Council of Europe** adopted the **European Charter for Regional or Minority Languages** (1992) and the **Framework Convention for the Protection of National Minorities** (1994).

Nairobi Forward-Looking Strategies for the Advancement of Women (UN)

The Nairobi Forward-Looking Strategies were adopted by the World Conference to Review and Appraise the Achievements of the United Nations Decade for Women: Equality, Development and Peace. This conference, which was held at Nairobi, Kenya, from 15 to 26 July 1985 brought the **United Nations Decade for Women: Equality, Development and Peace**, to a close. The Strategies provided a policy framework for improving the status of women during the period 1986-2000 and for eliminating all forms of inequality between men and women which is essential for strengthening peace and security. Governments were requested to adopt concrete measures to promoting the integration of women at all levels of public and private life. In bried, the strategies reaffirm the international concern regarding the status of women and provide a framework for renewed commitment by the international community to the advancement of women and for the elimination of gender-based **discrimination**. By resolution 40/108 of 13 December 1985, the **United Nations General Assembly** endorsed the Strategies and called upon States to take concrete and effective measures to: establish or strengthen, as appropriate, national mechanisms to ensure the advancement of women; to monitor the implementation of the Strategies with a view to ensuring the full integration of women in the political, economic, social and cultural life of their countries. Furthermore, the General Assembly entrusted the implementation of the Strategies to the **Commission on the Status of Women** and urged all organizations of the **United Nations system** to cooperate with the Commission in this work. The Commission called upon States to ensure that women become more aware of their rights and to eliminate negative connotations associated with women from textbooks and from the education system in general. It also called for action to combat acts of violence against women.

For more information see:
http://www.un.org/womenwatch/confer/nfls.htm

Naples Political Declaration and Global Action Plan against Organized Transnational Crime (UN)

On 23 December 1994, the **United Nations General Assembly** (A/RES/49/159) recognized the need to strengthen and improve international cooperation at all levels to assist States in their fight against transnational **organized crime** and approved the Naples Political Declaration and Global Action Plan against Organized Transnational Crime. These instruments were developed by the World Ministerial Conference on Organized Transnational Crime held in Naples, Italy, in November 1994. They proclaimed the resolve of the participants to the Conference to "protect their societies from organized crime in all its forms through strict and effective legislative measures and operational instruments, always consistent with internationally recognized human rights and fundamental freedoms" (para. 1). They also declared that the participants will join forces and fight together against the expansion and diversification of transnational organized crime (para. 2), in particular directing their efforts towards defeating the social and economic power of criminal organizations and their ability to infiltrate legitimate economies, to launder their criminal proceeds and to use violence and terror (para. 3). The Declaration and Action Plan urged States to achieve more effective international cooperation through: closer alignment of legislative texts concerning organized crime (para. 32); strengthening international cooperation at the investigative, prosecution and judicial levels in operational matters (paras. 23-27); establishing modalities and basic principles for international cooperation at the regional and global levels (para. 9); elaborating international agreements on organized transnational crime (para. 9); and establishing measures and strategies to prevent and combat money-laundering and to control the use of the proceeds of crime (paras. 35-39). States are also asked to increase their knowledge of criminal organizations and their dynamics by collecting, analysing and disseminating reliable statistics and information on the phenomenon (para. 13). In order to strengthen the struggle against organized crime, the General Assembly adopted on 15 November 2000, by its resolution 55/25, the following new instruments: **United Nations Convention against Transnational Organized Crime**, the **Protocol to Prevent, Suppress and Punish Trafficking in Persons, Especially Women and Children**, and the **Protocol against the Smuggling of Migrants by Land, Sea and Air**. The **Protocol Against the Illicit Manufacturing of and Trafficking in Firearms, Their Parts and Components and Ammunition** was adopted by the General Assembly on 31 May 2001 and is the third protocol to the Convention against Transnational Organized Crime.

National human rights institutions – NHRI

A great number of organizations are concerned with the promotion and protection of human rights. Among them, national human rights institutions (NHRI) have a special place. The role and functions of national institutions are described in the **United Nations Secretary-General**'s report entitled "National institutions for the protection and promotion of human rights", prepared at the request of the **United Nations General Assembly** resolution 40/123. NHRI can be defined as bodies established under the constitution or by law, whose functions are specifically designed to protect human rights. They should hear and investigate individual charges of human rights violations or discriminatory acts committed in violation of existing law. One of their most important functions is their systematic monitoring of existing government policy toward human rights and presenting suggestions concerning improvements in this regard. Furthermore, national institutions are engaged in educating the public about important issues in the field of human rights as well as in monitoring State compliance with existing human rights law. Their organization varies from country to country as well as their procedures in investigation and resolution of complaints. While no two institutions are the same, many share a number of important similarities. They are administrative in nature and are not judicial or law-making bodies. They have an ongoing advisory authority regarding the implementation of human rights at national and international levels. While many national institutions are attached, in some way, to the executive branch of government, the actual level of their independence depends on a number of factors including membership and the manner in which they operate.

The majority of existing national institutions take the form of either a human rights commission or an **ombudsperson**. Less common, are the 'specialized' national institutions which function to protect the rights of a **vulnerable group[s]** such as women, children or persons belonging to national or ethnic, religious and linguistic **minorities**. NHRI, as a rule do not have the power to take binding decisions in resolving a complaint. Therefore, to be effective, a strong connection between the law, the NHRI and the courts is necessary.

The United Nations Principles relating to the Status and Functioning of National Institutions for the Promotion and Protection of Human Rights are a comprehensive series of recommendations on the role, composition, status and functions of human rights institutions. Known as the **Paris Principles**, they comprise the criteria concerning the establishment and functioning of national institutions.

National human rights institutions exist in more than 100 countries. About one half of them are recognized as corresponding to criteria established by the Paris Principles.

Non-derogatory human rights

Non-derogatory human rights are those rights which are so basic that they can never be suspended by legal acts of governments, not even in times of public emergencies. They are enshrined in Article 4, para. 2, of the **International Covenant on Civil and Political Rights** and include: the **right to life**; the prohibition of torture and cruel, inhuman or degrading treatment of punishment; the prohibition of slavery, slave trade, and other forms of servitude; the right not to be imprisoned merely on the ground of inability to fulfil a contractual obligation; the prohibition of retroactive application of penal law; the **right to recognition as a person before the law**; and the **right to freedom of thought, conscience and religion**.

Non-governmental organizations in the field of human rights

The first non-governmental organizations (NGOs) were created in the 19th century. Since the end of the Second World War, their number has greatly expanded. NGOs may be of an international, regional, national, local or grassroots character. Several thousand of them deal with human rights issues and contribute significantly to the promotion and protection of human rights and to the daily struggle against their violations. They play an outstanding role in sensitizing civil society and the general public on threats and challenges to human rights. NGOs participate regularly in the meetings of the **Commission on Human Rights**, the **Sub-Commission on the Promotion and Protection of Human Rights** (formerly the **Sub-Commission on Prevention of Discrimination and Protection of Minorities**), the **Commission on the Status of Women** and other bodies dealing with human rights issues. Furthermore, non-governmental organizations participate in and often initiate the drafting of international standard-setting instruments. Article 71 of the **United Nations Charter** provides that "the **Economic and Social Council (ECOSOC)** may make suitable arrangements for consultation with non-governmental organizations which are concerned with matters within its competence". ECOSOC resolution on consultative relationship between the United Nations and non-governmental organizations (E/1996/31 of 25 July 1996), updating its previous resolution 1296 of 23 May 1968, divides NGOs into three categories: organizations in general consultative status, which are concerned with most of the activities of ECOSOC and whose membership is broadly representative in a large number of countries; organizations in special consultative status, which are concerned specifically with only a few activities and are known internationally within those fields; and organizations on the Roster, which can make occasional and useful contributions to the work of ECOSOC. All three categories of NGOs may have representatives present at meetings of ECOSOC and its subsidiary bodies (those on the Roster only at meetings concerned with matters within their competence). Furthermore, written statements, relevant to the work of ECOSOC, may be submitted by all three categories of NGOs and circulated if it does not exceed 2,000 words for organizations in general consultative status and 500 words for the others. Moreover, the first category may even propose to include items of special interest in the provisional agenda of the ECOSOC sessions. Many **United Nations specialized agencies**, programmes and funds have followed the example of ECOSOC and granted consultative status to NGOs. Over 1,500 NGOs maintain official relations with ECOSOC; more than 340 are admitted into official relations with the **United Nations Educational, Scientific and Cultural Organization (UNESCO)**, of them about one-quarter deals with human rights. The total number of NGOs having general or regional consultative status with the ILO reached 25 by the middle of 2003. Moreover, by that time 163 NGOs were included in the ILO Special List, set up to establish working relations with international NGOs other than employers' and workers' organizations. NGOs actively cooperate with the **Inter-American Commission on Human Rights** and the **Inter-American Court of Human Rights**, the **Council of Europe**, the **European Court of**

Human Rights, the **African Commission on Human and Peoples' Rights** and the **Organization for Security and Cooperation in Europe (OSCE)**. There has been a broad participation of NGOs in major conferences in the field of human rights. More than 800 NGOs were accredited to the **World Conference on Human Rights** (Vienna, 1993) and some 2,500 attended its parallel NGO Forum. The **World Conference against Racism, Racial Discrimination, Xenophobia and Related Intolerance** saw the participation of over 10,000 representatives from NGOs. Moreover, information from NGOs has official status in the **human rights treaty bodies**. They also play a major role in the promotion of **human rights education**.

One of the most wellknown NGOs in the field of human rights is **Amnesty International**. It was awarded the Nobel Peace Prize in 1977.

Nuremberg International Human Rights Award

The City of Nuremberg (Germany) established the Nuremberg International Human Rights Award in 1995 in order to contribute to the international sensitization on human rights issues and as a call for commitment and responsibility towards human rights. The Award is endowed with 15,000 Euros and is given every two years to an individual or a group demonstrating in an exemplary manner, their commitment to the respect of human rights, sometimes at considerable personal risk. An international jury selects the winner of the Award.

The first Award was given on 17 September 1995, almost 60 years after the passing of the National Socialist racial laws in Germany and 50 years after the end of the Second World War. The Award symbolizes the current image of Nuremberg, which has proclaimed itself a "City of Peace and Human Rights". The Award should serve to promote a lasting peace, implementation of human rights and mutual understanding.

Awardees include: 1995 – Serguei Kovalev (Russia); 1997 – Khemais Chammari (Tunisia) and Abe J. Nathan (Israel) for their peace activities in the Middle East; 1999 – Fatimata M'Baye (Mauritania) for her fight against discrimination of black African ethnic groups; 2001 – Bishop Samuel Ruiz Garcia (Mexico) for his struggle for the rights of **indigenous peoples**; 2003 – Teesta Setalvad (India) and Ibn Abdur Rehman (Pakistan) for their committed fight against prejudice, hatred and violence.

The City of Nuremberg was the first municipality worldwide to receive the **UNESCO Prize for Human Rights Education** for its tireless efforts and numerous activities to promote and protect human rights. The City of Nuremberg also plays a leading role in the movement **"Cities for Human Rights"**.

Office for Democratic Institutions and Human Rights – ODIHR (OSCE)

As part of the **Organization for Security and Cooperation in Europe (OSCE)**, the Office for Democratic Institutions and Human Rights (ODIHR) assists the participating States in the building of democratic institutions, in the monitoring of elections and in the implementation of their commitments in the field of human rights. It is the primary OSCE institution in the human dimension field. These activities and related projects focus particularly on: capacity building supporting the rule of law; combating trafficking in human beings; promoting gender equality; migration and freedom of movement issues; freedom of religion and preventing torture. The Office, situated in Warsaw, focuses mainly on three priorities. First, it is the focal point for OSCE election-related matters and monitors elections based on the OSCE election commitments made at the Copenhagen Meeting in 1990. Secondly, the Office carries out a number of programmes aimed at promoting civil society, democratic institutions and the rule of law, through providing training and technical assistance to national human rights institutions, State institutions and **non-governmental organizations**. In fulfilling its tasks, it works not only with other OSCE institutions, but also coordinates its activities with other intergovernmental organizations and non-governmental organizations. Finally, the ODIHR fulfils a monitoring function regarding the implementation of commitments by OSCE participating States in the field of human rights. As a separate function, the ODIHR also serves as the OSCE Contact Point for Roma and Sinti Issues.

For more information see: http://www.osce.org/odihr

Office of the United Nations High Commissioner for Human Rights – OHCHR

The mandate of the Office of the **United Nations High Commissioner for Human Rights (OHCHR)** derives from Articles 1, 13 and 55 of the **Charter of the United Nations**, the provisions of the **Vienna Declaration and Programme of Action**, and the **United Nations General Assembly** resolution 48/141 of 20 December 1993, by which the General Assembly established the post of a United Nations High Commissioner for the promotion and protection of all human rights, commonly called the High Commissioner for Human Rights. The Office is situated in Geneva and has a liaison office in New York.

In connection with the programme for reform of the **United Nations**, the OHCHR and the **United Nations Centre for Human Rights (UNCHR),** created on 18 December 1982 by the United Nations General Assembly in its redesignation of the former Division of Human Rights, became an integral part of the OHCHR on 15 September 1997. The Office is divided into organizational units and headed by a High Commissioner with the rank of Under-Secretary-General. Its functions are the following: promotion of universal enjoyment of all human rights by giving practical effect to the will and resolve of the world community as expressed by the UN; playing the leading role on human rights issues and emphasizing the importance of human rights at the international and national levels; promotion of international cooperation on human rights; stimulation and coordination of action for human rights throughout the **United Nations system**; promotion of universal ratification and implementation of international standards; assistance in the development of new norms; support for **human rights treaty monitoring bodies** and organs; response to serious violations of human rights; the undertaking of preventive human rights action; promotion of the establishment of national human rights infrastructures; the undertaking of human rights field activities and operations; and provision of education, information advisory services and technical assistance in the field of human rights.

For more information see: http://www.unhchr.ch

Office of the United Nations High Commissioner for Refugees – UNHCR

The Office of the United Nations High Commissioner for Refugees (UNHCR) was established by the **United Nations General Assembly** resolution 428(V) of 14 December 1950. It has its headquarters in Geneva and is mandated to lead and co-ordinate international action to protect refugees and resolve refugee problems worldwide. About 5000 people in more than 120 countries are working for UNHCR. Under the terms of its Statute a "refugee" is any person "who is outside the country of his nationality or, if he has no nationality, the country of his former habitual residence, because he has or had well-founded fear of persecution by reason of his race, religion, nationality, or political opinion and is unable or, because of such fear, is unwilling to avail himself of the protection of the government of the country of his former habitual residence" (para. 6). The Statute further provides that the function of the UNHCR shall be to seek permanent solutions for the problem of refugees "by assisting Governments and, subject to the approval of the Governments concerned, private organizations to facilitate the voluntary repatriation of such refugees, or their assimilation within new national communities" (para. 1). Where appropriate, UNHCR actively supports all efforts in favour of the return of refugees to their country of origin or former habitual residence by means of voluntary repatriation. However, in many cases of continued asylum, local integration forms the bulk of UNHCR assistance and in cases where durable solutions are not possible in countries of first asylum, resettlement in third countries becomes necessary. The ever-increasing number of refugees throughout the world, and the requests for assistance by the governments concerned, have contributed to a considerable development of the activities of UNHCR with respect to facilitating voluntary repatriation, resettling refugees in countries of asylum and various forms of material assistance for refugees, aimed primarily at durable solutions in the country of asylum. The UNHCR is also increasingly concerned with the root causes of conflicts and with the need for early-warning and preventative strategies to avert and resolve refugee flows and internal displacement. The 1951 **Convention relating to the Status of Refugees** and 1967 Protocol thereto are the key legal instruments dealing with refugee protection.

For more information see: http://www.unhcr.ch

Older persons

The **United Nations** has adopted a number of resolutions to ensure the full enjoyment by older persons of their human rights. In 1982, the First **World Assembly on Ageing** adopted the **Vienna International Plan of Action on Ageing**, which the **United Nations General Assembly** endorsed later that year in its resolution 37/51. The Plan calls for action in such areas as health and nutrition, housing, employment and social security, education and social welfare. A Second World Assembly on Ageing was held in Madrid, Spain in April 2002 on the twentieth anniversary of the Vienna World Assembly. In its resolution 1987/41, the **Economic and Social Council (ECOSOC)** authorized the creation of the International Institute on Ageing (INIA), which was established in Valletta, Malta, on 9 October 1987. It is an autonomous body operating under the auspices of the United Nations. It provides, in developing countries, education and training in gerontology, to policy makers, planners, programme executives, educators, professionals and para-professionals. It also acts as a catalyst as regards the exchange of information on issues connected with ageing.

In 1991, the General Assembly adopted the **United Nations Principles for Older Persons** which provides for five universal standards specific to the status of older persons: independence, participation, care, self-fulfilment and dignity of senior citizens. Subsequently, in its resolution 47/5 of 16 October 1992, the General Assembly proclaimed the year 1999 as the **International Year of Older Persons**.

Ombudsperson

The role and function of the institution of an ombudsperson are described in the **United Nations Secretary-General**'s report entitled National Institutions for the Protection and Promotion of Human Rights (E/CN.4/1993/33). Pursuant to it, the ombudsperson (the term "ombudsman" is still used but is considered by some as sexist) is an independent mediator – and, in some cases, a collegiate body – whose primary role is to protect the rights of the individual who believes that he/she is the victim of unjust acts on the part of the public administration. Generally appointed to office by the legislative body, the ombudsperson in many instances functions in a supervisory capacity on behalf of parliament, acting on complaints received from aggrieved persons against abuses or arbitrary acts by government officials or agencies. As an ombudsperson cannot be classified as a legislative, judicial or administrative organ, he/she is rather an institution of a *sui generis* nature with a multi-faceted character. Having had its beginnings in the early 19th century in Scandinavia (first created in Sweden in 1809), ombudspersons or similar offices have been established in a number of countries in various continents. The ombudsperson's office is an independent organ for the protection of human rights, which can be adapted to various political and social systems. Its title varies from country to country (for example in France – "Médiateur de la République"; in Austria – "Volksanwaltschaft"; in Spain – "Defensor del Pueblo" and in the United Kingdom – "Parliamentary Commissioner for Administration"). Procedures of access to the ombudsperson by an individual complainant also differ from country to country. Complaints are generally confidential and the identity of the complainant is not disclosed without the ombudsperson's consent. The first International Conference of Ombudsmen, held in Edmonton, Canada, in 1976, resulted in the establishment in 1978 of the International Ombudsman Institute with headquarters at the Law Center for the University of Alberta, Edmonton. It promotes the concept of ombudsmanship by conducting research on problems confronting ombudspersons and by organizing conferences and seminars. The post of ombudsperson has also been established at the regional level. In March 1994, the **European Union (EU)** created the post of a European Ombudsperson who can consider complaints from individuals or residents in the EU Member States. The Statute of the European Ombudsperson was laid down by the **European Parliament**, in accordance with community treaties.

Optional Protocol to the Convention against Torture and other Cruel, Inhuman or Degrading Treatment or Punishment (UN)

This Optional Protocol was adopted by the **United Nations General Assembly** (A/RES/57/199) on 18 December 2002. By the middle of 2003 it had not yet entered into force. The objective of the Protocol is "to establish a system of regular visits undertaken by independent international and national bodies to places where people are deprived of their liberty, in order to prevent torture and other cruel, inhuman or degrading treatment or punishment" (Article 1). The Protocol envisages the establishment of a Sub-Committee on Prevention of Torture and Other Cruel, Inhuman or Degrading Treatment or Punishment of the **Committee against Torture**. The Sub-Committee shall carry out its work "within the framework of the **Charter of the United Nations**" and "shall be guided by the "principles of confidentiality, impartiality, non-selectivity, universality and objectivity" (Article 2). The mandate of the Sub-Committee is presented in detail in Part III of the Protocol (Articles 11-16), while Part II

(Articles 5-10) concerns the composition of the body, which will consist first of 10 members, and, after the ratification of the Protocol by 50 States, will enlarge its membership to 25. The members of the Sub-Committee will be elected by the States Parties to the Convention against Torture among persons of high moral character with proven professional experience. They should act in their individual capacity and be independent and impartial.

Article 3 of the Protocol obliges States Parties to "set up, designate or maintain at the domestic level one or several visiting bodies for the prevention of torture and other cruel, inhuman or degrading treatment or punishment". The "national preventive mechanisms" (Part IV, Articles 17-23) should be established with due consideration to the Principles relating to the Status and Functioning of National Institutions for the Promotion and Protection of Human Rights, commonly known as the **Paris Principles**. The national preventive mechanisms shall be granted the powers to "regularly examine the treatment of the persons deprived of their liberty... with a view to strengthening their protection from torture" and to "make recommendations to the relevant authorities with the aim of improving the treatment and conditions of the persons deprived of their liberty" (Article 19). In order to fulfil their mandate, States Parties to the Protocol undertake to grant these mechanisms access to "all places of detention and their installations and facilities" and provide them with "access to all information referring to the treatment of these persons as well as their conditions of detention" (Article 20). Furthermore, each State Party shall allow visits by such mechanisms "to any place under its jurisdiction and control where persons are or may be deprived of their liberty" (Article 4).

Part VI of the Protocol concerns financial provisions and Part VII contains final provisions, including procedures of ratification of the Protocol and its entry into force.

Optional Protocol to the Convention on the Elimination of All Forms of Discrimination against Women (UN)

On 6 October 1999, the **United Nations General Assembly** adopted the Optional Protocol to the **Convention on the Elimination of All Forms of Discrimination against Women**. It was opened for signature on 10 December 1999, **Human Rights Day**, and entered into force on 22 December 2000. By the middle of 2003, it had been ratified by about 50 Member States. The aim of the Optional Protocol, elaborated upon the recommendation of the **World Conference on Human Rights** (Vienna, 1993), is to strengthen the implementation of the human rights of women. To this end, it gives individuals and groups of individuals the right to complain to the **Committee on the Elimination of Discrimination against Women (CEDAW)** about violations of the rights protected under the Convention. The Optional Protocol establishes the procedure called the "communications procedure" (Articles 1 and 2) and determines the conditions under which communications shall be admissible. Furthermore, it enables CEDAW to conduct inquiries into grave or systematic violations of women's rights by States Parties to the Optional Protocol (Article 8). The Optional Protocol sets out the first gender-specific international complaints procedure, and reinforces human rights monitoring within the **United Nations system**.

Optional Protocol to the Convention on the Rights of the Child on the Involvement of Children in Armed Conflict (UN)

The Optional Protocol was adopted by the **United Nations General Assembly** on 25 May 2000 and entered into force on 12 February 2002. By the middle of 2003, it had been signed by 76 States and ratified by 51 of them. The Protocol, in reaffirming the provisions of the **Convention on the Rights of the Child** reiterates that the rights of children require special protection to ensure their development and education in conditions of peace and security. In particular, States Parties shall ensure that those who have not attained the age of 18 years are not compulsorily recruited into the armed forces and take all feasible measures to ensure that voluntary members of the armed forces who have not attained the age of 18 years do not take a direct part in hostilities. The **Committee on the Rights of the Child** considers information concerning measures taken by States Parties to the Protocol to implement its provisions. Reports to this effect have to be submitted within two years after ratification.

Optional Protocol to the Convention on the Rights of the Child on the Sale of Children, Child Prostitution and Child Pornography (UN)

This Optional Protocol was adopted by the **United Nations General Assembly** on 25 May 2000 and entered into force on 18 January 2002. By the middle of 2003, it had been signed by 70 States and ratified by 50 of them. Its main objective is to extend the measures that States Parties undertake in order to guarantee the protection of the child from the sale of children, child prostitution and child pornography, and contains a detailed definition of such offences (Article 2). The Protocol, in its Article 3, enumerates acts which should be considered as criminal and punishable by law, including sexual exploitation of the child and transfer of organs of the child for profit. It contains a clause concerning the extradition of persons guilty of such offences. The **Committee on the Rights of the Child** considers information regarding the implementation of the Protocol, which should be submitted by States Parties to the Protocol initially two years after their acceding to it and every five years thereafter.

Optional Protocol to the International Covenant on Civil and Political Rights (UN)

An Optional Protocol to the International Covenant on Civil and Political Rights was adopted by the **United Nations General Assembly** on 16 December 1966 and entered into force on 23 March 1976. By the middle of 2003, it had been ratified by more than 100 Member States. Under Articles 1 to 6 of the Protocol, a State Party to the International Covenant that becomes a Party to the Protocol recognizes the competence of the **Human Rights Committee** to receive and consider communications from individuals subject to its jurisdiction who claim to be victims of a violation by that State. Such individuals, who have exhausted all available domestic remedies, may submit written communications to the Human Rights Committee for consideration. However, no communication may be received by the Committee if it concerns a State Party to the Covenant which is not also a Party to the Optional Protocol. The Committee then considers these communications at closed meetings, in the light of all written information made available to it by the individual and by the State Party concerned, and forwards its view to that State Party and to the individual.

Organisation for Economic Co-operation and Development – OECD

On 14 December 1960, 18 European States (Austria, Belgium, Denmark, France, Germany, Greece, Iceland, Ireland, Italy, Luxembourg, Netherlands, Norway, Portugal, Spain, Sweden, Switzerland, Turkey, United Kingdom), the United States and Canada signed the Convention establishing OECD, which entered into force on 30 September 1961. OECD succeeded the Organisation for European Economic Co-operation (OEEC) funded in 1948 to administer American and Canadian aid under the Marshall Plan for the Reconstruction of Europe after the Second World War. As of August 2003, 30 States are members of the

OECD and accept to share the values of open market economy, democratic pluralism and respect for human rights. (Japan, Australia, New Zealand, Finland, Mexico, Czech Republic, Hungary, Poland, Republic of Korea and Slovak Republic joined original members). As provided for by the 1960 Convention, OECD works to: build strong economies in its member countries, improve efficiency, stimulate market systems, liberalize international trade and contribute to development, not only in industrialized countries, but also in developing countries (Article 1 and Article 2 of the Convention). Member States meet and exchange information in committees, which are composed of their representatives. The governing body is the Council, which has decision-making powers. It provides general guidance to the Organisation and its work. It comprises one representative for each Member State, as well as a representative of the **European Commission**. Moreover, there are specialized committees dealing with specific areas of policy such as trade, public management, development cooperation or financial markets. Located in Paris, the OECD Secretariat is directed by a Secretary-General, assisted by four Deputy Secretaries-General. The Secretary-General also chairs the Council, providing the essential link between national delegations and the Secretariat. In 2000 OECD adopted the guidelines for Multinational Enterprises (see **Transnational corporations and human rights**).

For more information see: http://www.oecd.org

Organization for Security and Co-operation in Europe – OSCE

The Organization for Security and Co-operation in Europe (OSCE) was renamed on 1 January 1995 (taking effect on that date), emerging from the **Conference on Security and Co-operation in Europe (CSCE)** which was created in 1973 to serve as a multilateral forum for dialogue and negotiation between East and West. The Conference opened in Helsinki on 3 July 1973 and continued in Geneva from 18 September 1973 to 21 July 1975. It concluded in Helsinki on 1 August 1975 and was the first conference in the history of Europe with the participation of all European Countries, with the exception of Albania. It culminated in the signing of the **Helsinki Final Act**, recognizing the inviolability of the post-Second World War frontiers in Europe and committing the signatories to respect human rights and fundamental freedoms and to cooperate in scientific, cultural, and other fields. From 1975 to 1990, the CSCE functioned as a series of meetings and conferences setting norms and commitments and periodically reviewing their implementation. The Paris Summit Conference, which took place from 19 to 21 November 1990, formally recognized the end of the Cold War and can be considered as a historic event, concluding the the adoption of the **Charter of Paris for a New Europe**. Until that date the CSCE was a process without permanent institutions. In the following years, the development of the security situation in Europe led to fundamental changes in the CSCE. The Helsinki Document of July 1992 established a number of practical tools to strengthen the Conference's contribution to the protection of human rights and the management of the unprecedented changes in Europe. Reflecting the latter, and in order to give a new political impetus to the Conference, the 1994 Budapest Summit decided to change its name to the OSCE. Today it is an international organization playing a leading role in fostering security through cooperation in Europe. It comprises 55 States (Albania, Andorra, Armenia, Austria, Azerbaijan, Belarus, Belgium, Bosnia and Herzegovina, Bulgaria, Canada, Croatia, Cyprus, Czech Republic, Denmark, Estonia, Finland, France, Georgia, Germany, Greece, Holy See, Hungary, Iceland, Ireland, Italy, Kazakhstan, Kyrgyzstan, Latvia, Liechtenstein, Lithuania, Luxembourg, Malta, Moldova, Monaco, Netherlands, Norway, Poland, Portugal, Romania, Russian Federation, San Marino, Serbia and Montenegro, Slovak Republic, Slovenia, Spain, Sweden, Switzerland, Tajikistan, The former Yugoslav Republic of Macedonia, Turkey, Turkmenistan, Ukraine, United Kingdom, United States of America, Uzbekistan). It functions as an instrument for early warning, conflict prevention, crisis management, post-conflict rehabilitation and democratization in Europe. The OSCE's long-term involvement in conflict prevention and crisis management activities on the ground is embodied in its field missions in Participating States. Today, the OSCE has several political bodies and institutions. Its regular body for political consultation and decision-making is the Permanent Council which meets weekly in Vienna, Austria, where its Secretariat is based. The Forum for Security and Cooperation also meets weekly in Vienna to discuss arms control. High-ranking officials can meet at the Senior Council which convenes for political deliberations. The central decision-making and governing body is the Ministerial Council, which brings together the foreign ministers of the Participating States once a year. The Heads of State or Government meet at the OSCE Summits to assess the situation and provide new guidelines for the Organization's activities and may appoint Personal Representatives for specific functions. Consensus is the basis for OSCE decision-making. The post of Chairman-in-Office has overall responsibility for executive action and coordination of current OSCE activities. The post rotates annually and is held by the Foreign Minister of a Participating State.

The Organization's institutions comprise the Secretariat, the **Office for Democratic Institutions and Human Rights (ODIHR)**, the **High Commissioner on National Minorities (HCNM)** and the **OSCE Representative on Freedom of the Media**. OSCE-related bodies include the Court of Conciliation and Arbitration, the Joint Consultative Group and the Open Skies Consultative Commission. The OSCE is also characterized by a number of field missions located mainly in Eastern Europe and the former Soviet Union. In addition, there is an OSCE Parliamentary Assembly based in Copenhagen.

For more information see: http://www.osce.org

Organization of African Unity – OAU

The Organization of African Unity (OAU) was established on 25 May 1963, in Addis Ababa, Ethiopia, when 32 African Heads of State and Government signed the OAU Charter uniting States from all over Africa. By the middle of 2003, it comprised 53 members. The objectives of the Organization, as declared in Article II of the Charter, include the eradication of all forms of colonialism in Africa, the promotion of unity and solidarity of African States, the defence of the integrity, independence and national solidarity of African States, and the achievement of a better life for the People of Africa by means of promoting human rights, peace and mutual understanding. The OAU has two decision-making bodies. One is the Assembly of Heads of State and Government, which meets once a year and decides the general political guidelines. The other is the Council of Ministers which decides, inter alia, on budgetary matters. The Council, which meets twice a year, is composed of the Ministers of Foreign Affairs or other Ministers as are designated by the Governments of the Member States. A Secretariat, located in Addis Ababa and headed by a Secretary-General, carries out the daily work of the Organization. It is supported by and cooperates with a number of regional offices. The activities of the OAU cover a wide range of fields in the social, cultural, economic and political spheres, and are based upon a firm devotion to the promotion of human rights. The OAU has adopted several instruments in this field, including the **African Charter on Human and Peoples' Rights** (1981), the **Convention Governing the Specific Aspect of Refugee Problems in Africa** (1969) and the **African Charter on the Rights and Welfare of the Child** (1990). In September 1999 the **African Union** (AU) was created to effectively replace the OAU.

Organization of American States – OAS

The Organization of American States (OAS) is a regional inter-governmental organization that dates back to the First International Conference of American States held from

October 1889 to April 1890. This meeting approved the establishment of the International Union of American Republics, the forerunner to the OAS. On 30 April 1948, 21 Latin American Republics and the United States of America signed the Charter of the OAS, which established the Organization. The Charter entered into force in December 1951. The Charter was subsequently amended by the Protocol of Buenos Aires (1967), the Protocol of Cartagena de Indias (1985), the Protocol of Washington (1992) and the Protocol of Managua (1993). The OAS currently comprises 35 Member States, each with a single vote. In addition, Permanent Observer status has been granted to over 40 States, as well as to the **European Union**.

The main objectives of the OAS are, *inter alia*, to strengthen the peace and security of the continent, to promote and consolidate representative democracy, with due respect to the principle of non-intervention, to ensure the pacific settlement of disputes, and to promote, through means of cooperation, economic, social and cultural development. It is founded on the basic principles stipulated in Article 3 of the Charter stressing, among others, the importance of international law as the standard of conduct, international order, the effective exercise of democracy and, in particular, the fundamental rights of the individual without distinction as to race, nationality, creed or sex. The OAS Headquarters are in Washington, D.C. (U.S.A.). The main body of the OAS is its General Assembly which meets once a year and decides on the general lines of action and policy. The General Assembly is complemented by the Meeting of Consultation of Ministers of Foreign Affairs, which gathers at the request of any Member State or in the event of problems of an urgent nature. The standard-setting activities of the OAS in the field of human rights have resulted in a number of instruments, including the **American Declaration on the Rights and Duties of Man** (1948), the **American Convention on Human Rights** (1969), and the **Inter-American Convention to Prevent and Punish Torture** (1985).

For more information see: http://www.oas.org

Organized crime

Illegal activities conducted by organized crime, such as drug-trafficking or money-laundering, have an important adverse impact on human rights and the functioning of a democratic society. Smuggling of migrants, trafficking in women and children and other criminal acts present a major threat to human rights. To this end, the **Inter-American Convention on International Traffic in Minors** was adopted by the **Organization of American States (OAS)** on 18 March 1994 and entered into force on 15 August 1997. In 1996, the **Commission on Crime Prevention and Criminal Justice** established an open-ended working group to explore the links between transnational organized crime and terrorist criminal activities – "… a combination viewed as a severe threat to peace and development". The **United Nations General Assembly** adopted during its 51st session the **Declaration on Crime and Public Security** which states that Member States shall seek to protect the security and well-being of their citizens and all persons within their jurisdiction by taking effective national measures to combat serious transnational crime, including organized crime. The **United Nations Convention against Transnational Organized Crime**, the **Protocol to Prevent, Suppress and Punish Trafficking in Persons, Especially Women and Children**, and the **Protocol against the Smuggling of Migrants by Land, Sea and Air** were adopted by the United Nations General Assembly on 15 November 2000 by resolution 55/25. The **Protocol Against the Illicit Manufacturing of and Trafficking in Firearms, Their Parts and Components and Ammunition** was adopted by the General Assembly on 31 May 2001 and is the third Protocol to the Convention against Transnational Organized Crime.

OSCE Representative on Freedom of the Media (OSCE)

The post of the Representative on Freedom of the Media of the **Organization for Security and Co-operation in Europe**

(OSCE) was established on 5 November 1997 by the OSCE Permanent Council Decision N° 193. The Representative does not exercise a juridical function; his/her mandate is to observe relevant media developments in all Participating States and promote full compliance with OSCE principles and commitments concerning freedom of expression and the media. In this respect, he/she assumes an early-warning function and provides rapid response to serious issues such as obstruction of media activities and unfavourable working conditions for journalists (para. 2-3). To this end, the Representative seeks direct contacts with the Participating State and other parties concerned, assesses the facts, collects information on the situation of the media from all *bona fide* sources and, in particular, draws on information and assessments provided by the **Office of Democratic Institutions and Human Rights (ODIHR)** of the OSCE. The Representative consults regularly with the Chairman-in-Office and reports on a regular basis to the Permanent Council on matters concerning freedom of expression and free media; works with independence and impartiality and in close cooperation with the Participating States, relevant OSCE bodies, the **United Nations** and its specialized agencies, the **Council of Europe**, as well as with national and international media associations. The Representative is appointed for three years in accordance with OSCE procedures by the Ministerial Council upon the recommendation of the Chairman-in-Office after consultation with the Participating States.

For more information see: http://www.osce.org/fom

Pact of San José (OAS)

Common name for the **American Convention on Human Rights**, adopted by the **Organization of American States (OAS)** in 1969.

Paris Convention for the Protection of Industrial Property

The Paris Convention was adopted in 1883 and entered into force in 1884. It was the first major international treaty aiming to provide citizens of one country with protection for their intellectual creations in the form of industrial property in other countries. By the middle of 2003, it had been ratified by 164 States. Both the Paris Convention and the **Berne Convention for the Protection of Literary and Artistic Works** (1886) led to the creation of an international Organization called the United International Bureau for the Protection of Intellectual Property, best known by its French name *Bureaux internationaux réunis pour la protection de la propriété intellectuelle* (BIRPI). The **World Intellectual Property Organization (WIPO),** established in 1967, implements the functions formerly entrusted to BIRPI.

Paris Principles (UN)

The United Nations Principles relating to the status and functioning of national institutions for the promotion and protection of human rights, known as the Paris Principles, were adopted in October 1991 at an international workshop convened by the **United Nations Centre for Human Rights** (now the **Office of the United Nations High Commissioner for Human Rights**). This comprehensive set of recommendations concerns the role, composition, status and functions of human rights institutions. It was endorsed by the **Commission on Human Rights** (resolution 1992/54) in March 1992 and by the **United Nations General Assembly** (A/RES/48/134) in December 1993. A national human rights institution is defined as a body established under the constitution or by law, whose functions are specifically designed to protect human rights. Such an institution takes the form of either a human rights commission, **ombudsperson** or specialized national institution.

The four sections of the Principles outline: the competence and responsibilities of national institutions; composition and guarantees of independence and pluralism; methods of operation; and additional principles concerning the status of commissions with quasi-jurisdictional competence. The Principles stress the importance of a broad mandate and sphere of competence, a pluralistic and representative composition, adequate funding and effective cooperation with or through the presence of non-governmental human rights groups, trade unions, concerned social and professional organizations, eminent scientists, philosophers, religious leaders, professors and qualified experts, parliament and governmental departments.

The Principles contain an important section on the composition and guarantees of independence and pluralism of national human rights institutions. "The composition of the national institution shall be established in accordance with a procedure which affords all necessary guarantees to ensure the pluralist representation of the social forces (of civilian society) involved in the protection and promotion of human rights" (Section B, para. 1). In efforts to ensure the independence of these institutions, representatives of government departments should participate in the deliberations only in an advisory capacity (Section B, para. 2). Furthermore, the institutions shall be adequately funded so that they are able to have their own staff and premises in order to ensure independence from the government. "In order to ensure a stable mandate for the members of the institution, without which there can be no real independence, their appointment shall be effected by an official act which shall establish the specific duration of the mandate" (Section B, para. 3).

National human rights institutions in about 50 countries are recognized as corresponding to the Paris Principles. Their status is determined by the Accreditation Sub-Committee of the International Co-ordinating Committee of National Institutions for the Promotion and Protection of Human Rights, which is formed from representatives from various regional groups. The four regional groups: Africa; Americas; Asia/Pacific; and Europe develop and implement activities on a regional level and cooperate with other interested organizations. This network elects the Chairman and Vice Chairman of the International Co-ordinating Committee.

Peace and human rights

The importance of international peace to the realization of human rights and fundamental freedoms is made evident in the **Charter of the United Nations**. Its Preamble reads: "We the peoples of the **United Nations** determined to save succeeding generations from the scourge of war, ... and to reaffirm faith in fundamental human rights, in the dignity and worth of the human person, in the equal rights of men and women and of nations large and small, and to establish conditions under which justice and respect for the obligations arising from treaties and other sources of international law can be maintained, and to promote social progress and better standards of life in larger freedom, and for these ends to practice tolerance and live together in peace with one another as good neighbours, and to unite our strength to maintain international peace and security, and to ensure, by the acceptance of principles and the institution of methods, that armed force shall not be used, save in the common interest, and to employ international machinery for the promotion of the economic and social advancement of all peoples...". Similarly, Article 1 of the Charter sets out the purposes of the United Nations in the following terms: "To maintain international peace and security, and to that end: to take effective collective measures for the prevention and removal of threats to the peace, and for the suppression of acts of aggression or other breaches of the peace, and to bring about by peaceful means, and in conformity with the principles of justice and international law, adjustment or settlement of international disputes or situations which might lead to a breach of the peace".

That the maintenance of international peace is vital for the full realization of human rights is affirmed in a large number of instruments, including: the Declaration on Principles of International Law concerning Friendly Relations and Co-operation among States in accordance with the Charter of the United Nations (1970); the **Declaration on the Preparation of Societies for Life in Peace** (1978); in the **Declaration on the Participation of Women in Promoting International Peace and Co-operation** (1984). In declaring 1986 the **International Year of Peace** and in proclaiming the year 2000 as the **International Year for the Culture of Peace**, the **United Nations General Assembly** confirmed the inherent link between peace and human rights. United Nations bodies have also adopted resolutions linking the enjoyment of human rights with the maintenance of international peace and security. The **Commission on Human Rights** has considered the importance of international peace and security to the realization of human rights regularly since 1976 under the agenda item entitled "Human rights and scientific and technological developments". The prohibition of the threat or use of force in international relations is not an absolute one; the threat or use of force in self-defence against an armed attack, in achieving freedom and independence, and in rebelling against tyranny and oppression is legitimate.

In line with its constitutional objectives to contribute to peace and security by promoting collaboration among nations through education, science and culture, **UNESCO** adopted in 1974 the most comprehensive international instrument dealing with education for peace: the **Recommendation concerning Education for International Understanding, Co-operation and Peace and Education Relating to Human Rights and Fundamental Freedoms**. Furthermore, UNESCO has adopted a Transdisciplinary Project entitled "Towards a culture of peace" which is aimed at promoting values, attitudes and behaviours in people so that they will seek peaceful solutions to problems, and advancing a global movement for a culture of peace. UNESCO also plays a leading role in activities for the **International Decade for a Culture of Peace and Non-Violence for the Children of the World (2001-10)**.

Permanent Forum on Indigenous Issues (UN)

The creation of a Permanent Forum on Indigenous Issues was one of the central objectives of the programme of activities for the **International Decade of the World's Indigenous People (1995-2004)** and was first proposed at the United Nations **World Conference on Human Rights** (Vienna, Austria, 1993). Two **United Nations** workshops were held to discuss the possibility of a permanent forum. The first was held in Copenhagen, Denmark, in 1995 (relevant report: E/CN.4/Sub.2/AC.4/1995/7) the second in Santiago, Chile, in 1997 (E/CN.4/1998/11). In February 1999, an *ad hoc* working group of the **Commission on Human Rights** met in Geneva to elaborate proposals for the Forum. A second *ad hoc* working group met in February 2000 to finalize a proposal for the Commission. At its 56th session in 2000 the Commission on Human Rights recommended that the **Economic and Social Council** set up a permanent forum on indigenous issues.

On 28 July 2000 the Economic and Social Council adopted a resolution (E/RES/2000/22) establishing the Permanent Forum on Indigenous Issues. The Permanent Forum serves as an advisory body to the ECOSOC with a mandate to discuss indigenous issues relating to economic and social development, culture, the environment, education, health and human rights. It is also responsible for the dissemination of information on indigenous issues and promoting integration and coordination of activities relating to indigenous issues within the **United Nations system**.

The Forum is composed of 16 independent experts. Eight experts are nominated by governments and elected by the Council. The other eight members are appointed by the President of the Council on the basis of consultations with the Bureau and the regional groups through their coordinators, and on the basis of broad consultations with indigenous organizations. The composition of the Forum takes into account the diversity and geographical distribution of the indigenous people of the world. All members serve in their personal capacity for a period of three years with the possibility of re-election or re-appointment for one further period. The Forum meets once a year for ten working days and submits an annual report on its activities to the ECOSOC and other relevant United Nations organs. Participation in the Forum is open to the representatives of all indigenous organizations, even if the organizations are not in consultative status with ECOSOC.

The first session of the Forum was held at United Nations Headquarters in May 2002. A Secretariat for the Forum was established in March 2003 and will assist the body in carrying out its mandate.

For more information see:
http://www.unhchr.ch/indigenous/forum.htm

Political rights

Political rights refer to those rights and freedoms which allow people to participate in the public affairs of the society to which they belong. Political rights include: the right to **freedom of thought, conscience, religion or belief**, **opinion**, and **expression** and information; the right to peaceful assembly and to **freedom of association**; the right to take part in the conduct of public affairs directly or through freely chosen representatives; and the **right to vote and to be elected** and to have **equal access to public** service. The **International Covenant on Civil and Political Rights** (1966) provides that these rights are to be implemented without any **discrimination** and "without unreasonable restrictions" (Article 2). Political rights are, generally speaking, immediately applicable and directly enforceable, and are rights of the individual "against" the State, that is, against unlawful and unjust action of the State. Political rights require specific means and methods of implementation, namely through **communication procedures**. Among instruments whose purpose is either to proclaim political rights or to guarantee them are the **Universal Declaration of Human Rights** (1948) and the International Covenant on Civil and Political Rights, together with a number of specific instruments concerning particular political rights, such as the **Convention on the Political Rights of Women** (1952), as well as regional instruments such as: the **European Convention for the Protection of Human Rights and Fundamental Freedoms** (1950) and its Additional Protocol N° 1 (1952) which was amended by the Protocols N° 11 (1994) and N° 4 (1963); the **American Declaration of the Rights and Duties of Man** (1948); and the **American Convention on Human Rights** (1969).

Poverty

Poverty is a complex problem with various causes and manifestations. It remains a global problem of huge proportions since, as stated in the *World Development Report 2000/2001: Attacking Poverty* published by the World Bank, of the world's 6 billion people, 2.8 billion live on less than US$ 2 a day and 1.2 billion on less than US$ 1 a day. Poverty is characterized by: lack of income and productive resources sufficient to ensure a sustainable livelihood; hunger and malnutrition; ill health; increasing morbidity and mortality from illness; limited or lack of access to education and other basic services; homelessness and inadequate housing; lack of participation in decision-making and in civil, social and cultural life; unsafe environments; social **discrimination** and exclusion, etc. The multidimensional character of poverty explains that its elimination is a matter of priority for many bodies, programmes and agencies of the **United Nations system** including the **United Nations Development Programme (UNDP),** the World Bank Group, the International Monetary Fund (IMF), the **Food and Agriculture Organization of the United Nations (FAO)**, the World Food Programme (WFP), the **International Labour Organization (ILO)**, the **World Health Organization (WHO),** the **United Nations Educational, Scientific and Cultural Organization (UNESCO)**, the **United Nations Children's Fund (UNICEF)**, the **United Nations Population Fund (UNFPA)**, the **United Nations Centre for Human Settlements (Habitat)**, etc.

Moreover, the eradication of poverty has been a priority objective in many United Nations conferences held since the 1990s including the United Nations Conference on Environment and Development (UNCED) held in June 1992 in Rio de Janeiro, Brazil, and the International Conference on Population and Development (ICPD) held in Cairo, Egypt, in September 1994, which both recognized that combating poverty was an essential requirement for sustainable development and that poverty was irreconcilable with the concept of development. They called for action to implement the **right to development**, as reaffirmed by the **Declaration on the Right to Development** (1986). **The World Conference on Human Rights** (Vienna, Austria, 1993) underlined the importance of the implementation of the right to development and of the struggle against **extreme poverty**. It qualified poverty as one of the main obstacles to respect for human rights and declared that **extreme poverty** constitutes a violation of human dignity. The **World Summit for Social Development** (Copenhagen, Denmark, 1995) adopted the **Copenhagen Declaration on Social Development and Programme of Action**, which formulates a substantive framework for eradicating poverty. The fourth **World Conference[s] on Women** (Beijing, China, 1995) outlined expressly the increased feminization of poverty and stated that empowering women was an important factor in the eradication of poverty. The **World Summit for Sustainable Development** (Johannesburg, South Africa, 2002) addressed issues of poverty eradication and adopted the Johannesburg Declaration on Sustainable Development and its Plan of Implementation.

Furthermore, the **United Nations General Assembly** has adopted many resolutions concerning poverty reduction, including: resolution 47/196 of 22 December 1992, by which it proclaimed 17 October **International Day for the Eradication of Poverty**; resolution 48/183 of 21 December 1993, by which it declared 1996 **International Year for the Eradication of Poverty**; and resolution 50/107 of 20 December 1995, by which it proclaimed the **United Nations Decade for the Eradication of Poverty (1997-2006).**

In 2000, the **United Nations Secretary-General** submitted to the General Assembly a report (document A/55 of 21 September 2000) on the progress achieved in the implementation of measures, recommendations and activities relating to the United Nations Decade for the Eradication of Poverty (1997-2006), including an examination of the impact of **globalization** on the elimination of poverty. The report outlines the progress made in global poverty reduction since the World Summit for Social Development, highlighting the need for more concerted and sustained efforts. The elimination of poverty has been acknowledged as a priority in the **United Nations Millennium Declaration** and the reduction in extreme poverty and hunger by half is one of the eight **Millennium Development Goals.**

Principles for the Protection of Persons with Mental Illness and the Improvement of Mental Health Care (UN)

On 17 December 1991, the **United Nations General Assembly** adopted these Principles. They (25 altogether) define the fundamental freedoms and basic rights of persons with a mental illness, or those being treated as such, and deal with such matters as the right to life in the community (Principle 3), means of determining mental illness (Principle 4), consent to treatment (Principle 11), admission to treatment facilities (Principle 15), medication and treatment (Principles 9 and 10), rights and conditions in mental health facilities (Principle 13) and procedural safeguards (Principle 18). The Principles are intended to serve, *inter alia*, as a guide to Governments, specialized agencies, national and international organizations, governmental and non-governmental, and individuals, and to stimulate endeavours to overcome economic and other practical difficulties affecting the application of standards for the protection of fundamental freedoms and the human and legal rights of persons with mental illness.

Principles of International Co-operation in the Detection, Arrest, Extradition and Punishment of Persons Guilty of War Crimes and Crimes against Humanity (UN)

The **United Nations General Assembly**, in response to the urgent need to ensure the prosecution and punishment of persons guilty of war crimes and crimes against humanity, adopted resolution 3074 (XXVIII) on 3 December 1973, which sets forth the above Principles. In accordance with them: "War crimes and crimes against humanity, wherever they are committed, shall be subject to investigation and the persons against whom there is evidence that they have committed such crimes shall be subject to tracing, arrest, trial and, if found guilty, to punishment". Hence, States shall cooperate with each other in conformity with the **Charter of the United Nations** and the **Declaration on Principles of International Law concerning Friendly Relations and Cooperation among States**, with a view to preventing war crimes and crimes against humanity, collecting information and evidence, arresting and bringing to trial persons suspected of their commission. The right to seek and enjoy asylum, as Article 1 of the **Declaration on Territorial Asylum** stipulates: "... may not be invoked by any person with respect to whom there are serious reasons for considering that he has committed a crime against peace, a war crime or a crime against humanity, as defined in the international instruments drawn up to make provision in respect of such crimes". In this connection, States shall not grant asylum to any person suspected of committing such acts. States have jurisdiction to try and punish acts constituting war crimes and crimes against humanity, committed by their own nationals as well as by non-nationals, especially if those acts were perpetrated on their territory. Therefore, States shall co-operate closely to facilitate the extradition of such persons and shall avoid taking measures which may be prejudicial to that end.

Principles of Medical Ethics relevant to the Role of Health Personnel, particularly Physicians, in the Protection of Prisoners and Detainees against Torture and other Cruel, Inhuman or Degrading Treatment or Punishment (UN)

Alarmed that members of the medical profession or other health personnel are often engaged in activities which are difficult to reconcile with medical ethics, the **United Nations General Assembly** adopted these Principles on 18 December 1982 (Resolution 37/194). The instrument, which is comprised of six Principles, states that "health personnel, particularly physicians, charged with the medical care of prisoners and detainees have a duty to provide them with protection of their physical and mental health and treatment of disease of the same quality and standard as is afforded to those who are not imprisoned or detained" (Principle 1). It states further that: "It is a gross contravention of medical ethics, as well as an offense under applicable international instruments, for health personnel, particularly physicians, to engage, actively or passively, in acts which constitute participation in, complicity in, incitement to or attempts to commit torture or other cruel, inhuman or degrading treatment or punishment" (Principle 2) or to apply their knowledge and skills in order to assist in the interrogation of prisoners and detainees (Principle 4). Principle 6 stresses that there may be no derogation from the Principles contained in this instrument on any ground whatsoever, including public emergency.

Principles on the Effective Investigation and Documentation of Torture and other Cruel, Inhuman or Degrading Treatment or Punishment (UN)

Adopted by the **United Nations General Assembly** (A/RES/55/89) on 4 December 2000, these Principles outline measures necessary for an effective investigation and documentation of torture and other cruel, inhuman or degrading treatment or punishment. The purpose of an investigation "is the clarification of facts and establishment of individual and State responsibility for victims and their families; the identification of measures needed to prevent re-occurrence; and the facilitation of prosecution and/or disciplinary sanctions for those indicated by the investigation as being responsible…" (Principle 1). It includes fair and adequate financial compensation and provision of the means for medical care and rehabilitation. States shall ensure that "complaints and reports of torture or ill-treatment are promptly and effectively investigated" (Principle 2).

The investigative authority and relevant experts are to "have at their disposal all necessary budgetary and technical resources for effective investigation" (Principle 3) and medical experts involved shall "behave at all times in conformity with the highest ethical standards" (Principle 6). Principle 6 also provides a detailed outline of the responsibility of medical professionals involved in an investigation, including the preparation of a confidential written report which includes a detailed account of the subject's story, a record of the physical and psychological examination and the opinion of the medical expert as to the physical and psychological findings.

In cases where due to a lack of expertise or suspected bias the established mechanisms are unable to sufficiently investigate claims, States should ensure that investigations are undertaken through an independent commission of inquiry or similar procedure (Principle 5).

Principles on the Effective Prevention and Investigation of Extra-legal, Arbitrary and Summary Executions (UN)

On 24 May 1989, the **Economic and Social Council (ECOSOC)** adopted these Principles. Governments were requested to take them into account and respect them within the framework of their national legislation and practices. The instrument should also be brought to the attention of law enforcement and criminal justice officials, military personnel, lawyers, members of the executive and legislative bodies of the government and the public in general. The **Committee on Crime Prevention and Control** is requested to keep the Principles under constant review, including their implementation. The section on "Prevention" comprises eight Principles. Principle 1 states that: "Governments shall prohibit by law all extra-legal, arbitrary and summary executions and shall ensure that any such executions are recognized as offences under their criminal laws …". The second section on "Investigation" contains nine Principles. Principle 9 states that: "There shall be thorough, prompt and impartial investigation of all suspected cases of extra-legal, arbitrary and summary executions …". The last section is entitled "Legal proceedings" and comprises three Principles.

Proclamation of Tehran (UN)

The Proclamation of Tehran was adopted on 13 May 1968 by the **United Nations International Conference on Human Rights** held in Tehran, Iran, with a view to reviewing the progress made in the twenty years since the adoption of the **Universal Declaration of Human Rights** and to making recommendations for the future. The Proclamation states that despite substantial progress in developing international instruments of protection of human rights and fundamental freedoms, the implementation of those instruments is still to be achieved (para. 4). Therefore, the international community was urged to redouble its efforts to promote and encourage respect for human rights and fundamental freedoms, as set forth in the Universal Declaration of Human Rights and in other international instruments. In particular, national laws are required to provide for all, irrespective of race, sex, language, religion or political belief, freedom of expression, of information, of conscience and of religion, as well as the right to participate in the political, economic, cultural and social life of their country (para. 5). Furthermore, the Proclamation places a special emphasis on the struggle against **apartheid**, all ideologies based on racial superiority and intolerance, and colonialism (paras. 7-9). The Proclamation also enumerates major obstacles to the full realization of human rights: aggression or armed conflict; **discrimination** on grounds of race, religion, belief or expressions of opinion; economic and social problems in developing countries; illiteracy, etc. (paras. 10-14). The international community is urged to cooperate in eradicating such obstacles and in strengthening the protection of women, the family, the child, the younger generation (paras. 15-17). Issues concerning technological advances monitoring, and general and complete disarmament are also recognized as requiring adequate attention (paras. 18-19).

Protocol against the Illicit Manufacturing of and Trafficking in Firearms, Their Parts and Components and Ammunition (UN)

This third Protocol to the **United Nations Convention against Transnational Organized Crime** was adopted by the **United Nations**

General Assembly (A/RES/55/255) on 31 May 2001. It is designed to promote, facilitate and strengthen cooperation among States Parties in order to prevent, combat and eradicate the illicit manufacturing of and trafficking in firearms, their parts and components and ammunition. The Protocol, in its Article 5, requires States Parties to "adopt such legislative and other measures as may be necessary to establish as criminal offences the following conduct, when committed internationally: illicit manufacturing of firearms, their parts and components and ammunition; illicit trafficking in firearms, their parts and components and ammunition; and falsifying or illicitly obliterating, removing or altering the marking(s) on firearms" (as required by article 8 of the Protocol). States Parties "must ensure the maintenance, for not less than ten years, of information in relation to firearms and, whcrc appropriate and feasible, their parts and components and ammunition in order to identify and trace those firearms" (Article 7). The Protocol also establishes general requirements for export, import and transit licensing or authorization systems for the transfer of firearms (Article 10).

Protocol against the Smuggling of Migrants by Land, Sea and Air (UN)

This Protocol to the **United Nations Convention against Transnational Organized Crime** was adopted on the same day as the Convention, that is 15 November 2000, by **United Nations General Assembly** resolution 55/25. It deals with the growing international problem of the smuggling of migrants by organized criminal groups – often at high risk to the migrants and at great profit for the offenders. It supplements the more general measures stipulated in the Convention. States must become parties to the Convention itself before they can become parties to the Protocol. By the middle of 2003, the Protocol had not yet entered into force.

Protocol Amending the 1926 Slavery Convention (UN)

The **Slavery Convention** was signed in Geneva on 25 September 1926. It entrusted the **League of Nations** with certain duties and functions. Believing that these duties and functions should be continued and entrusted upon the **United Nations**, the **United Nations General Assembly** approved the Protocol Amending the 1926 Slavery Convention on 23 October 1953. It entered into force on 7 December 1953. By the middle of 2003, about 60 States are parties to it. Without changing the content of the Convention, the Protocol charges the **United Nations Secretary-General** and the **International Court of Justice** with monitoring the implementation of the Convention.

Protocol Instituting a Conciliation and Good Offices Commission to Be Responsible for Seeking a Settlement of Any Disputes which May Arise between States Parties to the Convention against Discrimination in Education (UNESCO)

On 10 December 1962, the General Conference of **UNESCO** adopted this Protocol. It entered into force on 24 October 1968 and had been ratified by more than 30 Member States by the middle of 2003. The Commission instituted by the Protocol consists of 11 members elected by the General Conference of UNESCO for a term of six years to serve in their personal capacity (Articles 2 and 5). Recourse to the Commission is limited to States Parties to the Protocol. If one of those States considers that another is not giving effect to the provisions of the Convention, it may, by written communication, bring the matter to the attention of that State (Article 12). If the matter is not adjusted to the satisfaction of both States within six months, either State has the right to refer it to the Commission (Article 12). The function of the Commission is essentially to ascertain the facts and make available its good offices to the States concerned, with a view to an amicable solution of the matter on the basis of respect for the Convention (Article 17). If no settlement of the dispute is reached, a report is prepared and sent to the States concerned with an indication of the recommendations which have been formulated (Article 17).

Protocol No. 13 to the Convention for the Protection of Human Rights and Fundamental Freedoms, concerning the Abolition of the Death Penalty in All Circumstances (Council of Europe)

This Protocol was adopted and opened for signature on 3 May 2002 to the Member States of the **Council of Europe** which had signed the **European Convention for the Protection of Human Rights and Fundamental Freedoms**. It entered into force on 1 July 2003 and had been ratified by 17 Member States by the middle of 2003. The Protocol bans the death penalty in all circumstances including its abolition for crimes committed in times of war or imminent threat of war. While Protocol 6 to the Convention also concerns the abolition of the death penalty, it does not exclude the death penalty with respect to acts committed in time of war or of imminent threat of war. The Protocol is considered the "final step in order to abolish the death penalty in all circumstances" (Preamble).

Protocol of San Salvador (OAS)

Common name for the **Additional Protocol to the American Convention on Human Rights in the Area of Economic, Social and Cultural Rights**, adopted by the **Organization of American States (OAS)** in 1988.

Protocol relating to the Status of Refugees (UN)

This Protocol was adopted in 1966 and entered into force in 1967 in order to modify, *inter alia*, the definition of the word "refugee", contained in the Convention relating to the Status of Refugees, adopted by the United Nations in 1951.

Protocol to Prevent, Suppress and Punish Trafficking in Persons, especially Women and Children (UN)

This Protocol to the **United Nations Convention against Transnational Organized Crime** was adopted on 15 November 2000, the same day as the Convention, by **United Nations General Assembly** resolution 55/25. It deals with the problem of modern slavery whereby organized criminal groups take advantage of the desire of people to seek a better life. Migrants are often confined or coerced into exploitative or oppressive forms of employment, often in the sex industry or dangerous occupations, with the illicit incomes generated going to organized crime. The Protocol commits States Parties to making its basic subject a criminal offence, and to adopting specific measures to combat such offences. States must become parties to the Convention itself before they can become parties to the Protocol. By the middle of 2003, the Protocol had not yet entered into force.

Protocol to the African Charter on Human and Peoples' Rights on the Establishment of an African Court on Human and Peoples' Rights (AU/OAU)

This Protocol, signed in Ouagadougou, Burkina Faso, on 9 June 1998, provides for the creation of the **African Court on Human and People's Rights**. The Protocol enters into force after its ratification by 15 States. By the middle of 2003, it had been ratified by 6 States and had not yet entered into force.

Protocol to the African Charter on Human and Peoples' Rights on the Rights of Women in Africa (AU/OAU)

Adopted on 11 July 2003, at the second summit of the **African Union** (AU) in Maputo, Mozambique, the Protocol is aimed at ensuring equality between women and men and at promoting human rights of women in Africa. The Protocol invites States Parties to adopt all appropriate measures to eliminate all forms of **discrimination** and violence against women in Africa and to integrate a gender perspective in their policy decisions, legislation and in all other spheres of life. Moreover States Parties are invited to commit themselves to modify the social and cultural patterns of conduct of women and men through public education, information and communication strategies, with a view to achieving the elimination of harmful cultural and traditional practices and all other practices which are based on the idea of the inferiority or the superiority of either of the sexes, or on stereotyped roles for women and men. The Protocol will enter into force thirty days after the deposit of the fifteenth instrument of ratification

In Articles 3-24, the Protocol enumerates the human rights of women as well as the measures which should be taken to implement these rights, in particular the right to participate in the political and decision-making process, **right to education** and training, right to food security, **right to adequate housing**, right to a healthy and sustainable environment, right to inheritance, right to access to justice and equal protection before the law as well as economic and social welfare rights. Furthermore, the instrument deals with marriage, separation and divorce and the protection of women in armed conflict. States Parties commit themselves to provide for appropriate remedies to any woman whose rights or freedoms, as recognized in the Protocol, have been violated (Article 25).

The **African Commission on Human and Peoples' Rights**, as in the case of other human rights treaties, shall be responsible for the monitoring of the implementation of the Protocol by the States Parties. States Parties undertake to submit to the Commission periodic reports on legislative and other measures they have taken to implement the Protocol. After the establishment of the **African Court on Human and Peoples' Rights**, the Court shall complement the protective mandate of the African Commission and deal with matters of interpretation arising from the application or implementation of the Protocol.

Protocol to the American Convention on Human Rights to Abolish the Death Penalty (OAS)

The second additional protocol to the **American Convention on Human Rights** is the Protocol to the American Convention on Human Rights to Abolish the Death Penalty. It was adopted in 1990 and enters into force immediately for the States that ratify or accede to it. By the middle of 2003, it had been ratified by 8 States.

Protocols Additional to the Geneva Conventions of 12 August 1949, and relating to the Protection of Victims of International Armed Conflicts (Protocol I) and Victims of Non-international Armed Conflicts (Protocol II) (ICRC)

Due to the changing nature of armed struggle, the Diplomatic Conference on the Reaffirmation and Development of **International Humanitarian Law** Applicable in Armed Conflicts adopted on 8 June 1977 two Additional Protocols to the 1949 Geneva Conventions. The Protocols, which entered into force on 7 December 1978, extend the protection to all persons affected by armed conflict, be it internal or international, and forbid attacks on civilian populations and objects. In Protocol I, which had been ratified by over 160 States by the middle of 2003, the basic provision concerning respect for the civilian population specifies that "the Parties to the conflict shall at all times distinguish between the civilian population and combatants and between civilian objects and military objectives and accordingly shall direct their operations only against military objectives" (Article 48). It prohibits "acts or threats of violence the primary purpose of which is to spread terror among the civilian population" (Article 51) as well as indiscriminate attacks and reprisals. Protocol I also sets out special measures for the protection of women and children, notably against rape, forced prostitution and any other form of indecent assault (Articles 76-78). It also sets out measures for the implementation of the Conventions and the Protocol and for repression of breaches of their provisions (Article 90).

Protocol II, which had been ratified by more than 150 States by the middle of 2003, develops and supplements the Geneva Conventions without modifying their existing conditions of application. Pursuant to Article 1, para. 1 of this Protocol, it shall apply to all armed conflicts which are not covered by Protocol I and which "take place in the territory of a High Contracting Party between its armed forces and dissident armed forces or other organized armed groups". However, it "shall not apply to situations of internal disturbances and tensions, such as riots, isolated and sporadic acts of violence and other acts of a similar nature, as not being armed conflicts" (Article 1, para. 2). Article 2 lays down the Protocol's application to all victims of armed conflicts without any kind of **discrimination**. The instrument calls for humane treatment (Part II), without adverse distinction, of "all persons who do not take a direct part or who have ceased to take part in hostilities" (Article 4). Furthermore, it lists a number of acts, such as murder, torture, mutilation and corporal punishment which are totally prohibited (Article 4). Article 5 establishes minimum standards and rules for the treatment of persons deprived of their liberty for reasons related to armed conflict. Part III of this Protocol deals with wounded, sick and shipwrecked. In Part IV (Articles 13-18), it further sets out special measures for the protection of the civilian population against acts or threats of violence (Article 13), against starvation as a method of combat (Article 14), and against forced movement from the population's territory (Article 17).

Protocols to the European Convention for the Protection of Human Rights and Fundamental Freedoms (Council of Europe)

Since the entry into force of the **European Convention for the Protection of Human Rights and Fundamental Freedoms** in 1953, thirteen Protocols have been adopted. Protocols Nos. 1, 4, 6, 7, 12 and 13 to the Convention added further rights and freedoms not included in the original text, while Protocols Nos. 2 and 9 improved mechanisms for its implementation. From 1980 onward, the steady growth in the number of cases brought before the Convention institutions made it increasingly difficult to keep the length of proceedings within acceptable limits. Consequently, in 1994, Protocol No. 11 was adopted to restructure the control machinery. Its aim was to simplify the structure with a view to shortening the length of proceedings and to strengthening the judicial character of the system by creating a single full-time court. Protocol No. 11 entered into force in 1998. Protocol No. 12, opened to signature in 2000, aims at strengthening the combat against **discrimination** and ensuring equality before the law for all. By the middle of 2003, it had received 5 ratifications. This Protocol will enter into force once ratified by 10 contracting States. Protocol No. 13 provides for the abolition of the death penalty in all circumstances. It entered into force on 1 July 2003.

Racism

The **International Convention on the Elimination of All Forms of Racial Discrimination** (1965) states: "In this Convention, the term 'racial discrimination' shall mean any distinction, exclusion, restriction or preference based on race, colour, descent, or national or ethnic origin which has the purpose or effect of nullifying or impairing the recognition, enjoyment or exercise, on an equal footing, of human rights and fundamental freedoms in the political, economic, social, cultural or any other field of public life" (Article 1).

The **United Nations General Assembly**, the **Economic and Social Council (ECOSOC)**, the **Commission on Human Rights** and its **Sub-Commission on the Promotion and Protection of Human Rights** (formerly the **Sub-Commission on Prevention of Discrimination and Protection of Minorities**) are engaged in the struggle against racism and racial discrimination. The General Assembly proclaimed the year 1971 as the **International Year for Action to Combat Racism and Racial Discrimination** and the three **Decades for Action to Combat Racism and Racial Discrimination (1973-1983, 1983-1993, 1993-2003)**.

UNESCO's stand against racism was determined by its Constitution which declares: "... the great and terrible war which has now ended was a war made possible by the denial of the democratic principles of the dignity, equality and mutual respect of men, and by the propagation, in their place, through ignorance and prejudice, of the doctrine of the inequality of men and races" (Preamble). In Article 1, the Organization engaged to further universal respect "... for the human rights and fundamental freedoms, which are affirmed for the peoples of the world, without distinction of race, sex, language or religion ...". In 1978, UNESCO adopted the **Declaration on Race and Racial Prejudice**.

On 12 December 1997, the General Assembly decided by its resolution 52/111 to convene a **World Conference against Racism, Racial Discrimination, Xenophobia and Related Intolerance**. In its resolution 53/132 of 23 February 1999, the General Assembly proclaimed the Year 2001 as the **International Year of Mobilization against Racism, Racial Discrimination, Xenophobia and Related Intolerance**, to draw "... the world's attention to the objectives of the World Conference". The World Conference was held in Durban, South Africa, in 2001 and adopted the **Durban Declaration and Programme of Action**, which presented to the international community a common plan for eradicating all forms of racism.

Recommendation concerning Education for International Understanding, Co-operation and Peace and Education relating to Human Rights and Fundamental Freedoms (UNESCO)

This Recommendation was adopted by the General Conference of **UNESCO** on 19 November 1974. It is directed to the implementation of Article 26, para. 2, of the **Universal Declaration of Human Rights** and Article 13, paragraph 1, of the **International Covenant on Economic, Social and Cultural Rights**. The Recommendation reaffirms, in particular, the responsibility of Member States to encourage and support any activity designed to ensure the education for all for the advancement of justice, freedom, human rights and peace. It applies to all stages and forms of education and determines general guidelines and specific actions in order to ensure better understanding of human rights. Among the principles set out in the Recommendation are that education should be so conceived as to promote "understanding and respect for all peoples, their cultures, civilizations, values and ways of life including domestic ethnic cultures and cultures of other nations"; "awareness of the increasing global interdependence between peoples and nations"; and understanding of "the inadmissibility of recourse to war for the purposes of expansion, aggression and domination, or to the use of force and violence for purposes of repression" (Principle III). In compliance with the Recommendation, Member States of UNESCO are urged to "take steps to ensure that the principles of the Universal Declaration of Human Rights and of the **International Convention on the Elimination of All Forms of Racial Discrimination** become an integral part of the developing personality of each child, adolescent, young person and adult by applying these principles in the daily conduct of education at each level and in all its forms" (Principle V).

In 1985, the General Conference of UNESCO, at its 23rd session, decided that the permanent system of reporting should apply to this Recommendation. Accordingly, the first synthesis of national reports was submitted to the General Conference at its 25th session in 1989.

Recommendation concerning the Status of Higher-Education Teaching Personnel (UNESCO)

This Recommendation is the outcome of a lengthy process that started with the adoption in 1966 of the **Recommendation concerning the Status of Teachers**. The latter set out a number of general principles applicable to teachers at the primary and secondary levels of education; it did not deal with teaching personnel at the tertiary level. Some 30 years of discussion and reflection involving UNESCO, the **International Labour Organization (ILO),** and national and international higher education teachers' organizations resulted in the Recommendation concerning the Status of Higher-Education Teaching Personnel, adopted by the General Conference of UNESCO at its 29th session, on 11 November 1997.

Because it is complementary to the 1966 Recommendation, the new Recommendation has a relatively similar structure. It starts by setting a number of general principles and definitions as well as common objectives and policies pertaining to the area of higher education. Sections dealing with institutional rights, duties and responsibilities and, for the first time, with the issues and concepts of institutional autonomy and accountability in higher education follow these. It then goes on to elaborate individual rights and freedoms, with particular emphasis on academic freedom as a basic pillar and guiding principle for the recognition of the status of teachers in higher education. It goes into considerable detail regarding the duties and responsibilities of higher-education teaching personnel, preparation for and entry into the academic profession, and conditions needed for effective teaching, research and scholarship such as security of employment, appraisal, discipline and dismissal, salaries, workload and social security. It also recommends measures to be taken to insure equal working opportunities for specific categories of higher-education teaching personnel, including those working part-time. The Recommendation's seventy-seven paragraphs cover an extensive and complex field of basic professional and social conditions of teaching personnel in higher education vital to the quality and the advancement of knowledge at that educational level.

Recommendation concerning the Status of Teachers (UNESCO/ILO)

The text of the Recommendation was adopted by an Intergovernmental Conference convened by **UNESCO** at which the **International Labour Organization (ILO)** was represented by a tripartite delegation of its Governing Body. It was the outcome of a process of some twenty years of discussion and reflection in governmental organizations, primarily UNESCO and ILO, and in national and international organizations of teachers.

After setting out a number of general principles applicable to the status of teachers and to educational objectives and policies, the Recommendation deals with preparation for the teaching profession, further education for teachers, employment and career, the rights and responsibilities of teachers, conditions for effective teaching and learning, teachers' salaries, social security for teachers and, finally, measures to be taken in the event of teacher shortage. It contains 146 paragraphs which cover an extensive field of teachers' professional and social conditions.

In conformity with the desire expressed by the 1966 Intergovernmental Conference a joint ILO/UNESCO Committee was set up to examine the reports of Member States on the application of the Recommendation, on the basis of questionnaires. The joint Committee then reports to the competent organs of the two organizations.

Recommendation concerning the Status of the Artist (UNESCO)

UNESCO has been concerned with the status of the artist since the Organization's creation. Convinced that artists play an important role in the life and evolution of society, and recognizing that the vigour and vitality of the arts depend, *inter alia*, on the well-being of artists both individually and collectively and that, as a result of recent economic, social and technological developments, their situation is passing through a crisis to which it is becoming urgent to find a remedy, UNESCO has organized various surveys, symposia, studies and meetings for the purpose of determining the political, economic, social and moral situation of the artist in contemporary society.

The **International Labour Organization (ILO)** was associated with this preliminary stage because problems relating to artists' work, conditions of employment and professional and trade-union organizations fell within ILO's competence. It became clear that the preparation of a recommendation would mark an important stage in this work on behalf of a professional group which has an essential role to play in safeguarding and developing culture.

The Recommendation, adopted by consensus by the UNESCO General Conference at its 21st session in 1980, defines the status of the artist in detail, with particular reference to conventions governing copyright and the rights of performers. It lays down some guiding principles for the action of governments in this matter and deals with the vocation and training of the artist and with measures designed to encourage them. It asks Member States to promote and protect the status of artists, both economic and social, by encouraging artistic activity, including innovation and research, and by providing the necessary safeguards of their creative freedom. Member States are invited to improve the social recognition of artists and to see that they are closely associated with decisions relating to the formulation and execution of cultural policies.

Recommendation N° R(92)6 on a Coherent Policy for People with Disabilities (Council of Europe)

The Recommendation N° R(92)6 was adopted by the Committee of Ministers of the **Council of Europe** on 9 April 1992 for the purpose of enhancing the protection of people with disabilities. A general policy in favour of people with disabilities must cover a wide range of issues including: prevention and health education, identification and diagnosis, treatment and therapeutic aids, education, vocational guidance and training, employment, social integration and daily environment, social, economic and legal protection, training of persons involved in the rehabilitation and integration of people with disabilities, information, statistics and research. States are requested to refer to the definitions formulated by the **World Health Organization (WHO)** concerning the concepts of impairment, disability, and handicap in order to ensure individualized programmes of rehabilitation, which take into account each individual's specific problems. Moreover States agreed to intensify their efforts to guarantee the right of people with disabilities to an independent life and full integration into society. It is envisaged that programmes of rehabilitation be initiated early and involve the persons with disabilities and their families, the general public, professionals and social partners.

Recommendation on Consent to Marriage, Minimum Age for Marriage and Registration of Marriages (UN)

This Recommendation, adopted by the **United Nations General Assembly** (resolution 2018 (XX) of 1 November 1965), aims to encourage the implementation of the **Convention on Consent to Marriage, Minimum Age for Marriage and Registration of Marriages** (1962).

Recommendation on Participation by the People at Large in Cultural Life and Their Contribution to It (UNESCO)

Adopted on 26 November 1976 by the General Conference of **UNESCO** at its 19th session held in Nairobi, this Recommendation is the result of a series of declarations adopted at intergovernmental conferences on cultural policies convened by UNESCO, which testify to the growing concern of Member States to ensure the promotion of **cultural rights** as human rights.

Similarly, the **United Nations General Assembly**, at its 28th session in 1973, urged governments to give attention to the involvement of the population in the elaboration and implementation of measures ensuring the preservation and further development of cultural and moral values (resolution 3148 (XXVIII).

The Recommendation concerns every measure that should be taken by Member States to democratize the means and instruments of cultural activity, so as to enable individuals to participate freely and fully in cultural creation and enjoy its benefits, in accordance with the requirements of social progress. It enumerates the ultimate aims which should be pursued through measures of a legislative or regulatory character. Among the technical, administrative, economic and financial measures, means of cultural action and key policies contributing to the attainment of the goal are set out. Finally measures recommended within the framework of international cooperation are directed towards strengthening mutual understanding and respect, the mobilization of resources, the combining of efforts and the circulation of people, knowledge and ideas.

Recommendation on the Development of Adult Education (UNESCO)

Adopted on 26 November 1976 by the nineteenth session of the General Conference of **UNESCO**, this Recommendation is the first international standard-setting instrument on the subject of adult education. It is elaborated in full accordance with the principles set forth in Articles 26 and 27 of the **Universal Declaration of Human Rights** guaranteeing the right to education and the right to participate freely in cultural, artistic and scientific life, and the norms established by Articles 13 and 15 of the **International Covenant on Economic, Social and Cultural Rights**. The document reaffirms that adult education is an "integral part of life-long education and can contribute decisively to economic and cultural development, social progress and world peace" (Preamble). The term "adult education" denotes the entire body of organized educational processes, whereby persons regarded as adult by the society to which they belong develop their abilities, enrich their knowledge or bring about change in their attitudes and behaviour, in the interest of personal development and participation in balanced and independent social, economic and cultural development (Part 1).

Part II of the instrument outlining the objectives and strategy, stresses that adult education should contribute to the promotion of peace, international understanding and cooperation. It specifically notes that adult education, while taking into account the social, cultural, economic and institutional factors in each country should contribute to the economic and social development of the entire community. Member States are called upon to promote adult education without restriction or **discrimination**, and to work towards ensuring equality of access and full participation in the entire range of adult education activities, particularly for women and members of under-privileged groups. The recommendation describes the content of adult education (Part III), as well as the structures of adult education (Part V), training and status of persons engaged in adult education work (Part VI), relations between adult education and youth education (Part VII), relations between adult education and work (Part VIII), and management, administration, coordination and financing of adult education (Part IX).

Recommendation on the Status of Scientific Researchers (UNESCO)

On 20 November 1974 the General Conference of **UNESCO** adopted the Recommendation on the Status of Scientific Researchers. After a first substantive section defining the scope of application of the text and explaining that "scientific research" signifies those "processes of study, experiment, conceptualization and theory-testing involved in the generation of scientific knowledge", there follows a section devoted to the role of scientific researchers in the context of national policy-making. The third section deals with the initial education and training of researchers. The fourth section speaks about the vocation of the scientific researcher, as regards the civic, ethical and international aspects of such research. The fifth and longest section presents nine specific and concrete elements of the conditions necessary for the conduct of successful research and experimentation. The sixth section contains recommendations as to the utilization and exploitation of the Recommendation. The seventh and final provision is designed to preserve the status already acquired by researchers.

Regional Conferences on Human Rights Education (UNESCO)

In conformity with the Plan of Action for the **United Nations Decade for Human Rights Education (1995-2004)**, UNESCO, "… by means of its long experience in education, educational methodology and human rights and through its network of UNESCO schools, clubs, human rights chairs and national commissions, shall play a central role in the design, implementation and evaluation of projects under this plan of action". In order to give an impetus to the promotion of education for human rights at the national and regional levels, UNESCO, in cooperation with the **Office of the United Nations High Commissioner for Human Rights (OHCHR),** organized a series of regional conferences on human rights education. It started in 1997 when a regional conference for Europe was organized in Turku (Abo), Finland. This meeting was followed by conferences for Africa (Dakar, Senegal, 1998), Asia and the Pacific (Pune, India, 1999) and the Arab States (Rabat, Morocco, 1999). The cycle of regional conferences was completed in 2001, by the organization of a conference for Latin America and the Carribean in Mexico City. Concrete recommendations were proposed in the final documents adopted by each conference in order to promote human rights education at national and regional levels, to enrich its content and improve methodology. In particular, it was underlined that educational programmes on human rights should be introduced in cooperation with the target groups for which they are designed. Special attention should be paid to the rights of women, children and persons belonging to vulnerable groups, including their more active involvement in human rights education, and to the preparation of special educational aids. The promotion of gender equality and the empowerment of women to participate on a non-discriminatory basis in all spheres of life were recognized as matters of priority within the context of human rights education. All five conferences appealed to governments to expedite the elaboration and implementation of national plans for human rights education and to ensure adequate funding.

Reports of States as a means of evaluation and control for the implementation of human rights standards

Reports periodically made by States concerning the implementation of an agreement's provisions are means of evaluation and control. This is necessary in order to find out whether subjects of international law comply with the duties they assumed. It is legitimated by Article 2 of the **Charter of the United Nations** stipulating that States should "fulfil in good faith the obligations assumed by them". In this connection, the principle *pacta sunt servanda* must also be mentioned as provision for the binding character of international agreements and as legitimization for a system of control over their implementation.

Submission of reports is foreseen by the **International Covenants on Human Rights,** the **International Convention on the Elimination of All Forms of Racial Discrimination,** the **Convention on the Elimination of All Forms of Discrimination against Women,** the **Convention against Torture,** the **Convention on the Rights of the Child** and the **International Convention on the Protection of the Rights of All Migrant Workers and Members of Their Families**. One or two years after ratifying an instrument, a State must furnish the **human rights treaty monitoring body** (normally called the Committee) established thereunder with a report on the treaty's implementation and on the exercise of the rights set forth therein. Subsequently, periodic reports must be submitted. Some **United Nations** human rights instruments provide for the participation of specialized agencies in considering the reports of the States Parties. **Non-governmental organizations** can also make direct or indirect contributions to the reviews of the reports.

The **International Labour Organization (ILO)** provides in Article 22 of its Constitution that "each of the Members agrees to make an annual report to the International Labour Office on the measures which it has taken to give effect to the provisions of Conventions to which it is a party". In the case of a non-ratified convention, the ILO Member States undertake to report on "the difficulties which prevent or delay the ratification of such convention" (ILO Constitution, Article 19, para. 5 (e)).

Article IV, paragraph 6, of the **UNESCO** Constitution foresees that the General Conference receives and considers reports sent to UNESCO by Member States on actions taken upon its recommendations and conventions. Apart from this general provision, more specific reporting procedures may be formulated by UNESCO standard-setting instruments, i.e. the **Convention against Discrimination in Education** and the **Recommendation concerning the Status of Teachers**.

Some regional intergovernmental organizations have their own (often similar to the **United Nations system**) procedures to monitor the implementation of human rights standards.

Right of parents to choose education for their children

The **Universal Declaration of Human Rights** proclaimed the right of parents to choose education for their children: "Parents have a prior right to choose the kind of education that shall be given to their children" (Article 26). This right is further elaborated in the **International Covenant on Economic, Social and Cultural Rights**. According to its Article 13, paragraph 3, States Parties have the obligation "... to have respect for the liberty of parents and, when applicable, legal guardians to choose for their children schools, other than those established by the public authorities, which conform to such minimum educational standards as may be laid down or approved by the State and to ensure the religious and moral education of their children in conformity with their own convictions". The **Additional Protocol** to the American Convention on Human Rights in the Area of Economic, Social and Cultural Rights "Protocol of San Salvador" (1988), in its Article 13, para. 4, stipulates that: "In conformity with the domestic legislation of the States Parties, parents should have the right to select the type of education to be given to their children …". **The Convention on the Rights of the Child** (1989) is aimed at providing protection of children's rights and ensuring the continuous improvement of the situation of children as well as their development and education in conditions of peace and security. In protecting the rights of the child, States Parties should take into account "… the rights and duties of his or her parents, legal guardians, or other individuals legally responsible for him or her, and, to this end, shall take all appropriate legislative and administrative measures" (Article 3, para. 2). Article 5 lays down that States Parties shall respect the responsibilities, rights and duties of parents in a manner consistent with the evolving capacities of the child.

Right of self-determination

The principle of self-determination is laid down in the **Charter of the United Nations** as one of the purposes of the Organization. It states that friendly relations among nations are based on respect for the principle of equal rights and self-determination of peoples (Article 1, para. 2). This principle is proclaimed in a comprehensive manner in the **Declaration on the Granting of Independence to Colonial Countries and Peoples (1960).** This historic instrument marks the beginning of the irreversible trend towards full decolonization. The **International Covenants on Human Rights** contain an identical provision on the right of self-determination. Common Article 1, para. 1, stipulates that: "All peoples have the right of self-determination. By virtue of that right they freely determine their political status and freely pursue their economic, social and cultural development". It further states that: "All peoples may, for their own ends, freely dispose of their natural wealth and resources without prejudice to any obligations arising out of international economic co-operation, based upon the principle of mutual benefit, and international law. In no case may a people be deprived of its own means of subsistence" (common Article 1, para. 2). Furthermore, common Article 1, para. 3, imposes on States Parties the obligation to "...promote the realization of the right of self-determination". The right of peoples to self-determination is also enshrined in the Declaration on the Inadmissibility of Intervention and Interference in the Internal Affairs of States, the **Declaration on Principles of International Law concerning Friendly Relations and Cooperation Among States**, the **Declaration on the Right to Development**, the **Declaration on Social Progress and Development** and the **African Charter on Human and Peoples' Rights**. The **United Nations International Conference on Human Rights** (Tehran, 1968) adopted a resolution on "the importance of the universal realization of the right of peoples to self-determination and of the speedy granting of independence to colonial countries and peoples for the effective guarantee and observance of human rights". In 1978, a study entitled "The right to self-determination: implementation of United Nations resolutions" was prepared by the **Special Rapporteur[s]** of the United Nations **Sub-Commission on Prevention of Discrimination and Protection of Minorities** (now **Sub-Commission on the Promotion and Protection of Human Rights**). Another special study, also submitted to the Sub-Commission in 1978, was concerned with the historical and current development of the right of self-determination. Furthermore, the **Vienna Declaration and Programme of Action**, in its Part I, paragraph 2, states that: "All peoples have the right of self-determination. By virtue of that right they freely determine their political status, and freely pursue their economic, social and cultural development...". The denial of the right of self-determination is considered as a violation of human rights.

In this context, the **International Decade for the Eradication of Colonialism** was declared by the **United Nations General Assembly** for the period 1990-2000 and the **Week of**

Solidarity with the Peoples of Non-Self-Governing Territories is celebrated each year on the week commencing 25 May.

Rights of refugees

The status of refugees is a matter of international concern. The Office of the **United Nations High Commissioner for Refugees (UNHCR)** has, since its establishment in January 1951, been charged with the international protection of these persons. Moreover, specific international instruments, notably the **Convention Relating to the Status of Refugees** (1951), have been elaborated in order to assure for refugees the widest possible exercise of human rights and fundamental freedoms. Two principles are the basis of such international instruments: first, that there should be as little distinction as possible between nationals, on the one hand, and refugees on the other; second, that there should be no discrimination based on race, religion or country of origin among refugees. Two rights are of particular importance. One is the principle of non-refoulement, which means, that refugees may not under any condition be expelled or returned to a country where their life or freedom would be threatened on account of their race, religion, nationality, membership of a particular group or political opinion. The second right is the **right to asylum**. The **Universal Declaration of Human Rights** proclaims that everyone has the right to seek and to enjoy in other countries asylum from persecution (Article 14). The right to territorial asylum is further elaborated in the **Declaration on Territorial Asylum** (1967). Among the regional organizations, the **Organization of American States (OAS)** has dealt with the matter of refugees by drafting numerous instruments concerning them, such as the **Convention on Asylum** (1928), supplemented by the **Convention on Political Asylum** (1933) and, more recently, by the **Convention on Territorial Asylum** (1954). In addition, it is to be noted that, owing to the deterioration of the refugee problem in Africa, the **Organization of African Unity (OAU)** has drawn up the

Convention Governing the Specific Aspects of Refugee Problems in Africa (1969).

Right to adequate food

The **Universal Declaration of Human Rights** proclaimed the right to adequate food as an indispensable element of the right of everyone to: "… a standard of living adequate for the health and well-being of himself and of his family" (Article 25). This right was further developed in Article 11 of the **International Covenant on Economic, Social and Cultural Rights**, which imposes on its States Parties the obligation to take appropriate steps to ensure the realization of the right of everyone to an adequate standard of living for himself and his family, including adequate food, clothing and housing, and to the continuous improvement of living conditions. Moreover, according to this article, States Parties recognize the fundamental right of everyone to be free from hunger and make an obligation: "(a) To improve methods of production, conservation and distribution of food by making full use of technical and scientific knowledge, by disseminating knowledge of the principles of nutrition and by developing or reforming agrarian systems in such a way as to achieve the most efficient development and utilization of natural resources; (b) Taking into account the problems of both food-importing and food-exporting countries, to ensure an equitable distribution of world food supplies in relation to need" (Article 11, para. 2). A great deal of effort aimed at raising standards of living and the level of nutrition has been made by the **Food and Agriculture Organization of the United Nations (FAO)**. It has undertaken concrete steps to alleviate poverty and hunger, through its work on food quality, safety and standards, monitoring nutritional situations and requirements, advice to Member States on improving food security and nutritional status, and through technical assistance to Member States, including under its Special Programme on Food Security for Low-Income Food-Deficit

Countries. At the International Conference on Nutrition (Rome, 1992), convened jointly by the FAO and the **World Health Organization (WHO),** strategies were set forth to reduce global hunger and malnutrition. At the **World Food Summit** (Rome, 1996), world leaders established the goal of reducing the number of the chronically undernourished population in developing countries (800 million at that time) by half by the year 2015. In June 2002, the participants assembled in Rome at the *World Food Summit: five years later*, reaffirmed the commitments assumed at the previous Summit and called for an international alliance to accelerate action to reduce world hunger.

The World Food Summit entrusted the **United Nations High Commissioner for Human Rights** with the mandate to clarify the content of the rights related to food and the ways of implementing them. Subsequently expert consultations were organized in 1997, 1998 and 2001. The **Committee on Economic, Social and Cultural Rights** adopted a General Comment N° 12 on the right to adequate food on 12 May 1999. The **Sub-Commission on the Promotion and Protection of Human Rights** (formerly the **Sub-Commission for Prevention of Discrimination and Protection of Minorities**) conducted several studies on the right to adequate food as a human right. By its resolution 2000/10, the **Commission on Human Rights** established the mandate of the **Special Rapporteur[s]** on the right to food. Since 2001, each year a report on the right to food has been submitted to the Commission on Human Rights.

FAO published *The Right to Food in Theory and Practice* in 1998 and issued in 1999 a trilingual brochure containing extracts from international and regional instruments and declarations and other authoritative texts addressing the right to food.

Right to adequate housing

The right to adequate housing is provided for in the **Universal Declaration of Human Rights** as an indispensable part of an adequate standard of living (Article 25, para. 1). This right was reaffirmed in the **International Covenant on Economic, Social and Cultural Rights** which states that: "The States Parties ... recognize the right of everyone to an adequate standard of living for himself and his family, including adequate food, clothing and housing ..." (Article 11, para. 1). This right is also confirmed in the **International Convention on the Elimination of All Forms of Racial Discrimination** (Article 5) and the **Convention on the Elimination of All Forms of Discrimination against Women** (Article 14, para. 2), the **Convention on the Rights of the Child** (Article 27, para. 3) and others.

The **Committee on Economic, Social and Cultural Rights** adopted, during its sixth session in 1991, General Comment N° 4 on the right to adequate housing. A **Special Rapporteur[s]** on the right to adequate housing, as a component of the **right to an adequate standard of living**, was appointed by the **Commission on Human Rights** in April 2000 (resolution 2000/9). The first **United Nations** Conference on Human Settlements was held in Vancouver, Canada, in 1976. At the second United Nations Conference on Human Settlements (Habitat II: Istanbul, Turkey, 3-14 June 1996), Heads of State or Government endorsed the universal goals of ensuring adequate shelter for all and making human settlements safer, healthier and more livable, and adopted the Habitat Agenda (Global Plan of Action). In June 2001, the **United Nations General Assembly** held a special session (Istanbul +5) to review and appraise the implementation of the Habitat Agenda and renewed the commitments made at Habitat II. **UNESCO** encourages intergovernmental and interdisciplinary research and sharing of knowledge on urban issues. The Organization ensures the implementation of the Habitat II Global Plan of Action. Its programme on **Management of Social Transformations (MOST)** facilitates exchange between public policy-makers and social scientists and supports a variety of comparative research with practical applications.

Right to a fair and public hearing

The basic principle of equality for all in the administration of justice, including the right to a fair and public hearing, is set out in Article 10 of the **Universal Declaration of Human Rights**. According to it: "Everyone is entitled in full equality to a fair and public hearing by an independent and impartial tribunal, in the determination of his rights and obligations and of any criminal charge against him". It is further elaborated in the **International Covenant on Civil and Political Rights** which stipulates that: "… everyone shall be entitled to a fair and public hearing by a competent, independent and impartial tribunal established by law" (Article 14, para. 1). This principle refers not only to criminal cases but also to civil disputes where one person sues another. The right is also confirmed in Article 5 of the **International Convention on the Elimination of All Forms of Racial Discrimination** and in Article 16 of both the **Convention Relating to the Status of Refugees** and the **Convention Relating to the Status of Stateless Persons**. This right is also formulated by various regional instruments. The **European Convention for the Protection of Human Rights and Fundamental Freedoms**, in its Article 6, states that: "Everyone is entitled to a fair and public hearing within a reasonable time by an independent and impartial tribunal established by law".

Right to a fair trial

The right to a fair trial is an indispensable element of the procedural guarantees. Certain principles relating to procedural guarantees are set out in Articles 6, 10, and 11 of the **Universal Declaration of Human Rights**. According to the **International Covenant on Civil and Political Rights** (Article 2, para. 3), States Parties undertake to ensure: that any person whose rights or freedoms are violated shall have an effective remedy, notwithstanding that the violation has been committed by persons acting in an official capacity; that any person claiming such a remedy shall have his right thereto determined by competent judicial, administrative or legislative authorities, or by any other competent authority provided for by the legal system of the State, and to develop the possibilities of judicial remedy; and that the competent authorities shall enforce such remedies when granted. This subject is also extensively dealt with in Articles 14 to 16 of the Covenant.

The right to a fair trial is recognized by the **American Convention on Human Rights** which provides that: "Every person has the right to a hearing, with due guarantees and within reasonable time, by a competent, independent and impartial tribunal, previously established by law, in the substantiation of any accusations of a criminal nature made against him or for the determination of his rights and obligations of a civil, labor, fiscal, or any other nature" (Article 8, para. 1). Similarly the **European Convention for the Protection of Human Rights and Fundamental Freedoms** states that: "In the determination of his civil rights and obligations or of any criminal charge against him, everyone is entitled to a fair and public hearing within a reasonable time by an independent and impartial tribunal established by law" (Article 6, para. 1).

Right to a healthy environment

The right to a healthy environment is recognized in several international instruments. The Declaration of the **United Nations** Conference on the Human Environment (Stockholm, 1972) states that men and women have the fundamental right to adequate conditions of life in an environment of a quality that permits a life of dignity and well-being, and that they bear a solemn responsibility to protect and improve the environment for present and future generations (Preamble). The **African Charter of Human and Peoples' Rights** declares that: "All peoples shall have the right to a general satisfactory environment favourable to their development" (Article 24). The **Additional Protocol to the American Convention on Human Rights in the Area of Economic, Social and Cultural Rights "Protocol of San Salvador"**

(1988) provides that: "Everyone shall have the right to live in a healthy environment and to have access to basic public services" (Article 11, para. 1). It further affirms that: "The States Parties shall promote the protection, preservation and improvement of the environment" (Article 11, para. 2). Concern for the protection of the environment can also be found in the realm of **international humanitarian law**. Article 35, para. 3 of the **Protocol[s] Additional to the Geneva Conventions of 12 August 1949, and relating to the Protection of Victims of International Armed Conflicts (Protocol I)** states that "it is prohibited to employ methods or means of warfare which...cause widespread, long-term and severe damage to the natural environment".

On 14 December 1990, the **United Nations General Assembly** adopted a resolution on the need to ensure a healthy environment for the well-being of individuals. To this end, the resolution calls upon United Nations Member States and intergovernmental and **non-governmental organizations** dealing with environmental questions to enhance their efforts towards ensuring a better and healthier environment (para. 2). Several reports were submitted to the **Sub-Commission on the Promotion and Protection of Human Rights** (formerly **Sub-Commission on Prevention of Discrimination and Protection of Minorities**) by its rapporteur on human rights and the environment. The 1994 final report analyses the legal foundations of the right to the environment, the impact of environmental degradation on **vulnerable groups** and on the enjoyment of fundamental rights and other aspects of the relationship between human rights and the environment. In submitting the Draft Declaration of Draft Principles on Human Rights and the Environment, contained in the annex to this report, the rapporteur expressed the hope that "the draft will help the United Nations to adopt...a set of norms consolidating the right to a satisfactory environment...". With its resolution 1995/81 the **Commission on Human Rights** decided to appoint a **Special Rapporteur[s]** on the adverse effects of the illicit movement and dumping of toxic and dangerous products and wastes on the enjoyment of human rights.

The United Nations Conference on Environment and Development (UNCED), held in Brazil in 1992, as a follow-up to the first global meeting on the environment (Stockholm, 1972), adopted the Rio Declaration on Environment and Development, also known as the Rio Principles. The Declaration states that "human beings...are entitled to a healthy and productive life in harmony with nature" (Principle I). The Declaration, together with Agenda 21, a comprehensive plan of action adopted by the Rio Conference, influenced all subsequent United Nations conferences, which have examined the relationship between human rights and the need for environmentally sustainable development. The commitments to the full implementation of Agenda 21 and the Rio Principles, were strongly reaffirmed at the **World Summit on Sustainable Development** (WSSD) held in Johannesburg, South Africa, in 2002.

UNESCO, in its **Declaration on the Responsibilities of the Present Generations towards Future Generations** (1997) acknowledged the importance of the right to a clean and healthy environment and stressed that present generations should strive for sustainable development and preserve living conditions, particularly the quality and integrity of the environment (Article 5).

Right to a just social and international order

The right to a just social and international order is provided for in Article 28 of the **Universal Declaration of Human Rights** which stipulates: "Everyone is entitled to a social and international order in which the rights and freedoms set forth in this Declaration can be fully realized". This right is crucial to the progressive development and implementation of the **right to democracy**.

Right to an adequate standard of living

The right to an adequate standard of living is dealt with in the **Universal Declaration of Human Rights** which in its Article 25, para. 1, states that: "Everyone has the right to a standard of living adequate for the health and well-being of himself and of his family, including food, clothing, housing and medical care and necessary social services, and the right to security in the event of unemployment…". The right was reaffirmed by Article 11, para. 1, of the **International Covenant on Economic, Social and Cultural Rights**. Under Article 27 of the **Convention on the Rights of the Child**: "States Parties recognize the right of every child to a standard of living adequate for the child's mental, physical, spiritual, moral and social development". The **European Social Charter**, in its Part I (4), speaks about the right of all workers to a fair remuneration sufficient "… for a decent standard of living for themselves and their families". The **World Summit for Social Development** (Copenhagen, 1995) adopted the **Copenhagen Declaration and Programme of Action** which underlined the urgent need to address profound social problems, including **poverty** which is a denial of chances to lead healthy, creative and long lives and to enjoy a decent standard of living, freedom and dignity. The World Summit recognized the goal of eradicating poverty as an ethical, social, political and moral imperative of humankind. On 22 December 1992, the **United Nations General Assembly** proclaimed 17 October as the **International Day for the Eradication of Poverty**; it then proclaimed on 21 December 1993 the year 1996 as the **International Year for the Eradication of Poverty;** by its resolution 50/107 II of 20 December 1995, the decade 1997–2006 was proclaimed the **United Nations Decade for the Eradication of Poverty**.

Right to a nationality

The **Universal Declaration of Human Rights** in its Article 15 proclaimed that: "Everyone has the right to a nationality" (para. 1) and that: "No one shall be arbitrarily deprived of his nationality nor denied the right to change his nationality" (para. 2). Concerning this right, the **International Covenant on Civil and Political Rights** provides that: "Every child has the right to acquire a nationality" (Article 24, para. 3). The **International Convention on the Elimination of All Forms of Racial Discrimination** provides that States Parties undertake to guarantee the right of everyone without any discrimination to equality before the law, which includes the enjoyment of the right to a nationality (Article 5 (d)(iii)). The **Convention on the Elimination of All Forms of Discrimination Against Women** states that: " States Parties shall grant women equal rights with men to acquire, change or retain their nationality …" (Article 9, para. 1). The right to a nationality is also provided for in Article 20 of the **American Convention on Human Rights**. In order to ensure married women equality with men in the exercise of the right to a nationality and to prevent them from becoming stateless, the **Convention on the Nationality of Married Women** was adopted in 1957. The **Convention relating to the Status of Stateless Persons** (1954) calls for stateless persons to be given the same treatment as that accorded to refugees under the **Convention Relating to the Status of Refugees**. Under the **Convention on the Reduction of Statelessness** (1954), a Contracting State shall grant its nationality to a person born in its territory who would otherwise be stateless.

Right to an effective remedy by tribunals

The right to an effective remedy by tribunals is proclaimed in the **Universal Declaration of Human Rights**, stating in its Article 8 that: "Everyone has the right to an effective remedy by the competent national tribunals for acts violating the fundamental rights granted him by the constitution or by law".

It is reaffirmed in the **International Covenant on Civil and Political Rights** which states that each State Party shall: "… ensure that any person whose rights or freedoms … are violated shall have an effective remedy…" (Article 2, para. 3(a)). Provisions on the subject also appear in Article 6 of the **International Convention on the Elimination of All Forms of Racial Discrimination** and in Articles 13 and 14 of the **Convention Against Torture and Other Cruel, Inhuman or Degrading Treatment or Punishment.** This right is also dealt with in regional normative instruments such as the **American Convention on Human Rights** (Article 10) and the **European Convention for the Protection of Human Rights and Fundamental Freedoms** (Article 13).

Right to appeal

The right to appeal is set out in Article 14, para. 5, of the **International Covenant on Civil and Political Rights** as follows: "Everyone convicted of a crime shall have the right to his conviction and sentence being reviewed by a higher tribunal according to law". The **Sub-Commission on Prevention of Discrimination and Protection of Minorities** (now **Sub-Commission on the Promotion and Protection of Human Rights**) of the **United Nations** formulated and adopted Draft Principles on Equality in the Administration of Justice on the basis of texts proposed by the **Special Rapporteur[s]** in 1969. In the Principle 16, paragraph X, the right to appeal is stipulated. The right to appeal is also foreseen by regional instruments. The **American Convention on Human Rights** (1969) in Article 8, para. 2h, provides "the right to appeal the judgment to a higher court". The **African Charter on Human and Peoples' Rights** (1981) speaks in Article 7, para. 1a, about "the right to an appeal to competent national organs …".

Right to asylum

The right to asylum is embodied in the **Universal Declaration of Human Rights**, which in Article 14, para. 2, states that: "Everyone has the right to seek and to enjoy in other countries asylum from persecution". Article 14, para. 2, stipulates that: "This right may not be invoked in the case of prosecutions genuinely arising from non-political crimes or from acts contrary to the purposes and principles of the **United Nations**". The right to asylum falls into two basic categories: territorial and extraterritorial or diplomatic asylum. The right is not yet fully codified universally. At the regional level binding instruments were adopted by the **Organization of American States (OAS):** the **Convention on Asylum** (1928), the **Convention on Political Asylum** (1933), the **Convention on Diplomatic Asylum** (1954) and the **Convention on Territorial Asylum** (1954). The right to asylum is also mentioned by the **American Declaration of the Rights and Duties of Man** (1948) which in Article XXVII provides: "Every person has the right, in case of pursuit not resulting from ordinary crimes, to seek and receive asylum in foreign territory, in accordance with the laws of each country and with international agreements". The first world debate on the right to asylum was carried out in 1961-1962 at the Vienna Conferences on Diplomatic Relations and Consular Matters. In 1967, the **United Nations General Assembly** adopted the **Declaration on Territorial Asylum** which sets out principles related to the granting or refusal of asylum by States. Furthermore, it makes clear that the international community has not yet resolved the question of asylum.

Right to benefit from the protection of the moral and material interests resulting from scientific, literary or artistic production

The **Universal Declaration of Human Rights**, in its Article 27, para. 2, proclaims that: "Everyone has the right to the protection of the moral and material interests resulting from any scientific, literary or artistic production of which he is the author". This subject is dealt with in the **International Covenant on Economic, Social and Cultural Rights** which recognizes the right of everyone "to benefit from the protection of the moral and material interests resulting from any scientific, literary or artistic production of which he is the author" (Article 15, para. 1(c)). An identical wording is repeated by the **Additional Protocol to the American Convention on Human Rights in the Area of Economic, Social and Cultural Rights "Protocol of San Salvador"** in its Article 14, para. 1(c). This right is one of the cultural rights which **UNESCO** protects and is dealt with in several UNESCO declarations and recommendations concerning various cultural rights. The principal normative instrument with direct relevance to the right to benefit from the protection of the moral and material interests resulting from scientific, literary or artistic production is the UNESCO **Universal Copyright Convention (1952) and the Universal Copyright Convention as revised in 1971.** Article I of both instruments stipulates that "Each Contracting State undertakes to provide for the adequate and effective protection of the rights of authors and other copyright proprietors in literary, scientific and artistic works, including writings, musical, dramatic and cinematographic works, and paintings, engravings and sculpture".

The **World Intellectual Property Organization (WIPO)**, a **United Nations** specialized agency, promotes the protection of intellectual property throughout the world through cooperation among States and, where appropriate, in collaboration with other international organizations. It monitors several international treaties dealing with the legal and administrative aspects of the protection of intellectual property, harmonizes and simplifies relevant rules and practices, and provides governments, organizations and the private sector with legal and technical assistance.

Right to be presumed innocent

The principle of presumption of innocence is fundamental to the protection of human rights. Relating to procedural guarantees, it is set out in the **Universal Declaration of Human Rights,** which states that: "Everyone charged with a penal offence has the right to be presumed innocent until proved guilty according to law in a public trial at which he has had all the guarantees necessary for his defence" (Article 11, para. 1). Thus, the presumption of innocence implies a right to be treated in accordance with this principle. Therefore, it is a duty for all public authorities to refrain from prejudging the outcome of a trial. The presumption of innocence is also dealt with in the **International Covenant on Civil and Political Rights** (Article 14, para. 2). The **American Convention on Human Rights** provides that: "Every person accused of a criminal offence has the right to be presumed innocent so long as his guilt has not been proven according to law" (Article 8, para. 2). The **African Charter on Human and Peoples' Rights** contains the same provision in its Article 7, para. 1(b), as does the **European Convention for the Protection of Human Rights and Fundamental Freedoms** in its Article 6, para. 2.

Right to compensation

The right to compensation is set out in the **International Covenant on Civil and Political Rights**, which states that: "Anyone who has been the victim of unlawful arrest or detention shall have an enforceable right to compensation" (Article 9, para. 5). Protocol N° 7 (amended by Protocol N° 11) to the **European Convention for the Protection of Human Rights and Fundamental Freedoms** provides, in its Article 3, that a person who has suffered punishment as a result of a miscarriage of justice "…shall be compensated according to the law or the practice of the State concerned". The meaning of this right is explained in Articles 12 and 13 of the **Declaration of Basic Principles of Justice for Victims of Crime and Abuse of Power** (adopted by the **United Nations General Assembly** resolution 40/34), which recommends that States should endeavour to provide financial compensation when compensation from the offender or other sources is not fully available, and that national funds for this purpose should be established and strengthened. The **Basic Principles and Guidelines on the Right to a Remedy and Reparation for**

Victims of Violations of International Human Rights and Humanitarian Law** provide for the right to reparation, which includes the right to compensation "for any economically assessable damage resulting from violations of human rights and humanitarian law" (Part X). The **Sub-Commission on Prevention of Discrimination and Protection of Minorities** (now **Sub-Commission on the Promotion and Protection of Human Rights**) confirmed in resolution 1988/11 the right to fair and just compensation.

Right to creativity

The right to creativity is formulated by human rights instruments in the context of freedom of scientific and artistic activities from limitation and external interventions. The **International Covenant on Economic, Social and Cultural Rights**, in its Article 15, para. 3, provides that: "The States Parties to the present Covenant undertake to respect the freedom indispensable for scientific research and creative activity". Creativity lays stress on the maintenance and development of individual and group aptitudes and opportunities, rather than on the product of their activities. Part V, para. 31 of the **Recommendation on the Status of Scientific Researchers**, adopted by **UNESCO** in 1974, stipulates that Member States should "stimulate creative performance in the field of science and technology by all scientific researchers". The **Recommendation concerning the Status of the Artist** adopted by UNESCO on 27 October 1980 calls upon Member States to encourage all measures tending to strengthen respect for artistic creation. It emphasized that governments should help to create and sustain not only a climate encouraging freedom of artistic expression but also the material conditions facilitating the release of creative talents. It stipulates that: "Since freedom of expression and communication is the essential prerequisite for all artistic activities, Member States should see that artists are unequivocally accorded the protection provided for in this respect by international and national legislation concerning human rights" (Part III, para 6).

Right to cultural identity

This right is indirectly formulated in Article 27 of the **International Covenant on Civil and Political Rights** which stipulates that persons belonging to **minorities** have the right to enjoy their own culture. During the World Conference on Cultural Policies, organized by **UNESCO** in Mexico City, in 1982, delegates emphasized people's growing awareness of their cultural identity, of the pluralism stemming from it, of their right to be different and of the mutual respect of one culture for another, including that of minorities. In its recommendation on cultural identity, the Conference called upon States to respect and work to preserve the cultural identity of all countries, regions and peoples and oppose any **discrimination** with regard to the cultural identity of other countries, regions and peoples; and promote the development of cultural identity through all appropriate means. The **Mexico City Declaration on Cultural Policies** (1982) states, *inter alia*, that the assertion of cultural identity contributes to the liberation of peoples. Furthermore, cultural identity is a treasure which vitalizes mankind's possibilities for self-fulfillment by encouraging every people and every group to seek nurture in the past, to welcome contributions from outside compatible with their own characteristics, and so to continue the process of their own creation.

The right to cultural identity is recognized in human rights instruments. Article 29(c) of the **Convention on the Rights of the Child** (1989) provides that the education of the child shall be directed to: "The development of respect for … his or her own cultural identity, language and values …". The right to respect for cultural identity means that everyone alone or in a community with others may freely choose his or her cultural identity in its various aspects such as language, religion, heritage, traditions, etc. Everyone may have one or several cultural identities and may freely decide whether or not to identify with one or more cultural communities. Nobody can be subjected against his or her will to forced assimilation.

The **Declaration on the Rights of Persons Belonging to National or Ethnic, Religious and Linguistic Minorities** (1992) provides that: "States shall protect the existence and the national or ethnic, cultural, religious and linguistic identity of minorities within their respective territories and shall encourage conditions for the promotion of that identity" (Article 1, para. 1). The **Framework Convention for the Protection of National Minorities** adopted by the **Council of Europe** in 1995 stipulates that: "The Parties undertake to promote the conditions necessary for persons belonging to national minorities to maintain and develop their culture, and to preserve the essential elements of their identity, namely their religion, language, tradition and cultural heritage" (Article 5).

UNESCO has undertaken many activities in order to promote and further develop **cultural rights**. In 1976, the Organization adopted the **Recommendation on Participation by the People at Large in Cultural Life and their Contribution to It**, which aims at ensuring the promotion and protection of cultural rights as an integral part of human rights. Its Article 4(f) recommends that Member States adopt legislation in order to "… ensure that national minorities and foreign minorities have full opportunities for gaining access to and participating in the cultural life of the countries in which they find themselves in order to enrich it with their specific contributions, while safeguarding their right to preserve their cultural identity". In 2001, the General Conference of UNESCO adopted the **Universal Declaration on Cultural Diversity**.

Right to democracy

Though the right to democracy is not explicitly codified in human rights instruments, many fundamental principles of democracy are embodied in international human rights law. The **Universal Declaration of Human Rights** confirms the cornerstone principle of democracy, stipulating that: "The will of the people shall be the basis of the authority of government; this will shall be expressed in periodic and genuine elections which shall be by universal and equal suffrage and shall be held by secret vote or by equivalent free voting procedures" (Article 21, para. 3). The Universal Declaration proclaims the **right** [of everyone] **to take part in the government** of his country, directly or through freely chosen representatives, as well as the **right to equal access to public service**. International human rights instruments guarantee a number of freedoms and rights, which are crucial for the functioning of democracy, such as **freedom of opinion and expression, freedom to seek, receive and impart information, freedom of association, freedom of peaceful assembly, freedom from arbitrary arrest, freedom from arbitrary interference with privacy, right to a fair public hearing, right to a fair trial, right to be presumed innocent, right to liberty and security of person, right to own property, right to strike, right to take part in government, right to vote and to be elected.** Moreover, the Universal Declaration proclaims: "Everyone is entitled to a social and international order in which the rights and freedoms set forth in this Declaration can be fully realized" (Article 28).

The inherent link between human rights and democracy was underlined by the **World Conference on Human Rights** (Vienna, Austria, 1993) which in the **Vienna Declaration and Programme of Action** (Part I, para. 8) declares that "Democracy, development and respect for human rights and fundamental freedoms are interdependent and mutually reinforcing. Democracy is based on the freely expressed will of the people to determine their own political, economic, social and cultural systems and their full participation in all aspects of their lives …". In recent years, resolutions on the right to democracy have been adopted by the **Commission on Human Rights**. In resolution 1999/57 entitled "Promotion of the right to democracy", it is affirmed that "… democracy fosters the full realization of all human rights, and vice versa …" (para. 1).

The interdependence of democracy and human rights was reaffirmed in the **United Nations Millennium Declaration**, adopted by the **United Nations General Assembly** in September 2000 by its resolution 55/2. It stipulated that: "Men and women have the right to live their lives and raise their children in dignity, free from hunger and from the fear of violence, oppression or injustice. Democratic and participatory governance based on the will of the people best assures these rights". The Heads of State and Government also expressed in the Millennium Declaration their resolution "… to strengthen the capacity of all our countries to implement the principles and practices of democracy and respect for human rights…".

Right to development

This right is defined in the **Declaration on the Right to Development**, an instrument of a non-binding character adopted by the **United Nations General Assembly** in 1986, as "an inalienable human right by virtue of which every human person and all peoples are entitled to participate in, contribute to, and enjoy economic, social, cultural, and political development, in which all human rights and fundamental freedoms can be fully realized" (Article 1). The Declaration further states that "the human person is the central subject of development and should be the active participant and beneficiary of the right to development" (Article 2).

The **United Nations High Commissioner for Human Rights** has a responsibility to promote and protect the realization of the right to development and enhance support from relevant bodies of the **United Nations system** for this purpose (A/RES/48/141).

In 1998, the **Economic and Social Council (ECOSOC)**, by its decision 1998/269, endorsed the recommendation contained in **Commission on Human Rights** resolution 1998/72, to establish a dual mechanism to make further progress towards the realization of the right to development as elaborated in the Declaration. An open-ended Working Group on the Right to Development was set up to monitor the progress made in the promotion and implementation of the right to development.

Furthermore its mandate includes to review any information submitted by States, **United Nations specialized agencies**, other intergovernmental organizations and **non-governmental organizations** on the relationship between their activities and the right to development, and to present a sessional report to the Commission on Human Rights, including, *inter alia*, recommendations to the **Office of the United Nations High Commissioner for Human Rights** with regard to the implementation of the right to development. By the middle of 2003, four sessions of this working group had taken place. Moreover, an independent expert on the right to development was appointed with the mandate to present to the Working Group at each of its sessions a study on the current state of progress in the implementation of the right to development as a basis for focused discussion. The Commission also requested the independent expert to focus on specific topics and to prepare additional studies. By 2003, five reports and a preliminary study on the impact of international economic, financial and trading issues on the enjoyment of human rights had been submitted.

The objective of making the right to development a reality for everyone is set out in the **United Nations Millennium Declaration.**

The importance of the right to development has also been reaffirmed at a number of United Nations conferences, including the **World Conference on Human Rights** (Vienna, 1993), the fourth **World Conference[s] on Women** (Beijing, 1995), the **World Summit for Social Development** (Copenhagen, 1995), the **World Conference against Racism, Racial Discrimination, Xenophobia and Related Intolerance** (Durban, 2001) and the **World Summit on Sustainable Development** (Johannesburg, 2002).

Right to education

The right to education was proclaimed and defined in Article 26 of the **Universal Declaration of Human Rights.** The **International Covenant on Economic, Social and Cultural Rights** further elaborates the content of this right. It stipulates that: "The States Parties to the present Covenant recognize the right of everyone to education. They agree that education shall be directed to the full development of the human personality and the sense of its dignity, and shall strengthen the respect for human rights and fundamental freedoms. They further agree that education shall enable all persons to participate effectively in a free society, promote understanding, tolerance and friendship among all nations and all racial, ethnic or religious groups, and further the activities of the **United Nations** for the maintenance of peace" (Article 13, para. 1). With a view to achieving the full realization of this right, the States Parties to the Covenant recognize that: "(a) Primary education shall be compulsory and available free to all; (b) Secondary education in its different forms, including technical and vocational secondary education, shall be made generally available and accessible to all by every appropriate means, and in particular by the progressive introduction of free education; (c) Higher education shall be made equally accessible to all, on the basis of capacity, by every appropriate means, and in particular by the progressive introduction of free education; (d) Fundamental education shall be encouraged or intensified as far as possible for those persons who have not received or completed the whole period of their primary education; (e) The development of a system of schools at all levels shall be actively pursued, an adequate fellowship system shall be established, and the material conditions of teaching staff shall be continuously improved" (Article 13, para. 2). The Covenant also confirms and further develops the **right of parents to choose education for their children** (Article 13, para. 3). The right to education is among others provided for by the **Convention on the Rights of the Child** (Articles 28 and 29), the **Additional Protocol to the American Convention on Human Rights in the Area of Economic, Social and Cultural Rights "Protocol of San Salvador"** (Article 13), the Protocol to the **European Convention for the Protection of Human Rights and Fundamental Freedoms** (Article 2), the **African Charter on Human and Peoples' Rights** (Article 17).

During the general discussion by the **Committee on Economic, Social and Cultural Rights** on the right to education (1998), an agreement was reached that four elements define its core content: No one shall be denied a right to education; Everyone is entitled to basic (primary) education in one form or another, this includes basic education for adults; Primary education must be compulsory and free; No one may withhold a child from primary education. A State has an obligation to protect this right from encroachment by third persons; there is a free choice of education without interference by the State or a third person; and minorities have the right to be taught in the language of their choice in institutions outside the official system of public education. The Committee, during its twenty-first session in 1999, adopted General Comment N° 13 on the right to education which declares that "Education is both a human right in itself and an indispensable means of realizing other human rights". The mandate of the **Special Rapporteur[s]** of the **Commission on Human Rights** on the right to education was established in 1998 (resolution 1998/33). In one of the reports submitted to the Commission is stated that the realization of the right to education is a prerequisite for the eradication of **poverty** and that it is essential for the exercise of all other human rights, **political**, **civil**, **economic**, **social** and **cultural rights** (E/CN.4/2001/52). In the **United Nations Millennium Declaration** (2000) it is resolved that, by 2015, "children everywhere, boys and girls alike, will be able to complete a full course of primary schooling and that girls and boys will have equal access to all levels of education". In December 2001, the **United Nations General Assembly** proclaimed the 10-year period beginning on 1 January 2003 the **United Nations Literacy Decade**.

Within the **United Nations system** UNESCO has a primary responsibility in the field of education. In accordance with its mandate, **UNESCO** gives priority to the implementation of the right to education and, in particular, to basic education for girls and boys. The Organization has adopted a number of instruments ensuring the enjoyment of the right to education for everyone. The best known among these is the **Convention against Discrimination in Education** (1960). Several instruments establish guarantees for the rights of teaching personnel, vital to the advancement of the right to education: the **Recommendation concerning the Status of Teachers** (1966) and the **Recommendation concerning the Status of Higher-Education Teaching Personnel** (1997). UNESCO's programmes are aimed at assuring access to education for all, including persons belonging to **vulnerable groups**. In April 2000, UNESCO organized the **World Education Forum** in Dakar, Senegal. The participants of the Forum adopted the **Dakar Framework for Action**, a collective commitment to achieve "Education for All". The Organization also plays an important role in promoting the right to **human rights education** as a human right and as an integral part of education.

Right to enjoy the benefits from scientific progress and its applications

This right, though in a general form, is recognized by the **International Bill of Rights** and by regional instruments. The **Universal Declaration of Human Rights**, in its Article 27, para. 1, proclaims that: "Everyone has the right … to share in scientific advancement and its benefits". The **International Covenant on Economic, Social and Cultural Rights**, in its Article 15, para. 1(b), reiterates the right of everyone: "To enjoy the benefits of scientific progress and its applications". The **Additional Protocol to the American Convention on Human Rights in the Area of Economic, Social and Cultural Rights** "Protocol of San Salvador", in its Article 14, para. 1(b) recognizes the right of everyone "to enjoy the benefits of scientific and technological progress". For the promotion of this right, several standard-setting instruments have been adopted by **UNESCO**. The **Recommendation on the Status of Scientific Researchers** (1974) underlines that each Member State should use scientific and technological knowledge for the enhancement of the cultural and natural well-being of its citizens and to further the ideals and objectives of the **United Nations**. In the field of bioethics, UNESCO adopted the **Universal Declaration on the Human Genome and Human Rights** in 1997.

Right to equal access to public service

The right to equal access to public service is provided for in the **Universal Declaration of Human Rights** which states: "Everyone has the right to equal access to public service in his country" (Article 21, para. 2). This right, which is intimately linked with the **right to take part in government**, is further elaborated in Article 25 of the **International Covenant on Civil and Political Rights** which states that: "Every citizen shall have the rights and the opportunity, without any of the distinctions mentioned in Article 2 and without unreasonable restrictions ... to have access, on general terms of equality, to public service in his country". The **American Convention on Human Rights**, in its Article 23, confirms that every citizen shall enjoy the right and opportunity "to have access, under general conditions of equality, to the public service of his country". A similar provision is contained in the **African Charter on Human and Peoples' Rights** (Article 13, para. 1c).

Right to equal pay for equal work

The **Universal Declaration of Human Rights** stipulates that: "Everyone, without any discrimination, has the right to equal pay for equal work" (Article 23, para. 2). The **International Covenant on Economic, Social and Cultural Rights** contains a similar provision which states that the States Parties to the Covenant recognize the right of everyone "to the enjoyment of just and favourable conditions of work" which ensure, in particular remuneration which provides all workers, as a minimum, with "fair wages and equal remuneration for work of equal value without distinction of any kind, in particular women being guaranteed conditions of work not inferior to those enjoyed by men, with equal pay for equal work" (Article 7). Furthermore, the **International Convention on the Elimination of All Forms of Racial Discrimination** provides for equal pay for equal work in Article 5 as does the **Convention on the Elimination of All Forms of Discrimination Against Women** in its Article 11, para. 1(d). Article 15 of the **African Charter on Human and Peoples' Rights** also contains provisions on this subject. Within the **United Nations system**, the **International Labour Organization (ILO)** has the primary responsibility for the supervision of international measures relating to the field of work. Under the ILO **Convention (N° 100) concerning Equal Remuneration for Men and Women Workers for Work of Equal Value** (1951), the Contracting States agree to enforce the basic principle – embodied in the Preamble to the ILO Constitution – of equal pay for equal work.

Right to equal protection of the law without discrimination

The principle of elementary justice is proclaimed in Article 7 of the **Universal Declaration of Human Rights,** which states that: "All are equal before the law and are entitled without any discrimination to equal protection of the law. All are entitled to equal protection against any discrimination in violation of this Declaration and against any incitement to such discrimination". The **International Covenant on Civil and Political Rights** contains a similar provision: "All persons are equal before the law and are entitled without any discrimination to the equal protection of the law ..." (Article 26). The right to equal protection of the law without discrimination is also contained in the **American Convention on Human Rights** (Article 1), the **African Charter on Human and Peoples' Rights** (Articles 2 and 3), and the **European Convention on Human Rights** (Articles 1 and 14).

Right to form and join trade unions

The **Universal Declaration of Human Rights** stipulates that: "Everyone has the right to form and to join trade unions for the protection of his interests" (Article 23, para. 4). This right is further elaborated in both **International Covenants on Human Rights**. Article 8 of the **International Covenant on Economic, Social and Cultural Rights** sets out that States Parties should ensure "the right of everyone to form trade unions..." (Article 8, para. 1(a)). The **International Covenant on Civil and Political Rights** provides that: "Everyone shall have the right to **freedom of association** with others, including the right to form and join trade unions for the protection of his interests" (Article 22, para. 1). Trade union rights constitute an important aspect of the right to **freedom of peaceful assembly** and **association**. Within the **United Nations system**, the lead agency concerned with these rights is the **International Labour Organization (ILO)** which adopted the **Convention (N° 87) concerning Freedom of Association and Protection of the Right to Organise** in 1948. This instrument was followed closely by the **Convention (N° 98) concerning the Application of the Principles of the Right to Organise and Bargain Collectively** of 1949, and supplemented later by the **Convention (N° 135) concerning Protection and Facilities to be Afforded to Workers' Representatives in the Undertaking** (1971), **Convention (N° 141) concerning Organisations of Rural Workers and their Role in Economic and Social Development** (1975) and **Convention (N° 151) concerning Protection of the Right to Organise and Procedures for Determining Conditions of Employment in the Public Service** (1978).

Right to free choice of employment

The right of everyone to free choice of employment is proclaimed in the **Universal Declaration of Human Rights,** which stipulates that: "Everyone has the **right to work**, to free choice of employment ..." (Article 23, para. 1). The **International Covenant on Economic, Social and Cultural Rights** contains a similar provision which states that States Parties "... recognize the right to work, which includes the right of everyone to the opportunity to gain his living by work which he freely chooses or accepts ..." (Article 6, para. 1). The **International Convention on the Elimination of All Forms of Racial Discrimination** provides for non-discrimination on racial grounds in respect of the right to free choice of employment (Article 5), as does the **Convention on the Elimination of All Forms of Discrimination against Women** on the ground of sex (Article 11). The basic instruments adopted by the **International Labour Organization (ILO)** in this field are the **Convention (N° 111) concerning Discrimination in Respect of Employment and Occupation** (1958) and the **Convention (N° 122) concerning Employment Policy** (1964).

Right to health and medical services

The **Universal Declaration of Human Rights** proclaims that: "Everyone has the right to a standard of living adequate for the health and well-being of himself and of his family including ... medical care and necessary social services ..." (Article 25, para. 1). The **Convention on the Elimination of All Forms of Discrimination against Women** ensures non-discrimination in this respect on the ground of sex stating that: "States Parties shall take all appropriate measures to eliminate discrimination against women in the field of health care in order to ensure, on a basis of equality of men and women, access to health care services, including those related to family planning" (Article 12, para. 1). The **African Charter on Human and Peoples' Rights** provides that its States Parties "... shall take the necessary measures to protect the health of their people and to ensure that they receive medical attention when they are sick" (Article 16, para. 2). Provisions to this end are contained in other regional instruments.

The **World Health Organization (WHO),** by its Constitution, is defined as the directing and coordinating authority on international health work. It considers that the basic health services essential for the provision of adequate health protection to the community should cover: care of mothers and children including midwifery; nutrition; prevention and control of communicable diseases; sanitation and water supply; health education; and occupational health. In 1981, the World Health Assembly adopted by its resolution 34/36 the "Global Strategy for Health for All by the Year 2000". In November 1999, WHO adopted the Kobe Declaration concerning the avoidance of a tobacco epidemic in women and **youth**. Furthermore the Framework Convention on Tobacco Control was adopted unanimously by the 56th Word Health Assembly on 21 May 2003. The objective of this Convention is "to protect present and future generations from the devastating health, social, environmental and economic consequences of tobacco consumption and exposure to tobacco smoke by providing a framework for tobacco control measures... in order to reduce continually and substantially the prevalence of tobacco use and exposure to tobacco smoke" (Article 3).

Right to highest attainable standard of physical and mental health

According to the **International Covenant on Economic, Social and Cultural Rights**, States Parties "... recognize the right of everyone to the enjoyment of the highest attainable standard of physical and mental health" (Article 12, para. 1). The Covenant imposes on States Parties the obligation to undertake steps "... to achieve the full realization of this right ..." including those necessary for: "(a) The provision for the reduction of the stillbirth-rate and of infant mortality and for the healthy development of the child; (b) The improvement of all aspects of environmental and industrial hygiene; (c) The prevention, treatment and control of epidemic, endemic, occupational and other diseases; (d) The creation of conditions which would assure to all medical service and medical attention in the event of sickness" (Article 12, para. 2). The **European Social Charter** provides in its Article 11 that: "Everyone has the right to benefit from any measures enabling him to enjoy the highest possible standard of health attainable". The **African Charter on Human and Peoples' Rights** stipulates in its Article 16, para. 1, that: "Every individual shall have the right to enjoy the best attainable state of physical and mental health". The **Additional Protocol to the American Convention on Human Rights in the Area of Economic, Social and Cultural Rights "Protocol of San Salvador"** (1988), in its Article 10, para. 1, declares that: "Everyone shall have the right to health, understood to mean the enjoyment of the highest level of physical, mental and social well-being". Further standards relating to specific groups are set out in other instruments, such as **Principles for the Protection of Persons with Mental Illness and the Improvement of Mental Health Care** and the **Declaration on the Elimination of Violence against Women**.

The **Committee on Economic, Social and Cultural Rights** adopted in 2000 General Comment N° 14 on the right to the highest attainable standard of health, which declares that this right is closely related to and dependent upon the realization of other human rights, including the **right to adequate food, right to adequate housing, right to work, right to education, right to life**, right to non-discrimination, **freedom of association, freedom of peaceful assembly, freedom from the subjection to torture and to cruel, inhuman or degrading treatment, freedom from arbitrary interference with privacy** and **freedom to seek, receive and impart information**. At its 1989 session, the **Commission on Human Rights** reaffirmed (resolution 1989/11) the right to enjoy the highest attainable standard of physical and mental health and recalled that all human rights apply to all patients without exception. In 2002, by its resolution 2002/31, the Commission established the mandate of the **Special Rapporteur[s]** on the right of everyone to the enjoyment of the highest attainable standard of physical and mental health. In the preliminary report of February 2003, the Special Rapporteur declares that he wishes to devote particular attention to the specific role of the right to health in **poverty** reduction, as well as to the linkage between the realization of this right and aspects of **discrimination** and stigma, with special focus on **vulnerable groups** such as women, persons with disabilities, **HIV-infected people or people with AIDS** and persons belonging to national or ethnic, religious and linguistic **minorities.**

Within the **United Nations system**, the **World Health Organization (WHO)** is primarily responsible for the preparation and supervision of international measures relating to the right to health. The Preamble of its Constitution states: "The enjoyment of the highest attainable standard of health is one of the fundamental rights of every human being without distinction of race, religion, political belief, economic and social conditions". WHO's definition of health includes "physical, mental and social well-being".

Right to just and favourable conditions of work

The **Universal Declaration of Human Rights** proclaims that everyone has the right to work and to just and favourable conditions of work (Article 23, para. 1). According to Article 7 of the **International Covenant on Economic, Social and Cultural Rights**, States Parties "…recognize the right of everyone to the enjoyment of just and favourable conditions of work…" which ensure the **right to just and favourable remuneration**; safe and healthy working conditions; equal opportunity for everyone to be promoted in his employment to an appropriate higher level, subject to no considerations other than those of seniority and competence; and rest, leisure and reasonable limitation of working hours and periodic holidays with pay, as well as remuneration for public holidays. The **International Convention on the Elimination of All Forms of Racial Discrimination** as well as the **Convention on the Elimination of All Forms of Discrimination Against Women** contain provisions concerning the right to just and favourable conditions of work. Primary responsibility to ensure respect for this right lies with the **International Labour Organization (ILO)** which adopted binding instruments relevant to the right to just and favourable conditions of work, among them the **Convention (N° 100) concerning Equal Remuneration for Men and Women Workers for Work of Equal Value** (1951), the Convention (N° 155) concerning Occupational Safety and Health and the Working Environment (1981), and the Convention (N° 162) concerning Safety in the Use of Asbestos (1986).

Right to just and favourable remuneration

The **Universal Declaration of Human Rights** states that: "Everyone who works has the right to just and favourable remuneration…" (Article 23, para. 3). According to Article 7 of the **International Covenant on Economic, Social and Cultural Rights**, remuneration is a part of the **right to just and favourable conditions of work**. It means that such remuneration should provide workers with fair wages, equal remuneration for work of equal value and a decent living for themselves and their families. The **International Convention on the Elimination of All Forms of Racial Discrimination** provides for non-discrimination on racial grounds also in regard of just and favourable remuneration (Article 5) as does the **Convention on the Elimination of All Forms of Discrimination Against Women** on the ground of sex (Article 11). The principal conventions of the **International Labour Organization (ILO)** related to this right include: **the Convention (N° 100) concerning Equal Remuneration for Men and Women Workers for Work of Equal Value** (1951) and the Convention (N° 131) concerning Minimum Wage Fixing, with Special Reference to Developing Countries (1970).

Right to leave any country, including one's own, and to return to one's own country

The **Universal Declaration of Human Rights** proclaims that: "Everyone has the right to leave any country, including his own, and to return to his country" (Article 13, para. 2). Article 12 of the **International Covenant on Civil and Political Rights** further elaborated this right and added that the only possible restrictions are those "... which are provided by law, are necessary to protect national security, public order (*ordre public*), public health or morals or the rights and freedoms of others ... ". The right is also provided for in Article 22, para. 2, of the **American Convention on Human Rights** and in Article 12, para. 2, of the **African Charter on Human and Peoples' Rights**. Protocol N° 4 (1963) to the **European Convention for the Protection of Human Rights and Fundamental Freedoms** states that: "Everyone shall be free to leave any country, including his own" (Article 2, para. 2). The **International Convention on the Elimination of All Forms of Racial Discrimination** stipulates in its Article 5 the guarantee of the right of everyone, without **discrimination** on the grounds of race, colour or national or ethnic origin, "... to equality before the law..." including the right to leave any country, including his own, and to return to one's country.

Right to liberty and security of person

The **Universal Declaration of Human Rights** stipulates that: "Everyone has the right to life, liberty and security of person" (Article 3). This right is further elaborated in Article 9 of the **International Covenant on Civil and Political Rights** concerning the **freedom from arbitrary arrest** or detention. The **Human Rights Committee** pointed out in its General Comment N° 8 that the provisions of this Article (with the exception of its para. 3) are applicable to all deprivations of liberty, whether in criminal cases or in other cases such as mental illness, vagrancy, drug addiction, educational purposes and immigration control. Article 10 of the Covenant affirms that: "All persons deprived of their liberty shall be treated with humanity and with respect for the inherent dignity of the human person". The Human Rights Committee stated that this provision imposes on States Parties a positive obligation towards all persons held in prisons, hospitals, detention camps, correctional institutions or elsewhere, who are particularly vulnerable because of their status as persons deprived of their liberty (General Comment N° 21). The **United Nations General Assembly**, in order to increase protection of all persons deprived of their liberty, adopted the **Body of Principles for the Protection of All Persons under Any Form of Detention or Imprisonment** (resolution 43/173 of 9 December 1988). The Working Group on Arbitrary Detention, composed of five independent experts, was established in 1991 by the **Commission on Human Rights** (resolution 1991/42). Its mandate provides, *inter alia*, for the consideration of complaints of individuals against the arbitrary deprivation of liberty. Several reports were submitted to the Commission and an "urgent action" procedure has been developed for cases in which the continuation of the alleged arbitrary detention may constitute a serious danger to the detained person's health or life.

The right to liberty and security of person is confirmed by the regional instruments. The **European Convention for the Protection of Human Rights and Fundamental Freedoms,** in its Article 5, enumerates only six situations in which a person may be deprived of his/her liberty in accordance with procedures prescribed by law. The **American Convention on Human Rights** contains Article 7 entitled "Right to personal liberty". Similarly, Article 6 of the **African Charter on Human and Peoples' Rights** stipulates that: "Every individual shall have the right to liberty and to the security of his person. No one may be deprived of his freedom except for reasons and conditions previously laid down by law. In particular, no one may be arbitrarily arrested or detained".

Right to life

Article 3 of the **Universal Declaration of Human Rights** states that: "Everyone has the right to life, liberty and security of person". Article 6, para. 1, of the **International Covenant on Civil and Political Rights** stipulates that: "Every human being has the inherent right to life. This right shall be protected by law. No one shall be arbitrarily deprived of his life". Furthermore,

Article 6, para. 2, imposes on countries which have not abolished the death penalty the obligation that "... sentence of death may be imposed only for the most serious crimes in accordance with the law in force at the time of the commission of the crime and not contrary to the provisions of the present Covenant and to the **Convention on the Prevention and Punishment of the Crime of Genocide**. This penalty can only be carried out pursuant to a final judgement rendered by a competent court". Article 6, para. 3, lays down that: "When deprivation of life constitutes the crime of genocide, it is understood that nothing in this article shall authorize any State Party to the present Covenant to derogate in any way from any obligation assumed under the provisions of the Convention on the Prevention and Punishment of the Crime of Genocide". Furthermore, "Anyone sentenced to death shall have the right to seek pardon or commutation of the sentence. Amnesty, pardon or commutation of the sentence of death may be granted in all cases" (Article 6, para. 4) and "Sentence of death shall not be imposed for crimes committed by persons below 18 years of age and shall not be carried out on pregnant women" (Article 6, para. 5). Finally, it stipulates: "Nothing in this article shall be invoked to delay or to prevent the abolition of capital punishment by any State Party to the present Covenant (Article 6, para. 6). The **United Nations** presents regular reports on enforced or involuntary disappearances and arbitrary and extra-judicial executions in many countries of the world. The **Human Rights Committee** adopted at its 23rd session General Comment N° 14 on the right to life, by which it confirmed that the right to life is the supreme right from which no derogation is permitted even in time of public emergency. Several international instruments aimed at the abolition of the death penalty have also been adopted, among them the **Second Optional Protocol to the International Covenant on Civil and Political Rights**, the **Protocol to the American Convention on Human Rights to Abolish the Death Penalty** and Protocols N° 6 and N° 13 to the **European**

Convention for the Protection of Human Rights and Fundamental Freedoms.

Right to marry and to found a family

The **Universal Declaration of Human Rights** stipulates in its Article 16, para. 1, that: "Men and women of full age, without any limitation due to race, nationality or religion, have the right to marry and to found a family. They are entitled to equal rights as to marriage, during marriage and at its dissolution". Furthermore, "Marriage shall be entered into only with the free and full consent of the intending spouses" (Article 16, para. 2). Under Article 16, para. 3: "The family is the natural and fundamental group unit of society and is entitled to protection by society and the State". The **International Covenant on Economic, Social and Cultural Rights** provides for special measures to be taken aimed at the protection of the family, mothers and children. Its Article 10, para. 1, imposes on States Parties the obligation that: "The widest possible protection and assistance should be accorded to the family, which is the natural and fundamental group unit of society, particularly for its establishment and while it is responsible for the care and education of dependent children. Marriage must be entered into with the free consent of the intending spouses". The **International Covenant on Civil and Political Rights** also calls for special measures to be taken to protect the family. Its Article 23 considers that the family, as the natural and fundamental group unit of society, is entitled to protection by society and the State. Under its Article 23, "The right of men and women of marriageable age to marry and to found a family shall be recognized" and "No marriage shall be entered into without the free and full consent of the intending spouses". The same Article stipulates that States Parties "… shall take appropriate steps to ensure equality of rights and responsibilities of spouses as to marriage, during marriage and at its dissolution …". The **International Convention on the Elimination of All Forms of Racial Discrimination**

(Article 5 (d)(iv)), the **Convention on the Elimination of All Forms of Discrimination Against Women** (Articles 4, 12 and 16), as well as several regional instruments, contain provisions concerning marriage and the family. The **Convention on Consent to Marriage, Minimum Age for Marriage, and Registration of Marriages** (1962) set out measures aimed at ensuring that no marriage shall be legally entered into without the full and free consent of both parties. In 1989, the **United Nations General Assembly** proclaimed 1994 as the **International Year of the Family** in order to increase awareness of family issues.

Right to own property

The right of everyone to own property is provided for in the **Universal Declaration of Human Rights**, which stipulates in its Article 17, that: "Everyone has the right to own property alone as well as in association with others" and that: "No one shall be arbitrarily deprived of his property". The right to own property is not mentioned in the **International Covenants on Human Rights**. However, this right is dealt with in several other international conventions, such as the **International Convention on the Elimination of All Forms of Discrimination** (Article 5(d)(v)) and the **Convention on the Elimination of Discrimination Against Women** (Article 13), the Protocol to the **European Convention for the Protection of Human Rights and Fundamental Freedoms** (Article 1) the **American Convention on Human Rights** (Article 21) as well as the **African Charter on Human and Peoples' Rights** (Article 14). The **Declaration on Social Progress and Development** (1969) assigns a role to property in the implementation of human rights. A number of instruments are aimed at the protection of intellectual property, such as the **Berne Convention for the Protection of Literary and Artistic Works** and the **Paris Convention for the Protection of Industrial Property**.

Right to peace

The human right to peace is formulated in a number of international instruments which, however, are of a non-binding character and have to be qualified as so-called "soft law". The Istanbul Declaration, adopted in 1969 during the 21st International Conference of the Red Cross, proclaimed the right to lasting peace as a human right. In 1976, the right to life in peace was recognized as a human right by resolution 5/XXXII of the **Commission on Human Rights**. In 1978, the **United Nations General Assembly** adopted, in its resolution 33/73, the Declaration on the Preparation of Societies for Life in Peace which provides, in its Article 1, that: "Every nation and every human being, regardless of race, conscience, language or sex, has the inherent right to life in peace. Respect for that right, as well as for the other human rights, is in the common interest of all mankind and an indispensable condition of advancement of all nations, large and small, in all fields". The **Declaration of Principles on Tolerance**, adopted by the General Conference of **UNESCO** in 1995, in its Article 1, para. 1.4, states that human beings "… have the right to live in peace". The right to peace is also proposed as the right of peoples. Thus, the General Assembly adopted in 1984 (with 34 abstentions) the **Declaration on the Right of Peoples to Peace** which "solemnly proclaims that the peoples of our planet have a sacred right to peace" and "solemnly declares that the preservation of the right of peoples to peace and the promotion of its implementation constitute a fundamental obligation of each State". The right of peoples to peace was recognized by the **African Charter on Human and Peoples' Rights** which, in its Article 23, provides that "All peoples shall have the right to national and international peace and security".

Right to recognition as a person before the law

Article 6 of the **Universal Declaration of Human Rights** proclaimed that: "Everyone has the right to recognition everywhere as a person before the law". The **International Covenant on Civil and Political Rights** also recognizes this right (Article 16), which is an indispensable element of procedural guarantees as set out in Articles 14 to 16. The **American Convention on Human Rights** (Article 3) and the **African Charter on Human and Peoples' Rights** (Article 5) contain provisions relating to this right. In 1984, the **Human Rights Committee** adopted a general comment on Article 14 of the **International Covenant on Civil and Political Rights** in which it set out the Committee's views on the use of procedural guarantees to ensure the proper administration of justice.

Right to rest and leisure

The **Universal Declaration of Human Rights**, in its Article 24, proclaims that: "Everyone has the right to rest and leisure, including reasonable limitation of working hours and periodic holidays with pay". The right to rest and leisure was further elaborated in the **International Covenant on Economic, Social and Cultural Rights** (Article 7) which stipulates that States Parties are obliged to recognize the **right to just and favourable conditions of work**, which includes in particular "rest, leisure and reasonable limitation of working hours and periodic holidays with pay, as well as remuneration for public holidays". Furthermore, in 1970 the **International Labour Organization (ILO)** adopted the Convention (N° 132) concerning Annual Holidays with Pay (Revised) which provides that all employed persons in a Contracting State are entitled to annual paid holidays of not less than three working weeks for one year of service. However, by the middle of 2003, the Convention had been ratified by only 32 States.

Right to security in the event of unemployment or other lack of livelihood

Apart from the **right to an adequate standard of living**, the **Universal Declaration of Human Rights** proclaims the right of everyone "... to security in the event of unemployment ... or other lack of livelihood in circumstances beyond his control" (Article 25, para. 1). According to the **International Convention on the Elimination of All Forms of Racial Discrimination**, States Parties are obliged to prohibit and to eliminate racial **discrimination** and to guarantee the right of everyone "to protection against unemployment" (Article 5(e)(i)). The **Convention on the Elimination of All Forms of Discrimination against Women** provides for non-discrimination on the grounds of sex in respect of: "The **right to social security**, particularly in cases of ... unemployment ..." (Article 11, para. 1(e)). The **Convention (N° 122) concerning Employment Policy** (1964), adopted by the **International Labour Organization (ILO)**, stipulates in Article 1 that States shall declare and pursue an active policy with a view to overcoming unemployment and underemployment.

Right to social security

The right of everyone to social security is proclaimed in the **Universal Declaration of Human Rights** which, in its Article 22, stipulates that: "Everyone, as a member of society, has the right to social security and is entitled to realization, through national effort and international cooperation and in accordance with the organization and resources of each State, of the **economic, social** and **cultural rights** indispensable for his dignity and the free development of his personality". Furthermore, Article 9 of the **International Covenant on Economic, Social and Cultural Rights** (1966) imposes on its States Parties the obligation to "... recognize the right of everyone to social security, including social insurance". The **International Convention on the Elimination of Racial**

Discrimination (1965) ensures non-discrimination on racial grounds in regard to the right to public health, medical care, social security and social services (Article 5 (e)(iv)) and the **Convention on the Elimination of All Forms of Discrimination Against Women** (1979) ensures non-discrimination on the ground of sex in regard to the right to social security (Article 11, paragraph 1(e)). The **European Code of Social Security – revised** (1990) is aimed at encouraging the development of social security in all Member States of the **Council of Europe**. Within the **United Nations system**, the **International Labour Organization (ILO)** has special responsibility concerning the right to social security. Its basic instruments in this field are the **Convention (N° 102) concerning Minimum Standards of Social Security** (1952) and **Convention (N° 118) concerning Equality of Treatment of Nationals and Non-Nationals in Social Security** (1962).

Right to strike

A strike is a collective refusal by employees to work under the conditions imposed by their employers. The right to strike is granted principally in nearly all industrial countries. The **International Covenant on Economic, Social and Cultural Rights** imposes on the States Parties the obligation to undertake to ensure: "The right to strike, provided that it is exercised in conformity with the laws of the particular country" (Article 8, para. 1(d)). "This Article shall not prevent the imposition of lawful restrictions on the exercise of these rights by members of the armed forces or of the police or of the administration of the State" (Article 8, para. 2). Article 8, para. 3, states that "Nothing ... shall authorize States Parties to the International Labour Organisation **Convention (N° 87) concerning Freedom of Association and Protection of the Right to Organise** to take legislative measures which would prejudice, or apply the law in such a manner as would prejudice the guarantees provided for in that Convention". The **Additional Protocol to the American Convention on Human Rights in the Area of Economic, Social and Cultural**

Rights **"Protocol of San Salvador"** imposes on States Parties the obligation to ensure the right to strike (Article 8, para. 1(b)). It further explains that members of the armed forces and the police and of other essential services shall be subject to limitations and restrictions established by law. In accordance with the **European Social Charter - revised**, the Contracting Parties recognize "… the right of workers and employers to collective action in cases of conflicts of interest, including the right to strike, subject to obligations that might arise out of collective agreements previously entered into" (Article 6, para. 4). The right to strike is closely linked with the **right to form and join trade unions, freedom of association** and **freedom of peaceful assembly.**

Right to take part in cultural life

The **Universal Declaration of Human Rights**, in its Article 27, para. 1, states that: "Everyone has the right freely to participate in the cultural life of the community …". It also provides in Article 22 that everyone is entitled to the realization of the economic, social and cultural rights indispensable for his dignity and the free development of his personality. The **International Covenant on Economic, Social and Cultural Rights** recognizes the right of everyone to take part in cultural life (Article 15, para. 1). Furthermore, States Parties should undertake steps in order to fully realize this right. Those steps shall "… include those necessary for the conservation, the development and the diffusion of science and culture" (Article 15, para. 2). Furthermore, the **American Declaration of the Rights and Duties of Man** (1948) as well as the **African Charter on Human and Peoples' Rights** (1981) formulate the right to take part in cultural life. The UNESCO **Recommendation on Participation by the People at Large in Cultural Life and their Contribution to It** (1978) explains both the active and passive aspects of the right. It encourages Member States to undertake efforts in order to democratize the means and instruments of cultural activity.

Right to take part in the government

The right of everyone to take part in government is proclaimed in the **Universal Declaration of Human Rights**: "Everyone has the right to take part in the government of his country, directly or through freely chosen representatives" (Article 21, para. 1). This political right is also dealt with in Article 25 of the **International Covenant on Civil and Political Rights** which stipulates that: "Every citizen shall have the right and the opportunity, without any of the distinctions mentioned in Article 2 and without unreasonable restrictions: (a) To take part in the conduct of public affairs, directly or through freely chosen representatives ...". The **International Convention on the Elimination of All Forms of Racial Discrimination** also provides for the right to take part in government (Article 5(c)), as well as the **Convention on the Elimination of All Forms of Discrimination Against Women** (Articles 7(b) and 8). The **American Convention on Human Rights** (Article 23, para. 1(a)) and the **African Charter on Human and Peoples' Rights** (Article 13, para. 1) contain provisions relating to this field. The right to take part in government is crucial for the implementation of the **right to democracy**.

Right to the protection of the law against interference and attacks on privacy

The right to the protection of the law against interference and attacks on privacy is provided for in the **Universal Declaration of Human Rights**, which stipulates in its Article 12 that: "No one shall be subjected to arbitrary interference with his privacy, family, home or correspondence, nor to attacks upon his honour and reputation. Everyone has the right to the protection of the law against such interference or attacks". The **International Covenant on Civil and Political Rights** contains a similar provision stipulating that: "No one shall be subjected to arbitrary or unlawful interference with his privacy, family, home or correspondence ..." (Article 17, para. 1) and "Everyone has the right to the protection of the law against such interference or attacks" (Article 17, para. 2). The **American Convention on Human Rights** deals with this subject in Article 11 and the **European Convention for the Protection of Human Rights and Fundamental Freedoms** in Article 8. In 1988, the **Human Rights Committee** adopted a general comment setting out its views on the meaning of the right as formulated in Article 17 of the **International Covenant on Civil and Political Rights.**

Right to vote and to be elected

The right to vote and to be elected is a political right which is set out in the **Universal Declaration of Human Rights** stating that "The will of the people shall be the basis of the authority of government; this will shall be expressed in periodic and genuine elections which shall be by universal and equal suffrage and shall be held by secret vote or by equivalent free voting procedures" (Article 21, para. 3). This provision reflects the basic principles of democracy. The right to vote and to be elected is further elaborated in the **International Covenant on Civil and Political Rights** which lays down that: "Every citizen shall have the right and the opportunity, without any of the distinctions mentioned in Article 2 and without unreasonable restrictions to vote and to be elected at genuine periodic elections which shall be by universal and equal suffrage and shall be held by secret ballot, guaranteeing the free expression of the will of the electors" (Article 25). The **International Convention on the Elimination of All Forms of Racial Discrimination** also contains a provision relating to this political right (Article 5(c)) as does the **Convention on the Elimination of All Forms of Discrimination Against Women** (Article 7(a)). The **American Convention on Human Rights** (Article 23, para. 1(b)) provides for the right to vote and to be elected. This right is enshrined in other universal and regional instruments. The **United Nations General Assembly** has recalled repeatedly the necessity and indispensability of periodic and genuine elections and reaffirmed that the systematic denial or abridgement of the right to vote on grounds of race or colour is a gross violation of human rights.

Right to work

The right of everyone to work is proclaimed in Article 23, para. 1, of the **Universal Declaration of Human Rights**. This provision is codified in the **International Covenant on Economic, Social and Cultural Rights**. Pursuant to its Article 6, para. 1, States Parties have the obligation to "... recognize the right to work, which includes the right of everyone to the opportunity to gain his living by work which he freely chooses or accepts, and will take appropriate steps to safeguard this right". Furthermore, in order to realize fully the right to work, Article 6, para. 2, prescribes a series of specific steps to be taken by States Parties which "... include technical and vocational guidance and training programmes, policies and techniques to achieve steady economic, social and cultural development and full and productive employment under conditions safeguarding fundamental political and economic freedoms to the individual". The right to work is also dealt with in the **International Convention on the Elimination of All Forms of Racial Discrimination** (Article 5(e)(i)) and the **Convention on the Elimination of All Forms of Discrimination against Women** (Article 11, para. 1(a)) as well as the **European Social Charter** (Article 1) and the **African Charter on Human and Peoples' Rights** (Article 15). The **International Labour Organization (ILO)** has the special responsibility of protecting the right to work. Its basic instruments in this field are the **Convention (N° 111) concerning Discrimination in respect of Employment and Occupation** (1958) and the **Convention (N° 122) concerning Employment Policy** (1964).

Riyadh Guidelines (UN)

Common name for the **United Nations Guidelines for the Prevention of Juvenile Delinquency**.

Rome Statute of the International Criminal Court – ICC (UN)

The Rome Statute of the International Criminal Court (ICC) was adopted on 17 July 1998 by the United Nations Diplomatic Conference of Plenipotentiaries on the Establishment of an International Criminal Court. The Statute entered into force on 1 July 2002, 60 days after the 60th instrument of ratification was deposited with the **United Nations Secretary-General**.

The establishment of a permanent **International Criminal Court (ICC)** represents a great advance in the international protection of human rights. Built on the examples set by the **International Criminal Tribunal for Rwanda (ICTR)** and the **International Criminal Tribunal for the Former Yugoslavia (ICTY)**, the ICC complements national criminal law systems and acts as a deterrent against massive violations of human rights throughout the world.

Safeguards Guaranteeing Protection of the Rights of Those Facing the Death Penalty (UN)

The Safeguards were adopted by the **Economic and Social Council (ECOSOC)** on 25 May 1984 (resolution 1984/50). According to them, capital punishment – in countries which have not abolished the death penalty – may be imposed only for the most serious crimes and only for a crime for which the death penalty is prescribed by law at the time of its commission. The guilt of the person charged must be based upon clear and convincing evidence. Persons under 18 years shall not be sentenced to death nor shall the death sentence be carried out on pregnant women, or on new mothers, or on persons who have become insane (Safeguard 3). Those sentenced to death shall have the **right to appeal** to a court of higher jurisdiction and to seek pardon or commutation of sentence (Safeguards 6-7). Where capital punishment occurs, it shall be carried out so as to inflict the minimum possible suffering (Safeguard 9).

Second Optional Protocol to the International Covenant on Civil and Political Rights, Aiming at the Abolition of the Death Penalty (UN)

The Second Optional Protocol to the International Covenant on Civil and Political Rights, aiming at the abolition of the death penalty was adopted by the **United Nations General Assembly** on 15 December 1989 and entered into force on 11 July 1991. By the middle of 2003 it had been ratified by 49 States. It is based on the belief that the abolition of the death penalty contributes to the enhancement of human dignity and the progressive development of human rights and that all measures of abolition of the death penalty should be considered as progress in the enjoyment of the **right to life** (Preamble). According to Article 1, States Parties to the Protocol agree that no one within their jurisdiction shall be executed and that all necessary measures to abolish the death penalty shall be taken. In the reports submitted to the **Human Rights Committee**, States Parties must include information on the measures they have adopted to give effect to the Protocol (Article 3). The competence of the Committee to receive complaints from States under Article 41 of the **International Covenant on Civil and Political Rights** and from individuals subject to the jurisdiction of States that have ratified the first **Optional Protocol** to the Covenant shall extend to the provisions of the Second Optional Protocol unless the State Party concerned has made a statement to the contrary at the moment of ratification or accession (Articles 4-5).

Security Council (UN)

The Security Council was set up under Article 7 of the **Charter of the United Nations**. It is the organ to which the Charter gives primary responsibility for the maintenance of international peace and security (Article 24). The Council comprises 15 members. Five of these (China, France, the Russian Federation, the United Kingdom, and the United States) are permanent members. The other ten are elected by the **United Nations General Assembly** for two-year terms. The Security Council can be convened at any time, whenever peace is threatened.

Article 34 of the Charter entrusts the Security Council to investigate any dispute or any situation which might lead to international friction. Since such "situations" too often stem in part from, or are accompanied by, massive and persistent human rights violations, the Security Council deals with human rights violations. When fighting breaks out, the Council tries to secure a ceasefire to prevent wider hostilities. On some occasions, the Security Council can decide to establish peace-keeping operations in an area of conflict. It defines the operation's size, its overall objectives and its time-frame. Between June 1948 and May 2003, there were 56 **United Nations** peacekeeping operations. In extreme cases, if a situation constitutes a serious threat to peace, and when peaceful means of settling a dispute have been exhausted, Article 39 of the Charter authorizes the Security Council to decide on enforcement measures, economic sanctions (such as trade embargoes) or collective military actions. While other organs of the United Nations provide recommendations for Governments, the Security Council alone is vested with power to compel action by Governments. Hence, under the Charter, Member States are obliged to accept and carry out the Security Council's decisions. Decisions on procedural matters require an affirmative vote of nine of the fifteen members (Article 27, para. 2, of the Charter). However, decisions on all other matters shall be made by an affirmative vote of nine members, including the concurring votes of all five permanent members (Article 27, para. 3, of the Charter). This is the rule of "Great Powers unanimity", often referred to as the "veto" power. The Security Council has also set up **International Criminal Tribunals** to prosecute persons accused of serious violations of **international humanitarian law** and **genocide**.

For more information see: http://www.un.org/Docs/sc/

Slave Route Project (UNESCO)

At the proposal of Haiti and some African countries, the General Conference of **UNESCO** approved, at its 27th Session in 1993, the inter-regional and intercultural Slave Route Project. The project was officially launched in September 1994 in Benin, one of the former pivots of the slave trade in the Gulf of Guinea. Bearing in mind the cost in human lives of the slave trade and the ideology that served to justify it, as well as its far-reaching effect in the economic, social and cultural sphere in the continents involved, the Slave Route Project has a twofold objective. On the one hand, it aims at bringing to universal attention the issue of the transatlantic slave trade and slavery in the Indian Ocean and Mediterranean by elucidating, through scientific research, their underlying causes and *modus operandi*. On the other hand, it should emphasize objectively its consequences and especially the interactions between the peoples concerned in Europe, Africa and the Caribbean. Hence the issues at stake concerning the Slave Route Project are: historical truth; peace; development; human rights; memory; and intercultural dialogue. The UNESCO General Conference, at its 29th session in 1997, proclaimed 23 August of every year as **International Day for the Remembrance of the Slave Trade and its Abolition**. This was the day in 1791 when the slaves of Santo Domingo and Haiti rose up in rebellion, thus taking the first step towards the abolition of the slave trade.

For more information see:
www.unesco.org/culture/dialogue/slave/index.shtml

Slavery

Prohibition of slavery, slave trade and similar practices is proclaimed among others in Article 4 of the **Universal Declaration of Human Rights**, Article 8 of the **International Covenant on Civil and Political Rights**, Article 6 of the **American Convention on Human Rights**, Article 5 of the **African Charter on Human and Peoples' Rights**, and Article 4 of the **European Convention for the Protection of Human Rights and Fundamental Freedoms**. Furthermore, several international conventions are directly related to the issue of slavery. In 1949, the **United Nations General Assembly** adopted the **Convention for the Suppression of the Traffic in Persons and of the Exploitation of the Prostitution of Others**. The **Slavery Convention** of 1926 became a **United Nations** instrument when the **Protocol Amending the 1926 Slavery Convention** entered into force in 1953. According to it and to the **Supplementary Convention on the Abolition of Slavery, the Slave Trade, and Institutions and Practices Similar to Slavery** of 1956, the term "slavery" means "... the status or condition of a person over whom any or all of the powers attaching to the right of ownership are exercised ..." (Article 1, para. 1 of the Slavery Convention and Article 7 (a) of the Supplementary Convention). The Working Group on Contemporary Forms of Slavery is the United Nations body which receives information from States on the steps they have taken to implement the three slavery-related Conventions. Meeting for the first time in 1975 as the Working Group on Slavery, the group was renamed in 1988 and has the general responsibility in the United Nations for the study of slavery in all its aspects. It comprises five independent experts chosen from the members of the **Sub-Commission on the Promotion and Protection of Human Rights** (formerly the **Sub-Commission on Prevention of Discrimination and Protection of Minorities**) and reports to it. The **Durban Declaration and Programme of Action** acknowledged slavery and the slave trade, especially the transatlantic slave trade, as a crime against humanity and a major source and manifestation of **racism** and racial **discrimination** (para. 13 of the Declaration).

Deeply rooted in economic and social structures, **poverty**, discrimination, prejudice, tradition and greed, slavery practices remain extremely difficult to eliminate. Today, they cover a wide variety of human rights violations. In addition to traditional slavery and the slave trade, abuses include the sale of children, child prostitution, child pornography, the exploitation of child labour, the sexual mutilation of female children, the use of children in armed conflicts, debt bondage, the traffic in persons and the sale of human organs, adult prostitution, and certain practices under **apartheid** and colonial regimes. Each year the **International Day for the Abolition of Slavery** is observed on 2 December and the **International Day for the Remembrance of the Slave Trade and its Abolition** is commemorated on 23 August.

Slavery Convention (League of Nations)

International instruments aimed at the abolishment of slavery, slavery-like practices and the slave trade were among the first human rights instruments. Some of them were adopted under the auspices of the **League of Nations**. The Slavery Convention, which was signed in Geneva on 25 September 1926 and entered into force on 9 March 1927, is one such instrument. Its Article 1 defines slavery as "the status or condition of a person over whom any or all of the powers attaching to the right of ownership are exercised", while the slave trade is defined as including "all acts involved in the capture, acquisition or disposal of a person with intent to reduce him to slavery; all acts involved in the acquisition of a slave with a view to selling or exchanging him; all acts of disposal by sale or exchange of a slave acquired with a view to being sold or exchanged, and, in general, every act of trade or transport in slaves". Parties to the Convention undertake "to prevent and suppress the slave trade" and "to bring about, progressively and as soon as possible, the complete abolition of slavery in all its forms" (Article 2). They undertake further "to adopt all appropriate measures with a view to preventing and suppressing the embarkation, disembarkation and transport of slaves in their territorial waters and upon all vessels flying their respective flags" (Article 3). On 27 April 1953, the **Economic and Social Council (ECOSOC)** recommended the functions undertaken by the League of Nations under the 1926 Convention be transferred to the **United Nations**. On 23 October 1953, the **United Nations General Assembly** approved the **Protocol Amending the 1926 Slavery Convention**, urged all States Parties to the Slavery Convention of 1926 to sign and accept the Protocol, and recommended that all other States accede to the Convention as amended by the Protocol at the earliest opportunity. The Slavery Convention of 1926 was ratified by over 40 States by the middle of 2003, the provisions of the Convention amended by the 1953 Protocol having become binding for 59 States.

Social rights

Social rights include: the **right to social security**; the **right to rest and leisure**; the **right to adequate food,** clothing, housing, medical and social services; the **right to an adequate standard of living**; and the **right to health**. The **right to education** is often listed among social rights although some experts consider it to be an **economic right[s]** and others a **cultural right[s]**. Each State Party undertakes to take steps, through international assistance and cooperation, to the maximum of its available resources, to achieving progressively the full realization of these rights. In other words, they are envisaged as a result of the progressive development of national social policies, legislation and practical programmes. Provision is made for social rights in the **United Nations Charter**. Chapter IX of the Charter, entitled "International Economic and Social Co-operation", states that one of the primary goals of the **United Nations** is "higher standards of living, full employment, and conditions of economic and social progress and development; solutions of international economic, social, health and related problems; and international cultural and educational cooperation ...". The **Universal Declaration of Human Rights** (1948) contains an extended and specific list of social rights (Articles 22-27). Furthermore these rights are expressed more fully in the **International Covenant on Economic, Social and Cultural Rights** (1966) whose provisions are designed to create binding obligations for States Parties to it. There are several regional instruments relating to social rights, in particular: the **American Declaration on the Rights and Duties of Man** and the **Inter-American Charter of Social Guarantees** (both of 1948); the **European Social Charter** (1961) and the **European Social Charter – revised** (1996); the **European Code of Social Security** (1964); the **American Convention on Human Rights** (1969).

Special Rapporteurs (UN)

Special Rapporteurs do not derive their mandate from a particular human rights instrument, but they are established by resolutions of the **Commission on Human Rights** or the **Sub-Commission on the Promotion and Protection of Human Rights** (formely the **Sub-Commission on Prevention of Discrimination and Protection of Minorities**) and subject to the approval by the **Economic and Social Council (ECOSOC)**. They can be generally divided into two categories: those who address human rights issues on a global basis by theme, the Thematic Rapporteurs, and those which focus on the overall human rights situation in a specific country, the Country Rapporteurs. The Special Rapporteurs are independent experts, not Government representatives, and do not receive any remuneration. They report regularly to the Commission and these reports can serve as a basis for relevant resolutions or decisions. They also provide the treaty bodies with information on the human rights situation in the countries whose reports are being considered.

The first Thematic Rapporteur was established in 1980 on enforced and involuntary disappearances. Afterwards, the Commission established Thematic Rapporteurs on for example extrajudicial, summary or arbitrary executions, torture, the right to freedom of religion, the right to freedom of expression, the **right to education** and the right to food, contemporary forms of racism, violence against women, independent judges and lawyers, human rights of migrants, etc. Several Rapporteurs, for example the ones on torture and on extrajudicial, summary or arbitrary executions, have an urgent action procedure, whereby they can promptly react to situations of concern by requesting governments to take immediate action to rectify or clarify a case. The Sub-Commission on the Promotion and Protection of Human Rights also nominated a number of Special Rapporteurs.

For more information see:
http://www.unhchr.ch/html/menu2/xtraconv.htm
http://www.unhchr.ch/html/menu2/2/liststudrepts.htm

Standard Minimum Rules for the Treatment of Prisoners (UN)

On 30 August 1955, the First **United Nations Congress[es] on the Prevention of Crime and the Treatment of Offenders** adopted the Standard Minimum Rules for the Treatment of Prisoners. The Rules aim to ensure that all persons deprived of their liberty are treated with humanity and with respect. These Rules, which are not binding on States, are aimed at setting out "what is generally accepted as being good principle and practice in the treatment of prisoners and the management of institutions" (Preliminary Observations), without however precluding new methods and practices, provided that they are consonant with the principles governing the protection of human dignity. Of these Rules, mention should be made of non-**discrimination** and respect of religious beliefs (Rule 6), accommodation (Rules 9-14), personal hygiene (Rules 15-16), clothing and bedding (Rules 17-19), food (Rule 20), exercise and sport (Rule 21), medical services (Rules 22-26). Provisions concerning discipline and punishment (Rules 27-32) are aimed at the protection of prisoners against arbitrary punishment, corporal punishment, etc. The right to make requests or complaints to the prison administration is clarified in detail in Rules 35 and 36. The instrument also prescribes special rules for certain categories of prisoners and persons under detention. In particular, accused minors and young delinquents should be separated from adults (Rule 8). Similarly, accused persons should be segregated from convicted persons (Rule 8). Finally, a number of rules are aimed at the establishment of a liberal penitentiary system, the goal of which should be the reformation and social rehabilitation of prisoners (Rules 56-95).

Standard Rules on the Equalization of Opportunities for Persons with Disabilities (UN)

On 20 December 1993, the **United Nations General Assembly** adopted the Standard Rules on the Equalization of Opportunities for Persons with Disabilities and requested Member States to apply the Standard Rules in developing national disability programmes. Their purpose is to ensure that girls, boys, women and men with disabilities, as citizens of their societies, may exercise the same rights and obligations as others. Although not compulsory, the 22 Rules set forth in this instrument impose on States a strong moral and political commitment to take appropriate action to remove obstacles preventing persons with disabilities from exercising their rights and freedoms and making it difficult for them to participate fully in the activities of their societies. For example, States agree to take action to raise awareness in society about persons with disabilities, their rights, their needs, their potential and their contribution (Rule 1), and to ensure disabled persons access to effective medical care (Rule 2), rehabilitation services (Rule 3), education (Rule 6), employment (Rule 7), recreation and sports (Rule 11), religion (Rule 12), and policy-making and planning (Rule 14). The Standard Rules were adopted in order to: stress that all action in the field of disability presupposes adequate knowledge of the special needs of persons with disabilities; emphasize that making every aspect of societal organization accessible to all is a basic objective of socio-economic development; outline crucial aspects of social policies in the field of disability; provide models for the political decision-making process required for the attainment of equal opportunities; propose national mechanisms for close collaboration among States, the organs of the **United Nations system**, other intergovernmental bodies and organizations of persons with disabilities; and propose an effective machinery for monitoring the process by which States seek to attain the equalization of opportunities for persons with disabilities.

Sub-Commission on Prevention of Discrimination and Protection of Minorities (UN)

This subsidiary body of the **Commission on Human Rights** was established in 1947. In 1999, it became the **Sub-Commission on the Promotion and Protection of Human Rights**.

Sub-Commission on the Promotion and Protection of Human Rights (UN)

The Sub-Commission on the Promotion and Protection of Human Rights existed until 1999 under the title **Sub-Commission on Prevention of Discrimination and Protection of Minorities**. It is the main subsidiary body of the **Commission on Human Rights**. Established in 1947, the Sub-Commission's functions are to "undertake studies, particularly in the light of the **Universal Declaration of Human Rights**, and to make recommendations to the Commission on Human Rights concerning the prevention of **discrimination** of any kind relating to human rights and fundamental freedoms and the protection of racial, national, religious and linguistic minorities" and "to perform any other functions which may be entrusted to it by the **Economic and Social Council (ECOSOC)** or the Commission on Human Rights" (ECOSOC resolution 9(II) of 21 June 1946). Studies prepared by the Sub-Commission include those on harmful practices affecting the health of women and children, freedom of expression, discrimination against people with AIDS, the **right to a fair trial**, the human rights of detained juveniles, human rights and the environment, the rights of minorities and **indigenous peoples**, the question of impunity of violators of human rights and the **right to adequate housing**. The Sub-Commission is composed of experts acting in their personal capacity, elected by the Commission with due regard for equitable geographical representation. It was originally composed of twelve experts, but the number has been increased progressively over the years and now stands at 26. Its annual session (four weeks until 2000 and three since 2000) is attended by members and their alternatives, representatives of States which are members of the **United Nations, United Nations specialized agencies**, other intergovernmental organizations, national liberation movements and **non-governmental organizations** in consultative status with ECOSOC. Currently, the Sub-Commission has six working groups which meet before or during each session to assist it with certain tasks. These are the Working Group on Communications (see: **Communications procedures**), the Working Group on Contemporary Forms of **Slavery**, the Working group on Indigenous Populations, the Working Group on **Minorities**, the Working group on Administration of Justice and the Working group on **Transnational Corporations**. In addition, the Sub-Commission may establish working groups to meet during the session to focus on matters requiring special attention. Special Rapporteurs of the Sub-Commission are working on such subjects as "**Terrorism** and human rights", "**Globalization** and its impact on the full enjoyment of all human rights", "The rights of non-citizens", etc.

For more information see:
http://www.unhchr.ch/html/menu2/2/sc.htm

Supervisory procedures of the International Labour Organisation (ILO)

A regular machinery for supervising the observance of obligations arising under or relating to International Labour Conventions and Recommendations has been established since 1926. The Committee of Experts on the Application of Conventions and Recommendations (20 members appointed by the Governing Body in a personal capacity among impartial persons of technical competence and independent standing) and the Conference Committee on the Application of Standards (a tripartite body consisting of representatives of governments, employers and workers) examine each year the reports submitted by governments on ratified conventions as well as information from employers' and workers' organizations. Some 2,000 government reports are examined annually. In addition, the Constitution provides for a procedure of representation as to the observance of ratified Conventions allowing any employers' or workers' organizations to present to the **International Labour Organisation (ILO)** a claim that a Member State has failed to comply with its obligations in respect of a convention it has ratified. A second procedure allows a Member State – or a delegate to the ILO Conference – to make a complaint against another Member State if it considers that the latter is not securing effective observance of any convention which they have both ratified. In addition, complaints concerning the infringements of **freedom of association** may be filed by governments or by employers' or workers' organizations, regardless of whether the country concerned is bound by any of the conventions in the field of freedom of association. The Committee on Freedom of Association examines the complaints and submits its conclusions and recommendations to the Governing Body, which may ask the Government concerned to take the necessary meassures.

Supplementary Convention on the Abolition of Slavery, the Slave Trade and Institutions and Practices Similar to Slavery (UN)

The Supplementary Convention on the Abolition of Slavery, the Slave Trade and Institutions and Practices Similar to Slavery was adopted on 30 April 1956 and entered into force on 30 April 1957. By the middle of 2003, it had been ratified by 119 States. Article 1 of the Supplementary Convention provides that each State Party shall "take all practicable and necessary legislative and other measures to bring about ... the complete abolition or abandonment of certain institutions and practices, where they still exist and whether or not they are covered by the definition of slavery contained in Article 1 of the **Slavery Convention** signed at Geneva on 25 September 1926". These practices and institutions as set out in Article 1 of the

Supplementary Convention are: "debt bondage"; "serfdom"; "any institution or practice whereby (i) a woman, without the right to refuse, is promised or given in marriage on payment of a consideration in money or in kind to her parents, guardian, family or any other person or group; or (ii) the husband of a woman, his family, or his clan, has the right to transfer her to another person for value received or otherwise; or (iii) a woman on the death of her husband is liable to be inherited by another person"; and "any institution or practice whereby a child or young person under the age of 18 years is delivered by either or both of his natural parents or by his guardian to another person, whether for reward or not, with a view to the exploitation of the child or young person or of his labour". "States Parties should cooperate with each other and with the **United Nations**. They undertake to communicate to the **United Nations Secretary-General**" copies of any laws, regulations and administrative measures enacted or put into effect to implement the provisions of this Convention" (Article 8, para.2).

Terrorism

The rise of terrorist practices made evident the need for international cooperation in order to combat it. The first step was undertaken by the **League of Nations**, which qualified terrorism as an international crime. In the early 1970s, the **United Nations General Assembly** became preoccupied with this subject, which led to the establishment of an *ad hoc* Committee. Several international conventions relating to various aspects of international terrorism have been adopted by the **United Nations system**.

The General Assembly adopted the Convention on the Prevention and Punishment of Crimes against Internationally Protected Persons, including Diplomatic Agents (1973), the **International Convention against the Taking of Hostages** (1979), the **International Convention for the Suppression of Terrorist Bombings** (1997) and **International Convention for the Suppression of the Financing of Terrorism** (1999).

The **International Civil Aviation Organization** (ICAO) adopted the following instruments: **Convention for the Suppression of Unlawful Acts against the Safety of Civil Aviation** (1971); **Convention for the Suppression of Unlawful Seizure of Aircraft** (1970); **Convention on Offences and Certain Other Acts Committed on Board Aircraft** (1963); Protocol for the Suppression of Unlawful Acts of Violence at Airports Serving International Civil Aviation, Supplementary to the Convention for the Suppression of Unlawful Acts against the Safety of Civil Aviation (1988), Convention on the Marking of Plastic Explosives for the Purpose of Detection (1991).

The International Maritime Organization adopted the Convention for the Suppression of Unlawful Acts Against the Safety of Maritime Navigation (1988) and the Protocol for the

Suppression of Unlawful Acts against the Safety of Fixed Platforms Located on the Continental Shelf (1988).

The International Atomic Energy Agency elaborated the Convention on the Physical Protection of Nuclear Material (1979).

Moreover, several instruments against terrorism have been elaborated at regional level. The **Convention to Prevent and Punish the Acts of Terrorism taking the Forms of Crimes against Persons and Related Extortion that are of International Significance** was adopted by the **Organization of American States (OAS)** in 1971, the **European Convention on the Suppression of Terrorism** was adopted by the **Council of Europe** in 1977. The League of Arab States adopted the Arab Convention on the Suppression of Terrorism (1998), the Organization of the Islamic Conference adopted the Convention on Combating International Terrorism (1999) and the **African Union** (formerly Organization of African Unity) adopted the **Convention on the Prevention and Combating of Terrorism** (1999).

The common feature of all the above instruments is the absence of a general and comprehensive definition of terrorism. They are limited to outlawing certain criminal acts whose inclusion in the concept of terrorism raised no objection.

The direct linkage between terrorism and violations of human rights was recognized by the **World Conference on Human Rights** (Vienna, 1993). The **Vienna Declaration and Programme of Action** affirm that "the acts, methods and practices of terrorism in all its forms and manifestations as well as linkage in some countries to drug trafficking are activities aimed at the destruction of human rights, fundamental freedoms and democracy, threatening territorial integrity, security of States and destabilizing legitimately constituted Governments" (Part I, para. 17). It concluded that "the international community should take the necessary steps to enhance cooperation to prevent and combat terrorism".

The United Nations General Assembly has repeatedly expressed in a number of resolutions (48/122, 49/185, 50/186,

52/133, 54/164) its unequivocal condemnation of the acts of terrorism.

The terrorist attacks of 11 September 2001 put the question of the prevention and elimination of terrorism at the top of the agenda of the international community. The Security Council unanimously adopted resolutions 1368 (2001) and 1373 (2001) condemning terrorism. The latter resolution established a Counter-Terrorism Committee, composed of all members of the Security Council, to monitor the implementation of the provisions of this resolution. The General Assembly convened a special session in 2001 and adopted by consensus resolution 56/1. In all the resolutions adopted since then by the Security Council and the General Assembly it was underlined that a shared international commitment is needed to find an effective, sustainable and multilateral response to the problem of terrorism. In resolution 56/160, the General Assembly expressed its concern about the persistence of the phenomenon of terrorism despite efforts at national and international levels. Moreover, it noted the growing consciousness within the international community of the negative effects of terrorism on the full enjoyment of human rights and the establishment of the rule of law and democratic freedoms and called for intensification of measures at the national level and for an enhanced international cooperation in preventing, combating and eliminating all acts of terrorism.

In October 2001, the **United Nations Secretary-General** established the Policy Working Group on the **United Nations and Terrorism**. It was supposed to identify the longer-term implications and broad policy dimensions of terrorism for the United Nations and to formulate recommendations on the steps to be taken by the United Nations system to address the issue. In its report presented to the General Assembly in 2002 (document A/57/2743-S/2002/875) the Working Group stressed that terrorism is undermining and threatening the core principles and purposes of the United Nations Charter. It also stipulated that action should be strengthened to combat violations of human rights, since terrorism often flourishes where human rights are violated. It underlined that terrorism is an assault on basic rights. The Working Group, however, also stressed that the fight against terrorism should be respectful of international human rights obligations. In resolution 57/219 the General Assembly recalling the provisions of article 4 of ICCPR, according to which certain rights are non-derogable in any circumstances, affirmed that States must ensure that any measure taken to combat terrorism complies with their obligations under international law, in particular international human rights and **international humanitarian law**. At the same time, it requested the **United Nations High Commissioner for Human Rights** to study the question, as well as to make general recommendations to Member States and provide them assistance and advice in this regard.

The United Nations system, regional inter-governmental organizations and a great number of organizations and institutions working in the field of human rights are paying an increased attention to the issues linked with the struggle against terrorism. The **Commission on Human Rights**, as well as the **Sub-Commission on Prevention of Discrimination and Protection of Minorities** adopted several resolutions on human rights and terrorism. A **Special Rapporteur[s]** of the Sub-Commission conducts a thorough study on the question of terrorism and human rights.

Tokyo Rules (UN)

Common name for the **United Nations Standard Minimum Rules for Non-Custodial Measures**.

Transnational corporations and human rights

According to international human rights standards, States have the primary responsibility to protect and promote human rights. However, in the era of **globalization**, many other actors are playing an important role in the field of human rights and the full realization of all human rights cannot be achieved without their commitment. Bearing in mind the large influence and impact that businesses, in particular transnational corporations, have on the economy, on societies and on the well-being of people, the question of the responsibility and accountability of transnational corporations with regard to human rights became a priority.

Several international principles, guidelines or codes of conduct, which all have a non-binding character, have been developed to determine the responsibility of corporations in the field of human rights. Already in 1977, the **International Labour Organization** (ILO) adopted the Tripartite Declaration of Principles concerning Multinational Enterprises and Social Policy, amended in 2000, which is a set of principles in the field of employment and labour standards to be observed by States, workers' and employer's organizations and multinational corporations. The **Organisation for Economic Co-operation and Development** (OECD) adopted in 2000 the revised version of its Guidelines for Multinational Enterprises, which are voluntary principles and standards for responsible business conduct in areas such as employment, human rights, environment, competition taxation, science and technology.

In August 2003, at its 55th session, the United Nations **Sub-Commission on the Promotion and Protection of Human Rights** adopted, after several years of work, the "United Nations Norms and Commentary on the Responsibilities of Transnational Corporations and Other Business Enterprises with Regard to Human Rights" (E/CN.4/Sub.2/2003/38/Rev.1). This document and the accompanying interpretive commentary, recalls that the **Universal Declaration of Human Rights** applies not only to States and individuals, but also to 'organs of society', including businesses. In addition to the major human rights treaties, the new Norms rely upon and reconfirm the relevant principles from a wide range of instruments in the field of labour, protection of the environment, consumer protection, and the struggle against

corruption. They also endorse methods of independent monitoring and other implementation mechanisms to hold businesses accountable for violations of human rights, and for non-respect for humanitarian, labour, environmental, and other international principles. These more detailed Norms are complementary to the **Global Compact** of the United Nations. The United Nations Norms and Commentary on the Responsibilities of Transnational Corporations and Other Business Enterprises with Regard to Human Rights will be submitted to the **Commission on Human Rights** for deliberation and eventual adoption.

Treaty of Amsterdam (EU)

The Treaty of Amsterdam was signed on 2 October 1997 and entered into force on 1 May 1999 after ratification by all 15 Member States of the **European Union (EU)**. The aim of the Treaty was to create the political and institutional conditions to enable the European Union to meet the challenges of the future such as the rapid evolution of the international situation; the **globalization** of the economy and its impact on jobs; the fight against terrorism, international crime and drug trafficking, ecological problems and threats to public health. It states unequivocally that the EU is founded on the principles of liberty, democracy, respect for human rights and fundamental freedoms, and the rule of law, and is attached to fundamental **social rights**.

Therefore the Treaty of Amsterdam widens some of the main tasks of the EU related to the protection of human rights and fundamental freedoms. More effective action is envisaged to fight against all forms of **discrimination** and to prevent and eliminate **racism** and xenophobia. Furthermore it incorporates a stronger social agreement with a commitment to tackle social exclusion and uphold equality between men and women.

UNESCO

Acronym for the **United Nations Educational, Scientific and Cultural Organization**.

UNESCO Chairs in Human Rights, Democracy, Peace and Tolerance

The UNITWIN/UNESCO Chairs Programme was launched by the General Conference of **UNESCO** at its 26th session in 1991 as an international plan of action for strengthening higher education, particularly in developing countries, through inter-university cooperation. The Chairs serve as major channels to establish networks of universities, first of all North/South but also South/South and East/West, and to enhance cooperation between higher education and scientific institutions, for the ultimate goal of fostering a more equitable sharing of knowledge. The programme became operational in 1992 and has developed rapidly. By the middle of 2003, more than 420 Chairs and about 60 networks existed in all regions of the world. The Chairs exist in various areas: social sciences, applied sciences, education, environment, engineering and technology, culture, communication, etc. The network of UNESCO Chairs in Human Rights, Democracy, Peace and Tolerance comprised in June 2003 56 Chairs in 48 countries and has proved to be a reliable partner in implementing the activities of UNESCO in these fields.

These Chairs play an important role in the promotion of education, research and dissemination of information on human rights. They participate in the elaboration and implementation of national plans for human rights education in accordance with the Plan of Action for the **United Nations Decade for Human Rights Education (1995-2004)**. They participated actively in the series of **Regional Conferences on Human Rights Education** organized by UNESCO in close cooperation with the **Office of the United Nations High Commissioner for Human Rights**.

The first meeting of the Representatives of UNESCO Chairs on Human Rights, Democracy, Peace and Tolerance (Stadtschlaining, Austria, 1998) was an important step towards the strengthening of cooperation between the Chairs themselves and between them and UNESCO. To this end, two major documents were adopted: the "Stadtschlaining Appeal to Promote Human Rights, Democracy, Peace, Tolerance and International Understanding" and the "Statement on the Role of UNESCO Chairs in the Promotion of a Culture of Peace". A Memorandum of Co-operation between UNESCO Chairs on Human Rights, Democracy, Peace and Tolerance was also signed at that time. The second meeting of chairholders, convened in Stadtschlaining (Austria) in 2000, marked a new step in strengthening the interaction of the Chairs. A new Agreement of Cooperation enlarging the interaction of the Chairs and their relations with other partners was signed. A third meeting of chairholders held in April 2002 led to a new Agreement on modalities of cooperation among UNESCO Chairs in Human Rights, Democracy, Peace and Tolerance which should further increase the contribution of the Chairs to human rights education and research activities and co-ordination of their efforts in this regard. The meeting also adopted the Declaration on the Contribution of UNESCO Chairs to the Promotion of Human Rights, Democracy, Peace and Tolerance. At the World Forum of UNESCO Chairs (Paris, November 2002) four Chairs in Human Rights, Democracy, Peace and Tolerance were awarded for their outstanding contribution to the promotion of education and research in their respective fields.

UNESCO/Madanjeet Singh Prize for the Promotion of Tolerance and Non-Violence

The UNESCO/Madanjeet Singh Prize for the Promotion of Tolerance and Non-Violence was created in 1995, on the occasion of the **International Year for Tolerance** and in commemoration of the 125th anniversary of Mahatma Gandhi's birth. It honours outstanding creative achievements in the promotion of tolerance and non-violence in science, the arts, education, culture and communication. Its donor, the Indian artist, writer and diplomat, Madanjeet Singh, was imprisoned during Mahatma Gandhi's non-violent Quit India movement against British colonial rule. The prize of US $40,000 (increased to US $100,000 in 2002) is awarded every two years at a ceremony held at **UNESCO** Headquarters on 16 November, the **International Day for Tolerance**. Candidates may be nationals of Member States of UNESCO or institutions or organizations with their headquarters in those States. A five-member international jury examines the submitted candidates and makes a suggestion to the Director-General of UNESCO concerning the nomination of the laureate. The Prize was first awarded in 1996 to Pro-femmes Twese Hamwe, a collective of 32 NGOs of Rwandese women, for their outstanding contributions to the rehabilitation of families and communities devastated by mass violence in Rwanda. The 1998 award was attributed to two laureates. One was the Joint Action Committee for People's Rights (Pakistan), a coalition of 30 non-governmental organizations and individuals that campaign for women's rights and religious tolerance, and against the nuclear arms race. The other was Mr Narayan Desai (India) for his work in promoting education and youth training camps with his Shanti Sena (Peace Brigade). In 2000, Pope Shenouda III, the head of Egypt's Coptic Orthodox Church, was laureate. Aung San Suu Kyi (Myanmar) was named laureate of the Prize in 2002 by the unanimous recommendation of the jury. Aung San Suu Kyi was also the laureate of the 1991 Nobel Peace Prize for having attempted to establish democracy in Burma. An international symbol of peaceful resistance, she is still pursuing her non-violent struggle for democracy in Myanmar. The jury also attributed 5 honorable mentions, which included two posthumous ones, the first going to Daniel Pearl, a reporter for *The Wall Street Journal* who was murdered in Pakistan while investigating Moslem fundamentalist networks, and the second going to eight journalists killed in Afghanistan in the exercise of their profession in 2001: Johanne Sutton (France, Radio France Internationale), Pierre Billaud (France, RTL), Volker Handloik (Germany, *Stern*), Ulf Stromberg (Sweden, TV4), Maria Grazia Cutuli (Italy, *Corriere della Sera*), Harry Burton (Australia, Reuters), Azizullah Haidar (Afghanistan, Reuters) and Julio Fuentes (Spain, *El Mundo*). Simon Wiesenthal and the Simon Wiesenthal Centre in Austria, recieved the third honourable mention for their denunciation of the crimes committed by the Nazis during the Second World War and their work in education for tolerance and non-violence. The fourth honourable mention was given to the Ramakrishna Mission (India) for its unrelenting efforts to promote the principles of tolerance and non-violence in assisting disadvantaged groups, and the fifth mention was given to Kids Can Free the Children (Canada), a youth network which transforms children into local and international peace activists.

UNESCO Prize for Human Rights Education

The **UNESCO** Prize for Human Rights Education was created in 1978 to mark the 30th anniversary of the **Universal Declaration of Human Rights**. Pursuant to its Constitution, UNESCO seeks "... to further universal respect for justice, for the rule of law and for the human rights and fundamental freedoms". Promoting human rights through teaching and training has thus become one of the priorities of the Organization. Through this prize, awarded every two years, UNESCO encourages activities aimed at developing human rights education. Since 1990, apart from the nomination of laureates, honourable mentions have been awarded in recognition of remarkable contributions to the development of human rights education. The decisions concerning laureates and honourable mentions are taken by the Director-General of UNESCO upon the recommendation of the International Jury, composed of six public personalities representing the different regions of the world. The Prize is awarded to institutions, organizations or persons having made a particularly efficient and exemplary contribution to the promotion of human rights. The names of the laureates are announced on 10 December, on the occasion of **Human Rights Day**. Since the Prize was created, it has been awarded to a number of personalities, human rights specialists and activists as well as institutions in the field, among them: Felix Ermacora (Austria – 1983); *Asamblea Permanente de los Derechos Humanos* (Bolivia – 1988); Vaclav Havel (Czech Republic – 1990); Arab Institute of Human Rights (Tunisia – 1992); Michael Kirby (Australia – 1998); and the City of Nuremberg (Germany – 2000). In 2002 it was awarded to *Academia Mexicana de Derechos Humanos* for pioneering the spread of human rights education in Mexico and in the region. Since 2002 the winner of the prize receives, apart from a financial award, a sculpture created by Toshimi Ishii, a Japanese artist known under her artistic name "Toshi", who is also the creator of the trophy for the **UNESCO/Madanjeet Singh Prize for the Promotion of Tolerance and Non-Violence**.

UNICEF

Acronym for the **United Nations Children's Fund**

United Nations – UN

The United Nations officially came into existence on 24 October 1945. It has six main organs: the **United Nations General Assembly,** the main deliberative body in which all 191 Member States are represented and have one vote; the **Security Council**, the organ to which the **United Nations Charter** gives primary responsibility for maintaining peace and security; the **Economic and Social Council (ECOSOC),** responsible for co-ordinating the economic and social work of the **United Nations** and its specialized agencies and institutions; the Trusteeship Council, established to ensure that governments responsible for administering Trust Territories take adequate steps to prepare them for self-government or independence; the **International Court of Justice**, the main judicial organ of the United Nations; and the Secretariat, which works for all the other organs of the United Nations and administers their programmes. The deep concern of the international community for the promotion and protection of human rights is clearly expressed in the United Nations Charter, in which the peoples of the United Nations express their determination "to reaffirm faith in fundamental human rights, in dignity and worth of the human person, in the equal rights of men and women and of nations large and small", and for this purpose "to practice tolerance and live together in peace with one another as good neighbours" and "to employ international machinery for the promotion of the economic and social advancement of all peoples". The Charter authorizes a number of organs to deal with questions of human rights. The main organs have undertaken and undertake activities in this field since their establishment. Specialized agencies such as the **International Labour Organisation (ILO), United Nations Educational, Scientific and Cultural Organization (UNESCO), World Health Organization (WHO)** and others implement manifold activities in order to ensure a meaningful contribution of the **United Nations system** to the promotion and protection of human rights and to ensure the enjoyment of human rights and fundamental freedoms by everyone without distinction. The **United Nations High Commissioner for Human Rights** co-ordinates human rights activities within the United Nations system.

For more information see: http://www.un.org

United Nations Centre for Human Rights – UNCHR

The United Nations Centre for Human Rights (UNCHR) was created on 18 December 1982 by the **United Nations General Assembly** as a re-designation of the former Division of Human Rights. As a part of the United Nations Secretariat, the Centre dealt with human rights issues. Located in Geneva, it had a Liaison Office at the United Nations in New York. It co-operated closely with other **United Nations** bodies and agencies which deal with human rights issues. At their request, it undertook relevant studies and publications. It also collected and disseminated information and material concerning human rights. Furthermore, the Centre provided advisory services and technical assistance, at the request of States concerned, to support their activities and programmes in such fields as: democratic elections; reforming national laws in line with human rights instruments; preparation of national reports; training of criminal justice personnel (judges, lawyers, prosecutors and police) on human rights matters.

In 1993, General Assembly resolution 48/141 of 20 December 1993 established the post of the **United Nations High Commissioner for Human Rights**. It entrusted the High Commissioner with specific functions concerning the promotion and protection of human rights. In September 1997, the Centre and the work of the High Commissioner for Human Rights became a part of a single unit called the **Office of the United Nations High Commissioner for Human Rights (OHCHR)**.

United Nations Centre for Human Settlements – Habitat

The United Nations Centre for Human Settlements, also known under the name "Habitat", was established in 1978 as the leading agency within the **United Nations system** for co-ordinating activities in the field of human settlements, following the recommendations of the United Nations Conference on

Human Settlements, known as "Habitat I" (Vancouver, Canada, 1976). This Conference adopted the Vancouver Declaration on Human Settlements and the Vancouver Plan of Action in order to promote sustainable development of human settlements.

The Centre works to ensure the implementation of the **right to adequate housing**, enshrined in the **Universal Declaration of Human Rights** (Article 25, para. 1) and the **International Covenant on Economic, Social and Cultural Rights** (Article 11, para. 1). Its activities related to the implementation of this right for all focus mainly on: reducing urban poverty; improving urban governance and the living environment and infrastructure; providing technical assistance to government programmes; and disseminating information about human settlements issues.

It served as the secretariat for the Second United Nations Conference on Human Settlements, known as "Habitat II" (Istanbul, Turkey, 1996). This Conference adopted the Habitat Agenda and the Istanbul Declaration in which governments committed themselves to ensuring adequate shelter for all and sustainable urban development. Subsequently, the Habitat Agenda and the Istanbul Declaration were endorsed by the **United Nations General Assembly** in its resolution 51/177 of 16 December 1996, which designated the agency as the focal point for the implementation of the Habitat Agenda at local, national and regional levels.

The International Conference "Habitat + 5" took place in Nairobi in June 2001 and considered the progress achieved in the implementation of decisions of the Istanbul Conference five years after their adoption.

The Centre also plays a leading role in raising global awareness about shelter and urbanization issues. To this end, the **World Habitat Day** is celebrated on the first Monday of October and is dedicated each year to a different theme. Thus, the theme for 1998 was "Safer Cities", for 1999 "Cities for All", for 2000 "Urban Governance", for 2001 "Cities without Slums", for 2002

"City to City Cooperation" and for 2003 "Water and Sanitation for Cities" to highlight the world's urban water and sanitation crisis.

The Centre is based in Nairobi, Kenya. It is guided by the United Nations Commission on Human Settlements which comprises 58 members and meets every two years.

In January 2002, the agency's mandate was strengthened and its status elevated to that of a fully fledged programme of the **United Nations system**.

For more information see: http://www.unhabitat.org/

United Nations Charter

Title often used for the **Charter of the United Nations**.

United Nations Children's Fund – UNICEF

The United Nations International Children's Emergency Fund was established by the **United Nations General Assembly** on 11 December 1946 to assist children and adolescents in countries where they had been victims of aggression. Its aim was to provide help to those in need without discrimination on grounds of race, creed, national status or political belief. In 1950, its mandate was broadened to address the long-term needs of children and mothers in developing countries everywhere. On 6 October 1953, the General Assembly decided to continue the activities of the organization and changed its name to the United Nations Children's Fund, while retaining the acronym UNICEF. The basic function of UNICEF is to help the Governments of developing countries to improve the quality of life of children. Its approach to development aid is based on the conviction that children are the means as well as the beneficiaries of national development and that enlightened social policies benefiting children are a prerequisite for sustained economic and social progress. UNICEF plays a leading role within the **United Nations system** in assisting children and implements programmes all over the world. The Executive Board, governing body of UNICEF, adopts policies, reviews programmes and approves expenditures. UNICEF promotes actively the full implementation of the **Convention on the Rights of the Child** (1989). The Secretariat of UNICEF is headed by an Executive Director and its Headquarters are in New York.

For more information see: http://www.unicef.org

United Nations Congresses on the Prevention of Crime and Treatment of Offenders

By its resolution 415 (V) of 1 December 1950, the **United Nations General Assembly** authorized the convening every five years of a United Nations Congress on the Prevention of Crime and Treatment of Offenders. The Congresses are worldwide forums, influencing national policies and mobilizing public opinion; focusing attention on major issues of concern to Member States, the professional and scientific community; recommending lines of action at the national, regional and international levels; and facilitating cooperation between States and between practitioners in the various sectors and disciplines which deal with crime. The participants in the Congresses are criminologists, penologists, senior police officers, specialists in criminal law, human rights and rehabilitation.

In order to strengthen international cooperation in the field of crime prevention and criminal justice, the **Economic and Social Council (ECOSOC)** established the **Commission on Crime Prevention and Criminal Justice** in February 1992 as the principal policy recommending body of the **United Nations** in the field. The Commission is also the preparatory body for the Congresses, pursuant to General Assembly resolution 46/152. Ten Congresses have been held:
- First Congress (Geneva, 1955) adopted the **Standard Minimum Rules for the Treatment of Prisoners**, which ECOSOC approved in 1957;

- Second Congress (London, 1960) dealt with measures for preventing juvenile delinquency as well as with issues of prison labour, conditional release and post-penitential assistance;
- Third Congress (Stockholm, 1965) approved measures concerning crime prevention action by the community and measures for combating recidivism;
- Fourth Congress (Tokyo, 1970) stressed the need to take crime into account in development planning, particularly in view of the effects of urbanization, industrialization and the technological revolution on the human environment;
- Fifth Congress (Geneva, 1975) adopted the **Declaration on the Protection of All Persons From Being Subjected to Torture or Other Cruel, Inhuman and Degrading Treatment or Punishment**, which the General Assembly approved later the same year. The Congress also laid the basis for the **Code of Conduct for Law Enforcement Officials**, which was adopted by the General Assembly in 1979;
- Sixth Congress (Caracas, 1980) dealt with such topics as crime trends and crime prevention strategies, juvenile delinquency, crime and the abuse of power, and deinstitutionalization of corrections. The Caracas Declaration, adopted by the Congress, was endorsed later in 1980 by the General Assembly;
- Seventh Congress (Milan, 1985) adopted the Milan Plan of Action for strengthening international cooperation in the field of crime prevention and criminal justice, which was subsequently approved by the General Assembly. It also adopted various instruments, including: **Basic Principles on the Independence of the Judiciary**; **Declaration of Basic Principles of Justice for Victims of Crime and Abuse of Power** and the **United Nations Standard Minimum Rules for the Administration of Juvenile Justice - "The Beijing Rules"**, all of them approved later by the General Assembly;
- Eighth Congress (Havana, 1990) approved a number of important instruments which were adopted in the same year

by the General Assembly, including: **United Nations Standard Minimum Rules for Non-Custodial Measures - "The Tokyo Rules"**, **Basic Principles for the Treatment of Prisoners**, **United Nations Guidelines for the Protection of Juvenile Delinquency – "The Riyadh Guidelines"**; **United Nations Rules for the Protection of Juveniles Deprived of their Liberty**; **Basic Principles on the Use of Force and Firearms by Law Enforcement Officials**, as well as **Basic Principles on the Role of Lawyers** and **Guidelines on the Role of Prosecutors**;

- Ninth Congress (Cairo, 1995) adopted a resolution urging States to explicitly extend criminal justice and criminal sanctions to a number of specific acts of violence against women;
- Tenth Congress (Vienna, 2000) was devoted to international cooperation in combating transnational organized crime. It adopted the **Vienna Declaration on Crime and Justice** and stressed the need to accord high priority to the completion of negotiations on the **United Nations Convention against Transnational Organized Crime**. This instrument was subsequently adopted on 15 November 2000 by the General Assembly resolution 55/25, as were its two Protocols: the **Protocol against the Smuggling of Migrants by Land, Sea and Air** and the **Protocol to Prevent, Suppress and Punish Trafficking in Persons, Especially Women and Children**. A third Protocol to the Convention, the **Protocol against the Illicit Manufacturing of and Trafficking in Firearms, Their Parts and Components and Ammunition**, was adopted in May 2001 (A/Res/55/255).

United Nations Convention against Transnational Organized Crime

This Convention was adopted on 15 November 2000 by the **United Nations General Assembly** resolution 55/25. By the middle of 2003, the Convention had not yet entered into force.

The Convention is the first **United Nations** binding instrument to combat **organized crime**. It is also aimed against, *inter alia*, money laundering, **corruption** and the obstruction of justice. The objectives of the Convention should be achieved through international cooperation on such matters as extradition, mutual legal assistance, transfer of proceedings and joint investigations. It contains provisions for victim and witness protection and shielding legal markets from infiltration by organized criminal groups. Parties to the Convention may provide technical assistance to developing countries to help them take the necessary measures and upgrade their capacities for dealing with organized crime.

To supplement the Convention, two Protocols dealing with specific transnational criminal activities were also adopted on the same day by the same resolution: the **Protocol against the Smuggling of Migrants by Land, Sea and Air** and the **Protocol to Prevent, Suppress and Punish Trafficking in Persons, Especially Women and Children**. A third Protocol, the **Protocol against the Illicit Manufacturing of and Trafficking in Firearms, Their Parts and Components and Ammunition**, was adopted in May 2001 by the General Assembly resolution 55/255.

United Nations Crime Prevention Programme

The **United Nations** has been dealing with crime prevention and criminal matters since the first days of its existence. In 1948, it set up its first office fighting international crime. Today, the Centre for International Crime Prevention (CICP) is the United Nations office responsible for crime prevention, criminal justice and criminal law reform. The Centre is composed of 15 professional staff members and support personnel. The Centre is part of the United Nations Office for Drug Control and Crime Prevention (ODCCP). Its activities focus on three areas: the struggle against **corruption**, the combat against illicit trafficking in human beings, and control of

organized crime. In addition, the Centre cooperates with a network of international and regional institutions such as the United Nations Interregional Crime and Justice Research Institute (UNICRI) with the aim to cope more effectively with such issues as organized crime, money laundering and drug control.

The Centre's activities are carried out under the auspices of the intergovernmental **Commission on Crime Prevention and Criminal Justice,** which was created by the **Economic and Social Council (ECOSOC)** in 1992 (decision 1992/2). The Commission, comprising 40 Member States of the United Nations, provides guidance to the CICP by developing, monitoring and reviewing the Programme, by formulating international policies and coordinating activities in crime prevention and criminal justice. In addition, the Commission organizes every five years the **United Nations Congress[es] on the Prevention of Crime and the Treatment of Offenders** to provide a forum to exchange policies and to stimulate progress in the fight against crime. Participants in the Congresses (ten have been held up to 2003) include criminologists, penologists and senior police officers, as well as experts in criminal law, human rights and rehabilitation.

On 15 November 2000, by its resolution 55/25, following the Tenth Congress, the **United Nations General Assembly** adopted the **United Nations Convention against Transnational Organized Crime** and its two Protocols: the **Protocol against the Smuggling of Migrants by Land, Sea and Air** and the **Protocol to Prevent, Suppress and Punish Trafficking in Persons, Especially Women and Children.**

United Nations Day – 24 October

The anniversary of the entry into force of the **Charter of the United Nations** on 24 October 1945 has been celebrated as United Nations Day since 1948. The day is devoted to making known to the people of the world the aims and achievements of the **United Nations**, and to gaining their support for the work of the United Nations.

United Nations Day for Women's Rights and International Peace

In 1975, during the **International Women's Year**, the **United Nations** began celebrating 8 March as **International Women's Day**. Two years later on 16 December 1997, the **United Nations General Assembly** adopted resolution 32/142 proclaiming a **United Nations Day for Women's Rights and International Peace** to be observed every year on a date to be chosen by each Member State. The action came in the wake of the International Women's Year (1975) and the **United Nations Decade for Women: Equality, Development, Peace – 1976-1985.**

United Nations Decade against Drug Abuse – 1991-2000

This Decade was proclaimed by the **United Nations General Assembly** in 1990. A Global Programme of Action to fight illegal drugs on all levels, which focused on international cooperation against illicit production, supply, demand and trafficking in narcotic drugs and psychotropic substances was also adopted at that time. On 17 December 1999, the General Assembly reaffirmed by resolution 54/132 III the importance for Member States, the United Nations International Drug Control Programme and the **United Nations system** to achieve the objectives of the Decade, under the theme: "A global response to a global challenge". The **International Day against Drug Abuse and Illicit Trafficking** is marked every year on 26 June.

United Nations Decade for Human Rights Education – 1995-2004

In accordance with a proposal made by the **World Conference on Human Rights** (Vienna, 1993), the **United Nations General Assembly** proclaimed by its resolution 49/184 the ten-year period starting from 1 January 1995 the United Nations Decade for Human Rights Education. The General Assembly expressed its conviction that human rights education should constitute a life-long process, by which people learn respect for the dignity of others. The Plan of Action for the Decade (A/51/506/Add.1) contains a comprehensive definition of human rights education: "training, dissemination and information efforts aimed at the building of a universal culture of human rights through the imparting of knowledge and skills and the moulding of attitudes". These efforts are directed to "the strengthening of respect for human rights and fundamental freedoms; the full development of the human personality and the sense of its dignity; the promotion of understanding, tolerance, gender equality, and friendship among all nations, indigenous peoples, racial, national, ethnic, religious and linguistic groups; the enabling of all persons to participate effectively in a free society; and the furtherance of the activities of the **United Nations** for the maintenance of peace" (para. 2).

The general objectives of the Decade are as follows: assess the needs and formulate effective strategies for the furtherance of human rights education in both formal and non-formal learning; build and strengthen programmes and capacities for human rights education at the international, regional, national and local levels; develop human rights education materials; strengthen the role and capacity of the mass media in the furtherance of human rights education; and disseminate the **Universal Declaration of Human Rights** in the maximum possible number of languages, and in other forms appropriate for various levels of literacy and for the disabled (para. 10).

The **United Nations High Commissioner for Human Rights** is specifically responsible for coordinating education and public information programmes in the field of human rights (para. 14). **Human rights treaty bodies,** the **Commission on Human Rights** and other relevant United Nations human rights bodies and programmes are invited to encourage the furtherance of human rights education (para. 15). **United Nations specialized agencies**, units of the Secretariat and programmes involved in human rights education activities, including the **United Nations Children's Fund (UNICEF),** the **International Labour Organisation (ILO),** the **United Nations High Commissioner for Refugees (UNHCR),** the **United Nations Development Programme (UNDP), United Nations Environment Programme (UNEP),** etc., are encouraged to cooperate with the High Commissioner in achieving the objectives of the Decade (para. 18). **UNESCO,** by reason of its long experience in education, educational methodology and human rights and through its network of UNESCO Associated Schools, Clubs and Chairs in Human Rights as well as its National Commissions, is entrusted with a central role in the design, implementation and evaluation of projects under the Plan of Action (para. 17). In order to contribute to the implementation of the Plan of Action, UNESCO organized, in cooperation with **Office of the United Nations High Commissioner for Human Rights (OHCHR)**, a series of **Regional Conferences on Human Rights Education** (for Europe, 1997; for Africa, 1998; for Asia and the Pacific, 1999; for the Arab States, 1999; and for Latin America and the Caribbean, 2001), and prepared a number of educational and information materials.

A mid-term evaluation of the Decade, organized by the Office of the High Commissioner for Human Rights in cooperation with UNESCO took place in 2000.

For more information see:
http://www.unhchr.ch/html/menu6/1/edudec.htm

United Nations Decade for the Eradication of Poverty – 1997-2006

The **United Nations General Assembly** proclaimed by its resolution 50/107 II of 20 December 1995 the ten-year period beginning in 1997 as the first United Nations Decade for the Eradication of **Poverty**. In its resolution 51/178 the General Assembly declared the theme for the Decade to be "Eradicating poverty as an ethical, social, political and economic imperative of humankind". The objective of the Decade is to eradicate absolute poverty and reduce substantially overall poverty in the world through decisive national actions and international cooperation in implementing fully and effectively all agreements, commitments and recommendations of major **United Nations** conferences and summits organized since 1990 as they relate to poverty eradication (para. 17). On 11 February 1997, the United Nations General Assembly recommended that, during the Decade, the causes of poverty be addressed in the context of sectoral strategies such as those on environment, security, migration, shelter, fresh water and productive employment, and by examining the specific needs of **vulnerable groups** (para. 5). All efforts should aim at the social and economic integration of people living in poverty (para. 5). The same resolution also recommends that donor countries give greater priority to the eradication of poverty in their assistance programmes and budgets (para. 8) and that developed countries strive for the fulfillment of the agreed target of allotting 0.7% of their gross national product for overall official development assistance (para. 15). Throughout the Decade and beyond, people living in poverty and their associations should be empowered by being fully involved in the setting of targets and in the design, implementation, monitoring and assessment of national strategies, activities and programmes for poverty eradication (para. 11). The **United Nations system** is actively involved in actions aimed at the eradication of poverty. **UNESCO** has proclaimed among its priorities for the years 2002-2007 the eradication of poverty and, especially, **extreme poverty**. The **International Year for the Eradication of Poverty** was observed in 1996.

United Nations Decade for Women: Equality, Development and Peace – 1976-1985

On 15 December 1975, the **United Nations General Assembly** proclaimed the period from 1976 to 1985 United Nations Decade for Women: Equality, Development and Peace.

The Decade was devoted to effective and sustained national, regional and international action to implement the resolutions of the World Conference of the **International Women's Year** (1975). At the mid-term of the Decade, a World Conference was held in Copenhagen, Denmark, from 14 to 30 July 1980. It formulated the Programme of Action for the Second Half of the United Nations Decade for Women, 1980-1985. The Programme of Action was designed to promote the attainment of three objectives: equality, development and peace, with special emphasis on the improvement of women's access to employment, health and education. It aimed at strengthening comprehensive and effective strategies to remove obstacles and constraints on women's full and equal participation in development, including actions to solve the problems of underdevelopment and of socio-economic structures which place women in an inferior position, and to increase women's contribution to the strengthening of world peace. The Decade concluded with the World Conference to Review and Appraise the Achievements of the United Nations Decade for Women: Equality, Development and Peace (1976-1985), held in Nairobi in 1985. This Conference adopted the **Nairobi Forward-Looking Strategies for the Advancement of Women** which were based on the assumption that an essential contribution to the strengthening of international peace and security would be made by the elimination of all forms of inequality between men and women in all spheres of public and civil life in their countries. The Strategies were endorsed by the United Nations General Assembly which entrusted the promotion of their implementation to the **Commission on the Status of Women**.

United Nations Decade of Disabled Persons – 1983-1992

On 3 December 1982, the **United Nations General Assembly** proclaimed the period 1983-1992 **United Nations** Decade of Disabled Persons. It encouraged Member States to implement within this period the **World Programme of Action**

Concerning Disabled Persons that had been adopted on the same day. The aims of the Decade were to give new impetus to the protection of disabled persons, to provide them with proper assistance, education, care and guidance as well as to educate and inform the public of the rights of such persons. In particular, all organs, organizations and agencies of the **United Nations system** were urged to undertake new measures or expedite those already under way to improve employment opportunities for disabled persons within these bodies at all levels and to improve access to their buildings and facilities and to their information sources. The need for an elaboration of national programmes for the training of rehabilitation personnel and for the production of prosthetic appliances and aids using locally available resources was stressed. At the mid-point of the Decade, in August 1987, the Secretary-General convened in Stockholm a global meeting of experts to review the implementation of the World Programme of Action concerning disabled persons. A second meeting, the International Meeting on Human Resources in the Field of Disability, was held in Tallinn, Estonia, in August 1989. It adopted a nine-point strategy, known as the Tallinn Guidelines for Action on Human Resources Development in the Field of Disability, to promote the participation, training and employment of disabled persons, especially in developing countries. To mark the end of the Decade, an agenda for action beyond the end of the Decade and a preliminary outline of a long-term strategy to the year 2000 were developed by the United Nations General Assembly in 1990.

United Nations Development Fund for Women – UNIFEM

The **United Nations** Development Fund for Women (UNIFEM) was created in 1985 by the **United Nations General Assembly** resolution 39/125 as a catalyst within the **United Nations system**, with the goal of ensuring women's self-realization and full participation in all spheres of life. To that end, UNIFEM focuses on: strengthening the capacity of national and regional women's organizations to advocate for women's human rights at the national and international levels; increasing women's participation in decision-making processes that shape their lives; promoting women's human rights in order to eliminate all forms of violence against women and transform development into a more peaceful, equitable and sustainable process. UNIFEM's projects are developed and overseen at the regional and country level by its 12 Regional Programme Advisors who represent the frontline of contact between UNIFEM and its partners. Furthermore, since the 1995 **World Conference[s] on Women** in Beijing, UNIFEM has placed a strong emphasis on providing assistance to governments and non-governmental organizations in developing national action plans and widely disseminating information. In particular, UNIFEM supports the implementation of the **Beijing Declaration and Platform for Action** which aimed at strengthening women's empowerment, improving women's health, advancing women's education and training, promoting women's marital and sexual rights, and eliminating gender-based violence. UNIFEM administers the Trust Fund in Support of Actions to Eliminate Violence against Women which was created in 1996 in accordance with General Assembly resolution 50/166.

For more information see: http://www.unifem.org

United Nations Development Programme – UNDP

The United Nations Development Programme (UNDP) was created in 1965 through merging two former **United Nations** technical cooperation programmes. In addition to being the world's largest multilateral source of grant funding for development co-operation, the UNDP is also the chief coordinating agency for operational development activities undertaken by the entire **United Nations system.** Funded by voluntary contributions of Member States of the United Nations and its specialized agencies, UNDP has three overriding goals: to help the United Nations become a powerful and cohesive force for sustainable human development; to focus its own resources on a series of objectives central to sustainable human development – elimination of poverty, environmental regeneration, job creation, and the advancement of women; to strengthen international cooperation for sustainable human development and serve as a major substantive resource on how to achieve it. UNDP works through a network of over 160 offices worldwide. Its major programmes and policy decisions are determined by an Executive Board composed of representatives from 36 nations, which operates on a rotating basis. It is the responsibility of the Board to ensure that UNDP's focus remains on six priority themes: Democratic Governance; **Poverty** reduction; Crisis Prevention and Recovery; Energy and Environment; Information and Communications Technology and HIV/AIDS. The UNDP Human Development Report, published yearly since 1990, assists the international community in developing new, practical and pragmatic concepts, measures and policy instruments to further promote human-oriented development.

For more information see: http://www.undp.org

United Nations Division for the Advancement of Women – UNDAW

The Section on the Status of Women was established in the Secretariat of the United Nations in 1946. It was transformed into the Branch for the Promotion of Equality of Men and Women in 1972, and in 1978 it changed its title and became the Branch for the Advancement of Women. In August 1993, the Division moved to New York where it formed part of the Department of Policy Coordination and Sustainable Development (DPCSD), which, as a result of restructuring in 1996, is now the Department of Economic and Social Affairs (DESA).

The Division's aims are the improvement of the status of women and the achievement of their equality with men. Through cooperation with governments, civil society and partners in the **United Nations system**, the Division works to ensure an equal participation of women in sustainable development, maintenance of peace and security, promotion of good governance and human rights and to make them full beneficiaries of these processes. In addition to conducting research, developing policy options and raising awareness, the Division supports the implementation of the **Nairobi Forward-Looking Strategies for the Advancement of Women**, and the **Beijing Platform for Action**.

The Division and its predecessors were in charge of the preparations of the first three **World Conferences on Women** held in Mexico City (1975), Copenhagen (1980) and Nairobi (1985). The UNDAW acted as the secretariat for the Fourth World Conference on Women in Beijing (1995).

United Nations Educational, Scientific and Cultural Organization – UNESCO

The United Nations Educational, Scientific and Cultural Organization (UNESCO) came into being on 4 November 1946. Its main organs are: the General Conference, which meets every two years and in which all Member States – 189 by the middle of 2003 – and the 6 Associate Member States are represented; the Executive Board, elected by the Conference, consisting of 58 Member States; and the Secretariat, headed by the Director-General. The purpose of UNESCO, as stated in Article 1 of its Constitution, is "to contribute to peace and security by promoting collaboration among the nations through education, science and culture in order to further universal respect for justice, for the rule of law and for the human rights and fundamental freedoms which are affirmed for the peoples of the world, without distinction of race, sex, language or religion, by the **Charter of the United Nations**". To achieve these aims, UNESCO establishes and supervises the application of standards; gathers and disseminates information of educational, scientific or cultural interest; provides advisory services and technical assistance; assists in the establishment of educational, scientific and cultural institutions and centres; organizes congresses, seminars and symposia, etc.

Within the framework of its standard-setting activity, UNESCO has adopted a number of international instruments aimed at the promotion of human rights, including, the **Convention against Discrimination in Education** (1960), the Declaration on Race and Racial Prejudice (1976), the **Declaration of Principles on Tolerance** (1995), the **Universal Declaration on the Human Genome and Human Rights** (1997), and the **Universal Declaration on Cultural Diversity** (2001).

Article IV, paragraph 6, of the UNESCO Constitution stipulates that the General Conference shall receive and consider reports of Member States on actions taken upon its recommendations and conventions. Apart from this general provision, more specific reporting procedures are formulated by several UNESCO standard-setting instruments. UNESCO also has a procedure (Executive Board Decision 104 EX 3.3) for the examination of complaints received by the Organization concerning alleged violations of human rights in its field of competence, namely education, science, culture and information. The complaints are considered by the Committee on Conventions and Recommendations, a subsidiary body of the Executive Board of UNESCO. As of May 2003, 503 cases have been examined and 314 have been resolved. As of that date, no questions of massive, systematic or flagrant violations of human rights and fundamental freedoms falling within the Organization's competence have been examined in public meetings, as laid down in Paragraph 18 of the Decision.

For more information see: http://www.unesco.org/

United Nations Environmental Programme – UNEP

The United Nations Environmental Programme (UNEP) was established in 1972 by the **United Nations General Assembly** (resolution 2997 [XXVII]). It serves as the lead agency in the field of environment within the **United Nations system**. It provides machinery for international cooperation on the problems of the human environment in order to enable nations and peoples to improve their quality of life without compromising that of future generations.

UNEP's principal functions are: to assess the state of the world's environment and to identify issues requiring international cooperation; to promote the development of international environmental law; to provide scientific knowledge and information on the environment, as well as education and training for the management of the environment. Raising public awareness on environmental issues guides most of UNEP's activities. The ultimate aim is not only to change the attitudes of people but also to motivate and empower them to act for the protection of the environment. Furthermore, UNEP has established various systems to protect and improve the environment, including: the Global Environment Monitoring System (GEMS), which deals with such environmental issues as climate and atmosphere, oceans, renewable resources, transboundary pollution and the health consequences of pollution; the Global Resource Information Database (GRID) which provides for environmental information; and the International Register of Potentially Toxic Chemicals (IRPTC) which provides practical information for chemical safety decisions.

Located in Nairobi, Kenya, UNEP is administered by a Governing Council which analyses the state of the world environment, determines UNEP's programme priorities, and approves its budget. The Governing Council comprises 58 members elected by the United Nations General Assembly for a four-year term.

For more information see: http://www.unep.org

United Nations General Assembly

The United Nations General Assembly is essentially a deliberative, supervisory and reviewing organ of the **United Nations**. It discusses any question or any matter within the scope of the **Charter of the United Nations** or relating to the powers and functions of organs provided for in the Charter. It may make recommendations to Member States and to the **Security Council** (Article 10 of the Charter). As provided by Article 13, para. 1, of the Charter: "The General Assembly shall initiate studies and make recommendations for the purpose of ... promoting international cooperation in the economic, social, cultural, educational, and health fields, and assisting in the realization of human rights and fundamental freedoms for all without distinction as to race, sex, language, or religion". The General Assembly consists of all the States Members of the United Nations (Article 9), with each Member having one vote (Article 18). Decisions on certain categories of important questions, such as recommendations concerning the maintenance of international peace and security, require a two-thirds majority of the Members present and voting. Decisions on other questions require a majority of the Members present and voting. The General Assembly meets in regular annual sessions and in such special sessions as occasion may require (Article 20). It adopts its own rules of procedure (Article 21) and generally holds its meetings at the Headquarters of the United Nations, New York. The Main Committees of the General Assembly are the following: Political and Security Committee (First Committee); Special Political Committee; Economic and Financial Committee (Second Committee); Social, Humanitarian and Cultural Committee (Third Committee); Trusteeship Committee (Fourth Committee); Administrative and Budgetary Committee (Fifth Committee); and Legal Committee (Sixth Committee). Normally, items relating to human rights are referred to the Third Committee. However, such items have also been directed to the First Committee, the Special Political Committee, the Sixth Committee or have been considered directly by the General Assembly. The General Assembly prepares and adopts standard-setting instruments and programmes of action to promote and protect particular rights and freedoms.

For more information see: http://www.un.org/ga/57/

United Nations Guidelines for the Prevention of Juvenile Delinquency – Riyadh Guidelines (UN)

The **United Nations** Guidelines for the Prevention of Juvenile Delinquency, known as the "Riyadh Guidelines", were adopted by the **United Nations General Assembly** by resolution 45/112 of 14 December 1990. The Guidelines set out standards for the prevention of juvenile delinquency, which is an essential part of crime prevention in society, including measures for the protection of young persons who are abandoned, neglected, abused or find themselves in marginal circumstances, in other words at "social risk". They are based on the premise that it is necessary to offset those conditions which adversely influence and impinge on the healthy development of children and young persons. To this end, comprehensive multidisciplinary measures are suggested to ensure for young persons a life free from crime, victimization and conflict with the law. In particular, the Guidelines urge that policies and measures adopted by States involve educational and other opportunities to serve as a supportive framework for the personal development of young persons. The Guidelines aim at promoting a positive role on the part of various social actors, including the family, the education system, the community and the mass media, as well as the young persons themselves.

United Nations High Commissioner for Human Rights

In recognition of the need to adapt the **United Nations** machinery for the promotion and protection of human rights to current and future needs and following the recommendations of the **World Conference on Human Rights** (Vienna, 1993), the **United Nations General Assembly** established on 20 December 1993, by its resolution 48/141, the post of a High Commissioner for the promotion and protection of all human rights – the United Nations High Commissioner for Human Rights. Since 5 April 1994, the High Commissioner has become the United Nations official with principal responsibility for human rights activities. Appointed for four years with the possibility of one renewal, the High Commissioner must function within the framework of the **United Nations Charter,** the **Universal Declaration of Human Rights** and other relevant instruments to promote universal respect for and observance of all human rights, and must be guided by the recognition that "all human rights – civil, cultural, economic, political and social – are universal, indivisible, interdependent and interrelated" (United Nations General Assembly resolution 48/141, para. 3b.), and that the promotion and protection of human rights is the legitimate concern of the international community. Among the High Commissioner's responsibilities are: coordinating human rights promotion and protection activities throughout the **United Nations system**; providing advisory services and technical and financial assistance through the **United Nations Centre for Human Rights** (now the **Office of the United Nations High Commissioner for Human Rights**); rationalization, adaption, strengthening and streamlining of the United Nations human rights machinery with a view to improving its efficiency and effectiveness; engaging in dialogue with all Governments in order to ensure respect for all human rights; and playing an active role in preventing the continuation of human rights violations throughout the world.

For more information see: http://www.unhchr.ch/

United Nations High Commissioner for Refugees – UNHCR

The post of the **United Nations** High Commissioner for Refugees was established by **United Nations General Assembly** resolution 428 (V) of 14 December 1950 on the statute of the **Office of the United Nations High Commissioner for Refugees**. The High Commissioner reports annually to the United Nations General Assembly through the **Economic and Social Council (ECOSOC)**. The Statute of the Office provides that the work of the High Commissioner, elected by the United Nations General Assembly, "... shall be of an entirely non-political character; it shall be humanitarian and social" (para. 2). It further provides that "the United Nations High Commissioner for Refugees ... shall assume the function of providing international protection, under the auspices of the United Nations, to refugees who fall within the scope of the present Statute" (para. 1). The High Commissioner promotes: the conclusion and ratification of international conventions for the protection of refugees, supervises their application and proposes amendments thereto; promotes the execution of any measures calculated to improve the situation of refugees and to reduce the number requiring protection; assists governmental and private efforts to promote voluntary repatriation or assimilation within new national communities; obtains from Governments information concerning the number and conditions of refugees in their territories and the laws and regulations concerning them; and facilitates the coordination of the efforts of private organizations concerned with the welfare of refugees (para. 8). In addition, paragraphs 9 and 10 of the Statute provide that the High Commissioner "shall engage in such additional activities, including repatriation and resettlement, as the United Nations General Assembly may determine, within the limits of the resources placed at his disposal". In recent years, as the size and complexity of the refugee problem in many parts of the world have grown dramatically, the provisions of paragraphs 9 and 10 have played a more prominent role. The High Commissioner's responsibilities have increased to include: assistance to **displaced persons** who are in a refugee-like situation; the prevention of refoulement (the return of a person to a country where he/she has reason to fear persecution); the granting of asylum, at least on a temporary basis; and the observance of the traditional obligations to rescue those in distress at sea.

United Nations International Conference on Human Rights

The International Conference on Human Rights was held in Tehran, Iran, from 22 April to 13 May 1968. It adopted the **Proclamation of Tehran** which underlined that peace and justice are indispensable to the full realization of human rights and fundamental freedoms. The Conference reviewed the progress made in the 20 years since the adoption of the **Universal Declaration of Human Rights** and formulated a programme for the future. It affirmed "its faith in the principles of the Universal Declaration of Human Rights and other international instruments in this field" and urged "all peoples and governments to dedicate themselves to the principles enshrined in the Universal Declaration of Human Rights and to redouble their efforts to provide for all human beings a life consonant with freedom and dignity and conducive to physical, mental, social and spiritual welfare". Twenty-five years after Tehran, the **World Conference on Human Rights** was organized in Vienna, Austria.

United Nations Literacy Decade – 2003-2012

While the information and knowledge society becomes a modern reality and technologies develop and spread at rapid speed, 860 million adults are illiterate and 100 million children have no access to school. Based on current estimates, by the year 2010, one of 6 adults will be illiterate. Considering that "literacy is crucial to the acquisition, by every child, youth and adult, of essential life skills that enable them to address the challenges they face in life" the **United Nations General Assembly** (A/RES/56/116) proclaimed on 19 December 2001 the period beginning 1 January 2003 the United Nations Literacy Decade. The Decade is aimed at the promotion of literacy for all, which is at the heart of basic education and social and human development. Literacy – the use of written communication – is an integral part of the global effort towards education for all.

The Decade is accompanied by a Plan of Action which reaffirms the **Dakar Framework for Action**, in which commitment was made to achieve a 50 percent improvement in levels of adult literacy by 2015 (Operative part, para. 3). The Plan also stresses the connection between literacy and poverty eradication, reducing child mortality, curbing population growth, achieving gender equality and ensuring sustainable development, peace and democracy (para. 7). Member States, specialized agencies and United Nations organs and bodies, as well as relevant intergovernmental and **non-governmental organizations** are called upon to increase their contributions to development within the Framework of the Decade (para. 9). **UNESCO** should take on the coordinating role in stimulating and catalyzing the activities within the framework of the Decade (para 10).

Literacy promotion is a central part of the overall strategy of education for all and is at the heart of the **Millennium Development Goals**. The **right to education**, of which literacy is a key element, is enshrined in a number of universal and regional standard-setting instruments including the **Universal Declaration of Human Rights** (Article 26), the **International Covenant on Economic, Social and Cultural Rights** (Article 13) and the **Convention on the Rights of the Child** (Articles 28 and 29).

International Literacy Day is observed on 8 September since 1966.

United Nations Millennium Declaration

The beginning of the 21st century and of the Third Millennium was a unique and symbolically compelling moment for the Member States of the **United Nations** to articulate and affirm an animating vision for the new era. The 55th session of the **United Nations General Assembly** was therefore designated "The Millennium Assembly of the United Nations" and opened on 5 September 2000. Subsequently, on 8 September, the General Assembly adopted, by its resolution 55/2, the United Nations Millennium Declaration. In it, the Heads of State and Government reaffirmed their commitment to the purposes and principles of the **Charter of the United Nations** and, in Part I of the Declaration, expressed their resolution to "... support all efforts to uphold the sovereign equality of all States, respect for their territorial integrity and political independence, resolution of disputes by peaceful means and in conformity with the principles of justice and international law, the right to self-determination of peoples which remain under colonial domination and foreign occupation, non-interference in the internal affairs of States, respect for human rights and fundamental freedoms, respect for the equal rights of all without distinction as to race, sex, language or religion and international cooperation in solving international problems of an economic, social, cultural or humanitarian character" (para. 4). They expressed the opinion that the central challenge in contemporary work is to ensure that **globalization** becomes a positive force for all the world's people (para. 5). They considered that certain fundamental values are essential to international relations in the 21st century, including freedom, equality, solidarity, tolerance, respect for nature and shared responsibility (para. 6).

Part II of the Declaration deals with peace, security and disarmament; Part III with development and **poverty** eradication, Part IV with the protection of our common environment.

Part V, which deals with human rights, democracy and good governance, resolves "to respect fully and uphold the **Universal Declaration of Human Rights**; to strive for the full protection and promotion ... of **civil, political, economic, social** and **cultural rights** for all; to strengthen the capacity ... to implement the principles and practices of **democracy** and respect for human rights, including minority rights; to combat all forms of violence against women and to implement the **Convention on the Elimination of All Forms of Discrimination Against Women**; to take measures to ensure respect for and protection of the human rights of migrants, **migrant workers** and their families, to eliminate the increasing acts of **racism** and xenophobia in many societies and to promote greater harmony and tolerance in all societies; to work collectively for more inclusive political processes, allowing genuine participation by all citizens; to ensure the freedom of the media to perform their essential role and the right of the public to have access to information" (para. 25).

The Millennium Declaration also deals with the protection of the vulnerable (Part VI), meeting the special needs of Africa (Part VII) and strengthening the United Nations (Part VIII).

United Nations Population Fund – UNFPA

UNFPA helps developing countries find solutions to their population problems. UNFPA began operations in 1969. It is the world's largest international source of population assistance: a great part of international assistance from donor nations to developing countries is channelled through UNFPA. The number of donors reached 135 countries in 2002 (in 1999, there were 69 countries). UNFPA is wholly funded by contributions, which are voluntary, and not part of the regular **United Nations** budget. The objectives of UNFPA are:

- to assist developing countries in providing quality reproductive health and family planning services on the basis of individual choice, and in formulating population policies that support sustainable development;
- to advance the strategy endorsed by the 1994 International Conference on Population and Development (ICPD) and reviewed by a special session of the **United Nations General Assembly** in 1999 (ICPD+5);
- to focus on meeting the needs of individual women and men rather than achieving demographic targets. Central to this approach is empowering women and providing them with more choices through expanded access to education, health services and employment opportunities;
- to promote cooperation and coordination among United Nations organizations, bilateral agencies, governments, non-governmental organizations (NGOs) and the private sector in addressing issues of population and development, reproductive health, gender equality and women's empowerment.

UNFPA has three main programme areas:
- Reproductive health including family planning and sexual health. UNFPA supports the provision of reproductive health care including wider choice of family planning methods and information. Reproductive health care includes: family planning; safe motherhood; counselling and prevention of infertility; preventing and treating reproductive tract infections and sexually transmitted diseases. It also deals with **HIV-infected people or people with AIDS** and with the health consequences of unsafe abortion;
- Population and Development Strategy, through which it helps countries formulate, implement and evaluate comprehensive population policies as a central part of sustainable development strategies. This includes support for data collection, analysis and research;
- Advocacy of the following: reproductive health and rights; improvement of the status of women; longer life expectancy; lower infant and maternal mortality; closing the gender gap in education; strengthening national capacity to formulate and implement population and development strategies; and increasing awareness and resources for population and development.

UNFPA offers assistance only at a country's own request. While there is international agreement on population and development goals, each country determines its own approach.

For more information see: http://www.unfpa.org

United Nations Principles for Older Persons

The United Nations Principles for Older Persons were adopted by the **United Nations General Assembly** in 1991 (A/RES/46/91). They aim to ensure that priority attention be given to the situation of older persons and provide a broad framework for governments to take action on ageing. They were approved in pursuance of the **Vienna International Plan of Action on Ageing** adopted by the **World Assembly on Ageing** and endorsed by the General Assembly in its resolution 37/51 of

3 December 1982. The 18 Principles are designed to ensure: independence of older persons through guaranteeing their basic rights: to adequate food, shelter, income-generating activities, etc.; their integration in society, including participation in the adoption and implementation of policies affecting their well-being; adequate protection and care, including health care, to maintain or regain the optimum level of physical, mental and emotional well-being; and opportunities for the full development of the potential of older persons, including access to educational, cultural and recreational activities. The final clauses states that: "Older persons should be able to live in dignity and security and be free of exploitation and physical or mental abuse" (Principle 17) and that "Older persons should be treated fairly regardless of age, gender, racial or ethnic background, disability or other status, and be valued independently of their economic contribution" (Principle 18).

United Nations Principles relating to the Status and Functioning of National Institutions for the Promotion and Protection of Human Rights

See **Paris Principles**.

United Nations Prize in the Field of Human Rights

The United Nations Prize in the Field of Human Rights was instituted by the **United Nations General Assembly** resolution 2217/XXI of 19 December 1966. For the first time, the Prize was awarded on 10 December 1968 on the occasion of the 20th Anniversary of the **Universal Declaration of Human Rights**. Thereafter, the prizes have been awarded in 1973, 1978, 1988, 1993 and 1998. The award of the prize has a particular significance since the 10th of December marked the 50th Anniversary of the Universal Declaration. A Special Committee is entrusted with selecting the laureates of the Prize; it is composed of the President of the United Nations General Assembly, the President of the

Economic and Social Council (ECOSOC), the Chair of the Commission on Human Rights, the Chair of the Commission on the Status of Women and the Chair of the Sub-Commission on the Promotion and Protection of Human Rights (formerly the Sub-Commission on Prevention of Discrimination and Protection of Minorities). Eleanor Roosevelt, the International Committee of the Red Cross and Amnesty International were among laureates.

United Nations Rules for the Protection of Juveniles Deprived of Their Liberty

The Rules were adopted by the **United Nations General Assembly** on 14 December 1990 by resolution 45/113. They advocate the least possible use of deprivation of liberty with regard to juveniles, especially in prison and other closed institutions, and provide specific principles which apply to all juveniles held in any form of detention and in any type of facility. Its fundamental perspective is that the justice system should uphold the rights and safety and promote their physical and mental well-being. The Rules call for the separation of juveniles from adults in detention and the classification of juveniles according to their sex, age, personality and type of offence, with a view to ensuring their protection from harmful influences and risk situations. The rules set forth special provisions covering various aspects of institutional life, such as the physical environment and accommodation, education, vocational training, work, recreation, religion, medical care, contacts with the wider community, limitations of physical restraint and the use of force, disciplinary procedures, inspection, complaints and return to the community. The Rules should be made available to juvenile justice personnel in their national languages and juveniles who are not fluent in the language spoken by the personnel should have the right to the services of an interpreter (Rule 6). The Rules should be implemented in the context of the economic, social and cultural conditions prevailing in each Member State (Rule 16).

United Nations Secretary-General

The United Nations Secretariat, in conformity with Article 7 of the **Charter of the United Nations**, is one of the six principal organs of the **United Nations**. It comprises "a Secretary-General and such staff as the Organization may require" (Article 97). The functions of the Secretariat and the Secretary-General are defined in Chapter XV of the Charter (Articles 97-101). The Charter defines the Secretary-General as the chief administrative officer of the Organization and entrusts him to bring to the attention of the **Security Council** any matter which, in his opinion, threatens international peace and security and to perform such other functions as requested by the Security Council, the **United Nations General Assembly, the Economic and Social Council (ECOSOC)** and other United Nations organs. The Secretary-General is appointed by the General Assembly upon the recommendation of the Security Council. Article 100 of the Charter prohibits the Secretary-General from seeking or receiving instructions from any government or from any other authority external to the Organization. At the same time, Member States are invited to respect the exclusively international character of the responsibilities of the Secretary-General and his staff and not to seek to influence them in the discharge of their responsibilities. The Secretary-General issues annually a report to the General Assembly on the work of the Organization and outlines its future priorities. Furthermore, he is known to the general public for using his good offices, (steps taken publicly and privately, drawing upon his independence, impartiality and integrity, to prevent international disputes from arising, escalating or spreading). The Secretary-General appoints all the staff of the United Nations Secretariat in conformity with regulations established by the General Assembly (Article 101 of the Charter).

For more information see:
http://www.un.org/News/ossg/sg

United Nations Specialized Agencies

The United Nations specialized agencies, created with few exceptions after the Second World War, comprise: **International Labour Organisation (ILO)** established in 1919; **Food and Agriculture Organization of the United Nations (FAO); United Nations Educational, Scientific and Cultural Organization (UNESCO); World Health Organization (WHO);** World Bank Group; International Monetary Fund (IMF); International Civil Aviation Organization (ICAO); Universal Postal Union (UPU) established in 1874; International Telecommunication Union (ITU); World Meteorological Organization (WMO); International Maritime Organization (IMO); **World Intellectual Property Organization (WIPO);** International Fund for Agricultural Development (IFAD); United Nations Industrial Development Organization (UNIDO).

All specialized agencies are linked to the United Nations through cooperative agreements. Established by intergovernmental agreements, they are autonomous bodies. The United Nations specialized agencies have their own governing bodies, budgets and secretariats. Their membership may differ from that of the United Nations. A number of specialized agencies, such as the International Labour Organization (ILO) and UNESCO, deal actively with the promotion and protection of human rights. United Nations specialized agencies form an integral part of the **United Nations system.**

United Nations Special Session on Children (UN)

More than a decade after the adoption of the **Convention on the Rights of the Child** (1989) and the **World Summit for Children** (1990), the **United Nations General Assembly** held a Special Session on Children. Originally planned for 19 to 21 September 2001, the Special Session was rescheduled and held from 8 to 10 May 2002. It was attended by Heads of State and Government, **United Nations** officials, representatives of other intergovernmental organizations, child rights' advocates and children from around the world. The Special Session was held in order to review the progress of the previous decade in improving the lives of children and to reach agreement on future action for renewing a global commitment to children.

The Special Session adopted a far-reaching plan entitled "A World Fit for Children" which includes a Declaration; Review of Progress and Lessons Learned; and Plan of Action. In the Declaration, participants stressed their commitment to create "a world fit for children" in which "sustainable human development, taking into account the interests of the child is founded on principles of democracy, equality, non-discrimination, peace and social justice and the universality, indivisibility, interdependence and interrelatedness of all human rights, including the **right to development**" (para. 5). While recognizing that much progress has been made in improving the lives of children since the 1990 World Summit, the Declaration notes that many obstacles remain, particularly in developing countries. It reaffirms commitment to the unfinished agenda of the World Summit, and underlines the need to address other emerging issues vital to the achievement of the longer-term goals endorsed at recent major summits and conferences, in particular the goals of the **United Nations Millennium Declaration**.

The Plan of Action stipulates that "all children get the best possible start in life and have access to a quality basic education" and have the opportunity to "develop their individual capacities in a safe and supportive environment" and that the "physical, psychological, spiritual, social, emotional, cognitive and cultural development of children is a matter of national and global priority" (para. 4). The Plan of Action enumerates goals, strategies and actions, which include: promoting healthy lives of children; providing quality education; protecting against abuse, exploitation and violence; and combating HIV/AIDS. A separate section of the Plan is devoted to the mobilization of human, financial and material resources (para. 48-58) and is followed by a final section concerning follow-up assessments which call for the strengthening of national and, where appropriate, regional action plans, to facilitate the implementation of the Document (para. 59-62).

United Nations Standard Minimum Rules for Non-Custodial Measures – Tokyo Rules

The **United Nations** Standard Minimum Rules for Non-Custodial Measures, commonly referred to as the "Tokyo Rules" were adopted by the **United Nations General Assembly** on 14 December 1990. They aim at the greater use of alternatives to imprisonment (or, in other words, non-custodial measures) and at the creation of minimum legal safeguards for persons subject to them. When implementing the Rules, Member States : "... shall endeavour to ensure a proper balance between the rights of individual offenders, the rights of victims, and the concern of society for public safety and crime prevention" (Rule 1.4). The Rules are intended to promote greater community involvement in the management of criminal justice and to promote among offenders a sense of responsibility towards society. Similarly, they are intended to be used in accordance with the minimum intervention and the use of informal community measures in the discharge of criminal proceedings. They apply to all persons subject to prosecution, trial or terms of sentencing. They seek to ensure that the criminal justice system provides a wide range of non-custodial measures, from pre-trial to post-sentencing dispositions, to allow flexibility while maintaining a capacity for consistent sentencing. To this end, the Rules provide that: judicial discretion is to be exercised to ensure accordance with the law; non-custodial measures imposing an obligation on the offenders shall require the offender's consent; the offender is entitled to make a request or complaint regarding the implementation of non-custodial measures; grievances related to violation of internationally recognized human rights shall be redressed; and non-custodial measures shall not involve medical or psychological experimentation or undue risk of injury and shall respect the dignity and privacy of the offender.

United Nations Standard Minimum Rules for the Administration of Juvenile Justice – Beijing Rules

The **United Nations** Standard Minimum Rules for the Administration of Juvenile Justice were adopted by the **United Nations General Assembly** on 29 November 1985 by resolution 40/33. On the same day, the General Assembly also approved the recommendation of the Seventh **United Nations Congress[es] on the Prevention of Crime and the Treatment of Offenders** held in Beijing, China, from 14-18 May 1984. For this reason the rules are known as the "Beijing Rules". The Rules relate to such matters as the minimum age of criminal responsibility, the objectives of juvenile justice administration, the exercise of discretionary power, the human rights principles to be applied and protection of privacy (Part I). They also cover matters relating to investigation and prosecution of crimes committed by juveniles, including the question of detention (part II), and matters relating to the adjudication and disposition of cases against juvenile offenders (Part III). In general, they recommend the least possible use of incarceration, stating that "the placement of a juvenile in an institution shall always be a disposition of last resort and for the minimum necessary period" (Part III). The rules, however, set out some essential elements of protection for juvenile offenders placed in penitentiary institutions, such as placing juveniles under detention separate from adults, and ensuring that such juveniles receive care, protection, education and vocational training (Part V). The **United Nations General Assembly** invited Member States to adapt to the Rules, wherever necessary, their national legislation, policies and practices, particularly in the training of juvenile justice personnel, and to bring these Rules to the attention of the relevant authorities and the public in general.

United Nations System

The **United Nations** system comprises the Organization of the United Nations, its bodies, **United Nations specialized agencies**, as well as programmes and funds. The United Nations programmes and funds work under the authority of the **United Nations General Assembly** and the **Economic and Social Council (ECOSOC)** in carrying out the Organization's mandate. The **United Nations Children's Fund (UNICEF)** is the lead United Nations entity working for the promotion and protection of the rights of children. The **United Nations Development Programme (UNDP)** strives to ensure economic and social development that respects the human rights of individuals. The **Office of the United Nations High Commissioner for Refugees (UNHCR)** deals with problems of refugees and internally **displaced persons**. The **United Nations Drug Control Programme (UNDCP),** the **United Nations Environment Programme (UNEP),** the **United Nations Population Fund (UNFPA),** the World Food Programme (WFP), and several other programmes also deal with some aspects of human rights. Programmes and funds have their own budgets and governing bodies. Four organizations are related to the United Nations system: the International Atomic Energy Agency (IAEA), the World Trade Organization (WTO), the World Tourism Organization (WTO) and the Organization for the Prohibition of Chemical Weapons (OPCW).

A number of activities within the United Nations system are coordinated. Principal responsibility for coordination of human rights activities within the United Nations system is entrusted upon the **Office of the United Nations High Commissioner for Human Rights (OHCHR)**, which is a part of the United Nations itself.

United Nations Year of Dialogue among Civilizations – 2001

The year 2001 was proclaimed as the **United Nations** Year of Dialogue among Civilizations by the **United Nations General**

Assembly (resolution 53/22 of 4 November 1998). The purpose of the Year is to enhance the understanding through constructive dialogue among civilizations. The resolution emphasized the importance of tolerance in international relations and the significant role of dialogue as a means to reach understanding, to remove threats to peace and to strengthen interaction and exchange among civilizations. It invited governments, the **United Nations system**, including **UNESCO**, and other relevant intergovernmental and **non-governmental organizations** to plan and to implement cultural, educational and social programmes to promote the concept of dialogue among civilizations, including through organizing conferences and seminars and disseminating information and scholarly material. In its subsequent resolutions concerning the Year, the United Nations General Assembly noted with interest the activities undertaken and proposals made by Member States, UNESCO and other organizations, encouraged States, regional and international organizations, civil society and non-governmental organizations to continue to develop appropriate initiatives at all levels to promote dialogue in all fields with a view to fostering mutual recognition and understanding among and within civilizations (resolution 55/23, paras. 6 and 7). Governments were invited to encourage all members of society to participate in promoting such dialogue and provide them with an opportunity to make contributions to the Year (resolution 54/113, para. 4).

The promotion of dialogue among civilizations is intimately linked with the issue of human rights and cultural diversity. In its resolution 55/91 on this subject, the United Nations General Assembly reaffirmed that cultural diversity and the pursuit of cultural development by all peoples and nations are a source of mutual enrichment for the cultural life of humankind, and that all cultures and civilizations share a common set of universal values. It reaffirmed the **right to take part in cultural life** and the **right to enjoy the benefits of scientific progress and its applications**. It states that intercultural dialogue enriches essentially the common understanding of human rights and that respect for cultural diversity and the cultural rights of all enhances cultural pluralism and contributes to a wider exchange of knowledge and understanding of cultural background advancing the application and enjoyment of universally accepted human rights and to fostering stable friendly relations among peoples and nations worldwide.

Universal Children's Day – 20 November (UN)

On 14 December 1954, the **United Nations General Assembly** (resolution 836 [IX]) recommended that a Universal Children's Day be observed by all countries as a day of worldwide fraternity and understanding between children, and of activities devoted to promoting the welfare of the world's children. It also proposed to Member States that the Day be observed on the date and in the way which each considers appropriate. Universal Children's Day is usually celebrated on 20 November, because on that day the 1959 **Declaration of the Rights of the Child** and the 1989 **Convention on the Rights of the Child** were adopted.

Universal Copyright Convention (1952) and the Universal Copyright Convention as revised in 1971 (UNESCO)

The Universal Copyright Convention was adopted in Geneva on 6 September 1952 by the Intergovernmental Copyright Conference convened by **UNESCO**. It came into force on 16 September 1955 and, by the middle of 2003, had been ratified by 98 States. Until 10 July 1974, when the Revised Universal Convention came into force, it was open to ratification, acceptance or accession by any State. Since that date, no State has been able to accede solely to the 1952 Convention, but accession to the Revised Convention by a State not party to the first Convention constitutes, in addition, accession to the latter. The purpose of the 1952 Convention is to improve copyright protection worldwide and to establish a basis for common action in this respect between countries with widely differing civilizations, cultures, legal systems and administrative practices, and sometimes conflicting interests. With a view to introducing a preferential system to benefit the developing countries, the Convention was revised by the Conference for the Revision of the Universal Copyright Convention, convened by UNESCO. Adopted by that Conference in Paris on 24 July 1971, the Revised Convention came into force on 10 July 1974 and had been ratified by 63 States by the middle of 2003. Its purpose is also to establish standard copyright provisions in all the States Parties. The revised Convention covers not only the protection of the rights of authors, but also the rights of other copyright proprietors in literary, scientific and artistic works (Article I). Article IV bis extends these rights to the basic rights ensuring the author's economic interests, including the exclusive right to authorize reproduction by any means, public performance and broadcasting. Two Protocols to the Universal Copyright Convention as revised in Paris on 24 July 1971 came also into force on 10 July 1971. Protocol 1, which had been ratified by 38 States as of the middle of 2003, concerns the application of that Convention to works of stateless persons and refugees, whereas Protocol 2, which had been ratified by 41 States by the middle of 2003, concerns the application of that Convention to the works of certain international organizations.

Universal Declaration of Human Rights (UN)

On 10 December 1948, the **United Nations General Assembly** adopted and proclaimed the **Universal Declaration of Human Rights** "as a common standard of achievement for all peoples and all nations, to the end that every individual and every organ of society, keeping this Declaration constantly in mind, shall strive by teaching and education to promote respect for these rights and freedoms and by progressive measures, national and international, to secure their universal and effective recognition and observance..." (Preamble). The Universal

Declaration consists of a Preamble and 30 Articles setting forth the basic human rights and fundamental freedoms to which all human beings everywhere in the world are entitled without **discrimination**. Article 1 lays down the philosophical postulates upon which the Declaration is based: "All human beings are born free and equal in dignity and rights. They are endowed with reason and conscience and should act towards one another in a spirit of brotherhood". Article 2, para. 1, affirms the principle of non-discrimination, stipulating that: "Everyone is entitled to all the rights and freedoms set forth in this Declaration, without distinction of any kind, such as race, colour, sex, language, religion, political or other opinion, national or social origin, property, birth or other status". The Declaration lays down fundamental **civil, cultural, economic, political** and **social rights**, among which (Articles 3 to 27): the **right to life**, liberty and security of person; **freedom from subjection to torture and cruel, inhuman or degrading treatment** or punishment; the **right to recognition as a person before the law**; the **right to an effective remedy by the tribunals**; the **right to marry and to found a family**; freedom of movement; the **right of asylum**; the **right to a nationality**; **freedom of thought, conscience and religion**; the **right to own property**; the right of association and of assembly; the **right of equal access to public service**; the **right to social security**; the **right to work**; the **right to rest and leisure**; the right to a standard of living adequate for health and well-being; the **right to education**; and the **right to take part in cultural life** of the community. Article 28 stipulates that: "Everyone is entitled to a social and international order in which the rights and freedoms set forth in the Declaration can be fully realized". Article 29 contains two important provisions. Paragraph 1 states: "Everyone has duties to the community in which alone the free and full development of his personality is possible". Paragraph 2 stipulates that: "In the exercise of his rights and freedoms, everyone shall be subject only to such limitations as are determined by law solely for the purpose of securing due recognition and respect for the rights and freedoms of others and of meeting the just requirements of morality, public order and the general welfare in a democratic society". Article 30 proclaims: "Nothing in this Declaration may be interpreted as implying for any State, group or person any right to engage in any activity or to perform any act aimed at the destruction of any of the rights and freedoms set forth herein".

The Universal Declaration forms the very basis of the **International Bill of Human Rights** and has become the cornerstone instrument of human rights law. It has inspired the adoption of numerous standard-setting instruments and influenced national laws in a number of States.

For more information see:
http://www.unhchr.ch/udhr/index.htm

Universal Declaration on Cultural Diversity (UNESCO)

Adopted on 2 November 2001 by the 31st Session of the General Conference on **UNESCO**, the Universal Declaration on Cultural Diversity accompanied by an Action Plan, is aimed towards "humanizing the process of **globalization** and ensuring the preservation and promotion of the fruitful diversity of cultures" (Preamble). Member States adopted the Declaration by acclamation thus affirming their conviction that intercultural dialogue is the best guarantee of peace and categorically rejecting the idea that conflicts between cultures are inevitable.

For the purposes of the Declaration, culture should be regarded as "the set of distinctive spiritual, material, intellectual and emotional features of a society or a social group, and that it encompasses, in addition to art and literature, lifestyles, ways of living together, value systems, traditions and beliefs" (Preamble). The defence of cultural diversity is an ethical imperative inseparable from respect for human dignity and implies a commitment to fundamental freedoms (Article 4). Furthermore, cultural rights (defined in Article 27 of the **Universal Declaration of Human**

Rights and in Articles 13 and 15 of the **International Covenant on Economic, Social and Cultural Rights**) are viewed as an integral part of human rights, which are universal, indivisible and interdependent (Article 5).

Universal Declaration on Democracy (IPU)

The Universal Declaration on Democracy was adopted on 16 September 1997 by the Inter-Parliamentary Council, the plenary body of the **Inter-Parliamentary Union (IPU)**. The Declaration is the result of a process started in 1995 when the Inter-Parliamentary Council decided to prepare such a Declaration in order to advance international standards and contribute to the process of democratization under way in the world.

The Declaration first sets out the principles of democracy, describing it as a universally recognized ideal and goal aiming essentially to preserve and promote the dignity and fundamental rights of the individual, to achieve social justice and to foster the economic and social development of the community, as well as a mode of government best suited to achieving these objectives. As a mode of government, democracy "is to be applied according to modalities which reflect the diversity of experience and cultural particularities without derogating from internationally recognized principles, norms and standards". The Declaration affirms also that the "achievement of democracy presupposes a genuine partnership between men and women in the conduct of the affairs of society". Part II of the Declaration deals with the elements and exercise of democratic government, the guarantee of judicial institutions and independent and effective oversight mechanisms, the existence of an active civil society through education and satisfaction of the basic economic needs of the most disadvantaged. Finally, the Declaration stresses the importance of the international dimension of democracy. Part III of the declaration affirms that democracy "must be recognized as an international principle, applicable to international organizations and to States in their international relations".

Universal Declaration on the Eradication of Hunger and Malnutrition (UN)

The Universal Declaration on the Eradication of Hunger and Malnutrition was adopted on 16 November 1974 by the World Food Conference and was subsequently endorsed by the **United Nations General Assembly** in its resolution 3348 (XXIX) of 17 December 1974. The Declaration guarantees the **right to adequate food**, enshrined in Article 25 of the **Universal Declaration of Human Rights** and Article 11 of the **International Covenant on Social, Economic and Cultural Rights**.

The Conference proclaimed that: "every man, woman and child has the inalienable right to be free from hunger and malnutrition in order to develop fully and maintain their mental and physical faculties" (para. 1 of the Declaration). To ensure the enjoyment of this right, States should work together, in accordance with their sovereign judgement and internal legislation, for higher food production and a more equitable and efficient distribution of food between and within countries. In this connection, States undertook to collaborate for the establishment of an effective system of world food security by promoting, *inter alia*, the advancement of food production technology, as well as by providing additional technical and financial assistance to developing and least developed countries. It was stressed, however, that ensuring the right to adequate food should not be detrimental to the conservation of natural resources and, therefore, their rational exploitation as well as the preservation of the environment should be promoted.

The concept of food security was further elaborated and developed by the **World Food Summit** organized by the **Food and Agriculture Organization of the United Nations** in Rome in November 1996. In recognizing the fundamental right to adequate food, the World Food Summit Plan of Action underlined that "… food security exists when all people, at all times, have physical and economic access to sufficient, safe and nutritious food to meet their dietary needs and food preferences for an active and healthy life…" (Article 1).

Since 1980, **World Food Day** has been observed every year on 16 October. Its purpose is to increase public awareness of the world's food problems and strengthen solidarity in the struggle against hunger, malnutrition and **poverty**.

Universal Declaration on the Human Genome and Human Rights (UNESCO)

The Universal Declaration on the Human Genome and Human Rights was adopted unanimously and by acclamation by the General Conference of **UNESCO** at its 29th session on 11 November 1997, and endorsed by the **United Nations General Assembly** on 9 December 1998, as part of the celebration of the fiftieth anniversary of the **Universal Declaration of Human Rights**. The first universal instrument in the field of bioethics, it sets out ethical and legal principles to assist the progress of genetic research and its applications. Its purpose is to strike a balance between the freedom of scientific research and the protection of human dignity and human freedom against potential drifts in biomedical research.

The Declaration states that the human genome "…underlies the fundamental unity of all members of the human family …. In a symbolic sense, it is the heritage of humanity". The concept of the human genome refers to the genes of every individual as well as to the whole spectrum of genes constituting the human species. With its preamble and twenty-five articles, the Declaration is based on four pillars: human dignity, freedom of research, solidarity and international cooperation. It focuses, among others, on the prohibition of **discrimination** based on genetic characteristics, the consent of each individual, the protection of the confidentiality of genetic data, the freedom and responsibility of researchers, the sharing of benefits of advances in biomedicine, especially with developing countries, and the responsibility of States in the implementation of the Declaration.

It also entrusts the International Bioethics Committee of UNESCO (IBC) with the task of contributing to the dissemination of the principles set out in the Declaration, in particular through giving advice on its follow-up and further examining issues raised by its implementation.

Universal Forum of Cultures

The first Universal Forum of Cultures will take place in Barcelona (Spain) from 9 May to 26 September 2004. The Forum will bring together representatives from all of the world's cultures to promote study, reflection, and a process of dialogue intended to foster intercultural understanding and celebrate diversity. The Forum is structured around three core themes: cultural diversity; sustainable development; and conditions for peace.

The Forum is expected to draw between 3.5 and 4 million visitors. The 141 days of activities will include interactive events, exhibitions, informal gatherings, workshops and games and over 900 daily performances by theatre groups, musical groups, and other performing artists.

The Barcelona World Forum of Cultures is coorganized by the Barcelona City Council, the Catalan autonomous Government and the Spanish Government, with **UNESCO** as the main partner.

Vienna Declaration and Programme of Action (UN)

The Vienna Declaration and Programme of Action was adopted on 25 June 1993, by the **World Conference on Human Rights**, which took place in Vienna, Austria (14-25 June 1993). The World Conference brought together representatives of 171 States, as well as **United Nations specialized agencies**, bodies, programmes, other intergovernmental organizations and 800 **non-governmental organizations**. Its final document declares that the promotion and protection of human rights is a matter of priority for the international community and that all States are responsible for developing and encouraging respect for human rights and fundamental freedoms for all (Part I, para. 1). One of the most significant conclusions of the Vienna Declaration and Programme of Action, adopted by consensus, is the confirmation of the equal importance of all human rights. The Conference proclaimed that "all human rights are universal, indivisible and interdependent and interrelated" and that "the international community must treat human rights globally in a fair and equal manner, on the same footing, and with the same emphasis" (Part I, para. 5). It proclaims that democracy, development and respect for human rights and fundamental freedoms are interdependent and mutually reinforcing (Part I, para. 8). The Vienna Declaration and Programme of Action also underlined that "... the universal respect for, and observance of, human rights and fundamental freedoms for all, contribute to the stability and well-being necessary for peaceful and friendly relations among nations, and to improved conditions for peace and security, as well as social and economic development ..." (Part I, para. 6). It also reaffirms that States are duty-bound to ensure that education is aimed at strengthening the respect for human rights and fundamental freedoms (Part I, para. 33) and as such should include peace, democracy, development and social justice (Part II, para. 80). The Declaration and Programme of Action further recommends that States develop specific programmes and strategies for ensuring the widest **human rights education** and the dissemination of public information, taking particular account of the human rights needs of women (Part II, para. 81).

The document contains a separate section concerning increased coordination on human rights within the **United Nations system** (Part II, paras. 1-15) and the strengthening of the United Nations machinery for human rights, including the establishment of the post of the **United Nations High Commissioner for Human Rights** (Part II, paras. 17-18). The Programme of Action (Part II) also deals specifically with the struggle against **discrimination** (paras. 19-24), protection of persons belonging to **minorities** (paras. 25-27); **indigenous people** (paras. 28-32), **migrant workers** (paras. 33-35) disabled persons (paras. 63-65). Special sections are devoted to the equal status and human rights of women (paras. 36-44) and the rights of the child (paras. 45-53). The Programme also enumerates measures to give priority to national and international action to promote human rights (paras. 66-77) and to strengthen the monitory mechanisms for their implementation (paras. 83-98). It also recommended the proclamation of a **United Nations Decade for Human Rights Education** (para. 82).

Vienna Declaration on Crime and Justice (UN)

This Declaration was adopted by the **United Nations General Assembly** in its resolution 55/59 of 4 December 2000. It had previously been approved on 17 April 2000 by the Tenth **United Nations Congress[es] on the Prevention of Crime and Treatment of Offenders** (Vienna, April 2000). This instrument has been described as a landmark document to serve as a guiding light for years to come.

The Declaration followed the adoption on 15 November 2000 by the General Assembly of the **Convention against Transnational Organized Crime**. Both these instruments will strengthen international cooperation in combating **organized crime**, including **corruption**, money laundering, and in achieving a significant decrease in trafficking in persons, especially women and children, as well as in the illicit manufacturing and trafficking of firearms.

Vienna International Plan of Action on Ageing (UN)

The Vienna Plan of Action on Ageing was drawn up by the **World Assembly on Ageing** (Vienna, Austria, 1982). It was later endorsed by the **United Nations General Assembly** by its resolution 37/51 of 3 December 1982. It aims primarily at strengthening the capacities of Governments and civil society to deal effectively with the ageing of populations and with the special concerns and needs of the elderly, and at promoting regional and international cooperation. The Plan includes 62 recommendations for action, addressing research, data collection and analysis, training and education as well as several areas of concern to ageing individuals, such as health and nutrition, housing and environment and social welfare. Nine years after the endorsement of the Plan, the General Assembly adopted the **United Nations Principles for Older Persons** (1991). These 18 Principles are designed to guarantee various rights for older persons and to ensure that they live in dignity and security.

Vulnerable Groups

Over the years relevant organs and agencies within the **United Nations system** have adopted special measures of protection and assistance to benefit members of groups whose human rights are very often neglected, for example the elderly, aliens, **migrant workers**, the handicapped, **HIV-infected people or people with AIDS**. Such special measures are necessary to ensure equality in the realization of human rights and fundamental freedoms of persons belonging to those groups. A few examples of such instruments are: the **Declaration on the Rights of Disabled Persons** (1975); the **Declaration on the Human Rights of Individuals who are not Nationals of the Country in which They Live** (1985); the **International Convention on the Protection of the Rights of All Migrant Workers and Members of Their Families** (1990); the **United Nations Principles for Older Persons** (1991) and the **Declaration on the Rights of Persons Belonging to National or Ethnic, Religious and Linguistic Minorities** (1992).

Some specialists prefer to give to the definition "vulnerable groups" a broader sense and to include in these groups children and women.

Week of Solidarity with the Peoples of Non-self-governing Territories – beginning 25 May (UN)

On 6 December 1999, the **United Nations General Assembly**, by its resolution 54/91, requested the Special Committee on Decolonization to observe annually the Week of Solidarity with the Peoples of Non-Self-Governing Territories, commencing in the week beginning 25 May – African Liberation Day. This Week had first been proclaimed in 1972 as a week of solidarity with colonial peoples fighting for their independence.

Week of Solidarity with the Peoples Struggling against Racism and Racial Discrimination – beginning 21 March (UN)

As part of its programme for the first Decade for Action to combat Racism and Racial **discrimination**, in 1979 the **United Nations General Assembly** called for the observance by all States of a Week of Solidarity with the Peoples Struggling against Racism and Racial Discrimination (resolution 34/24). This week begins each year on 21 March, the **International Day for the Elimination of Racial Discrimination**.

World AIDS Day – 1 December (WHO)

The World Aids Day was observed for the first time on 1 December 1988 in accordance with the decision of the **World Health Organization (WHO)**. Deep concern about the pandemic proportions of the acquired immunodeficiency syndrome (AIDS) has been expressed by the **United Nations General Assembly** and the human rights dimension of this problem is articulated in several international resolutions and decisions taken by United Nations bodies, programmes and agencies. Many international conferences and events have been devoted to the subject of **HIV infected people or people with AIDS.** Today over 50 million people are living with HIV/AIDS. "Stigma and **Discrimination**" became the theme of the World AIDS Day Campaign for 2002-2003.

World Assembly on Ageing (UN)

The first World Assembly on Ageing took place in Vienna, Austria, in 1982 and resulted in the adoption of the **Vienna Plan of Action on Ageing.** This Plan was later endorsed by the **United Nations General Assembly** by its resolution 37/51 of 3 December 1982. The Assembly was a first step towards drafting and adopting the **United Nations Principles for Older Persons** (1991).

The General Assembly decided, at its 54th session, to convene a Second World Assembly on Ageing. Held in Madrid, Spain (April 8-12, 2002) on the twentieth anniversary of the Vienna World Assembly, it was devoted to the review of the outcome of the first World Assembly as well as the adoption of a revised plan of action and a long term strategy on ageing.

The General Assembly (A/RES/45/106) designated 1 October the **International Day of Older Persons.**

World Conference against Racism, Racial Discrimination, Xenophobia and Related Intolerance – WCAR (UN)

Noting with grave concern the persistence of all forms of racism in many parts of the world, the **United Nations General Assembly** decided (resolution 52/111 of 12 December 1997) to convene a World Conference against **Racism**, Racial **Discrimination**, Xenophobia and Related Intolerance (WCAR). Regional experts seminars to discuss the issues of priority concern were held from 1999 to 2000 in Addis Ababa, Bangkok, Geneva, Santiago de Chile and Warsaw. Regional intergovernmental meetings were also held for Europe (Strasbourg, October 2000); for the Americas (Santiago de Chile, December 2000); for Africa (Dakar, January 2001); and for Asia (Tehran, February 2001). The United Nations **Commission on Human Rights** acted as the preparatory committee for the World Conference. Three sessions of the preparatory committee were held in Geneva in May 2000, June 2001 and July/August 2001. These meetings made decisions concerning the provisional agenda for the Conference, its draft rules of procedure, and contributed to the preparation of the draft documents.

The Conference, held in Durban, South Africa, from 31 August to 8 September 2001 was a landmark event in the struggle to eradicate all forms of racism and related intolerance. It marked both the International Year – and the Third Decade – for the Elimination of Racial Discrimination. The Conference was attended by a great number of Heads of State and Government, representatives from 194 States and about 10,000 representatives of **non-governmental organizations**. The **United Nations specialized agencies** and bodies as well as regional non-governmental organizations also took part in the Conference.

The objectives of the Conference were: to produce a document recognizing the damage caused by past expressions of racism and outlining modern forms of racism and xenophobia; to reach agreement on a strong practical programme of action; and to forge an alliance of governments and civil society to fight racism. Five main themes formed the core of the Conference's agenda: sources, causes, forms and contemporary manifestations of racism; victims; measures of prevention, education and protection aimed at the eradication of racism, racial discrimination, xenophobia and related intolerance at the national, regional and international levels; provision for effective remedies, recourse, redress (compensation) and other measures at all levels; and strategies to achieve full and effective equality, including enhancement of international cooperation and the role of **United Nations** and other international mechanisms.

The **Durban Declaration and Programme of Action** were adopted at the Conference and presented to the international community as a common plan for eradicating all forms of racism and discrimination.

The **International Day for the Elimination of Racial Discrimination** is observed each year on 21 March and the **Week of Solidarity with the Peoples Struggling against Racism and Racial Discrimination** starts the same day.

For more information see :
http://www.unhchr.ch/html/racism/

World Conference of the International Women's Year (UN)

The World Conference of the **International Women's Year** took place in Mexico from 19 June to 2 July 1975. Through the adoption of the **Declaration of Mexico on the Equality of Women and Their Contribution to Development and Peace**, the **World Plan of Action for the Implementation of the Objectives of the International Women's Year** and related resolutions, the World Conference made a valuable contribution towards the achievement of the threefold objectives of the Year, namely, to promote equality between men and women, to ensure the full integration of women in the total development effort and to promote women's contribution to the development of friendly relations and cooperation among States and to the strengthening of world peace. This Conference proved to be a first milestone in the **United Nations** work regarding women at all levels of society, including civil society, governments, international and inter-governmental organizations.

World Conference on Human Rights (UN)

The World Conference on Human Rights was convened by the **United Nations** and held in Vienna, Austria, from 14 to 25 June 1993. It was attended by more than 7,000 participants, including delegates from 171 States and 800 **non-governmental**

organizations, as well as by representatives of **United Nations specialized agencies**, bodies, programmes and other intergovernmental organizations. On 25 June 1993, the **Vienna Declaration and Programme of Action** was adopted by consensus, successfully closing the World Conference and presenting to the international community a common plan for strengthening human rights activities around the world. It was then endorsed by the **United Nations General Assembly**. The document marks not only the culmination of a long process of review and debate, but also the beginning of a renewed effort to reinforce and further implement the body of human rights instruments. Thus, the Vienna Declaration recommends strengthening and harmonizing the monitoring capacity of the **United Nations system** and calls for the establishment of the post of the **United Nations High Commissioner for Human Rights**. The World Conference confirmed that all human rights – civil, cultural, economic, political and social – are universal, indivisible and interrelated and interdependent. It also confirmed an inherent link between human rights, peace, democracy and development. It emphasized the need for speedy ratification of all human rights instruments. The World Conference recommended the proclamation by the **United Nations General Assembly** of the **United Nations Decade for Human Rights Education** and the **International Decade of the World's Indigenous People**.

For more information see:
http://www.unhchr.ch/html/menu5/wchr.htm

World Conferences on Women (UN)

The **World Conference of the International Women's Year** held in Mexico City in 1975, was the first **United Nations** World Conference on Women. Pursuant to the proposals made by this Conference, the **United Nations General Assembly** proclaimed the **United Nations Decade for Women: Equality, Development and Peace (1976-1985)**.

In July 1980, at the mid-point of the Decade, the second World Conference of the United Nations Decade for Women: Equality, Development and Peace, was held in Copenhagen, Denmark. This conference reviewed and evaluated the progress achieved and obstacles encountered in attaining the objectives of the Decade at the national, regional and international levels. It adopted the Programme of Action for the Second Half of the United Nations Decade for Women in order to promote the implementation of the three objectives of equality, development and peace. Special emphasis was placed on employment, health and education, which were considered as being significant elements to ensure the full and equal participation of women in development.

In July 1985, at the end of the Decade, the third World Conference to Review and Appraise the Achievements of the United Nations Decade for Women: Equality, Development and Peace was held in Nairobi, Kenya. It adopted the **Nairobi Forward-Looking Strategies for the Advancement of Women**, which provided a policy framework for improving the status of women during the period 1986-2000 and the elimination of all forms of inequality between men and women which is essential for strengthening peace and security.

The fourth World Conference on Women was held in Beijing, China, in September 1995. Its aim was to increase awareness of the gender dimensions of equality, development and peace and to further promote women's advancement worldwide. The fourth World Conference was attended by representatives of 189 countries and 2,600 **non-governmental organizations** (more than 30,000 people attended the parallel Non-Governmental Organization Forum). The Conference adopted the **Beijing Declaration and Platform for Action** in which the participating governments committed themselves to the effective inclusion of a gender dimension throughout all their institutions, policies, planning and decision-making. As the main **United Nations** intergovernmental entity entrusted with the responsibility of promoting the advancement of women and gender equality, the

Commission on the Status of Women was the preparatory body for all four World Conferences on Women.

In June 2000, the General Assembly held a special session to review and appraise the progress achieved in implementing the objectives of the Beijing Platform for Action and the Nairobi Forward Looking Strategies.

World Day for Water – 22 March (UN)

Considering that the promotion of water conservation and sustainable management requires public awareness at local, national, regional and international levels, the **United Nations General Assembly** adopted on 22 December 1992, resolution 47/193 by which 22 March of each year was declared World Day for Water. Coordinated by the World Meteorological Organization (WMO) and **UNESCO**, in conformity with the recommendations of the United Nations Conference on Environment and Development (UNCED) held in Brazil in 1992, the Day was first observed in 1993. States are invited to devote the Day to concrete activities related to the conservation and development of water resources and the implementation of the recommendations of Agenda 21, a comprehensive plan of action adopted at the UNCED. These activities may include the promotion of public awareness through the publication and diffusion of documentaries and the organization of conferences, round tables, seminars and expositions.

World Declaration on the Survival, Protection, and Development of Children (UN)

On 30 September 1990, the **World Summit for Children**, which met in New York, adopted the World Declaration on the Survival, Protection, and Development of Children. It was accompanied by a Plan of Action for Implementing the World Declaration. Both documents aim at giving a better future for every child, with respect to the **Convention on the Rights of the Child**. On 21 December 1990, the **United Nations General**

Assembly called on States and the international community to work towards achieving the objectives approved in them as an integral part of their national plans and international co-operation. The World Declaration states that the political leaders are aware of the challenges to be met, have the means and the knowledge (Articles 4-8) to fulfil the tasks listed in Articles 10-17, such as the "enhancement of children's health and nutrition" (Article 10) or "strengthening the role of women in general and ensuring their equal rights" (Article 12). Therefore, the Declaration contains in its Article 21 a ten-point programme, to which the political leaders committed themselves, to protect the rights of children and to improve their lives. The Plan of Action, as a framework for more specific national and international undertakings, calls for specific action to be taken by national Governments, international organizations, bilateral aid agencies, **non-governmental organizations** and all other sectors of society. It calls for specific action on questions such as child health; food and nutrition; role of women and the family, maternal health, and family planning; basic education and literacy; children in especially difficult situations; protection of children during armed conflicts; children and the environment; and alleviation of **poverty** and revitalization of economic growth.

The **United Nations Special Session on Children** was held from 8 to 10 May 2002 in order to review the progress of the previous decade in improving the lives of children and the achievements in the implementation of the Declaration and Plan of Action adopted at the 1990 World Summit. Participants also renewed their commitment for action for children in the next decade.

World Education Forum (UNESCO)

The Forum was convened by **UNESCO** in Dakar, Senegal, from 26 to 28 April 2000. It was the most important event in the field of education at the dawn of the new century. By adopting the **Dakar Framework for Action**, the 1,100 participants of the

Forum reaffirmed their commitment to achieving the goals of "Education for All" for every citizen and every society.

World Food Day – 16 October (FAO)

On 28 November 1979, the **Food and Agriculture Organization (FAO)** Conference unanimously decided that World Food Day should be observed for the first time on 16 October 1981 and annually thereafter. The objectives of this Day are to heighten public awareness of the nature and dimensions of the world food problem and to mobilize support for the long-term effort to overcome widespread chronic malnutrition. The **United Nations General Assembly**, on 5 December 1980, welcomed the observance of World Food Day and urged Governments and international, regional and national organizations to contribute to its annual commemoration. On 17 November 1997, the FAO Conference mandated, within the framework of World Food Day, the TeleFood Programme to raise public awareness of the issues underlying food security and to mobilize support in the struggle against world hunger and malnutrition. In 2002, the World Food Day/TeleFood theme was "Water: source of food security".

World Food Summit (FAO)

Noting with grave concern the continued existence of widespread malnutrition and the failure to meet the goals set by the World Food Conference held in 1974, the Conference of the **Food and Agriculture Organization of the United Nations (FAO)** decided, at its 28th session in October 1995, to convene a World Food Summit. Subsequently this decision was endorsed unanimously by the **United Nations General Assembly**. The Summit took place from 13 to 17 November 1996 in Rome, and was attended by high-level representatives from 185 countries and from the **European Community**. The objective of the Summit was to renew global commitment at the highest political level to eliminate hunger and malnutrition and to achieve sustainable food security for all. The Rome Declaration on World Food Security and the Plan of Action adopted by the Summit reaffirmed the commitments of the **Universal Declaration on the Eradication of Hunger and Malnutrition** and provided a framework for bringing about important changes in policies and programmes needed to achieve "Food for All". FAO's Committee on World Food Security (CFS) has the responsibility to monitor and appraise the implementation of the Plan of Action.

The "World Food Summit: five years later" was called for by the FAO Council in October 2001 when it became clear that the original Summit goal of cutting the number of hungry in half by the year 2015 would not be met without renewed effort. The Summit was held from 10 to 13 June 2002 and adopted the Declaration of the "World Food Summit: five years later", whereby States Parties pledged to renew commitments to end hunger and called for an international alliance to accelerate efforts towards that goal.

For more information see:
http://www.fao.org/wfs/homepage.htm

World Habitat Day
– 1st Monday of October (UN)

In 1985, the **United Nations General Assembly** by its resolution 40/202 designated the first Monday of October as World Habitat Day. The first observance of the Day, in 1986, marked the 10th anniversary of the first international conference on the issue – Habitat: **United Nations** Conference on Human Settlements (Vancouver, Canada, 1976).

Ten years later, the second United Nations Conference on Human Settlements (Habitat II, Istanbul, Turkey, 1996) adopted the Habitat Agenda (principles, commitments and plan of action) for addressing questions relating to human settlements, both urban and rural. In his message on the occasion of World Habitat Day in 2000 – whose theme was "Women in Urban Governance" – the **United Nations Secretary-General** said that: "In theory, the poor are excluded from governance regardless of gender. In practice, it is women, even more than men, who must confront the consequences of other peoples decisions". He therefore called for the further involvement of women in the governance of urban neighbourhoods. Every year, on the occasion of the Day, the "Habitat Scroll of Honour" is awarded to organizations, individuals or projects having made an outstanding contribution to human settlements development. The theme for World Habitat Day 2002 was "City-to-City Cooperation."

World Health Day – 7 April (WHO)

The **World Health Organization (WHO)** designated 7 April each year as World Health Day. The objective of the Day is to raise global awareness of a specific health theme to highlight a priority area of concern for WHO. The Day serves to launch long-term advocacy programmes for which activities are undertaken and resources provided. In 2003, the theme of the Day was "Healthy Environments for Children". **World Mental Health Day** is observed on 10 October each year.

World Health Organization – WHO

The Constitution of the World Health Organization (WHO) was adopted on 22 July 1946 by the International Health Conference. WHO came into being officially on 7 April 1948 and on 10 July of the same year it became a **United Nations specialized agency**. The objective of WHO, as stated in Article 1 of its Constitution, is "the attainment by all peoples of the highest possible level of health". It defines "health" as "a state of complete physical, mental and social well-being and not merely the absence of disease or infirmity". WHO's efforts are concerned not only with the provision of health care to everyone, but also with the provision of care throughout the entire life of each individual (Preamble). To attain this objective, the functions of WHO are: to act as the directing and coördinating authority on international health work; to transmit policy decisions on international health matters; to promote international agreement on health policies; to promote the rationalization and mobilization of resources for health and to support developing countries identifying their needs for external resources; to serve as a neutral ground for absorbing, distilling, synthesizing and widely disseminating information that has practical value for countries in solving their health problems; and to identify or generate health technology that is appropriate (Article 2). Since its establishment, WHO has cooperated closely with the **United Nations** in matters relating to the **right to health**. In 1981, the **United Nations General Assembly** endorsed the Global Strategy for Health for All by the Year 2000 which had been adopted earlier by the World Health Assembly (the main body of WHO). In 1982, the General Assembly adopted the **Principles of Medical Ethics relevant to the Role of Health Personnel, particularly Physicians, in the Protection of Prisoners and Detainees against Torture and Other Cruel, Inhuman or Degrading Treatment or Punishment**, which it had invited WHO to prepare. The World Health Assembly has adopted various regulations designed to prevent the international spread of disease and several resolutions on subjects related to the realization of rights provided in the **International Covenants on Human Rights**, such as nutrition, family health and medical research.

For more information see: http://www.who.int/en/

World Heritage Committee (UNESCO)

The Intergovernmental Committee for the Protection of the World Cultural and Natural Heritage of Outstanding Universal Value commonly called the World Heritage Committee, was established pursuant to Article 8 of the **Convention concerning the Protection of the World Cultural and Natural Heritage** of 1972. The Committee comprises 21 States Parties elected for a term of six years by the **UNESCO** General Conference. It meets annually and is responsible for the implementation of the Convention. It determines the inclusion of sites on the **World Heritage List and List of World Heritage in Danger.** The Committee defines the criteria on the basis of which a property belonging to the cultural or natural heritage may be included in either list. Furthermore the Convention states that "The World Heritage Committee shall receive and study requests for international assistance formulated by States Parties to the Convention …" (Article 13).

For more information see:
http://whc.unesco.org/ab_comm.htm

World Heritage List and List of World Heritage in Danger (UNESCO)

The World Heritage List is compiled by the **World Heritage Committee** of **UNESCO**, pursuant to the **Convention concerning the Protection of the World Cultural and Natural Heritage,** which was adopted by the General Conference of UNESCO in 1972. By July 2003, the Committee had inscribed on the World Heritage List 754 properties (582 cultural, 149 natural and 23 mixed properties in 128 States Parties). Furthermore, 35 properties have been inscribed on the List of the World Heritage in Danger.

For more information see:
http://whc.unesco.org/heritage.htm

World Intellectual Property Organization – WIPO (UN)

The Convention Establishing the World Intellectual Property Organization was signed in Stockholm on 14 July 1967 and entered into force in April 1970. In December 1974, the World Intellectual Property Organization (WIPO) became a **United Nations specialized agency.** By the middle of 2003, 179 States were members of the Organization.

The origins of WIPO go back to the adoption of the **Paris Convention for the Protection of Industrial Property** in 1883, which entered into force in 1884 and was the first major international treaty aiming to provide citizens of one country with protection in other countries for their intellectual creations in the form of industrial property rights. By the middle of 2003, 164 States had ratified the Paris Convention. In 1886, the **Berne Convention for the Protection of Literary and Artistic Works** was adopted to guarantee international protection of the rights of authors in their literary and artistic works. By the middle of 2003, it had been ratified by about 150 States. Both the 1883 Paris Convention and the 1886 Berne Convention created an international bureau to deal with administrative tasks. In 1893, these two bureaux united to form an international organization called the United International Bureaux for the Protection of Intellectual Property, best known by its French name *Bureaux internationaux réunis pour la protection de la propriété intellectuelle* (BIRPI). In 1967, WIPO succeeded BIRPI with the same headquarters in Geneva and with a larger structure.

The overall objective of WIPO is to promote the protection of intellectual property throughout the world through cooperation among States and, where appropriate, in collaboration with other international organizations. WIPO monitors several international treaties dealing with the legal and administrative aspects of intellectual property, harmonizes and simplifies relevant rules and practices, and provides governments, organizations and the private sector with legal and technical assistance. The 1967 Convention defines the term "intellectual property" as including the rights concerning "literary, artistic and scientific works; performances of performing artists, phonograms, and broadcasts; inventions in all fields of human endeavour; scientific discoveries; industrial designs; trademarks, service marks, and commercial names and designations; protection against unfair competition; and all other rights resulting from intellectual activity in the industrial, scientific, literary or artistic fields".

WIPO is governed by a General Assembly and a Conference, each composed of all its Member States; a Co-ordination Committee, and a secretariat called the International Bureau headed by the

Director-General. It also comprises an Arbitration and Mediation Center set up in 1994 to resolve commercial disputes between private parties concerning intellectual property.

World Mental Health Day – 10 October (WHO)

World Mental Health Day was first proclaimed by the World Federation for Mental Health in 1992 and is co-sponsored by the **World Health Organization (WHO)**. WHO requests Member States to promote mental health and healthy behaviour using the commemoration of the World Mental Health Day. In 2003, the theme "The Effects of Trauma and Violence on Children" was selected for the Day.

World Plan of Action for the Implementation of the Objectives of the International Women's Year (UN)

Like the **Declaration of Mexico on the Equality of Women and Their Contribution to Development and Peace**, the World Plan of Action for the Implementation of the Objectives of the **International Women's Year** was adopted by the **World Conference of the International Women's Year**, held in Mexico City, from 19 June to 2 July 1975. The objectives of the World Plan of Action were: to reinforce the implementation of the instruments and programmes which have been adopted concerning the status of women, and to broaden and place them in a more timely context; to encourage national and international action to solve the problems of under-development and the socio-economic structure which place women in an inferior position, in order to achieve the aims of the **International Women's Year**. With a view to promote equality between women and men the Plan recommended that Governments ensure both women and men: equality before the law; equality of educational training and opportunities; equality in conditions of employment, including remuneration; and adequate social security. Moreover, the Plan provided specific guidelines for national action and made recommendations for international and regional action. In brief, the Plan was drawn up with a view to integrating fully women into an international community based on equality and reflecting the many-sided contribution that women can make. The World Plan of Action was later endorsed by the **United Nations General Assembly** (resolution 3520 (XXX) of 15 December 1975) which proclaimed the period 1976-1985 the **United Nations Decade for Women: Equality, Development and Peace.**

World Plan of Action on Education for Human Rights and Democracy (UNESCO/UN)

The World Plan of Action on Education for Human Rights and Democracy was adopted by the **International Congress on Education for Human Rights and Democracy** (Montreal, Canada, 1993), organized by **UNESCO** in cooperation with the **United Nations Centre of Human Rights** (now the **Office of the United Nations High Commissioner for Human Rights**) and the Canadian Commission for UNESCO. The objectives of the Montreal Congress were: to highlight the achievements and identify the obstacles to be overcome in the field of **human rights education**; to introduce education for democracy as a complementary aspect; and to encourage the elaboration of tools and ideas, in particular educational methods, pedagogic approaches and didactic materials, so as to give a new impetus to education for human rights and democracy.

The World Plan is addressed to various social actors: individuals, families, States, **non-governmental organizations**, and the **United Nations system**. It proposed major strategies for concerted action to promote education for human rights and democracy. UNESCO was called for the development and distribution of a standard form for planning, implementing and assessing the Plan, the strengthening of UNESCO's Voluntary Fund for the Development of Knowledge of Human Rights through Education and Information, and the establishment of a follow-up committee (the UNESCO Advisory Committee on Education for Peace, Human Rights, International Understanding and Tolerance was established in 1994 and held five sessions). The World Plan's ultimate purpose is to create a culture of human rights. Its main lines of action include the identification of the most appropriate target groups, the design of the cost-effective and sustainable education programmes and a global commitment to increase resources to make education for human rights and democracy effective and comprehensive worldwide.

In order to ensure a broad and comprehensive implementation of the World Plan, the following activities are foreseen: the inclusion of human rights and democracy in the curricula of all levels of the school system and the promotion of education for human rights and democracy in a non-formal setting. The World Plan underlined that UNESCO bears special responsibility for enhancing the quality of publications in the area of human rights education and for the best use and distribution of information, documentation and materials. The World Plan acknowledged that education for human rights is itself a human right.

The World Plan was noted by the **World Conference on Human Rights** (Vienna, Austria, 1993). With reference to the World Plan, the **Vienna Declaration and Programme of Action** recommended that "… States develop specific programmes and strategies for ensuring the widest human rights education and the dissemination of public information, taking particular account of the human rights of women" (Part II, para. 81).

World Population Day – 11 July (UN)

In 1989, the **United Nations Development Programme (UNDP)** recommended that 11 July be observed as World Population Day. The Day seeks to focus attention on the urgency and importance of population issues, particularly in the context of overall development plans and programmes, and the need to find solutions for these issues. In 2003, the world population was estimated at over 6 billion.

World Press Freedom Day – 3 May (UNESCO)

On 20 December 1993, the **United Nations General Assembly** declared 3 May as World Press Freedom Day. The initiative of proclaiming the Day stemmed from the General Conference of **UNESCO**, which had adopted, on 6 November 1991, the resolution "Promotion of press freedom in the world" in which it recognized that a free, pluralistic and independent press was an essential component of any democratic society. The date had been chosen to commemorate the adoption by the Seminar on Promoting an Independent and Pluralistic African Press, in Windhoek, Namibia, on 3 May 1991 of the **Declaration of Windhoek on Promoting an Independent and Pluralistic African Press**. This Day is also the occasion for the awarding of the **World Press Freedom Prize**.

World Press Freedom Prize (UNESCO)

The **Guillermo Cano World Press Freedom Prize**, was first awarded by **UNESCO** in 1997. It honours each year a person, organization or institution that has made an outstanding contribution to the defence and/or promotion of the freedom of the press anywhere in the world, especially if this involved risk or punishment. It is formally conferred by the Director-General of UNESCO on the occasion of **World Press Freedom Day – 3 May**.

This Prize was instituted in 1997 and is named after Guillermo Cano Isaza, a Colombian journalist who was assassinated by the drug cartels in 1986.

World Programme of Action concerning Disabled Persons (UN)

The World Programme of Action concerning Disabled Persons was adopted by the **United Nations General Assembly** in its resolution 37/52 of 3 December 1982 as a principal outcome of the **International Year of Disabled Persons** (1981). The World Programme of Action is a global strategy to strengthen disability prevention and rehabilitation of disabled persons and to promote their rights to the same opportunities as other citizens and to equal share in the improvements in living conditions resulting from economic and social development. The ultimate goal is to ensure the full participation of disabled persons in all aspects of social and economic life of their countries.

Having defined principles and concepts relating to disabilities, the Programme stresses the necessity to treat disability issues from a human rights perspective and provides recommendations for action at the national, regional and international levels in the fields of disability prevention, rehabilitation of disabled persons and equalization of opportunities for them. It therefore calls for technical and economic cooperation among countries, all relevant **non-governmental organizations**, organizations of disabled persons, and all organs of the **United Nations system**.

The World Programme of Action provided a strong impetus for progress concerning the rights of persons with disabilities. On 3 December 1982, the **United Nations** General Assembly adopted resolution 37/53 on the implementation of the World Programme of Action concerning Disabled Persons, in which, *inter alia*, it proclaimed the period 1983-1992 the **United Nations Decade of Disabled Persons**. On 20 December 1993, the General Assembly adopted resolution 48/96 regarding the **Standard Rules on the Equalization of Opportunities for Persons with Disabilities** which are essentially built on the concepts enshrined in the World Programme of Action concerning

Disabled Persons and which aim at improving the opportunities for full participation and equality for people with disabilities.

World Public Information Campaign for Human Rights (UN)

The World Public Information Campaign for Human Rights was launched by the **United Nations General Assembly** (resolution 43/128 of 8 December 1988). The Campaign, which started on 10 December 1988, is aimed at increasing understanding and awareness on human rights and on the international machinery to promote and protect them. Through education and information, the Campaign should foster the development of a universal culture of human rights. The activities within it include: the preparation and dissemination of printed and audio-visual information and reference materials; organization of training courses; and the observance of special human rights events and promotional activities. Among the main targets of the Campaign are governments, **non-governmental organizations**, the mass media, education and research communities, national and regional human rights institutions and interested individuals. The **World Conference on Human Rights** (Vienna, Austria, 1993) confirmed the importance of public information and related activities for promoting respect for human rights. Public information is also an important means to ensure the implementation of human rights and to affirm the principles of non-**discrimination**, equality of opportunities, universality and indivisibility of human rights which have been repeatedly underlined in recent General Assembly resolutions.

World Refugee Day – 20 June (UN)

On 4 December 2000 the **United Nations General Assembly** (A/RES/55/76) decided that as from 2001, 20 June would be celebrated as World Refugee Day. The year 2001 marked the 50th anniversary of the **Convention Relating to the**

Status of Refugees (1951). Africa Refugee Day is also observed on 20 June.

World Social Forum

Developed in response to the growing international movement against neo-liberal economic policies and the negative impact of **globalization**, the World Social Forum is not a group or organization, but a permanent world process guided by a Charter of Principles. According to Principle 1 of the Charter, the World Social Forum is "an open meeting place for reflective thinking, democratic debate of ideas, formulation of proposals, free-exchange of experiences and interlinking for effective action, by groups and movements of civil society that are opposed to neo-liberalism and to domination of the world by capital and any form of imperialism, and are committed to building a planetary society directed towards fruitful relationships among Mankind and between it and the Earth".

Three Forums have taken place, all in Porto Alegre, Brazil. The first was held in January 2001 and was attended by over 20,000 participants (of whom 4,702 were registered delegates), representing over 500 national and international organizations from more than 100 countries. The success of the event and the enthusiasm it generated led to the decision to make the World Social Forum an annual event. Held in January 2002, the second Forum was even larger and saw the participation of over 50,000 participants, including 15,000 registered delegates, from 123 countries. Debates were organized around four major themes: production of wealth; access to wealth; affirmation of civil society and the public arena; and political and ethical power. The most recent, and the largest and most diverse World Social Forum was held on 23-28 January 2003. Attendance reached 100,000 – double that of the previous year. Nearly 30,000 delegates representing 4,962 organizations from 121 countries were present. During the 6 day event there were 37 panels, 10 conferences, 4 roundtables and 1,700 workshops and seminars. The 5 areas of focus during the Forum were: democratic and sustainable development; principles and values, human rights and diversity and equality; media, culture and counter hegemony; political power, civil society and democracy; democratic world order, fight against militarism and promoting peace.

In efforts to encourage and facilitate the participation of Asian and African entities and organizations, whose access to the meetings in Porto Alegre has been difficult due to financial reasons and geographical distance, it was decided to hold the fourth World Social Forum in 2004 in India.

World Summit for Children (UN)

The World Summit for Children was held at the **United Nations** Headquarters in New York in September 1990 and was attended by more than 70 Heads of State or Government and representatives of 152 countries.

The Summit adopted the **World Declaration on the Survival, Protection and Development of Children** as well as a Plan of Action in the context of each country. It is intended as a guide for national governments, international organizations, bilateral aid agencies, **non-governmental organizations**, and all other actors of civil society in formulating their own programmes to ensure the implementation of the Declaration. Its major goals were: reduction of infant and child mortality; reduction of maternal mortality; reduction of severe and moderate malnutrition among children under five years old; universal access to safe drinking water and to sanitary means of excreta disposal; and universal access to basic education and completion of primary education.

From 8 to 10 May 2002, more than 7,000 people participated in the Special Session of the **United Nations General Assembly** on Children. It was convened to review progress made since the World Summit for Children in 1990 and to re-energize global commitment to children's rights. The Special Session culminated in the adoption of the Declaration and Plan of Action,

"A World Fit for Children", setting 21 specific goals and four key priorities: promoting healthy lives; providing quality education for all; protecting children against abuse, exploitation and violence; and combating HIV/AIDS (A/RES/S-27/2). As the world's leading agency for children, **UNICEF**, was requested to prepare and disseminate information on the progress made in the implementation of the Declaration and the Plan of Action.

For more information see: http://www.unicef.org/wsc

World Summit for Social Development (UN)

The World Summit for Social Development was held in Copenhagen, Denmark, from 6 to 12 March 1995, with the participation of many Heads of State or Government. It adopted the **Copenhagen Declaration on Social Development and Programme of Action**. The World Summit elaborated a major international agreement with a view to concentrating the efforts of the international community on meeting three global challenges: eradicating **poverty**; creating jobs; and enhancing social integration. The agreement produced a consensus on development objectives, which should be people-oriented, promote well-being for all, recognize the central role of women, and empower civil society. The Programme of Action outlines policies and measures to fulfil the commitments enunciated in the Declaration, including: the creation of an environment favourable for social development; elimination of poverty; expansion of productive employment and reduction of unemployment; and building solidarity. Subsequently the **United Nations General Assembly** endorsed both documents in its resolution 50/161 of 22 December 1995.

Five years later, the General Assembly convened a Special Session in Geneva (26 June–1 July 2000) to reconfirm the commitments made in Copenhagen, to assess the achievements since the World Summit, and to agree on further initiatives for social development. The "Copenhagen + 5" session discussed a large number of issues, including health and AIDS problems,

globalization, corporate social responsibility, new resources for social development, poverty, decent conditions of work, etc.

World Summit on Sustainable Development – WSSD (UN)

The **United Nations** World Summit on Sustainable Development, also known as the Johannesburg Summit, was held in Johannesburg, South Africa, from 26 August to 4 September 2002. Ten years after the United Nations Conference on Environment and Development (UNCED) held in Rio de Janeiro, Brazil, from 3 to 14 June 1992, the Johannesburg Summit brought together tens of thousands of participants including Heads of State and Government, national delegates, representatives of **non-governmental organizations**, business and industry, children and **youth**, **indigenous people**, local authorities, women and union workers.

The Summit addressed such issues as **poverty** eradication, unsustainable patterns of consumption and production, the natural resource base of economic and social development, increasing challenges posed by **globalization**, objectives and frameworks of sustainable development and the role of the United Nations.

Two important documents were produced at the Summit: the Plan of Implementation and the Johannesburg Declaration on Sustainable Development, both reaffirming commitment to the Rio Declaration on Environment and Development and the Plan of Action "Agenda 21", adopted in 1992. The Plan of Implementation confirms commitment to achieving internationally agreed development goals including those contained in the **United Nations Millennium Declaration** and in the outcomes of the major United Nations conferences and international agreements since 1992 (Paragraph 1). Furthermore it calls for States to ensure good governance and insists that respect for human rights and fundamental freedoms, including the **right to development**, is essential for achieving sustainable development and ensuring that sustainable development benefits all (Paragraphs 4-5). The Declaration on Sustainable Development recognizes the need to produce a "practical and visible plan that should bring about poverty eradication and human development" (Preamble). It addresses issues of women's empowerment, poverty eradication and the role of indigenous peoples in sustainable development.

World Teachers' Day – 5 October (UNESCO)

In 1994, the General Conference of **UNESCO**, at its 25th session, proclaimed 5 October World Teachers' Day in order to mark the day of the adoption of the joint **International Labour Organization (ILO)/UNESCO Recommendation concerning the Status of Teachers** in 1966. The Day pays tribute to the role of teachers in promoting education in its most basic dimensions and encourages the enhancement of their status and their work conditions, in accordance with the guidelines provided by the 1966 Recommendation and, subsequently, the **Recommendation concerning the Status of Higher-Education Teaching Personnel** adopted by UNESCO in 1997. The theme of World Teachers' Day in 2002 was "Teachers Create Dialogue Every Day", to highlight the key role of teachers as promoters of dialogue, understanding, mutual respect and solidarity, which constitute the basic values of democratic societies. In their joint message on the occasion of the Day in 2002, the Director-General of **UNESCO** and the Director-General of the **ILO**, the Administrator of the **United Nations Development Programme (UNDP)** and the Executive Director of **UNICEF** stressed that "teachers are central to any process that aims to raise educational levels, promote learning to live together in peace and eliminate **discrimination**". Furthermore, taking into account the alarming shortage of teachers, Governments were urged to ensure for them good physical, moral, and remunerative conditions to work and live.

Youth

The **United Nations General Assembly** defined 'youth' as those persons falling between the ages of 15 and 24 years inclusive. It has approved numerous decisions and activities concerning youth. On 7 December 1965, it adopted the **Declaration on the Promotion among Youth of the Ideals of Peace, Mutual Respect and the Understanding between Peoples**, which highlights the importance of the role of youth in today's world.

Two decades later, the General Assembly proclaimed the year 1985 as **International Youth Year: Participation, Development, Peace**, to increase the involvement of young people in the overall development of society. The General Assembly provided guidelines for further action and appropriate follow-up, with particular emphasis on youth work. The **United Nations** has subsequently supported Governments' activities concerning youth and has enhanced cooperation with youth organizations.

In 1995, on the 10th anniversary of the Year, the United Nations adopted the World Programme of Action for Youth to the Year 2000 and Beyond, which aimed at increasing awareness of youth-related issues and promoting youth rights. The Programme formulates guidelines for national and international action to improve opportunities for the participation of youth in society. In particular, it envisaged the convening of World Conferences of Ministers Responsible for Youth and of youth **non-governmental organizations**. Accordingly, in 1998, the first World Conference was convened in Lisbon by Portugal, in cooperation with the United Nations. On this occasion, the Lisbon Declaration on Youth was adopted to promote actions at national and international levels in the field of youth. Concerning the World

Youth Forum of the **United Nations system**, the third session of the Forum was organized in partnership with the Portuguese National Youth Committee in Braga, Portugal, in August 1998. The Forum adopted the Braga Youth Action Plan which formulates recommendations to empower young people to participate in human development and to improve opportunities available to young people. The Forum brought together representatives of youth organizations, and representatives of the United Nations system and other intergovernmental organizations, to discuss enhanced cooperation. In August 2001, the fourth session of the World Youth Forum of the United Nations system was held in Senegal. At this Forum, the Dakar Youth Empowerment Strategy was adopted, which was designed to strengthen the implementation of the Braga Youth Action Plan. The main points of concern are: education, employment, hunger and **poverty**, health, environment, drug abuse, juvenile delinquency, leisure-time activities, girls and young women, and full and effective participation of youth in the life of society and in decision-making. Every year, **International Youth Day** is celebrated on 12 August.

Annexes

I UNIVERSAL DECLARATION OF HUMAN RIGHTS*

Adopted and proclaimed by the United Nations General Assembly resolution 217 A (III) of 10 December 1948.

Preamble

Whereas recognition of the inherent dignity and of the equal and inalienable rights of all members of the human family is the foundation of freedom, justice and peace in the world,

Whereas disregard and contempt for human rights have resulted in barbarous acts which have outraged the conscience of mankind, and the advent of a world in which human beings shall enjoy freedom of speech and belief and freedom from fear and want has been proclaimed as the highest aspiration of the common people,

Whereas it is essential, if man is not to be compelled to have recourse, as a last resort, to rebellion against tyranny and oppression, that human rights should be protected by the rule of law,

Whereas it is essential to promote the development of friendly relations between nations,

Whereas the people of the United Nations have in the Charter reaffirmed their faith in fundamental human rights, in the dignity and worth of the human person and in the equal rights of men and women and have determined to promote social progress and better standards of life in larger freedom,

---

* The text of this instrument has been downloaded from the relevant United Nations web-site.

Whereas Member States have pledged themselves to achieve, in co-operation with the United Nations, the promotion of universal respect for and observance of human rights and fundamental freedoms,

Whereas a common understanding of these rights and freedoms is of the greatest importance for the full realization of this pledge,

Now, therefore,
The General Assembly,

Proclaims this Universal Declaration of Human Rights as a common standard of achievement for all peoples and all nations, to the end that every individual and every organ of society, keeping this Declaration constantly in mind, shall strive by teaching and education to promote respect for these rights and freedoms and by progressive measures, national and international, to secure their universal and effective recognition and observance, both among the peoples of Member States themselves and among the peoples of territories under their jurisdiction.

Article 1

All human beings are born free and equal in dignity and rights. They are endowed with reason and conscience and should act towards one another in a spirit of brotherhood.

Article 2

Everyone is entitled to all the rights and freedoms set forth in this Declaration, without distinction of any kind, such as race, colour, sex, language, religion, political or other opinion, national or social origin, property, birth or other status.

Furthermore, no distinction shall be made on the basis of the political, jurisdictional or international status of the country or territory to which a person belongs, whether it be independent, trust, non-self-governing or under any other limitation of sovereignty.

Article 3

Everyone has the right to life, liberty and security of person.

Article 4

No one shall be held in slavery or servitude; slavery and the slave trade shall be prohibited in all their forms.

Article 5

No one shall be subjected to torture or to cruel, inhuman or degrading treatment or punishment.

Article 6

Everyone has the right to recognition everywhere as a person before the law.

Article 7

All are equal before the law and are entitled without any discrimination to equal protection of the law. All are entitled to equal protection against any discrimination in violation of this Declaration and against any incitement to such discrimination.

Article 8

Everyone has the right to an effective remedy by the competent national tribunals for acts violating the fundamental rights granted him by the constitution or by law.

Article 9

No one shall be subjected to arbitrary arrest, detention or exile.

Article 10

Everyone is entitled in full equality to a fair and public hearing by an independent and impartial tribunal, in the determination of his rights and obligations and of any criminal charge against him.

Article 11

1. Everyone charged with a penal offence has the right to be presumed innocent until proved guilty according to law in a

public trial at which he has had all the guarantees necessary for his defence.

2. No one shall be held guilty of any penal offence on account of any act or omission which did not constitute a penal offence, under national or international law, at the time when it was committed. Nor shall a heavier penalty be imposed than the one that was applicable at the time the penal offence was committed.

Article 12

No one shall be subjected to arbitrary interference with his privacy, family, home or correspondence, nor to attacks upon his honour and reputation. Everyone has the right to the protection of the law against such interference or attacks.

Article 13

1. Everyone has the right to freedom of movement and residence within the borders of each State.
2. Everyone has the right to leave any country, including his own, and to return to his country.

Article 14

1. Everyone has the right to seek and to enjoy in other countries asylum from persecution.
2. This right may not be invoked in the case of prosecutions genuinely arising from non-political crimes or from acts contrary to the purposes and principles of the United Nations.

Article 15

1. Everyone has the right to a nationality.
2. No one shall be arbitrarily deprived of his nationality nor denied the right to change his nationality.

Article 16

1. Men and women of full age, without any limitation due to race, nationality or religion, have the right to marry and to found a

family. They are entitled to equal rights as to marriage, during marriage and at its dissolution.
2. Marriage shall be entered into only with the free and full consent of the intending spouses.
3. The family is the natural and fundamental group unit of society and is entitled to protection by society and the State.

Article 17

1. Everyone has the right to own property alone as well as in association with others.
2. No one shall be arbitrarily deprived of his property.

Article 18

Everyone has the right to freedom of thought, conscience and religion; this right includes freedom to change his religion or belief, and freedom, either alone or in community with others and in public or private, to manifest his religion or belief in teaching, practice, worship and observance.

Article 19

Everyone has the right to freedom of opinion and expression; this right includes freedom to hold opinions without interference and to seek, receive and impart information and ideas through any media and regardless of frontiers.

Article 20

1. Everyone has the right to freedom of peaceful assembly and association.
2. No one may be compelled to belong to an association.

Article 21

1. Everyone has the right to take part in the government of his country, directly or through freely chosen representatives.
2. Everyone has the right to equal access to public service in his country.
3. The will of the people shall be the basis of the authority of government; this will shall be expressed in periodic and

genuine elections which shall be by universal and equal suffrage and shall be held by secret vote or by equivalent free voting procedures.

Article 22

Everyone, as a member of society, has the right to social security and is entitled to realization, through national effort and international co-operation and in accordance with the organization and resources of each State, of the economic, social and cultural rights indispensable for his dignity and the free development of his personality.

Article 23

1. Everyone has the right to work, to free choice of employment, to just and favourable conditions of work and to protection against unemployment.
2. Everyone, without any discrimination, has the right to equal pay for equal work.
3. Everyone who works has the right to just and favourable remuneration ensuring for himself and his family an existence worthy of human dignity, and supplemented, if necessary, by other means of social protection.
4. Everyone has the right to form and to join trade unions for the protection of his interests.

Article 24

Everyone has the right to rest and leisure, including reasonable limitation of working hours and periodic holidays with pay.

Article 25

1. Everyone has the right to a standard of living adequate for the health and well-being of himself and of his family, including food, clothing, housing and medical care and necessary social services, and the right to security in the event of unemployment, sickness, disability, widowhood, old age or other lack of livelihood in circumstances beyond his control.

2. Motherhood and childhood are entitled to special care and assistance. All children, whether born in or out of wedlock, shall enjoy the same social protection.

Article 26

1. Everyone has the right to education. Education shall be free, at least in the elementary and fundamental stages. Elementary education shall be compulsory. Technical and professional education shall be made generally available and higher education shall be equally accessible to all on the basis of merit.
2. Education shall be directed to the full development of the human personality and to the strengthening of respect for human rights and fundamental freedoms. It shall promote understanding, tolerance and friendship among all nations, racial or religious groups, and shall further the activities of the United Nations for the maintenance of peace.
3. Parents have a prior right to choose the kind of education that shall be given to their children.

Article 27

1. Everyone has the right freely to participate in the cultural life of the community, to enjoy the arts and to share in scientific advancement and its benefits.
2. Everyone has the right to the protection of the moral and material interests resulting from any scientific, literary or artistic production of which he is the author.

Article 28

Everyone is entitled to a social and international order in which the rights and freedoms set forth in the Declaration can be fully realized.

Article 29

1. Everyone has duties to the community in which alone the free and full development of his personality is possible.
2. In the exercise of his rights and freedoms, everyone shall be subject only to such limitations as are determined by law solely

for the purpose of securing due recognition and respect for the rights and freedoms of others and of meeting the just requirements of morality, public order and the general welfare in a democratic society.

3. These rights and freedoms may in no case be exercised contrary to the purposes and principles of the United Nations.

Article 30

Nothing in this Declaration may be interpreted as implying for any State, group or person any right to engage in any activity or to perform any act aimed at the destruction of any of the rights and freedoms set forth herein.

II INTERNATIONAL COVENANT ON ECONOMIC, SOCIAL AND CULTURAL RIGHTS*

Adopted and opened for signature, ratification and accession by General Assembly resolution 2200A (XXI) of 16 December 1966.
Entered into force on 3 January 1976.

Preamble

The States Parties to the present Covenant,

Considering that, in accordance with the principles proclaimed in the Charter of the United Nations, recognition of the inherent dignity and of the equal and inalienable rights of all members of the human family is the foundation of freedom, justice and peace in the world,

Recognizing that these rights derive from the inherent dignity of the human person,

Recognizing that, in accordance with the Universal Declaration of Human Rights, the ideal of free human beings enjoying freedom from fear and want can only be achieved if conditions are created whereby everyone may enjoy his economic, social and cultural rights, as well as his civil and political rights,

Considering the obligation of States under the Charter of the United Nations to promote universal respect for, and observance of human rights and freedoms,

---

* The text of this instrument has been downloaded from the relevant United Nations web-site.

Realizing that the individual, having duties to other individuals and to the community to which he belongs, is under a responsibility to strive for the promotion and observance of the rights recognized in the present Covenant,

Agree upon the following articles:

PART I

Article 1

1. All peoples have the right of self-determination. By virtue of that right they freely determine their political status and freely pursue their economic, social and cultural development.
2. All peoples may, for their own ends, freely dispose of their natural wealth and resources without prejudice to any obligations arising out of international economic co-operation, based upon the principle of mutual benefit, and international law. In no case may a people be deprived of its own means of subsistence.
3. The States Parties to the present Covenant, including those having responsibility for the administration of Non-Self-Governing and Trust Territories, shall promote the realization of the right of self-determination, and shall respect that right, in conformity with the provisions of the Charter of the United Nations.

PART II

Article 2

1. Each State Party to the present Covenant undertakes to take steps, individually and through international assistance and co-operation, especially economic and technical, to the maximum of its available resources, with a view to achieving progressively the full realization of the rights recognized in the

present Covenant by all appropriate means, including particularly the adoption of legislative measures.

2. The States Parties to the present Covenant undertake to guarantee that the rights enunciated in the present Covenant will be exercised without discrimination of any kind as to race, colour, sex, language, religion, political or other opinion, national or social origin, property, birth or other status.

3. Developing countries, with due regard to human rights and their national economy, may determine to what extent they would guarantee the economic rights recognized in the present Covenant to non-nationals.

Article 3

The States Parties to the present Covenant undertake to ensure the equal right of men and women to the enjoyment of all economic, social and cultural rights set forth in the present Covenant.

Article 4

The States Parties to the present Covenant recognize that, in the enjoyment of those rights provided by the State in conformity with the present Covenant, the State may subject such rights only to such limitations as are determined by law only in so far as this may be compatible with the nature of these rights and solely for the purpose of promoting the general welfare in a democratic society.

Article 5

1. Nothing in the present Covenant may be interpreted as implying for any State, group or person any right to engage in any activity or to perform any act aimed at the destruction of any of the rights or freedoms recognized herein, or at their limitation to a greater extent than is provided for in the present Covenant.

2. No restriction upon or derogation from any of the fundamental human rights recognized or existing in any country in virtue of law, conventions, regulations or custom shall be admitted on

the pretext that the present Covenant does not recognize such rights or that it recognizes them to a lesser extent.

PART III

Article 6

1. The States Parties to the present Covenant recognize the right to work, which includes the right of everyone to the opportunity to gain his living by work which he freely chooses or accepts, and will take appropriate steps to safeguard this right.
2. The steps to be taken by a State Party to the present Covenant to achieve the full realization of this right shall include technical and vocational guidance and training programmes, policies and techniques to achieve steady economic, social and cultural development and full and productive employment under conditions safeguarding fundamental political and economic freedoms to the individual.

Article 7

The States Parties to the present Covenant recognize the right of everyone to the enjoyment of just and favourable conditions of work which ensure, in particular:

   (a) Remuneration which provides all workers, as a minimum, with:

   (i) Fair wages and equal remuneration for work of equal value without distinction of any kind, in particular women being guaranteed conditions of work not inferior to those enjoyed by men, with equal pay for equal work;

   (ii) A decent living for themselves and their families in accordance with the provisions of the present Covenant;

   (b) Safe and healthy working conditions;

(c) Equal opportunity for everyone to be promoted in his employment to an appropriate higher level, subject to no considerations other than those of seniority and competence;

(d) Rest, leisure and reasonable limitation of working hours and periodic holidays with pay, as well as remuneration for public holidays.

Article 8

1. The States Parties to the present Covenant undertake to ensure:

    (a) The right of everyone to form trade unions and join the trade union of his choice, subject only to the rules of the organization concerned, for the promotion and protection of his economic and social interests. No restrictions may be placed on the exercise of this right other than those prescribed by law and which are necessary in a democratic society in the interests of national security or public order or for the protection of the rights and freedoms of others;

    (b) The right of trade unions to establish national federations or confederations and the right of the latter to form or join international trade-union organizations;

    (c) The right of trade unions to function freely subject to no limitations other than those prescribed by law and which are necessary in a democratic society in the interests of national security or public order or for the protection of the rights and freedoms of others;

    (d) The right to strike, provided that it is exercised in conformity with the laws of the particular country.

2. This article shall not prevent the imposition of lawful restrictions on the exercise of these rights by members of the armed forces or of the police or of the administration of the State.

3. Nothing in this article shall authorize States Parties to the International Labour Organisation Convention of 1948 concerning Freedom of Association and Protection of the Right

to Organize to take legislative measures which would prejudice, or apply the law in such a manner as would prejudice, the guarantees provided for in that Convention.

Article 9

The States Parties to the present Covenant recognize the right of everyone to social security, including social insurance.

Article 10

The States Parties to the present Covenant recognize that:
1. The widest possible protection and assistance should be accorded to the family, which is the natural and fundamental group unit of society, particularly for its establishment and while it is responsible for the care and education of dependent children. Marriage must be entered into with the free consent of the intending spouses.
2. Special protection should be accorded to mothers during a reasonable period before and after childbirth. During such period working mothers should be accorded paid leave or leave with adequate social security benefits.
3. Special measures of protection and assistance should be taken on behalf of all children and young persons without any discrimination for reasons of parentage or other conditions. Children and young persons should be protected from economic and social exploitation. Their employment in work harmful to their morals or health or dangerous to life or likely to hamper their normal development should be punishable by law. States should also set age limits below which the paid employment of child labour should be prohibited and punishable by law.

Article 11

The States Parties to the present Covenant recognize the right of everyone to an adequate standard of living for himself and his family, including adequate food, clothing and housing, and to the continuous improvement of living conditions. The States Parties will take appropriate steps to ensure the realization of this right, recognizing to this effect the essential importance of international co-operation based on free consent.

The States Parties to the present Covenant, recognizing the fundamental right of everyone to be free from hunger, shall take, individually and through international co-operation, the measures, including specific programmes, which are needed:

(a) To improve methods of production, conservation and distribution of food by making full use of technical and scientific knowledge, by disseminating knowledge of the principles of nutrition and by developing or reforming agrarian systems in such a way as to achieve the most efficient development and utilization of natural resources;

(b) Taking into account the problems of both food-importing and food-exporting countries, to ensure an equitable distribution of world food supplies in relation to need.

Article 12

1. The States Parties to the present Covenant recognize the right of everyone to the enjoyment of the highest attainable standard of physical and mental health.

2. The steps to be taken by the States Parties to the present Covenant to achieve the full realization of this right shall include those necessary for:

   (a) The provision for the reduction of the stillbirth-rate and of infant mortality and for the healthy development of the child;

   (b) The improvement of all aspects of environmental and industrial hygiene;

   (c) The prevention, treatment and control of epidemic, endemic, occupational and other diseases;

   (d) The creation of conditions which would assure to all medical service and medical attention in the event of sickness.

Article 13

1. The States Parties to the present Covenant recognize the right of everyone to education. They agree that education shall be directed to the full development of the human personality and the sense of its dignity, and shall strengthen the respect for human rights and fundamental freedoms. They further agree that education shall enable all persons to participate effectively in a free society, promote understanding, tolerance and friendship among all nations and all racial, ethnic or religious groups, and further the activities of the United Nations for the maintenance of peace.
2. The States Parties to the present Covenant recognize that, with a view to achieving the full realization of this right:
   (a) Primary education shall be compulsory and available free to all;
   (b) Secondary education in its different forms, including technical and vocational secondary education, shall be made generally available and accessible to all by every appropriate means, and in particular by the progressive introduction of free education;
   (c) Higher education shall be made equally accessible to all, on the basis of capacity, by every appropriate means, and in particular by the progressive introduction of free education;
   (d) Fundamental education shall be encouraged or intensified as far as possible for those persons who have not received or completed the whole period of their primary education;
   (e) The development of a system of schools at all levels shall be actively pursued, an adequate fellowship system shall be established, and the material conditions of teaching staff shall be continuously improved.
3. The States Parties to the present Covenant undertake to have respect for the liberty of parents and, when applicable, legal guardians to choose for their children schools, other than those established by the public authorities, which conform to such minimum educational standards as may be laid down or

approved by the State and to ensure the religious and moral education of their children in conformity with their own convictions.

4. No part of this article shall be construed so as to interfere with the liberty of individuals and bodies to establish and direct educational institutions, subject always to the observance of the principles set forth in paragraph I of this article and to the requirement that the education given in such institutions shall conform to such minimum standards as may be laid down by the State.

Article 14

Each State Party to the present Covenant which, at the time of becoming a Party, has not been able to secure in its metropolitan territory or other territories under its jurisdiction compulsory primary education, free of charge, undertakes, within two years, to work out and adopt a detailed plan of action for the progressive implementation, within a reasonable number of years, to be fixed in the plan, of the principle of compulsory education free of charge for all.

Article 15

1. The States Parties to the present Covenant recognize the right of everyone:
    (a) To take part in cultural life;
    (b) To enjoy the benefits of scientific progress and its applications;
    (c) To benefit from the protection of the moral and material interests resulting from any scientific, literary or artistic production of which he is the author.
2. The steps to be taken by the States Parties to the present Covenant to achieve the full realization of this right shall include those necessary for the conservation, the development and the diffusion of science and culture.

3. The States Parties to the present Covenant undertake to respect the freedom indispensable for scientific research and creative activity.
4. The States Parties to the present Covenant recognize the benefits to be derived from the encouragement and development of international contacts and co-operation in the scientific and cultural fields.

PART IV

Article 16

1. The States Parties to the present Covenant undertake to submit in conformity with this part of the Covenant reports on the measures which they have adopted and the progress made in achieving the observance of the rights recognized herein.
2. (a) All reports shall be submitted to the Secretary-General of the United Nations, who shall transmit copies to the Economic and Social Council for consideration in accordance with the provisions of the present Covenant;
   (b) The Secretary-General of the United Nations shall also transmit to the specialized agencies copies of the reports, or any relevant parts therefrom, from States Parties to the present Covenant which are also members of these specialized agencies in so far as these reports, or parts therefrom, relate to any matters which fall within the responsibilities of the said agencies in accordance with their constitutional instruments.

Article 17

1. The States Parties to the present Covenant shall furnish their reports in stages, in accordance with a programme to be established by the Economic and Social Council within one year of the entry into force of the present Covenant after consultation with the States Parties and the specialized agencies concerned.

2. Reports may indicate factors and difficulties affecting the degree of fulfilment of obligations under the present Covenant.
3. Where relevant information has previously been furnished to the United Nations or to any specialized agency by any State Party to the present Covenant, it will not be necessary to reproduce that information, but a precise reference to the information so furnished will suffice.

Article 18

Pursuant to its responsibilities under the Charter of the United Nations in the field of human rights and fundamental freedoms, the Economic and Social Council may make arrangements with the specialized agencies in respect of their reporting to it on the progress made in achieving the observance of the provisions of the present Covenant falling within the scope of their activities. These reports may include particulars of decisions and recommendations on such implementation adopted by their competent organs.

Article 19

The Economic and Social Council may transmit to the Commission on Human Rights for study and general recommendation or, as appropriate, for information the reports concerning human rights submitted by States in accordance with articles 16 and 17, and those concerning human rights submitted by the specialized agencies in accordance with article 18.

Article 20

The States Parties to the present Covenant and the specialized agencies concerned may submit comments to the Economic and Social Council on any general recommendation under article 19 or reference to such general recommendation in any report of the Commission on Human Rights or any documentation referred to therein.

Article 21

The Economic and Social Council may submit from time to time to the General Assembly reports with recommendations of a general nature and a summary of the information received from the States Parties to the present Covenant and the specialized agencies on the measures taken and the progress made in achieving general observance of the rights recognized in the present Covenant.

Article 22

The Economic and Social Council may bring to the attention of other organs of the United Nations, their subsidiary organs and specialized agencies concerned with furnishing technical assistance any matters arising out of the reports referred to in this part of the present Covenant which may assist such bodies in deciding, each within its field of competence, on the advisability of international measures likely to contribute to the effective progressive implementation of the present Covenant.

Article 23

The States Parties to the present Covenant agree that international action for the achievement of the rights recognized in the present Covenant includes such methods as the conclusion of conventions, the adoption of recommendations, the furnishing of technical assistance and the holding of regional meetings and technical meetings for the purpose of consultation and study organized in conjunction with the Governments concerned.

Article 24

Nothing in the present Covenant shall be interpreted as impairing the provisions of the Charter of the United Nations and of the constitutions of the specialized agencies which define the respective responsibilities of the various organs of the United Nations and of the specialized agencies in regard to the matters dealt with in the present Covenant.

Article 25

Nothing in the present Covenant shall be interpreted as impairing the inherent right of all peoples to enjoy and utilize fully and freely their natural wealth and resources.

PART V

Article 26

1. The present Covenant is open for signature by any State Member of the United Nations or member of any of its specialized agencies, by any State Party to the Statute of the International Court of Justice, and by any other State which has been invited by the General Assembly of the United Nations to become a party to the present Covenant.
2. The present Covenant is subject to ratification. Instruments of ratification shall be deposited with the Secretary-General of the United Nations.
3. The present Covenant shall be open to accession by any State referred to in paragraph 1 of this article.
4. Accession shall be effected by the deposit of an instrument of accession with the Secretary-General of the United Nations.
5. The Secretary-General of the United Nations shall inform all States which have signed the present Covenant or acceded to it of the deposit of each instrument of ratification or accession.

Article 27

1. The present Covenant shall enter into force three months after the date of the deposit with the Secretary-General of the United Nations of the thirty-fifth instrument of ratification or instrument of accession.
2. For each State ratifying the present Covenant or acceding to it after the deposit of the thirty-fifth instrument of ratification or instrument of accession, the present Covenant shall enter into force three months after the date of the deposit of its own instrument of ratification or instrument of accession.

Article 28

The provisions of the present Covenant shall extend to all parts of federal States without any limitations or exceptions.

Article 29

1. Any State Party to the present Covenant may propose an amendment and file it with the Secretary-General of the United Nations. The Secretary-General shall thereupon communicate any proposed amendments to the States Parties to the present Covenant with a request that they notify him whether they favour a conference of States Parties for the purpose of considering and voting upon the proposals. In the event that at least one third of the States Parties favours such a conference, the Secretary-General shall convene the conference under the auspices of the United Nations. Any amendment adopted by a majority of the States Parties present and voting at the conference shall be submitted to the General Assembly of the United Nations for approval.
2. Amendments shall come into force when they have been approved by the General Assembly of the United Nations and accepted by a two-thirds majority of the States Parties to the present Covenant in accordance with their respective constitutional processes.
3. When amendments come into force they shall be binding on those States Parties which have accepted them, other States Parties still being bound by the provisions of the present Covenant and any earlier amendment which they have accepted.

Article 30

Irrespective of the notifications made under article 26, paragraph 5, the Secretary-General of the United Nations shall inform all States referred to in paragraph I of the same article of the following particulars:

(a) Signatures, ratifications and accessions under article 26;
(b) The date of the entry into force of the present Covenant under article 27 and the date of the entry into force of any amendments under article 29.

Article 31

1. The present Covenant, of which the Chinese, English, French, Russian and Spanish texts are equally authentic, shall be deposited in the archives of the United Nations.
2. The Secretary-General of the United Nations shall transmit certified copies of the present Covenant to all States referred to in article 26.

III INTERNATIONAL COVENANT ON CIVIL AND POLITICAL RIGHTS*

Adopted by the General Assembly resolution 2200A (XXI) of 16 December 1966. Entered into force 23 March 1976.

Preamble

The States Parties to the present Covenant,

Considering that, in accordance with the principles proclaimed in the Charter of the United Nations, recognition of the inherent dignity and of the equal and inalienable rights of all members of the human family is the foundation of freedom, justice and peace in the world,

Recognizing that these rights derive from the inherent dignity of the human person,

Recognizing that, in accordance with the Universal Declaration of Human Rights, the ideal of free human beings enjoying civil and political freedom and freedom from fear and want can only be achieved if conditions are created whereby everyone may enjoy his civil and political rights, as well as his economic, social and cultural rights,

Considering the obligation of States under the Charter of the United Nations to promote universal respect for, and observance of, human rights and freedoms,

---

* The text of this instrument has been downloaded from the relevant United Nations web-site.

Realizing that the individual, having duties to other individuals and to the community to which he belongs, is under a responsibility to strive for the promotion and observance of the rights recognized in the present Covenant,

Agree upon the following articles:

PART I

Article 1

1. All peoples have the right of self-determination. By virtue of that right they freely determine their political status and freely pursue their economic, social and cultural development.
2. All peoples may, for their own ends, freely dispose of their natural wealth and resources without prejudice to any obligations arising out of international economic co-operation, based upon the principle of mutual benefit, and international law. In no case may a people be deprived of its own means of subsistence.
3. The States Parties to the present Covenant, including those having responsibility for the administration of Non-Self-Governing and Trust Territories, shall promote the realization of the right of self-determination, and shall respect that right, in conformity with the provisions of the Charter of the United Nations.

PART II

Article 2

1. Each State Party to the present Covenant undertakes to respect and to ensure to all individuals within its territory and subject to its jurisdiction the rights recognized in the present Covenant, without distinction of any kind, such as race, colour, sex, language, religion, political or other opinion, national or social origin, property, birth or other status.

2. Where not already provided for by existing legislative or other measures, each State Party to the present Covenant undertakes to take the necessary steps, in accordance with its constitutional processes and with the provisions of the present Covenant, to adopt such laws or other measures as may be necessary to give effect to the rights recognized in the present Covenant.
3. Each State Party to the present Covenant undertakes:
   (a) To ensure that any person whose rights or freedoms as herein recognized are violated shall have an effective remedy, notwithstanding that the violation has been committed by persons acting in an official capacity;
   (b) To ensure that any person claiming such a remedy shall have his right thereto determined by competent judicial, administrative or legislative authorities, or by any other competent authority provided for by the legal system of the State, and to develop the possibilities of judicial remedy;
   (c) To ensure that the competent authorities shall enforce such remedies when granted.

Article 3

The States Parties to the present Covenant undertake to ensure the equal right of men and women to the enjoyment of all civil and political rights set forth in the present Covenant.

Article 4

1. In time of public emergency which threatens the life of the nation and the existence of which is officially proclaimed, the States Parties to the present Covenant may take measures derogating from their obligations under the present Covenant to the extent strictly required by the exigencies of the situation, provided that such measures are not inconsistent with their other obligations under international law and do not involve discrimination solely on the ground of race, colour, sex, language, religion or social origin.
2. No derogation from articles 6, 7, 8 (paragraphs I and 2), 11, 15, 16 and 18 may be made under this provision.

3. Any State Party to the present Covenant availing itself of the right of derogation shall immediately inform the other States Parties to the present Covenant, through the intermediary of the Secretary-General of the United Nations, of the provisions from which it has derogated and of the reasons by which it was actuated. A further communication shall be made, through the same intermediary, on the date on which it terminates such derogation.

Article 5

1. Nothing in the present Covenant may be interpreted as implying for any State, group or person any right to engage in any activity or perform any act aimed at the destruction of any of the rights and freedoms recognized herein or at their limitation to a greater extent than is provided for in the present Covenant.
2. There shall be no restriction upon or derogation from any of the fundamental human rights recognized or existing in any State Party to the present Covenant pursuant to law, conventions, regulations or custom on the pretext that the present Covenant does not recognize such rights or that it recognizes them to a lesser extent.

PART III

Article 6

1. Every human being has the inherent right to life. This right shall be protected by law. No one shall be arbitrarily deprived of his life.
2. In countries which have not abolished the death penalty, sentence of death may be imposed only for the most serious crimes in accordance with the law in force at the time of the commission of the crime and not contrary to the provisions of the present Covenant and to the Convention on the Prevention and Punishment of the Crime of Genocide. This penalty can

only be carried out pursuant to a final judgement rendered by a competent court.

3. When deprivation of life constitutes the crime of genocide, it is understood that nothing in this article shall authorize any State Party to the present Covenant to derogate in any way from any obligation assumed under the provisions of the Convention on the Prevention and Punishment of the Crime of Genocide.
4. Anyone sentenced to death shall have the right to seek pardon or commutation of the sentence. Amnesty, pardon or commutation of the sentence of death may be granted in all cases.
5. Sentence of death shall not be imposed for crimes committed by persons below eighteen years of age and shall not be carried out on pregnant women.
6. Nothing in this article shall be invoked to delay or to prevent the abolition of capital punishment by any State Party to the present Covenant.

Article 7

No one shall be subjected to torture or to cruel, inhuman or degrading treatment or punishment. In particular, no one shall be subjected without his free consent to medical or scientific experimentation.

Article 8

1. No one shall be held in slavery; slavery and the slave-trade in all their forms shall be prohibited.
2. No one shall be held in servitude.
3. (a) No one shall be required to perform forced or compulsory labour;
   (b) Paragraph 3 (a) shall not be held to preclude, in countries where imprisonment with hard labour may be imposed as a punishment for a crime, the performance of hard labour in pursuance of a sentence to such punishment by a competent court;
   (c) For the purpose of this paragraph the term "forced or compulsory labour" shall not include:

(i) Any work or service, not referred to in subparagraph (b), normally required of a person who is under detention in consequence of a lawful order of a court, or of a person during conditional release from such detention;
(ii) Any service of a military character and, in countries where conscientious objection is recognized, any national service required by law of conscientious objectors;
(iii) Any service exacted in cases of emergency or calamity threatening the life or well-being of the community;
(iv) Any work or service which forms part of normal civil obligations.

Article 9

1. Everyone has the right to liberty and security of person. No one shall be subjected to arbitrary arrest or detention. No one shall be deprived of his liberty except on such grounds and in accordance with such procedure as are established by law.
2. Anyone who is arrested shall be informed, at the time of arrest, of the reasons for his arrest and shall be promptly informed of any charges against him.
3. Anyone arrested or detained on a criminal charge shall be brought promptly before a judge or other officer authorized by law to exercise judicial power and shall be entitled to trial within a reasonable time or to release. It shall not be the general rule that persons awaiting trial shall be detained in custody, but release may be subject to guarantees to appear for trial, at any other stage of the judicial proceedings, and, should occasion arise, for execution of the judgement.
4. Anyone who is deprived of his liberty by arrest or detention shall be entitled to take proceedings before a court, in order that court may decide without delay on the lawfulness of his detention and order his release if the detention is not lawful.
5. Anyone who has been the victim of unlawful arrest or detention shall have an enforceable right to compensation.

Article 10

1. All persons deprived of their liberty shall be treated with humanity and with respect for the inherent dignity of the human person.
2. (a) Accused persons shall, save in exceptional circumstances, be segregated from convicted persons and shall be subject to separate treatment appropriate to their status as unconvicted persons;
   (b) Accused juvenile persons shall be separated from adults and brought as speedily as possible for adjudication.
3. The penitentiary system shall comprise treatment of prisoners the essential aim of which shall be their reformation and social rehabilitation. Juvenile offenders shall be segregated from adults and be accorded treatment appropriate to their age and legal status.

Article 11

No one shall be imprisoned merely on the ground of inability to fulfil a contractual obligation.

Article 12

1. Everyone lawfully within the territory of a State shall, within that territory, have the right to liberty of movement and freedom to choose his residence.
2. Everyone shall be free to leave any country, including his own.
3. The above-mentioned rights shall not be subject to any restrictions except those which are provided by law, are necessary to protect national security, public order *(ordre public)*, public health or morals or the rights and freedoms of others, and are consistent with the other rights recognized in the present Covenant.
4. No one shall be arbitrarily deprived of the right to enter his own country.

Article 13

An alien lawfully in the territory of a State Party to the present Covenant may be expelled therefrom only in pursuance of a decision reached in accordance with law and shall, except where compelling reasons of national security otherwise require, be allowed to submit the reasons against his expulsion and to have his case reviewed by, and be represented for the purpose before, the competent authority or a person or persons especially designated by the competent authority.

Article 14

1. All persons shall be equal before the courts and tribunals. In the determination of any criminal charge against him, or of his rights and obligations in a suit at law, everyone shall be entitled to a fair and public hearing by a competent, independent and impartial tribunal established by law. The press and the public may be excluded from all or part of a trial for reasons of morals, public order *(ordre public)* or national security in a democratic society, or when the interest of the private lives of the parties so requires, or to the extent strictly necessary in the opinion of the court in special circumstances where publicity would prejudice the interests of justice; but any judgement rendered in a criminal case or in a suit at law shall be made public except where the interest of juvenile persons otherwise requires or the proceedings concern matrimonial disputes or the guardianship of children.
2. Everyone charged with a criminal offence shall have the right to be presumed innocent until proved guilty according to law.
3. In the determination of any criminal charge against him, everyone shall be entitled to the following minimum guarantees, in full equality:
    (a) To be informed promptly and in detail in a language which he understands of the nature and cause of the charge against him;

(b) To have adequate time and facilities for the preparation of his defence and to communicate with counsel of his own choosing;
(c) To be tried without undue delay;
(d) To be tried in his presence, and to defend himself in person or through legal assistance of his own choosing; to be informed, if he does not have legal assistance, of this right; and to have legal assistance assigned to him, in any case where the interests of justice so require, and without payment by him in any such case if he does not have sufficient means to pay for it;
(e) To examine, or have examined, the witnesses against him and to obtain the attendance and examination of witnesses on his behalf under the same conditions as witnesses against him;
(f) To have the free assistance of an interpreter if he cannot understand or speak the language used in court;
(g) Not to be compelled to testify against himself or to confess guilt.

4. In the case of juvenile persons, the procedure shall be such as will take account of their age and the desirability of promoting their rehabilitation.
5. Everyone convicted of a crime shall have the right to his conviction and sentence being reviewed by a higher tribunal according to law.
6. When a person has by a final decision been convicted of a criminal offence and when subsequently his conviction has been reversed or he has been pardoned on the ground that a new or newly discovered fact shows conclusively that there has been a miscarriage of justice, the person who has suffered punishment as a result of such conviction shall be compensated according to law, unless it is proved that the non-disclosure of the unknown fact in time is wholly or partly attributable to him.
7. No one shall be liable to be tried or punished again for an offence for which he has already been finally convicted or

acquitted in accordance with the law and penal procedure of each country.

Article 15

1. No one shall be held guilty of any criminal offence on account of any act or omission which did not constitute a criminal offence, under national or international law, at the time when it was committed. Nor shall a heavier penalty be imposed than the one that was applicable at the time when the criminal offence was committed. If, subsequent to the commission of the offence, provision is made by law for the imposition of the lighter penalty, the offender shall benefit thereby.
2. Nothing in this article shall prejudice the trial and punishment of any person for any act or omission which, at the time when it was committed, was criminal according to the general principles of law recognized by the community of nations.

Article 16

Everyone shall have the right to recognition everywhere as a person before the law.

Article 17

1. No one shall be subjected to arbitrary or unlawful interference with his privacy, family, home or correspondence, nor to unlawful attacks on his honour and reputation.
2. Everyone has the right to the protection of the law against such interference or attacks.

Article 18

1. Everyone shall have the right to freedom of thought, conscience and religion. This right shall include freedom to have or to adopt a religion or belief of his choice, and freedom, either individually or in community with others and in public or private, to manifest his religion or belief in worship, observance, practice and teaching.
2. No one shall be subject to coercion which would impair his freedom to have or to adopt a religion or belief of his choice.

3. Freedom to manifest one's religion or beliefs may be subject only to such limitations as are prescribed by law and are necessary to protect public safety, order, health, or morals or the fundamental rights and freedoms of others.
4. The States Parties to the present Covenant undertake to have respect for the liberty of parents and, when applicable, legal guardians to ensure the religious and moral education of their children in conformity with their own convictions.

Article 19

1. Everyone shall have the right to hold opinions without interference.
2. Everyone shall have the right to freedom of expression; this right shall include freedom to seek, receive and impart information and ideas of all kinds, regardless of frontiers, either orally, in writing or in print, in the form of art, or through any other media of his choice.
3. The exercise of the rights provided for in paragraph 2 of this article carries with it special duties and responsibilities. It may therefore be subject to certain restrictions, but these shall only be such as are provided by law and are necessary:
   (a) For respect of the rights or reputations of others;
   (b) For the protection of national security or of public order *(ordre public)*, or of public health or morals.

Article 20

1. Any propaganda for war shall be prohibited by law.
2. Any advocacy of national, racial or religious hatred that constitutes incitement to discrimination, hostility or violence shall be prohibited by law.

Article 21

The right of peaceful assembly shall be recognized. No restrictions may be placed on the exercise of this right other than those imposed in conformity with the law and which are necessary in a democratic society in the interests of national security or public safety, public order *(ordre public)*, the protection of public health or morals or the protection of the rights and freedoms of others.

Article 22

1. Everyone shall have the right to freedom of association with others, including the right to form and join trade unions for the protection of his interests.
2. No restrictions may be placed on the exercise of this right other than those which are prescribed by law and which are necessary in a democratic society in the interests of national security or public safety, public order *(ordre public)*, the protection of public health or morals or the protection of the rights and freedoms of others. This article shall not prevent the imposition of lawful restrictions on members of the armed forces and of the police in their exercise of this right.
3. Nothing in this article shall authorize States Parties to the International Labour Organisation Convention of 1948 concerning Freedom of Association and Protection of the Right to Organize to take legislative measures which would prejudice, or to apply the law in such a manner as to prejudice, the guarantees provided for in that Convention.

Article 23

1. The family is the natural and fundamental group unit of society and is entitled to protection by society and the State.
2. The right of men and women of marriageable age to marry and to found a family shall be recognized.
3. No marriage shall be entered into without the free and full consent of the intending spouses.
4. States Parties to the present Covenant shall take appropriate steps to ensure equality of rights and responsibilities of spouses as to marriage, during marriage and at its dissolution. In the case of dissolution, provision shall be made for the necessary protection of any children.

Article 24

1. Every child shall have, without any discrimination as to race, colour, sex, language, religion, national or social origin, property or birth, the right to such measures of protection as are required by his status as a minor, on the part of his family, society and the State.
2. Every child shall be registered immediately after birth and shall have a name.
3. Every child has the right to acquire a nationality.

Article 25

Every citizen shall have the right and the opportunity, without any of the distinctions mentioned in article 2 and without unreasonable restrictions:

(a) To take part in the conduct of public affairs, directly or through freely chosen representatives;

(b) To vote and to be elected at genuine periodic elections which shall be by universal and equal suffrage and shall be held by secret ballot, guaranteeing the free expression of the will of the electors;

(c) To have access, on general terms of equality, to public service in his country.

Article 26

All persons are equal before the law and are entitled without any discrimination to the equal protection of the law. In this respect, the law shall prohibit any discrimination and guarantee to all persons equal and effective protection against discrimination on any ground such as race, colour, sex, language, religion, political or other opinion, national or social origin, property, birth or other status.

Article 27

In those States in which ethnic, religious or linguistic minorities exist, persons belonging to such minorities shall not be denied the right, in community with the other members of their group, to enjoy their own culture, to profess and practise their own religion, or to use their own language.

PART IV

Article 28

1. There shall be established a Human Rights Committee (hereafter referred to in the present Covenant as the Committee). It shall consist of eighteen members and shall carry out the functions hereinafter provided.
2. The Committee shall be composed of nationals of the States Parties to the present Covenant who shall be persons of high moral character and recognized competence in the field of human rights, consideration being given to the usefulness of the participation of some persons having legal experience.
3. The members of the Committee shall be elected and shall serve in their personal capacity.

Article 29

1. The members of the Committee shall be elected by secret ballot from a list of persons possessing the qualifications prescribed in article 28 and nominated for the purpose by the States Parties to the present Covenant.
2. Each State Party to the present Covenant may nominate not more than two persons. These persons shall be nationals of the nominating State.
3. A person shall be eligible for renomination.

Article 30

1. The initial election shall be held no later than six months after the date of the entry into force of the present Covenant.
2. At least four months before the date of each election to the Committee, other than an election to fill a vacancy declared in accordance with article 34, the Secretary-General of the United Nations shall address a written invitation to the States Parties

to the present Covenant to submit their nominations for membership of the Committee within three months.

3. The Secretary-General of the United Nations shall prepare a list in alphabetical order of all the persons thus nominated, with an indication of the States Parties which have nominated them, and shall submit it to the States Parties to the present Covenant no later than one month before the date of each election.

4. Elections of the members of the Committee shall be held at a meeting of the States Parties to the present Covenant convened by the Secretary General of the United Nations at the Headquarters of the United Nations. At that meeting, for which two thirds of the States Parties to the present Covenant shall constitute a quorum, the persons elected to the Committee shall be those nominees who obtain the largest number of votes and an absolute majority of the votes of the representatives of States Parties present and voting.

Article 31

1. The Committee may not include more than one national of the same State.

2. In the election of the Committee, consideration shall be given to equitable geographical distribution of membership and to the representation of the different forms of civilization and of the principal legal systems.

Article 32

1. The members of the Committee shall be elected for a term of four years. They shall be eligible for re-election if renominated. However, the terms of nine of the members elected at the first election shall expire at the end of two years; immediately after the first election, the names of these nine members shall be chosen by lot by the Chairman of the meeting referred to in article 30, paragraph 4.

2. Elections at the expiry of office shall be held in accordance with the preceding articles of this part of the present Covenant.

Article 33

1. If, in the unanimous opinion of the other members, a member of the Committee has ceased to carry out his functions for any cause other than absence of a temporary character, the Chairman of the Committee shall notify the Secretary-General of the United Nations, who shall then declare the seat of that member to be vacant.
2. In the event of the death or the resignation of a member of the Committee, the Chairman shall immediately notify the Secretary-General of the United Nations, who shall declare the seat vacant from the date of death or the date on which the resignation takes effect.

Article 34

1. When a vacancy is declared in accordance with article 33 and if the term of office of the member to be replaced does not expire within six months of the declaration of the vacancy, the Secretary-General of the United Nations shall notify each of the States Parties to the present Covenant, which may within two months submit nominations in accordance with article 29 for the purpose of filling the vacancy.
2. The Secretary-General of the United Nations shall prepare a list in alphabetical order of the persons thus nominated and shall submit it to the States Parties to the present Covenant. The election to fill the vacancy shall then take place in accordance with the relevant provisions of this part of the present Covenant.
3. A member of the Committee elected to fill a vacancy declared in accordance with article 33 shall hold office for the remainder of the term of the member who vacated the seat on the Committee under the provisions of that article.

Article 35

The members of the Committee shall, with the approval of the General Assembly of the United Nations, receive emoluments from United Nations resources on such terms and conditions as the General Assembly may decide, having regard to the importance of the Committee's responsibilities.

Article 36

The Secretary-General of the United Nations shall provide the necessary staff and facilities for the effective performance of the functions of the Committee under the present Covenant.

Article 37

1. The Secretary-General of the United Nations shall convene the initial meeting of the Committee at the Headquarters of the United Nations.
2. After its initial meeting, the Committee shall meet at such times as shall be provided in its rules of procedure.
3. The Committee shall normally meet at the Headquarters of the United Nations or at the United Nations Office at Geneva.

Article 38

Every member of the Committee shall, before taking up his duties, make a solemn declaration in open committee that he will perform his functions impartially and conscientiously.

Article 39

1. The Committee shall elect its officers for a term of two years. They may be re-elected.
2. The Committee shall establish its own rules of procedure, but these rules shall provide, inter alia, that:
   (a) Twelve members shall constitute a quorum;
   (b) Decisions of the Committee shall be made by a majority vote of the members present.

Article 40

1. The States Parties to the present Covenant undertake to submit reports on the measures they have adopted which give effect to the rights recognized herein and on the progress made in the enjoyment of those rights:

(a) Within one year of the entry into force of the present Covenant for the States Parties concerned;

(b) Thereafter whenever the Committee so requests.

2. All reports shall be submitted to the Secretary-General of the United Nations, who shall transmit them to the Committee for consideration. Reports shall indicate the factors and difficulties, if any, affecting the implementation of the present Covenant.

3. The Secretary-General of the United Nations may, after consultation with the Committee, transmit to the specialized agencies concerned copies of such parts of the reports as may fall within their field of competence.

4. The Committee shall study the reports submitted by the States Parties to the present Covenant. It shall transmit its reports, and such general comments as it may consider appropriate, to the States Parties. The Committee may also transmit to the Economic and Social Council these comments along with the copies of the reports it has received from States Parties to the present Covenant.

5. The States Parties to the present Covenant may submit to the Committee observations on any comments that may be made in accordance with paragraph 4 of this article.

Article 41

1. A State Party to the present Covenant may at any time declare under this article that it recognizes the competence of the Committee to receive and consider communications to the effect that a State Party claims that another State Party is not fulfilling its obligations under the present Covenant. Communications under this article may be received and considered only if submitted by a State Party which has made a declaration recognizing in regard to itself the competence of the Committee. No communication shall be received by the Committee if it concerns a State Party which has not made such a declaration. Communications received under this article shall be dealt with in accordance with the following procedure:

(a) If a State Party to the present Covenant considers that another State Party is not giving effect to the provisions of the present Covenant, it may, by written communication, bring the matter to the attention of that State Party. Within three months after the receipt of the communication the receiving State shall afford the State which sent the communication an explanation, or any other statement in writing clarifying the matter which should include, to the extent possible and pertinent, reference to domestic procedures and remedies taken, pending, or available in the matter;

(b) If the matter is not adjusted to the satisfaction of both States Parties concerned within six months after the receipt by the receiving State of the initial communication, either State shall have the right to refer the matter to the Committee, by notice given to the Committee and to the other State;

(c) The Committee shall deal with a matter referred to it only after it has ascertained that all available domestic remedies have been invoked and exhausted in the matter, in conformity with the generally recognized principles of international law. This shall not be the rule where the application of the remedies is unreasonably prolonged;

(d) The Committee shall hold closed meetings when examining communications under this article;

(e) Subject to the provisions of subparagraph (c), the Committee shall make available its good offices to the States Parties concerned with a view to a friendly solution of the matter on the basis of respect for human rights and fundamental freedoms as recognized in the present Covenant;

(f) In any matter referred to it, the Committee may call upon the States Parties concerned, referred to in subparagraph (b), to supply any relevant information;

(g) The States Parties concerned, referred to in subparagraph (b), shall have the right to be represented when the matter is being considered in the Committee and to make submissions orally and/or in writing;

(h) The Committee shall, within twelve months after the date of receipt of notice under subparagraph (b), submit a report:

(i) If a solution within the terms of subparagraph (e) is reached, the Committee shall confine its report to a brief statement of the facts and of the solution reached;

(ii) If a solution within the terms of subparagraph (e) is not reached, the Committee shall confine its report to a brief statement of the facts; the written submissions and record of the oral submissions made by the States Parties concerned shall be attached to the report.

In every matter, the report shall be communicated to the States Parties concerned.

2. The provisions of this article shall come into force when ten States Parties to the present Covenant have made declarations under paragraph I of this article. Such declarations shall be deposited by the States Parties with the Secretary-General of the United Nations, who shall transmit copies thereof to the other States Parties. A declaration may be withdrawn at any time by notification to the Secretary-General. Such a withdrawal shall not prejudice the consideration of any matter which is the subject of a communication already transmitted under this article; no further communication by any State Party shall be received after the notification of withdrawal of the declaration has been received by the Secretary-General, unless the State Party concerned has made a new declaration.

Article 42

1. (a) If a matter referred to the Committee in accordance with article 41 is not resolved to the satisfaction of the States Parties concerned, the Committee may, with the prior consent of the States Parties concerned, appoint an ad hoc Conciliation Commission (hereinafter referred to as the Commission). The good offices of the Commission shall be

made available to the States Parties concerned with a view to an amicable solution of the matter on the basis of respect for the present Covenant;

(b) The Commission shall consist of five persons acceptable to the States Parties concerned. If the States Parties concerned fail to reach agreement within three months on all or part of the composition of the Commission, the members of the Commission concerning whom no agreement has been reached shall be elected by secret ballot by a two-thirds majority vote of the Committee from among its members.

2. The members of the Commission shall serve in their personal capacity. They shall not be nationals of the States Parties concerned, or of a State not Party to the present Covenant, or of a State Party which has not made a declaration under article 41.

3. The Commission shall elect its own Chairman and adopt its own rules of procedure.

4. The meetings of the Commission shall normally be held at the Headquarters of the United Nations or at the United Nations Office at Geneva. However, they may be held at such other convenient places as the Commission may determine in consultation with the Secretary-General of the United Nations and the States Parties concerned.

5. The secretariat provided in accordance with article 36 shall also service the commissions appointed under this article.

6. The information received and collated by the Committee shall be made available to the Commission and the Commission may call upon the States Parties concerned to supply any other relevant information.

7. When the Commission has fully considered the matter, but in any event not later than twelve months after having been seized of the matter, it shall submit to the Chairman of the Committee a report for communication to the States Parties concerned:

(a) If the Commission is unable to complete its consideration of the matter within twelve months, it shall confine its report to a brief statement of the status of its consideration of the matter;

(b) If an amicable solution to the matter on tie basis of respect for human rights as recognized in the present Covenant is reached, the Commission shall confine its report to a brief statement of the facts and of the solution reached;

(c) If a solution within the terms of subparagraph (b) is not reached, the Commission's report shall embody its findings on all questions of fact relevant to the issues between the States Parties concerned, and its views on the possibilities of an amicable solution of the matter. This report shall also contain the written submissions and a record of the oral submissions made by the States Parties concerned;

(d) If the Commission's report is submitted under subparagraph (c), the States Parties concerned shall, within three months of the receipt of the report, notify the Chairman of the Committee whether or not they accept the contents of the report of the Commission.

8. The provisions of this article are without prejudice to the responsibilities of the Committee under article 41.

9. The States Parties concerned shall share equally all the expenses of the members of the Commission in accordance with estimates to be provided by the Secretary-General of the United Nations.

10. The Secretary-General of the United Nations shall be empowered to pay the expenses of the members of the Commission, if necessary, before reimbursement by the States Parties concerned, in accordance with paragraph 9 of this article.

Article 43

The members of the Committee, and of the ad hoc conciliation commissions which may be appointed under article 42, shall be entitled to the facilities, privileges and immunities of experts on mission for the United Nations as laid down in the relevant sections of the Convention on the Privileges and Immunities of the United Nations.

Article 44

The provisions for the implementation of the present Covenant shall apply without prejudice to the procedures prescribed in the field of human rights by or under the constituent instruments and the conventions of the United Nations and of the specialized agencies and shall not prevent the States Parties to the present Covenant from having recourse to other procedures for settling a dispute in accordance with general or special international agreements in force between them.

Article 45

The Committee shall submit to the General Assembly of the United Nations, through the Economic and Social Council, an annual report on its activities.

PART V

Article 46

Nothing in the present Covenant shall be interpreted as impairing the provisions of the Charter of the United Nations and of the constitutions of the specialized agencies which define the respective responsibilities of the various organs of the United Nations and of the specialized agencies in regard to the matters dealt with in the present Covenant.

Article 47

Nothing in the present Covenant shall be interpreted as impairing the inherent right of all peoples to enjoy and utilize fully and freely their natural wealth and resources.

PART VI

Article 48

1. The present Covenant is open for signature by any State Member of the United Nations or member of any of its specialized agencies, by any State Party to the Statute of the International Court of Justice, and by any other State which has been invited by the General Assembly of the United Nations to become a Party to the present Covenant.
2. The present Covenant is subject to ratification. Instruments of ratification shall be deposited with the Secretary-General of the United Nations.
3. The present Covenant shall be open to accession by any State referred to in paragraph 1 of this article.
4. Accession shall be effected by the deposit of an instrument of accession with the Secretary-General of the United Nations.
5. The Secretary-General of the United Nations shall inform all States which have signed this Covenant or acceded to it of the deposit of each instrument of ratification or accession.

Article 49

1. The present Covenant shall enter into force three months after the date of the deposit with the Secretary-General of the United Nations of the thirty-fifth instrument of ratification or instrument of accession.
2. For each State ratifying the present Covenant or acceding to it after the deposit of the thirty-fifth instrument of ratification or instrument of accession, the present Covenant shall enter into force three months after the date of the deposit of its own instrument of ratification or instrument of accession.

Article 50

The provisions of the present Covenant shall extend to all parts of federal States without any limitations or exceptions.

Article 51

1. Any State Party to the present Covenant may propose an amendment and file it with the Secretary-General of the United Nations. The Secretary-General of the United Nations shall thereupon communicate any proposed amendments to the States Parties to the present Covenant with a request that they notify him whether they favour a conference of States Parties for the purpose of considering and voting upon the proposals. In the event that at least one third of the States Parties favours such a conference, the Secretary-General shall convene the conference under the auspices of the United Nations. Any amendment adopted by a majority of the States Parties present and voting at the conference shall be submitted to the General Assembly of the United Nations for approval.
2. Amendments shall come into force when they have been approved by the General Assembly of the United Nations and accepted by a two-thirds majority of the States Parties to the present Covenant in accordance with their respective constitutional processes.
3. When amendments come into force, they shall be binding on those States Parties which have accepted them, other States Parties still being bound by the provisions of the present Covenant and any earlier amendment which they have accepted.

Article 52

Irrespective of the notifications made under article 48, paragraph 5, the Secretary-General of the United Nations shall inform all States referred to in paragraph 1 of the same article of the following particulars:

(a) Signatures, ratifications and accessions under article 48;
(b) The date of the entry into force of the present Covenant under article 49 and the date of the entry into force of any amendments under article 51.

Article 53

1. The present Covenant, of which the Chinese, English, French, Russian and Spanish texts are equally authentic, shall be deposited in the archives of the United Nations.
2. The Secretary-General of the United Nations shall transmit certified copies of the present Covenant to all States referred to in article 48.

IV VIENNA DECLARATION AND PROGRAMME OF ACTION*

Adopted by the World Conference on Human Rights, Vienna, Austria on 25 June 1993.

The World Conference on Human Rights,

Considering that the promotion and protection of human rights is a matter of priority for the international community, and that the Conference affords a unique opportunity to carry out a comprehensive analysis of the international human rights system and of the machinery for the protection of human rights, in order to enhance and thus promote a fuller observance of those rights, in a just and balanced manner,

Recognizing and affirming that all human rights derive from the dignity and worth inherent in the human person, and that the human person is the central subject of human rights and fundamental freedoms, and consequently should be the principal beneficiary and should participate actively in the realization of these rights and freedoms,

Reaffirming their commitment to the purposes and principles contained in the Charter of the United Nations and the Universal Declaration of Human Rights,

Reaffirming the commitment contained in Article 56 of the Charter of the United Nations to take joint and separate action, placing proper emphasis on developing effective international cooperation for the realization of the purposes set out in Article 55, including universal respect for, and observance of, human rights and fundamental freedoms for all,

---

* The text of this instrument has been downloaded from the relevant United Nations web-site.

Emphasizing the responsibilities of all States, in conformity with the Charter of the United Nations, to develop and encourage respect for human rights and fundamental freedoms for all, without distinction as to race, sex, language or religion,

Recalling the Preamble to the Charter of the United Nations, in particular the determination to reaffirm faith in fundamental human rights, in the dignity and worth of the human person, and in the equal rights of men and women and of nations large and small,

Recalling also the determination expressed in the Preamble of the Charter of the United Nations to save succeeding generations from the scourge of war, to establish conditions under which justice and respect for obligations arising from treaties and other sources of international law can be maintained, to promote social progress and better standards of life in larger freedom, to practice tolerance and good neighbourliness, and to employ international machinery for the promotion of the economic and social advancement of all peoples,

Emphasizing that the Universal Declaration of Human Rights, which constitutes a common standard of achievement for all peoples and all nations, is the source of inspiration and has been the basis for the United Nations in making advances in standard setting as contained in the existing international human rights instruments, in particular the International Covenant on Civil and Political Rights and the International Covenant on Economic, Social and Cultural Rights.

Considering the major changes taking place on the international scene and the aspirations of all the peoples for an international order based on the principles enshrined in the Charter of the United Nations, including promoting and encouraging respect for human rights and fundamental freedoms for all and respect for the principle of equal rights and self -determination of peoples, peace, democracy, justice, equality, rule of law, pluralism, development, better standards of living and solidarity,

Deeply concerned by various forms of discrimination and violence, to which women continue to be exposed all over the world,

Recognizing that the activities of the United Nations in the field of human rights should be rationalized and enhanced in order to strengthen the United Nations machinery in this field and to further the objectives of universal respect for observance of international human rights standards,

Having taken into account the Declarations adopted by the three regional meetings at Tunis, San José and Bangkok and the contributions made by Governments, and bearing in mind the suggestions made by intergovernmental and non-governmental organizations, as well as the studies prepared by independent experts during the preparatory process leading to the World Conference on Human Rights,

Welcoming the International Year of the World's Indigenous People 1993 as a reaffirmation of the commitment of the international community to ensure their enjoyment of all human rights and fundamental freedoms and to respect the value and diversity of their cultures and identities,

Recognizing also that the international community should devise ways and means to remove the current obstacles and meet challenges to the full realization of all human rights and to prevent the continuation of human rights violations resulting thereof throughout the world,

Invoking the spirit of our age and the realities of our time which call upon the peoples of the world and all States Members of the United Nations to rededicate themselves to the global task of promoting and protecting all human rights and fundamental freedoms so as to secure full and universal enjoyment of these rights,

Determined to take new steps forward in the commitment of the international community with a view to achieving substantial progress in human rights endeavours by an increased and sustained effort of international cooperation and solidarity,

Solemnly adopts the **Vienna Declaration and Programme of Action.**

I

1. The World Conference on Human Rights reaffirms the solemn commitment of all States to fulfil their obligations to promote universal respect for, and observance and protection of, all human rights and fundamental freedoms for all in accordance with the Charter of the United Nations, other instruments relating to human rights, and international law. The universal nature of these rights and freedoms is beyond question.

    In this framework, enhancement of international cooperation in the field of human rights is essential for the full achievement of the purposes of the United Nations.

    Human rights and fundamental freedoms are the birthright of all human beings; their protection and promotion is the first responsibility of Governments.

2. All peoples have the right of self-determination. By virtue of that right they freely determine their political status, and freely pursue their economic, social and cultural development.

    Taking into account the particular situation of peoples under colonial or other forms of alien domination or foreign occupation, the World Conference on Human Rights recognizes the right of peoples to take any legitimate action, in accordance with the Charter of the United Nations, to realize their inalienable right of self-determination. The World Conference on Human Rights considers the denial of the right of self-determination as a violation of human rights and underlines the importance of the effective realization of this right.

    In accordance with the Declaration on Principles of International Law concerning Friendly Relations and Cooperation Among States in accordance with the Charter of the United Nations, this shall not be construed as authorizing or encouraging any action which would dismember or impair, totally or in part, the territorial integrity or political unity of sovereign and independent States conducting themselves in compliance with the principle of equal rights and self-determination of peoples and thus possessed of a Government representing the whole people belonging to the territory without distinction of any kind.

3. Effective international measures to guarantee and monitor the implementation of human rights standards should be taken in respect of people under foreign occupation, and effective legal protection against the violation of their human rights should be provided, in accordance with human rights norms and international law, particularly the Geneva Convention relative to the Protection of Civilian Persons in Time of War, of 14 August 1949, and other applicable norms of humanitarian law.

4. The promotion and protection of all human rights and fundamental freedoms must be considered as a priority objective of the United Nations in accordance with its purposes and principles, in particular the purpose of international cooperation. In the framework of these purposes and principles, the promotion and protection of all human rights is a legitimate concern of the international community. The organs and specialized agencies related to human rights should therefore further enhance the coordination of their activities based on the consistent and objective application of international human rights instruments.

5. All human rights are universal, indivisible and interdependent and interrelated. The international community must treat human rights globally in a fair and equal manner, on the same footing, and with the same emphasis. While the significance of national and regional particularities and various historical, cultural and religious backgrounds must be borne in mind, it is the duty of States, regardless of their political, economic and cultural systems, to promote and protect all human rights and fundamental freedoms.

6. The efforts of the United Nations system towards the universal respect for, and observance of, human rights and fundamental

freedoms for all, contribute to the stability and well-being necessary for peaceful and friendly relations among nations, and to improved conditions for peace and security as well as social and economic development, in conformity with the Charter of the United Nations.

7. The processes of promoting and protecting human rights should be conducted in conformity with the purposes and principles of the Charter of the United Nations, and international law.

8. Democracy, development and respect for human rights and fundamental freedoms are interdependent and mutually reinforcing. Democracy is based on the freely expressed will of the people to determine their own political, economic, social and cultural systems and their full participation in all aspects of their lives. In the context of the above, the promotion and protection of human rights and fundamental freedoms at the national and international levels should be universal and conducted without conditions attached. The international community should support the strengthening and promoting of democracy, development and respect for human rights and fundamental freedoms in the entire world.

9. The World Conference on Human Rights reaffirms that least developed countries committed to the process of democratization and economic reforms, many of which are in Africa, should be supported by the international community in order to succeed in their transition to democracy and economic development.

10. The World Conference on Human Rights reaffirms the right to development, as established in the Declaration on the Right to Development, as a universal and inalienable right and an integral part of fundamental human rights.

    As stated in the Declaration on the Right to Development, the human person is the central subject of development.

    While development facilitates the enjoyment of all human rights, the lack of development may not be invoked to justify the abridgement of internationally recognized human rights.

States should cooperate with each other in ensuring development and eliminating obstacles to development. The international community should promote an effective international cooperation for the realization of the right to development and the elimination of obstacles to development.

Lasting progress towards the implementation of the right to development requires effective development policies at the national level, as well as equitable economic relations and a favourable economic environment at the international level.

11. The right to development should be fulfilled so as to meet equitably the developmental and environmental needs of present and future generations. The World Conference on Human Rights recognizes that illicit dumping of toxic and dangerous substances and waste potentially constitutes a serious threat to the human rights to life and health of everyone.

    Consequently, the World Conference on Human Rights calls on all States to adopt and vigorously implement existing conventions relating to the dumping of toxic and dangerous products and waste and to cooperate in the prevention of illicit dumping.

    Everyone has the right to enjoy the benefits of scientific progress and its applications. The World Conference on Human Rights notes that certain advances, notably in the biomedical and life sciences as well as in information technology, may have potentially adverse consequences for the integrity, dignity and human rights of the individual, and calls for international cooperation to ensure that human rights and dignity are fully respected in this area of universal concern.

12. The World Conference on Human Rights calls upon the international community to make all efforts to help alleviate the external debt burden of developing countries, in order to supplement the efforts of the Governments of such countries to attain the full realization of the economic, social and cultural rights of their people.

13. There is a need for States and international organizations, in cooperation with non-governmental organizations, to create favourable conditions at the national, regional and international levels to ensure the full and effective enjoyment of human rights. States should eliminate all violations of human rights and their causes, as well as obstacles to the enjoyment of these rights.
14. The existence of widespread extreme poverty inhibits the full and effective enjoyment of human rights; its immediate alleviation and eventual elimination must remain a high priority for the international community.
15. Respect for human rights and for fundamental freedoms without distinction of any kind is a fundamental rule of international human rights law. The speedy and comprehensive elimination of all forms of racism and racial discrimination, xenophobia and related intolerance is a priority task for the international community. Governments should take effective measures to prevent and combat them. Groups, institutions, intergovernmental and non-governmental organizations and individuals are urged to intensify their efforts in cooperating and coordinating their activities against these evils.
16. The World Conference on Human Rights welcomes the progress made in dismantling apartheid and calls upon the international community and the United Nations system to assist in this process.

    The World Conference on Human Rights also deplores the continuing acts of violence aimed at undermining the quest for a peaceful dismantling of apartheid.
17. The acts, methods and practices of terrorism in all its forms and manifestations as well as linkage in some countries to drug trafficking are activities aimed at the destruction of human rights, fundamental freedoms and democracy, threatening territorial integrity, security of States and destabilizing legitimately constituted Governments. The international community should

take the necessary steps to enhance cooperation to prevent and combat terrorism.

18. The human rights of women and of the girl-child are an inalienable, integral and indivisible part of universal human rights. The full and equal participation of women in political, civil, economic, social and cultural life, at the national, regional and international levels, and the eradication of all forms of discrimination on grounds of sex are priority objectives of the international community.

    Gender-based violence and all forms of sexual harassment and exploitation, including those resulting from cultural prejudice and international trafficking, are incompatible with the dignity and worth of the human person, and must be eliminated. This can be achieved by legal measures and through national action and international cooperation in such fields as economic and social development, education, safe maternity and health care, and social support.

    The human rights of women should form an integral part of the United Nations human rights activities, including the promotion of all human rights instruments relating to women.

    The World Conference on Human Rights urges Governments, institutions, intergovernmental and non-governmental organizations to intensify their efforts for the protection and promotion of human rights of women and the girl-child.

19. Considering the importance of the promotion and protection of the rights of persons belonging to minorities and the contribution of such promotion and protection to the political and social stability of the States in which such persons live,

    The World Conference on Human Rights reaffirms the obligation of States to ensure that persons belonging to minorities may exercise fully and effectively all human rights and fundamental freedoms without any discrimination and in full equality before the law in accordance with the Declaration on the Rights of Persons Belonging to National or Ethnic, Religious and Linguistic Minorities.

The persons belonging to minorities have the right to enjoy their own culture, to profess and practise their own religion and to use their own language in private and in public, freely and without interference or any form of discrimination.

20. The World Conference on Human Rights recognizes the inherent dignity and the unique contribution of indigenous people to the development and plurality of society and strongly reaffirms the commitment of the international community to their economic, social and cultural well-being and their enjoyment of the fruits of sustainable development. States should ensure the full and free participation of indigenous people in all aspects of society, in particular in matters of concern to them. Considering the importance of the promotion and protection of the rights of indigenous people, and the contribution of such promotion and protection to the political and social stability of the States in which such people live, States should, in accordance with international law, take concerted positive steps to ensure respect for all human rights and fundamental freedoms of indigenous people, on the basis of equality and non-discrimination, and recognize the value and diversity of their distinct identities, cultures and social organization.

21. The World Conference on Human Rights, welcoming the early ratification of the Convention on the Rights of the Child by a large number of States and noting the recognition of the human rights of children in the World Declaration on the Survival, Protection and Development of Children and Plan of Action adopted by the World Summit for Children, urges universal ratification of the Convention by 1995 and its effective implementation by States parties through the adoption of all the necessary legislative, administrative and other measures and the allocation to the maximum extent of the available resources. In all actions concerning children, non-discrimination and the best interest of the child should be primary considerations and

the views of the child given due weight. National and international mechanisms and programmes should be strengthened for the defence and protection of children, in particular, the girl-child, abandoned children, street children, economically and sexually exploited children, including through child pornography, child prostitution or sale of organs, children victims of diseases including acquired immunodeficiency syndrome, refugee and displaced children, children in detention, children in armed conflict, as well as children victims of famine and drought and other emergencies. International cooperation and solidarity should be promoted to support the implementation of the Convention and the rights of the child should be a priority in the United Nations system-wide action on human rights.

The World Conference on Human Rights also stresses that the child for the full and harmonious development of his or her personality should grow up in a family environment which accordingly merits broader protection.

22. Special attention needs to be paid to ensuring non-discrimination, and the equal enjoyment of all human rights and fundamental freedoms by disabled persons, including their active participation in all aspects of society.

23. The World Conference on Human Rights reaffirms that everyone, without distinction of any kind, is entitled to the right to seek and to enjoy in other countries asylum from persecution, as well as the right to return to one's own country. In this respect it stresses the importance of the Universal Declaration of Human Rights, the 1951 Convention relating to the Status of Refugees, its 1967 Protocol and regional instruments. It expresses its appreciation to States that continue to admit and host large numbers of refugees in their territories, and to the Office of the United Nations High Commissioner for Refugees for its dedication to its task. It also expresses its appreciation to the United Nations Relief and Works Agency for Palestine Refugees in the Near East.

The World Conference on Human Rights recognizes that gross violations of human rights, including in armed conflicts, are among the multiple and complex factors leading to displacement of people.

The World Conference on Human Rights recognizes that, in view of the complexities of the global refugee crisis and in accordance with the Charter of the United Nations, relevant international instruments and international solidarity and in the spirit of burden-sharing, a comprehensive approach by the international community is needed in coordination and cooperation with the countries concerned and relevant organizations, bearing in mind the mandate of the United Nations High Commissioner for Refugees. This should include the development of strategies to address the root causes and effects of movements of refugees and other displaced persons, the strengthening of emergency preparedness and response mechanisms, the provision of effective protection and assistance, bearing in mind the special needs of women and children, as well as the achievement of durable solutions, primarily through the preferred solution of dignified and safe voluntary repatriation, including solutions such as those adopted by the international refugee conferences. The World Conference on Human Rights underlines the responsibilities of States, particularly as they relate to the countries of origin.

In the light of the comprehensive approach, the World Conference on Human Rights emphasizes the importance of giving special attention including through intergovernmental and humanitarian organizations and finding lasting solutions to questions related to internally displaced persons including their voluntary and safe return and rehabilitation.

In accordance with the Charter of the United Nations and the principles of humanitarian law, the World Conference on Human Rights further emphasizes the importance of and the need for humanitarian assistance to victims of all natural and man-made disasters.

24. Great importance must be given to the promotion and protection of the human rights of persons belonging to groups which have been rendered vulnerable, including migrant workers, the elimination of all forms of discrimination against them, and the strengthening and more effective implementation of existing human rights instruments. States have an obligation to create and maintain adequate measures at the national level, in particular in the fields of education, health and social support, for the promotion and protection of the rights of persons in vulnerable sectors of their populations and to ensure the participation of those among them who are interested in finding a solution to their own problems.
25. The World Conference on Human Rights affirms that extreme poverty and social exclusion constitute a violation of human dignity and that urgent steps are necessary to achieve better knowledge of extreme poverty and its causes, including those related to the problem of development, in order to promote the human rights of the poorest, and to put an end to extreme poverty and social exclusion and to promote the enjoyment of the fruits of social progress. It is essential for States to foster participation by the poorest people in the decision-making process by the community in which they live, the promotion of human rights and efforts to combat extreme poverty.
26. The World Conference on Human Rights welcomes the progress made in the codification of human rights instruments, which is a dynamic and evolving process, and urges the universal ratification of human rights treaties. All States are encouraged to accede to these international instruments; all States are encouraged to avoid, as far as possible, the resort to reservations.
27. Every State should provide an effective framework of remedies to redress human rights grievances or violations. The administration of justice, including law enforcement and prosecutorial agencies and, especially, an independent judiciary and legal profession in full conformity with applicable standards contained in international human rights instruments, are

essential to the full and non-discriminatory realization of human rights and indispensable to the processes of democracy and sustainable development. In this context, institutions concerned with the administration of justice should be properly funded, and an increased level of both technical and financial assistance should be provided by the international community. It is incumbent upon the United Nations to make use of special programmes of advisory services on a priority basis for the achievement of a strong and independent administration of justice.

28. The World Conference on Human Rights expresses its dismay at massive violations of human rights especially in the form of genocide, "ethnic cleansing" and systematic rape of women in war situations, creating mass exodus of refugees and displaced persons. While strongly condemning such abhorrent practices it reiterates the call that perpetrators of such crimes be punished and such practices immediately stopped.

29. The World Conference on Human Rights expresses grave concern about continuing human rights violations in all parts of the world in disregard of standards as contained in international human rights instruments and international humanitarian law and about the lack of sufficient and effective remedies for the victims.

The World Conference on Human Rights is deeply concerned about violations of human rights during armed conflicts, affecting the civilian population, especially women, children, the elderly and the disabled. The Conference therefore calls upon States and all parties to armed conflicts strictly to observe international humanitarian law, as set forth in the Geneva Conventions of 1949 and other rules and principles of international law, as well as minimum standards for protection of human rights, as laid down in international conventions.

The World Conference on Human Rights reaffirms the right of the victims to be assisted by humanitarian organizations, as set forth in the Geneva Conventions of 1949 and other relevant instruments of international humanitarian law, and calls for the safe and timely access for such assistance.

30. The World Conference on Human Rights also expresses its dismay and condemnation that gross and systematic violations and situations that constitute serious obstacles to the full enjoyment of all human rights continue to occur in different parts of the world. Such violations and obstacles include, as well as torture and cruel, inhuman and degrading treatment or punishment, summary and arbitrary executions, disappearances, arbitrary detentions, all forms of racism, racial discrimination and apartheid, foreign occupation and alien domination, xenophobia, poverty, hunger and other denials of economic, social and cultural rights, religious intolerance, terrorism, discrimination against women and lack of the rule of law.

31. The World Conference on Human Rights calls upon States to refrain from any unilateral measure not in accordance with international law and the Charter of the United Nations that creates obstacles to trade relations among States and impedes the full realization of the human rights set forth in the Universal Declaration of Human Rights and international human rights instruments, in particular the rights of everyone to a standard of living adequate for their health and well-being, including food and medical care, housing and the necessary social services. The World Conference on Human Rights affirms that food should not be used as a tool for political pressure.

32. The World Conference on Human Rights reaffirms the importance of ensuring the universality, objectivity and non-selectivity of the consideration of human rights issues.

33. The World Conference on Human Rights reaffirms that States are duty-bound, as stipulated in the Universal Declaration of Human Rights and the International Covenant on Economic, Social and Cultural Rights and in other international human rights instruments, to ensure that education is aimed at strengthening the respect of human rights and fundamental freedoms. The World Conference on Human Rights emphasizes

the importance of incorporating the subject of human rights education programmes and calls upon States to do so. Education should promote understanding, tolerance, peace and friendly relations between the nations and all racial or religious groups and encourage the development of United Nations activities in pursuance of these objectives. Therefore, education on human rights and the dissemination of proper information, both theoretical and practical, play an important role in the promotion and respect of human rights with regard to all individuals without distinction of any kind such as race, sex, language or religion, and this should be integrated in the education policies at the national as well as international levels. The World Conference on Human Rights notes that resource constraints and institutional inadequacies may impede the immediate realization of these objectives.

34. Increased efforts should be made to assist countries which so request to create the conditions whereby each individual can enjoy universal human rights and fundamental freedoms. Governments, the United Nations system as well as other multilateral organizations are urged to increase considerably the resources allocated to programmes aiming at the establishment and strengthening of national legislation, national institutions and related infrastructures which uphold the rule of law and democracy, electoral assistance, human rights awareness through training, teaching and education, popular participation and civil society.

    The programmes of advisory services and technical cooperation under the Centre for Human Rights should be strengthened as well as made more efficient and transparent and thus become a major contribution to improving respect for human rights. States are called upon to increase their contributions to these programmes, both through promoting a larger allocation from the United Nations regular budget, and through voluntary contributions.

35. The full and effective implementation of United Nations activities to promote and protect human rights must reflect the high importance accorded to human rights by the Charter of the United Nations and the demands of the United Nations human rights activities, as mandated by Member States. To this end, United Nations human rights activities should be provided with increased resources.

36. The World Conference on Human Rights reaffirms the important and constructive role played by national institutions for the promotion and protection of human rights, in particular in their advisory capacity to the competent authorities, their role in remedying human rights violations, in the dissemination of human rights information, and education in human rights.

    The World Conference on Human Rights encourages the establishment and strengthening of national institutions, having regard to the "Principles relating to the status of national institutions" and recognizing that it is the right of each State to choose the framework which is best suited to its particular needs at the national level.

37. Regional arrangements play a fundamental role in promoting and protecting human rights. They should reinforce universal human rights standards, as contained in international human rights instruments, and their protection. The World Conference on Human Rights endorses efforts under way to strengthen these arrangements and to increase their effectiveness, while at the same time stressing the importance of cooperation with the United Nations human rights activities.

    The World Conference on Human Rights reiterates the need to consider the possibility of establishing regional and subregional arrangements for the promotion and protection of human rights where they do not already exist.

38. The World Conference on Human Rights recognizes the important role of non-governmental organizations in the promotion of all human rights and in humanitarian activities at national, regional and international levels. The World

Conference on Human Rights appreciates their contribution to increasing public awareness of human rights issues, to the conduct of education, training and research in this field, and to the promotion and protection of all human rights and fundamental freedoms. While recognizing that the primary responsibility for standard-setting lies with States, the conference also appreciates the contribution of non-governmental organizations to this process. In this respect, the World Conference on Human Rights emphasizes the importance of continued dialogue and cooperation between Governments and non-governmental organizations. Non-governmental organizations and their members genuinely involved in the field of human rights should enjoy the rights and freedoms recognized in the Universal Declaration of Human Rights, and the protection of the national law. These rights and freedoms may not be exercised contrary to the purposes and principles of the United Nations. Non-governmental organizations should be free to carry out their human rights activities, without interference, within the framework of national law and the Universal Declaration of Human Rights.

39. Underlining the importance of objective, responsible and impartial information about human rights and humanitarian issues, the World Conference on Human Rights encourages the increased involvement of the media, for whom freedom and protection should be guaranteed within the framework of national law.

II

A. Increased coordination on human rights within the United Nations system

1. The World Conference on Human Rights recommends increased coordination in support of human rights and fundamental freedoms within the United Nations system. To this end, the World Conference on Human Rights urges all United Nations organs, bodies and the specialized agencies whose activities deal with human rights to cooperate in order to strengthen, rationalize and streamline their activities, taking into account the need to avoid unnecessary duplication. The World Conference on Human Rights also recommends to the Secretary-General that high-level officials of relevant United Nations bodies and specialized agencies at their annual meeting, besides coordinating their activities, also assess the impact of their strategies and policies on the enjoyment of all human rights.
2. Furthermore, the World Conference on Human Rights calls on regional organizations and prominent international and regional finance and development institutions to assess also the impact of their policies and programmes on the enjoyment of human rights.
3. The World Conference on Human Rights recognizes that relevant specialized agencies and bodies and institutions of the United Nations system as well as other relevant intergovernmental organizations whose activities deal with human rights play a vital role in the formulation, promotion and implementation of human rights standards, within their respective mandates, and should take into account the outcome of the World Conference on Human Rights within their fields of competence.

4. The World Conference on Human Rights strongly recommends that a concerted effort be made to encourage and facilitate the ratification of and accession or succession to international human rights treaties and protocols adopted within the framework of the United Nations system with the aim of universal acceptance. The Secretary-General, in consultation with treaty bodies, should consider opening a dialogue with States not having acceded to these human rights treaties, in order to identify obstacles and to seek ways of overcoming them.
5. The World Conference on Human Rights encourages States to consider limiting the extent of any reservations they lodge to international human rights instruments, formulate any reservations as precisely and narrowly as possible, ensure that none is incompatible with the object and purpose of the relevant treaty and regularly review any reservations with a view to withdrawing them.
6. The World Conference on Human Rights, recognizing the need to maintain consistency with the high quality of existing international standards and to avoid proliferation of human rights instruments, reaffirms the guidelines relating to the elaboration of new international instruments contained in General Assembly resolution 41/120 of 4 December 1986 and calls on the United Nations human rights bodies, when considering the elaboration of new international standards, to keep those guidelines in mind, to consult with human rights treaty bodies on the necessity for drafting new standards and to request the Secretariat to carry out technical reviews of proposed new instruments.
7. The World Conference on Human Rights recommends that human rights officers be assigned if and when necessary to regional offices of the United Nations Organization with the purpose of disseminating information and offering training and other technical assistance in the field of human rights upon the request of concerned Member States. Human rights training for international civil servants who are assigned to work relating to human rights should be organized.

8. The World Conference on Human Rights welcomes the convening of emergency sessions of the Commission on Human Rights as a positive initiative and that other ways of responding to acute violations of human rights be considered by the relevant organs of the United Nations system.

Resources

9. The World Conference on Human Rights, concerned by the growing disparity between the activities of the Centre for Human Rights and the human, financial and other resources available to carry them out, and bearing in mind the resources needed for other important United Nations programmes, requests the Secretary-General and the General Assembly to take immediate steps to increase substantially the resources for the human rights programme from within the existing and future regular budgets of the United Nations, and to take urgent steps to seek increased extrabudgetary resources.

10. Within this framework, an increased proportion of the regular budget should be allocated directly to the Centre for Human Rights to cover its costs and all other costs borne by the Centre for Human Rights, including those related to the United Nations human rights bodies. Voluntary funding of the Centre's technical cooperation activities should reinforce this enhanced budget; the World Conference on Human Rights calls for generous contributions to the existing trust funds.

11. The World Conference on Human Rights requests the Secretary-General and the General Assembly to provide sufficient human, financial and other resources to the Centre for Human Rights to enable it effectively, efficiently and expeditiously to carry out its activities.

12. The World Conference on Human Rights, noting the need to ensure that human and financial resources are available to carry out the human rights activities, as mandated by intergovernmental bodies, urges the Secretary-General, in

accordance with Article 101 of the Charter of the United Nations, and Member States to adopt a coherent approach aimed at securing that resources commensurate to the increased mandates are allocated to the Secretariat. The World Conference on Human Rights invites the Secretary-General to consider whether adjustments to procedures in the programme budget cycle would be necessary or helpful to ensure the timely and effective implementation of human rights activities as mandated by Member States.

Centre for Human Rights

13. The World Conference on Human Rights stresses the importance of strengthening the United Nations Centre for Human Rights.
14. The Centre for Human Rights should play an important role in coordinating system-wide attention for human rights. The focal role of the Centre can best be realized if it is enabled to cooperate fully with other United Nations bodies and organs. The coordinating role of the Centre for Human Rights also implies that the office of the Centre for Human Rights in New York is strengthened.
15. The Centre for Human Rights should be assured adequate means for the system of thematic and country rapporteurs, experts, working groups and treaty bodies. Follow-up on recommendations should become a priority matter for consideration by the Commission on Human Rights.
16. The Centre for Human Rights should assume a larger role in the promotion of human rights. This role could be given shape through cooperation with Member States and by an enhanced programme of advisory services and technical assistance. The existing voluntary funds will have to be expanded substantially for these purposes and should be managed in a more efficient and coordinated way. All activities should follow strict and transparent project management rules and regular programme and project evaluations should be held periodically. To this end,

the results of such evaluation exercises and other relevant information should be made available regularly. The Centre should, in particular, organize at least once a year information meetings open to all Member States and organizations directly involved in these projects and programmes.

Adaptation and strengthening of the United Nations machinery for human rights, including the question of the establishment of a United Nations High Commissioner for Human Rights

17. The World Conference on Human Rights recognizes the necessity for a continuing adaptation of the United Nations human rights machinery to the current and future needs in the promotion and protection of human rights, as reflected in the present Declaration and within the framework of a balanced and sustainable development for all people. In particular, the United Nations human rights organs should improve their coordination, efficiency and effectiveness.

18. The World Conference on Human Rights recommends to the General Assembly that when examining the report of the Conference at its forty-eighth session, it begin, as a matter of priority, consideration of the question of the establishment of a High Commissioner for Human Rights for the promotion and protection of all human rights.

B. Equality, dignity and tolerance

1. Racism, racial discrimination, xenophobia and other forms of intolerance

19. The World Conference on Human Rights considers the elimination of racism and racial discrimination, in particular in their institutionalized forms such as apartheid or resulting from doctrines of racial superiority or exclusivity or contemporary

forms and manifestations of racism, as a primary objective for the international community and a worldwide promotion programme in the field of human rights. United Nations organs and agencies should strengthen their efforts to implement such a programme of action related to the third decade to combat racism and racial discrimination as well as subsequent mandates to the same end. The World Conference on Human Rights strongly appeals to the international community to contribute generously to the Trust Fund for the Programme for the Decade for Action to Combat Racism and Racial Discrimination.

20. The World Conference on Human Rights urges all Governments to take immediate measures and to develop strong policies to prevent and combat all forms and manifestations of racism, xenophobia or related intolerance, where necessary by enactment of appropriate legislation, including penal measures, and by the establishment of national institutions to combat such phenomena.

21. The World Conference on Human Rights welcomes the decision of the Commission on Human Rights to appoint a Special Rapporteur on contemporary forms of racism, racial discrimination, xenophobia and related intolerance. The World Conference on Human Rights also appeals to all States parties to the International Convention on the Elimination of All Forms of Racial Discrimination to consider making the declaration under article 14 of the Convention.

22. The World Conference on Human Rights calls upon all Governments to take all appropriate measures in compliance with their international obligations and with due regard to their respective legal systems to counter intolerance and related violence based on religion or belief, including practices of discrimination against women and including the desecration of religious sites, recognizing that every individual has the right to freedom of thought, conscience, expression and religion. The Conference also invites all States to put into practice the provisions of the Declaration on the Elimination of All Forms

of Intolerance and of Discrimination Based on Religion or Belief.

23. The World Conference on Human Rights stresses that all persons who perpetrate or authorize criminal acts associated with ethnic cleansing are individually responsible and accountable for such human rights violations, and that the international community should exert every effort to bring those legally responsible for such violations to justice.

24. The World Conference on Human Rights calls on all States to take immediate measures, individually and collectively, to combat the practice of ethnic cleansing to bring it quickly to an end. Victims of the abhorrent practice of ethnic cleansing are entitled to appropriate and effective remedies.

2. Persons belonging to national or ethnic, religious and linguistic minorities

25. The World Conference on Human Rights calls on the Commission on Human Rights to examine ways and means to promote and protect effectively the rights of persons belonging to minorities as set out in the Declaration on the Rights of Persons belonging to National or Ethnic, Religious and Linguistic Minorities. In this context, the World Conference on Human Rights calls upon the Centre for Human Rights to provide, at the request of Governments concerned and as part of its programme of advisory services and technical assistance, qualified expertise on minority issues and human rights, as well as on the prevention and resolution of disputes, to assist in existing or potential situations involving minorities.

26. The World Conference on Human Rights urges States and the international community to promote and protect the rights of persons belonging to national or ethnic, religious and linguistic minorities in accordance with the Declaration on the Rights of

Persons belonging to National or Ethnic, Religious and Linguistic Minorities.

27. Measures to be taken, where appropriate, should include facilitation of their full participation in all aspects of the political, economic, social, religious and cultural life of society and in the economic progress and development in their country.

Indigenous people

28. The World Conference on Human Rights calls on the Working Group on Indigenous Populations of the Sub-Commission on Prevention of Discrimination and Protection of Minorities to complete the drafting of a declaration on the rights of indigenous people at its eleventh session.

29. The World Conference on Human Rights recommends that the Commission on Human Rights consider the renewal and updating of the mandate of the Working Group on Indigenous Populations upon completion of the drafting of a declaration on the rights of indigenous people.

30. The World Conference on Human Rights also recommends that advisory services and technical assistance programmes within the United Nations system respond positively to requests by States for assistance which would be of direct benefit to indigenous people. The World Conference on Human Rights further recommends that adequate human and financial resources be made available to the Centre for Human Rights within the overall framework of strengthening the Centre's activities as envisaged by this document.

31. The World Conference on Human Rights urges States to ensure the full and free participation of indigenous people in all aspects of society, in particular in matters of concern to them.

32. The World Conference on Human Rights recommends that the General Assembly proclaim an international decade of the world's indigenous people, to begin from January 1994, including action-orientated programmes, to be decided upon in partnership

with indigenous people. An appropriate voluntary trust fund should be set up for this purpose. In the framework of such a decade, the establishment of a permanent forum for indigenous people in the United Nations system should be considered.

Migrant workers

33. The World Conference on Human Rights urges all States to guarantee the protection of the human rights of all migrant workers and their families.
34. The World Conference on Human Rights considers that the creation of conditions to foster greater harmony and tolerance between migrant workers and the rest of the society of the State in which they reside is of particular importance.
35. The World Conference on Human Rights invites States to consider the possibility of signing and ratifying, at the earliest possible time, the International Convention on the Rights of All Migrant Workers and Members of Their Families.

3. The equal status and human rights of women

36. The World Conference on Human Rights urges the full and equal enjoyment by women of all human rights and that this be a priority for Governments and for the United Nations. The World Conference on Human Rights also underlines the importance of the integration and full participation of women as both agents and beneficiaries in the development process, and reiterates the objectives established on global action for women towards sustainable and equitable development set forth in the Rio Declaration on Environment and Development and chapter 24 of Agenda 21, adopted by the United Nations Conference on Environment and Development (Rio de Janeiro, Brazil, 3-14 June 1992).
37. The equal status of women and the human rights of women should be integrated into the mainstream of United Nations

system-wide activity. These issues should be regularly and systematically addressed throughout relevant United Nations bodies and mechanisms. In particular, steps should be taken to increase cooperation and promote further integration of objectives and goals between the Commission on the Status of Women, the Commission on Human Rights, the Committee for the Elimination of Discrimination against Women, the United Nations Development Fund for Women, the United Nations Development Programme and other United Nations agencies. In this context, cooperation and coordination should be strengthened between the Centre for Human Rights and the Division for the Advancement of Women.

38. In particular, the World Conference on Human Rights stresses the importance of working towards the elimination of violence against women in public and private life, the elimination of all forms of sexual harassment, exploitation and trafficking in women, the elimination of gender bias in the administration of justice and the eradication of any conflicts which may arise between the rights of women and the harmful effects of certain traditional or customary practices, cultural prejudices and religious extremism. The World Conference on Human Rights calls upon the General Assembly to adopt the draft declaration on violence against women and urges States to combat violence against women in accordance with its provisions. Violations of the human rights of women in situations of armed conflict are violations of the fundamental principles of international human rights and humanitarian law. All violations of this kind, including in particular murder, systematic rape, sexual slavery, and forced pregnancy, require a particularly effective response.

39. The World Conference on Human Rights urges the eradication of all forms of discrimination against women, both hidden and overt. The United Nations should encourage the goal of universal ratification by all States of the Convention on the Elimination of All Forms of Discrimination against Women by the year 2000. Ways and means of addressing the particularly large number

of reservations to the Convention should be encouraged. *Inter alia,* the Committee on the Elimination of Discrimination against Women should continue its review of reservations to the Convention. States are urged to withdraw reservations that are contrary to the object and purpose of the Convention or which are otherwise incompatible with international treaty law.

40. Treaty monitoring bodies should disseminate necessary information to enable women to make more effective use of existing implementation procedures in their pursuits of full and equal enjoyment of human rights and non-discrimination. New procedures should also be adopted to strengthen implementation of the commitment to women's equality and the human rights of women. The Commission on the Status of Women and the Committee on the Elimination of Discrimination against Women should quickly examine the possibility of introducing the right of petition through the preparation of an optional protocol to the Convention on the Elimination of All Forms of Discrimination against Women. The World Conference on Human Rights welcomes the decision of the Commission on Human Rights to consider the appointment of a special rapporteur on violence against women at its fiftieth session.

41. The World Conference on Human Rights recognizes the importance of the enjoyment by women of the highest standard of physical and mental health throughout their life span. In the context of the World Conference on Women and the Convention on the Elimination of All Forms of Discrimination against Women, as well as the Proclamation of Tehran of 1968, the World Conference on Human Rights reaffirms, on the basis of equality between women and men, a woman's right to accessible and adequate health care and the widest range of family planning services, as well as equal access to education at all levels.

42. Treaty monitoring bodies should include the status of women and the human rights of women in their deliberations and findings, making use of gender-specific data. States should be

encouraged to supply information on the situation of women *de jure* and de facto in their reports to treaty monitoring bodies. The World Conference on Human Rights notes with satisfaction that the Commission on Human Rights adopted at its forty-ninth session resolution 1993/46 of 8 March 1993 stating that rapporteurs and working groups in the field of human rights should also be encouraged to do so. Steps should also be taken by the Division for the Advancement of Women in cooperation with other United Nations bodies, specifically the Centre for Human Rights, to ensure that the human rights activities of the United Nations regularly address violations of women's human rights, including gender-specific abuses. Training for United Nations human rights and humanitarian relief personnel to assist them to recognize and deal with human rights abuses particular to women and to carry out their work without gender bias should be encouraged.

43. The World Conference on Human Rights urges Governments and regional and international organizations to facilitate the access of women to decision-making posts and their greater participation in the decision-making process. It encourages further steps within the United Nations Secretariat to appoint and promote women staff members in accordance with the Charter of the United Nations, and encourages other principal and subsidiary organs of the United Nations to guarantee the participation of women under conditions of equality.

44. The World Conference on Human Rights welcomes the World Conference on Women to be held in Beijing in 1995 and urges that human rights of women should play an important role in its deliberations, in accordance with the priority themes of the World Conference on Women of equality, development and peace.

4. The rights of the child

45. The World Conference on Human Rights reiterates the principle of "First Call for Children" and, in this respect, underlines the importance of major national and international efforts, especially those of the United Nations Children's Fund, for promoting respect for the rights of the child to survival, protection, development and participation.
46. Measures should be taken to achieve universal ratification of the Convention on the Rights of the Child by 1995 and the universal signing of the World Declaration on the Survival, Protection and Development of Children and Plan of Action adopted by the World Summit for Children, as well as their effective implementation. The World Conference on Human Rights urges States to withdraw reservations to the Convention on the Rights of the Child contrary to the object and purpose of the Convention or otherwise contrary to international treaty law.
47. The World Conference on Human Rights urges all nations to undertake measures to the maximum extent of their available resources, with the support of international cooperation, to achieve the goals in the World Summit Plan of Action. The Conference calls on States to integrate the Convention on the Rights of the Child into their national action plans. By means of these national action plans and through international efforts, particular priority should be placed on reducing infant and maternal mortality rates, reducing malnutrition and illiteracy rates and providing access to safe drinking water and to basic education. Whenever so called for, national plans of action should be devised to combat devastating emergencies resulting from natural disasters and armed conflicts and the equally grave problem of children in extreme poverty.
48. The World Conference on Human Rights urges all States, with the support of international cooperation, to address the acute problem of children under especially difficult circumstances.

Exploitation and abuse of children should be actively combated, including by addressing their root causes. Effective measures are required against female infanticide, harmful child labour, sale of children and organs, child prostitution, child pornography, as well as other forms of sexual abuse.

49. The World Conference on Human Rights supports all measures by the United Nations and its specialized agencies to ensure the effective protection and promotion of human rights of the girl child. The World Conference on Human Rights urges States to repeal existing laws and regulations and remove customs and practices which discriminate against and cause harm to the girl child.

50. The World Conference on Human Rights strongly supports the proposal that the Secretary-General initiate a study into means of improving the protection of children in armed conflicts. Humanitarian norms should be implemented and measures taken in order to protect and facilitate assistance to children in war zones. Measures should include protection for children against indiscriminate use of all weapons of war, especially anti-personnel mines. The need for aftercare and rehabilitation of children traumatized by war must be addressed urgently. The Conference calls on the Committee on the Rights of the Child to study the question of raising the minimum age of recruitment into armed forces.

51. The World Conference on Human Rights recommends that matters relating to human rights and the situation of children be regularly reviewed and monitored by all relevant organs and mechanisms of the United Nations system and by the supervisory bodies of the specialized agencies in accordance with their mandates.

52. The World Conference on Human Rights recognizes the important role played by non-governmental organizations in the effective implementation of all human rights instruments and, in particular, the Convention on the Rights of the Child.

53. The World Conference on Human Rights recommends that the Committee on the Rights of the Child, with the assistance of the Centre for Human Rights, be enabled expeditiously and effectively to meet its mandate, especially in view of the unprecedented extent of ratification and subsequent submission of country reports.

5. Freedom from torture

54. The World Conference on Human Rights welcomes the ratification by many Member States of the Convention against Torture and Other Cruel, Inhuman or Degrading Treatment or Punishment and encourages its speedy ratification by all other Member States.
55. The World Conference on Human Rights emphasizes that one of the most atrocious violations against human dignity is the act of torture, the result of which destroys the dignity and impairs the capability of victims to continue their lives and their activities.
56. The World Conference on Human Rights reaffirms that under human rights law and international humanitarian law, freedom from torture is a right which must be protected under all circumstances, including in times of internal or international disturbance or armed conflicts.
57. The World Conference on Human Rights therefore urges all States to put an immediate end to the practice of torture and eradicate this evil forever through full implementation of the Universal Declaration of Human Rights as well as the relevant conventions and, where necessary, strengthening of existing mechanisms. The World Conference on Human Rights calls on all States to cooperate fully with the Special Rapporteur on the question of torture in the fulfilment of his mandate.
58. Special attention should be given to ensure universal respect for, and effective implementation of, the Principles of Medical

Ethics relevant to the Role of Health Personnel, particularly Physicians, in the Protection of Prisoners and Detainees against Torture and other Cruel, Inhuman or Degrading Treatment or Punishment adopted by the General Assembly of the United Nations.

59. The World Conference on Human Rights stresses the importance of further concrete action within the framework of the United Nations with the view to providing assistance to victims of torture and ensure more effective remedies for their physical, psychological and social rehabilitation. Providing the necessary resources for this purpose should be given high priority, *inter alia*, by additional contributions to the United Nations Voluntary Fund for the Victims of Torture.

60. States should abrogate legislation leading to impunity for those responsible for grave violations of human rights such as torture and prosecute such violations, thereby providing a firm basis for the rule of law.

61. The World Conference on Human Rights reaffirms that efforts to eradicate torture should, first and foremost, be concentrated on prevention and, therefore, calls for the early adoption of an optional protocol to the Convention against Torture and Other Cruel, Inhuman and Degrading Treatment or Punishment, which is intended to establish a preventive system of regular visits to places of detention.

Enforced disappearances

62. The World Conference on Human Rights, welcoming the adoption by the General Assembly of the Declaration on the Protection of All Persons from Enforced Disappearance, calls upon all States to take effective legislative, administrative, judicial or other measures to prevent, terminate and punish acts of enforced disappearances. The World Conference on Human Rights reaffirms that it is the duty of all States, under any circumstances, to make investigations whenever there is reason

to believe that an enforced disappearance has taken place on a territory under their jurisdiction and, if allegations are confirmed, to prosecute its perpetrators.

6. The rights of the disabled person

63. The World Conference on Human Rights reaffirms that all human rights and fundamental freedoms are universal and thus unreservedly include persons with disabilities. Every person is born equal and has the same rights to life and welfare, education and work, living independently and active participation in all aspects of society. Any direct discrimination or other negative discriminatory treatment of a disabled person is therefore a violation of his or her rights. The World Conference on Human Rights calls on Governments, where necessary, to adopt or adjust legislation to assure access to these and other rights for disabled persons.
64. The place of disabled persons is everywhere. Persons with disabilities should be guaranteed equal opportunity through the elimination of all socially determined barriers, be they physical, financial, social or psychological, which exclude or restrict full participation in society.
65. Recalling the World Programme of Action concerning Disabled Persons, adopted by the General Assembly at its thirty-seventh session, the World Conference on Human Rights calls upon the General Assembly and the Economic and Social Council to adopt the draft standard rules on the equalization of opportunities for persons with disabilities, at their meetings in 1993

C. Cooperation, development and strengthening of human rights

66. The World Conference on Human Rights recommends that priority be given to national and international action to promote democracy, development and human rights.
67. Special emphasis should be given to measures to assist in the strengthening and building of institutions relating to human rights, strengthening of a pluralistic civil society and the protection of groups which have been rendered vulnerable. In this context, assistance provided upon the request of Governments for the conduct of free and fair elections, including assistance in the human rights aspects of elections and public information about elections, is of particular importance. Equally important is the assistance to be given to the strengthening of the rule of law, the promotion of freedom of expression and the administration of justice, and to the real and effective participation of the people in the decision-making processes.
68. The World Conference on Human Rights stresses the need for the implementation of strengthened advisory services and technical assistance activities by the Centre for Human Rights. The Centre should make available to States upon request assistance on specific human rights issues, including the preparation of reports under human rights treaties as well as for the implementation of coherent and comprehensive plans of action for the promotion and protection of human rights. Strengthening the institutions of human rights and democracy, the legal protection of human rights, training of officials and others, broad-based education and public information aimed at promoting respect for human rights should all be available as components of these programmes.
69. The World Conference on Human Rights strongly recommends that a comprehensive programme be established within the

United Nations in order to help States in the task of building and strengthening adequate national structures which have a direct impact on the overall observance of human rights and the maintenance of the rule of law. Such a programme, to be coordinated by the Centre for Human Rights, should be able to provide, upon the request of the interested Government, technical and financial assistance to national projects in reforming penal and correctional establishments, education and training of lawyers, judges and security forces in human rights, and any other sphere of activity relevant to the good functioning of the rule of law. That programme should make available to States assistance for the implementation of plans of action for the promotion and protection of human rights.

70. The World Conference on Human Rights requests the Secretary-General of the United Nations to submit proposals to the United Nations General Assembly, containing alternatives for the establishment, structure, operational modalities and funding of the proposed programme.

71. The World Conference on Human Rights recommends that each State consider the desirability of drawing up a national action plan identifying steps whereby that State would improve the promotion and protection of human rights.

72. The World Conference on Human Rights on Human Rights reaffirms that the universal and inalienable right to development, as established in the Declaration on the Right to Development, must be implemented and realized. In this context, the World Conference on Human Rights welcomes the appointment by the Commission on Human Rights of a thematic working group on the right to development and urges that the Working Group, in consultation and cooperation with other organs and agencies of the United Nations system, promptly formulate, for early consideration by the United Nations General Assembly, comprehensive and effective measures to eliminate obstacles to the implementation and realization of the Declaration on the Right to Development and recommending ways and means

towards the realization of the right to development by all States.

73. The World Conference on Human Rights recommends that non-governmental and other grass-roots organizations active in development and/or human rights should be enabled to play a major role on the national and international levels in the debate, activities and implementation relating to the right to development and, in cooperation with Governments, in all relevant aspects of development cooperation.

74. The World Conference on Human Rights appeals to Governments, competent agencies and institutions to increase considerably the resources devoted to building well-functioning legal systems able to protect human rights, and to national institutions working in this area. Actors in the field of development cooperation should bear in mind the mutually reinforcing interrelationship between development, democracy and human rights. Cooperation should be based on dialogue and transparency. The World Conference on Human Rights also calls for the establishment of comprehensive programmes, including resource banks of information and personnel with expertise relating to the strengthening of the rule of law and of democratic institutions.

75. The World Conference on Human Rights encourages the Commission on Human Rights, in cooperation with the Committee on Economic, Social and Cultural Rights, to continue the examination of optional protocols to the International Covenant on Economic, Social and Cultural Rights.

76. The World Conference on Human Rights recommends that more resources be made available for the strengthening or the establishment of regional arrangements for the promotion and protection of human rights under the programmes of advisory services and technical assistance of the Centre for Human Rights. States are encouraged to request assistance for such purposes as regional and subregional workshops, seminars and information exchanges designed to strengthen regional

arrangements for the promotion and protection of human rights in accord with universal human rights standards as contained in international human rights instruments.

77. The World Conference on Human Rights supports all measures by the United Nations and its relevant specialized agencies to ensure the effective promotion and protection of trade union rights, as stipulated in the International Covenant on Economic, Social and Cultural Rights and other relevant international instruments. It calls on all States to abide fully by their obligations in this regard contained in international instruments.

D. Human rights education

78. The World Conference on Human Rights considers human rights education, training and public information essential for the promotion and achievement of stable and harmonious relations among communities and for fostering mutual understanding, tolerance and peace.
79. States should strive to eradicate illiteracy and should direct education towards the full development of the human personality and to the strengthening of respect for human rights and fundamental freedoms. The World Conference on Human Rights calls on all States and institutions to include human rights, humanitarian law, democracy and rule of law as subjects in the curricula of all learning institutions in formal and non-formal settings.
80. Human rights education should include peace, democracy, development and social justice, as set forth in international and regional human rights instruments, in order to achieve common understanding and awareness with a view to strengthening universal commitment to human rights.
81. Taking into account the World Plan of Action on Education for Human Rights and Democracy, adopted in March 1993 by the International Congress on Education for Human Rights and

Democracy of the United Nations Educational, Scientific and Cultural Organization, and other human rights instruments, the World Conference on Human Rights recommends that States develop specific programmes and strategies for ensuring the widest human rights education and the dissemination of public information, taking particular account of the human rights needs of women.

82. Governments, with the assistance of intergovernmental organizations, national institutions and non-governmental organizations, should promote an increased awareness of human rights and mutual tolerance. The World Conference on Human Rights underlines the importance of strengthening the World Public Information Campaign for Human Rights carried out by the United Nations. They should initiate and support education in human rights and undertake effective dissemination of public information in this field. The advisory services and technical assistance programmes of the United Nations system should be able to respond immediately to requests from States for educational and training activities in the field of human rights as well as for special education concerning standards as contained in international human rights instruments and in humanitarian law and their application to special groups such as military forces, law enforcement personnel, police and the health profession. The proclamation of a United Nations decade for human rights education in order to promote, encourage and focus these educational activities should be considered.

E. Implementation and monitoring methods

83. The World Conference on Human Rights urges Governments to incorporate standards as contained in international human rights instruments in domestic legislation and to strengthen

national structures, institutions and organs of society which play a role in promoting and safeguarding human rights.

84. The World Conference on Human Rights recommends the strengthening of United Nations activities and programmes to meet requests for assistance by States which want to establish or strengthen their own national institutions for the promotion and protection of human rights.

85. The World Conference on Human Rights also encourages the strengthening of cooperation between national institutions for the promotion and protection of human rights, particularly through exchanges of information and experience, as well as cooperation with regional organizations and the United Nations.

86. The World Conference on Human Rights strongly recommends in this regard that representatives of national institutions for the promotion and protection of human rights convene periodic meetings under the auspices of the Centre for Human Rights to examine ways and means of improving their mechanisms and sharing experiences.

87. The World Conference on Human Rights recommends to the human rights treaty bodies, to the meetings of chairpersons of the treaty bodies and to the meetings of States parties that they continue to take steps aimed at coordinating the multiple reporting requirements and guidelines for preparing State reports under the respective human rights conventions and study the suggestion that the submission of one overall report on treaty obligations undertaken by each State would make these procedures more effective and increase their impact.

88. The World Conference on Human Rights recommends that the States parties to international human rights instruments, the General Assembly and the Economic and Social Council should consider studying the existing human rights treaty bodies and the various thematic mechanisms and procedures with a view to promoting greater efficiency and effectiveness through better coordination of the various bodies, mechanisms and procedures,

taking into account the need to avoid unnecessary duplication and overlapping of their mandates and tasks.

89. The World Conference on Human Rights recommends continued work on the improvement of the functioning, including the monitoring tasks, of the treaty bodies, taking into account multiple proposals made in this respect, in particular those made by the treaty bodies themselves and by the meetings of the chairpersons of the treaty bodies. The comprehensive national approach taken by the Committee on the Rights of the Child should also be encouraged.

90. The World Conference on Human Rights recommends that States parties to human rights treaties consider accepting all the available optional communication procedures.

91. The World Conference on Human Rights views with concern the issue of impunity of perpetrators of human rights violations, and supports the efforts of the Commission on Human Rights and the Sub-Commission on Prevention of Discrimination and Protection of Minorities to examine all aspects of the issue.

92. The World Conference on Human Rights recommends that the Commission on Human Rights examine the possibility for better implementation of existing human rights instruments at the international and regional levels and encourages the International Law Commission to continue its work on an international criminal court.

93. The World Conference on Human Rights appeals to States which have not yet done so to accede to the Geneva Conventions of 12 August 1949 and the Protocols thereto, and to take all appropriate national measures, including legislative ones, for their full implementation.

94. The World Conference on Human Rights recommends the speedy completion and adoption of the draft declaration on the right and responsibility of individuals, groups and organs of society to promote and protect universally recognized human rights and fundamental freedoms.

95. The World Conference on Human Rights underlines the importance of preserving and strengthening the system of special procedures, rapporteurs, representatives, experts and working groups of the Commission on Human Rights and the Sub-Commission on the Prevention of Discrimination and Protection of Minorities, in order to enable them to carry out their mandates in all countries throughout the world, providing them with the necessary human and financial resources. The procedures and mechanisms should be enabled to harmonize and rationalize their work through periodic meetings. All States are asked to cooperate fully with these procedures and mechanisms.

96. The World Conference on Human Rights recommends that the United Nations assume a more active role in the promotion and protection of human rights in ensuring full respect for international humanitarian law in all situations of armed conflict, in accordance with the purposes and principles of the Charter of the United Nations.

97. The World Conference on Human Rights, recognizing the important role of human rights components in specific arrangements concerning some peace-keeping operations by the United Nations, recommends that the Secretary-General take into account the reporting, experience and capabilities of the Centre for Human Rights and human rights mechanisms, in conformity with the Charter of the United Nations.

98. To strengthen the enjoyment of economic, social and cultural rights, additional approaches should be examined, such as a system of indicators to measure progress in the realization of the rights set forth in the International Covenant on Economic, Social and Cultural Rights. There must be a concerted effort to ensure recognition of economic, social and cultural rights at the national, regional and international levels.

F. Follow-up to the World Conference on Human Rights

99. The World Conference on Human Rights on Human Rights recommends that the General Assembly, the Commission on Human Rights and other organs and agencies of the United Nations system related to human rights consider ways and means for the full implementation, without delay, of the recommendations contained in the present Declaration, including the possibility of proclaiming a United Nations decade for human rights. The World Conference on Human Rights further recommends that the Commission on Human Rights annually review the progress towards this end.
100. The World Conference on Human Rights requests the Secretary-General of the United Nations to invite on the occasion of the fiftieth anniversary of the Universal Declaration of Human Rights all States, all organs and agencies of the United Nations system related to human rights, to report to him on the progress made in the implementation of the present Declaration and to submit a report to the General Assembly at its fifty-third session, through the Commission on Human Rights and the Economic and Social Council. Likewise, regional and, as appropriate, national human rights institutions, as well as non-governmental organizations, may present their views to the Secretary-General on the progress made in the implementation of the present Declaration. Special attention should be paid to assessing the progress towards the goal of universal ratification of international human rights treaties and protocols adopted within the framework of the United Nations system.

V LIST OF SELECTED HUMAN RIGHTS WEB-SITES

1. Web sites of the United Nations system

United Nations:
 http://www.un.org
United Nations Center for Human Settlements:
 http://www.unhabitat.org/en/archive.asp
United Nations Children's Fund:
 http://www.unicef.org
United Nations Development Fund for Women:
 http://www.unifem.org
United Nations Development Programme:
 http://www.undp.org
United Nations Educational, Scientific, Cultural Organization:
 http://www.unesco.org
United Nations Environment Programme:
 http://www.unep.org
United Nations General Assembly:
 http://www.un.org/ga
United Nations Population Fund:
 http://www.unfpa.org
United Nations Programme on HIV/AIDS:
 http://www.unaids.org
United Nations Secretary General:
 http://www.un.org/News/ossg/sg
United Nations Security Council:
 http://www.un.org/Docs/sc/
Economic and Social Council:
 http://www.un.org/esa/coordination/ecosoc
Food and Agriculture Organization of the United Nation:
 http://www.fao.org
International Civil Aviation Organization:
 http://www.icao.int
International Court of Justice:
 http://www.icj-cij.org

International Criminal Court:
  http://www.un.org/law/icc
International Labour Organization:
  http://www.ilo.org
Office of the United Nations High Commissioner for Human Rights:
  http://www.unhchr.ch
United Nations High Commissioner for Refugees:
  http://www.unhcr.ch
World Health Organization:
  http://www.who.int/en
World Intellectual Property Organization:
  http://www.wipo.org

2. **Web sites of regional organizations**

African Commission on Human and Peoples' Rights:
  http://www.achpr.org
Commissioner for Human Rights (CE):
  http://www.coe.int/T/E/Commissioner_H.R/Communication_Unit
Council of Europe:
  http://www.coe.int
Court of Justice of the European Communities:
  http://curia.eu.int
European Commission:
  http://europa.eu.int/comm/index_en.htm
European Court of Human Rights:
  http://www.echr.coe.int
European Parliament:
  http://www.europarl.eu.int
European Union:
  http://europa.eu.int
High Commissioner on National Minorities (OSCE):
  http://www.osce.org/hcnm
Inter-American Commission on Human Rights:
  http://www.cidh.oas.org
Inter-American Court of Human Rights:
  http://www.oas.org/EN/PINFO/OAS/court.htm
International Organization for Migration:
  http://www.iom.int

Office for Democratic Institutions and Human Rights (OSCE):
   http://www.osce.org/odihr
Organisation for Economic Co-operation and Development:
   http://www.oecd.org
Organization for Security and Co-operation in Europe:
   http://www.osce.org
Organization of African Unity:
   http://www.africa-union.org
Organization of American States:
   http://www.oas.org

3. Other human rights web sites

Amnesty International:
   http://www.amnesty.org
CARE:
   http://www.care.org
Derechos Human Rights:
   http://www.derechos.org
Human Rights Information and Documentation Systems, International:
   http://www.huridocs.org
Human Rights Internet:
   http://www.hri.ca
Human Rights Watch:
   http://www.hrw.org
International Committee of the Red Cross:
   http://www.icrc.org
International Federation for Human Rights:
   http://www.fidh.org
International Law and Human Rights:
   http://www.xs4all.nl/~ingel/c.ingelse/main.htm
Inter-Parliamentary Union:
   http://www.ipu.org
University of Minnesota Human Rights Library:
   http://www.umn.edu/humanrts
World Organization Against Torture:
   http://www.omct.org

VI LIST OF ABBREVIATIONS*
USED IN THIS PUBLICATION

ACHPR   African Commission on Human and Peoples' Rights
AI   Amnesty International
AIDS   acquired immune deficiency syndrome
ALECSO Arab League Educational, Cultural and Scientific Organization
AU   African Union

BIRPI   Bureaux internationaux réunis pour la protection
        de la propriété intellectuelle (International Bureau
        for the Protection of Intellectual Property)

CAT   Committee against Torture
CBSS   Council of the Baltic Sea States
CE   Council of Europe
CEDAW   Committee on the Elimination of Discrimination against Women
CERD   Committee on the Elimination of Racial Discrimination
CESCR   Committee on Economic, Social and Cultural Rights
CFS   Committee on World Food Security
CIM   Inter-American Commission of Women
CIOMS   Council for International Organizations of Medical Sciences
CJCE   Court of Justice of the European Communities
CPT   European Committee for the Prevention of Torture and
        Inhuman or Degrading Treatment or Punishment
CRC   Committee on the Rights of the Child
CSCE   Conference for Security and Co-operation in Europe

EC   European Community
ECHR   European Court of Human Rights
ECOSOC Economic and Social Council
ECRI   European Commission against Racism and Intolerance
ECSR   European Committee of Social Rights
EEC   European Economic Community
EIDHR   European Initiative for Democracy and Human Rights

---

* The list contains most of the abbreviations used in this publication which might be useful for a reader in further research on human rights related issues.

ESCAP	Economic and Social Commission for Asia and the Pacific
EU	European Union
FAO	Food and Agriculture Organization of the United Nations
GA	General Assembly (UN)
GEMS	Global Environment Monitoring System (UNEP)
GRID	Global Resource Information Data Base (UNEP)
HABITAT	United Nations Centre for Human Settlements
HCNM	High Commissioner on National Minorities (OSCE)
HIV	human immunodeficiency virus
HRC	Human Rights Committee
HRE	Human Rights Education
IBC	International Bioethics Convention (UNESCO)
ICAO	International Civil Aviation Organization
ICC	International Criminal Court (UN)
ICCPR	International Covenant on Civil and Political Rights (UN)
ICEM	Intergovernmental Committee for European Migration
ICESCR	International Covenant on Economic, Social and Cultural Rights
ICJ	International Court of Justice
ICPD	International Conference on Population and Development
ICRC	International Committee of the Red Cross
ICTR	International Criminal Tribunal for Rwanda
ICTY	International Criminal Tribunal for the former Yugoslavia
IGO	Intergovernmental organisation
ILO	International Labour Organization
IMF	International Monetary Fund
INIA	International Institute on Ageing
INSTRAW	International Research and Training Institute for the Advancement of Women
IOM	International Organization for Migration
IPU	Inter-Parliamentary Union
IRO	International Refugee Organization
MOST	Management of Social Transformations
NGO	non-governmental organization
NHRI	National Human Rights Institutions

OAS	Organization of American States
OAU	Organization of African Unity
ODIHR	Office for Democratic Institutions and Human Rights (OSCE)
OECD	Organisation for Economic Co-operation and Development
OHCHR	Office of the United Nations High Commissioner for Human Rights
OPCW	Organisation for the Prohibition of Chemical Weapons
OSCE	Organization for Security and Co-operation in Europe
PICMME	Provisional Intergovernmental Committee for the Movements of Migrants from Europe
POW	Prisoner of War
UDHR	Universal Declaration of Human Rights
UN	United Nations
UNAIDS	United Nations Programme on HIV/AIDS
UNCED	United Nations Conference on Environment and Development
UNCHR	United Nations Centre for Human Rights
UNDAW	United Nations Division for the Advancement of Women
UNDCP	United Nations Drug Control Programme
UNDP	United Nations Development Programme
UNEP	United Nations Environmental Programme
UNESCO	United Nations Educational, Scientific and Cultural Organization
UNFPA	United Nations Population Fund
UNGA	United Nations General Assembly
UNHCR	United Nations High Commissioner for Refugees
UNICEF	United Nations Children's Fund
UNIDO	United Nations Industrial Development Organization
UNIFEM	United Nations Development Fund for Women
VDPA	Vienna Declaration and Programme of Action
WCAR	World Conference against Racism, Racial Discrimination, Xenophobia and Related Intolerance
WFP	World Food Programme
WHO	World Health Organization
WIPO	World Intellectual Property Organization
WMA	World Medical Association
WSSD	World Summit for Sustainable Development
WTO	World Trade Organization